Internet Drama and
Mystery Television Series,
1996–2014

Internet Drama and Mystery Television Series, 1996–2014

VINCENT TERRACE

McFarland & Company, Inc., Publishers
Jefferson, North Carolina

LIBRARY OF CONGRESS CATALOGUING-IN-PUBLICATION DATA

Terrace, Vincent, 1948–
Internet drama and mystery television series, 1996–2014 / Vincent Terrace.
    p.   cm.
Includes index.

ISBN 978-0-7864-9581-8 (softcover : acid free paper) ∞
ISBN 978-1-4766-1930-9 (ebook)

1. Internet television—Encyclopedias.   2. Television programs—
Plots, themes, etc.—Encyclopedias.   3. Detective and mystery
television programs—Plots, themes, etc.—Encyclopedias.   I. Title.
PN1992.2.T54 2015   791.45'7503—dc23   2014042760

BRITISH LIBRARY CATALOGUING DATA ARE AVAILABLE

Cover image Antonio Guillem/ThinkStock

Printed in the United States of America

McFarland & Company, Inc., Publishers
Box 611, Jefferson, North Carolina 28640
www.mcfarlandpub.com

TABLE OF CONTENTS

PREFACE

Internet Drama and Mystery Television Series, 1996–2014, is the second of a multi-volume set of books that examines television programs produced exclusively for the Internet. An Internet or Web television series (as they are also termed) is usually independently produced and generally features talented but unknown performers. It is most often financed through an online fund-raising campaign at sites such as Kickstarter.com and entirely without product sponsor backing. Of course, there are exceptions and some such programs have backers (like Allstate Insurance producing *The Lines*) and others have major networks behind them (such as Showtime with *Secret Diary of a Call Girl Webisodes* and *Dexter Early Cuts*). In rare cases, well-known performers do star on such programs; e.g., Rosanna Arquette on *Rochelle* and Billy Miller (from *The Young and the Restless*) on *Enormous.*

No matter who produces them and who headlines them, Internet series are considered "no budget" or "low budget" productions (often created by borrowing equipment and utilizing volunteer casts and crews). Internet users interested in this relatively new format/venue of television generally find these Internet series by chance or through word of mouth. Up until now there has been no single guide in print or on the Internet that one can use (like *TV Guide*) to locate all the Web TV programs that fit a specific genre.

The programs contained within this book cover not only those produced in the U.S. but also those created in other countries (like England, Australia, and Canada) that have worldwide distribution (country of origin is indicated with each such program entry in the text). Most of the series listed in this volume are still available to be viewed although some are no longer active Internet television shows and, for the most part, have been withdrawn from public access (actual episodes are not viewable, but teasers or trailers often still remain online).

In this volume the genres of drama (including crime drama, soap operas, action, Western, adventure, anthology, and comedy-drama) and mystery (including suspense and thriller) are presented with detailed listings. Each of the 405 alphabetically arranged entries in this volume contains: 1) a detailed storyline; 2) a descriptive episode guide, performer and character casts, credits (producer, writer, and director) where available; 3) a website where episodes were viewable at the time of publication; 4) year(s) of production; and 5) commentary. Forty-four photographs and an index complete the book.

For this particular book, the drama and mystery genres are covered from their beginnings in 1996 through July 2014. It does *not* include broadcast and cable television programs that are streamed over the Internet (as these are *not* series produced exclusively for the Internet). Simple as it may sound, this book was not simple to write. For example, there was no available single source (including Google, Bing, and Yahoo) that tracked all the shows that fit within a specific genre. As such, finding and researching potential entries was a major hurdle. Once this difficulty was met, gathering specific program information proved to be an even greater challenge. Often story synopses and listings of episodes produced for a series were available but were too short to be informative. In many instances there were no episode descriptions and, sometimes, synopses did not match what the actual series (as available online) was really about. In addition, I found a considerable amount of conflicting data regarding the number of episodes, especially with those programs that appear on several sharing websites. (For example, episode listings, titles, and running times were not always identical; casts differed in name spellings; and synopsis information sometimes varied.) Actually viewing the episodes of American and foreign-produced series that could be found became the only viable solution to the researching problem. In fact, it was the only way a book such as this could be done effectively and accurately.

Regarding conflicting information, particularly with name spellings (as many are unusual), the final forms presented here were taken from the screen (where possible) as opposed to various other Internet sources (such as reviews and third party sharing websites). Unfortunately, some episode information has been removed from the Internet both before and during the research for this book. Thus it was not possible to present episode descriptions for every show.

Compiling this volume brought to light an exciting new world of television programming that, for the most part, has been overlooked—so far—by the general public. It is pleasantly surprising just how good many Internet series can be (better, in some cases, than what is available on broadcast and cable television). Delving into the genres presented in this book, one will discover murder mysteries (*Who Killed Jessica Lane?*, *Sam Had 7 Friends*), gorgeous cowgirls (*Cowgirl Up*), teenage mermaids (*A Splashy Tale*) and bad-to-the bone girls (*Bad Tara*). There are soap operas (*Empire*, *Beacon Hill*), anthologies (*Or So the Story Goes*, *The Midnight Room*), beautiful secret agents (*Tanya X*, *The Russian Spy*), mobsters (*Mob on the Run*), lesbian detectives (*B.J. Fletcher, Private Eye*), Westerns (*Thurston*, *Sundown*) and even misfit cops (*South Beach Undercover*).

If you have never seen an Internet-based series or you have based your judgment on a knee-jerk reaction to the new format itself, or just word-of-mouth, then watching what has been produced in the drama and mystery genres of Internet television may stir your interest to view other series presented in this book. It could change your perspective and make you wonder: why isn't this series on traditional television?

The author would like to thank James Robert Parish for his assistance on this project.

THE SERIES

1 *The After.* facebook.com. 2014 (Drama).

Eight strangers, all with the same birth date, are trapped in a building when the power fails following an unexplained event that virtually destroys the world as it was once known. Was it an apocalypse, a supernatural occurrence, an alien force? With no explanation as to why they were chosen (something unknown in common other than their birthdays?) and with no real plan on how to survive, the program charts their efforts to make sense as to what has happened and find a way to survive the chaos that is surrounding them.

Cast: Louise Monot (Gigi Genereau), Arielle Kebbel (Tammy), Sharon Lawrence (Frances), Sam Littlefield (Dark Shadow), Jamie Kennedy (David), Aldis Hodge (D. Love), Andrew Howard (McCormick), Jaina Lee Ortiz (Marly), Adrian Pasdar (Wade), Brynne Bowie (Marie Genereau), Jason Lewis (Gigi's husband). **Credits:** *Producer:* Chris Carter, Leon Clarence, Marc Rosen, Gabe Rotter. *Writer-Director:* Chris Carter. **Comment:** Although created by Chris Carter, the man responsible for TV's successful *The X-Files*, *The After* does not play as well as it can become a bit confusing at times (sort of like the TV series *Lost*). This may have been done on purpose to set up a mystery and introduce the characters that will become a part of the series. The special effects are good and the production values and acting also very good. Several possible regular characters are introduced (including a French actress, a Latina police woman, a gay clown, an old woman and an Irishman). There is chaos on the streets and a mystery has been established but the plot has been done before with the twist here being that selected people have something in common. There are some familiar names in the cast (Sharon Lawrence and Jamie Kennedy) but as far as pilot films go, the slow pacing and *Lost*-like confusion is the reason why such a series, even on the Internet, will not probably advance any further. *Lost* was good in its time, but the confusion it established with episodes also proved to be its downfall as it became a difficult series to sell into syndication.

Episodes:

1. The Pilot (54 min.). Establishes the somewhat murky storyline as eight strangers find themselves trapped and not fully aware as to what has happened.

2 *After the Beast: The Benjamin Walker Chronicle.* youtube.com. 2011 (Action).

Six years ago a regime called "The Beast" had taken over society as we know it and has declared that all citizens must adhere to its rules. Society however, suffered, with economic instability, violence and anarchy. Some, like Benjamin Walker, have chosen not to live by what the regime has proclaimed and have retreated to the wilderness to live off the land. The regime, however, despises such individuals and those who circumvent it have become targets of the Mark Bearers, agents loyal to the regime, who seek to destroy those who oppose "The Beast." Stories follow Benjamin's struggles for survival and efforts to avoid the Mark Bearers—a situation made more difficult when he encounters and attaches himself to a woman survivor (Jordan) and a child that accompanies her (called The Boy).

Cast: Jake Parker (Benjamin Walker), Mikjan Torrie (Jordan), Eric Mathews (The Boy), Jim "Bear" Martin (Trapper), Shawn York (Red Beaver), Amber York (Wicker Salwen). **Credits:** *Producer-Writer:* Rob York, Scott Baird. *Director:* Rob York. **Comment:** Totally filmed outdoors and striking in presentation. The acting is very good, especially the Trapper, and the story flows smoothly from beginning to end. The type of program that has a mysterious air about it that can draw the viewer into it and keep him hooked to see how the story progresses. It could easily be transformed into a network or basic cable TV series.

Episodes:

1. Wilderness (10 min., 40 sec.). Establishes the story line as Benjamin explains the predicament he is facing since the regime became law.

2. Trapper (6 min., 19 sec.). After injuring his ankle in a trap set by "The Trapper," for animals, the Trapper comes to his aid and releases him.

3. Faith (5 min., 37 sec.). As Benjamin's injury begins to heal he learns a bit more about the Trapper.

4. Hunted (5 min., 39 sec.). Sensing something is wrong, the Trapper leaves the camp to investigate.

5. Exile (8 min., 30 sec.). As Benjamin and the Trapper part company, Benjamin begins to again wander, hoping to avoid the Mark Bearers.

6. Refugees (3 min., 57 sec.). As Benjamin wanders he stumbles across two other fugitives wanted by the Mark Bearers—a woman (Jordan) and The Boy.

7. Companions (4 min., 57 sec.). Although a bit reluctant, Benjamin agrees to help Jordan and The Boy find safety at the nearest safe village.

8. The Tribe (5 min., 11 sec.). Benjamin and his companions find themselves being captured by a group of armed warriors and brought to their camp.

9. Flight (3 min., 43 sec.). Unknown to them, they are being watched by—and are shortly after attacked by the Mark Bearers.

10. The Mark (10 min., 31 sec.). The concluding unresolved episode finds Benjamin, Jordan and The Boy escaping from their captors and seeking safety in the forest.

3 *Aim High.* webserieschannel.com. 2011–2013 (Crime Drama).

Fairview High School is a typical educational institution in Chicago with a student body of typical young men and women. Or so it appears. One student, Nicholas Green is the exception—he has been recruited by the U.S. government as a special agent for sensitive, top secret missions. It all began when Nicholas, a seventh grader, joined a fitness program called DEPP (Department of Education Pilot Program) and took first honors. Little did he (or apparently anyone else) know that DEPP was a training program for future U.S. government spies. When Nicholas reached the age of 16, he was asked to join "the team." Believing it would be something different he did and now regrets it as it has totally changed his life. Nick, as he is called, may not be able to attend all his classes, pass all his tests or even complete all his homework assignments, but he is an effective, clever and deadly agent. As a student Nick has a crush on Amanda, the beautiful "wickedly cool rocker" who, to his dismay, is dating Derek, the captain of the school's swimming team. As an agent Nick is an underage version of James Bond and stories follow Nick as he struggles to keep his two worlds separate, maintain his grades and save the world from evil.

Cast: Jackson Rathbone (Nick Green), Aimee Teegarden (Amanda Miles), Natalie Dreyfuss (Dakota), Devon Bostick (Marcus Anderson), Chris Wylde (Terry), Tony Cavalero (Deuce), Natalie Lander (Marcy), Steve Kim (Sukarno), Johnny Pemberton (Marcus Anderson), Jonathan Mc-

After the Beast: The Benjamin Walker Chronicle. **Poster art from the series (copyright FireSpire Productions, 2012).**

Daniel (Derek), Jonathan Avigdori (Goombah), Matthew Moy (Scott Winelin), Greg Germann (Ockenhocker), Michelle Glavan (Trish), Ray Corasani (Gordon), Massi Fulan (Joey). **Credits:** *Producer:* McG, Richie Keen, Lance Sloane. *Director:* Thor Freudenthal. *Writer:* Richie Keen. **Comment:** Although not an original idea (the Fox TV series *The New Adventures of Beans Baxter* used the same teenage government agent idea), it is charming, well acted and produced. There are hints of comedy mixed with the assignments Nick must endure to save the world.

Episodes:

1. Episode 1 (7 min., 52 sec.). Introduces Nick Green, a student with an after school job like no other; Amanda, the girl on whom he has a crush; and Derek, his competition for Amanda's affections.

2. Episode (9 min., 36 sec.). Just as Nick manages to get close to Amanda, he receives an assignment to silence a Russian mercenary who is planning to steal a radioactive isotope to make a bomb.

3. Episode 3 (6 min., 29 sec.). An upcoming chemistry test complicates Nick's life as he must now chose between studying for the exam, continue his pursuit of Amanda, take out a mobster or silence the mercenary.

4. Episode 4 (10 min., 59 sec.). After taking out a mobster (but incurring the wrath of the crime boss), Nick also decides to quit his job as a teenage killer. For the first time in months Nick begins to enjoy life as an ordinary student—or at least he thinks.

5. Episode 5 (7 min., 19 sec.). Nick soon finds that he cannot escape his after school job and must return to it, leaving his and Amanda's relationship in peril when the Russian mercenary as well as the crime boss come gunning for him.

6. Episode 6 (8 min., 8 sec.). Nick's troubles have only just begun—his enemies have tracked him to the school and he must now protect the student body without revealing his secret identity. The program's concluding episode.

4 *All My Children.* sidereel.com. 2013 (Drama).

A web version of the ABC series *All My Children* (Jan. 1, 1970 to Sept. 23, 2011), that continues to relate events in the lives of the citizens of Pine Valley, Pennsylvania.

Cast: Julia Barr (Brooke English), Vincent Irizarry (Dr. David Hayward), Cady McClain (Dixie Cooney), Debbi Morgan (Dr. Angie Hubbard), Eden Riegel (Bianca Montgomery), Darnell Williams (Jesse Hubbard), Jill Larson (Opal Cortlandt), Thorsten Kaye (Zach Slater), Paula Garces (Lea Marquez), Lindsay Hartley (Dr. Cara Castillo), Ryan Bittle (Jr. Chandler), Saleisha Stowers (Cassandra Foster), Eric Nelson (AJ Chandler), Jordan Lane Price (Celia Fitzgerald), Denyse Tontz (Miranda Montgomery), Robert Scott Wilson (Peter Cortlandt). **Credits:** *Producer:* Ginger Smith. **Comment:** The program continued in the tradition set by the ABC version with excellent acting and production values.

Episodes: 220 episodes were planned, but only the following list resulted.

1. The Revolutionary Road Home. April 29, 2013.
2. The Nightmare Begins. April 30, 2013.
3. Ghosts from the Past. May 1, 2013.
4. Was It a Boy? Was It a Girl? May 2, 2013.
5. Eyes Wide Open. May 6, 2013.
6. Lessons from the Past. May 7, 2013.
7. Reunited. May 8, 2013.
8. Hung Up. May 9, 2013.
9. A Mother's Nightmare. May 13, 2013.
10. Sinnamon and Spice. May 14, 2013.
11. Stolen Innocence. May 15, 2013.
12. Baptized in That River and Born Again. May 16, 2013.
13. We'll Have Manhattan. May 20, 2013.
14. The Haunted Lullaby. May 22, 2013.
15. Your Every Fantasy. May 27, 2013.
16. Alert the Press. May 29, 2013.
17. Message of Hope. June 3, 2013.
18. Sibling Rivalry. June 5, 2013.
19. Damsel in Distress. June 10, 2013.
20. M.U.D. June 12, 2013.
21. Dead or Alive. June 17, 2013.
22. Out of the Nest. June 19, 2013.
23. Dirty, Sexy Love. June 24, 2013.
24. Pins and Needles. June 26, 2013.
25. Big Bullets and Small Bundles. July 1, 2013.
26. Straight Talk. July 1, 2013.
27. The Law of Passion. July 8, 2013.
28. Danger Becomes You. July 8, 2013.
29. A Mother's Love. July 15, 2013.
30. Secrets and Lies. July 15, 2013.
31. Nightmare on Cedar Street. July 22, 2013.
32. The Mask, the Makeover. July 22, 2013.
33. The Choice. July 29, 2013.
34. What's an Inch Between Friends? July 29, 2013.
35. A Guarded Heart. August 5, 2013.
36. An Enchanted Evening: The Gala Begins. August 5, 2013.
37. Stinky Pinkies and Sabotage. August 12, 2013.
38. Pie, Pitchers and Peanuts. August 12, 2013.
39. That's My Boy. August 19, 2013.
40. Frenemies and Forgery. August 19, 2013.
41. And We Call It Bella Notte. August 26, 2013.
42. Second Chances. August 26, 2013.
43. A Knight to Remember. September 2, 2013.

Note: The program originally aired Monday through Thursday with a Friday recap called *More All My Children* and hosted by Leslie Miller. It later aired new episodes only on Monday and Wednesdays (alternating with the revised *One Life to Live* on Tuesdays and Thursdays).

5 *Allegiance of Powers.* allegianceofpow ers.com. 2013 (Adventure).

A red rain caused when a meteor crashes into Dallas, changes ordinary good people into super heroes and people with criminal intent into villains. Two such good people, Egotan and Cybersting, join forces and form The Allegiance of Powers, an organization of costumed super heroes dedicated to the cause of destroying evil wherever it exists. While villains are evil, the heroes are a bit eccentric, but dedicated to stopping those who deviate from the norms of society. The program charts the heroes' activities as they not only deal with the distinction of being heroes, but their personal issues and, most importantly, adhering to the rules of society while dispensing justice.

Heroes: Egotan, possessed of super speed, considers recycling, talking about orphans and stopping crime (in that order) as his hobbies. He hates fellow crime fighter Benever Beaver and has a strong dislike of guns. His favorite quote is "Let's settle those jitters with a little crime stopping."

Cybersting, with the power of super strength, considers snapping pencils in half, breaking bad guys and writing poems his hobbies. He dislikes crimes and his weakness is constantly seeking but never finding love. His favorite saying is "Why did Cybersting cross the road? To Stop Crime!"

Benever Beaver, the second to join the Allegiance, cannot be killed. Miniature golf and avoiding pain he claims are his hobbies. He dislikes getting hurt and his weakness is "anything causing pain in any way."

Shy, with the power of telepathy, claims that writing and changing her hair color are her hobbies. Her note book is her weakness and anyone touching her note book is her greatest dislike.

Jason X, with the power of a concussion fist, likes video games and helping others. He dislikes evil and his main weakness is that he cares too much.

Jerry, with the ability to produce projectiles, loves ping pong and caring too much for humanity is his weakness.

Villains: Max, with the evil power of perception, hates Egotan and Cybersting. He claims his hobby is being evil and what he does not see is his weakness.

Clamp, with unknown hobbies, dislikes weaknesses and has the power of super strength. He often quotes "Let us tear this world apart."

Maze, a mysterious evil doer, is like Clamp, with a totally unknown history.

Metus, with the power to control by touch, claims his hobby is to plot ways to take over the world. He is angered that he can not fully use his left hand and dislikes anything that is normal.

Vale, whose hobbies include havoc and destruction, has a power called Ash Touch (able to burn anything on contact). He considers being heartless his weakness and hates his city.

Christi, an explosives expert, dislikes girly things but loves firearms and explosives and claims that, although she does not have a super power, blowing up things compensates for that flaw.

Kale, with the ability to dispense chains from his arms, dislikes anything that deviates from the norm. His weakness is that he loves Christi.

Assassin X, who can conjure blades from her body, likes dealing death but hates her profession. She has a child and she considers that her weakness.

KC, with the ability to use her tears to attract anyone, collects heads (her hobby). She dislikes bacon and conformity and considers the power she needs to produce her tears a weakness.

Kat Laveau, with the power of voodoo and her ability to resurrect the dead, has set her goal to become all powerful.

Crypt, who is dead (an ethereal), enjoys "messing with the living," and his greatest dislike is anything that lives.

Cast: Gerald Crum (Egotan), Alex Dunton (Cybersting), Shannon Snedden (Christi), Dylan Alford (Jerry), Justin Armstrong (Maze), Jason Dilworth (Jason X), Hugo Matz (Super Steve), Robert Cavazos (Benever Beaver), Kevin A. Green (Metus), Meredith LeDuc (Shy), Marc Colombo (Clamp), Larissa Holmes (Vale), Tex Marshall (Wayne), Crystal Chaney (Assassin X), Cody Duggan (Alan), Nicole Holt (Crypt), Amanda Marie (KC), Paula Marcenaro Solinger (Kat Laveau). **Credits:** *Producer:* Jason McRoberts, Gerald Crum, Joe Bucknam, Steven Barnes, Michael Crum, Terry Gilbert, Tristan Luyks. **Comment:** Good idea but badly presented. The close-ups are just too close (you just do not want to stare at faces that encompass the whole screen); many scenes are badly lit, the costumes are ridiculous, the annoying shaky (unsteady) camera is used too much and the acting is not convincing and can easily turn you off. If care had been taken to make costumes more in accord with what super heroes (and even villains) wear, immediately the viewer could make a connection and associate it with other such programs. Being an eccentric hero is okay, but making him embarrassingly stupid is not the way to go (as was done here). The program is different and for something different in the super hero vein, *The Allegiance of Powers* did accomplish that goal.

Episodes:

1. Egotan and Cybersting. Establishes the formation of the Allegiance following the meteor's crash into the heart of Dallas.

2. Requiem. As Egotan and Cybersting recruit members, the super villain Metus begins building his own army of evil doers.

3. Rise of an Empire. Believing all is normal in The City, Cybersting begins on-line dating unaware that Metus is ready to strike.

4. Shades of Ash. Metus strikes by capturing Egotan and Jerry and unleashing Vale on the city.

5. Round 1. The stage is set—The Allegiance

must now stand together and battle Metus and his evil army.

6. Death of a Hero. Jerry, trained by The Allegiance to encompass his powers, believes it is time for him to leave the organization and battle evil on his own.

7. Kale. A battle between good and evil leaves two heroes, Egotan and Cybersting not as all-powerful as they thought when they are wounded by Metus's agents.

8. Meeting of Powers. The battle did net the Allegiance a captive—Crypt, who through questioning, reveals incidents from his past that led him to becoming evil—beginning when he was a child and refused to eat his vegetables.

9. Allegiance. In the concluding episode the Allegiance must band together to fight an ever growing and increasingly evil enemy—Metus's army.

6 Almost a Turkish Soap Opera. almost aturkishsoapopera.com. 2011 (Comedy-Drama).

Adel and Kamil are friends living in Turkey and not economically stable, especially Adel. He and his family are living in poverty as a result of the mechanizations of his Grand Uncle Emre, who has manipulated the family's funds (seizing land and money left to them by their grandfather). When Adel is no longer able to abide by the conditions under which he lives (especially since his father fears standing up to his Grand Uncle to right the situation) he and Kamil embark on a journey to the U.S. to change their lives by becoming part of "The American Dream." The young men soon discover that what they heard and read about that dream is simply not handed to them on a silver platter and must earn it. The program charts their experiences, working first as shuttle cab drivers at Los Angeles International Airport, to Adel's deportation (when he is caught as an illegal alien) to their relocation to Canada where Adel discovers a way to turn the tables on his uncle and gain his rightful status—by marrying his uncle's obnoxious granddaughter (Yonka). All in all, the life of two young Turkish men whose journey to reinvent themselves almost becomes a Turkish soap opera, especially when, after marrying Yonka, Adel meets and falls in love with Nora, his English teacher.

Adel, the son of a middle-class Muslim family, lives in Istanbul and dreams of beginning a new life in America, having read of the wealth and opportunities that wait.

Kamil is Adel's best friend (since childhood). His father works as a chauffeur for Adele's Grand Uncle, making him a servant's son (although he is not treated like one by Adel and his family).

Grand Uncle (as he is called) is known as the Godfather of Istanbul. He is a greedy, selfish businessman who controls his family's money—money that rightfully belongs to Adel's spineless father.

Yonka is Adel's second cousin and the granddaughter of Adel's Grand Uncle. She is stubborn, rebellious and manipulative. Yonka moved to Canada when she was a teenager and has become so taken with the Canadian way of life that she has virtually abandoned the traditions of Turkish women.

Nora, the woman who captures Adel's heart, teaches English as a Second Language at the English Language Institute in Canada. She feels her life is heading nowhere (especially since she appears to be stuck in a boring relationship with her boss, Michael, the Academic Program Director) and dreams of traveling to exciting places.

Mirwan is Grand Uncle's underhanded, back-stabbing underling, the man who does all the dirty work.

Adel's mother is a devote Turkish woman who works hard and struggles to feed her family (of six children) as best she can on what little money they have (Adel's father works when he can in construction).

Ayca is Kamil's wife, a traditional Turkish housewife who is also like the American town gossip.

Mehmet is Kamil's friend and co-worker (in Canada); Sami is Adel's brother; Guy is Yonka's friend; Ms. Myrtle and Ms. Suarez are Nora's coworkers; Miguel is a fellow student of Adel's; Susan, Jenny and Guy work with Kamil at a hotel in Vancouver.

Cast: Jon Welch (Adel), Fatih Turan (Kamil), Kim Bennett (Nora), Donna Bonastella (Yonka), John Samaha (Grand Uncle), Seyhan Demir (Adel's father), Victoria Vice (Adel's mother), Sam Mansouri (Mirwan), Sera Malazi (Ayca), Tony Hoare (Michael), Farshad Taghizadeh-Roudposhti (Mehmet), Arif Guler (Sami), Victor Stapelberg (Guy), Drea King (Ms. Myrtle), Michelle Halldorson (Ms. Suarez), Andrew V. Cruz (Miguel), Rick Liciana (Moe), Linda McIntyre, Maki Matori (Jenny). **Credits:** *Producer:* Jospeh Khalil. *Writer-Director:* Anne-Rae Vasquez. **Comment:** The episodes play like an episode of a daily TV soap opera and are well acted (especially Grand Uncle) and produced. Although the program concludes in a cliff hanger, the doorway has been left open for more episodes to follow.

Episodes:

1. The Arrangement (6 min., 4 sec.). Grand Uncle pre-arranges a marriage between Adel and his niece, Yonka, in Canada.

2. The Wedding (4 min., 18 sec.). The marriage takes place but Adel temporarily abandons Yonka, and heads for California hoping to make enough money to get out from under his Grand Uncle's control.

3. Hollywood Here We Come (3 min., 37 sec.). Adel announces to his family that he and Kamil have decided to begin new lives in California.

4. Bad News (3 min., 17 sec.). Adel and Kamil arrive in Los Angeles and begin their search for a job. Kamil then announces he is thinking of moving to Canada to be with his family.

5. Welcome to Beverly Hills (5 min., 44 sec.). Adel and Kamil take in the sights of Beverly Hills but soon realize it was a foolish move as the money they brought with them is not going to last much longer.

6. Training Day at LA Airport (3 min., 58 sec.). Luck is with Adel and Kamil as they both acquire jobs as shuttle bus drivers at LAX Airport.

7. Adel's Lessons in Money Making (3 min., 19 sec.). Adel's enthusiasm and drive soon makes him the highest paid shuttle cab driver at the airport (seen in a training-like video).

8. Adel Meets His Hollywood Dream Girl (3 min., 59 sec.). While waiting for customers, Adel meets Nora, on vacation in Los Angeles (from Canada), and immediately falls in love with her.

9. Adel Is Arrested (3 min., 14 sec.). Adel is arrested by Immigration for residing and working in Los Angeles without the proper papers. He is deported back to Turkey, but elects to move to Canada and be with Yonka—and Nora.

7 Anacostia. webserieschannel.com. 2009–2012 (Drama).

Dramatic incidents in the lives of the citizens of Anacostia, a small residential community in Washington, D.C., where what appears on the outside (a peaceful town) only conceals its true nature where hidden secrets, deception and even murder rule and where some will stop at nothing to get what they want.

Cast: Anthony Anderson (Sean), Chante Bowser (Salina), Tamieka Chavis (Mia), Marion Akpan (Nancy), Pasha Diallo (Dominique), Kena Hodges (Nicole), Christopher Bair (Cliff), William Lash (Scott), Rabon Hutcherson (Andre), Deidra Taylor (Lashawn "Cherry" Alexander), Darnell Lamont Walker (Julian), Tia Dae (Deanna Grayson), Carey Green (Jack), Giselle Gant (Madison), Darnerien McCants (Cyrus), Tye Frazier (Brian), Tiana Harris (Ashley), Martha Byrne (Alexis Jordan), Kevin Cook (Ray), India Doy (Jennifer), Tandrea Parrott (Desiree). **Credits:** *Producer-Writer:* Anthony Anderson. *Director:* Anthony Anderson, Fran E. Jackson, Jr. **Comment:** An actual comment based on viewing is not possible but based on press release information, the program was inspired by the TV dramas *Dallas* and *Knots Landing* (and no doubt *Dynasty* and *Falcon Crest*) and appears to be more sex-oriented than its inspirations.

Episodes: All episodes have been taken off line. It appears that 30 episodes were produced although some sources indicate only 10 while others state 25. A listing follows.

Season 1: *1.* Covet Thy Neighbor. *2.* Breaking the Surface. *3.* Beware of the Fine Print. *4.* Always Bet on Black, Part 1. *5.* Always Bet on Black, Part 2. *6.* L.O.V.E. *7.* Bad Girl. *8.* You've Got the Look. *9.* Se Acerca El Final. *10.* Arrivals and Departures.

Season 2: *11.* Scar Tissue. *12.* What Will I Tell My Heart? *13.* Hello, Like Before. *14.* Wheels on the Bus. *15.* Checks and Balances. *16.* One for the Road. *17.* A House Is Not a Home. *18.* Business as Usual. *19.* Sins of the Past. *20.* And Justice for All.

Season 3: *21.* Where Do We Go From Here? *22.* Only in My Dreams. *23.* Sign Your Name. *24.* Helping Hands. *25.* The Bigger They Are. *26.* Show & Tell. *27.* The Gang's All Here. *28.* The Power of Goodbye. *29.* Break Up to Make Up. *30.* Til Death Do Us Part.

8 *And Boris.* andboris.com. 2011 (Adventure).

T.A.K.A. is a secretive unit of the U.S. government that tackles hazardous missions to ensure the safety of the country. It is composed of three members (Katerina, Peter and Charlie) and stories relate the assignments they tackle with the help of Boris Soronov, a former KGB agent turned CIA operative who is less-than enthusiastic to return to active duty as an agent for an under-staffed, under-funded organization and a sorry-looking group of operatives. While Boris is Russian and did serve with the KGB, he defected to the U.S. after his partner was killed and was recruited by the CIA to help in their operations at the time. He eventually retired and was set to live his life under the radar until his notorious nephew, Alexander, acquired a bio-chemical weapon and T.A.K.A. recruited him to help—to not only stop Alexander, but retrieve the bio weapon before it detonates and destroys Los Angeles.

Cast: J. Anthony McCarthy (Boris Soronov), Sarah Barton (Emily Holmes), Christie Insley (Katerina), Michael Proctor (Peter Mulligan), Joshua Hume (Charlie), Steven Braun (Alexander Soronov), Jenny Baek (Kimmy), Ari Levin (Snyder), Emy Coligado (Angelica), Susan Sloane (Margo), Jennifer Emily McLean (The Professor). **Credits:** *Producer-Director:* David Kronmiller. *Writer:* Jennifer Emily McLean, J. Anthony McCarthy. **Comment:** Well acted and produced program with an unlikely hero (Boris) coming out of retirement to once gain save the world—this time with a motley team of agents. The story is good and shows that heroes have flaws—like Boris when he battles the enemy but finds he is not the agent he once was. There are possibilities for more assignments but it has been several years now and that appears unlikely.

Episodes:

1. Episode 1 (10 min., 39 sec.). The team recruits Boris when it is learned his small-time Russian mobster nephew, Alexander, has acquired a bio chemical weapon.

2. The Valley and Boris (8 min., 16 sec.). Although reluctant, Boris joins the unit and finds he is a bit out of shape when it comes to dealing with the enemy. Meanwhile, Alexander has set his sights on detonating his Novochok bomb in Los Angeles.

3. Alexander and Boris (12 min., 54 sec.). The concluding first season episode that finds Boris as a full team member and out to stop Alexander and retrieve the bio-chemical weapon.

4. Season 2, Episode 1 (12 min., 49 sec.). After retrieving the weapon, the team tackles a case wherein they must find the missing daughter of a man who once fought against Boris.

5. Snyder and Boris (13 min., 14 sec.). The case becomes deadly when team member Katerina is killed and an old adversary, The Professor, enters the picture. Not only does she deal in bio weapons, but kidnapping people to sell their organs on the black market.

6. William and Boris (13 min., 18 sec.). A new agent joins the team (Emily) as the kidnapping case continues. Emily, however, has more than she can handle when she is kidnapped and brought to The Professor.

7. The Group and Boris, Part 1 (14 min., 55 sec.). Emily awakens in a room with another kidnap victim (a doctor) and learns that in a matter of hours her organs will be removed and sold to the highest bidder.

8. The Group and Boris, Part 2 (15 min., 56 sec.). The concluding episode wherein Emily finds an unexpected ally (the doctor) but The Professor and her agents appear to be more of a challenge not only for them, but for Boris and the team as they close in to stop her.

9 *Anyone but Me.* anyonebutme.com. 2008–2012 (Drama).

Vivian McMillan is a beautiful 16-year-old girl living in Manhattan. She is the daughter of Gabe, a firefighter who is suffering the after-effects (respiratory problems) of the 9/11 terrorist attacks (as he was actively involved in the Ground Zero search and recovery efforts). Vivian is also a lesbian (openly admitted) and in love with a stunning girl named Aster (whose parents are absent from her life and take little interest in what she does). Vivian's life with Aster is accepted and all is progressing well for Vivian until she is forced to move to the suburban community of Westchester (about 30 miles from Manhattan) and into the home of her aunt (Jodie) when Gabe feels it is necessary for Vivian to experience her adolescence without having to deal with the consequences of the terror attacks. Vivian's mother abandoned the family when Vivian was a young girl and Gabe, despite his failing health, had been raising Vivian alone. Now thrown into a new environment, Vivian is uncertain of her own destiny. She continues her relationship with Aster but conceals the fact of her sexuality from her aunt and those she encounters when she enrolls in Clarence High School (as she believes those around her will not accept who she really is). The program relates the various problems Vivian now encounters—from dealing with an aunt who is

finding it difficult to become a mother to her, secretly maintaining her love life with Aster and how she deals with the misconceptions she perceived when her "secret" life is slowly uncovered.

Cast: Rachael Hip-Flores (Vivian McMillan), Nicole Pacent (Aster Gaston), Jessy Hodges (Sophie), Alexis Slade (Elisabeth Matthews), Mitchell S. Adams (Jonathan Kerwin), Barbara Pitts (Jodie Nevan), Joshua Holland (Archibald Bishop), Dan Via (Gabe McMillan), Garrett Ross (Sterns), Russell Jordan (Principal Dennis), Amy Jackson Lewis (Jamie), Johnny Yoder (Breck), Helene Taylor (Mrs. Winters), Liza Weil (Dr. Glass), Marissa Skell (Carey). **Credits:** *Producer:* Susan Miller, Tina Cesa Ward, Lida Orzeck. *Director:* Tina Cesa Ward. *Writer:* Tina Cesa Ward, Susan Miller, Scott Alexander. **Comment:** Character-driven story with very good acting and production values. There are kissing scenes (but no nudity) and the program moves right along with touching moments encountered by Vivian and Aster as their relationship goes from good to bad.

Episodes:

1. Heavy Lifting (8 min., 15 sec.). Vivian and Aster face the prospect of losing each other as Vivian breaks the news to Aster that she is moving.

2. New Alliance (6 min., 16 sec.). Vivian begins classes at a new school where she meets a fellow student (Archibald) who shares her interest of drawing.

3. Countdown (8 min., 34 sec.). Vivian and Aster make plans to see each other in the city which results in them making love when Vivian stays over at Aster's apartment.

4. Vivian + Aster (9 min., 7 sec.). The scene opens with Vivian and Aster in bed together—but it is not the same as Vivian must once again leave Aster and return to her new home.

5. The Note, Part 1 (8 min., 50 sec.). As Aster begins to miss Vivian she realizes she must face a whole new world without her lover.

6. The Note, Part 2 (7 min., 52 sec.). As Aster devises a way to be with Vivian while at school, Archibald attempts to get closer to Elizabeth, a fellow student.

7. Welcome to the Party (7 min., 19 sec.). Aster, having moved to Westchester and transferred to Vivian's school, accompanies Vivian to a party.

8. Welcome to the Party, Part 2 (8 min., 18 sec.). The party aspect is continued with Aster meeting Vivian's new friends.

9. Out of the Gate (15 min., 47 sec.). The cast (out-of-character) discuss the events of the prior eight episodes.

10. Enormous Changes at the Last Minute (14 min., 14 sec.). A school field trip to the New York *Times* in Manhattan (to see the workings of a city desk) finds Vivian and Aster deserting the group for a romantic encounter.

11. The Real Thing (13 min., 4 sec.). A recap of what has happened so far.

Anyone but Me. Poster art from the series (copyright Anyone but Me, LLC, 2010).

12. Quickly, to the Exit (8 min., 17 sec.). Elizabeth and Archibald have become close but Vivian and Aster's relationship appears to be facing difficult times.

13. Identity Crisis (6 min., 27 sec.). Sophie, Vivian's friend, discovers her secret when she sees Vivian and Aster kissing.

14. Girl Talk (10 min., 10 sec.). Aster and Jodie (Vivian's aunt) spend time together with Aster revealing that she (and Vivian) are lovers.

15. One Step Forward, One Step Back (7 min., 48 sec.). Vivian confronts Aster about revealing the fact that she is a lesbian to her aunt.

16. The Things We Know (9 min., 39 sec.). Sophie, understanding Vivian's love for Aster, reveals that she too had a romantic encounter with an older man (a teacher named Ben).

17. Date Night (7 min., 23 sec.). Vivian and Aster attempt to salvage their relationship, which is slowly breaking up now that Vivian's sexuality is known.

18. Naming Things (10 min., 20 sec.). Vivian, a writer for the school newspaper (*The Gazette*) and Archibald devise a comic strip for the paper that will reveal the lives of students as if they were in an alternate universe.

19. Private Rooms and Public Spaces (9 min., 3 sec.). Gabe invites Jodie to Manhattan to meet his firemen friends while Aster, having previously been in therapy to control her attitude, returns to her therapist (Dr. Glass) for help in saving her relationship with Vivian.

20. Curtain's Up (9 min., 59 sec.). The first issue of Vivian and Archibald's comic is printed and seen by students as "a lesbian and a black dude trying to save the world" (with Vivian as "The Lesbian Reporter Chick"). Meanwhile, Archibald becomes interested in Elizabeth's acting ambitions by helping her rehearse for a school play.

21. Stick Figures (7 min., 53 sec.). Vivian, having used incidents from her past to create the comic strip, finds that those memories are now manifesting themselves and causing her to now face things she had tried to forget.

22. Far Away (12 min., 17 sec.). As Aster and Vivian's relationship appears to be on the verge of collapse, Aster feels it is best if she and Vivian stop seeing each other. Shortly after, Aster, now in Los Angeles, meets a beautiful college student (Carey) who becomes attracted to her.

23. Something Old, Something New (8 min., 57 sec.). Sophie's secret comes to light when Ben approaches her in the school hallway, concerned about their one night stand and that if she is okay. Meanwhile, Carey, on a week-long school break, invites Aster to her dorm room. It is at this time that Vivian learns that Ben is Sophie's secret affair.

24. Mapping Home (8 min., 43 sec.). It is a week later and Aster feels that even though she and Carey were intimate, she still has feelings for Vivian.

25. 2,500 Miles to You (9 min., 41 sec.). Aster returns to Westchester hoping to rekindle her love for Vivian.

26. We Went Down to Battery Park (10 min., 3 sec.). Vivian and Aster confront their past to work for a future together in the concluding episode.

10 *Are Fishy Little Secret.* youtube.com. 2013 (Comedy-Drama).

When cousins Brooke and Ember decide to go swimming they do so in a public pool. Unknown to them, the treated water is special to them and activates a recessed Mermaid gene. While nothing happens at first, it is when they return home and come in contact with water that they transform into Mermaids. Now, with no choice but to encompass what they have become, Brooke and Ember must conceal their secret identities and learn to lead lives as normal school girls.

Cast (as credited): Bridgette (Brooke), Rachel (Ember). **Credits** are not given. **Comment:** Typical of virtually all the Internet Mermaid series: poor sound and photography although the young girls handle their roles well.

Episodes:

1. Episode 1 (5 min., 14 sec.). The story line is established as Ember and Brooke become Mermaids.
2. Episode 2 (6 min., 43 sec.). Ember and Brooke encounter an unusual adventure when they are whisked back in time to the 1800s and must find a way to return to the present.

11 *Ariana Mermaids.* youtube.com. 2014 (Comedy-Drama).

Kimi, a mysterious young girl (a Mermaid) with what appears to be an unnatural fear of water and the full moon, transfers to a new school where she meets two girls, Aubree and Marina. The girls quickly become friends, but unknown to Aubree and Marina, they have come under a spell that enhances Kimi. The spell magically transports Aubree and Marina to Kimi's backyard swimming pool and like Kimi, are transformed into Mermaids—and into a world where they must protect their secret while also attempting to lead normal lives as typical school girls.

Cast (as credited): Jillian (Aubree Henshaw), Isa (Marina Anderson), Jae (Kimi O'Connor). **Credits** are not given. **Comment:** Only one episode has thus far been produced. The sound and photography are poor but the project does show potential for some intrigue as the girls cope with what has happened to them.

Episodes:

1. A New Tail. The pilot film that establishes the series story line as Aubree and Marina discover their new friend is a Mermaid.

12 *The Arksville Homicides.* snobbyrobot. com. 2013 (Animated Thriller).

Arksville, a small town in Pennsylvania tucked away in its forests and thriving on tourism is suddenly plagued by a series of unexplained and horrific murders. The residents are on edge and the police department's top detective, Mike Eidalman, has been assigned to find the killer. The program charts Mike's seemingly fruitless investigation as the further he digs, the more mysterious it becomes with his belief being that the killer is far more sinister and could be something beyond this world.

Mike is a seasoned, rather grizzled cop and is currently a Lieutenant. He is a family man, devoted to his community and often takes unnecessary risks.

Frank Wepps is a police Sergeant (married to Lucy and the father of Patricia) whose career was almost ruined in an arrest that went bad. But it was that mistake that has reinforced his goal to continue in his job and see that criminals are put behind bars.

Rick Hoffman is the Police Captain who is looked upon by fellow officers as a father figure as well as their leader.

Margaret Hurston is a reporter for the town's newspaper, *The Arksville Telegraph*. While she is struggling to make her mark in the male-dominated field, she often takes risks to acquire stories and has joined with Mike in tracking down the mysterious killer that is stalking the town.

Jimmy Luciano is the local crime boss, not as powerful as the big city bosses, but who will achieve his goals by any means he can.

Father William Langston is the town's parish priest, who cares for his parishioners, is devoted to his religion, but hides a mysterious past.

Voice Cast: Lewis Roscoe (Lt. Mike Eidalman), Chriss Anglin (Sgt. Frank Wepps), Dallas Barnett (Capt. Rick Hoffman), Natalie Beran (Margaret Hurston), Barry Duffield (Jimmy Luciano), Steven Richards (Father William Langston), Anna Hewett (Patricia Wepps), Jennifer Bainbridge (Lucy Wepps). **Credits:** *Producer-Writer-Director:* Lewis Roscoe. **Comment:** Computer (CGI) animated project that has life-like characters in a well plotted story that holds interest.

Episodes:

1. Prologue (3 min., 32 sec.). Explores the history of Arksville, which dates back to the Spanish explorer Francisco Vasquez de Coronado when, under orders from the Vatican, was charged with finding the most remote spot on earth and bury a mysterious box (presumably containing evil) where it could never be found. He chose would be eventually become Arksville.

2. Arrival and Murder (5 min., 53 sec.). As the Wepps family head for Arksville, hoping to begin a new life, mysterious happenings are beginning to affect the town.

13 *L'Assassin.* webserieschannel.com. 2013 (Action).

The hits performed by a nameless Assassin who shows little compassion for the targets he is assigned.

Cast: Shing Ka (Assassin), Spawn (James). The following performers do not appear in the program, but are credited on the website: Tsveta Dimova, Tak

Wah Eng, Joe Chan. **Credits:** *Producer:* Shing Ka, Douglas A. Ferguson. *Writer-Director:* Douglas A. Ferguson. **Comment:** Filmed in black and white and rather talkative (complete with foul language). The "action" is a dinner conversation between the Assassin and his target (James) with the viewer left to wonder will he or won't he shoot him. It is difficult to judge the program based on only one episode being produced. Although it is tagged as an action series, there is none and could suffer if additional episodes are planned and follow the same premise. Web material indicates that James was killed and that the Assassin is now on the run, being pursued by a detective who was also a friend of the victim (episodes however, have not yet been released).

Episodes:
1. Dinner with a Friend (9 min., 53 sec.). The Assassin's target: His former partner and childhood friend.

14 *Assassin's Creed: Lineage.* youtube.com. 2009 (Adventure).

A three-part French-Canadian series produced as a prequel to the video game *Assassin's Creed II* that is set in 15th century Renaissance Italy. It tells of an assassin (Giovanni Auditore, the father of the game's principal character, Ezio Auditire da Firenze), as he attempts to stop a plot by enemies of the powerful Medici family (the Borgias) from overthrowing them and destroying a unified Italy.

Cast: Romano Orzari (Giovanni Auditore), Manuel Tadros (Rodrigo Borgia), Claudia Ferri (Maria Auditore), Jesse Rath (Federico Auditore), Devon Bostick (Ezio Auditore), Alex Ivanovici (Lorenzo de' Medici), Michel Perron (Uberto Alberti), Arthur Grosser (Pope Sixtus IV), Shawn Baichoo (Father Antonio Maffei), Peter Miller (Galeazzo Maria Sforza), Harry Standjofsky (Silvio Barbarigo), Frank Fontaine (Marco Barbarigo). **Credits:** *Producer:* Serge Hascoet, Yannis Mallat, Yves Guillemot. *Director:* Yves Simineau. *Writer:* William Reymond, Yves Simineau.

Comment: Authentic costumes and scenery (accomplished through green screen technology) highlight a program that is actually a promotional gimmick for its producing company, Ubisoft, to break into film making.

Episodes:
1. Episode 1. The fact is established that in Florence (1476) as the Renaissance grows, the city is also plagued by corruption, betrayal and murder and an overwhelming desire by the Borgia family to become its leaders. On behalf of Lorenzo de' Medici, Giovanni begins his quest to bring down his enemies, especially the power-hungry Rodrigo Borgia.
2. Episode 2. A shift in power occurs when the Duke of Milan is assassinated and Giovanni, who was unable to stop it, seeks the culprit, which also brings him closer to a face-to-face confrontation with Rodrigo.

3. Episode 3. In Venice, Rodrigo, head of the Barbarigos, prepares himself for battle; it is learned that Lorenzo's refusal to bow to Pope Sixtus IV's authority and live by the Church's rules, is what started the conflict. The Pope has spiritually aided Rodrigo in his effort to restore order in Florence and dethrone the de' Medici family. While a confrontation does ensue and Giovanni is wounded (and recovers) the program ends unresolved (with the message, "The conclusion ... is in your hands") thus leaving the doorway open for the video game Assassin's Creed II.

15 *Atarax.* ataraxthewebseries.com. 2013 (Crime Drama).

The killing of a girl (Kait) has an affect on two men: Carter, his sister and Sid, her fiancé, police detectives who have vowed to find her killer and the reason why. Although it appears the girl did not use drugs or was involved with them, she may have been the target of a drug addict or mistaken for someone else. The program relates Carter and Sid's hell-bent-on-revenge efforts to find a killer by doing whatever it takes, including breaking every rule in the book. The title refers to a rare condition that strips a person (Carter in this case) of an ability to show emotion no matter what situation they face.

Cast: Ryan Garcia (Carter), David Crane (Sid), Ernest Briggs (Teddy), Amanda Wing (Kait), Rhyan Shwartz (Ian), Greg Wyszynski (Hank). **Credits:** *Producer-Writer-Director:* Christopher Lee.

Comment: The definition of Atarax that appears before each episode begins helps (especially in the first episode) to know why Carter is so unaffected emotionally by what is happening around him. The acting and production values are good, but the program is rather violent and contains strong language.

Episodes:
1. Episode 1 (Pilot, Parts 1 and 2; 9 min., 47 sec.). The storyline is established with Carter and Sid beginning their investigation into Kait's mysterious death.
2. Episode 3 (6 min., 30 sec.). Linking Kait's murder to a local drug dealer (Ian), Carter and Sid set up a sting operation in an effort to get the evidence they need.
3. Episode 4 (6 min., 40 sec.). The concluding, unresolved episode, wherein Carter and Sid find questionable responses after talking to Ian leading them to conclude that the mystery is more complex than they originally thought.

16 *B.J. Fletcher, Private Eye.* bjfletcherprivateeye.com. 2008–2012 (Crime Drama).

Beatrix Jane (B.J.) Fletcher is a pretty but somewhat lonely young woman. She is a lesbian and has a girlfriend (Georgia "George" Drew") a bartender at Milligan's Bar, who looks out for her simply because B.J. will not do it herself. B.J. works as a private detective, but charges only eight dollars an hour for her services. She wishes for cases that would bring a higher income, but such cases never seem to come her way. Stories follow B.J. as she and her self-proclaimed assistant (and lover) Georgia acquire cases—and attempt to solve them with as little fanfare as possible.

Cast: Lindy Zucker (B.J. Fletcher), Dana Puddicombe (Georgia Drew), Vanessa Dunn (Jenna Watson), Karim Morgan (Joe Magnum), Natasha Gordon (Marjorie Matlock), Jonathan Thomas (Doyle), Sean Tasson (Louis), Maria Heidler (Mrs. Watson), Patricia Yeatman (Mrs. Drew), Stewart Dowling (Dominic Christie), Kimwun Perehinec (Samantha Steele), Stavroula Logothettis (Katerina Kinsey), Kesta Graham (Christine, the Baker). **Credits:** *Producer:* Regan Latimer, Rochell Dancel *Director:* Regan Latimer. *Writer:* Regan Latimer, Alys Latimer. **Comment:** A light-hearted, enjoyable approach to crime solving with a lesbian theme. There are scenes of affection (including kissing) but nothing that is objectionable. The program is well acted and filmed and the cases interesting. Well worth watching.

Episodes:

1. Episode 1. A girl from B.J.'s past—her ex-girlfriend, Marjorie Matlock, hires B.J. to uncover the source of a leak in her office that has been supplying information to her competitors.

2. Episode 2. B.J. and Georgia begin their investigation of case they call "Agatha and her Leaky Empire."

3. Episode 3. B.J.'s questioning of Marjorie leads her to believe that she is more involved in the case than she is letting on.

4. Episode 4. Just as B.J. and Georgia resolve their first televised case, B.J. finds little time for herself when she is hired by a wife (Marilyn) to discover if her photographer husband (Dominic) is cheating on her.

5. Episode 5. B.J., accompanied by Georgia, begins her investigation of a case they call "Mr. Christie and His Wandering Aperture."

6. Episode 6. Posing as a model, Georgia goes undercover at Dominic's studio in an attempt to get the goods on him.

7. Episode 7. B.J.'s plan to entrap Dominic doesn't go as planned. With Georgia's life now in danger, B.J. asks her friend, police detective Joe Magnum for assistance.

B.J. Fletcher, Private Eye. **Lindy Zucker (left) and Dana Puddicombe (copyright Bee Chamber Productions, 2014).**

8. Episode 8. Dominic is exposed and the case is solved, but soon thereafter, B.J. acquires something more in line with her sexuality when she takes on the case of "The Little Lost Lesbian: Run, Jenna, Run."

9. Episode 9. B.J.'s attempt to find the missing daughter (Jenna Watson) of a local politician's wife places her and Georgia in a dangerous situation when they become involved in a game of dirty politics.

10. Episode 10. B.J. and Georgia discover they have competition from two men (Doyle, B.J.'s old nemesis, and his partner Louis) who are seeking to find Jenna first (to expose her as a lesbian and hopefully ruin her father's political career).

11. Episode 11. The case concludes and takes an unexpected turn when Jenna is found and she and Georgia become attracted to each other.

12. Episode 12. Before accepting another case ("Mrs. Lacey and Her Hidden Gems") B.J. and Georgia reflect on their relationship now that another woman has entered the picture (Jenna). After B.J. and Georgia discover that gems were stolen by a bicycle-napping gang, they host a dinner party for the gang in an effort to uncover more information.

13. Episode 13. At the party, B.J. and Georgia's investigation reveals that the gang has an affiliation with the local mafia.

14. Episode 14. B.J. and Georgia's discovery places them in extreme danger. Unknowingly they are being observed by Joe Magnum (who becomes their rescuer).

15. Episode 15. As Jenna and Georgia grow closer, B.J. tackles a case called "Bitter Batter at the Dip 'n' Sip Bakery" (wherein she is hired to find a saboteur whose actions are threatening to close a bakery).

16. Episode 16. As clues to the saboteur's identity become increasingly slimmer, Georgia recruits Jenna's help on the case.

17. Episode 17. Jenna's assistance helps resolve the case but B.J. appears to becoming a bit jealous over her and Georgia's relationship, especially when she learns Georgia and Jenna are going to luncheon with each other's mother (Maria Heidler and Patricia Yeatman).

18. Episode 18. The case of "Wheelings and Dealings at the Watson Warehouse" finds B.J. and Georgia becoming involved with the mafia and stolen diamonds.

19. Episode 19. B.J. becomes angered when she learns that Doyle (her nemesis) is responsible for the theft of the diamonds and has put her and Georgia's life in jeopardy.

20. Episode 20. Discovering that Doyle (and his mafia associates) has captured B.J., Georgia and Jenna begin a race against time to save her.

21. Episode 21. With B.J. rescued and the diamonds recovered, B.J. next becomes involved with the case of "The Elusive Husband of Katarina Kinsey" (wherein she and Georgia seek a missing—and elusive husband [Frank]).

22. Episode 22. As B.J. and Georgia continue their investigation, an outside investigator (Samantha Steele) becomes part of the case—and a source of concern for Georgia, whose plans for the future could change her relationship with Jenna and B.J.

23. Episode 23. Finding the elusive husband (Frank) begins to take its toll on B.J. and Georgia as tracking him down has become more of a problem than they previously thought.

24. Episode 24. Georgia's future plans (moving to England) have her a bit on edge during a stakeout in which she and B.J. hope to capture Frank.

25. Episode 25. The concluding episode wherein the case is solved but what will become of B.J. and Georgia's relationship as Georgia prepares to leave for England is left unresolved.

17 Bad Tara. webserieschannel.com. 2012 (Thriller).

A beautiful young Asian woman, known only as Bad Tara, is a woman of mystery. She is a ruthless, vengeful gangster (possibly an ex-mob member) whose fierce reputation has earned her the nickname "Bad." Tara appears to want to break ties with the mob, but she is too well connected and that does not appear to be an option. While she tries to live under the radar, circumstances force her to deal with problems (usually helping someone in trouble) that brings her above ground and not only makes her a crusader, but angers the mob bosses who would like to silence her. Tara is first seen as a young girl in 1977, where she shows signs of being a rebel, wanting to do what she wants to do, not being told what to do. For the actual program, it is 2012 when Tara is seen as a

seemingly ordinary woman (although working as a debt collector for persons unknown) until she becomes involved with the wife of a murder victim (Maria) and her own plight to avoid becoming a target of the mob.

Cast: Celia Au (Bad Tara), Mya Lazar (Kitty Kat), Terri-Ann Peters (Pamela Reid), Shing Ka (Mr. One), Annemijn Nieuwkoop (Jennifer Entin), Princess Lam (Young Tara), Molly Ebasu (Young Kitty). **Credits:** *Producer-Writer-Director:* Julio Thillet. **Comment:** Fast-moving program with good acting and production values. The lead (Celia Au) however, appears too young for the role (based on the flashback to 1977 wherein Tara was 8 or 9 years old, Tara would be in her early 40s in 2012; Celia looks to be in her early 20s).

Episodes:

1. They're Trying to Kill You Bad Tara (9 min., 2 sec.). The story begins as Tara becomes involved in a murder (of Rodrigo Perez) and finds herself being sought by the police as the killer.

2. Bad Tara Needs Answers (13 min., 10 sec.). Tara's predicament takes a turn for the worse when she is shot by members of Mr. Tone's mob, who believe she possesses something that could destroy them (a computer disk).

3. Bad Tara Gotta See Mr. Tone (12 min., 13 sec.). The disk, made by Rodrigo (who double-crossed the mob) is now possessed by his widow (Maria). Fearing for her life, Maria contacts Tara for help.

4. Bullets Fly (8 min., 5 sec.). Tara, now in possession of the disk, seeks a way to clear her name before Mr. Tone takes her out. Meanwhile, rival mob leader, the Mysterious White Lady (Jennifer Entin) takes an interest and has Tara followed.

5. The Wild Rabbit (13 min., 22 sec.). Tara confronts Jennifer to make a deal to end the contract on her life in the concluding episode.

18 Bad to the Jones. badtothejones.com. 2011 (Action).

An unexplained virus ("a class 4 outbreak" but of what?) has turned people into zombie-like creatures and survivors must now battle a new enemy to survive. Craig and Tyrone Jones are two such survivors, brothers who have lost track of their sister and must now find her before she becomes one of the affected. The program follows Craig and Tyrone as they begin their search, destroying what gets in their way as they are not only bad to the bone "but bad to the Jones."

Cast: Marlon Ladd (Craig Jones), Chris Paul (Tyrone Jones), Cara Black (Laila), Philip Borghee (Mario), Jude Cutter (Ricci Jett), Kelly Edwards (Gretchen Jones), Kenneth Nolan (Daniel Jones), Nothemba Huddleston (Lareefa), Will Jordan (Dennis). **Credits:** *Producer:* Weston Denny, Andrea Jarman. *Writer-Director:* Marlon Ladd. **Comment:** The brothers are argumentative; there is violence, vulgar language and numerous zombies. But for some unknown reason the program is not tagged as a horror series, but as an action-adventure. It is an African-American production that, based on the first episode, will be an action-adventure. The acting and production values are good and the cliff-hanging first episode leaves the viewer to wonder how the brothers will ever escape a horde of approaching zombies.

Episodes:

1. The Black Horizon (10 min.). Establishes a story line wherein the brothers are Midwest zombie hunters just struggling to survive the chaos that surrounds them.

19 Badge Ladies. youtube.com. 2009 (Drama).

Billed as "Inside the Lady Cops Division of the N.Y.P.D." that is presented like a documentary with the two very attractive police women addressing the camera to discuss aspects of their police work.

Cast: Janie Haddad (Off. Haddad), Samantha McIntire (Off. McIntire). **Comment:** The title is a bit deceiving as one would expect to see two sexy ladies battling evil. What results is an interesting take on normal female-oriented crime dramas with discussions as opposed to the squad car chases, shootouts, investigations and arrests.

Episodes:

1. Episode 1 (2 min., 51 sec.). Haddad and McIntire (as they are seen in identifying titles) discuss how each became a police officer.

2. Episode 2 (2 min., 1 sec.). Each reveals aspects of arrest cases in which they were active participants.

3. Episode 3 (2 min., 2 sec.). What each requires of the other as being partners is discussed.

4. Episode 4 (3 min., 22 sec.). The women discuss the first cases to which they were assigned.

5. Episode 5 (2 min., 16 sec.). How each woman sees the justice system is revealed.

6. Episode 6 (2 min., 2 sec.). Haddad and McIntire discuss their working and personal relationships.

20 The Bannen Way. webserieschannel.com. 2009–2010 (Crime Drama).

Neal Bannen, the son of a police chief (Bannen) and the nephew of a mob boss (Mr. B.) grew up to become a man who strayed from the justice side of the family to embellish the benefits of the criminal side as a con artist. Neal is addicted to gambling, has a weakness for women and sincerely wants to change his life around and become a decent citizen. Fate, however, will prevent that from happening as he has incurred a huge gambling debt (to Sonny Carr) that, to pay off, he must perform one last assignment for Mr. B.: retrieve a mysterious box to cancel his debt. The program follows Neal as he enlists the help of a beautiful thief (Madison), and a technical wizard (Zeke) to accomplish his goal.

Cast: Mark Gantt (Neal Bannen), Vanessa Marcil (Madison), Robert Forster (Mr. B.), Michael Ironside (Chief Bannen), Gabriel Tigerman (Zeke), Ski Carr (Sonny Carr), Michael Lerner (The Mensch). **Credits:** *Producer:* Bailey Williams. *Director:* Jesse Warren. *Writer:* Jesse Warren, Mark Gantt. **Comment:** Fast-moving story that is well produced (Sony Pictures Television is behind it) with some familiar TV faces (Michael Ironside, Vanessa Marcil, Robert Forster and Michael Lerner). The acting is above par for an Internet series and worth watching as an above-average crime story.

Episodes:

1. The Criminal Lifestyle. A serious losing streak in a poker game forces Neal to perform an assignment for Sonny to pay off a gambling debt: steal $100,000.

2. The Offer. Getting wind of what his nephew is up to, Mr. B. offers Neal one million dollars to steal a mysterious box.

3. The Third Strike. Neal begins planning his heist with the help of Madison and Zeke.

4. The Proposition. Things begin to turn sour when Sonny learns what Neal is up to and wants "a piece of the action."

5. The Assassin Trio. "The Box Job," as it is called, takes another turn for the worse when Neal learns that a trio of three beautiful assassins is out to stop him.

6. The Unpaid Debt. Sonny's continued "vested interest" in Neal (wanting his money) could complicate "The Box Job."

7. The Prep Day. As Neal eludes Sonny and his threats, he, Madison and Zeke, plan the final stages of the heist.

8. The Sex Party. Neal, Madison and Zeke begin their caper by infiltrating a party in the home where the box is kept—and where one of the three beautiful assassins is also waiting.

9. The Bait. Neal's plans are foiled when he is recognized by the first assassin (Brynn Thayer) while, at a club to drown his sorrows, Neal encounters the second assassin (Autumn Reeser).

10. The Chase. As Neal escapes the clutches of the assassin, it is leaned that Madison had managed to steal the box—but she is not as free as she thinks when she encounters the third assassin (Brianne Davis).

11. The Drop. With the illegal side of the law closing in on him, Neal decides to play it straight.

12. The Rivalry. Neal's decision opens old wounds as his father and uncle have a confrontation.

13. The Grudge. Sonny, acquiring the box from the assassin who persuaded Madison to give it to her, returns it to Neal.

14. The Family Secret. Information regarding the Bannen family history is revealed.

15. The Truth. Neal learns additional information about his father when he is summoned by Mr. B.

16. The New Bannen. "The Box Caper" has

changed Neal's life and now, with a new start, seeks to remain above the law and start a new life (if he can).

21 *Barbie: Water Tails*. youtube.com. 2012 (Drama).

The Mattel series of Barbie Dolls are encompassed to explore the life of Lizzie, a teenage girl who attends Miami Day School and who, though not very much liked by the other girls at school (through unflattering rumors spread by Chrissy) finds her life changing forever when, during a hike in the woods, she stumbles upon a glowing object and is transported to an enchanted, glass-like cave. As Lizzie explores her surroundings, she is drawn to and swims in its waters. At that exact moment, rays from the moon enter the cave and illuminate the water. Magically she is transported back home and appears to be unaffected—at first. She soon learns that her experience in the woods was extraordinary, perhaps supernatural as her first contact with water (taking a bath) transforms her into a beautiful Mermaid—something that boosts Lizzie's self confidence and makes her more respectful of who she is—but a self-confidence that only appears when she is a Mermaid. The program follows Lizzie as she struggles to adjust to a new (and secret) life while also trying to live her normal life—at school and at home with a "Barbie psycho freak" mother and her younger sister Kassidy.

Voice Cast: Lizzie Summers (Lizzie/Narrator; Kassidy), Chrissy Carson (Chrissy), Louis Summers, Jason Shaw. **Credits** (as listed): *Writer-Director:* Kenzie. **Comment:** Lizzie Summers' voice is captivating and she does make the series work. She also handles the dolls and her pain as Lizzie can be felt by the viewer. With the actual Barbie Dolls as "the stars," it does present something different and it does come with a parental warning as it is not a comedy series but a dramatic look at real problems faced by teenage girls (although told through dolls) from eating disorders (possessed by Lizzie) to bullying and romance (it also warns against the hazards of swimming with marine life without supervision).

Episodes: Only a handful of episodes remain on line (the exact number of produced episodes is unknown) and the list is as follows: *1.* Mysterious Waters. *2.* Safety First. *3.* The Chosen Ones. *4.* Thank You. *5.* Blown Away. *6.* The End of the Tail.

22 *Bay State*. sidereel.com. 1991–Present (Drama).

Fictional Beacon Hill College in Boston provides the setting for a look at college life—not just on its students and their academic achievements, but on its "back-stabbing, angst-ridden students." Borrowing aspects from the TV soap operas of the day (including *The Guiding Light*, *As the World Turns*, *All My Children* and *Days of Our Lives*) Bay State holds the record as not only being the earliest Internet drama, but the longest-running, continually broadcast student produced soap opera.

Cast: Michelle Sammartino (Brooke Shepard Taylor), Chris Bell (Davis), Victoria Price (Grace), Emily Africk (Alexis), Kelsey Labrot (Jamie), Wendy Seyb (Miranda Davis), Valentina Monte (Olivia), Liz Breen (Whitney), Jenn Ficarra (Robin), Madison Durbin (Mason), Tom Rotolo (Scott Taylor), Erika Brannan (Laura Surrett), Joan Ritchey (Leigh Capetta), Graeme Rattray (Russell Wilson), Bill McGlynn (Jeff Corbin), Len Webber (Marc Schiffer), James Simone (Sebastian), Gus Herrera (Max), Joshua Clark (Nick), Alex Hawley (Kyle), Rebecca Boll (Paige Davenport), Laura Montorio (Claire), Cody Brotter (Zack), Leah Garvin (Jess), Alex DeLeon (Ethan), Brian Latimer (Jacob), Alex Verlage (Declan), Michael Apgar (Ben), Melody Tran (Camryn), Audrey Reuben (Nora), Donna Williams (Danielle Clark), Amanda Garant (Bailey), Sean Collins (Asher Forbes), Andrew Smith (Sean Lawrence), Angelica Allen (Michelle), Farrell Parker (Mercedes), Brian Reichelt (Eric Martin), Timothy Shivers (Brandon), Lindsey Mann (Britney), Chloe Director (Lily), Rasila Schroeder (Sonja Campbell), Wendy Stewart (Naomi Chapman), Elisabeth Apton (Cassie Roman), Charles Heinemann (Max), Lee Rohrlich (Stephen), Wilson Cleveland (Jason Davenport), Suzanne Sorenson (Mallory), Brian Forte (Brock), Madelyn Strubelt (Ava), David Zamojski (Dr. Rotolo), Daniel James Blundell (Aaron), John Battaglino (President Dixon), Malia Moses (Marisa), Joshua Guite (Adam York), Carrie Pine (Avery Sands), Julia Gaynor (C.J. Dixon), Felipe Barraza (Felipe), Sarah Hartshorne (Samantha), Michelle Ellsworth (Sydney), Neil Anand (Hudson), Amanda Chivil (Blair), Jon Mayer (Trent), Roy Nygaard (Tyler Hawkins), Vail Schwarz (Marlena), Doris Jean (Meridian), Yolanda Vazquez (Kendal Foxmoore), Roman Graure (Alex Paley), Philip J. Tavares (Vincenzo Estante), Rich Southwick (Kyle Highland), Annie Dow (Emily), Danny Laplaza (Nik), Matt Maguire (Adrian), Melissa Abraham (Bethany Marshall), Terry McCrossan (Pierce), Lewis Barlow (Leo Capetta), Caitlin O'Neal (Tyler), Joe Sobalo, Jr. (Hunter), Christopher Soucey (Tyler Hawkins), Michael Butvinik (Derrick), Sandra Piha (Paige Davenport), Cara Shockley (Dr. Mara Wilkins), Anjua Warfield-Maximo (Devon Jones), Jarman Day-Bohn (James), Morgan Tara (Nina), Emilie Soghomonian (Genny), Kellie Terese Walker (Elaine), Paul Akl (Trent), Alex Reed (Dante), Claire Wasserman (Gail), Evan Tuohey (Richard), Craig Gering (Adam York), Elizabeth Leslie (Laura Surrett), Shannon Ennis (Shannon Brock), Elicia Eddington, Colleen Murray (Channing Brooks), Brian Feller (Davis Sands), Ian Bascetta, Britten West (Ian), Amanda Stanilla (Tracy Donovan), Jay Butler (Jake), Clay Cahoon (Alex Harris), John Ford Noonan (Cater James), David Riedel (Brian Herrerra), Jennifer

Dykes (Emma), Cat Markman (Jennifer Baines), Joah Wingate (Jackson Holligan), Jeff Farrow (Jordan Katz), Elizabeth Hope (Hope Sutton), Bebe Butler, Pilar Flynn (Marissa Lawson), Jane Gaffney (Ryan Hart), Linda Said (Kate Meadows), Doug Jaeger (Peter), Michelle Nishikawa (Marlena), Barbara Silva, Lara Nyman (Cassie Roman), Jennifer Waldorf (Elke Sinclair), Jim Eshom (Damon Atkins), Steven Lekowicz (Greg Harmon), Meghan McGuire (Jacqueline Lawson), Justin Kutcher (Foster Campbell), Megan Linder (Sarah), Nicole Rosenberg (Melissa), Hannah Burns (Maya), Zach Coseglia (Andy Miller), Elizabeth Tyson (Diana Shotlen), Jason Nadler (Craig), Erica Gerard (Skyler), Lauren McLaughlin (Rena Tyler), Matt Amore (Dennis), Ethan Clay (Will), Frances Cosico (Erica). **Credits:** *Producer:* Jac Woods, Delaina A. Dixon, Haewon Yom, Kim Mackey, Kristen McKittrick, Joshua Patrick Brown, Erin Conley, Maddie Staszak, Conrad Golovac, Melissa Raffalow, Lee Anne Carluccio, Arestia Rosenberg, Amanda Brown, Ryan Schreiner, Matt Cohen,Tom Rotolo, Catherine Burns, Molly Randall, David Kalbeitzer, Kate Spencer, Elizabeth Tyson. *Director:* David Foucher, Rachel Smith, Erin Forrest, Liz Olenski, Conrad Golovac, Jac Woods, Joshua Patrick Brown, Jenn Carroll, Liz Alfonso, Anthony Cifone, Chris Clemente, Maddie Staszak, Greg Fleming, Ryan Schreiner, Sam Hayes, Mike Lupia, Tessa Olson, Danny Laplaza, Gemma Vardy, Devin Silberfein, Ryan Berdan, Arestia Rosenberg. *Writer:* Tom Rotolo, Haewon Yom, Delaina A. Dixon, Dan Spiegel, Anthony Cifone, Joshua Patrick Brown, Nate Suri, Grace DeVuono, Jenn Carroll, Michele Farbman, Neil Swart, Hillary Richonne, Ariel Levine, Liz Breen, Jenn Ficarra, Mike Lupia, Zoe Owens, Evan Tuohey, Michael Shapiro, Michael Apgar, Rachel Appelle, Isabel Shanahan, Keya Vakil, Catherine Burns, Carrie Regan, Hiko Mitsuzuka, Lynley Kozinski, Michelle Kohanloo, Josh Fox. **Comment:** With a tag-line like "Sex, drugs and murder," *Bay State* has covered virtually everything possible story line wise and, over the years has had many students perform and write and direct episodes (the cast and credits listing represents what information still appears on line). And, just like TV soap operas, *Bay State* has its share of good and bad episodes, although many produced episodes are no longer viewable (as seen by the episode listing). The program has also become a favorite of TV soap opera stars and many, such as *Days of Our Lives* stars Kristian Alfonso, Alison Sweeney, Austin Peck and Lisa Rinna have appeared as guests on the program.

Episodes: Following is a list of known episodes.

Season 1 (1991): *1.* In the Beginning. *2.* Truth and Consequences. *3.* Unpleasant Encounters. *4.* Final Confrontations.

Season 2 (1991–1992): *1.* Sex, Lies and Video Tape. *2.* Dangerous Liaisons. *3.* Life of the Party. *4.* Party Games. *5.* Another Fine Mess. *6.* A Turn for the Worse. *7.* The Plot Thickens. *8.* Calm Before the Storm. *9.* Till Death Do Us Part.

Season 3 (1992–1993): *1.* Rising from the Ashes. *2.* Strange Bedfellows. *3.* Lights, Camera, Action. *4.* Exit Stage Left. *5.* Disquiet on the Set. *6.* Haunted by the Past. *7.* Hide and Seek. *8.* Mirror, Mirror. *9.* Reunion. *10.* Finale.

Season 4 (1993): Unknown.

Season 5 (1994): *1.* To Tell the Truth. *2.* Double Trouble.

Seasons 6–16 (1994–2006): Unknown.

Season 17 (2007): *1.* Rebound. *2.* Red All Over. *3.* Blow Out. *4.* Feel Your Pain. *5.* Still Dreaming.

Season 18 (2008): *1.* Leave It All Behind. *2.* While You Were Sleeping. *3.* Love Me Not. *4.* All's Fair. *5.* Loose Ends.

Season 19 (2009): *1.* Second Chances. *2.* The Celluloid Closet. *3.* Et' Tu, Brute? *4.* Expose, Showdown.

Season 20 (2009–2010): *1.* Too Late. *2.* We Can Go to My Room. *3.* Keep It Together. *4.* Out of Sight Haunted. *5.* Redemption,

Season 21 (2010–2011): *1.* No Big Deal. *2.* Smashed. *3.* Blood Ties. *4.* Hold It Against Me. *5.* Blood on the Moon. *6.* From the Ashes.

Season 22 (2011–2012): *1.* Lift Off. *2.* Mind Eraser. *3.* Practically Tragic. *4.* Dazed. *5.* New Beginnings. *6.* Have a Nice Life.

Season 23 (2012–2013): *1.* A New Pledge. *2.* A Change in Tide. *3.* Winter Is Coming. *4.* Playing with Fire. *5.* Checkmate. *6.* A Cinderella Story.

Season 24 (2013): *1.* Family Matters. *2.* The Big Fish. *3.* Beers and Fears.

23 Beacon Hill. beconhilltheseries.com. 2014 (Drama).

Sara Preston, a young woman working as a reporter in New York City, suddenly finds her life changing when her grandfather, Senior Massachusetts Senator William Preston, suffers a stroke and she returns home to Boston after a six year absence to be with her family: Claire, a mother who finds comfort in alcohol; Eric, her brother; and, to her surprise, William's much younger wife, Evelyn, a woman who is as ruthless as William. Stories, presented in the serial style of television soap operas (like *The Young and the Restless*) portray the events that spark Sara's life—from a former lover (Katherine, now a State Representative seeking a Senatorial seat), political intrigue and the "cat and mouse game" controlled by her grandfather (a staunch Democrat who gets what he wants, no matter what means he needs to secure it).

Other Characters: Senator Tom Wesley, a Republican and William's rival, who is seeking the Presidency; Andrew Miller, Katherine's Chief of Staff, a man with his own political ambitions; Laura Parker, Katherine's best friend and current lover (although Sara's return has stirred old feelings in Katherine);

Emily Tanner, a friend to both Sara and Katherine, owns the local coffeehouse; Diane Hamilton is Sara's current lover, the girl who finds herself with a possible rival when Katherine re-enters Sara's life; Louise Casell, Emily's partner in the coffeehouse.

Cast: Alicia Minshew (Sara Preston), Sarah Brown (Katherine Wesley), Melissa Archer (Evelyn Preston), John-Paul Lavoisier (Eric Preston), Scott Bryce (Tom Wesley), Jessica Morris (Diane Hamilton), Ron Raines (William Preston), Louise Sorel (Emily Tanner), Ricky Paull Goldin (Andrew Miller), Crystal Chappell (Claire Preston), Rebecca Mozo (Laura Parker), Tina Sloan (Louise Casell). **Credits:** *Producer:* Crystal Chappell, Hillary B. Smith, Christa Morris, Linda Hill, Jessica Hill, Ricky Paull Goldin. *Director:* Albert Alarr. *Writer:* Jessica Hill, Linda Hill, Skip Shea. **Comment:** Lavishly produced in the style of network television soap operas with very good acting and production values. The program is not a copy of or related to a prior CBS series called *Beacon Hill* and has enough intrigue (including the lesbian aspect) to draw viewers to it although episodes are only available through a subscription service and not posted for free on the Internet.

Episodes (available for free):
1. Season One Highlights (1 min., 41 sec.).
2. Season One Finale Preview (37 sec.).
3. Episode 11 Preview (22 sec.).
4. Episode 10 Preview (23 sec.).
5. Episode 9 Preview (28 sec.).
6. Episode 1 (13 min., 1 sec.).
7. Episode 7 Preview (28 sec.).
8. Episode 8 Preview (28 sec.).
9. Thank You from the Cast of Beacon Hill (2 min., 38 sec.).
10. Season One Introduction (33 sec.).
11. Behind the Scenes: About Season 2 (2 min., 58 sec.).
12. Behind the Scenes: About Web Series (2 min., 51 sec.).
13. Behind the Scenes: About the Production (3 min., 55 sec.).
14. Season One Promo: Power & Politics (1 min., 11 sec.).

Beat Girl. **Poster art from the series (copyright beActive Entertainment).**

15. About the Characters (4 min., 48 sec.).
16. Behind the Scenes: Here We Go (1 min., 15 sec.).
17. Behind the Scenes: The Beginning (2 min., 6 sec.).
18. Season One Promo: Will History Repeat Itself? (1 min., 42 sec.).
19. Season One Teaser: Meet the Cast (1 min., 2 sec.).

24 *Beat Girl.* webserieschannel.com. 2013 (Drama).

Following the death of her mother, a young woman (Heather) finds her dreams of following in her mother's footsteps and becoming a concert pianist shattered. It was actually her mother's dream to see Heather achieve the same status and had mentored her toward that goal. With no other choice at present Heather moves in with her estranged father and half-brother. With the grand piano left to her by her mother, Heather is still able to practice, but is unsure her upcoming audition at the Julliard School of Music will gain her acceptance into the prestigious institution. Shortly after, Heather's life takes a turn for the better when she enters a music store and meets Toby, the owner who, after learning of her plight, suggests she delve into the world of DJ-ing and electronic dance music. Seeing this as an opportunity to acquire money, Heather agrees and soon finds herself immersed in a world she really never knew existed. The program follows Heather as she pursues a new musical choice—but must ultimately decide which one to choose—her dream or what she is currently doing.

Cast: Louise Dylan (Heather), Craig Daniel Adams (Toby), Michael Higgs (Tom). **Credits:** *Producer:* John McDonnell, Nuno Bernardo, Triona Campbell, Mairtin de Barra. *Writer:* Nuno Bernardo, Melanie Martinez, Susana Tavares. **Comment:** Louise Dylan is captivating as Heather. The decision to have Heather face the camera and relate what happens to her (with brief scenes exploring this) works well as Louise is so honest and believable that you are immediately drawn into her world. The acting and production values are very good and the only complaint might be is that the episodes are way too short.

Episodes:

1. Music Is Everything (2 min., 1 sec.). An introduction to Heather as she explains how music is her life and how she has hopes of attending Julliard.

2. My New Life (1 min., 52 sec.). How life has changed for Heather since moving in with her father and step-brother is explored.

3. Shoplifting (2 min., 6 sec.). Heather helps a friend (Tom) who has been arrested for shoplifting.

4. My Best Friend (2 min., 32 sec.). As her audition nears, Amy, Heather's friend (a boutique owner) helps her choose a wardrobe.

5. My Big Dream (1 min., 53 sec.). Heather relates her feelings and hopes about being accepted into Julliard.

6. My First Rave (1 min., 44 sec.). A new world of music awaits Heather as Toby arranges for her to attend a Rave party and Toby talks her into trying her hand at DJ-ing.

7. Taking Risks (1 min., 26 sec.). As Amy puts everything on the line to showcase her designs at the Young Designer's Fashion Show, Heather agrees to provide the music.

8. Struggling (2 min., 26 sec.). Heather reflects on how she may have to give up her dream if she is accepted into Julliard and is unable to pay the tuition.

9. My First Gig (1 min., 32 sec.). After finding a job DJ-ing Heather relates her difficulties in adjusting to the situation—from missed cues to bad transitions—"it was a complete disaster," she says.

10. Refocus (1 min., 44 sec.). Heather relates her feelings about what happened and whether she should just focus on the piano or continue DJ-ing to earn money, which she feels may become a distraction to her goal.

11. Toby's Secret (1 min., 52 sec.). While discussing matters with Toby, Heather discovers that he has a law degree but abandoned going into practice when music became a part of his life.

12. Never Give Up (1 min., 42 sec.). Although Heather had vowed to give up DJ-ing, she finds that, despite what happened, she is in demand and now must find a way to balance her world as she does not want to give up Julliard—or her DJ-ing.

25 ***Behind the 8 Ball.*** webserieschannel. com. 2012 (Drama).

Rain (artist), Kat (photographer), Case (rapper), Matty (actor) and Levi (undecided and hooked on drugs) are friends who do not always see eye-to-eye on everything, but are usually there for each other in times of need. The program charts their individual experiences as they navigate a world in which they are still not quite sure of their future ambitions.

Cast: Kerrie Gee (Rain), Cadence Tom Gao (Case), Meighan Visser (Kat), Garrett Black (Levi), Eric Allen Buelow (Matty), Derek Lawrence Kemle (Bruce). **Credits:** *Producer:* Drew B.E. Hutchinson, Serge Lashchuk. *Writer:* Serge Lushchuk. *Director:* Drew B.E. Hutchinson. **Comment:** If the unsteady (shaky) camera style of filming bothers you, avoid this series entirely. From start to finish the director has chosen to bounce scenes up and down and from side to side for "style" that just falls flat. The production suffers because of it (some steady scenes would have been a nice touch) and makes the whole project look like an amateur attempt at filmmaking. The story ideas and acting are good although at times you get the feeling that they are just acting (especially with Levi in the first episode). The characters of Kat and Rain shine above the rest and their conflicts over boyfriend issues (despite the vulgar language) are very well done.

Episodes:

1. Everyone (20 min., 15 sec.). Five young people are introduced with a particular focus on Levi and his drug habit.

2. Levi (20 min., 35 sec.). The focus continues on Levi as his uncaring attitude and aimless drifting force his parents to cut off his financial support.

3. Case (20 min., 46 sec.). Matty becomes the center of focus as he joins with a friend from film school to produce a music video.

4. Rain (18 min., 15 sec.). Rain is the center of attention as she is commissioned to do a painting but finds the assignment occupying much of her time and alienating herself from her friends.

5. Matty (22 min., 20 sec.). Matty's attempts to secure acting roles is the principal focus of the

episode, beginning with his audition for a role that he later discovers is for gay porn.

6. Kat (22 min., 58 sec.). Kat's experiences with producers and musicians are explored as she tries to recover after her manipulative ways cause her to be bounced from a music production.

26 *Best Friend Dad.* webserieschannel.com. 2012 (Drama).

Diane is a divorcee with a son (Jackie) who marries a man (Spencer) half her age and a former classmate of Jackie's, a kid Jackie considered psychotic. Diane figured Jackie needed a male influence in his life, although her choice was not a wise one. Now Spencer is Jackie's stepfather and the program relates what happens when a psychotic becomes a member of a family with its own share of problems. **Cast:** Johnny Jacapraro (Jackie Gentles), June Mandeville (Diane Cribowski-Gentles), Noah Wesley (Spencer Gentles). **Credits:** *Producer:* Noah Wesley, Mark Walsh. *Writer-Director:* Noah Wesley, Caleb Ellison. **Comment:** Unpleasant program that is a turn off from the very beginning. The characters are not only unbelievable but unlikable; there is vulgar language, the annoying shaky camera (here coupled with the even more nauseating panning back and forth as characters speak) and sexual situations that are forced upon the viewer. The idea is a bit different but its presentation is badly executed.

Episodes:

1. Pilot (14 min., 41 sec.). After completing his first year of college Jackie finds that his life is changing for the worse—his mother has married his former high school classmate.

2. Campout (12 min., 43 sec.). Spencer attempts to bond with Jackie by forming a camping trip.

3. Working Stiff (18 min., 41 sec.). Having skipped college to get a job, Spencer tries to instill the value of work in Jackie.

4. Daddy Issues (12 min., 15 sec.). To overcome the resentment Jackie has toward him, Spencer attempts to show Jackie how to be a good son.

5. Double Date (16 min., 20 sec.). The episode (perhaps due to "the orgy scene at the end" has been taken off line; "This Video Is Private" will appear).

6. Spare the Rod (16 min., 20 sec.). Spencer's continual abuse of Jackie has unforeseen consequences when Jackie turns to drugs.

7. Nanna (11 min., 16 sec.). Spencer fears a visit from Diane's mother, who is intent on breaking up her daughter's new marriage.

8. Bad Vibrations (14 min., 2 sec.). The program concludes with Jackie becoming more involved with drugs while Spencer attempts to have sex with an unwilling Diane.

27 *The Better Half.* thebetterhalfseries. com. 2013 (Drama).

Lindsay, a blonde, and Amy, a brunette, meet on a subway train, make eye contact and it becomes a case of love at first sight. They date, fall in love and, after graduating from college, move in together. They are each self-sufficient although they each feel they have not reached the height of the goals they have set for themselves. The program charts the problems they encounter and how they overcome them in a time when maintaining such a relationship is more difficult than ever. **Cast:** Lindsay Hicks (Lindsay), Amy Jackson Lewis (Amy), Adriana DeGirolami (Angel), Katie Hartman (Diane), Todd Briscoe (Sandy), Leah Rudick (Cherry). **Credits:** *Producer:* Christine Ng, Leyla Perez. *Director:* Leyla Perez. *Writer:* Lindsay Hicks, Amy Jackson Lewis. **Comment:** Enjoyable lesbian-themed program with very good acting and production qualities. Both leads, a real-life couple, have a chemistry that spills over from their real lives and onto the screen as anyone can relate to the problems they are facing as they are problems, for the most part, that can be faced by anyone.

Episodes:

1. Going Out. Long-term girlfriends Lindsay and Amy are introduced and first seen as being in a nesting slump. To hopefully add some excitement into their lives, they plan an evening out with Lindsay's indecision about what to wear to a ladies' bar only setting the scene for a night out that does not exactly go as planned.

2. Sunny Side Up. Still believing that they are be-

The Better Half. **Lindsay Hicks (left) and Amy Jackson Lewis (copyright www.theverbproject.com).**

coming too comfortable with each other, Amy and Lindsay decide to indulge in things they have never attempted before. Their first choice is to visit a karaoke bar.

3. Lesbifriends. Amy and Lindsay join their friends, Angel and Cherry, to discuss matters concerning their next "great" adventure: a camping trip or the Lesbian Cheese Cave.

4. Pure Camp. Having chosen the camping trip, a totally unprepared Amy and Lindsay must now contend with Mother Nature.

5. Early Retirement. Amy's desire to have a child changes the course of her and Lindsay's lives when each feels they are working in dead-end jobs and, unknown the each other, quit at the same time—putting a damper on not only paying the bills but how to afford a baby.

28 *BFF Mermaids.* youtube.com. 2013 (Comedy-Drama).

While in her bedroom, a teenage girl (Reeva) and her friend Ashley discover a clear plastic box that appears to contain gumballs. Believing they have something to do with Mermaids, Reeva and Ashley take one. The box mysteriously disappears and Reeva and Ashley are transformed into Mermaids. They now not only fear water and a full moon (which can begin their transformation) but an evil Siren whose anger they later arouse when they disturb her peace after discovering and exploring an abandoned house. **Cast (as credited):** Alyssa (Ashley), Phoebe (Reeva). **Credits** are not given. **Comment:** The introduction of a Siren adds some intrigue in the Mermaid saga but the sound is poor and the photography just acceptable. **Episode List:** *1.* Tail Scale Change. *2.* The Bag. *3.* Episode 3. *4.* Not Understood. *5.* New Moon (Parts 1, 2, 3, 4). *6.* The Siren.

29 *Big Country Blues.* blip.tv. 2011 (Drama).

Grayson Ricker, a young man with a talent for singing, is stuck working a double shift in the local (Kentucky) railroad yard while not only attempting to support himself, but his destructive mother and his burned-out brother. When his girlfriend (Brooke) learns that a reality competition TV show is seeking musicians for contestants, she persuades Grayson to enter and leave his despicable life behind and pursue the chance of a lifetime—stardom as a country and western singer. The program charts Grayson's challenges as he, accompanied by his own entourage (Brooke and their friend Walt) seek a one-in-a-million chance at success in an industry filled with more heartache than joy. **Cast:** Jeremy McComb (Grayson Ricker), Sarah Jacobs (Brooke Massey), Shane Allen (Walt Wheeler), Alicia Levy (Marissa Phillips), Sally Purifoy (Grayson's mother), Bryan Schany (Grayson's brother), Jef-frey Rutkowski (Garyson's father), Jason Shebiro (TJ). **Credits:** *Producer:* Annie Gillies, Sandra Kampf, Jonathan Rippon, Brian A. Ross, Andrew Galloway. *Director:* Brian A. Ross, Jonathan Rippon. *Writer:* Brian A. Ross. **Comment:** Music-filled drama that takes viewers on a not-so-typical tour of Nashville (the not-so-glamorous look) as Grayson seeks to become a success. The acting and production values are good and the program is something different, more suited for a network TV drama rather than an Internet drama. **Episodes:**

1. Home of the Blues. On the urging of his girlfriend and best friend, Grayson enters the TV show competition.

2. Your Good Girl's Gonna Go Bad. Grayson, Brooke and Walt leave their past behind and head for Nashville.

3. Stand by Your Man. Grayson faces his first challenge when he auditions for the *American Idol*–like TV show.

4. He Stopped Loving Her Today. Life in the big city appears to be slowly affecting the friends as they accustom themselves to a style they have never before experienced.

5. Sing Me Back Home. The program concludes but sets the stage for the possibility of future episodes wherein Grayson (as well as Brooke and Walt) must decide on their own futures when Grayson is rejected by the TV show.

30 *Bleeder.* bleederseries.com. 2009 (Thriller).

Alex Daub is a young man afflicted with hemophilia, a genetic condition that causes excessive bleeding due a lack of a clotting factor in the blood. He also requires fresh blood to sustain himself. To acquire blood, Alex has befriended a hospital nurse that supplies him with what he needs for a price. But, as Alex's finances begin to dwindle down his life changes, first losing his wife, his supplier and the cheap apartment he rented. One night, while wandering the streets of Philadelphia, Alex encounters a female vampire (Charlotte) and a life-changing decision—all the blood he requires if he will make her pregnant. A friendship is begun and Alex is soon taken in by Charlotte and her sexy group of female vampires (Lizzie, Daisy and Marlene). The program follows Alex as he allies himself with vampires who appear to want more than they express (especially when they discover that Alex is not only a hemophilic but possesses "a rare gene" that they apparently need). **Cast:** Mark Kochanowicz (Alex Daub), Brea Bee (Charlotte), Sarah Croce (Daisy), Lisa Roman (Lizzie), Katie Foster (Marlene), Brian Anthony Wilson (Detective Gardner), William Spangler (Det. Abel), Jennifer Butler (Karin Weatherstone), Omar Wilder (Mookie), Jason Bentley Jones (Off. Auxeter), Jeremy Peter Axworthy (John). **Credits:**

Producer-Writer-Director: Wade Balance, Mark Kochanowicz. **Comment:** Although only three episodes were produced and the story ends unresolved, it is well acted and produced. The story line leaves several unanswered questions, including Alex's fate and what the rare gene is.

Episodes:

1. Necessities (9 min., 40 sec.). The story line is introduced as Alex crosses the path of Charlotte for the first time.

2. Common Ground (9 min., 35 sec.). As Alex becomes accustomed to his new living arrangements, Charlotte discovers that he possesses "a rare gene" that will apparently benefit a vampire's thirst for human blood.

3. Episode 3 (8 min., 3 sec.). A sudden rise in the death rate brings police detectives into a case wherein the victims are discovered to have strange bite marks on the neck.

31 *Blink the Series.* youtube.com. 2013 (Drama).

Jon, a young man born in Vancouver, Canada, has moved to Berlin, Germany, to get inspiration and

Bleeder. **Poster art from the series (copyright Liberty Bell Films, 2009).**

hopefully further his career as an artist. Kat, his girlfriend, born in Seattle, Washington, is a photographer who learned her craft from her grandfather. She and Jon met in Vancouver and she decided to accompany Jon to Berlin in the hope of furthering her career. Life changes for them one day when Jon finds himself in a park with no idea as to how he got there. Seeing that Jon is somewhat in a daze, a young woman (Annie) comes to his rescue and, learning where he lives, takes him home. Kat's jealousy is aroused when she sees "what" Jon has brought home, and becomes even more so when she learns that Jon and Annie have bonded over something they both possess: a rare gene that transforms them into capeless super heroes. Although their powers have not fully developed, Jon has taken advantage of the situation and begun selling a line of super hero underwear. The program follows Jon as he continually connects with Annie (upsetting Kat) to learn more about what is happening and what his and Annie's ultimate mission will be. **Cast:** Jon Amar (Jon), Vanessa Locke (Annie), Christine Utterberg (Kat), David Masterson (Crow). **Credits:** *Producer:* Jon Amar, Vanessa Locke, Christine Utterberg. *Director:* Glenn Conroy, Malachi Rempen. *Writer:* Jon Amar, Glenn Conroy, Andrea Ingloff, Andrew James, Vanessa Locke, Korey Powell, Christine Utterberg. **Comment:** While not a super hero series in the true vein (like *Batman*) it could develop into a similar idea as Jon and Annie help each other understand the powers they appear to be developing (the episodes end without really explaining anything). The acting and production values are good and the doorway is left open for additional episodes.

Episodes:

1. Episode 1. Jon, awakening in a park, begins to wander and meets Annie, the girl that will soon change the course of his life.

2. Episode 2. Kat is distraught when Jon returns home and learns what has happened; more so about the woman who helped him.

3. Episode 3. Feeling that something is not right, Jon goes back to the park, hoping to find Annie.

4. Episode 4. Unknown to Jon, Kat follows him—and becomes a bit jealous when she sees him with Annie.

5. Episode 5. Jon finds he is uncontrollably forced to help save an old man from a mugging.

6. Episode 6. Although he wanted no reward for his actions, Jon's finds that his intervention was captured on video and posted on the Internet.

7. Episode 7. As strange sensations begin to manifest themselves in Jon, he realizes that he has the power to tele-transport himself from one place to another.

8. Episode 8. Re-connecting with Annie, Jon finds that she too has a similar power—but Kat is not pleased that they are becoming close. The program's concluding episode.

32 *Blood Cell.* webserieschannel.com. 2010 (Thriller).

It is 3:30 a.m. when a young woman (Julia) receives a phone call from her friend, Susan, with a frightening message: "I've been kidnapped. Help me. Don't call the cops and don't turn off your cell phone. He'll kill me if you do." The tense program follows Julia, the only apparent hope Susan has, as she seeks to find Susan before her cell phone battery wears down and she loses all contact with her kidnapper. **Cast:** Jessica Rose (Julia), Sara Sanderson (Alex), Robert Mammana (The Bad Man). **Credits:** *Producer-Writer-Director:* Eduardo Rodriquez. **Comment:** Effective, fast-paced thriller that captures your interest from the beginning and keeps you hooked, with twists and turns as Julia seeks to save Susan's life. The program originally aired on the WB.com.
Episodes:
1. I've Been Kidnapped (4 min., 10 sec.). A phone call from her friend Susan begins Julia's ordeal as she learns that Susan has been kidnapped and she is her only hope to save her. It also appears that Julia has only as long as her cell phone battery lasts to save Susan.

2. Cell = Dead Friend Kidnapped (4 min., 3 sec.). Julia's first clue arrives when the kidnapper (Bad Man) sends her a cell phone message: "Dead Cell = Dead Friend."

3. Alex, I'll Be at Your Place Soon (3 min., 30 sec.). Feeling that she cannot help Susan by herself, Julia seeks the help of her friend, Alex.

4. Where Are You Alex? (3 min., 36 sec.). As Julia seeks Alex, she is unknowingly being tracked by the Bad Man.

5. He Wants to Listen (3 min., 18 sec.). Shortly after Julia finds Alex, Julia receives a phone call from the Bad Man with a strange message: "learn how to listen to others."

6. Finally, Susan's Place (4 min., 14 sec.). Julia and Alex begin a search of Susan's apartment hoping to find clues.

7. Who's the Redhead in the Picture? (4 min., 22 sec.). As they search Susan's home, Julia finds a photo album with pictures of a mysterious red haired woman.

8. It's All Gonna Be Okay (3 min., 18 sec.). Unknown to Julia and Alex, they are being observed (from behind the closet door) by the Bad Man.

9. You'll Know What I Want in 30 min. (2 min.,

54 sec.). A cell phone call alerts Julia that she has only 30 minutes left to locate Susan or she will die.

10. Susan Mentioned a Big Bird (3 min., 11 sec.). As time begins to dwindle down, Julia recalls that Susan mentioned meeting a man at a restaurant with a big bird entrance.

11. Can You Give Me a Hand? (5 min., 47 sec.). Believing that the restaurant holds the key to saving Susan, Julia heads for it, but finds trouble of her own when her car breaks down.

12. The Picture Is Fake (4 min., 10 sec.). As Julia begins walking to the restaurant, Alex is confronted by the Bad Man in a desolate parking lot.

13. I Could Use a Ride (3 min., 26 sec.). An apparent Good Samaritan offers Julia a ride.

14. Stop the Car (4 min., 50 sec.). Julia's fears begin to grow as she feels it was not a wise decision to accept a ride from a stranger.

15. I'm Coming Susan (4 min., 21 sec.). Julia's fears are eased as she arrives, safe and sound at the restaurant.

16. Julia Where Are You? (2 min., 49 sec.). As Julia enters the restaurant she receives as phone call from Susan telling her that she is in the right place.

17. Get Me Out of Here (1 min., 56 sec.). Julia begins her search of the restaurant for Susan and her kidnapper.

18. Oh, My God (6 min., 4 sec.). The program concludes with Julia confronting the kidnapper.

33 *Blue.* watchwigs.com. 2012 (Drama).

Blue (no other name given) is a young woman and the single mother of a 13-year-old son (Josh). She appears to be leading a normal life but is secretly living two lives—that of a working mother during the day (at an accounting firm) and a high-priced call girl at night (earning as much as $900 per client) for her madam (Cynthia). Blue has not had an easy life, being abused as a child and having had an affair with an older man when she was a teenager. She is very protective of Josh, struggling to keep her secret from him (and everyone else around her), and has apparently become a prostitute to make ends meet. The program charts Blue's double life, mostly her experiences with the men who seek her services and her continual efforts to keep both lives secret, especially from Josh. **Cast:** Julia Stiles (Blue), Uriah Sheltn (Josh), Kathleen Quinlan (Jessica), Brooklyn Lowe (Francesca), Carla Gallo (Rose), Jacob Vargas (Roy), Brian Shortall (Will), James Morrison (Olsen), David Harbour (Cooper), Sarah Paulson (Lavinia), Taylor Nichols (Bill), Wanda De Jesus (Cynthia). **Credits:** *Producer:* Jacob Avnet, Jon Avnet, Rodrigo Garcia, Marsha Ogesby. *Director:* Rodrigo Garcia. *Writer:* Rodrigo Garcia, Karen Graci. **Comment:** Lavishly filmed and well-acted story that plays like a soap opera. Although the idea is not new (cable's *Secret*

Diary of a Call Girl is an example) the program flows smoothly and is interesting.

Episodes:

1. Mom (8 min., 30 sec.). Introduces Blue, a woman you would never suspect of leading a double life, and Josh, her rather brilliant (but troublesome anti-social) son.

2. Son (7 min., 32 sec.). Josh becomes more of a concern to Blue when she returns home earlier than expected and catches him watching Internet pornography.

3. You Rule (9 min., 51 sec.). Blue's daytime job and her relationship with some of her co-workers are explored.

4. Long Day, Blue? (7 min., 38 sec.). A meeting with her mother (Jessica) has Blue a bit on edge as she fears she will learn about her secret life.

5. You're Good (8 min., 24 sec.). Blue meets with a client and finds herself in an awkward situation when he becomes fascinated by her and begins inquiring about her private life.

6. Jack the Ripper (7 min., 13 sec.). Blue's acquaintance with an old friend (Cooper) who served time in jail for embezzlement has Josh worried that his mother is seeing a Jack the Ripper type of felon.

7. Paying for Sex (8 min.). Blue becomes a bit unsettled when Cooper confides in her that he has intimacy issues when it comes to women.

8. See and Be Seen (11 min., 43 sec.). Blue and her mother (Jessica) meet for a luncheon date in an attempt to repair their strained relationship.

9. What Kind of Name Is Blue? (8 min., 29 sec.). Blue attempts to ease a tense situation after Josh insults a fellow student by meeting with the boy's parents.

10. It's Just a Crutch (6 min., 16 sec.). Josh's continual disruptive behavior forces Blue to send him to a therapist if he is to remain in school.

11. Everything Is a Test (8 min., 3 sec.). A meeting between Blue and her madam (Cynthia) is showcased.

12. How Do You Do? (7 min., 26 sec.). Blue's talk with Josh after she caught him watching porn apparently didn't help when she finds he is tutoring an older girl (Francesca) igniting memories of her affair with an older man.

13. Glue and Lubricant (7 min., 16 sec.). A public relations job opening at the accounting firm has Blue and her co-worker (Rose) discussing issues, including personal ones (like Rose fearing that as she grows older men will no longer be interested in her).

14. Wow, Wow, Wow (9 min., 19 sec.). Blue is shocked to learn that the father of the boy Josh insulted is the son of the older man she dated as a teenager.

15. On My Own (8 min., 37 sec.). As Josh begins his therapy sessions, he begins to realize that his mother is hiding something from him.

16. The Truth Hurts (8 min., 45 sec.). In an attempt to better understand Josh, Blue opens up to the therapist (Will) about her troubled upbringing.

17. A Man's Permission (8 min., 45 sec.). Knowing that one of three men she dated 13 years earlier is Josh's father, Blue seeks advice on how to have a paternity test done without the men knowing to determine the father.

18. Make Yourself at Home (7 min., 35 sec.). With Josh not yet home from school, Blue takes the opportunity to get to know a bit more about Francesca.

19. Old Habits Die Hard (8 min., 15 sec.). Olsen, the older man Blue dated as a teenager, has Blue rejecting his friendship when he re-enters her life (as she suspects he may be the father).

20. Doubling the Equation (7 min., 57 sec.). Blue's decision to leave Josh and Francesca alone in the house during a tutoring session turns into romantic temptation for Josh.

21. Are You Clean? (11 min., 39 sec.). Explores one Blue's client meetings when things get out of hand and Blue faces the temper of an angry customer.

22. In the Running (7 min., 38 sec.). Blue faces a choice: accept the public relations job offer at the firm and give up her secret life, or continue as a call girl (as it has now become an obsession with her).

23. Hard Time (9 min., 3 sec.). Some insight into Blue's childhood is given when she meets with her father (who is serving time in prison).

24. The Details (10 min., 29 sec.). As Josh returns to therapy he learns about his mother's troubled life before his birth.

25. You're Not a Freak, Are You? (6 min., 32 sec.). Blue suspects that Josh and Francesca may have engaged in sex and struggles to find a way to approach him about it.

26. Getting to the Point (6 min., 47 sec.). As Blue confronts Josh about Francesca, it is leaned that Blue was offered the higher paying job but rejected it.

27. I'm Not a Stalker (7 min., 3 sec.). Blue receives an unexpected suitor—the plumber (Roy) who unclogged her garbage disposal, who asks her out on a date.

28. Savages (8 min., 38 sec.). Although she has an opportunity to give up her secret life, Blue continues, this time picking up a client at a bar—a once famous actor who was previously Cynthia's (her madam) client.

29. Role Play (9 min., 48 sec.). Josh meets Olsen but is unaware that he may be his father.

30. Winning With (8 min., 17 sec.). A normal experience for Blue is explored when she and Roy embark on a date, but they are plagued by numerous mishaps.

31. A Straight Answer (6 min., 3 sec.). Blue confides in Josh about her date with Roy.

32. Choices Add Up (6 min., 50 sec.). Blue and her mother (who dates younger men) catch Josh and Francesca in a compromising situation.

33. Where Were You? (6 min., 59 sec.). Blue and Jessica begin arguing about Josh's upbringing with Josh overhearing what is being said—and learning even more about his mother's past. The program's concluding episode.

34 Blue Belle. youtube.com. 2010 (Drama).

Blue Smith, the daughter of a Caucasian mother (Judy) and an African-American father (Malcolm), never wanted for anything in her life growing up. She was the perfect child and excelled in school. But, as a teenager, she became obsessed with sex, freely giving of herself, but never becoming totally satisfied. As time passed she became interested in teaching, and pursued those ambitions, eventually becoming a high school teacher. She lives in Santa Barbara, California and has a seemingly good life. But the neurosis she developed earlier in life has manifested itself to a point where Blue has begun living a second, secret life: that of a weekend high-class Las Vegas prostitute. Blue has successfully managed to live two separate lives until a paraplegic student (Marcus) becomes infatuated with her and begins stalking her. The program not only details Blue's secret life and the men she encounters, but on Marcus, when he steals the flight itinerary from her purse and realizes something is not right. Complicating the situation is Quinn, Marcus's sex-obsessed friend, who helps him uncover Blue's secret and the confrontation that follows when Marcus attempts to understand why Blue is selling her body for money.

Cast: Tessa Thompson (Blue Smith), Calvin Pijlman (Marcus), Michael Karman (Quinn), Henry Brown (Malcolm), Sharon Lawrence (Judy), Leigh Dunham (Amy), Sage Parker (Janice), Michael Cassidy (Daniel), Josh Heosler (Stephen), Perry Lang (David), Gregory Smith (Jackson), Shannon Sullivan (Jaci), Hailey Rosenberg (Hayley). **Credits:** *Producer:* Judy Trotter. *Writer-Director:* Perry Lang. **Comment:** Outstanding production with stunning cinematography and superior acting. The program draws you in from the very beginning with Tessa Thompson becoming an example of how an African-American themed production should be done: tastefully; not what most others present: trashy stories with non-likeable characters and an excessive use of vulgar language. Although the idea is not original (shades of the TV series *Secret Diary of a Call Girl* will come to mind), it is unique for its depiction of an African-American protagonist.

Episodes:

1. As Little Soiled as Possible. Blue, attired in a sexy bikini, is at the beach with her dog (Cash) and unknowingly being observed by Marcus and Quinn.

2. Alone. Seizing the opportunity to learn more about Blue, Marcus searches through Blue's purse and discovers her Las Vegas itinerary.

3. Your Whack-Off Fantasy. After showing Quinn what he has found, Marcus convinces Quinn to follow Blue to Las Vegas.

4. Goin' to Vegas. Blue's secret begins to unravel when her parents, Judy and Malcolm, discover she is going to Las Vegas. Incidents about Blue's troubled past as being an only child are also revealed.

5. Komshe Thunder-f**k. Explores Blue's prior life with her parents as a child.

6. Ready or Not. The trip to Las Vegas has a different meaning for Marcus, who desperately wants to discover what Blue does, while Quinn feels he can fulfill his sexual needs.

7. A Dude in Vegas. Daniel, one of Blue's regular customers, is introduced as an actor who appears to have fallen in love with her.

8. But I Was Hungry. At her hotel Blue meets with other call girls who have gathered to prepare for the evening ahead.

9. More and More Secrets. Blue and a fellow prostitute (Jaci) discuss their lives and what they hope for the future.

10. Into the Night, Part 1. The conversations between Blue and Jaci bring back memories of Jackson, whom Blue thought was the man of her dreams.

11. Into the Night, Part 2. Blue and Jaci venture outside of their hotel room to begin their evening's activities.

12. It's Time Either Way. As Blue enters the night life of Las Vegas to meet with clients, Marcus continues his probe of Blue's actions.

13. The Top Half. As Blue meets with a client (David), Marcus becomes increasingly concerned about Blue.

14. e-Harmony. Introduces the character of Hayley, a lady of the evening Blue befriends and who will later become a part of her life.

15. Honey, You're on Your Own. Focuses on Marcus, wheelchair bound, as he becomes increasingly frustrated over his inability to uncover Blue's secret.

16. The Pioneer Spirit. Blue's meeting with a client who is becoming increasingly intoxicated, causes Blue to have doubts about what she is doing.

17. You Don't Know Me. Despite what she is thinking, Blue succumbs to her neurosis but is later overcome by feelings of self hate; a flashback to better times with Jackson is also seen.

18. I'm Not Like Some Painting. The flashback continues with Blue now regretting that not kissing Jackson on an afternoon she shared with him may have been a mistake and caused a rift in their relationship.

19. Mr. Smith Goes to Vegas. Marcus, able to build up the courage he needs, confronts Blue.

20. I Suppose That's the Question Isn't It? Now that he has broken the ice, Marcus asks the one question he needs the answer to—Why?

21. As Little Soiled as Possible. Concludes the series with the same title that opened it with Blue facing Marcus and finding it difficult to not only tell him, but what to do about her own future.

35 Body Politic. blip.tv. 2013 (Drama).

Los Angeles provides the setting for a political drama that focuses on Joseph Nevin, a charismatic city councilman and his bid for mayor in an upcoming race—an race for Nevin wherein his peers resent him but a race wherein private interests see him as someone they may be able to manipulate for their own needs.

Cast: Scott Laska (Joseph Nevin), Jen Drohan (Holly McHale), Marina Valle (Angelica Nevin), Mike Romo (Dan "Ace" Kampman), Chris Lee (Billy Weatherford), Randa Walker (Dawn Irving). **Credits:** *Producer:* Steve Rousseau, Seth Soloway, Jae Trevits. *Writer-Director:* Steve Rousseau. **Comment:** Even on broadcast and cable TV, politically-themed programs are a hard sell. There is either interest or not. Most often it is not. And, although the acting and production values are good here, the limited appeal program is well done and intriguing.

Episodes:

1. Viral/Iconoclast. Nevin comes under the scrutiny of Holly McHale, a TV journalist following the campaign.

2. Tamale. Holly and show segment producer Dawn Irving, cover the story of a grisly crime in Echo Park that has ramifications for the City Council.

3. Idealist. As Holly's personal interview takes shape, feathers are ruffled when the topic of energy giant Western Jupiter is raised and linked with corporate influence over the city's politics.

4. What Do You Want, Billy? Dan Kampman, called Ace, is introduced as Nevin's aggressive campaign manager.

5. Honest. Anjelica, Nevin's wife, becomes the subject of Holly's continuing exclusive on the Joseph Nevin story.

6. Everything. As a video emerges that appears to implicate Nevin in an uncompromising situation, Ace tries to suppress it with an "We can explain this" scenario as it being a fake.

7. Swimming. As Holly's probe continues, she uncovers evidence that Nevin may not be the upright citizen he pretends to be.

8. Running. The season finale wherein the door is left open for future episodes when Holly reveals to Nevin the information she has just found—and what the consequences could be if it were made public.

36 *Borderline Coyotes.* webserieschannel. com. 2012 (Crime Drama).

A Coyote, when referring to humans, is a person who traffics in illegal human smuggling (illegally bringing people across borders). Gregory, Mike and Rick Stone are brothers who are also Coyotes and working for a mob boss known as Rico. They operate along the Southern borders (between the U.S. and Mexico) and stories follow their illegal activities as they attempt to avoid the law and earn the big bucks such operations net.

Cast: Victor Kelso (Gregory Stone, Jr.), Exie Booker (Mike Stone), Sean Riggs (Rick Stone), Roberto Sanchez (Rico Martinez), Max Decker (Det.

Jason Santiago), Atheana Ritchie (Natasha), Franco Vega (Diego Ortega), Janelle Froehlich (Sara), Samantha Carro (Alexis Martinez), Chris Abdou (Zaid Torysan), Bruno Oliver (Det. Charles Johnson), Chris Pardal (Franky), Gev Khal (Arman), Amy Wray (Det. Harris). **Credits:** *Producer:* Victor Kelso, Exie Booker, India Love. *Director:* Victor Kelso. *Writer:* Victor Kelso, Exie Booker. **Comment:** Imaginative program with good acting and production values. The premise is somewhat different and the program flows smoothly from beginning to end.

Episodes:

1. Dead or Alive. A detective (Charles Johnson) begins the hunt for mob boss Rico and the three brothers that work for him.

2. Flashback. As the Stone brothers receive their first payment from Rico, trouble enters the scene when rival Coyotes threaten Rico's business.

3. The Pick Up. As things begin to heat up the brothers decide to head to Mexico to avoid Johnson and his agents.

4. A Night Out. Johnson's associate, Santiago, starts building a case against Rico and his human smuggling operations.

5. Betrayal. Rick begins a side business with Armenians causing a rift between Rico and his brothers Mike and Gregory in the concluding episode.

37 *Breaking Point.* breakingpointshow. com. 2011–2012 (Drama).

Serial-like program that charts the lives of a group of friends as they seek to follow their dreams and how, to maintain their relationships, jobs and even their sanity, must also deal with the triumphs, heartaches and struggles required to do so.

Cast: Jessica Tome (Gabby Edwards), Crystal Coney (Crystal Woods), Olivia Dunkley (Det. Dana Parker), Kyle Steven Templin (Ben Campbell), Dennis Teh (Dennis Edwards), Keena Ferguson (Imani Clarke), Claudia Perea (Lynette Kelly), Jillian Peterson (Tory Scott), Cardell Jackson (Victor Brown), Mark Harley (Wes), Wesley Alan Johnson (Tate Kelly), Haile D'Alan (Rick Hubbard), Brian Ceponis (Dr. James Woods), Jordan Preston (Det. Patrick Chase), Joe Komara (Zach Scott), Katrina Nelson (Amber), Essa Thiry (Sheyl Hubbard), Brianna Colleen Marton (Val Brown), Noah J. Smith (T.J.), Etalvia Cashin (Cinnamon), Neto DePaula Pimenta (Emilio), Gichi Gamba (Owens), Kiana Rene (Monica Rhodes), Samantha Sadoff (Aja Woods), Sheilynn Wactor (Chandelier). **Credits:** *Producer:* Caryn K. Hayes, Carolyn O. Jacobs. *Writer-Director:* Caryn K. Hayes. **Comment:** Impressively filmed and expertly acted, but very difficult show to follow with many characters, interconnected stories and numerous plot twists and turns (why only an episode listing is presented). The program is more complex than TV soap operas like *General Hospital* and *The Young*

Breaking Point. **Logo art from the series (copyright Hardly Working Entertainment, LLC).**

and the Restless due, possibly to its squeezing too much into each short episode. Stretching each episode by a minute or two would have helped as scenes could have been made less complex and the story much easier to follow.

Season 1 Episode List: *1.* Full Disclosure. *2.* House of Cards. *3.* The Return. *4.* Necessary Roughness. *5.* In Too Deep.

Season 2 Episode List: *6.* Unforgiven. *7.* Stand By Me. *8.* Strictly Business. *9.* About a Boy. *10.* Sucker Punch. *11.* Waiting to Exhale. *12.* Catch Me if You Can. *13.* The Trap. *14.* True Colors. *15.* Betrayed.

38 *Broken.* blip.tv. 2012 (Drama).

The Elam Marshal Community Center in Raleigh, North Carolina, is a struggling, financially strapped youth center now run by Allie Gray. She inherited the position from her mother when she became gravely ill and has only one ambition: to keep the center open despite a major hurdle she is facing from the state which is threatening to close what they consider a bottomless money pit. Allie believes in the project her mother started but acquiring the money she needs has led her to embezzling funds from her and her husband's personal bank accounts.

Allie's marriage to Rick, an attorney is slowly breaking up and when he discovers what Allie has been doing, he vows to close the center without regard to the consequences that may occur in his family. Allie believes the youth of Raleigh need the center and stories relate the intrigue that follows as Allie and Rick each conspire to achieve a goal that could eventually destroy both of their lives.

Cast: Je T'aime (Allie Gray), Connie Rogers (Crystal), T.J. Swann (Rick), Donnell Millsaps (Parker), Andre G. Smith (Morgan), Jalonda Clax (Tessa), Kevin J. Stone (David), Markita McNair (Dominique KaClair), Tara Sarpe (Mrs. Bone), Saprina Willis (Portia Karr), Quentin Johnson (Roc), Ashley V. Bagley (Samantha Bone), Fatima Smith (Yolanda), Michael Buie (Don Sharpe), La-Don Brown (Fish), Terry Johnson (Craig), Bruce Davis (Det. McKay). **Credits:** *Producer:* Rose Wilder. *Director:* Tamika Morris. *Writer:* Andre G. Smith. **Comment:** There is some mild violence and vulgar language but overall a well-produced and acted program that ends unresolved but leaves the possibility open for future stories.

Episodes:

1. Pilot (32 min., 50 sec.). Introduces Allie as her mother becomes ill and she must now continue her legacy of running the youth center.

2. The Re-Naming (36 min., 28 sec.). Allie's takeover begins on a good note when the center is renamed in honor of its founder (Allie's mother).

3. Where Is Parker? (19 min., 28 sec.). Parker, Allie's always-in-trouble brother, is arrested, booked—and "lost" in the justice system when Allie posts bail but he can't be found.

4. Making New Friends (20 min., 57 sec.). More light is shed on Rick and his determination to shut down the center as well as his involvement with Don Sharp, an unsavory hoodlum.

5. Love Is in the Air. Focuses on various romantically themed incidents Allie encounters while attempting to deal with the problems she is facing.

6. The Battle Within. Rick faces harsh words from Sam, a friend of Allie's father who warns him to back down or he will live to regret what he is doing. The program's concluding episode.

39 *Broken at Love.* brokenatlovetheseries. com. 2012–2014 (Drama).

Vivienne Taylor, called Vivie, is a very attractive college senior (at the Cinematic School of the Arts) facing a slight dilemma: what subject to encompass for a film-making class. While lunching with her mother (Ava) at The Veggie Grill Ava suggests a documentary-like project that would reveal incidents in the life of a celebrity. She calls it "A Day in the Life" and, because Vivie watches tennis on TV, suggests she contact up-and-coming star Holden Gregory. Although a bit reluctant at first, Vivie does e-mail Holden and much to her surprise, he does respond with a positive attitude about the project. Shortly after, as Vivie meets with Holden to plan the project, she finds herself becoming attracted to him and stories relate Vivie's ups and downs as she contemplates a romance with Holden but finds it is something that fate has intended not to happen.

Cast: Karolina Sivas (Vivienne "Vivie" Taylor), Rob Healy (Holden Gregory), Pamela Bowen (Ava Taylor), Carly Reeves (Olivia), Kelsey Long (Sandy), Bobby Quinn Rice (Darin), Joanna Tiwald (Deana Taylor), Sarah Strazi (Rebecca), Amber Smith (Audrey), Tobie Elizabeth Easton (Lauren), Patrick Morgan (Noah), Shea Buckner (Montgomery), Ben Reed (Dr. Eduardo Taylor), Sharon Farrell (Grandma Geraldine), Marcia Rodd (Grandma Lulu). **Credits:** *Producer:* Karolina Sivas, Ida Sivas. *Director:* Karolina Sivas, Savannah Bloch, Mark Marchillo, Viral Shah, Robert Hollocks, Ivan Silvestrini. *Writer:* Karolina Sivas. **Comment:** Enjoyable program that will capture your attention from the very beginning. Karolina Sivas is delightful as Vivienne that your heart goes out to her for the misery Holden causes her. The acting is very good and the writing and directing comparable to any comedy-drama television series. The program also features veteran TV actresses Sharon Farrell and Marcia Rodd.

Episodes:

1. Dear Mr. Holden Gregory. Vivie is introduced as her mother suggests a subject for her film class.

2. First Round. After acquiring Holden's permis-

Broken at Love. **Episode title card featuring Karolina Sivas (copyright Karolina Sivas).**

sion to film him, Vivie faces the prospect of meeting Holden in person.

3. Evening Session. To get to know his director, Holden invites Vivie to dinner to discuss aspects of her project.

4. Court Date. As Vivie begins filming her documentary it is becoming apparent that she is becoming more interested in him than the game of tennis.

5. Holden at Love. Vivie's love life becomes more complicated when her former boyfriend, Tristan, returns to her after a year overseas.

6. Follow Through. Vivie faces disappointment when she screens her film but its star fails to show up.

7. Return Game. After a month away (playing in tennis matches) Holden returns and arranges a meeting with Vivie. Holden, a bit apprehensive, tells Vivie that he is moving (will stay with friends) as much traveling is involved in playing tennis. As they talk, Vivie also has her heart broken when Holden tells her he is not the marrying kind.

8. Player's Party. To get her mind off what has happened, Vivie attends a house party given by Darin, the school's rugby team captain, only to find further disappointment when she discovers Holden has blocked her from his Facebook page ("unfriended me" as she says).

9. On Court Meltdown. When Vivie decides to surprise Holden by showing up unannounced at one of his tennis matches, she sees that he is with another girl and realizes that she is the other woman in his life.

10. Post-Match Analysis. At her graduation party, family members begin offering opinions about Vivie and Holden's relationship.

11. Bashing the Opponent. At another party Vivie finds additional "Holden girlfriend bashing" although her girlfriends, Olivia and Audrey attempt to help her understand the situation she is facing.

12. Deciding Point. Holden's recent breakup with the girl he had been seeing has Vivie believing she may be able to rekindle her relationship with him.

13. Taken to the Woodshed. As Holden hooks up with a new girl, Vive becomes jealous, but struggles to control her emotions so as not to ruin any chances she may have with him.

14. Game, Set, Heartbreak. Realizing that her chances with Holden now appear unlikely, especially since he has blocked her from accessing her Facebook page, Vivie decides that a sequel to her film is her next step—to tell the true story of Holden Gregory. The program's concluding episode.

40 Brooklyn Is in Love. plentertainment.com. 2011–2012 (Drama).

Brooklyn, New York, provides the backdrop for a story about three friends (Diane, Nikki and Bryan) and their struggles to find love—a situation made more difficult for Diane after the murder of her boyfriend (Jeremy) and the effect it also has on Nikki and Bryan.

Cast: Miranda McCauley (Diane), Katka Gerz (Nikki), Nadia Serantes (Aimee), Kather Sei (Bryan), Terrence Ruggiero (Kevin), Evan Baker (Charlie), Blaine Pennington (Henry), Benedict Mazurek (Benny), Rahmel Reid (DJ Rodney), Keil Christine Laing (Kim), Renee Kay (Alex). **Credits:** *Producer-Director:* Danielle Earle. *Writer:* Danielle Earle, Stephanie Lazorchak. **Comment:** Like-able characters, a well-developed story line and good acting coupled with good production values makes for a change of pace program about people (especially Diane here) seeking to find love amidst trying circumstances.

Episode List:

1. The Beginning, Part 1 (12 min., 37 sec.).
2. The Beginning, Part 2 (13 min., 43 sec.).
3. Old Friends, Old Flame (15 min., 42 sec.).
4. Hate That I Love You (17 min., 6 sec.).
5. Catch Me (16 min., 14 sec.).
6. My Mistakes (19 min., 40 sec.).
7. The Things That Are (11 min., 38 sec.).
8. Hearts and Arrows (14 min., 39 sec.).
9. Happy Birthday, Diane, Part 1 (16 min., 50 sec.).
10. Happy Birthday, Diane, Part 2 (13 min., 36 sec.).
11. Skydive for Love, Part 1 (11 min., 46 sec.).
12. Skydive for Love, Part 2 (18 min., 49 sec.).
13. Say What You Mean (14 min., 59 sec.).
14. Honesty Can Get Sticky, Part 1 (7 min., 2 sec.).
15. Honesty Can Get Sticky, Part 2 (16 min., 14 sec.).
16. Mixed Feelings (15 min., 32 sec.).
17. Breakdown to a New Start (8 min., 15 sec.).
18. Underneath the Surface (6 min., 15 sec.).
19. Make Me Hallow (10 min., 32 sec.).
20. Season Finale (9 min., 38 sec.).

41 Bullets. bulletstv.com. 2012 (Crime Drama).

Hugo Roosa is a man in his early thirties who is addicted to gambling, especially poker. His addiction started in high school and, after graduating from college and acquiring a job as a Wall Street banker, Hugo found that the temptation to gamble became the most important thing in his life. As his addiction grew, it not only cost him the money he had saved, but his wife (Ashley, who could no longer deal with him) and career. Although it appears he is just unlucky, Hugo decides to go pro with stories following what happens when his continual unlucky streak forces him into a life of crime to make ends meet.

Mark Metzger is Hugo's college friend (majored with Hugo in finance) and now works as a bank teller. Like Hugo, he too is a loser and always in trouble—and always being bailed out by Hugo.

Manny Sanco is the feared mafia boss who oversees gambling, money-laundering and loan sharking. It is his annual big stakes poker games that draw Hugo into the underworld and trouble when he loses and needs to acquire money for the next big tournament.

Micky Valentine is a money launderer for Manny, a bit of a screw-up who hopes to one day break free of Manny and go into business for himself.

Detective Swartz is an embittered cop who has set his goal to get Manny for causing the death of his partner. Although he is smart and cunning, he is unable to get the goods on Manny and send him to prison.

Detective Hunts is a rookie and Swartz's partner. He has just been promoted and his eagerness to prove himself often complicates the cases he and Swartz investigate.

Keith Obermeir is the psychiatrist attempting to help Swartz overcome the psychological effects he is suffering due to his partner's death.

Frank McCourt is the absent-minded bank manager responsible for Manny's money-laundering operations.

Jesse is the drug dealer with ties to Manny. George is the aspiring gangster seeking to work his way into Manny's organization. Jason is a poker player with a serious attitude problem when he loses. Al is the eldest of the poker players. Ralph is Manny's right-hand man.

Cast: Clint Keepin (Hugo Roosa), Zach Silverman (Mark Metzger), Ed Morrone (Manny Sanco), Brian Majestic (Det. Swartz), Maxwell Glick (Dr. Keith Obermeir), Rudy Casillas (Micky Valentine), Jimmy Freivogul (Frank Higgins), Sam Proof (Ralph), Dennis O'Mahoney (Al), Dave Baez (Miguel), Julian Grabt (George), Somya von Eames (Ashley Roosa). **Credits:** *Producer:* Ty Leisher, Alexis Edelman. *Writer-Director:* Ty Leisher. **Comment:** Harsh portrayal of how an addiction can ruin lives. The acting and production values are good and the story, although unresolved, is well done and more for those interested in character studies rather than extreme violence and action.

Episodes:

1. The Flop (11 min., 59 sec.). Tired of his job as a banker, Mark convinces Hugo to steal a million dollars from a bank account to enable them to play in a high-stakes poker game.

2. The Turn (12 min., 52 sec.). Having stolen the money, Hugo must now inch his way into Manny's illegal gambling den. He begins by convincing his drug-dealer friend (Jesse) to introduce him.

3. The River (10 min.). As Det. Swartz investigates a murder, he finds his life taking another turn for the worse when he is teamed with the less-than professional Det. Hunts. Hugo has made his way into Manny's high-stakes poker tournament.

4. Squeezed (13 min., 1 sec.). For the first time, Hugo appears to have a winning hand—but faces a dilemma in his first game with Manny—fold or let Manny win to gain his confidence.

5. Cracked (7 min., 59 sec.). Hugo's decision to fold appears to have been a wise decision. The stakes are growing and players are bowing out, leaving Hugo to face Manny in a two man game. Meanwhile, Swartz appears to have uncovered evidence he needs to nail Manny. The program's concluding episode.

42 *Café Kremlin.* webserieschannel.com. 2012–2013 (Drama).

Michael and Banks are men addicted to gambling. But instead of continually indulging in a losing career they decide to turn their vice into a business and establish an illegal underground gambling den. All is progressing well until they start taking bets from a man named Serge, a ruthless Russian gambler who plans to rig the betting system so the odds are in his favor. When Michael and Banks discover what is happening but are powerless to stop it, they seek help from their mentor, Carmine, a family friend with connections to the mob. The program follows Michael and Banks as they, with Carmine's help, seek to stop Serge's take over of their small but progressing empire.

Michael is a thinker and will do whatever it takes to get something done. Banks is ambitious, a playboy and usually follows Michael's lead. Jake is Michael's older brother and the man who looks out for Michael.

Serge appears to be a legitimate businessman (as he operates a cab stand and coffee shop that serve as fronts for his underground businesses). Lazarus, newly arrived in Chicago (the program's setting) from New York, works alongside Serge. Carmine, once a top-ranking mob member, now lives a somewhat non-descript life, but sometimes yearns to get back in the game.

Viktoria is Serge's niece, a deadly assassin. Isabella is Carmine's highly-educated daughter. Lisa is Banks younger sister, an aspiring professional poker player. Katie is Lisa and Banks older sister. Mia is a party girl and Lisa's best friend. Jessica is the hostess at Michael and Banks club; Traci is a childhood friend of Michael and Banks.

Vlad is Serge's enforcer. Sal is the owner of the club frequented by Michael and Banks. Kyle, front man for a band, is a friend of Michael and Banks. Don "Da Bomb" George is Chicago's World Ranked Super Middle Weight Contender who trains with Jake. The Russian Hostess (no other name given) works the counter at the Russian Coffee Shop. Pierce is the off-the-wall friend of Michael and Banks.

Cast: Jon Kasunic (Michael), Ariel Grigas (Banks), Vernon A. Hintt III (Serge), Harry W. Walters (Carmine), Jordan Miczek (Jake), Eric Bland (Vlad), Caitlin Costello (Alyssa), Lorell Edelberg (Mia), Erik Kennedy (Pierce), Hank Stahlecker (Kyle), Elena Chernyakova (Viktoria), Manya Niman (Isabella), Rachel Joy Mazza (Lisa), Heather Dorff (Katie), Peter George (Michael's father), Michael Apa (Sal), Amanda Powell (Traci), Jessica DuPlessis (Jessica), Hank Stahlecker (Kyle), Don "Da Bomb" George (Himself), Emma Pope (Russian Hostess), Joette Waters (Michael's mother), Erik Kennedy (Pierce). **Credits:** *Producer:* Joseph Graziani, Joseph Lampugnano. *Director:* Joseph Graziani. *Writer:* Joseph Graziani, Karl Hafner, Jon Kasunic, Joseph Lampugnano. **Comment:** Fast-moving story with good acting, believable characters and television series–like production values. Well worth watching even though there are traces of vulgar language (although far less than many other good guy vs. bad guy web programs).

Episodes:

1. A Very Beautiful Friendship (5 min., 21 sec.). The story begins as Michael and Banks plan their business venture.

2. Weird KGB Vibe (8 min.). Michael and Banks approach Serge for the money they need to open their club.

3. Knocking D Zero Off (8 min., 40 sec.). Things are looking up for Michael and Banks as they throw a party to celebrate the opening of their club.

4. Little Russian Guru (5 min., 51 sec.). Unknown to Michael and Banks, professional gamblers, posing as amateurs, make large bets on the outcome of a soccer game.

5. It Is What It Is (6 min., 9 sec.). The bets pay off for the gamblers, leaving Michael and Banks owing money they don't have ($600,000).

6. Short Notice (6 min., 1 sec.). Without the funds and with threats from Serge to pay up, Michael and Banks seek the help of their friend Carmine.

7. The Trial (5 min., 16 sec.). Carmine manages to call off Serge's pressure in a plan to have both sides meet and tell their sides of the story (Michael insisting Serge's associates cheated by opening two accounts under the same name to increase winnings).

8. My New Soldier (7 min., 18 sec.). To insure that he gets the money due, Serge kidnaps Banks in a ploy to take over the club. Unaware as to what has happened, Michael begins calling in favors to raise the money.

9. No Other Choice (6 min., 10 sec.). Michael finds a letter (placed on his doorstep) from Banks telling him that he has left town (leading Michael to believe he bailed out on him). In actuality, the letter was placed there to cover up Banks' kidnapping.

10. Bigger Picture (8 min., 58 sec.). At a party, originally planned for Banks, Michael covers for him by saying that Banks has ventured onto a spiritual retreat while the viewer sees that Banks is still being held captive by Serge's goons.

11. Your Revenge (7 min., 28 sec.). The concluding episode wherein Michael suspects foul play and confronts the Russian Hostess, as she was the last person to see Banks, in an effort to find Banks.

43 *California Heaven.* californiaheaven. com. 2005–2006 (Drama).

California Heaven & Surf, the largest chain of swimwear and surf stores in the U.S., is owned by the wealthy but mysterious Corrigan family. Incorporating the format of a daily network television soap opera, the program focuses primarily on two intertwining story lines: the conflict that exists between the Corrigan and Hutton families and a mystery that begins when Heaven Corrigan, having been away from the family for several years (living in Oklahoma), returns to Malibu to investigate the circumstances surrounding her mother's sudden death when it appears natural to authorities but seems unnatural to her. As she probes, she begins to uncover unnerving facts about her family and slowly comes to realize she has become the victim of a plot to drive her out of Malibu (by convincing everyone she is insane) and conceal the facts that killed her mother.

Cast: Jacqueline Bradley (Heaven Corrigan), Bruce Blauer (James Corrigan), Kali Cook (K.C. Corrigan), Bram Hoover (Dominic Corrigan), Brianna Rose (Lexy Corrigan), Michael Myracle (Virginia Corrigan), Maya Waterman (Rebecca Corrigan), Tanya Gorlow (Nicolette Tibbets), Ciera Rose Allen (Alicia Gabaldon), Ashley Keene (Brooke Kinkaid), Will Stanfill (Christian Hutton), John Stanfill (Walt Hutton), Jan Stewart (Dottie Hutton), Angelique Mermet (Olivia Hutton). **Credits:** *Producer:* Stewart St. John, Todd Fisher. *Writer-Director:* Stewart St. John. **Comment:** A personal judgment is not possible, but based on existing reviews of the program, it was intriguing, exceptionally well-acted (especially Jacqueline Bradley as Heaven) and very well produced (captures attention from the very beginning; "If you watch *California Heaven* once, you'll probably watch it again").

Episodes: All episodes (including the official website) have been taken off line. Following is a listing of known titles: *1.* Heaven in Malibu, Part 1. *2.* Heaven in Malibu, Part 2. *3.* The Last Supper. *4.* Wicked at 23. *5.* Winners and Losers. *6.* Eye for an Eye. *7.* The Lyin', the Switch and the Videotape. *8.* The Trojan Horse. *9.* Back to Oklahoma? *10.* Checkmate. *11.* Crazy Heaven.

44 *Caper.* youtube.com. 2014 (Comical Adventure).

In the City of Angles ("Where everyone has an angle"), reside four friends—Penny, Alexia, Dagr and Luke—friends who are actually underpaid and under-appreciated super heroes. They share the rent and reside in a rather cheap "rat palace" ("something you wouldn't wish on your worst enemy," says Penny). They are always behind in rent, always face eviction, risk their lives to protect the innocent, get no respect and stories chart their escapades as they plan the ultimate caper—posing as "bad guys" to infiltrate the heavily secured Clark Industries, crack a vault and relieve it of all its money.

Penny, alias The Machine, is a very pretty young woman and the only human living with three immortals. She previously worked for Clark Industries where she developed a specialized space suit that is capable of enabling its wearer to fly and acquire incredible strength. She stole the suit (which Clark Industries wants back) is on the run and encompasses the power of the suit to become a super hero. While keeping under the radar is her main problem, she does not have the necessary equipment or parts to maintain the suit and relies on her father's old tool box and what replacement parts she can get a Radio Shack. Her identity is always hidden by the face helmet and most people believe that The Machine is a man.

Alexia is a gorgeous Amazon who gave up her royal blood at the age of 13 when she joined the Assassins Guild hoping for glory. When all she got was a deflated ego, she chose to go straight. She now works on the side of good, is strong, mean and someone you do not want to get angry.

Luke Washington, known as The Trooper gave up his low-paying job as a journalist for an even lower paying job as a blogger (as he now gets paid via page views). He is the son of an earth mother and an alien (Starman) and has the ability to fly.

Dagr is the 12th son of 12 sons and from an alternate dimension where Vikings still rule. Penny considers him "Euro-trash and a pain in the butt" and has been sent to earth "on a quest for some sacred something" which he still hasn't found. He works as a handyman (charges $50 to change a light bulb) and is the one whose income helps the friends meet the rent (well, almost always).

Cast: Abby Miller (Penny Blue), Beth Riesgraf (Alexia), Hartley Sawyer (Dagr), Harry Shum, Jr. (Luke), Yuri Lowenthal (Blake Anders), Tara Platt (Cherry Storm), Joel Gretsch (Sam Clarke), James Callis (Doc English), Robert Craighead (Chief Stebbins), Cullen Douglas (Landlord). **Credits:** *Producer:* Felicia Day, Sheri Bryant. Mike Sizemore, Amy Berg. *Director:* Donald Murphy. *Writer:* Amy Berg, Mike Sizemore. **Comment:** Enjoyable super hero spoof with good acting and production values; would make a great transition to network or basic cable TV. The story flows from beginning to end and the use of animated comic book panels adds to the fun.

Episodes:

1. City of Angles (10 min., 36 sec.). The characters are introduced through Penny's narration.

2. The Kilt Brahs (11 min., 24 sec.). With the rent due, and their usual inability to meet it, the team becomes sidetracked when they join forces to rescue hostages being held by a gunman at a mini mart.

3. Psycho Path (8 min., 48 sec.). The group plans a caper, but in order for it to work Penny believes they have to become bad and seek the help of a bad

dude named Psycho to teach them the ins and outs of becoming despicable.

4. The British Guy (9 min., 28 sec.). As the team trains to become bad, they learn a number of things—like not using guns (as Alexia accidentally shoots Dagr).

5. Lasers and Feelings (7 min., 12 sec.). With the knowledge of how to be bad encompassed (at least the team hopes so) they now plan a "Mission: Impossible"–like caper to rob an impenetrable vault.

6. Southpaw's Always Right (8 min., 33 sec.). Penny receives a visit from Southpaw, an East Coast hero (with the East Coast 6) with an offer to join their team in New York.

7. Histgrectory (11 min., 3 sec.). Unaware that Southpaw was a ploy by Clark Industries to trap Penny and get the suit back, Penny seeks the advice of her father, Pete (Scott Bakula) as his decision could change the course of not only her life—but the roommates as well.

45 The Captive. webserieschannel.com. 2008 (Thriller).

A young man, standing on the street and waiting for a bus, is mysteriously kidnapped (he is somehow whisked away when a car passes) and confined to an area from which there appears to be no escape. The program relates his plight as he faces harsh interrogation while seeking way to escape.

Cast: Brian Greer (The Captive), Michael Gladis. **Credits:** *Creator:* Karin Diann Williams, Hynson Culpepper. **Comment:** The program is well produced and worth watching. It is an obvious take-off on the TV series *The Prisoner* (its original title) but not as fantasy-like. The acting is good but some scenes are very dark and it is difficult to make out what is happening. The actors used for the program perform their chores well, but for reasons that are unknown, they are not credited and the printed visuals that appear at the end of each program are either an inside joke for the producers or some sort of code that even Sherlock Holmes would have trouble deciphering. It varies with each episode, but there is no spacing between words that appear and a series of numbers appears where the cast would normally be seen. The crew involved with the show also lack credit. The two names that appear in the cast were found on a sharing website; unfortunately, the beautiful Trustee that was part of the program remains a mystery.

Episodes:

1. Red Yellow Green (4 min., 13 sec.). The story line is set up as the Captive (as he is called) is kidnapped and placed in an unknown location.

2. Scratch My Back (4 min.). A beautiful Trustee warns the Captive to do what he is told and not make waves.

3. Meatloaf Night (2 min., 40 sec.). The Captive is introduced to other prisoners.

4. Water Water (2 min., 48 sec.). The Captive faces another round of harsh questioning for a crime he has no idea he committed.

5. Freedom to Freedom From (3 min., 34 sec.). Unable to get answers from brutal questioning, the Interrogator changes direction, hoping a softer approach will get results.

6. The Secret (3 min., 6 sec.). The Captive discovers a secret door that leads to the Interrogator's lair.

7. Written in Blood (7 min., 38 sec.). The Captive uncovers new evidence about the Interrogator while exploring his office.

8. The Riddle (3 min., 13 sec.). With his information, the Captive meets with the Trustee he befriended in episode 2.

9. Trust Me (2 min., 5 sec.). The Captive is unexpectedly promoted to a Trustee. He says to himself he must have done something right, but what?

10. Meals on Wheels (2 min., 34 sec.). The Captive begins his new job of providing meals to the prisoners.

11. Liberty (3 min., 57 sec.). With his new found freedom, the Captive manages to elude guards and escape.

12. Liberty (3 min., 57 sec.). The Captive is puzzled—as his escape has led him into the heart of Manhattan (as seen by the Statue of Liberty).

13. Call Waiting (3 min., 11 sec.). As the Captive returns to his apartment he receives a phone call (apparently from the female Trustee) telling him that he is not free, that he did not escape, but was let go on purpose.

46 Caribe Road. cariberoad.com. 2011– 2013 (Action Drama).

Mark Caribe (pronounced Ka-re-bay, Spanish for Caribbean) is a former U.S. Special Forces Airborne Commander. During a mission in South America to stop rebels led by a Colombian terrorist (Carlos Saldana), Mark's unit not only suffered loses but his daughter (Alina) was possibly kidnapped by Saldana. Rather than continue the fight and risk his daughter's life, the unit retreated and Mark resigned. Sometime later, when it is learned that Saldana is about to strike again, this time in a plot to destroy Los Angeles in a nuclear attack, the Secretary of Defense (Williams) approaches Mark and asks him to head an elite combat unit to stop Saldana. Mark is reluctant at first until Williams' hints that the government knows Alina's whereabouts and in return for his services will assist in her retrieval. Figuring this is his best chance of rescuing Alina, he agrees and the story follows Mark as he and his unit set out on a deadly mission to stop Saldana once and for all.

Cast: Hector Luis Bustamante (Mark Caribe), Ransford Doherty (James Crews), Thom Tran (Thom Chen), Alexandra Manea (Allie Cortez), Mike Pfaff (Nick O'Neil), Marlene Forte (Capt. Garcia),

Caribe Road. Logo art from the series (copyright HELU Films).

Jennifer Field (Ashley Belle), Don R. Williams (Sec. of Defense Williams), Jeannie Bolet (Ms. Honeycutt), Alina Herrera (Alina Caribe), Julian Scott Urena (Carlos Saldana), Carlos Antonio (Fred Piaget). **Credits:** *Show Creator:* H. Bustamante. *Executive Producer:* Louise Wu, Cherish McDowell. *Co-Executive Producer:* Milton Wu, Lisa Banks, Geno Nicholas. *Contributing Producer:* Alex O. Gaynor, Jeremy Rush, Mike Pfaff, Carlos Amselle. *Director:* Hector Luis Bustamante, Alex Gaynor, Jeremy Rush. *Writer:* Joseph Sheridan, Anne Eston, H. Bustamante. *Technical Support*: Justin Aguirre, Reid Gibian, Adam Sperry. **Comment:** The program was created "out of a deep desire to say thank you and show appreciation to all the men and women and their families who sacrificed so much." It is well acted and produced and, although it remains unresolved at the time of publication, has set the pace for an intriguing, action oriented race against time.

Episodes:

1. Rise from the Ashes. An unexpected call from the Department of Defense brings retired U.S. Special Forces commander Mark Caribe back to Washington, D.C. to meet with the Secretary of Defense and acquire the information he needs to lead him back to his daughter. But it is not as simple as Mark first believes.

2. Without Trust There Is Nothing. Mark, meeting with the Secretary, learns about a terrorist plot by Carlos Saldana to destroy Los Angeles. He also learns that Saldana is responsible for his daughter's kidnapping and what he must do to get her back.

3. Blood Patriots. Mark accepts the assignment to stop Saldana by taking command of a counter terrorism unit called SFT1.

4. Another Day. The stage is set: Mark acquires his mission: lead a top secret counter-terrorist unit with the primary object being to destroy Saldana's network and either capture or kill Saldana.

5. Present and Collide. Mark and his former team from his days with the Los Angeles P.D. SWAT division are reunited when one of their own is killed in a car-bomb explosion that was meant to send a message: a bomb has been hidden in the city and set to go off in a matter of hours.

6. Lone Wolf, Part 1. Could the bomb and the killing be the work of Saldana? Mark (and authorities believe so) and, as Mark rejoins the L.A.P.D., he begins the daunting task of finding the bomb before it detonates. The concluding (filmed) episode as of July 2014.

47 *Casters.* casterstheshow.com. 2011–2012 (Drama).

Bring It On is a fictional podcast (downloadable digital media audio and video files) that is based in Queens, New York and controlled by three friends: Cal and Ronnie (the hosts) and Owen (the engineer). Each episode looks at their attempts to produce a weekly episode, focusing in particular on their efforts to acquire guests to appear with them. The program also details the behind-the-scene conflicts as it delves into the personal lives of the friends as they deal with romantic relationships, addiction and family problems.

Cast: Jason Griffith (Cal), Miriam Pultro (Ronnie), Joshua Tussin (Owen), Claire Buckingham (Emily), Erin Zapcic (Liza), Adam Henry Garcia (Clarke), Dawn Yanek (Anne), Brian Faherty (Brian), Dana Segal (Dana), Shea Davies (Julie). **Credits:** *Producer:* Marc Berman. *Writer-Director:* Erin Gould. **Comment:** Well-acted and produced program that is basically just a podcast with some drama and guests thrown into the mix.

Episodes:

1. Bring It Up, Part 1 (11 min., 32 sec.). Introduces the three regulars as they figure change is best for their podcast but Cal is reluctant to do so when he feels what they have is already successful.

2. Bring It Up, Part 2 (11 min., 21 sec.). Despite some squabbles, a podcast airs with guests Joe Jung and Brian Frank.

3. The Assist, Part 1 (11 min., 6 sec.). As the situation with Cal worsens (reluctant to change the format), Ronnie and Cal attempt to produce the show without him.

4. The Assist, Part 2 (12 min., 56 sec.). Owen makes contact with Dana, a girl with her own podcast, and seeks her advice about the situation.

5. Emily, Part 1 (12 min., 59 sec.). A look at podcast hookups as Cal and Owen explore the possibility of meeting women; meanwhile, Ronnie prepares to have lunch with her sister, Julie, who disapproves of her on air activities and wishes she would just concentrate on her job as a bartender.

6. Emily, Part 2 (9 min., 55 sec.). Owen meets with Dana while Cal talks with his podcast date, Emily in the concluding episode.

48 *Celeste Bright.* ovguide.com. 2010 (Drama).

Celeste Bright, an investment broker for Bright and Associates, is a young woman who plays by her own rules (like charging excessive amounts of interest on loans). She is beautiful, cunning and "able to take care of myself." Celeste, however, has one serious flaw: she is too trusting of others, especially Gordon Tate, a promising new client, who sees her enthusiasm as an escape goat for himself when he sets her up as a person of interest in a murder he committed. Celeste's life suddenly changes for the worse when an FBI Special Agent (Rick Taylor) begins an investigation into the murder and becomes overly suspicious of Celeste wondering who she really is and what she is hiding. The program follows Celeste's efforts to clear her name and, with Rick's help, find the actual murderer.

Cast: Ryan Michelle Bathe (Celeste Bright), Eddie

Goines (Rick Taylor), Anita Dashiell (Trudy Alexander), Barry Ford (Benjamin Carrington), Dionne Lea (Madam Lila), Joyce Chow (Joyce Liu), Brad Raider (Gordon Tate), Edward Singletary (Murray Stover). **Credits:** *Producer:* Joseph Doughrity, Sonya Steele. *Director:* Joseph Doughrity, Gregory Storm. *Writer:* Judy Dent, Sonya Steele. **Comment:** Well-acted and produced program that hints at dishonesty from the very beginning and how one woman attempts to justify what she does. Adding her as the leading suspect in a murder case adds to her trauma and makes for a well presented series.

Episodes:

1. Person of Interest. Celeste and her seemingly normal business activities are seen for the first time.

2. T.M.I. Celeste is not as ethical as she seems when a client (Henry) requiring $100,000 to make good money he embezzled, is charged $10,000 a week interest until the money is repaid.

3. The Company She Keeps. Celeste, a person of interest in an FBI case, comes under scrutiny when Agent Rick Taylor begins questioning her about her business practices.

4. True Colors. At a party Celeste finds that her worst enemy is Gordon Tate, a client who is setting her up for a killing.

5. Fear No Evil. Agent Taylor approaches Celeste with advice to detach herself from Gordon before the situation gets out of control. She refuses, saying she can take care of herself.

6. S.O.L. Celeste feels threatened when Gordon approaches and tells her not to make waves—because if he goes down, so will she.

7. Revelations. Agent Taylor begins questioning Celeste's psychic friend (Madam Lila) hoping to gather information on what she has told her.

8. The Heart Wants. In a conversation with Agent Taylor, it is learned that Celeste's father was swindled by the very people he tried to help. When he died and Celeste took over the company, she used her trust fund to continue the business and make her high interest loans to the same type of crooks who ripped her father off.

9. Things Fall Apart. Everything appears to be going well for Celeste—until she is attacked by Gordon (seeking not only money—but her father's gun).

10. No Regrets. In a surprise turn of events, Gordon frames Celeste for a killing with her father's gun; Agent Taylor, having fallen in love with Celeste, approaches her and gives her a passport and money to leave town—and not tell him where she is going. The episode concludes with Celeste at the airport and about to depart.

49 Central Division. cerntraldivisiontvseries.com. 2009 (Crime Drama).

Los Angeles provides the backdrop for a gritty program (sort of inspired by *N.Y.P.D. Blue*) that follows two police detectives (Alan Edwards and Frank Hodge) as they seek an elusive killer that planted the body of his victim in the trunk of their squad car.

Cast: Brian Silverman (Det. Alan Edwards), Clay Wilcox (Det. Frank Hodge), Marcele Kutkauskaite (Sarah). **Credits:** *Producer-Writer-Director:* Aleem Hossain. **Comment:** The program is a bit dark at times and a bit talkative as Alan and Frank plot their investigation. Only the first two episodes are on line with episodes 3 ("The Full Number," 2 min., 5 sec.) and 4 ("The Recorder," 1 min., 37 sec.) no longer available for viewing.

Episodes:

1. Feels Like a Situation (2 min., 40 sec.). Alan and Frank's investigation of a crime connected with the Serbian mob takes an unsuspected turn of events when Internal Affairs begins investigating them.

2. The Trunk (2 min., 40 sec.). With evidence of possible wrong doing being probed, Alan and Frank believe they are being set up by the Serbian mob.

50 The Centre. youtube.com. 2013 (Anthology).

German-produced program of stories about how African-American women cope with life in Berlin, Germany. Each story revolves around The Centre, a refuge for women started by a Namibian social worker (Leoni) after finding disenchantment with the German Bureaucracy. With the help of a doctor (Jessi) she befriended years ago in a refugee camp in Lesotho, she helps the troubled women (apparently to be lesbians) with no place else to go.

Cast: Naomi Beukes-Meyer (Leoni), Brigit Stauber (Jessi). **Credits:** *Producer:* Brigit Stauber, Mirya Kalmuth, Lucia Luciano, Julia Stenke, Timalen Jose. *Director:* Amber Palmer, Eddy Balardi. *Writer:* Naomi Beukes-Meyer. **Comment:** Thus far only one episode (a pilot) has been produced and, without a doubt, the most unusual of all the lesbian series that have been produced for the Internet. The program has English subtitles and its subject matter, while different, may also have little appeal to American audiences.

Episodes:

1. I'm Still Down Here. A young woman (Sanaa) seeks help when her love for a German punk girl (Janis) is opposed by her very religious family. Starring: Lucia Luciano as Sanaa and Julia Stenke as Julia.

51 Chapel. iverpictures.com. 2008 (Crime Drama).

It has been said that, although prison is punishment for those who break the law, it is also a school. Ashley Banks is one of its students. Although a charge is not stated, Ashley is first seen as a young, plain–Jane type of woman who is totally out of place in prison (The Women's Correctional Facility). She has been sentenced to six years and she is not only a bit nerdy, but mousy and apparently without any friends (as the only correspondence she receives is a post card with the picture of a chapel on the front). As Ashley attempts to fit into the prison society, she becomes abused by the other inmates and given the nickname "Chapel" based on the postcard she displays near her bed. The abuse and beatings toughen Chapel (her "schooling"), so much so that when she is released she is a totally different woman—a bitch with a vicious attitude. Chapel also changes her nerdy appearance (to that of a butch-like lesbian) and begins a new career—drug dealer. Drugs were forced upon her in prison and learning of the drug business from inmates, Chapel now feels she is ready to start her own dealership. The program follows Chapel as she does what she must to remain in business—killing anyone that stands in her way.

Cast: Emily Mills (Chapel), Kelly Maxwell (Burke), Meghan Rose (Yvonne), Cameron Shimniok (Benny), Geri Matsushita (Christine Church), Dana Pellebon (Stone), Matt Fanale (Butch), Dylan Brogan (Leifield). **Credits:** *Producer-Writer-Director:* Rob Matsushita. **Comment:** Emily Mills is captivating as Chapel. Though vicious and involved in the drug trade, she is also the hero of the story, wanting to be independent and not letting anything stand in her way. Although not the best message to send, it is well produced and acted. It is also very violent and contains vulgar language.

Episodes:
1. Audited (6 min., 50 sec.). Begins the story as Chapel, just released from prison, makes plans to begin a new life.
2. Battered, Part 1 (10 min.). Finding that no one is willing to hire an ex-con, Chapel hooks up with a small-time drug dealer (Benny) who operates from a skate park.
3. Battered, Part 2 (10 min., 55 sec.). Chapel's new business venture is anything but pleasing to her when she begins to have doubts about selling drugs to kids.
4. Complicated (5 min., 30 sec.). Chapel finds her life threatened when she teams with a crooked cop (whom she later has to kill) when a drug deal doesn't go as planned.
5. Distracted (6 min., 6 sec.). Chapel takes to the road, hoping to put what just happened behind her and start anew elsewhere.
6. Extremed (8 min., 29 sec.). Chapel encounters a new enemy (Burke) when she begins selling a new drug (Extremed) on which he wants exclusive rights.
7. Famed (19 min., 51 sec.). Unable to defeat Burke, Chapel finds herself out of the drug business but in a new predicament when she is blackmailed into helping a has-been actress desperately trying to revive her career.
8. Guilted (16 min., 55 sec.). Chapel is kidnapped by a madman who mistakes her for his former lover. Strapped to a bed and facing certain death, Chapel manages to turn the tables and kill him.

9. Handcuffed (14 min., 45 sec.). A figure from Chapel's past appears and offers her a chance at something better.
10. Inked (14 min., 25 sec.). Chapel's situation appears to be improving until she over-doses on a new hallucinogenic and begins envisioning her past enemies teaming up to get her. The episode is presented as a comic book with the cast providing voices over their drawn images.
11. Jacked, Part 1 (10 min., 52 sec.). Chapel travels to New York City, where she hopes to make a new beginning—until she discovers her nemesis, Burke, has also set up shop.
12. Jacked, Part 2 (16 min., 16 sec.). A rival dealer, Christine Church, sets her plans to eliminate Chapel. Concludes in a cliffhanger with Chapel defeating Christine, but Christine vowing to return and finish what she started.

52 *Chica Busca Chica (Girl Seeks Girl).* afterellen.com. 2007 (Comedy-Drama).

Madrid, Spain, provides the exotic backdrop for a look at the lives, loves and personal issues faced by a group of gorgeous women who are also lesbians: Nines, a flirtatious bartender at the local lesbian bar, Chica Busca Chica, who romances every woman she meets although she has an on-again, off-again romance with her boss, Rosi (the editor of a publishing house wherein Nines is hoping to produce a book about a super heroine). Her lame pick-up line, "You have an eyelash on your cheek," grants her the girl she has set her sights on; Ana, a young woman new to the lesbian scene (and desperate for Nines to teach her the techniques of lesbian dating and love); Monica, a judo coach called "The Psycho" at clubs (as she can't quite give up the prospect of losing a girlfriend), and Carmen, a heterosexual who is drawn mostly to women after she discovers she has a cheating boyfriend (Jorge).

Cast: Celia Freijeiro (Nines), Cristina Pons (Monica), Almudena Gallego (Ana), Sandra Collantes (Carmen), Karola Sanchez (Victoria), Paloma Arimon (Rosi), Paco Manzanedo (Jorge), Jimena Fernandez (Michelle), Cristina Camison (Yoyo), Inma Cuesta (Roberta), Maribel Luis (Carla), Isabel Prinz (La Paciente), Eva Pallares (Maite).

Comment: Premiering on the Internet while the TV series *The L-Word* was still current, *Girl Seeks Girl* offered a more focused look at the relationships encountered by the cast. There are sexual situations, numerous kissing scenes and a look at life in a lesbian community outside of the United States. The same can be said for both—the women are gorgeous and the problems they encounter—whether from infidelity to one night stands are the same.

Episodes: Sixteen untitled episodes were produced, each of which is produced in Spanish with English subtitles, making for a difficult-to-follow story (as it distracts from the striking visual elements of the series). The acting is top rate and the production values as comparable to any television series.

53 *Circle-Drawers.* circledrawers.com. 2009 (Drama).

Circle-Drawers are earth bound angels living among humans and, in essence, "lowly janitors of the Almighty's imperfect system" (they perform mundane tasks and receive their assignments from an organizational system that includes the Internal or from their messengers, the Human Protectors). Once human, but having lived a lackluster or unproductive life, they have been reborn as angels and condemned to remain as such until they perform 1571 tasks to earn the privilege of rebirth as humans. Oleg, a special emissary of the Almighty, has been assigned a most difficult task: provide a detailed semi-centennial analysis of the Circle-Drawer system. As Oleg establishes himself in Iceland (a central transmission center), it is learned that a young man in New York (Lewis) fell through the cracks in the system and, for 20 years, was reborn and raised as a human. To correct the system's mistake, Lewis is stripped of his human life and placed in the custody of seasoned Circle-Drawers Marcus and Moses; he must now begin possible eternity as a Circle-Drawer. The program follows Lewis as he makes the transition, but also struggles with his inability to leave his human life behind (it is also hinted that Lewis may be something more than just a Circle-Drawer but someone being geared for a higher calling).

Cast: Hilmir Snaer Guonason (Oleg), Logan Huffman (Lewis), Ashley Springer (Moses), Stefan C. Schaefer (Marcus), Sharon Angela (Judy), Diana De La Cruz (Rita), Steve Schirripa (Human Protector). **Credits:** *Producer:* Olaf de Fleur Johannesson, Diane Crespo, Victoria Imperioli. *Director:* Olaf de Fleur Johannesson. *Writer:* Olaf de Fleur Johannesson, Rune Kippervik, Hrafnkell Stefansson, Stefan C. Schaefer. **Comment:** Intriguing program that focuses on an aspect of Angels that has not been tackled before. The program, produced in Iceland, is well acted and produced and the last episode leaves the doorway open for addition episodes as it follows Lewis's plight to complete his tasks and return to his life as a human.

Episodes:
1. Central Transmission Station (2 min., 32 sec.). Establishes the format as Oleg begins his assignment in Iceland.
2. Angel's Daily Deeds (8 min., 23 sec.). Explores Oleg as he explains his assignment and detects a flaw in the system.
3. A Boy Named Lewis (8 min., 43 sec.). Lewis, the human who was accidentally overlooked by the system, is detected.
4. Marcus and Moses (8 min., 55 sec.). Angels Marcus and Moses are assigned the task of initiating Lewis into the Circle-Drawers system.

5. You're an Angel Now (9 min.). Lewis begins his new life as a Circle-Drawer.
6. The Human Protector (9 min., 49 sec.). Lewis, now a member of the New York Circle-Drawer division, meets his commander, The Human Protector.
7. The Women (8 min., 28 sec.). Lewis is introduced to The Women, the governors of the Circle-Drawer system.
8. Departure (8 min., 28 sec.). The New York based Women's Unit begins its job of preparing a group of Circle-Drawers for an assignment, including Lewis.
9. The Future (8 min., 52 sec.). As Oleg completes his assignment in Iceland, Lewis is stripped of his human life and embarks on his first mission as a Circle-Drawer.

54 *Claddagh: The Series.* claddaghtheseries.com. 2012 (Crime Drama).

James McGovern, a native of Northern Ireland, is 35 years old and a member of organized crime. He is very loyal (Claddagh) and has a reputation for being dangerous—but also fair and respectful in following orders—even if it means killing family rivals. Life changes for James when on a mission to Montreal to recruit Canadians, he is implicated in a crime (the murder of a priest) and his presence made known to the police. The priest is revealed to have been an undercover crime boss and James's uncle, Frank, seizes upon the opportunity to become the new head of "the family." To avoid capture, James escapes to Belfast and finds that he has been stripped of his authority and the respect he had achieved. Now, working as a petty cash collector for the Montreal Irish mob, James vows to rebuild his life and regain the status and authority he once had. The program charts his efforts to find the person responsible for his plight and once again become a loyal family member.

James was born in Northern Ireland and raised as a Catholic by various relatives (his mother mysteriously disappeared when he was very young and his father was either in prison or on business for the mob). Despite what he does, James attends mass every Sunday, is respectful of women, children and his elders. He has an obsession for black women, loves R&B, reggae and hip-hop music and is also wanted for questioning by the police in several unsolved beating cases.

Frank McQuire, James's mob boss uncle, is well rooted in the Irish mob. He is all about respect and loyalty and has spent much time in jail. He is connected to both the old and new world mobs and "knows where all the bodies are buried." The ghosts from his past often haunt him and his one dream is to win the lottery and disappear to Costa Rica. Frank never married, has no children and his given his entire life to the mob.

Kieran O'Malley, a mob member and faithful to both Frank and James, is ambitious but vicious when threatened. His old world connections have earned him trust in the Irish mob—as he is loyal to the present, not the past.

Mo McCann, a mob enforcer and ex-boxer, also works as a trainer. He is African-Irish-Canadian, quick-witted and charming—but also deceptively dangerous.

Grace O'Neil is an ambitious and tough police detective that heads the Canadian Task Force (battles organized crime). She is African-Irish-Canadian and was raised by a single mother (who became pregnant by a black Irish rock star). Law enforcement is Grace's life and she has a chip on her shoulder—which she takes out on criminals.

Gerry Donnelly is an Irish-Canadian mobster who can't quite make things happen the way he would like (could be considered a screw up). While women appear to like him, his involvement with them causes him nothing but trouble.

Alister Simms is a corrupt prison warden and involved in illegal drugs. While he appears well dressed and well-manicured, he is very dangerous and, through his prison connections, acquires and uses information for his own gain.

Jimmy G represents the new face of organized crime—sees himself as a businessman, not a mobster. He is always well dressed, possesses degrees in law and accounting and he sees the mob as a game—something you set out to win.

Silent Sal is a man of mystery as virtually nothing is known about him; he is quiet, but when he speaks people listen. He appears to have no friends, no lovers and is quick to use violence to solve problems. He has become an urban legend in a way, with myths surrounding him. His job is simple: set up meetings and do the dirty work.

Cast: Alan Duggan (James McGovern), James McGowan (Frank McGuire), Patricia McKenzie (Grace O'Neil), Adam Lolacher (Kieran O'Malley), Marlon Lon (Mo McCann), Trevor Hayes (Mickey Finn), Nick Baillie (Gerry Donnelly), Richard Zeman (Alister Simms), Donny Quinn (Jimmy G), Anthony Mancini (Silent Sal), Dawn Ford (Mother O'Malley), Jonathan Higgins (Sean O'Malley), Dan Bingham (Patrick O'Malley), John Griffin (Liam O'Malley). **Credits:** *Producer:* Alan Duggan, Tressia Walter, Louis Fairbain. *Director:* Cormac McGrath, Alan Duggan. *Writer:* Anthony Mancini, Alan Duggan. **Comment:** Although the entire series cannot be watched it is still possible to enjoy the program as the overall theme can be picked up as the story unfolds. The acting and production values are good but it does take a few minutes to adjust to the Irish accents encountered as some characters speak.

Episodes: An episode listing follows as not all episodes remain on line and a sequential description is not possible (no episode descriptions are on line to make up for the missing information). *1.* Deception. *2.* The Call. *3.* The Test. *4.* Crossing the Line. *5.* The Cover-Up. *6.* Home Coming. *7.* Wrong Place, Wrong Time. *8.* The Reunion. *9.* Word from the Grave. *10.* The Mission. *11.* Order in the House. *12.* The Favor. *13.* Old World, New World. *14.* Taking Care of Business. *15.* The Big Picture. *16.* Payback. *17.* The Fix. *18.* Choose Your Drug. *19.* War. *20.* The Set-Up.

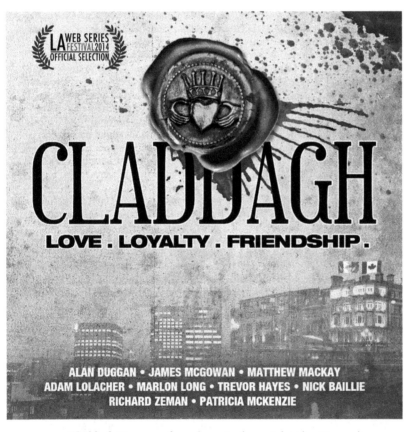

Claddagh. **Poster art from the series (copyright Alan Duggan).**

55 *Clutch.* clutchtheseries.com. 2011–2013 (Crime Drama).

Kylie is a beautiful young woman who acquires money as a pick pocket. She is self-taught and the life she leads suits her. She is dating Matt, a courier for a crime boss (Marcel) and, although Matt is seemingly not her type (cowardly and wimpy) she appears to love him. Life changes for Kylie when Matt loses $50,000 in a trade for drugs and Kylie becomes the pawn in an effort by Marcel to recover the money. She is suddenly drawn into the underworld and becomes a fugitive of sorts, hiding from Marcel and struggling to continue her prior life as best she can.

Kylie is a professional pickpocket but suffers from an inability to spot a wealthy mark. She relies on relieving "lonely males on barstools" of their money and stealing just enough to get by. In school Kylie was the girl no one could figure out and was ignored; she is now a woman of few words who lives under the radar and appears to be happy doing what she does.

Mike is a professional, street-smart thief. He knows how to spot a mark, stalk and then strike when the time is right. He keeps his past a secret and it is wise not to dig into that past. He is an expert in the use of firearms and military tactics and has a soft-spot for women, especially Kylie.

Matt is (although he tries to hide it) a coward at heart and will say and do whatever is needed "to the guy in charge to save his skin."

Bridgette is a prostitute by her own choosing (possibly initiated when she was rejected by society—and her foster family) and owns her own Cathouse as a safe haven for prostitutes who operate independently.

Marcel, a self-proclaimed Mafia-like boss with his own group of thugs, controls the city's drug traffic and sex trade. He is a master manipulator and smarter than he lets on. He is simply a thug who gets what he wants when he wants it.

Raven is a dominatrix who owns her own fetish dungeon (of which Marcel is her best customer). Although she appears tough, Raven cares for her girls and her clients, who must obey her rules, include politicians and police officials.

Michelle is the "Fetish Guide" in Raven's dungeon. She has a crush on Raven and also serves as the receptionist (helping new clients match a girl to their fetishes).

Cast: Elitsa Bako (Kylie), Matthew Carvery (Matt), Lea Lawrynowicz (Bridgette), Jeff Sinasac (Mike), Buzz Koffman (Hatchet Man), Peter Hodgins (Marcel Obertovitch), Alexandra Elle (Raven), Emily Schooley (Michelle), Caitlynne Medrek (Lex), Katherine Fogler (Jordan), Katya Gardner (FBI Agent Kriss), Jillian Clare (Nicole), Tom Konkle (Darius). **Credits:** *Producer:* Jonathan Robbins, Will Wong, Matthew Carvery. *Director:* Jonathan Robbins. *Wri-*

ter: Jonathan Robbins, Matthew Carvery, Charles Barangan, Lea Lawrynowicz, Alex Gheorghe. **Comment:** Well produced, fast-moving story that contains nudity, violence and foul language. A parental warning is posted before episodes begin.

Episodes:

1. Your Ex-Lover Is Dead, Part 1 (7 min., 25 sec.). Kylie's life takes a turn for the worse when Matt botches a drug deal and she becomes the pawn in a mob boss's efforts to recover his money.

2. Your Ex-Lover Is Dead, Part 2 (6 min., 18 sec.). Kylie, now having to live under the radar, befriends a hooker named Bridgette at the seedy hotel at which she resides.

3. Pick a Pocket or Two (8 min., 12 sec.). Needing money, but still having to keep a low profile, Kylie returns to the streets, where she encounters another pick pocket (Mike).

4. A Mentor (9 min., 27 sec.). Kylie learns that Mike is more than he appears to be when she learns he is sizing her up for a caper that will net a fortune (steal money possessed by Marcel).

5. Know Your Target (9 min., 21 sec.). The caper begins with Kylie infiltrating the fetish boutique frequented by Marcel to observe (to later impersonate) a dominatrix (Raven).

6. Whip It (11 min., 2 sec.). The plan appears to be running smoothly. Kylie has distracted Marcel, allowing Mike and Bridgette to enter the boutique.

7. It Always Catches Up to You (9 min., 16 sec.). The situation becomes tense as Kylie sizes up the situation with Mike secretly overseeing the plan.

8. Balance Due (8 min., 37 sec.). Things change drastically when Marcel's thugs realize Kylie has infiltrated the boutique and an all-out war erupts. Lives are lost but Kylie, Mike and Bridgette manage to escape.

9. Aftermath (5 min., 49 sec.). Kylie is now in hiding as Mike returns to his nefarious ways. In a strange twist, Matt has been secretly recruited by Marcel (and becomes involved with Lex, Marcel's daughter). Raven finds herself out of work and becoming Marcel's personal dominatrix.

10. Debt Collectors (7 min., 37 sec.). Marcel begins torturing Bridgette, hoping to extract information as to where Kylie may be hiding.

11. La Malinche (8 min., 25 sec.). Bridgette is forced into Marcel's prostitution ring while Matt and Lex are sent on a mission: collect a debt from Mike.

12. Inamorata (5 min., 37 sec.). Although Bridgette appears to have overcome Marcel's interrogation and seems to be happy that she has begun a relationship with a fellow prostitute (Jordan), feelings of guilt for revealing information about Kylie prompts her to commit suicide.

13. Catsup (5 min., 58 sec.). Angered by Bridgette's death, Jordan vows to bring Marcel down and make him pay for what he did to Bridgette.

14. Peripeteia (10 min., 19 sec.). Jordan and Raven seek a way to get even with Marcel for what

he has done to them. Kylie, in the meantime, has been captured by Marcel and held captive (to be sold as a sex slave).

15. Living in Fear (10 min., 52 sec.). Raven and Jordan find Mike who, after learning of Bridgette's death, and himself feeling guilty for plotting the earlier failed robbery, joins with them to get Marcel.

16. Digging Your Own Grave (8 min., 53 sec.). Matt and Mike learn where Kylie is being held (but getting to her and avoiding Marcel's henchmen poses a problem).

17. Unlikely Allies (7 min., 33 sec.). The situation intensifies as Mike, having access to a gun trafficking connection, arms his newly formed team with weapons.

18. Traffic Jam (9 min., 16 sec.). During a sex trafficking sale, Marcel's girls', aided by Mike, rebel, causing Marcel to flee for his life.

19. The Lucky Ones (13 min., 51 sec.). Hoping to find Kylie, Matt and Mike pose as buyers and infiltrate the house. Unknown to them, the FBI has also staked out the house, hoping to capture the head of the trafficking ring (Darius). As things go from bad to worse, Matt and Mike, helped by a kidnap victim (Nicole) manage to escape—but Agent Kriss is wounded and Kylie is nowhere to be found. The program concludes in a cliff hanger.

56 Coastal Dreams. nbc.com. 2007 (Drama).

Zoe Charles, a young woman who hopes to become a jewelry designer, lives in Plano, Texas. She has a best friend, Stacey (since childhood), a boyfriend (Sebastian) and a future full of dreams. Life changes suddenly for Zoe during her senior year at college when Sebastian becomes overly obsessed with her and begins stalking her. The situation has unnerved Zoe so much so, that after graduating, she accepts an invitation from her wealthy cousin April (an ex-model and international businesswoman) for her and Stacey to move to Southern California and live with her at her seaside home in Pacific Shores. The program follows the three women and the problems each faces: Zoe trying to move on and find someone new; Stacey adjusting to the new world in which she lives; and April, raised by a father (Gabriel) after her mother abandoned the family when she was an infant, now struggling to overcome the recent death of her father and run his billion-dollar business empire.

Other Regulars: Christian, a mysterious surfer who has made Pacific Shores his temporary home is the man who earns money performing odd jobs for April, and to whom Zoe becomes attracted. Will, born and raised in Pacific Shores, is the son of the town police chief and himself a police officer.

Cast: Danica Stewart (Zoe), Tanee McCall (Stacey), Kam Heskin (April), Charlie Koznick (Christian), Ken Luckey (Will Crawford). **Comment:**

With NBC behind it, the serial-like soap opera was no doubt well produced and acted. Unfortunately, programs produced by major companies (like NBC and WB) do not survive long after their initial runs, making compiling information more difficult and the removal of even trailers from YouTube places such programs in a situation that is common to most network series: once their run is completed they are withdrawn and in most cases, never seen again.

Episode List: All episodes have been taken offline.

1. Hello Pacific Shores (Oct. 2, 2007).
2. Meeting the Caretaker (Oct. 4, 2007).
3. Stacey Gets a Hot Date (Oct. 9, 2007).
4. The Key (Oct. 11, 2007).
5. Sebastian's on the Loose (Oct. 16, 2007).
6. The Ring (Oct. 18, 2007).
7. Who Turned Out the Lights? (Oct. 23, 2007).
8. The Intruder (Oct. 25, 2007).
9. Date Interrupted (Oct. 30, 2007).
10. Two Virgins (Nov. 1, 2007).
11. A Murder in Pacific Shores? (Nov. 6, 2007).
12. Seduction and Investigation (Nov. 8, 2007).
13. April Gets Suspicious (Nov., 13, 2007).
14. The Map (Nov. 15, 2007).
15. April's Showdown (Nov. 20, 2007).
16. Getting Rid of Christian (Nov. 22, 2007).
17. Will's No Saint (Nov. 27, 2007).
18. April's Big Mistake (Nov. 29, 2007).
19. Into the Cellar (Dec. 4, 2007).
20. Christian's Mom (Dec. 6, 2007).
21. Sisters (Dec. 11, 2007).
22. The Skeleton in the Cellar (Dec. 13, 2007).
23. The Rescue (Dec. 18, 2007).
24. A Voice from Beyond the Grave (Dec. 20, 2007).

57 Compulsions. compulsions.tv. 2009 (Thriller).

Tense character study of Mark Sandler, an admitted sadist who leads a double life: office worker by day; professional (but brutal) interrogator by night. The program follows his less-than-professional efforts to extract crucial information from the less-than-reputable people who hire him. Justine Davis, a beautiful woman who is described as "a trophy hunter and retrieval specialist," supplies Mark with the unwilling people he interrogates. Cassandra Morrisey, another beautiful woman in Mark's life, is an IT technician with a strange compulsion—to spy on people through their personal computers (which are altered by her when brought to her for repair).

Cast: Craig Frank (Mark Sandler), Seth Caskey (Adam Creedy), Janna Bossier (Justine Davis), Taryn O'Neill (Sara Flannery), Andrew Clemons (David), Annemarie Pazmino (Cassandra Morrissey), RC Ormond (James), Elizabeth Tsing (Lacey), Sean Spence (Randy), Ping Wu (Brian). **Credits:** *Producer-Writer:*

Bernie Su. *Director:* Nathan Atkinson. **Comment:** Not for everyone as the interrogation scenes can be quite upsetting (although they do not faze Mark in the least). The program does a good job showing how one person can be two different people—seemingly normal and somewhat laid back by day and cruel and vicious at night. The program is well produced and acted and recommended for mature audiences only.

Episodes:

1. Unleash (5 min., 12 sec.). Mark is hired to break a man (Adam Creedy) into revealing what he knows about a missing woman being sought by his contact's client.

2. Friends (4 min., 35 sec.). Shows how Mark can lead two lives and manage to keep both separate. Although it is not what he is seeking, Mark reveals what he has thus far learned from Adam to Justine.

3. Fairy Tale (2 min., 59 sec.). Justine follows Mark's lead and takes a young woman (Sara) into custody.

4. Solutions (4 min., 29 sec.). Mark sees no distinction between clients and proceeds to mercilessly interrogate Sara (Adam's girlfriend). Mark, however, becomes distracted when a nagging problem at work begins to interfere with his questioning.

5. Only I Can See (4 min., 2 sec.). Introduces Cassandra (the voyeur) and how she "fixes" clients computers for her own desires.

6. Ripen (5 min., 31 sec.). Mark continues his harsh interrogation of Sara. Meanwhile, Mark's problem at work intensifies as his co-worker (Randy) urges him to approach their pretty co-worker, Lacey.

7. Obsessed with a Crush (3 min., 24 sec.). Cassandra's spying on Mark has her wondering exactly who he is.

8. Promise Kept (3 min., 12 sec.). Justine finds herself in a jam when she is unable to provide her client (Bryan) with the information she promised Mark would extract from Adam. The program concludes in a cliff hanger.

58 *The Confession.* webserieschannel.com. 2011 (Thriller).

As a child he (name not revealed) and his family were abused by their father. The abuse caused their mother to commit suicide and he, after accidentally breaking a bottle of his father's whiskey, was punished by having his hand burned over the stove. The father, who had an addiction to alcohol, abandoned the family and the boy was raised in various foster homes. The boy grew up bitter and turned to a life of crime by becoming a hit man, killing people who deserve to die and not feeling any remorse over what he has done. Many years later the man (called The Confessor) enters a Catholic church to confess his sins. At first the priest refuses to hear The Confessor's sins until the Confessor tells him that if he refuses he will kill again. Flashbacks are used to explore

The Confessor's past as he and the priest become involved in an argument over God, good vs. evil and whether or not certain people deserve to die. As their conversation continues, The Confessor manipulates the priest into revealing his past—that he was married, had a son, was an alcoholic, punished his son by burning his hand and later abandoned him. The priest tries to get The Confessor to admit what he is doing is wrong, but it appears The Confessor is not looking for forgiveness. The Confessor then shows the priest a scar on his hand—the result of being burned on the stove. The priest realizes that The Confessor is his son—but The Confessor was not sure if the priest was his father, having only seen him a few days before. However, when he looked the priest straight into the eyes, he knew for sure. The Confessor's true intent is revealed—he will not kill the priest, nor will he forgive him for what he did to him and his mother—but he will continue to kill and send the priest newspaper clippings of the killings to punish the priest as the priest made him who he is and he is responsible for their deaths.

Cast: Kiefer Sutherland (Confessor), John Hurt (Priest). **Credits:** *Producer:* Kiefer Sutherland, Chris Young, Joseph Gomes, Chip Russo, Maura Mandt. *Writer-Director:* Brad Mirman. **Comment:** Although the actual episodes cannot be watched (due to the DVD release of the series) the program is well acted and produced and captivating. The original shortness of the episodes (5 to 7 min.) made for a compelling story and held your interest from the beginning.

Episodes: Ten episodes were produced but have been taken off line.

59 *Connection Lost: A Love Story.* web serieschannel.com. 2012 (Thriller).

It is Valentine's Day and a young woman (Ophelia) who truly loves her boyfriend (Greg) feels that he is too connected to the information highway to love her back. As Greg sits at his computer and witnesses a warning stating that the world is ending, he suddenly faces a nightmare when his Internet connection is lost. He then receives a phone call from Ophelia warning him not to use his cell phone. Moments later Ophelia, apparently covered in blood, arrives at his home. She warns Greg that "they" have come and the world has ended. Only a few, like herself and Greg have managed to survive and that "they" thrive on electricity, even that which is derived from batteries (hence why not to use his cell phone). To protect themselves, Ophelia insists they wrap the room in aluminum foil to prevent them from being detected by "them." The program charts Ophelia's efforts to convince a disbelieving Greg that the apocalypse has occurred and they must do what they can to survive.

Cast: Rachel Parsons (Ophelia), Rolland Walsh (Greg). **Credits:** *Producer:* Malarkey Films. *Director:*

Anna Callahan. *Writer:* Vladimir Zelevinsky. **Comment:** Delightful, well produced and well-acted mystery-thriller that although who "they" are is never revealed, keeps you interested from the very beginning.

Episodes:

1. Disconnect (3 min., 16 sec.). Greg's life suddenly changes when he loses his Internet connection and receives a frantic call from Ophelia telling him not to use his cell phone.

2. Lock Every Lock (5 min., 3 sec.). Unable to fully accept what Ophelia has told him, Greg agrees to help her barricade themselves in.

3. They're Here (6 min., 35 sec.). Ophelia explains that "they" have come and the world has ended as they know it.

4. Face to Face (5 min., 38 sec.). Ophelia explains that the blood on her clothes is that of her roommate, who used her cell phone and "exploded." Ophelia then tells Greg she must go outside to see what is happening.

5. Connect (6 min., 17 sec.). As Ophelia makes it safely back, it finally dawns on Greg that what he as been told actually happened.

6. Occam's Razor (6 min., 48 sec.). After a romantic dinner Ophelia reveals that she loves Greg and that the world still exists (to get Greg to see her as she sees him, she disconnected his Internet and electrical connections hoping to make him see that there are other things more important than his obsession with the Internet).

60 Cops and Monsters. copsandmonster swebseries.com. 2013 (Thriller).

The Paranormal Investigative Team Scotland (PITS) is a special unit of a futuristic Scotland police department that protects not only humans, but creatures once feared and thought to be evil: vampires, werewolves and zombies. Five years ago, when supernatural creatures chose to come out of hiding and live among humans, Scotland's Prime Minister created PITS as a means to keep the balance between the two factions and ensure the safety of each. Eve Mitchell, assigned to head the team, is assisted by Jack Stone, Alia Carmichael and Tom Middleton. The program follows the team as they investigate the crimes and incidents that occur in the supernatural and human communities as well as their efforts to deal with their own problems—both personally and professionally.

Eve, born in Texas, moved with her family to England when she was a teenager. Educated at the finest schools, she turned her attention to fighting crime and became a police officer. Her exceptional performance came to the attention of Charles Sloan who recruited her (when she was 30) to head the PITS unit.

Jack, 29 years old, was a police detective whose reckless behavior cost him his job. When Eve discovered that Jack was a weapons expert, she recruited him to build her unit's defense arsenal to battle supernatural beings.

Alia, the team's youngest member (21), was a police constable when Eve recruited her to act as a negotiator between vampires, zombies and werewolves. She is experienced in research and communication and can speak several languages; she is also a werewolf (having been scratched by one as a teenager) and can live freely in the open since such creatures joined the human race.

Hank, a 29-year-old computer expert, monitors supernatural activity for the unit.

Crystal, neither human or supernatural, is an in-between and serves as the conduit between the unit and the underworld leaders.

Julia is a seductive vampire who often violates the zoning laws that separate humans from creatures. She is also a major concern of the PITS team as they believe Julia possesses key information about the mysterious "Weapon," something that could destroy the peace treaty between vampires and humans and open the doorway to something beyond imagining.

Tom, 26 years old, replaced Hank after he was killed by vampires (although Tom also has his share of problems as a female vampire is stalking him). He is trained in all forms of self-defense and is literally learning the ropes as the team's newest recruit.

The Cult of Many Faces is a mysterious figure, apparently guided by an unknown force that lurks in the shadows and manipulates others in his attempt to acquire knowledge and power.

Norris Fletcher, a Deputy Chief Constable, oversees the unit, which he believes is useless and mainly responsible for all the problems that arise in the city. While he'd rather deal with the human-type criminal, he handles the paperwork involved and has one goal: limit the unit to causing as little damage as possible.

Young Alexis is very pretty girl whose looks are deceiving. She is a werewolf with mysterious origins and connected to the PITS unit (as the series progresses, information about her will be revealed and her transformation from adolescent to adult will be explored).

Captain Roberts, Jack's former commanding officer (Army), is now a bounty hunter tracking down rogue creatures for their posted rewards.

Cast: Kirsty Strain (Eve Mitchell), Mark Harvey (Jack Stone), Caitlin Gillespie (Alia Carmichael), Rhys Teare-Williams (Tom Middleton), Alan Mackenzie (Hank Stevenson), Anne Nicholson (Crystal), Simon Weir (Norris Fletcher), Sarah Louise Madison (Julia), Billy Kirkwood (The Cult of Many Faces), Caitlin Blackwood (Young Alexis), Tam Toye (Captain Roberts). **Credits:** *Producer:* Emer O'Donovan. *Writer:* Fraser Coull, Amanda Kane, Ian Smith **Comment:** Although only a first episode has thus far been produced, it is well acted and produced. There are minimal and well done special effects and judging by the pilot, *Cops and Monsters* looks to be a fascinating series that has the qualities to make its way onto the Syfy network (should the producers decide to pursue a cable broadcaster).

Episodes:

1. The Weapon (8 min., 49 sec.). Eve explains the purpose of PITS and how it was created. The pilot also explores the team's efforts to acquire information about a mysterious "Weapon" through the interrogation of the vampire Julia.

61 Cost of Capital. mergersandinquistions.com. 2012 (Drama).

A behind-the-scenes look at investing—from the viewpoint of a young man (Jason), a newly hired investment firm equity associate as he is given an assignment by his boss (David): find a company for his firm to buy. With the help of his friends (Todd and Leonard), he chooses IonX, a small company owned by a woman named Nancy, and the pitfalls that arise as he attempts to acquire it.

Cast: Sam C. Martin (Jason Shaw), Jordan Butcher (Todd), Sharon Jordan (Susan), Josh Shibata (Leonard), Kevin Ashworth (David), Sharon Gardner (Nancy), Timothy Guest (Robert), Don Robb (Grandpa), Eamon Sheehan (Scott), Derek Meacham (Martin), Jason Weiss (Byron), Marsha Walter (Paula). **Credits:** *Producer:* Goldie Chan, Brian DeChesare, Allison Vanore. *Director:* Jorge L. Urbina. *Writer:* Goldie Chan, Brian DeChesare. **Comment:** Well-acted and produced program that takes a slightly different approach by focusing on the associates and their efforts to make big money deals. The problems, as opposed to the successes, are profiled and the story is tightly constructed to make for a smooth flowing presentation.

Episodes:

1. The Idea. Establishes the story line as Jason struggles to balance his new assignment (finding a firm in which to invest) with caring for his ill grandfather.

2. The Fundraising. Jason arranges a meeting with Nancy, the CEO of IonX, but finds she is a bit reluctant to sell her company—at first—until Nancy and her business partner (Scott) figure the money will give them the opportunity to start a new business venture.

3. The Reversal. As Jason discovers that his grandfather's condition has worsened and he will be responsible for all medical bills, Robert, the head of Jason's firm, becomes skeptical of Jason's choice of IonX and its viability.

4. The Deal. As Nancy finds her proposals are not going to be met, she demands (from Jason) to see not only David (his boss), but Robert (the company president).

5. The Negotiations. Nancy's demands—$60 million and 20 percent interest, has Robert and David negotiating and counter offering of $50 mil-

lion and 10 percent ownership. Plays a bit like ABC's *Shark Tank* with Nancy walking away from the deal.

6. The Dotted Line. The concluding episode wherein Robert and David discuss Nancy's original offer but find, now that they are desperate to own the company, they must accept even more demands from Nancy.

62 Cowgirl Up. onemorelesbian.com. 2011–2013 (Comic Western).

"Wanna see funny and hot girls ridin' horses, shootin' guns and playin' Cowgirl?" is a tag line used to introduce a lesbian western parody about the gorgeous girls who have booked accommodations at the Double D Ranch, an all-girl dude ranch nestled in the heart of the Cochella Valley and "just a stone's throw" away from the resorts, restaurants and shopping centers of a large metropolitan city in California. Cricket and Lu are the co-owners and among the sexy cowgirls are Savannah, the adopted daughter of Lu and Cricket; Dakota, a young woman out to win every competition offered at the ranch; Maddie, Dakota's best friend (tough and mean—and doesn't take anything from anyone; she not only gets mad but she gets even); Robbie, star of the TV series *Spur*, who has come to the ranch to learn all there is to be a professional cowgirl and do all her own stunts. Maeve and Snapper are con artists who, after learning that oil is sitting on ranch property are seeking to acquire it for themselves; Babe and Bitsy (a man in drag) are the law officers (called "The Cagney and Lacey of Cochella" [referring to the 1980s CBS TV series *Cagney and Lacey*]); Buckshot Betty has an eye for Cricket and also wants to take over the ranch; Dee and Rusty are Double D wranglers and Coon-Ass Kate, can't see "the lesbian thing" and prefers real dudes. The program relates the competition, the cat-fights, the kissing and the shenanigans that occur at the Double D Ranch as girls attempt to enjoy themselves and have some fun.

Cast: Mandy Musgrave (Dakota), Bridget McManus (Babe), Marnie Alton (Abby), Kodi Kitchen (Dee), Melissa Denton (Lu), Linda Miller (Cricket), Shannan Leigh Reeve (Rusty), Kate McCoy (Coon Ass Kate), Nicole Travolta (Eager Beaver), Niki Lindgren (Jo), Maribeth Monroe (Merideth), Treisa Gary (Sunny Trails), Aasha Davis (Robbie), Butch Jerinic (Chief Morning Wind), Brandy Howard (Snapper), Valery M. Ortiz (Maddie), Maeve Quinlan (Buckshot Betty), Hannah Madison Taylor (Savannah), Matt Cohen (Sheriff Bitsy Calhoun), Pam Pierce (Hooch McCarthy), Nancylee Myatt (The Boss). **Credits:** *Producer:* Nancylee Myatt, Paige Bernhardt, Matt Cohen, Christin Mell, Nicole Valentine. *Director:* Paige Bernhardt, Matt Cohen, Nancylee Myatt, Christin Mell, Courtney Rowe. *Writer:* Paige Bernhardt, Nancylee Myatt. **Comment:** Enjoyable eye candy series just based on the available free episodes. The girls really appear to be doing their own stunts and the competition sequences, though somewhat campy, are fun to watch. The acting and production values, as with all Tello Film productions are first rate.

Episodes: Episodes are available only through a pay subscription service. The following episodes are available for free on the official website.

1. Cowgirl Up: Season 1, Episode 1: The Good, the Bad and the Pretty.
2. Cowgirl Up: Girls Gone Wild: Meredith and Dakota.
3. Cowgirl Up: Girls Gone Wild West: Jo and Eager Beaver.
4. Cowgirl Up Extra: Girls Gone Wild West: Dee and Abby.
5. Cowgirl Up: Girls Gone Wild West: Wrangler Fight.

63 *Creature of the Deep.* youtube.com. 2012 (Comedy-Drama).

Erin is a young girl who finds a recipe ("Glass of fresh water in a magic Mermaid shell") and follows its instructions. Within 30 minutes after drinking the mixture, she is magically transformed into a Mermaid and her adventure as she struggles to live two different lives becomes the focal point of stories.

Cast (as credited): Wiebits (Erin), Jabba (Ruby), Peck (Tessa), Sweetheart (Kirsten). **Comment:** The girls perform their roles well but the sound and photography are poor.

Episode List: *1.* Ocean Potion. *2.* The Voice of Ruby. *3.* Ruby Befriends Erin. *4.* A Twist in the Tail. *5.* Power Hour. *6.* Hide-and-Go-Seek-a-Tail. *7.* Swimming with Fins. *8.* Tail Fever. *9.* Lake Swim. *10.* Season Finale, Parts 1 and 2. *11.* Moonstruck (Season 2 begins). *12.* A Weird Discovery. *13.* An Unexpected Dive. *14.* Potion Commotion. *15.* A Storm Is Rising. *16.* A Tail of Trouble. *17.* And Then There Were Four. *18.* A Secret Revealed. *19.* Christmas Creature. *20.* Moonlight Swim (concludes Season 2). *21.* Accidents Happen (Begins Season 3). *22.* Mermaids Cove. *23.* The Mysterious Realm. *24.* The Capture. *25.* Evil Unleashed. *26.* Split Personalities. *27.* Twins! *28.* Mini Episode. *29.* Fairly Magical. *30.* Party Pooper.

64 *Crew: The Web Series.* thecrewwebseries.com. 2013 (Crime Drama).

Johnny Gallagher, Anthony Lombardi and Steve Petriceli are mob connected errand boys for Nicholas "Nicky" Greco, head of a ruthless New York City crime family. Johnny, Anthony and Steve however, are dissatisfied doing someone else's bidding and devise a plan to become as important as Nicky by starting their own "family" (crew) and, in time, make inroads into the New York City–based underworld. The program charts their efforts to achieve that goal as they encompass the resources of Nicky's "family"

while at the same time trying to keep what they are doing from Nicky and rival gangs.

Cast: Greg Acceta (Steve Petriceli), Ezie Cotler (Johnny Gallager), Stephen Medvidick (Anthony Lombardi), Elisa Santamaria (Heather), Skip Johnson (Nicky Greco), Nick Dubanos (Jackie Ricci), David Mohr (Jojo). **Credits:** *Producer-Writer-Director:* Tony Napolitano. **Comment:** With its vulgar language, strong violence, female nudity and strong sexual situations you would think you are watching a theatrical film, not a web series. But a web series it is and so well produced and acted that it plays like a feature film. Although there is a parental warning, all sharing websites permit viewing without blocking scenes.

Episodes:

1. The Drop (15 min., 31 sec.). Johnny, Anthony and Steve have decided to split from Nicky and begin their operations by muscling in on Nicky's territory and stealing a $100,000 drug payoff.
2. Aftermath (14 min., 6 sec.). The new crew encounters Nicky's wrath first hand when the currier (from whom the money was stolen) is killed and Nicky vows to get those responsible.
3. Slick Willie James (17 min., 28 sec.). Now fearing for their lives if Nicky should discover they are the culprits, the crew figure it is best to get the money back to Nicky—until they learn Anthony's cousin has stolen it and they are without funds.
4. No Strings Attached (16 min., 32 sec.). To "raise" the money they need, the crew plans a drug heist—again hitting Nicky's territory.
5. Sunshine Escorts (17 min., 35 sec.). The guys figure they need help and take on a new crew member—Heather, a gorgeous girl who poses as a high-priced call girl to extract information from marks.
6. This Is My City (14 min., 13 sec.). As the crew begins to establish themselves, they make themselves known to other crime families—and let it be believed that they are working for Nicky.
7. You Got 48 Hours (21 min., 20 sec.). Nicky, believing that a rival family is responsible for the drug heist, gives the two couriers who were robbed 48 hours to find the culprits or face execution.
8. I'm No Gangster (21 min., 9 sec.). Continues from where the last episode left off with a slightly different side of Nicky seen—a pastry chef for a legit business called Mario's Pastry Shop, but also a man who becomes easily angered and violent when someone rips him off.
9. You Think Jackie's Loyal (20 min.). The crew, now with bags of uncut dope and a potential fortune, are stymied about who to trust to cut the dope for them for street sales.
10. Meeting with the Families (19 min., 59 sec.). A meeting with various New York family heads has negative results as each now believes the other is responsible for the thefts and killings that have been occurring.
11. It's Hot Out There (21 min., 17 sec.). Feeling

that their small time operations need to be taken to a higher level, Johnny, Anthony and Steve begin plans to increase their crew.

12. Take Me to See Bill (19 min., 59 sec.). Murder has now become a part of their life when Johnny, Steve and Anthony resort to murder to acquire a suit-case filled with millions of dollars-worth of Jewels. The theft, however, has angered mob families who now believe the recent thefts/killings are related to Nicky and feel that he should be eliminated as he has lost control of his family. The program's concluding episode.

65 The Crews. youtube.com. 2011 (Crime Drama).

Tommy Granger and Mick Turner are lifelong friends and notorious crime figures (mobsters) in Glasgow (Scotland). Over the years they obtained a reputation as being ruthless but as time passed, circumstances changed and Tommy elected to retire from the mob while Mick remained, becoming a high-ranking crime lord. The program follows both men and the situations they face: Tommy as he struggles to lead a new life despite circumstances that threaten to return him to his former life, and Mick, growing older, as he seeks a way to ease his way out of the mob before circumstances prevent him from doing so. The main characters were introduced in a 2006 short film called *Sandwich*.

Cast: Robert Harrison (Tommy Granger), Jim Sweeney (Mick Turner), Jennifer Byrne (Patricia Coulter), Andrew McIntosh (Stevie Turner), Sean O'Kane (Det. Strachan), Joe Cassidy (John Drummond), John Gaffney (Dougie Fallon), Stuart Hepburn (Det. Watt), Scott Kyle (Kenny McFadden), Lauren Lamarr (Anne Paterson), Rebekah Lamb (Emma Harrison), Ross Maxwell (Jake Ferguson), Joy McAvoy (Dawn). **Credits:** *Producer-Director:* Colin Ross Smith. *Writer:* Colin Ross Smith, Kolin Ferguson. **Comment:** The program is produced in Scotland and suffers at times with difficult-to-understand Scottish accents. The production values and acting are good but the story line is not new and rather lame compared to American versions of the same theme.

Episodes:

1. Sandwich (16 min.). The story line as described above is established.

2. The Dutch Connection (16 min., 25 sec.). A drug deal in Amsterdam spells trouble for Mick when the situation takes a turn for the worse.

3. The Old Firm (19 min., 6 sec.). Tommy finds himself in a precarious situation of returning to his old ways when a former associate (Pepe) seeks his help.

4. The Young Team (18 min., 23 sec.). Patricia Coulter, a female police detective, is introduced as she begins her first day on the job. Stevie Turner, from the original film, is re-introduced as a mobster

now seeking to get even with Jimmy Kergan for the beating he sustained in the film.

5. The Prodigal Son (18 min., 56 sec.). Mick's son, Stevie becomes an active member of the mob.

6. Just Another Day in Paradise (18 min., 15 sec.). Learning that Tommy was responsible for the death of her brother years ago, Patricia plots to seek revenge.

7. Guess Who's Coming to Dinner? (17 min., 25 sec.). Tommy seeks revenge against Stevie and incurs the wrath of Mick in the concluding episode.

66 Cuckoo. vimeo.com. 2013 (Drama).

In 1999 while a mother went about shopping, her three-year-old child was taken from her stroller by an unknown person (the mother or kidnapper were not fully seen). A police investigation was conducted but the child and her kidnapper were never found. It is 14 years later when the series begins and viewers first see Niamh Keegan, a pretty but rebellious 17-year-old girl who feels her life is boring and her family does not understand her and her need to make life exciting. Life changes for Niamh when a newspaper story reopens that cold kidnapping case and a digitally aged picture of what that baby would look like today is published. Niamh is immediately struck by how the picture looks exactly like her and begins to wonder if she was that kidnapped baby. As her imagination runs wild and she believes that she could be someone else, Niamh begins a series of probes to literally re-open the case and find out the truth for herself. The program charts her investigation to uncover the truth about who she really is.

Cast: Pagan McGrath (Niamh Keegan), Denise McCormack (Tina Vickers), Brian Fortune (Brendan Keegan), Orla Gildea (Maureen Keegan), Erin McEnery (Young Niamh), Laura O. Leary (Sarah), Jeff Doyle (Kieran). **Credits:** *Producer:* Marie Caffrey. *Director:* Danann Breathnach. *Writer:* Nikki Racklin, Danann Breathnach. **Comment:** Irish produced program that is well acted and produced. It is a fast moving program that is well worth watching as a young girl attempts to discover her true being.

Episodes:

1. Episode 1 (6 min., 9 sec.). Establishes the storyline as the kidnapping occurs and introduces, in 2013, a 17-year-old girl named Niamh, who finds she may not be whom she believes when she sees a digitally aged photograph in the paper of a baby that was kidnapped 14 years earlier.

2. Episode 2 (6 min., 15 sec.). After becoming mesmerized with the picture, Niamh sketches on eyeglasses (which she needs to wear) and sees a striking resemblance to herself.

3. Episode 3 (7 min., 21 sec.). Convinced that she is that kidnapped child, Niamh begins to envision women she sees as being her mother—more so than ever when she crosses one in a mall and is struck by her likeness to her.

Cuckoo. Clockwise from top left: Pagan McGrath; Denise McCormack; Brian Fortune (back of head) and Jeff Doyle; Brian Fortune, Orla Gildea (used by permission of Marie Caffrey).

4. Episode 4 (7 min., 47 sec.). Although Niamh's initial approach to the woman was uneasy (as the woman didn't believe that she was her daughter), the woman agrees to talk with her. Whether or not the woman was convinced or Niamh was mistaken is left unexplored (for future episodes) as the program concludes with Niamh returning home and seemingly accepting who she is and her parents as her parents (Brendan and Maureen).

Note: With the exception of vimeo.com, where all the episodes can be viewed, other sharing websites present only an edited (to 27 minutes and 14 seconds) version of the program that showcases the story in one single viewing.

67 *Cultural Differences.* webserieschannel. com. 2013 (Comedy-Drama).

London, England provides the backdrop for a look at two families and the cultural differences that separate and define them: The Campbell's (Jamaican) and the Tobiloba's (Nigerian) and how their lives intertwine when Michelle, raised by two parents, and Tasha, born out of wedlock when her mother was 17, meet and befriend each other.

Cast: Deborah Kolade (Michelle Tobiloba), Tatiana Braganca (Tasha Campbell), Adolphus George (Michael Tobiloba), Ibiye Ikuku (Natalie), Sharron Spice (Ms. Campbell), Eleanor Agala (Mrs. O. Tobiloba), Onosky Ukorha (Mr. Tobiloba). **Credits:** *Producer-Writer-Director:* Deborah Kolade. **Comment:** The program ends unresolved and may have only limited appeal due to the ethnic groups portrayed. The acting and production values are good and it is not stated whether additional episodes will be produced.

Episodes:
1. The Beginning of a Friendship (20 min., 12 sec.). Michelle is introduced as she begins her first year of college and befriends Tasha.
2. The Day After Tasha's Stay Over (20 min., 8 sec.). Michael, Michelle's brother, becomes attracted to Tasha and seeks a way to build the confidence he needs to ask her for a date—without Michelle finding out.
3. The Mystery Phone Call (19 min., 47 sec.). Someone has apparently discovered that Michael and Tasha are seeing each other and sending strange messages to Tasha's mother. Meanwhile, it appears that Tasha's mother opposes her seeing Michael, as she feels he is not worthy of her (although Tasha feels she has the right to see Michael and will not make the same mistake her mother did when she was 17). The program's concluding episode.

68 *Curse of the Crimson Mask.* hulu.com. 2012–2013 (Thriller).

Jack Parker is currently a wrestler who performs as The Crimson Mask. He was born in Brooklyn, New York and achieved fame as a boxer (called "Brooklyn's Bad-Fisted Brawler" and "The Ravaging Right Hook from Red Hook"). But his temper, his constant need for money (to pay off gambling debts) and his inability to follow the rules cost him not only his boxing profession, but his later job as a masked wrestler called The Crimson Mask. Now without an income and large sums of money owed to ruthless bookies, Jack figures it is best to skip town until he meets Thomas Caine, a businessman on the brink of losing his business—but who sees Jack as a means by which to regain control of his company by eliminating the competition. Jack has already killed (a girl he apparently loved, but she knew of his plans to skip town and, fearing the mob would use her to get to him, shot her). The program follows two desperate men and their efforts to help each other destroy the demons that are haunting them.

Cast: Robert Clohessy (Jack Parker), Frank Paige (Eddie), Lee R. Sellars (Jeffries), Debra Jans (Karen), Joshua Burrow (Thomas Caine), Ed Kershen (Jefe), Judas Young (Johnny Jericho), Arthur Acuria (Mr. Kuo), Matthew Conlon (Faustus), Rachel Cornish (Ashley), Robert C. Kirk (Det. Jones), Danny Kuo (Chow Wing Wang), Richard Mawe (Jonathan Caine). **Credits:** *Producer:* Michael Gonzalez Wallace, Robert Clohessy, Ed Plagianos. *Director:* Elias Plagianos. *Writer:* Elias Plagianos, Jason Plagianos.

Comment: Harsh program with good acting and production values but violent. Robert Clohessy is good as the troubled wrestler although what happens to him and the crimes her commits is left unresolved.

Episodes:

1. The Book (20 min.). Introduces Jack as a wrestler—but also how his temper gets him fired and why he must now flee town.

2. The Banker (21 min). Thomas Caine, the businessman on the brink of losing his company to bankruptcy, is introduced as he finds Jack his escape goat.

3. Who Pulls the Puppet Strings? (24 min.). Jack and Caine come to terms on what needs to be done—but Jack is not all that happy when Caine takes charge. The program's concluding episode.

69 Cybergeddon. webserieschannel.com. 2012 (Thriller).

It is the present day and virtually everyone is connected through some sort of electronic devise. There are cyber attacks and there is cyber crime. Although authorities attempt to track cyber criminals, it appears to be a losing battle and such criminals bilk the American public out of more than $600 million a year. Threats are faced from every direction and the speculative program is an attempt to establish a scenario wherein a Cybergeddon is possible but is the world prepared for such an event? The intent is to focus on Chloe Jocelyn, an FBI Special Agent who is framed for a cyber-crime she did not commit and must prove her innocence by exposing the real culprit, the master cyber-criminal Gustov Dobreff.

Cast: Missy Peregrym (Chloe Jocelyn), Kick Gurry (Rabbit Rosen), Efran Elias Edraki (Konrad), Olivier Martinez (Gustov Dobreff), Tonya Lee Williams (Donna Berg), Manny Montana (Frank Parker), Sonja Smits (Amanda Jocelyn), Joel Keller (Jim McCluskey), Christine Horne (Irina). **Credits:** *Producer:* Anthony E. Zuiker, Bill O'Dowd, Javier Riera, Joshua Caldwell, Anthony Leo. *Director:* Diego Velasco. *Writer:* Miles Chapman, Anthony E. Zuiker. **Comment:** Missy Peregrym is a looker and she helps propel a slow-moving concept with numerous can happen issues into a watch-able program. The special effects and direction are good and it is well done technically (meant to show what could happen as it appears most people do not believe that such a danger lurks).

Episodes: Nine episodes have been produced but are no longer available. Only a one minute and 36 second trailer remains that highlights the series premise. The Episode Titles: *1.* The Push of a Button. *2.* Disappear. *3.* The Rabbit Hole. *4.* Slash and Burn. *5.* A Billion Devices. *6.* Look at Me Now. *7.* The Preview. *8.* Revenge. *9.* Cybergeddon.

70 Danger 5: The Diamond Girls. you tube.com. 2011 (Action Comedy).

Danger 5 is a 2012 Australian television series, set in a fantasy-like World War II era, wherein a team of spies (Danger 5) have been assigned a dangerous mission: stop Adolph Hitler's plans of world domination. The web program aired as a prequel to the TV series. It appears that Hitler will stop at nothing to become ruler of the world. His scientists have been experimenting with unleashing dinosaur-like creatures on the Allies, but those efforts have not been successful. When he discovers that a rare black diamond can give him an invincible army (of She-Nazis) he has the diamonds stolen, ground into a powder-like substance and applied like make-up to a group of gorgeous women—women who are impervious to bullets. Danger 5, an Australian-based unit of fearless spies (Ilsa, Claire, Jackson, Pierre and Tucker), led by Colonel Chestbridge, are assigned the task of recovering the diamonds and stop another devious plot by Hitler as he slowly gains inroads on his ultimate goal (here to infiltrate the Allied command of the World President, Massimiliano Importanta).

Cast: Natasa Ristic (Ilsa), Amanda Simons (Claire), David Ashby (Jackson), Aldo Mignone (Pierre), Sean James Murphy (Tucker), Tilman Vogler (Chestbridge), Carmine Russo (Adolph Hitler), Anna Cashman (Nazi Hostess), Ryan Cortazzo (Gunther), Susanna Dekker (Madam Julietta), Caitlin McCreanor (Nazi Priestess), Cameron Pike (Hein), Peter Powell (Gibraltar). **Credits:** *Producer:* Kate Croser, Dario Russo. *Director:* Dario Russo. *Writer:* David Ashby, Dario Russo. **Comment:** Enjoyable World War II spoof that presents Hitler in a totally new light (a megalomaniac with ways of defeating the Allies the real Hitler never imagined). The acting and production values are outstanding and the use of miniature sets to establish outdoor scenes is very well done.

Episodes:

1. Episode 1 (5 min., 50 sec.). Danger 5 receives their first assignment: stop the thefts of rare black diamonds (known as Carbonado) which are being horded by the Nazis.

2. Episode 2 (4 min., 27 sec.). The team begins operations by plotting to impersonate the Nazi team (Unit 6) assigned by Hitler to steal the diamonds.

3. Episode 3 (4 min., 24 sec.). With their initial plan enacted, Danger 5 overtakes Unit 6 and must now convince Hitler they are the real Unit 6.

4. Episode 4 (4 min., 34 sec.). Danger 5, alias Unit 6, arrives in Germany and must now find their Nazi connection.

5. Episode 5 (5 min., 54 sec.). Hitler's experiment with the black diamond dust has produced a group of invincible female Super Nazis that Danger 5 must somehow defeat or perish. The program ends in a cliff hanger.

71 *Dangerous Women.* blip.tv. 2009 (Drama).

Cheryl, Shelly and Linda are three women stuck in a routine of being ordinary housewives leading ordinary lives. They care for their kids, the house and have even became soccer moms. While the women have their own inner demons to contend with they also have doubles—evil doubles that torment them, commit criminal acts in their likeness and lead others to believe they are the actual culprits. Even though they have alibis for the crimes committed and are under constant suspicion by the police, Cheryl, Linda and Shelly are innocent and the program follows their efforts to track down and expose the three women who are posing as them.

Cast: Betsy Baker (Linda), Ellen Sandweiss (Cheryl), Theresa Tilly (Shelly), Maddy Kennedy (Erika), Cynthia Dallas (Detective), Fred Ochs (Det. Kravitz), Ashley Ann-Michaels (Vanessa). **Credits:** *Producer:* David O'Malley, Ellen Sandweiss. *Director:* Lee Miller. *Writer:* David O'Malley. **Comment:** Interesting concept that has been done numerous times on television with shows like *F Troop*, *Wonder Woman* and *The Bionic Woman* wherein an evil look-a-like causes havoc. But tripling the effect adds more interest and even more situations wherein three women must prove they are not the culprits by exposing the real imposters. As the tag line states, "They look exactly like you—but it's not you."

Episodes: Only the first episode remains on line. Following is an episode and date listing.

1. Heart in a Jar. Jan. 22, 2009.
2. Take Your Book. Jan. 30, 2009.
3. Come with Us. Feb. 6, 2009.
4. Slut. Feb. 13, 2009.
5. No Refunds, No Autographs. Feb. 20, 2009.
6. That's Not Me. Feb. 27, 2009.

72 *Darkest Times.* youtube.com. 2013 (Thriller).

In an unspecified time, a Super Collider experiment goes horribly wrong, causing great destruction. Everything has changed—"People you knew are gone. But something is out there. It wants to take you. And everyone has become one of your Darkest Times." Many people have escaped the catastrophe and have banned together in small groups in an effort to survive—and battle an unknown enemy that seeks only to kill (people affected by the Collider). The program focuses on one small group of survivors (Steel, Tibbie, Clover, Miller and Weasel) as they not only battle the enemy, but their own inner demons as they struggle to make sense of the world as it has now become.

Cast: Dennis Barham (Steel), Patrice Henry (Tibbie), Allan Michael Brunet (The Old Man), Madelyn Rogers (Bitsy), Danny F. Santos (Weasel), Holly Sarchfield (Lane), Janine Short (Newcomer), Emma Jean Sutherland (Clover), Vanessa Tavares (Sticks), Agata Waclawska (Notes), David Walpole (Miller). **Credits:** *Producer-Writer-Director:* Sam Winterson. **Comment:** The production is well filmed to give a very good impression of what the survivors are experiencing (especially with the earth slowly losing its daylight). The acting is also very good and the last episode leaves the doorway open to continue the suspenseful story.

Episodes:

1. Episode 1. A small group of survivors have banned together and establish a stronghold in an abandoned building.

2. Episode 2. Mysterious light beams appear to be the key to something that is happening but Lane and Steel, unable to figure out what, become more concerned about Tibbie, who is pregnant and what effects the beams could have on her.

3. Episode 3. As time passes, the survivors come to realize that time no longer has the same meaning (as it did before the apocalypse). Meanwhile the light beams are becoming more of a concern and what they could mean and Bitsy, a Newcomer (a person apparently not affected) makes her way to the compound. She is accepted—but Bitsy appears to be something evil.

4. Episode 4. The concluding episode wherein The Old Man, an apparent scientist responsible for the Collider accident, explains that in February of 2013, five years after the accident, most of the world's population is gone and it appears that those beams of light where the sun's dying rays as the earth is becoming increasingly dark and twilight is all that remains.

73 *Dates Like This.* dateslikethis.com. 2012 (Comedy-Drama).

Meg and Alicia are young women in their early

twenties seeking romance although not with each other. While Meg is a lesbian and Alicia is straight, Meg has chosen not to pursue Alicia although she is attracted to her. Meg is a bit unpredictable and will devise elaborate schemes to find a mate while Alicia is just seeking a down-to-earth man with whom she can spend the rest of her life with. The program charts the women's efforts to find romance, with a particular focus on Meg as she devises and attempts to follow through on The 30 Days Project—date a different woman each night in 30 days.

Cast: Hannah Vaughn (Meg), Leigh Poulos (Alicia), Natalie Fehlner (Gwen), Keiko Green (Theresa), Katie Hammond (Claire), Jillian Green (Amber), William G. Kean (Scott), Colin Aarons (Owen), Brittany Anne Oman (Allison), Kristen Lazzarini (Vera), Katie Rose Spence (Jessie), Jill Wurzburg (Norah), Rachel Sussman (Melody), Jenny Donoghue (Kelsey), Amanda Gardner (Stephanie), Samantha Cooper (Jacquelyn), Michelle Polera (Emily). **Credits:** *Producer-Director:* Hannah Vaughn, Leigh Poulos. **Comment:** Meg and Alicia are smartly portrayed as down-to-earth girls in a well-acted and produced program. There are several kissing scenes but nothing objectionable. Several scenes are a bit hard to understand due to an annoying background noise that overpowers the dialogue.

Episodes:

1. Episode 1 (9 min., 53 sec.). Meg and Alicia are introduced as Alicia devises her 30 days of dating project.

2. Episode 2 (7 min., 42 sec.). As Meg continues her dating spree, Alicia seeks to begin a relationship of her own.

3. Episode 3 (11 min., 53 sec.). Alicia finds romance with Scott while Meg feels a spark when she dates Vera for the second time.

4. Episode 4 (9 min., 49 sec.). Alicia uncovers a secret about Scott while Meg tries to deal with a date (Laura) who has become too controlling.

5. Episode 5 (10 min., 50 sec.). Alicia confronts Scott about his secret (that he has a child from a previous marriage).

6. Episode 6 (10 min., 13 sec.). Unable to deal with what Scott has hidden from her, Alicia feels she and Scott need time apart. Meanwhile, Meg becomes attracted to her latest date (Lindsay).

7. Episode 7 (13 min., 21 sec.). Alicia turns to Meg for comfort over her breakup with Scott.

8. Episode 8 (13 min., 21 sec.). Delves into Alicia's feelings (that she still loves Scott) while Meg begins to rethink her dating project.

9. Episode 9. 14 min., 55 sec.). Meg appears to have found romance with a new girl (Julie) while Alicia seeks a way to rekindle the romance she had with Scott in the concluding episode.

74 *Dead Man's Trigger.* webserieschannel.com. 2012 (Thriller).

A terrorist (Khalim), escaping the clutches of Homeland Security, makes his way to New York City. Three FBI agents (Patel, Owens and Thomas), assigned to capture him, do so, but encounter a deadly problem when Patel and Owens learn that Agent Thomas has been kidnapped and that her life is in peril (imprisoned in an unknown location with a ticking bomb). The program charts the desperate race against time as Patel and Owens seek to find Thomas before it is too late.

Cast: Hassan Johnson (Agent Patel), Rick Zahn (Agent Owens), Khalil Gonzales-Garcia (Khalim), Leila Sbitani (Agent Thomas). **Credits:** *Producer-Writer-Director:* Juan Reinoso. **Comment:** Fast-moving, well done combination of action, suspense and drama that holds your attention from the first episode. The acting is good and the program is open-ended leaving the possibility of additional cases to be solved by the three agents.

Episodes:

1. The Chase. Agents Patel and Owens track terrorist Khalim to Manhattan where their pursuit begins.

2. The Information. Khalim's capture reveals that a fellow agent (Thomas) has been abducted and that her life is in danger.

3. Time. Patel and Owens learn of Khalim's diabolical plan and of a bomb that they must diffuse to save Thomas.

4. Where There's a Goon. Patel and Owens find the site where Thomas is being held, but exactly where in the complex is the mystery.

5. The Shootout. As Patel and Owens close in on Thomas's whereabouts they find themselves involved in a shootout with Khalim's men.

6. God, That Stupid Face. Patel locates the room wherein Thomas is being held—but can he diffuse the bomb and save her—and himself, all within a 4 minute and 32 second window before the bomb explodes.

75 *Decrypted.* vimeo.com. 2012 (Drama).

Camilla Reed, a computer hacker known as The Locksmith, tackles jobs for people who want to remain anonymous and who do not like questions. Her life is progressing well until a businessman named Hunter hires her to decrypt a hard drive linked to something called Project Paradise. The program relates what happens when Camilla decodes the disk and uncovers evidence of a bizarre medical experiment that went horribly wrong—and her efforts to escape those seeking to stop her before she uncovers the secret of Project Paradise.

Cast: Cat Davidson (Camilla Reed), Walt Sloan (Prof. Mitchell Powers), Scott Bailey (Hunter), Walter Kartman (Austin Sellers), Melissa Walker (Jennifer Baxter), David Vogel (Dr. Douglas Baxter), Doris Grice (Lisa), Quincy Joyner (Det. Carlos King). **Credits:** *Producer:* Lisa Walker England,

Bobby Schmidt, Quincy Joyner, Jeff Wieck, Rubin Whitmore II. *Director:* Bobby Schmidt, Rubin Whitmore II, Sergio Espino, Quincy Joyner. *Writer:* Rebekah Conrad, Lisa Walker England, Bobby Schmidt. **Comment:** Well-acted and produced suspense drama that holds interest from the very beginning. The concept is also intriguing and is well worth checking out for that alone.

Episodes:

1. Wizard. Camilla's plight begins as she accepts a job from Hunter to decrypt a hard drive disk.

2. Deep Magic. After encountering difficulty with the disk, Camilla seeks the help of her college mentor, Professor Mitchell Powers.

3. Deadlock. Camilla's nightmare begins when Hunter discovers that Camilla has broken his trust and consulted someone else.

4. Bit Bucket. As Hunter retrieves the disk from Camilla, Camilla and Mitchell decide to continue their investigation to uncover what the disk contains.

5. Phase of the Moon. Knowing they must stop Hunter from covering up a bizarre medical experiment, Camilla and Mitchell seek information about Project Paradise.

6. Coke Bottle. Camilla and Mitchell's search leads them to Austin Sellers, a quirky character who is somehow connected to the project.

7. Never-Never Land. Strange as he may be, Austin reveals information about the project to Camilla and Mitchell (that he was terminally ill—until he was given a drug that not only cured him, but changed his physical appearance).

8. Catatonia. Unknown to Camilla, her comatose mother may hold the key to uncovering the mystery of what happened. Meanwhile, Camilla and Mitchell are being shadowed by a mysterious figure (Dr. Jennifer Baxter).

9. Terminal Illness. Camilla uncovers information that forces Austin to confess his true connection to Project Paradise (a flashback is used to see how the drug changed Austin's life).

10. Smoke and Mirrors. As Camilla and Mitchell delve further into Austin's past, they discover that the drug has serious side-effects and while it can cure disease, it also causes mental problems.

11. Daemon. Camilla and Mitchell find help when a doctor associated with the project (Jennifer Baxter) approaches them (she had been following them to make sure she could trust them). With Jennifer's help, Camilla and Mitchell could have the means to uncovering the mystery. Complications set in when Camilla receives a phone call threatening her mother if she doesn't back off. The program ends, unresolved, with Camilla attempting to get to her mother before it is too late.

76 *Deep Blue Mermaids.* youtube.com. 2012 (Comedy-Drama).

As the result of a weird dream, two young girls, Lea and Nicole, learn they are descended from Mermaids when contact with water causes their transformation. Stories follow the girls as they struggle to protect their secret identities while attempting to live normal lives.

Cast (as credited): Te'a/Lynor04 (Lea Opale), Alisia (Nicole Aigue-Marine), Kailey (Catalina/Winda), Emily (Liv Walters). **Credits** are not given. **Comment:** Poor sound but acceptable photography with capable acting by the young female leads.

Episodes:

1. The Beginning (5 min., 14 sec.). The story line is established as Lea and Nicole become Mermaids.

2. A Fishy Family (5 min., 17 sec.). As Lea and Nicole attempt to adjust to the fact that they are now Mermaids, Lea learns that her great-grandmother was also a Mermaid.

3. New Life, New Moon (4 min., 22 sec.). Just as Nicole and Lea believe they are now able to control their powers, they find that the full moon can also affect them and turn them into Mermaids.

4. Episode 4 (Untitled; 3 min., 47 sec.). Nicole and Lea, under the influence of a full moon, attempt their first swim as Mermaids.

5. Episode 5 (Untitled; 3 min., 35 sec.). The girls make a startling discovery while swimming—another Mermaid (Winda).

6. Episode 6 (Untitled; 4 min., 52 sec.). Frustrated that they cannot make contact with the elusive Winda, Nicole and Lea devise a plan to meet her.

7. Episode 7 (Untitled; 1 min., 47 sec.). Nicole and Lea's plan to attract Winda works and they make first contact with her.

8. Episode 8 (Untitled; 4 min., 4 sec.). Obsessed with becoming a Mermaid, Nicole and Lea's friend, Catalina, seeks a way to do so by finding a spell that will initiate the change.

9. Episode 9 (Untitled; 4 min., 23 sec.). Nicole and Lea ponder what to do when a rainstorm prevents them from leaving the house for school.

10. Episode 10 (Untitled; 5 min., 15 sec.). The concluding episode wherein Nicole and Lea discover another Mermaid lives among them—their friend Liv, who has successfully concealed her powers for some time.

77 *Deep Sea Tails.* youtube.com. 2012 (Comedy-Drama).

While in a public swimming pool, a young girl (Synde) finds a mysterious turquoise gemstone and takes it home with her. Curious about what she has found, and believing it may be related to Mermaids, Synde conducts an Internet search and learns that all Mermaids have a gem in the ocean and whoever finds one will become a Mermaid (how the gem found its way into a public pool is not stated). Synde soon discovers that she is a Mermaid (with a turquoise tail) when water spills on her and she transforms. By drying her tail she regains her legs and stories follow her adventures—as she attempts to encompass her new abilities and keep, as best she can, her secret from others (her friend, Ruby, discovers her secret in the second episode and vows to not only help her but protect her).

Cast (as credited): Meredith G. (Sydne), Caroline M. (Ruby), Kayla G. (Hailey), Giny A. (Cassidy), Sophie V. (Sofia), Mariah K. (McKayla), Sam Y. (Teddy). **Credits** are not given. **Comment:** Camera microphones do not provide the best sound and the production suffers because of it. The girls are good and the photography acceptable.

Episode List: *1.* Fish Out of Water. *2.* House Maid. *3.* Halloween Special. *4.* Hypnotized Half Tail. *5.* Water Wastage. *6.* Stranger Than the Average Strange. *7.* Fishy Letters. *8.* Truth Be Told. *9.* Dive Deep. *10.* Season 1 Finale. *11.* Full Moon Despair (Begins Season 2). *12.* One Letter Too Far. *13.* New Girl in Town. *14.* Déjà vu. *15.* Fish Over Fed (Concluding episode).

78 Desenterrados (The Unearthed). de senterrados.com. 2012 (Thriller).

In an effort to save his dying daughter (Barbara), a scientist (Dr. Samuel) has begun experimenting with resurrecting the dead. His efforts have been unsuccessful and have produced horrifying side effects: deceased people (The Unearthed) have been brought back to life although they are unaware of who or what they were previously. Unable to reverse his process, the doctor has created an isolated community to house them and has hired a psychologist (Nicole) to watch over them and hopefully learn through their progression what he needs to do to perfect his research. The program relates what happens when both the doctor and Nicole begin to experience strange dreams and hear mysterious noises and conduct an investigation to discover their source.

Nataly is a rarity in the Unearthed community. She is the only one whose dreams bring to light memories of her past. Barbara is the only daughter of the doctor and is kept alive on a breathing machine. She is his obsession to perfect his procedure. Albert is Dr. Samuel's assistant and an expert on exhumation (which is critical to Samuel's experiments). Unknown to the doctor, Albert has plans to profit from the technology. Oliver can hear mysterious voices that no one can perceive. He is seeking to discover the meaning of life without memories and assists Nataly in her quest to return to the real world.

Cast: Christian Stamm (Dr. Samuel), Maria Minaya (Nicole), Jessica Alonso (Nataly), Juanma Mallen (Albert), Ines Padilla (Barbara), Juanan Lucena (Oliver). **Credits:** *Producer-Writer-Director:* Xavi Cortes. **Comment:** While not an original idea (shades of it can be seen in the feature film *She Demons* and the TV series *Strange Paradise*) it is well done and intriguing and the cast is appealing.

Episodes: Five untitled episodes were produced, all of which are in Spanish with no English subtitles or English captioning available thus following the story line is quite difficult without knowledge of the Spanish language.

79 DeVanity. devanity.com. 2011–2014 (Drama).

Los Angeles provides the backdrop for a look at the diverse lives of the DeVanity family, owners of a jewelry empire, and the problems they attempt to overcome when Richard, the family patriarch is murdered (by his psychotic lover) and his heirs must take over the business and keep it from falling into ruins.

Cast: Michael Caruso (Jason DeVanity), Alexis Zibolis (Lara Muller DeVanity), Katie Caprio (Bianca DeVanity Regis), Mike Dirksen (Alexander Roth), Erin Christine Buckley (Jackie DeVanity Crowne), Katie Apicella (Dr. Portia Muller Roth), Chris Parke, Jason Christopher (Byron DeVanity), Kyle Lowder (Andrew Regis), Jaclyn Lyons (Isabelle Roth DeVanity), John Brody (Dr. Sebastian Crowne), Robin Riker (Angelica Roth), Gordon Thomson (Preston Regis), Maxwell Caulfield (Richard DeVanity), Arianne Zucker (Julia Regis), Charlene Tilton (Francesca DeVanity), Steve Kanaly (Charles Kane), Andrea Evans (Vivian Price), Sheree J. Wilson (Claudia Muller). **Credits:** *Producer-Writer:* Michael Caruso. *Director:* Kelly Portier. **Comment:** Presented like a daily television soap opera with good acting and production values. The program also sports some TV veterans: Steve Kanaly, Andrea Evans, Sherrie J. Wilson, Gordon Thomson, Charlene Tilton and Robin Riker.

Episode List: *1.* Broken Bitches. *2.* My Brother's Humper. *3.* Too Many Pricks. *4.* Better Things to Swallow. *5.* Bad Seeds. *6.* Sparing No Expense. *7.* Fake Jewels. *8.* Shock Therapy. *9.* Crash and Burn. *10.* Mommy Dearest. *11.* Holly Through Your Heart. *12.* Battle of the Brides. *13.* Surprise, Surprise. *14.* Other People's Bodies. *15.* Payback's a Bitch. *16.* Sleeping Giant. *17.* Clash of the Tyrants. *18.* Broken Promises. *19.* Shattered Future. *20.* Aftermath. *21.* Baby Bumps. *22.* A Matter of Timing. *23.* Death Becomes Him, Part 1. *24.* Death Becomes Him, Part 2. *25.* Phoenix Rising. *26.* Revelations. *27.* Homecoming. *28.* Blood of Diamonds.

80 Dexter: Early Cuts. sho.com. 2009–2012 (Crime Drama).

Animated Internet prequel to the Showtime TV series *Dexter* about a blood splatter specialist (Dexter Morgan) for the Miami-Dade Police Department. Dexter is not an ordinary police detective and leads a secret life by eliminating criminals as a mysterious and vicious serial killer. If the police are unable to catch a killer or the culprit beats the system, Dexter makes sure they receive their just desserts—with no trace left as to who killed them—"I'm a very neat monster," he says. Dexter, an orphan, was raised by Harry Morgan, a police detective. When Harry noticed Dexter had an unnatural urge to kill, he encouraged Dexter and taught him how to focus on criminals, especially serial killers, and how not to leave any evidence behind. Stories follow Dexter as he chooses a victim and how he goes about eliminating his target.

Cast: Michael C. Hall (Dexter/Narrator). **Credits:** *Producer:* Michael C. Hall. *Illustrator:* David Mack, Bill Sienkiewicz. *Writer:* Tim Schlattman. **Comment:** Almost still-like animation is encompassed to present a program just as creepy (in atmosphere) as the live-action series. Although Dexter is the only voice heard (sort of narrating what is happening) it plays well although some episodes, especially on YouTube, require a sign-in to certify that you are over 18 years of age due to the bloody aspects of some episodes.

Episodes:

1. Alex Timmons (8 min., 9 sec.). Dexter's first target is Alex Timmons, a despicable Gulf War veteran who used the cover of war to kill innocent people.

2. Gene Marshall (7 min., 47 sec.). An arsonist becomes Dexter's next target.

3. Cindy Landon (8 min., 45 sec.). A black widow (Cindy Landon) gets a dose of her own medicine when she encounters Dexter.

4. Dark Echo, Chapter 1 (2 min., 33 sec.). Explores Dexter's life after his father passes and he enrolls in college.

5. Dark Echo, Chapter 2 (2 min., 19 sec.). An evil criminology professor (Robert Milson) becomes Dexter's new target.

6. Dark Echo, Chapter 3 (2 min., 44 sec.). It is January and for the New Year Dexter chooses Jenna Lincoln, a young woman who arranged for the death of her family so she could inherit a fortune.

7. Dark Echo, Chapter 4 (3 min., 12 sec.). Jenna is killed—but not by Dexter as Dexter now fears a copy-cat killer is on the loose.

8. All in the Family, Chapter 1 (1 min., 53 sec.). It is New Year's Eve and Dexter sets his sights on a hooker and must then find a way to dispose of her body.

9. All in the Family, Chapter 2 (3 min). Continues the story that shows Dexter disposing of bodies (dumping them in the ocean) then setting his sights on Tony Rodriquez—accused of murdering his best friend but freed when the D.A. claims there is not enough evidence to convict him.

81 *Diary of a Black Widow.* timberwolf west.com. 2011 (Crime Drama).

Color mixes with black and white film footage to eerily explore the world of a beautiful woman (Hope) who seduces men and women then plots to kill them in ways only the mind of a depraved person can devise.

Cast: Hannah Townsend (Hope), Shannan Leigh Reeve (Esperanza), Randall Shea (John Clarke), Kim Irwin Dildine (Landlord), Julia Bantner (Tasha), Shaela Cook (Jessica), Rydell Danzie (Mark), Jessica Haro-Predes (Alice), Nikole Howell (Veronica), Marie Joelyn (Bikini girl), Nicole Pacent (Lori), Bridget McManus (Diana). **Credits:** *Producer:* Rydell Danzie, Timothy Whitfield, Shannan Leigh Reeve. *Director:* Rydell Danzie, Timothy Whitfield, Darin Mangan. *Writer:* Rydell Danzie. **Comment:** Billed as "Twisted tales of seduction and murder," two trailers and what is called "A Preview Episode" do remain on line and from them one can gather the essence of the program. It is well acted and produced and, although it has nudity, violence, sexual situations and gore, these sequences have been removed from the trailers.

Episodes: All episodes have been taken off line due to release of a DVD version of the program (edited to form a feature film). The episode titles: *1.* The Eve. *2.* Vacation. *3.* Demons. *4.* The Apprentice, Part 1. *5.* The Apprentice, Part 2. *6.* Dreamscape. *7.* Empowerment of New Life. *8.* Journey. *9.* Classified. *10.* New Beginnings.

82 *Diary of a Single Mom.* pic.tv. 2009–2011 (Drama).

The program is actually a profile of three single mothers and their families and how they face the challenges of their individual situations and deal with issues such as finances, education, childcare and healthcare. Principal focus is on Ocean Jackson, a 27-year-old mother of two (Trina and Sammy; Mike is their father) struggling against all odds to acquire her GED, enroll in college and establishing her own business (she is currently employed as the manager of her three flat apartment building). Lupe is a young mother with health issues and two children (each of which has a different father); and Peggy, an older woman (50) who, after the death of her wealthy husband, suddenly finds herself broke and the guardian to her only grandchild (Ian); she later develops her own culinary business.

Cast: Monica Calhoun (Ocean Jackson), Valery M. Ortiz (Lupe), Janice Lynde (Peggy), Jonathan Biggs (Sammy), Nieko Mann (Trina), Zach Callison (Ian), Richard Roundtree (Lou Bailey), Billy Dee Williams (Uncle Bo), Aya Marie Easter (Kayla), Logan Grove (J.J.), China Anderson (Sophie), Diahann Carroll (Therapist), Brooklyn McLinn (Sam, Sr.), Irma P. Hall (Dessa) Leon (as credited) (Mike). **Credits:** *Producer:* Robert Townsend, Rey Ramsey, Aaron Steele, Messiah Jacobs. *Director:* Robert Townsend. *Writer:* Cheryl L. West. **Comment:** Television quality production overseen by actor-comedian

Robert Townsend and featuring some prominent names (Richard Roundtree, Diahann Carroll, Billy Dee Williams and Janice Lynde). Only third season episodes remain on line due to a release of the first two seasons on DVD.

Season 1 Episode List: *1.* Life Raft. *2.* School Maze. *3.* Creating a Village. *4.* Eyes Don't Lie. *5.* Halloween Ghosts. *6.* Aftermath. *7.* Solstice. *8.* Thanksgiving's End.

Season 2 Episode List: *9.* Anybody for a Miracle? *10.* Trick Play. *11.* Flexing. *12.* The Meek Shall Inherit the Earth. *13.* Hiding Out. *14.* Snap Back. *15.* Promise Keeper. *16.* Emasculated.

Season 3 Episode List: *17.* By Omission. *18.* Struggling or Surviving. *19.* Running on Empty. *20.* Burnt Dreams. *21.* The Gift of Rosary. *22.* Aplomb. *23.* Paradox. *24.* In the Meantime. *25.* Dream Cart. *26.* Friday.

83 *Die Monsters Die.* blip.tv. 2012 (Adventure).

"A post-apocalyptic world, an evil corporation, mutants, the living dead, beautiful women with swords.... What more could you want?" (the series tag line). It is the year 2041, 50 years following two devastating events: the Great White Plague and a war with the Kyonshi (the Korean-like Mafia) that literally destroyed the world, leaving only the Asian race unscathed (as they are genetically immune). New San Francisco, as it is now called, is the setting. It is here that survivors blame the activities of the Wyatt Corporation for instituting the plague. Although the city is safe, half-human victims called Bleeders are still a threat as are the deadly Kyonshi, who seek to control the city. But from the ashes a group of young people called the Dianzu have emerged and, with their swords, have instituted a battle against the enemy, striking without mercy to free New San Francisco from the evil that now plagues it. The group is led by a single mother, and her comrades include a pair of identical twins, a male stripper, a man with a mysterious past and a former yakuza. **Cast:** Sandra Young (Hope), L.J. Batinas (Trent), Carolyn Hu, Nan Suphari (Zoey), Jean Franco (Dakota), Remmy Medlina (Evan/Eric), Kalinda Wang (Eve). **Credits:** *Producer:* Sandra Young, L.J. Batinas, K. Miyazoe. **Comment:** Presented in black and white and featuring an all Asian-American cast. The acting is very good and the story fast-moving and well produced.

Episodes:

1. Die Monsters Die Begins. Establishes the story line as New San Francisco becomes the headquarters for a group of survivors to bring down the evil Wyatt Corporation.

2. From Bangkok with Love. A woman's desperate efforts to send a message for help in a battle that will soon begin.

3. Someone in This Room Is Going to Die. Hope, a young woman with incredible bravery, initiates the battle for survival against the evils that resulted from the plague.

4. On the Beach. As Hope forms her group, the Identical Twins (called so but not related) become a part of her team.

5. Watch Over Me. Hope's band of warriors continues battling to defeat the enemy and restore their zombie-like plagued city to the way it once was. The program's concluding episode.

84 *The Discovery: Mountain Mermaid.* youtube.com. 2013 (Comedy Drama).

While on a hiking trip, two young girls (Kylie and Liz) take a wrong turn and find themselves on an apparently uncharted trail on the wrong side of a mountain. As they walk, Kylie falls through a grass-covered hole and into a sandy-like area near a cave. As Liz goes for help, Kylie enters the cave and finds herself waist-high in water—at the same time beams from the moon enhance the water. It is not shown how, but Kylie is magically transported back to her home—at the same time Liz had arrived to summon help. Kylie appears to be unaffected by her weird adventure until she comes in contact with water and is transformed into a Mermaid. With Liz witnessing the change, Kylie must now learn to adjust to her Mermaid abilities (with Liz's help) and live the life of a normal girl. **Cast (as credited):** Dani (Kylie), Kate (Liz). **Credits** are not given. **Comment:** Good underwater filming and acting by the girls but the program has poor sound and sometimes unsteady indoor scenes.

Episodes: Only three of four produced episodes remain on line. Each has no title and is listed as: "Episode 1," "Episode 2" and "Episode 3."

85 *The Division.* whatisthedivision.com. 2011–2012 (Action).

Nick Trever, a bodyguard at the Garner Security Group, is married to Michelle and they are the parents of Jeremy. Michelle is a drug researcher at Genesis Pharmaceuticals and has been working on a project that could cure brain dysfunctions (like Alzheimer's and dementia). The cost to continue, however, is astronomical ($20 billion) and no legitimate company is willing to take the risk. Unknown to Michelle, a shady organization called The Division, foots the bill so Michelle's work can continue. As Michelle works in secret (not even telling Nick), persons unknown breach the Genesis system's computer firewall and gain access to the entire project on which Michelle is working. When the Department of Defense learns what has happened, a U.S. Senator (Thomas Miller) orders Michelle's abduction (to protect her and uncover the people behind The Division) but her death is faked, leaving Michael and others to believe she is really dead. Two weeks later, while with Jeremy in the park, Nick receives a phone call that causes him to turn his back on Jeremy. Jeremy mysteriously disappears and Nick immediately receives a phone call telling him that Jeremy has been abducted and that to get him back he must kidnap a senator (Raymond Stanfield). It appears that Stanfield, who is running for President of the United States, has ties to The Division and he may be the key to uncovering the people behind it. The program follows what happens when Nick discovers that Michelle is alive and that what she has discovered "could change everything" (ends in a cliff hanger).

Cast: Andrew Bowen (Nick Trever), Ivana Shein (Michelle Trever), Tarik Ellinger (Jeremy Trever), Jessica Tome (Chloe), Thomas Blankenship (John McFadden), Tommy Evan Lee (Rick Chan), Kevin McCorkle (Senator Stanfield), Greg Philippi (Thomas Miller). **Credits:** *Producer:* Temara Melek, Javier Prato, Eric Won, Campbell McCorke. *Writer-Director:* Eric Won. **Comment:** Compelling, well-acted and produced series. The production is high caliber (comparable to any TV series) with visually impressive photography. The story moves right along and draws you in from the first few minutes of episode one. Worth watching even though there are only three episodes.

Episodes:
1. Taken (9 min., 19 sec.). Nick finds that after his son is abducted, he must kidnap a senator in order to get him back.
2. Genesis (11 min., 26 sec.). Nick performs his task, is reunited with Jeremy—and discovers that his wife, Michelle, is alive.
3. The Research (14 min., 40 sec.). Nick discovers that The Division is seeking Michelle's research papers on something she discovered (not disclosed) "that could change everything."

86 *Dr. Horrible's Sing-a-Long Blog.* dr horrible.com. 2007–2008 (Musical Comedy-Drama).

Billy, a seeming innocent, hard-working scientist, is secretly Dr. Horrible, an evil man who sees the world "as a mess" and wants to rule it. He believes that joining the Evil League of Evil will give him his greatest chance, but he has been rejected a number of times as his evil deeds are constantly foiled by the do-gooder Captain Hammer. The story relates Billy's attempts to become a member of the Evil League of Evil and the complication that sets in when he meets Penny, a girl who crusades for the underdog (like the homeless) and falls in love with her—a girl who is also the apple of Captain Hammer's eye.

Cast: Neil Patrick Harris (Dr. Horrible), Nathan Fillian (Captain Hammer), Felicia Day (Penny), Simon Helberg (Moist). **Credits:** *Producer:* David M. Burns, Michael Boretz, Joss Whedon. *Writer-Director:* Joss Wedon. *Music and Lyrics:* Jed Whedon,

Joss Whedon, Maurissa Tancharoen. **Comment:** Enjoyable take on super hero sagas with original music and songs. The entire production is well performed, written and directed. The 14 minute episodes were edited to form a TV special and aired on the CW network on October 9, 2012.

Episodes:
1. Act 1. Introduces Dr. Horrible as he receives word that his letter to the Evil League of Evil will be evaluated and they will be watching for his next crime. Needing "wonderflonium" for his next invention (his time-stopping Freeze Ray), Dr. Horrible opts to steal the material and make that his ultimate crime for acceptance into the League. As he begins, he runs into Penny, who is petitioning to turn a condemned building into a homeless shelter. Although smitten by her, he feels completing his mission is more important. Although he does re-connect with her in his true guise as Billy after he commits his crime as Dr. Horrible, he finds that he also has competition for her hand from Captain Hammer.
2. Act 2. After successfully building his Freeze Ray, Dr. Horrible posts a video blog that he will use the ray on the city. When his efforts fail (the blog had been watched by the police who stopped him) Dr. Horrible receives notice from the League that he has been reprimanded and for him to join, he must now kill someone of his own choosing. When Billy and Penny meet at a Laundromat and run into Captain Hammer, Billy decides to make him his target for assassination.
3. Act 3. Captain Hammer's sudden interest in joining Penny's crusade to help the homeless angers Billy as Captain Hammer has now become the city's new hero. As Captain Hammer begins delivering a speech to help the homeless, Dr. Horrible freezes him with his Freeze Ray then attempts to kill him with his Death Ray gun. But before he can do so, the freeze ray wears off and the Captain attacks Dr. Horrible. The Death Ray gun falls to the floor and is retrieved by the Captain. Ignoring Dr. Horrible's warnings not to fire the gun as the fall damaged it, the Captain pulls the trigger. The gun explodes, injuring the Captain and killing Penny (who is hit by shrapnel). Although Penny was not the intended victim, the League sees the killing as being what they ordered and Dr. Horrible is accepted into the League. He accomplished a goal at the cost of someone he loved and the Captain, having felt pain for the first time in his life, believes he has failed as a super hero (allowing Penny to die) and has sought psychiatric care.

87 *Downsized (2010).* webserieschannel. com. 2010–2011 (Comedy-Drama).

Reality-like presentation that focuses on a blended family of nine (the Bruce-Rumsey's) as they attempt to survive the demands of a sluggish economy.

Cast: Todd Bruce, Laura Bruce, Heather Bruce, Bailey Rumsey, Levi Bruce, Dylan Rumsey, Whitney

Rumsey, Rex Rumsey, Danielle Rumsey (Themselves). **Credits:** *Producer:* Suzanne Gladstone, Kris Curry, Kristy Wampole, Malachi McGlone, Scott Templeton, Monica Ramone, Tara Sandler, Russell Heldt. *Director:* Malachi McGlone, Daryn Strauss. *Writer:* Daryn Strauss. **Comment:** A different approach to a current situation that plays well with good acting and production values. Situations encountered by the real-life family are typically those that could be encountered by any family.

Episodes:

1. Down but Not Out. Introduces the family and the problems they face.

2. Reality Bites. Having lost his job, Todd and his wife (Laura) contemplate the fact that they may have to move but regret telling their children.

3. Cruel Cruel Summer. As the situation becomes tense, the family believes that to keep their home, they need to drastically cut expenses.

4. We're Working on It. Todd begins the task of finding a job.

5. Love Don't Cost a Thing. The family has added worries as Laura's upcoming MRI could destroy what is left of their finances.

6. Much Ado About Hoagies. In an attempt to make her family adhere to their situation, Laura institutes a family boot camp.

7. Call Me Dad. The challenges of a blended family are explored.

8. Kansas City Blues. The family situation appears to be improving as all family members are pitching in and cutting expenses.

9. A House Divided. Now that things are looking better, Todd and Laura must figure on the right way to start saving money.

10. Teenage Rampage. An injury suffered by Rex threatens to wipe out the family's savings.

11. Divorce Drama. Rex's medical bills are causing friction between Todd and Laura.

12. The Other Side of the Glass. Family problems increase as Cody, Todd's estranged son, pays a visit.

13. Fend for Yourself. To hopefully resolve issues, Todd institutes a "Fend for Yourself" policy.

14. Run for Your Life. The MRI reveals that Laura has MS.

15. Too Much Pressure. Laura's fears are expressed that her disease will cause her to lose her job.

16. No More Emergency Fund. With bills mounting, Laura feels she needs to sell her wedding ring to raise money.

17. Talk to Her. Mounting family problems force Laura and Todd to seek the help of a therapist.

18. At the Table. Bailey adds to the family woes when she and her boyfriend can't agree on anything. The program's concluding episode.

88 *Downsized* (2012). minglemedia.tv. 2012 (Comedy-Drama).

Explores the lives of several people struggling to survive the pressures of everyday life: Beth, a mid-level saleswoman who finds herself unemployed when her corporation downsizes her; Maura, her boss, who masterminded the corporation's downsizing program; Lowell, Maura's efficiency expert; Connor, Maura's ex-husband, an over-worked attorney who has fallen hopelessly in love with his Turkish cleaning lady (Leyla); Andy, an office temp struggling to fund a recession-based self-help program; Astrid, a beauty pageant coach and con-artist; Nate, a father she has conned; and Priscilla, Andy's ex-wife, who is facing a crisis when her investments bottom out and her privileged life style is suddenly in jeopardy.

Cast: Daryn Strauss (Beth), Michele Mavissakalian (Maura), Duncan Murdoch (Lowell), Chris Henry Coffey (Connor), Esra Gaffin (Leyla), Conan McCarty (Andy), Shannon Conley (Astrid), Kaipo Schwab (Nate), Meredith Zinner (Priscilla), Gerard Urciuoli (Hank), Anna Stone (Brenda). **Comment:** Gentle mix of comedy and drama that is well acted and produced. Like-able characters are mixed with a good story line that flows smoothly from beginning to end.

Episodes:

1. Duane (3 min., 17 sec.). Maura's downsizing plan causes Beth to lose her job.

2. Broken English (4 min., 23 sec.). Connor's infatuation with Leyla begins to take a turn for the worse when he finds difficulty in understanding her attempts at speaking English.

3. Pageantry (3 min., 14 sec.). Deeply in debt and needing to pay off her credit card bills, Astrid seeks a victim to con—Nate, by coaching his six-year-old daughter Poppy to become a beauty pageant queen.

4. Self-Help (5 min., 25 sec.). Andy's plans to present his program, E-Quad, to the corporation as a means of reinventing itself, falls short when he discovers his half-brother (Lowell) has stolen it (The E-Trinity).

5. Linguistics (3 min., 45 sec.). Connor devises a plan to help his situation with Leyla: get her to speak English through a series of DVD programs.

6. Unemployment Blues (2 min., 16 sec.). Beth's problems are explored as she tries to figure out her financial problems.

7. Grand Supreme (4 min., 33 sec.). Astrid's plan to increase her cash flow backfires when she double books an event and Poppy, becoming frightened, locks herself in the ladies room and refuses to come out.

8. Split Assets (4 min., 20 sec.). Andy, facing financial problems of his own attempts to sweet talk Priscilla into lending him money.

9. Valentine's Day (4 min., 39 sec.). Maura's Valentine's Day celebration becomes a bit too much when she becomes drunk and Connor finds himself coming to her rescue.

10. Creative Real Estate (4 min., 13 sec.). Priscilla seeks a way to save her home from foreclosure.

11. Employment (8 min., 27 sec.). Hank, Beth's fiancé, seeks a way to help Beth overcome her depression while Connor finds himself again sleeping with his estranged wife, Maura.

12. Clientele (5 min., 36 sec.). Astrid, convincing Nate to appear with Poppy in a "Daddy and Me" pageant, finds a stumbling block when Brenda, Nate's wife, feels something is not right. The program's concluding episode.

89 *Dyke Central.* youtube.com. 2012 (Comedy-Drama).

Alex and Gin, women in their early thirties, are also roommates and lesbians (in a style considered butch). Alex and Gin, however, are not lovers and pursue their own individual relationships. Alex is currently dating Jackie, while Gin pretends to be someone she is really not to impress girls. Her chameleon-like life style and Alex's inability to be more supportive of the women she loves have placed them in a situation where they need to change their ways, but are not totally capable of doing it on their own. The program relates what happens when Alex and Gin's friends step in and attempt to change them for the better.

Cast: Tai Rockett (Alex), Giovannie Espiritu (Gin), Comika Beaudry (Jackie), Carla Pauli (Fabiana), Amelia Mae Paradise (Molly), Andre LeBlanc (Mario), Tom Paul (Zack), Mahasin Munir (Sol). **Credits:** *Producer:* Florencia Manovil, Comika Beaudry, Lex Sloan, Alicia Kester, Arnetta Smith, Tammy Massa. *Director:* Florencia Manovil. *Writer:* Florencia Manovil, Arnetta Smith. **Comment:** Based on what has been released, a promising series that will detail the ups and downs of four friends. The acting and production values are very good and the mix of butch-type lesbians with the more feminine type works well.

Episodes:
1. Pilot (20 min., 49 sec.). Basically an introduction to the four main characters: Alex, Gin, Jackie and Fabiana (a girl from San Francisco, newly arrived in Oakland [the series setting] and hopeful actress, who becomes roommates with Alex and Gin in an area called Dyke Central).

90 *EastSiders.* eastsiderstheseries.com. 2012 (Drama).

It has been predicted that on December 21, 2012 the Mayan Apocalypse would occur. Four friends, Cal and Thom (a gay couple) and their friend Kathy and her boyfriend, Ian decide to make the best of it by attending an end-of-the-world party. The party results in Cal discovering that Thom has been unfaithful to him (with Jeremy) and the program explores a question of relationships and fidelity, not only in a gay couple, but in their straight couple friends as well.

Cast: Kit Williamson (Cal), Van Hansis (Thom), Constance Wu (Kathy), John Halbach (Ian), Matthew McKelligon (Jeremy), Stephen Guarino (Quincy). **Credits:** *Producer:* Chrissy Dodson, Kristyne Elizabeth Fetsic, Jonathan Stahl. *Writer-Director:* Kit Williamson. **Comment:** Comedy mixes with drama in a program that does not focus on the sexual aspects of a relationship but on the efforts of people to solve the problems they have and make a relationship work. The acting and production values are good and due to its gay theme, may have a limited audience.

Episodes:
1. Episode 1 (13 min., 49 sec.). An evening of enjoyment at a party turns to dismay when Cal discovers that Thom has been cheating on him and Kathy, a bit unstable, believes Ian, as nice as he is, is not in love with her (all of which she is imagining).

2. Episode 2 (10 min., 35 sec.). As Cal and Thom's relationship becomes strained when Cal objects to an article Thom has written about their relationship, Jeremy, who is bi-sexual, sets his sights on Kathy, causing Ian to dissuade him from asking her for a date.

91 *Easy Abby.* easyabby.com. 2012–2013 (Comedy-Drama).

Abby, a young woman seeking to find love with another woman is not as seductive as other lesbians she knows. She has an anxiety disorder, is a chronic seducer and does not appear to realize that her aggressiveness is often the reason why she cannot maintain a steady relationship. Abby's world is one of neurotic characters and stories follow Abby as she struggles to make ends meet (working in a bicycle shop) and find that one special woman.

Cast: Lisa Cordoleone (Abby), Emily Shain (Sara), Laura Chernicky (Eileen), Mouzam Makkar (Danielle), Karmine Byrne (Carolyn), Brian Plocharczyk (Charlie), Leeron Silberberg (Kelly), Lana Smithner (Laura), Fawzia Mirza (Bobbie), Haviland Stillwell (Lydia), Adria Dawn (Angela). **Credits:** *Writer-Director:* Wendy Jo Carlton. **Comment:** There are suggestive romantic encounters coupled with tender kissing scenes but nothing is taken to the point of being too racy even for broadcast TV. The acting and production values are very good and the program, although aimed at a specific audience, can be enjoyed by anyone.

Episodes:
1. Portable Feast (5 min., 13 sec.). Abby's accidental encounter with a former lover has her wondering if she has what it takes to fall in love when she can't remember the girl's name.

2. Pie's the Limit (7 min., 49 sec.). As Abby's friends Carolyn and Sara host a dinner party, Abby finds herself talked into a blind date with a woman she actually dated before.

3. Naming the Baby (6 min., 6 sec.). Abby's date

fosters a one night stand while Sara, believing Carolyn is cheating on her, decides to crash at Abby's apartment.

4. Bacon and Legs (4 min., 52 sec.). Abby tries to cheer up a depressed Sara by introducing her to a group of women at a mid-day brunch.

5. Danish Twist (6 min., 14 sec.). At a restaurant Abby encounters a girl she once dated, but never reconnected with (they make up for lost time by making out in the ladies' room).

6. Love Monkey (5 min., 34 sec.). While at work, Abby confides in her co-worker that her mother's arrival has put a damper on her dating life as her mother just doesn't understand her sexual preference.

7. No Fly Zone (5 min., 42 sec.). With her mother gone and her life seemingly back to normal, Abby finds another distraction when her neighbor, Lydia, interrupts a love-making session to complain that Abby leaves her household garbage on the side of the disposal rather than placing it inside.

8. Martini in the Closet (9 min., 44 sec.). With Sara still reeling over her breakup with Carolyn, Abby takes her to a lesbian bar—where a stranger (Eileen) makes a play for Sara.

9. Walk Before You Run (7 min., 33 sec.). After several beers, Sara warms up to Eileen and the two leave the bar together—without Abby.

10. Icing on the Sponge Cake (8 min., 58 sec.). Abby, tending bar at a wedding reception discovers what making love to an older woman is all about when the bride's mother seduces her and the two have a brief affair.

11. How to Travel Light (7 min., 49 sec.). Abby hooks up with Danielle, the pretty bartender she met in episode 8.

12. The Meatball Test (7 min., 39 sec.). After accidentally locking herself out of her apartment, Abby meets her lesbian neighbors (Bobbie and Lydia) for the first time as the program concludes.

92 Eighty-Six. webserieschannel.com. 2011–2012 (Crime Drama).

Tweety-La, a famous African-American recording artist, is represented by the prestigious (but somewhat shady) Casey-Mac Entertainment. The company, run by Alexander Mac, Maxine Casey and Jaxon Casey, are not the most upstanding people in the industry and although respected (and feared) they do what it takes to get their clients what they require. It is the evening of an important event—Tweety-La is about to sign a new contract with a competing label (Roman P. Jones) when she is found murdered and suspicion immediately falls on Alexander, Maxine and Jaxon, who sought to lose a fortune if Tweety-La jumped ship. The program, which ends unresolved, relates the intrigues, lies and personal issues facing those involved with Tweety-La as the police, under the supervision of L.A.P.D.

Detective Michelle Fournier, seek to find her killer.

Cast: Francesca Gailes (Maxine Casey), Adam Starks (Alex Mac), Coley Speaks (Jaxon Casey), Cherub Moore (Tweety-La), Shawn Singletary (DJ Krazy Kay), Anthony M. Bertram (Johnnie Wilcox), Heidi Lewandowski (Anastacia Joi), Jennifer Marshall (Barbara Davies), Blair Sharne (Det. Michelle Fournier), David Hunter, Jr. (Roman P. Jones). **Credits:** *Producer:* Antonio Moscatelli, Cameron Wallace, Brandy Starks, Francesca Gailes. *Director:* J.L. Walters. *Writer:* Francesca Gailes, Adam Starks. **Comment:** All episodes, including trailers and teasers have been taken off-line. Promotional information refers to the series as "high concept drama exposing the underbelly of success within the entertainment industry." The producers also state: "*Eighty-Six* will be the poster child for what happens when young, positive, and professional minority filmmakers get together in pursuit of a common goal. Our standard is nothing but the best in story-telling, so with our web series you won't find the stereotypical components that plague so many popular African-American projects. The better news is that this is a show everyone, regardless of race, will be captivated by." Five episodes were apparently planned but only two have surfaced.

Episodes:

1. The Beginning of the End (5 min., 20 sec.). Establishes the story line as Tweety-La is found murdered and suspicion falls on the heads of Casey-Mac Entertainment.

2. Ill-Gotten Gains (13 min., 20 sec.). With a police investigation begun and Alex and Max seeking to gain the most publicity for what has happened, Jaxon struggles to get the business back to normal.

93 Embers of War. blip.tv. 2012 (Adventure).

In a futuristic time Echo 7, a space patrolling orbital system designed to detect threats from outer space is destroyed by the Dakai, an evil alien race that plans to control the universe. While the Earth is not the first target, a peaceful planet called Kylene has just come under attack. To battle the enemy, a first response unit, the United Colonial Marine Force (UCMF), headed by General Maximus Provo, is sent into action. The program follows the battle that ensues as the Delta Force division of the UCMF soon discovers it is facing a deadly foe that appears unstoppable.

Cast: Andrew Garrettson (Lt. Ray McManus), Tim Harrold (Capt. Steve Collins), Megan Gamez (Princess Selena Veriana), Aris Juson (Lt. Rawly Gunnar), Ryan Findley (Vorenus Meyer), Tiffany Forni (Bex Roberts), Tim Harold (Capt. Steve Collins). **Credits:** *Producer:* Justin Lee. *Director:* Justin Lee, David Townsend. *Writer:* Justin Lee. **Comment:** Immediately you are struck by the special effects, outstanding for a web series. The story line, although not original, is well handled and the acting good for such a project (although it is a budgeted show, it appears that a majority of funds went to the special effects).

Episodes:

1. Arrival. An unknown alien race, seeking to rule the universe, plots a genocide attack on the peaceful planet Kylene.

2. Political Evacuation. Captain Collins and his Delta Force team enact a plan wherein they must outsmart the enemy and rescue Selena Veriana (Princess of Kylene).

3. No Angels Here. A mostly narrated episode wherein the destruction of Kylene cities is seen as well as re-grouping efforts on part of the UCMF, who are suffering casualties in a war against a deadly enemy.

94 *Emma Approved*. em maapproved.com. 2013–2014 (Comedy-Drama).

Emma Approved, run by Emma Woodhouse and Alex Knightley, is the match-making division of a developing company called The Highbury Partners Lifestyle Group. Emma has designated herself as the matchmaker while Alex handles "all the boring stuff" (like bookkeeping and business development). Emma knew, from the day that she graduated from college what she wanted to do—"I'm Emma Woodhouse and the People Need Me." Being a trained lifestyle expert it was only natural (at least to Emma) that she put her abilities to work and joined with Alex to begin their upstart business. The program follows Emma as she speaks directly to a camera, talks about her job, her matches and how she hopes what she is doing (documenting everything she does—"My Greatness") will win her a future Life Achievement Award for Lifestyle Excellence.

Emma was born in Southern California and raised in what she considers a perfect family. She is pretty, smart, idealistic and doesn't consider what she does to be a job ("My job isn't a job. It's a higher calling"). She is an expert life coach and believes she can fix people's problems—even problems people do not realize they have. Emma stays with her clients (a perfect 19 out 19 in the first episode) and says "Emma Approved" when a match works. She also says "I make your life better—I never fail."

Alex is not only Emma's business partner but her life-long friend. He is more in tune with business and reality than Emma and has the skill to become a For-

Emma Approved. Poster art from the series featuring, left to right: Dayeanne Hutton, Joanna Sotomura and Brent Bailey (used by permission of Pemberley Digital).

tune 500 CEO. While Emma is a bit disorganized, Alex is "cool, collected and organized." He is "The Ying to her Yang" and the one that keeps her in check.

Harriet Smith, a young woman who idolizes Emma, is her assistant and protégé and her eagerness to please Emma often depicts her as being a bit unsure of exactly what she is doing.

Annie Taylor is Emma's friend and former assistant who left the business to become a homemaker. She married Ryan Weston (a match arranged by Emma), the CEO of Cuddly Cupcakes (for which Annie is also a pastry chef).

Bobby Martin is the IT Contractor at Emma Approved (he has a passion for poker and bird watching).

James Elton is Emma's most prestigious client, a state senator and the city's most eligible bachelor, who is seeking that perfect mate.

Izzy Knightley is Emma's older sister and married to Alex's brother John. She is a total opposite of Emma and the mother of two children.

Frank Churchill is Ryan's brother-in-law, a high profile entrepreneur.

Maddy Bates, a friend of the Woodhouse family, is CEO of Bates Financial Services, but her business suffers on occasion as she is much too generous supporting various charities.

Cast: Joanna Sotomura (Emma Woodhouse), Brent Bailey (Alex Knightley), Dayeanne Hutton (Harriet Smith), Alexis Boozer (Annie Taylor), James Brent Isaacs (Bobby Martin), Paul Stuart (James Elton), Gabriel Voss (Ryan Weston), Stephen Chang (Frank Churchill) **Credits:** *Producer:* Bernie Su, Hank Green, Tracy Bitterolf. *Director:* Bernie Su. *Writer:* Bernie Su, Kate Rorick. **Comment:** Charming program with an adorable lead and excellent photography. Programs presented in this nature (basically addressing the camera rarely work unless the lead is truly appealing and stories being told are interesting). The team responsible for *The Lizzie Bennet Diaries* and *Welcome to Sanditon* has achieved the same charm here.

Episodes: (each is a video chat by Emma, explaining an aspect of her life or company with other regulars making brief appearances).
1. I Am Emma Woodhouse. Oct. 7. 2013.
2. Imminent Success. Oct. 10, 2013.
3. Self Sufficient. Oct. 14, 2013.
4. The Right Decision. Oct. 17, 2013.
5. Do What's Best. Oct. 21, 2013.
6. Let's Be Frank. Oct. 24, 2013.
7. What Really Matters. Oct. 28, 2013.
8. Being a Great Friend. Oct. 31, 2013.
9. A Worthy Subject. Nov. 4, 2013.
10. Wind in the Sails. Nov. 7, 2013.
11. Under-Whelmed. Nov. 11, 2013.
12. The Rooster Obstacle. Nov. 14, 2013.
13. Tweetception. Nov. 17, 2003.
14. Hash-Tag Miracle Worker. Nov. 21, 2013.
15. Ambition and Fruition. Nov. 25, 2013.
16. Giving Thanks. Nov. 28, 2103.
17. First Impressions. Dec. 2, 2013.
18. Practice Date. Dec. 5, 2013.
19. The Proof Is in the Yogurt. Dec. 9, 2013.
20. For a Very Special Lady. Dec. 12, 2013.
21. Fine Tuning. Dec. 16, 2013.
22. Planning Perfection. Dec. 19, 2013.
23. Moment of Triumph. Dec. 23, 2013.
24. Vingt-et-un. Dec. 26, 2013.
25. Should Have Listened. Feb. 3, 2014.
26. New Direction. Feb. 6, 2014.
27. The Need to Help. Feb. 10, 2014.
28. Sister Attack. Feb. 13, 2013.
29. Change of Plans. Feb. 17, 2014.
30. Winners and Losers. Feb. 20, 2014.
31. Listening, Again. Feb. 24, 2014.
32. Back in Business. Feb. 27, 2014.
33. Back in the Saddle. Mar. 3, 2014.
34. Attitude and Gratitude. Mar. 6, 2014.
35. Flies to Honey. Mar. 10, 2014.
36. Internal Troubles. Mar. 13, 2014.
37. Cinderella in the Making. Mar. 17, 2014.
38. Surprise, Surprise. Mar. 20, 2014.
39. Benefiting the Greater Good. Mar. 24, 2014.
40. Two for Two. Mar. 27, 2014.
41. Karma Is a... Mar. 31, 2014.
42. No, No and No. April 3, 2014.
43. To New Heights. April 7, 2014.
44. A Little Too Familiar. April 10, 2014.

95 Emma Stahl. onemorelesbian.com. 2010 (Drama).

Emma Stahl is a beautiful young woman, attracted to women and addicted to adventure, who is secretly a German government special agent whose assignments, battling terrorism and organized crime, brings her in contact with both. The program charts Emma's escapades—with other women and battling evil.

Cast: Meike Gottschalk (Emma Stahl), Gerrit Spangenberg (Emma's partner), Uwe Rapschlaeger (Regie), Matthias Van Denberg (Bornheim), Mira Herold (Fria Bornheim). **Credits:** *Producer:* Sandra Viedot. **Comment:** It appears that only a teaser has been released. It is well acted and produced and shows great potential as being an intriguing series. It is produced in Germany and has subtitles for American audiences.

Episodes:
1. Pilot Teaser (5 min., 26 sec.). Sets up the series proposed first story as Emma is assigned to assist local police in uncovering a band of terrorists whose strikes have been killing innocent people.

96 Empire. empiretheseries.com.com. 2010 (Drama).

Ensemble-like TV cast and production about a powerful and wealthy Long Island, New York family (the Havens), the owners of the society magazine *Empire* and how they struggle to keep their publishing empire afloat amidst the secrets they hide that could eventually destroy them.

Cubbie Haven, the second born son, took over Empire when Arthur, his older brother, showed no interest in following in their father's footsteps. Cubbie attended Harvard where he met and later married Sandra (with whom he believes he had three sons, Thomas, Evan and Cane; in actuality, Thomas and Evan resulted from an affair Sandra had with Arthur).

Thomas Haven, the eldest of the sons, is the family's black sheep. He was arrested and convicted for statutory rape (a tryst with a 15-year-old male hooker). He served time in prison and later tricked a young woman (Marin Lively) into marrying him. Disgraced by what he had done with his life, Thomas simply vanished and his whereabouts are unknown.

Ethan Haven, the middle son, has set his goal to prove to his father that he is capable of running *Empire* magazine but living in the shadow of his older, more successful brother, Thomas, has put a damper on that desire.

Cane Haven, the youngest of the three brothers, was disavowed by the family when it was discovered he was gay. He works as a private detective and had a relationship with Alex Russo.

Sandra Haven, Cubbie's wife, is the daughter of a wealthy New England family and met Cubbie while at Harvard. Their marriage flourished until Sandra learned Cubbie had an affair with Theodora and left him.

Katherine Valentine is the girl who was cared for by Cubbie and Sandra Haven after her mother, a maid to the Havens, died (she became their new maid when she was a teenager). Unknown to Katherine, Cubbie is her biological father (through an affair he had with Katherine's mother while still married to Sandra).

Theodora Grant Haven, the daughter of West Coast publishing legend Theodore Grant, is also the widow of Arthur Haven (Cubbie's older brother) and has set her goal to destroy Sandra and Cubbie's marriage—and acquire Empire in the process (a goal set in motion when she discovered that Sandra fathered two sons with Arthur [Thomas and Evan] while he was married to her).

Marin Lively is the girl who grew up with the Haven brothers (Evan has always been her best friend), but it was Thomas she had been set to marry—until his tryst with an underage male prostitute temporarily ended their relationship. When Thomas was released from prison, he and Marin reconnected and they married when Marin discovered that her marriage would allow Evan (whom she really loved) to take full control of Empire. Her plan backfired when Evan found out she married Thomas (unaware of her original intent) and, to get even, exposed Marin's teen sister's pregnancy in *Empire* and forced Marin to leave Thomas and Long Island.

Irving Reed is Cubbie's friend and rival from his college days. He now works as a high-powered attorney (although his practices have him under investigation for fraud and embezzlement) and is married to Kinky (her real name), his second wife, a former stripper.

Colleen Lively, the single mother of Lucy, was a promising actress who traded fame and fortune for marriage to a popular politician.

Lucy Lively, Colleen's pampered daughter, was on the road to becoming a beauty pageant winner (under Colleen's tutorage) until she became pregnant by her gay best friend (Jake Harper) and ruined her chances; she is how having to face the harsh realities of the world by caring for a child.

Valerie is an old friend of Colleen; Leslie is Irving's first wife and the father of Landon; Lance is Theodora's right-hand man; Norma is Empire's trusted cleaning lady; Lisa, a girl who wants the finer things in life, is Theodora's biggest fan; Bailey is the detective who has had legal tangles with both Cubbie and Irving; Bag Lady is the woman seen hanging out at the entrance to Empire—a psychic who appears to know more than she is letting on.

Cast: Nick Lewis (Evan Haven), Tina Sloan (Theodora Grant Haven), Kathryn Neville Browne (Sandra Haven), Chris Douros (Thomas Haven), Ryan Clardy (Cane Haven), Richard Flight (Cubbie Haven), Annalisa Derr (Katherine Valentine), Josh Davis (Jesse Jordan), Lise Fisher (Rachel Stone), Christian Barber (Rodney Dillon), Orlagh Cassidy (Colleen Lively), Afton Boggiano (Lucy Lively), Kate Forsatz (Marin Lively), Toby Levin (Jake Harper), Yvonne Perry (Valerie), Harlan J. Strauss (Irving Reed), Mary Leggio (Leslie Reed), Kevin DeBacker (Landon Reed), Heidi Jane Sparks (Kinky Reed), Chris J. Handley (Lance), Morgan Lindsey Tachco (Norma Morton), Molly Bennett (Lisa), Mark Hapka (Trevor), Lauren B. Martin (Bailey), Ellen Dolan (Bag Lady), Von Hottie (Herself), Casey Jon Deidrick (Gabe), Shane Zeigler (Wesley). **Credits:** *Producer-Director:* Steven Slate, Greg Turner, Brian Hewson. *Writer:* Brian Hewson, Craig Turner.

Comment: Well-acted serial-like soap opera whose format has been done numerous times before on television—from 1970s shows like *Beacon Hill* to 2000s *Dirt.*

YouTube Episode List: The exact number of episodes is unknown. Below is a list of what appears on YouTube and the show's official website.

Season 1: Untitled Episodes 1 through 10 (July 12, 2009–Aug. 6, 2009).

Season 2: Untitled Episodes 11 through 20 (Sept. 12, 2009–June 29, 2010). Episode 3 is off-line.

Season 3: Episodes 21–28 (Nov. 8, 2010–Jan. 10, 2011). Episode 25 is off-line. Titled episodes are *Bedfellows* (23; Dec. 29, 2010), *A New Normal* (24; Dec. 7, 2010), *Part of the Family* (26; Dec. 20, 2010), *Kiss and Show* (27; Jan. 3, 2011), *Cover Girls* (28; Jan. 10, 2011).

Season 4: Episodes 29–33 (July 23, 2011–Aug. 13, 2011). Titles: *Where's the Party?* (29; July 31, 2012), *Causing a Commotion* (30; July 24, 2012), *Live to Tell* (31; July 30, 2012), *I Don't Give a...* (32; Aug. 16, 2012), *Don't Tell Me* (33; Aug. 13, 2012).

Empire Website Episodes:

1. Season 1: The Beginning (3 min., 21 sec.).
2. Season 2: Sex, Secrets, Secret Rooms (1 min., 38 sec.).
3. Season 3: Trysts and Takeover (11 min., 53 sec.).
4. Season 4: Sex, Scandal, Soap (1 min., 15 sec.).

Note: With the exception of season three, which is more of a recap, the other episodes are teasers for the season and what to expect. Actual episodes are not available for viewing.

97 *End Result*. webserieschannel.com. 2010 (Crime Drama).

A big money heist, pulled by three mobsters (Reece, Eddie and Gabriel) goes awry when Reece double crosses his partners and disappears with the money. Eddie, a big time crime boss, seeks to recoup the money and kidnaps Reece's wife, Natalie, as a ploy to get Reece to come out of hiding—but is

Natalie as innocent as she appears to be or is she a part of a more devious plot? And why would Reece, a loyal mobster suddenly betray his associates and risk his life to keep the heist money? The story follows Reece as he seeks to rescue Natalie and the twists and turns he encounters as he infiltrates the crime syndicate to find the end result.

Cast: Seth Caskey (Reece Simmons), Elizabeth Stenson (Natalie Williams), Rogba Norris (Merrick Vaughn), Mo Darwiche (Gabriel Reign), Cameron Alexander (Darren Jacobs), Sarah Beth Cook (Lily Gordon), Gabriella Rodriquez (Kayla Gordon), Jamie Fishback (Eric Larsen), Zack Beseda (Connor Stevens), Jason Grasl (Edward Davian), Anastasia Savko (Eva Davian). **Credits:** *Producer-Writer-Director:* Heath Vinyard, James Callahan. **Comment:** The story flows smoothly and the acting and production values are good. While the series literally has no place left to go after the last episode, it is still worth watching for the action and thrills that it does present.

Episodes:

1. You Must Be Merrek. Begins the story as Reece's wife (Natalie) is kidnapped and he begins the search to find her.

2. Where Is She? Reece learns the identity of the man who kidnapped Natalie—Merrek.

3. What I Think Is Right. Reece tracks down Merrek but is unable to get any information out of him.

4. Not as Innocent as You Think. At gunpoint, Merrek reveals Natalie's whereabouts but when Reece confronts her he finds that she wants Reece to take the money and run. When he refuses, Natalie devises a plan to keep the money for herself.

5. The Retirement He Deserves. Natalie's plan is foiled when Merrek's boss, Gabriel, plots to get Reece for shooting him and stealing the heist money.

6. Once You're In, You're In. Gabriel and Edward plan to use Natalie as a lure to trap Reece.

7. The Whole Story. Believing that Merrek is a traitor, Gabriel and Edward order his execution.

8. There's Another Way. With Natalie's life hanging in the balance, Reece must devise a way to save not only her but himself.

9. I Can't Forgive Myself. Reece faces the wrath of Gabriel and his thugs in the concluding episode.

Note: There is also a Trailer (2 min., 2 sec.) that highlights mostly action-adventure scenes.

98 *English Teachers.* englishteachersthe series.com. 2010 (Drama).

Be Yes! is an educational institution in Nagoya, Japan, that has instituted a course requiring English as a second language. Tom Kellerman, a somewhat inexperienced American teacher, accepts a one-year contract to relocate to Japan and teach English. The program charts Tom's experiences—not only as he attempts to provide quality lessons for his students, but how his students provide life lessons for him.

Tom was born in Kansas and raised in the shadow of his parents, both of whom were educators. Tom's future was set by his parents and he believed teaching was a sacred profession. After acquiring his teaching degree Tom realized that he did not have an identity of his own and, when he learned of teachers being needed in Japan, immediately applied, hoping to find the identity that has eluded him in Kansas.

Other Teachers: Jodie is a free spirit and wise beyond her years. She was born in Oregon and has been a free thinker since she was a child. She has a natural flair for teaching, is unaffected by trends (or the status quo) and her relaxed teaching methods (from reading to playing her beat-up guitar) differ greatly from those who follow the book.

Mark, born in England, is a graduate of the London School of Business, but his penchant for sleeping with his female colleagues managed to get him dismissed from several institutions. The situation also caused his wife to divorce him and with no job and no money Mark figured a change of direction was needed and applied for a teaching job in Japan (where his misconception that Japanese woman "are easy" is anything but true).

Neville, born in Australia, had a childhood dream to travel to Japan to meet his idol Bruce Lee (although he didn't realize Bruce didn't live there). Although Neville is a teacher, it is not explained how, after traveling to Japan to immerse himself in its culture, he went from martial arts student to Buddhist philosopher before becoming an educator.

Roberto, a faculty trainer at Be Yes! incorporates a sock puppet as a teaching aide. He was born in Spain but all that is known about his past history is that he was expelled from a South American clown college for his involvement in "the clown car fire."

Ashley, born in San Dusky, Ohio, and voted "Most Likely to Succeed," is a staunch feminist. She is a graduate of Brown University (earning two degrees) and ended up at Be Yes! at the insistence of her father, who felt she needed people skills and could learn how to discipline herself by being exposed to a more refined culture.

Suzuki, a master of patience and ambition, is of both Japanese and Filipino descent. She had always dreamed of becoming a teacher and now that she has achieved that goal, she accepts the traditions of her culture, hoping to implement them on her students, but deep down she conceals inklings of rebellion (as she feels the world is spinning around her and she is just standing still accepting the hand that fate has dealt her).

Sawaguchi is the school administrator. She was raised in a traditional Japanese household but vowed at an early age not to be controlled by a male-dominated culture. Sawaguchi had dedicated herself to achieving her degrees and now finds herself constantly struggling to deal with the numerous problems that arise from both students and teachers.

Cast: Jonathan Sherr (Tom), Ananda Jacobs

(Jodi), Naoko Nakano (Suzuki), Michael Walker (Neville), Lindsay Sakamoto (Ashley), Trevor David (Victor), Chiaki Miaow (Sawaguchi), Michael Kruse (Mark), Gaetano Totaro (Roberto). **Credits:** *Producer-Director:* Anthony Gilmore. *Writer:* Ryan Smith, Kelly Quinn, Cameron Smith, Brandon Kennison. **Comment:** Shades of the feature film *To Sir with Love* (which dealt with an American teacher at a British school) will come to mind. The program is filmed in Japan and the acting, writing and directing are very good. It is a bit of an unusual setting for a web series but the story is well done and the program plays like a TV sitcom, with the possibility of more episodes to follow.

Episodes:

1. First Days Suck (5 min., 2 sec.). Explores Tom's first days at the Be Yes! school and his first meeting with Jodi.

2. (Un)equilibrium (5 min., 55 sec.). While the new teachers believe they have finally adjusted to their surroundings, Sawaguchi informs them that the school's future may be compromised by a lack of government support.

3. Hail Mary (5 min., 38 sec.). With the threat of the school closing becoming more of a reality, the staff seeks ways to save their institution with the only hope resting with Sawaguchi and an important figure from the schools past (Roberto).

4. Not in Kansas (6 min., 54 sec.). With the school saved, it now must face the unusual teaching style of "The Roberto," a former professor as he attempts to implement his strange methods of instructing students. The program's concluding episode.

99 Enormous. screenrant.com. 2014 (Thriller).

It is a time when an ecological disaster (E-Day) has changed the course of life on Earth. Man is no longer the dominant species, having been replaced by giant and deadly mutated insects—once tiny creatures that now threaten the very existence of the humans that survived. The program begins several years after the initial disaster to focus on a United Nations Search and Rescue team as they patrol the devastated areas of the country, seeking to find survivors and battle the giant insects that see humans as a food source. **Cast:** Erica Gimpel (Caroline), Billy Miller (Billy), Ceran Lee (Ellen), Steven Brand (Hopkins), Garrett Coffey (Thomas), Charles Melton (Lee). **Credits:** *Producer:* Andre Ovredal, Andy Shapiro, Joshua R. Wexler, Ian Moffitt, Roger Houben. *Director:* Ben David Grabinski. *Writer:* Andre Ovredal. **Comment:** Although the "stars" of the program will be the monsters, only a small glimpse of one is seen in the pilot. The program is well produced and acted (encompasses Erica Gimpel from *Veronica Mars* and Billy Miller from *The Young and the Rest-*

less) and captures your attention from the very beginning. It is based on the graphic novel by Tim Daniel and Mehdi Cheggour and, just based on the initial presentation, looks to be a standout among Internet television series.

Episode:

1. Pilot (9 min., 36 sec.). Something has happened to devastate the planet. A search and rescue team is then seen seeking survivors but facing a threat from marauders and a giant insect.

100 Entangled with You. entangledwith you.com. 2013 (Drama).

Rocky and Jaliyah are a lesbian couple having a difficult time as Rocky seeks a commitment but Jaliyah is fearful of doing so. Alisha and Craig, a straight couple living together appear to have a happy relationship until Craig reveals that he has a sexually transmitted disease (Gonorrhea) and has passed it onto her. Feeling betrayed that he not only cheated on her but waited to tell her about it on their anniversary, Alisha breaks up with Craig. In a strange twist of fate, Alisha and Jaliyah, total strangers to each other, become roommates. Alisha and Jaliyah, however, find separating is not easy as Craig seeks to win Alisha back and Rocky becomes jealous of her lost love's (Jaliyah) new roommate (Alisha). The program follows the four individuals as they deal with the circumstances of what has happened and try to move on but always realizing that their true loves are still in the picture.

Cast: Loren Lillian (Jaliyah), Kathryn Taylor (Alisha), Jessica Meza (Rocky), Shannan Leigh Reeve (Jen), Al Thompson (Craig), David Spates (Darrell), Vana Bell (Mickey), Crystal Coney (Candice). **Credits:** *Producer:* Caryn K. Hayes, Carolyn O. Jacobs. *Writer-Director:* Caryn K. Hayes **Comment:** Although the program ends unresolved, it is well produced and acted. While tame by some Internet series, it does contain adult situations.

Episodes:

1. Just Say It. As Alisha and Craig celebrate their anniversary, Craig revels that he has Gonorrhea. Meanwhile Jaliyah is reluctant to give into Rocky's demands of making a commitment.

2. Moving Out, Moving In, Moving On? Rocky feels that she may have been too demanding with Jaliyah and seeks to change that. Meanwhile Alisha and Jaliyah have decided to become roommates.

3. Your Blues Ain't Mine. As Jaliyah and Rocky attempt to move on, they find that leaving the past behind is not as easy as they thought as their ex-s are still a part of their lives.

4. Got 'Til It's Gone. Craig's persistent attempts to win Alisha back are causing more harm than good while Rocky's efforts are making Jaliyha uneasy and having a negative effect on her (affecting her work as a writer). The program's concluding episode.

Entangled with You (copyright Hardly Working Entertainment, LLC).

101 Epic Day. epicwebseries.com. 2012 (Drama).

The small town of Trewick provides the backdrop for a look at the lives of a group of young people (in their mid-twenties) who, after years of separation, are reunited at a sixth-year class reunion party. Particular focus is on Brian and Serena, a couple who broke up at their graduation party and what happens when the two reconnect.

Cast: Brandon Lavon Hightower, Sylvia Nicole, Desmond Thorne, Nigil Whyte, Whitney Peaks, Jazzmyne Morrison, Ashley WiMoni, Aaron Bryan, Melissa Montalvo, Ian Petersen, Paul LaTorre, Justin Dickerson, Genese Martin, Jackson Scalera, Emeka Nwafor. There are no cast/character match-ups on screen or on the website. **Credits:** *Producer-Director:* Cris Thorne. *Writer:* Cris Thorne, Matthew Lee. **Comment:** Well done program that explores how people deal with and try to resolve personal issues and relationships that had been avoided for several years. Their efforts to put the past behind them and move forward are also a pivotal point of the program.

Episodes:

1. Six Years Later (14 min., 39 sec.). Brian returns to town hoping to make amends for leaving and alienating everyone after the graduation party in 2006.

2. Long Time, No Talk (13 min., 11 sec.). After an uneasy reunion with Selena, Brian attempts to reconnect with his former best friend, Caleb.

3. A Twisted Trewick Tale (4 min., 29 sec.). A comic tale (meant to appear between episodes 1 and 2) that finds one of the graduates, Gloria, seeking how to deal with a perplexing situation—the dog she had been pet sitting is dead.

4. The Reunion (14 min., 3 sec.). The reunion party begins with Brian attempting to adjust to the fact that Serena is now pregnant and with another problem: Caleb has admitted that he is gay and attracted to Brian.

5. Last Call (14 min., 3 sec.). The concluding episode wherein tensions begin to mount as each of the graduates discovers that you can't go back to a time when all was right with each other and the world.

102 Eternal. webserieschannel.com. 2012 (Thriller).

Joshua Davis is a man in his late twenties who has always dreamed of becoming a pool shark. He currently lives in Atlanta, has a pregnant girlfriend (Naudia), a long-time friend (Smoke) and a dead-end job. Life changes suddenly for Joshua when he meets an old friend that offers him a better job if he is willing to relocate to New Orleans. Joshua takes him up on his offer but soon regrets the decision when he learns that he is being sought by the Eternals, a covet of vampires led by a woman named Natasha. Joshua is the scion of a powerful force that Natasha requires for her Eternals to begin their quest of mankind. Before Natasha can infect Joshua with her bite (the Influence) and bring him to her cause, Joshua is rescued by Sundiatta, the head of an opposing covet of vampires. Joshua is now caught between two vampire realms and the program relates the battle to acquire his soul—not to become one of the undead (as vampire lore relates) but to come under the spell of the Influence (which no longer sentences a victim to eternal damnation; instead a person is only cursed if they are willing to let themselves be consumed with the darkness. Here, the one promise of eternity is redemption).

Cast: Corey Hines, Red Summer, Herman Caheej McCloun, Meka Leshae, Hannah Lewis, Naylon Mitchell, Felita Lawrence. **Credits:** *Producer:* Malik Salaam. **Comment:** Although the program is marked as a thriller series (and not horror) it deviates from the traditional vampire legend in an attempt to take an established concept (vampires) and present it in a different light (a good vs. evil situation) involving a mortal whose untapped power is more significant than any force on earth. Although the concept sounds good, the presented episodes do not delve into the real heart of what the series could present and basically only establish a premise as what is to follow (if more episodes are produced).

Episodes:

1. Episode 1: Pilot (9 min., 50 sec.). Joshua is introduced as a man at his wits end with apparently no hope of achieving any goal in life.

2. Ain't Looking for No Trouble (13 min., 18 sec.). An old friend offers Joshua a job that could change his life.

3. Enough Blood to Get It Up (9 min., 51 sec.). Joshua's move is anything but normal when he learns what the future holds for him.

103 Ever After High. everafterhigh.com. 2013 (Animated Comedy-Drama).

In the fairytale world, the children of famous characters attend Ever After High School and make their own decisions. Raven Queen, for example, yearns to lead her own life and not remain a fairytale character forever, while Apple White wants to remain loyal to her fairytale heritage. Their decisions have caused a conflict as others feel as they do and two factions have grown: The Royals and The Rebels. The Royals believe all fairytale characters must remain true to what they are or else their stories will disappear forever while The Rebels oppose their "happily ever-after" world and must become their own individuals. Stories relate the conflicts that such characters face as they contemplate the lives they now have and what awaits them if they should deviate from what they have become.

Characters: Apple White, the daughter of Snow White, is a Royal (and leader of the Royal Faction). An incident from her childhood (falling down a well) has made her afraid of a different future and will do what it takes to keep the world she loves (Happily Ever After) from disappearing forever.

Raven Queen, Apple White's roommate, is the daughter of the Evil Queen and the Good King. Although she is a Rebel and leader of that faction, she has a good heart but is not interested in assuming the role destiny has planned for her.

Briar Beauty, the daughter of Sleeping Beauty, is Apple White's best friend and a Royal (she fears the prospect of sleeping for 100 years and suffers from sleeping spells at inopportune moments). It appears Briar's goal is to acquire as much knowledge as possible before falling under that sleeping spell.

Madeline Hatter, called Maddie, is the daughter of the Mad Hatter and Raven's best friend. Although Maddie is a Royal and is looking forward to her destiny in *Alice and Wonderland* she sides with the Rebels as believes everyone should have the right of free choice. She and her father live in the village of Book End and run a tea shop together.

C.C. Cupid, the adopted daughter of the gods Eros and Psyche, believes the conflict between the Royals and Rebels is foolish but sides with the Rebels as she believes destiny should not get in the way of love. She has the power to unite people through love and has become the school's advisor on romantic problems.

Ashlynn Ella, the daughter of Cinderella, is a Royal who owns the Glass Slipper shoe store. Like her mother, she is a nature lover and, because a slipper brought her mother and Prince Charming together, she is only interested in fashion if there are sensational shoes to go along with it. She is sweet and kind and fears she will lose her heritage if the Rebels get their way.

Hunter Huntsman, the son of The Huntsman (a character in *Snow White* and *Little Red Riding Hood*) is a Rebel and the boyfriend of Ashlynn Ella, something he must hide as he is not a part of her story and characters are not permitted to become a part of a story for which they were not written.

Blondie Locks, the daughter of Goldilocks, is a Royal and Cupid's roommate (she is also best friends with Apple White and Briar Beauty). At school she runs a Mirror-Cast Show (a newscast) and loves to gossip and has the uncanny ability to open any lock.

Cedar Wood is a Rebel and the daughter of Pinocchio. She is a life-size puppet made of Cedar and cursed to telling the truth (which will be lifted when she graduates). Although she is a Royal and looking forward to her destiny, she feels for the Rebels and believes they have the right to choose their own destiny.

Cerise Hood, the daughter of Little Red Riding Hood and The Big Bad Wolf (can only happen in cartoons) conceals the fact of who her father actually is. She wears a red hood to cover her wolf ears, has a strong craving for meat and wolf-like instincts. Her red hood also gives her the ability to secretly travel through shadows.

Dexter Charming, the son of King Charming and the brother of Daring Charming, is a Royal and more down-to-earth-than his older brother. He likes Raven but is unaware that Cupid has a crush on him. Daring is the first son of King Charming and is destined to become the prince who will save Apple White.

Other Characters: Hopper Croakington (son of the Frog Prince), Lizzie Hearts (daughter of the Queen of Hearts), Kitty Cheshire (daughter of the Cheshire Cat), Tiny (the son of the Giant from *Jack and the Beanstalk*), Duchess Swan (daughter of Odette, the Swan Princess from *Swan Lake*), Sparrow Hood (the son of Robin Hood and Maid Marian), Milton Grimm (the founder and Headmaster of Ever After High. He and his brother, Giles are named after the Brothers Grimm).

Voice Cast: Erin Fitzgerald (Raven Queen/C.A. Cupid), Jonquil Goode (Apple White/Cedar Wood), Kate Higgins (Briar Beauty) Cindy Robinson (Madeline Hatter), Laura Bailey (Ashlynn Ella), Grant George (Hunter Huntsman), Julie Maddalena (Blondie Locks), Rena S. Mandel (Cerise Hood), Evan Smith (Dexter Charming), Cam Clarke (Hopper/Giles Grimm), Wendee Lee (Lizzie Hearts), Bekks Prewitt (Kitty Cheshire), Malcolm Danare (Tiny), Stephanie Sheh (Duchess Swan), Todd Haberkorn (Sparrow Hood), Jamieson Price (Milton Grimm), Valerie Arem, Joe Sanfelipo (Narrators).

Comment: Based on the series of dolls released by Mattel, the program is well animated and the voice cast well chosen. The episodes are rather short (under 3 minutes) and the stories quick and right to the point.

Episodes: Most episodes have been taken off line. Following is a list of titles still available (as of July 2014): *1.* Hatter Makeup Tutorial. *2.* True Hearts Day (Parts 1, 2 and 3). *3.* Apple's Tale: The Story of a Royal. *4.* Raven's Story: The Story of a Rebel. *5.* The Tale of a Legacy Day. *6.* The Cat Who Cried Wolf. *7.* After High Parents. *8.* Here Comes Cupid. *9.* True Reflections. *10.* Bratzillaz. *11.* Class Confusion. *12.* Replacing Raven. *13.* Maddie-in-Chief. *14.* Cedar Wood Would Love to Lie. *15.* Stark Raven. *16.* The Shoe Must Go On. *17.* Stark Raven Mad. *18.* The Day Ever After. *19.* Briar's Study Party.

104 *The Ex-Box.* webserieschannel.com. 2012 (Comedy-Drama).

Shortly after graduating from college, sweethearts Nate and Allie relocate to Hollywood to pursue their dreams of becoming a director and leading lady. All begins well and they take out a one year lease on an apartment. Three months later their dreams begin to fold when they find they cannot live together and

decide it is best to end their relationship. A problem arises when they are stuck with a lease with nine months left to go and, unable to afford other living quarters, decide to remain where they are—but in a divided apartment, each with their own space. The program charts the mishaps that follow as two ex-lovers try to live together and still pursue their dreams.

Cast: Adam Kitchen (Nate Reed), Emily Brownell (Allie Burke), Richard Riehle (Mr. Reed), Laura Sheehy (Laura), Alix Van Aernam (The Hunk), John Forest (Dave), Juliette Hing-Lee (Jezebel), Brad Lee (Mr. Antoni). **Credits:** *Producer:* Kristyn Macready, Emily Brownell. *Director:* Annie Lukowski. *Writer:* Emily Brownell. **Comment:** Charming tale of two people just struggling to do their own thing. The acting, writing and directing are good and the program could continue as the story line is left open for additional episodes.

Episodes:

1. This Is Yours, This Is Mine (5 min., 15 sec.). Nate and Allie decide to share their apartment when each discovers there is still nine months left on their lease.

2. How to Get Over Your Be-Otch (5 min., 5 sec.). Now that they have broken up, Allie and Nat attempt to move on with their lives, although they are still living together.

3. The Break-Up Rules (6 min., 3 sec.). Feeling they need some ground rules, Allie devises a series of rules for them to live by.

4. Devil in Disguise (5 min., 25 sec.). While seeking an audition Allie discovers that Nate is secretly producing a short film ("Wiggle Room") and plots to land a role in it.

5. The Seduction (7 min., 7 sec.). Allie feels her chances for a role may be lost when she sees that Nate has fallen for his leading lady (Jezebel) and can see no one but her.

6. It's Broke, Fix It (5 min., 23 sec.). Allie's plan to seduce Nate for a film roll fails when Nate goes out on a date with Jezebel—and everything that can go wrong does.

7. The Proposition (6 min., 17 sec.). Nate's romance with Jezebel appears to be progressing well until she suggests a three-some and Nate can't get Allie's image out of his head. Meanwhile Allie has been signed on by her dream agency—the Garsh Agency. The program's concluding episode.

105 *Exposure.* exposurewebseries.com. 2013 (Drama).

Natalie D'Angelo is a young, star-struck woman who dreams of becoming a big time Hollywood actress. Her life, however, is controlled by her powerful father (Richard), a New York City lawyer, who opposes her becoming an actress. Natalie, however, has plans of her own and deserts her family when she learns that Jacksonville, Florida, "The Hollywood

East" is where the film industry is taking root. As Natalie establishes herself in Jacksonville, she moves in with a former college friend (Kansas) and manages to land a role in a film being directed by a noted Hollywood director (Stephen Day). The program follows Natalie as she encounters intrigue, deceit and disappointment as she attempts to achieve her dream, all the time unaware that her father has hired her ex-boyfriend, Greg, to convince her to return home.

Cast: Janine Anzalone, Cindy Hogan, Kent Lindsey, Kevin Porter, Jesse Malinowski. There are no character match-ups on screen or on the website. **Credits:** *Producer:* Janine Anzalone, Daniel R. Solomon. *Director:* Daniel R. Solomon. *Writer:* Janine Anzalone. **Comment:** Smooth running drama from beginning to end with good acting, writing and directing. Although the program ends unresolved, it is worth watching as the doorway is left open for additional episodes to follow as Natalie contemplates the future.

Episodes:

1. Episode 1 (11 min., 17 sec.). Establishes the story line as Natalie defies her father and moves to Jacksonville.

2. Episode 2 (10 min., 33 sec.). Unknown to Natalie, her father hires Greg to follow Natalie and bring her back to New York.

3. Episode 3 (11 min., 37 sec.). Natalie's dreams are about to be realized when she auditions for Stephen and a role in his blockbuster movie.

4. Episode 4. Unknown to Natalie, Stephen is not the professional he appears to be and has other plans for Natalie.

5. Episode 5 (8 min., 16 sec.). In an attempt to once again get on Natalie's good side, Greg helps Natalie out of a financial situation by paying her back rent. It appears to work until Greg, an actor also, and Natalie clash at an acting class.

6. Episode 6 (7 min., 4 sec.). Unknown to Natalie, Kansas secretly auditions for a part in the same film.

7. Episode 7 (10 min., 7 sec.). Richard continues to put the pressure on Greg to convince Natalie to return home.

8. Episode 8 (11 min., 38 sec.). As Kansas leaves Natalie and heads to California to further her career, Natalie's family begins to fear that Natalie will not give up her desire to become an actress.

9. Episode 9 (10 min., 18 sec.). The concluding episode where it is learned, through a conversation with Natalie and her grandmother (who resides in Jacksonville) that Natalie did not get a role in the movie and that she "is sick of all these games" (manipulation by her father) and needs to get her life back on the right track.

106 *The Extent.* webserieschannel.com. 2013 (Thriller).

Eight people, unknown to each other and from different walks of life, awaken one day to find themselves mysteriously transported to what appears to be an inescapable room. With no knowledge of where they are or who (or what) is responsible, the group begins plotting a way to find a way out with the program charting not only their efforts to escape but the toll the situation begins to take on the individual group members.

Cast: D.B. Dewdney (Tom Hunter), Leslie McCurdy (Mary), Allie Boak (Rebecca Jenkins), Melissa Amlin (Jessica), Maggie Yoell (Samantha Johanson), Steve Markou (Luther Vanette), Jamell VanDusen (Adam Dollarhyde), Marvin Ramos (Aman Anumpama). **Credits:** *Producer:* Jason Nassr, Ryan Rogers. *Writer-Director:* Jason Nassr. **Comment:** Similar to *The Twilight Zone* episode "Six Characters in Search of an Exit" although this version is much more elaborate and compelling with good acting, suspenseful scenes and a mystery that is not easy to solve without more episodes.

Episodes:

1. Pilot (5 min., 36 sec.). The story line as described above is established.

2. Arizona (7 min., 19 sec.). With Tommy as the principal focus, the strangers try and figure out what is happening to them.

3. Solus (10 min.). The strangers contemplate what has happened and that they must work together to figure out where they are and how to escape.

4. Collateral Damage (8 min., 56 sec.). Jenkins becomes the center of attention as she tries to convince the others that she should lead them.

5. Jessica's Sadness (9 min., 29 sec.). A new captive (Jessica) is introduced into the group and like the others she does not know how she came to be there and believes she was drugged.

6. Trust Find Baby (9 min., 35 sec.). A search of their surroundings reveals a hidden gun which has the captives wondering how it can be used to help them escape.

7. The Exorcism of Samantha Johanson (8 min., 5 sec.). Another captive (Samantha) is brought into the mix—and like the others believes she had been drugged by persons unknown.

8. What I Think of You (9 min., 14 sec.). The captives reflect on what has happened and what connection they have to each other.

9. Breakdown (7 min., 15 sec.). Their continuing inability to escape has members of the group believing that must accept what has happened and do what they are told by their captors.

10. King of the Sandbox (9 min., 44 sec.). As resistance begins to grow, Luther tries to convince the others that they need to work together.

11. Survival of the Fittest (10 min.). Desperation sets in as the food supply dwindles.

12. The Message Home (6 min., 7 sec.). A plan is devised to learn more about the camera that is watching them and how it might be used as a means for their escape.

13. Exodus (10 min., 1 sec.). A plan of escape is devised with Adam volunteering to find a way out. His efforts are followed as he does find a way out—and in an area surrounded by windmills. The program ends unresolved.

107 F to 7th. fto7th.com. 2013 (Comedy-Drama).

Ingrid is a woman, enjoying relationships with other women when she suddenly realizes she is approaching middle age and the world around her is swiftly changing and passing her by. She has not made a serious commitment and now finds herself in a time where gender and sexuality have "left her old-fashioned lesbianism behind." The program charts Ingrid's struggles as she must now embrace who she is and deal with her descent into pre–middle-age. **Cast:** Ingrid Jungermann (Ingrid), Casey Legler (Simone), Ashlie Atkinson (Alex), Ann Carr (Ann), R.J. Foster (Ron), Elizabeth Gifford (Evelyn), Gaby Hoffmann (Devon), Hye Mee Na (Mel), Amy Sedaris (Kate), Michael Showalter (Ben), Brandi Ryans (Lila), Isaiah Stokes (Alan), Kathleen Wise (Liz), Stewart Thorndike (Dr. Thorndike). **Credits:** *Producer:* Jason Klorfein. *Writer-Director:* Ingrid Jungermann. **Comment:** Light drama mixes with comedy in an attempt to show an older woman facing life in a lesbian community (sort of akin to the adult film industry's glamorizing older women in its series of MILF [Middle-Aged Housewives] series of XXX Videos). The program is well acted and produced and a change of pace in the many lesbian-themed programs on television and the Internet.
Episodes:
1. Off-Leash Hours. The pilot episode that introduces Ingrid and the situation she encounters—helping decide which of the two men she meets better cares for his dog.
2. Tweener. At a Wet Lips (all-girl) softball game in Prospect Park, Ingrid and her girlfriend Alex debate whether or not Ingrid should admit she is a butch-type lesbian.
3. Interchangeable. Feeling a bit lonely, Ingrid hooks up with another girl (Ann) and finds her evening turning from talking to romancing.
4. Family. A visit from Ingrid's aunt (Kate) finds Ingrid becoming uneasy when Kate takes an unexpected and vested interest in her life style.
5. Straight Talk. A conversation between Ingrid and her friend Devon, a mother who loves to flirt, reveals that straight women only seduce lesbians when there is no other option.
6. Gyno. An uncomfortable time for Ingrid when she pays a visit to her gynecologist only to discover he has been replaced by a rather unorthodox doctor (Thorndike).
7. Gowanus. Realizing that she has "transphobia" (trouble accepting transvestites), Ingrid talks Alex

into helping her overcome her problem by attending a "hip trans party" in Gowanus, Brooklyn.
8. Intersex. Recalling her earlier conversation with Alex, Ingrid finally comes to terms with the fact that she is a butch lesbian.

108 The Fall. thefallwebseries.com. 2013 (Drama).

A look at the formative years in the lives of seven friends (Chloe, Izzy, Nick, April, Mark, Orlando and Kieran) as they attempt to come to terms with the issues that surround them—from identity crisis to relationships to their own individual sexuality.

Chloe, the most popular girl in high school is not as perfect as she pretends to be and is silently suffering from an identity crisis.

Izzy, tough and reckless, has a misconception that she is invincible and can have any boy she desires. She is being cared for by her older brother, Nick, who, although currently unemployed, finds extraditing her from the troublesome situations she creates is his biggest problem.

Orlando, an undergrad, is seeing Izzy (still in high school) but is tempted by the girls he shares classes with in grad school.

April, sweet and adorable, is the friend who is always there for those that are close to her, but finds her life changing when she falls for Kieran and doesn't quite know how to handle her new found feelings of love.

Mark, officially cut off financially by his parents for his lack of motivation (he has no job and yearns to be a rap singer) is an optimist and believes he will find his calling without his parent's money.

Kieran, seeing Chloe, is what one would call "a preppy boy" (which he detests being called) as he comes from an upscale family and dislikes hanging out with "socialite wannabes" (he would ditch his society upbringing for some down-to-earth fun as a regular guy). **Cast:** Rebecca Gismondi (Chloe), Kelly Paoli (Izzy), Charis Ann Wiens (April), Brendan Flynn (Mark), Jared Bronstein (Kieran), Brock Duke (Nick), Dylan Crewe-Young (Orlando). **Credits:** *Producer:* Kelly Paoli, Tanner Zurkoski, Steffi Tupe, Lester Millado. *Director:* Steffi Tupe. *Writer:* Kelly Paoli. **Comment:** Don't expect *Sweet Valley High* or *Saved by the Bell* as this teen-oriented program is anything but a sugary coated view of high school life. With its unnecessary use of foul language and depressing situations the characters encounter, it is more of an adult-themed, in (and after) high school look at the lives of a group of friends. It is exceptionally well-produced and acted and a totally different look at the lives of young adults.
Episodes:
1. Pilot (5 min., 36 sec.). Izzy and April strike up a drug deal with their classmates Chloe and Kieran.
2. Roommates (7 min., 28 sec.). The relationship

between Orlando and his roommate Kieran is explored.

3. Between the Sheets (6 min., 16 sec.). Mishaps abound as April and Kieran attempt to spend some quality time together.

4. Ditched (8 min., 7 sec.). Izzy tries to comfort Chloe when she learns her boyfriend (Kieran) has cheated on her.

5. Therapy (6 min., 56 sec.). Feeling depressed that, at age 27 he is without a job, Nick believes therapy may be the road he needs to take.

6. Breakups (4 min., 34 sec.). Chloe and Kieran confront each other over what happened.

7. Siblings (6 min., 18 sec.). Nick uncovers Izzy's secret: she is hooked on drugs.

8. Rash Decisions (6 min., 59 sec.). Events leading to each of the teen's downfall are explored in the concluding episode.

109 Family Problems. angelwoodpictures. com. 2013 (Mystery).

A young woman, Jennifer Grady, is murdered and her body secretly buried in the woods. But who did it? Jennifer was the daughter of Molly Grady, now remarried (to Henry, a lawyer) and the mother of Missy and Connor. But in the 1990s, when Molly divorced her first husband, she was left to take care of Jennifer. Jennifer showed little respect towards her mother, was defiant and had a bad attitude. As the situation worsened, Molly turned to drinking while Jennifer began to experiment with drugs. Jennifer was insistent that she wanted to become a model while Molly struggled but failed to convince her to finish high school first. Shortly after when Molly discovers drugs in Jennifer's room and confronts her about it, Jennifer loses control and assaults her (punches her in the face). Fearing for her safety, Molly calls the police and Jennifer is sent to juvenile hall. Molly has made up her mind to start a new life with a man she recently met (Henry) and Jennifer is not to be a part of it. Following Jennifer's release from juvenile hall, Molly tells her she is old enough to be on her own and presents her with a key to an apartment she had rented for her. She then drives off and abandons Jennifer. As time passes Molly and Henry marry, move to Boston and become the parents of Missy and Connor. It is 2011 when their lives change: Jennifer, now in her thirties, has tracked down Molly and now wants to become a part of her life. But before anything can happen, Jennifer is murdered (by someone in the family?) and the family members become involved in concealing the crime and burying her body in the woods. The program, which encompasses flashbacks (to 1995 and 1996) and flash-forwards (to 2044) while dealing with issues in the present, relates clues to a mystery—who killed Jennifer?

Cast: Theresa Chiasson (Molly Solloway), Peter Morse (Henry Solloway), Natasha Hatalsky (Det.

Christina Elliot), Vicky Lynch (Jennifer Grady), Wendy Hartman (Det. Rebecca Ellison), Sarah Alfano (Missy Solloway), Alex Dhima (Connor Solloway), Christopher Ferreira (Aaron), Mary Paolino (Dolores), John Samela (Chief Alexander Hudson), Paula Dellatte (D.A. Cheryl Waller), Alex Pires (Off. Randal Holmes), Marie Brandt (Detective Lanetello), Lisa J. Coleman Hatsy (Kathy), Stacey Forbes-Iwanicki (Det. Elizabeth Hunt). **Credits:** *Producer:* Seth Chitwood, Theresa Chiasson. *Writer-Director:* Seth Chitwood. **Comment:** Although not resolved, the program keeps you guessing with twists and turns making for a very good who-dun-it. The acting and production values are good although the violence and vulgar language makes it unsuitable for all ages.

Episodes:

1. Start (16 min., 42 sec.). Jennifer is murdered and her body buried in the woods. But who did it?

2. Smoked (11 min., 53 sec.). Has someone (Aaron) been observing the family? Molly's neighbor (Dolores) notices cigarette butts on her lawn.

3. Accused (12 min., 1 sec.). The pressure of what she and her family did appears to be affecting Missy, who refuses to go to school.

4. Threat (11 min., 30 sec.). Missy's sudden disappearance (she snuck out of the house to get away from what is happening) has Molly worried that she may reveal what has happened.

5. Judgment (10 min., 35 sec.). A police detective (Elliot) becomes suspicious of Molly's strange behavior and questions her about Jennifer's disappearance.

6. Guilt (12 min.). A flashback to 1995 that shows the tension that existed between Molly and Jennifer. In the present, Molly receives a disturbing package in the mail—a box containing three severed fingers.

7. Disturbance (11 min.). In 1995, Molly and Henry meet for the first time; in 2012, Molly tries to deal with what she received in the mail, a situation that intensifies when Missy learns about it.

8. Decisions (12 min., 35 sec.). A flashback to 1995 shows Molly and Henry discussing their future plans. Back in 2012, Coco, the family dog disappears as Missy and Connor prepare to visit their Aunt Trudy.

9. Searching (12 min., 9 sec.). Further information is revealed about Molly and Jennifer in 1995 while in the present Molly begins a search for Coco—who is found tied to a tree next to Jennifer's unmarked grave.

10. Biological (13 min., 16 sec.). In 1995, as Molly and Henry become close, Molly feels it is necessary to tell him about Jennifer.

11. Confrontation (11 min., 50 sec.). It is 1996 when Henry tells Molly that he passed his bar exam. In the present, Missy asks Molly who Jennifer was.

12. Unburied (16 min., 42 sec.). In 1996 Henry proposes to Molly; in 2012 the pressure of what has

happened forces Henry to confront an old detective friend in the hope that she can help. In 2044, Molly is questioned by Christina Elliot about Jennifer's disappearance 30 years earlier. The program's concluding episode.

110 *Far Out*. youtube.com. 2009 (Drama).

London, England provides the backdrop for a program billed as both "Britain's first-ever Lesbian web series" and "The Lesbian Queer as Folk." It is the story of a group of women, some of whom are lesbians while others are bi-sexual, and their experiences in life coping with who they are and who they want to be with romantically.

Cast: Grace Wendy Allen (Grace), Faye Hughes (Kat). **Credits:** *Producer-Writer-Creator:* Faye Hughes. **Comment:** All the episodes have been withdrawn from the Internet as well as virtually all text information, including the cast and credits. Based on the only visual evidence that exists (the trailer on the official site and on YouTube), the series appears to be quite provocative and well-acted although with an echoing-like sound track and thick British accents it is difficult to understand dialogue at times. Drama appears to mix with comedy and no specific reason is given as to why the series was taken off-line. The women are very attractive and Grace Wendy Allen and Faye Hughes are the only cast members listed with Faye Hughes also being the creator and writer. There are several lesbian web series (for example, *We Have to Stop Now* and *Seeking Simone*) and it appears that *Far Out* is the more sexually explicit of the group.

111 *Feed*. webserieschannel.com. 2008 (Drama).

Maura Knight is a young woman who works as a news blogger for True World, an on-line website. One night, while watching the news on CBN, a story is broadcast covering a beheading in Iraq that shows the incident in graphic detail (the result of someone hacking into the CBN server and releasing the raw, uncut footage). The incident has an adverse effect on Maura and sets her on a path to do something about injustice, beginning in her home town of Los Angeles. Hiding her true identity, Maura posts a video to tell people about the atrocities that are occurring around them and how it needs to be stopped. Her posts soon earn her the name The Vigilante Journalist (also called The Digital Vigilante) and, armed with her camera she begins a one-woman mission to expose the crime and what is really happening on the streets of Los Angeles through the Internet.

Cast: Amanda Deibert (Maura Knight), Sarah Maine (Charlie Hampton), Daniel Miller (Mike Vitorro), Alexandree Antoine (Tanya Edwards), Jennifer Morton (Lisa Dobbyn), Christi Castellande (Bianca), Erin Kelly (Tara), Mike Myers (Mario Car-

rera). **Credits:** *Producer:* Heroine Films. *Writer-Director:* Mel Robertson. **Comment:** Captivating story line with good acting and production values (although it is a bit vague at times). Although billed as "A Lesbian Web Series," it is not in the traditional sense as there are no sexual situations. There is vulgar language but it has been edited indicating that producers felt it would play better this way as opposed to leaving it in. Editing might also explain the story line inconsistencies stated in the episode listing.

Episodes:

1. Beheading (4 min., 55 sec.). Maura is introduced as the CBN newscast of a beheading in Iraq sets her on a path to do something about criminal activity in Los Angeles.

2. Lorna Michales Exclusive (7 min., 19 sec.). Maura, in disguise, allows CBN news reporter Lorna Michaels (who dubbed her The Digital Vigilante) to interview her in a further attempt to get her message to the people.

3. Lorna Goes Down (5 min., 55 sec.). As the interview continues, Lorna is blindfolded and taken to a secret location to see that a digital underground is being formed to expose crime and bring the guilty to justice.

4. Maura's Reality (6 min., 28 sec.). A flashback explores Maura's life before she became a news blogger to the night of the CBN newscast.

5. On the Fence (9 min., 45 sec.). Reveals that Maura is sexually attracted to her sexy female coworker, Charlie (and vice versa) and how, after sharing a drink, they are starting to become intimate.

6. Going Down (5 min., 42 sec.). After working late into the night, Maura and Charlie give into their sexual desires and spend the night together. Unknown to them, they have been observed by a fellow worker at True World.

7. Escape Plan (5 min., 49 sec.). While it shouldn't matter what Maura and Charlie did together, it causes a ripple at True World and Maura is fired.

8. The Breaks (9 min., 51 sec.). With bills to pay, Maura finds a job at a restaurant but has not yet resumed her secret alias as The Digital Vigilante.

9. Surveillance (9 min., 3 sec.). Events will soon change the course of Maura's life. Maura and Tara (a waitress) are alone in the restaurant when two men enter. Maura is in the kitchen when she hears a ruckus and sees the men attempting to rape Tara. Maura, with camera in hand, decides to record what is happening rather than interfere (Tara is saved when a third man, Mike, standing guard outside the restaurant sees what is happening and puts an end to the situation).

10. The Family Problem (9 min., 20 sec.). While it is not explained exactly how CBN acquired Maura's video of the attempted rape, it is broadcast by CBN and puts Maura's and Mike's lives in jeopardy when one of the men who attempted to rape Tara is exposed as the son of a crime boss—a crime

boss who now wants Maura dead and puts a contract out on her.

11. Uninvited Guests (10 min., 23 sec.). Although it is not made clear how it is known to others that Maura shot the attempted rape footage (especially when she was hiding under a table at the time), Maura and Mike are now on the run for their lives as mob hit men are seeking them (how Mike knows this is also not made clear).

12. Underground (9 min., 38 min). The concluding unresolved episode wherein Maura and Mike attempt to make their way to the underground vigilante headquarters to establish a new base and expose "The Family."

112 *Fifty Shades of Blue*. disparrowfilms.com. 2013 (Action Comedy).

Jia and Katja are a lesbian couple who are not only lovers, but friends with two morons: Frederico Blue and Arnoldo, would-be hoodlums who have the illusion they are gangsters and living in the 1950s. Frederico believes, that blue is the color and not only dresses in such, but everything associated with him is in blue (even his gun); Arnoldo, on the other hand, appears to thrive on bananas and even incorporates them as weapons. The program, billed as "a test" follows the disillusioned gangsters as they become involved in a plot to retrieve a mysterious suitcase from the real underworld; unknown to them, Jia and Katja are only friendly with them to help them achieve their goal—the suitcase for themselves.

Cast: Lukas DiSparrow (Frederico Blue), Jordan Adriano Brown (Arnoldo), Suan-Li Ong (Jia), Taly Vasilyev (Katja), Ricky Rajpal (Banana Dealer). **Credits:** *Producer-Writer-Director:* Lukas DiSparrow. **Comment:** Frederico and Arnoldo, although living disillusioned lives, really believe they are gangsters and are not afraid to do what it takes to achieve a goal (even kill if they have too). Based on the two episodes that have been produced, the program shows signs of being a real change from the typical gangster-themed programs of the past. Throwing in two beautiful lesbians, their kissing scenes and some comical action, *Fifty Shades of Blue* could easily become a fan favorite.

Episodes:

1. The Pilot. Frederico and his "left-hand man," Arnoldo begin a dangerous quest—find the culprit who not only stole milk from Frederico's refrigerator but left the oven burning in his kitchen.

2. The Stranger. After questioning several suspects, Frederico and Arnoldo find that they have stumbled onto a case involving the real mob and a missing suitcase. The episode also introduces Arnold's "gun" supplier—the Banana Dealer.

113 *Fins and Flippers*. youtube.com. 2013 (Comedy-Drama).

As two friends (Tracy and Skyeia) discover what appears to be a hidden pond, emanating wave's first causes Skyeia then Tracy to experience a headache. As the water in the pool begins to bubble, it produces a magic mist that transforms the girls into Mermaids and now, learning that contact with water will transform them into Mermaids, Tracy and Skyeia must keep their Mermaid abilities a secret while living lives as normal girls.

Cast (as credited): Isabella (Skyeia), Sara (Tracy), Gabby (Selena). **Credits** are not given. **Comment:** Very well done with good acting, photography and even special effects.

Episodes:

1. The Beginning of a New Life. The story line is introduced as Skeia discovers a hidden pond.

2. Have a Tail—Now You Don't. Skyeia is unaffected at first—until she returns home and comes in contact with water.

3. Season 1 Episode 3. A flashback sequence is used to show Skyeia and Tracy as Mermaids—possibly indicating that they are descended from such creatures of the sea.

4. Season 1 Episode 4. Reveals that Tracy is also a Mermaid—but she was not aware of it until Skyeia found the pond.

5. Um, Your Hair Is Green. Skyeia and Tracy attempt to deal with a new problem: their hair changing color without them being in their Mermaid state. The program's concluding episode.

114 *Flock*. youtube.com. 2012 (Drama).

"Need help but the church won't listen? God doesn't discriminate and neither do we. Discreet and Respectful" are the fliers posted (usually in car windshield wipers) by Paul, a Bible School dropout, and his assistant, his wife Beverly, con artists who use manipulation to sell door-to-door salvation. They are discreet and they are respectful—and, as Beverly says at the conclusion of a salvation—"Will that be cash or a check." The program charts the souls Paul "saves" but the consequences of his actions when he begins to believe he is more powerful than the con artist that he actually is.

Cast: Dean Strober (Paul), Alexandra Boylan (Beverly), Meggie Maddock (Alice), J. Ryan Montenery (Frank), Matt Page (Wyatt). **Credits:** *Producer:* Dan Mathis, Catherine Doughty. *Director:* Dan Mathis. *Writer:* Dan Mathis, Catherine Doughty, Malik Daniels, Justyn E. James. **Comment:** Well done, effective drama with good acting and production values.

Episodes:

1. Cash or Check (5 min., 47 sec.). The story begins as Paul and Beverly seek easy prey.

2. Filthy Young Man (6 min., 6 sec.). Pastor Paul and Beverly come to the aid of a mother who needs help for her son to overcome his obsession with gay internet porn. He and Beverly then meet Alice, the

brother's mysterious sister, who becomes attracted to Paul (and vice versa).

3. Sweet Tea (4 min., 57 sec.). Pastor Paul tries to help a disillusioned young man see that he is not a vampire (by making him face the light of day).

4. Black and White (5 min., 50 sec.). As Beverly sees that there is a potential problem with Alice, she arranges for Alice to meet with her—as a surprise to Paul (who sees her as evil and attacks her).

5. Poor in Spirit (8 min., 8 sec.). In the aftermath of the attack, Paul attempts to apologize to Alice but gets more than he expected when she tells him not to pretend to be something he already is. Now, confused, Paul has doubts about what he has done and realizes that he is a fraud. But will he change? The program's concluding episode.

115 *Foreign Body.* youtube.com. 2008 (Drama).

On August 5, 2008 the book *Foreign Body* by Robin Cook was released. Prior to this and running from May 27 to August 4, 2008, a web series called *Foreign Body* was produced as a back story to where the novel would pick up. The program's tag line, establishes the story: "From best-selling author Robin Cook, the master of the medical thriller, comes the prologue to his soon-to-be-released summer blockbuster, *Foreign Body*. A series like no other."

The program opens in Delhi (India) where a group of beautiful women, yearning for the American dream, are transported to Santa Monica in Southern California but not for what they had hoped. Instead, they are brought to a secret location where a group of nefarious medical entrepreneurs with United Medical Health Care plan to train them and use their nursing skills for their own means (create a rather questionable overseas surgery unit as an alternative to the high cost of medical care in the U.S.). Cal Morgan is the ambitious charmer who appears to control the women; Veena Chandra is the Indian beauty for whom he lusts, but finds unattainable. His desire to have her and her refusal to succumb to his wishes soon leads her to uncover a conspiracy and what happens as the true nature of United Medical is slowly exposed leads into the story continuing in the pages of the novel.

Cast: Pranidhi Varshney (Veena Chandra), Wes McGee (Cal Morgan), Terasa Livingstone (Petra Danderoff), Rachna Khatau (Samira Patel), Keith Arthur Bolden (Durell Williams), Jennifer Dorogi (Santana Ramos), Jasleen Singh (Dharini), Lisha Yakub (Supriya), Ranjit Johal (Amala), Faraaz Siddiqi (Taj), Kateland Carr (Denise), Tim Coyne (Ridley), Kara Michelle Hyatt (Rachelle), John Kerry (Raymond Housman), Charles Pacello (Dr. Own Tomlinson), Amol Shah (Dr. Sanjay). **Credits:** *Producer:* Douglas Cheney, Michael Eisner, Chris Hampel, Chris McCaleb. *Director:* Douglas Cheney,

Chris Hampel, Chris McCaleb, Ryan Wise. *Writer:* Douglas Cheney, Robin Cook, Chris Hampel, Chris McCaleb, Ryan Wise. **Comment:** The book and series were actually done as an experiment to tie two different mediums together for the first time. Unfortunately, all video information has been taken off line and presenting an even more detailed story line or episode descriptions is not possible.

Episodes: 50 episodes, each running two minutes, were produced but have since been taken off line. Following is a listing.

1. Boundaries of Desire: The Story Begins. May 27, 2008.
2. Sex and Death. May 28, 2008.
3. Nurses International. May 29, 2008.
4. Fishing Off the Company Pier. May 30, 2008.
5. Filthy American Ways. June 2, 2008.
6. Dirty Secret. June 2, 2008.
7. Blowing Smoke. June 2, 2008.
8. Taking Advantage. June 4, 2008.
9. Young and Attractive. June 6, 2008.
10. Girls Talk English. June 9, 2008.
11. Sexy Indian Nurses. June 9, 2008.
12. Easy Sleazy. June 11, 2008.
13. Girls Behaving Badly. June 11, 2008.
14. Night on the Town. June 11, 2008.
15. Training Day. June 11, 2008.
16. Don't Touch. June 11, 2008.
17. Flirting Disaster. June 11, 2008.
18. Out of Control. June 12, 2008.
19. High Alert. June 12, 2008.
20. Blow Off Steam. June 23, 2008.
21. Ride the Ride. June 24, 2008.
22. Feeling Something. June 25, 2008.
23. Stripping the Data. June 26, 2008.
24. Unfinished Business. June 27, 2008.
25. Tell Them the Truth. June 30, 2008.
26. Drooling for the Story. July 1, 2008.
27. Please and Thank You. July 2, 2008.
28. Party Favors. July 3, 2008.
29. Tardiness Issues. July 3, 2008.
30. Welcome Home. July 7, 2008.
31. Decisions. July 8, 2008.
32. The Real Deal. July 9, 2008.
33. Bungalow Blues. July 10, 2008.
34. Morality Rates. July 11, 2008.
35. Outside the Box. July 14, 2008.
36. Coming Undone. July 15, 2008.
37. Man of the House. July 16, 2008.
38. Girl in Trouble. July 17, 2008.
39. The Meeting. July 18, 2008.
40. Kill for You. July 21, 2008.
41. Betrayed. July 22, 2008.
42. Living in Fear. July 23, 2008.
43. Promise Me. July 24, 2008.
44. Requiem. July 25, 2008.
45. Watch Her Die. July 28, 2008.
46. Once in My Life. July 29, 2008.
47. Taste of Your Own Medicine. July 30, 2008.
48. Monsters in the Dark. July 31, 2008.

49. Because I Care. Aug. 1, 2008.
50. Naked. Aug. 4, 2008.

116 *The Fosters: Girls United.* afterellen. com. 2014 (Drama).

An Internet spin off from the ABC Family series *The Fosters* (about a multi-ethnic family mix of foster and biological children being raised by two mothers: Stefanie "Stef" Foster [Teri Polo], a dedicated police officer, and her wife Lena Adams Foster [Sherri Saum]). Brandon (David Lambert) is Stef's biological son from a prior marriage and twins Jesus (Jake T. Austin) and Mariana (Cierra Ramirez) are their adopted children. The family lives in San Diego, California and when the series begins, they have adopted two troubled foster children: Callie (Maia Mitchell) and her younger brother Jude (Hayden Byerly). As the Internet program begins, Callie, a troublesome teenage girl, is caught shoplifting and sent back to her foster home (Girls United) when it is felt she requires additional rehabilitation. Stef and Lena will welcome her back if and when she changes her ways. Life at Girls United now becomes the program's focus and presents a mystery: Gabi, one of the girls, mysteriously disappears with each member of the house attempting to find her before time runs out (the police are called) and she is sent to juvenile hall.

Cast: Maia Mitchell (Callie), Daffany Clark (Daphne), Cherinda Kincherlow (Kiara), Annmarie Kenoyer (Becca), Alicia Sixtos (Carmen), Hayley Kiyoko (Gabi), Angela Gibbs (Michelle). **Comment:** With ABC Family behind it, it is like watching the actual series with excellent acting and production values.

Episodes:

1. Run Baby Run (4 min., 36 sec.). Establishes the story line as Gabi runs away and it is learned that the house does not track down runaways—they have to come back on their own.

2. Stab in the Back (3 min., 48 sec.). A pregnancy test is found leading to the theory that Gabi left because she is pregnant.

3. Got Your Back (4 min., 29 sec.). Each of the girls begins to theorize what happened to Gabi and why she ran away; meanwhile Callie tries to help a friend who has turned to cutting herself.

4. Scorpion Kings (2 min., 54 sec.). Gabi's father comes looking for his daughter; Gabi has only eight hours left before authorities must be called and she will be sent to juvenile hall when found.

5. United We Stand (5 min., 15 sec.). While throwing out the garbage, Callie sees Gabi and convinces her to return. She is welcomed back into the group and it is shown that, like the home in which they live, they are strongest when united (Gabi, it is learned used drugs and believes she caught AIDS by sharing a needle).

117 *4 Cambridge Center.* webserieschan nel.com. 2011 (Drama).

4 Cambridge Center is the street address of a home shared by three friends (David, Victor and Andrew). A young woman named Robin has been murdered. She was the girlfriend of David, but David has awoken to find he has no memory of what happened the previous day or of Robin during that time. With the help of a psychologist (Victor) to help David remember what happened, the program charts the intrigues that occur as David slowly regains his memories, but begins suffering from hallucinations and must come to the realization that Robin may not have been the girl she pretended to be and he may be responsible for her death.

Cast: Steven Trothen (Andrew), Evan Konstantine (David), Joe Sobalo, Jr. (Victor), David J. Curtis (Scott), Stacy Caswell (Meg), Michael T. Francis (Dr. Brant), Ron Leo (Killer), Caryn May (Jean), Maria Natapov (Receptionist), Zinnia Politzer (June), Susan T. Travers (Robin), Steven Trothen (Andrew). **Credits:** *Producer:* Domenico Eramo. *Writer-Director:* Sam Luddy, Zak Ray. **Comment:** Although the program is well acted and produced, the lack of additional episodes being made available is somewhat of a deterrent to even watch as it just ends in the middle of nowhere and leaves the viewer unsatisfied.

Episodes: 8 episodes were produced, but only the following three remain on line.

1. Episode 1 (11 min., 25 sec.). As Andrew moves in with David and Scott, David visits a psychologist (Victor) in the hope of regaining his lost memory.

2. Episode 2 (6 min., 26 sec.). The mystery surrounding Robin's death deepens with David discovering he has lost more time than he realized.

3. Episode 3 (6 min., 6 sec.). David appears to be regaining his memory but Andrew's strange behavior has David concerned that Andrew may somehow be connected to Robin's death.

118 *444 The Series.* webserieschannel. com. 2013 (Thriller).

It is 4:44 a.m. when Kyle Cooper, a seemingly average working man, awakens from a nightmare (wherein he witnessed the killing of a young woman) to see a shadowy figure standing by the foot of his bed. The image appears to suddenly vanish but leaves Kyle wondering if he actually saw a figure and why such a nightmare. Kyle's search of his home turns up nothing but the viewer learns, from a TV newscast, that several young women have been murdered and that the police believe a serial killer is responsible. Did Kyle see the killer in his nightmare? Who or what is the shadowy figure that appeared after the nightmare? Unfortunately, only two episodes were produced and they present more questions than answers (even a more specific storyline cannot be developed based on what has been released).

Cast: Brett Lamarque (Kyle Cooper), Lauren Helling (Amy Cooper), Laura Flannery (Susan Malba), Hunter McGregor (Cory Park), Jon McCarthy (Gus Leamati). **Credits:** *Producer-Director:* Charles Bodenheimer. *Writer:* Charles Bodenheimer, Edward V. Joubert, Keith Dunn. **Comment:** Suspenseful, well produced and acted program that appears to border on being a mystery and a thriller based on what has been released. The potential for a good program exists but additional episodes have not been released.

Episodes:
1. Four, Four, Four (4 min., 20 sec.). Establishes the storyline as Kyle Cooper becomes the first to realize that something is not right when he awakens from a nightmare and encounters a dark figure in his room.
2. The Fuss with Gus (7 min., 8 sec.). Kyle discusses his nightmare with his girlfriend (Susan) while a new neighbor (Gus) does not appear to be just an ordinary man (the episode leads to the conclusion that there is something sinister about him).

119 *Four Tails.* youtube.com. 2012 (Comedy-Drama).

Bree, Claire, Skyler and Lauren are four young girls who, while walking their dogs, find a strange bottle, which they believe contains soda. Without really thinking first, they each take a sip, unaware that it is a magic Mermaid potion. Later that day, when the girls go swimming, they discover the effects of the "soda": each becomes a Mermaid and now must keep their abilities a secret—while still trying to be ordinary young girls.

Cast (as credited): RunningLuver-4Ever (Bree), Sillygal4Ever (Claire), 04ever (Skyler), Friend 1 (Lauren). **Credits** are not given. **Comment:** Poorly presented Mermaid series due to unexplained reasons why most of the girls do not show their faces on camera and are seen from the back only.

Episodes: All episodes have been taken off line ("This Video Is Private" or "This Video Does Not Exist" will appear). Following is a list. *1.* Mermaids? *2.* The Powers. *3.* The Necklaces. *4.* Bad Luc. *5.* Necklace. *6.* Mermaid. *7.* Rose. *8.* New Tail.

120 *Friday Night Dykes.* onemorelesbian. com. 2008 (Comedy-Drama).

Siobhan, Andrea, Roxie and Geri are neighbors in what appears to be a California housing complex. Siobhan, Andrea and Roxie are gorgeous while Geri is a bit overweight and not as attractive. While it wouldn't seem likely, the four are friends and all have one thing in common—they are lesbians. The program follows the women, focusing not only on the hookups made by Siobhan, Roxie and Andrea (even

among themselves) but on Geri as she too seeks romance—with women who fall more into her category than the more desirable, gorgeous women encountered by her friends.

Cast: Maeve Quinlan (Siobhan McGarry), Jill Bennett (Andrea Bailey), Cathy Shim (Roxie Lautzenheiser), Maile Flanagan (Geri O'Flanagn), Elizabeth Keener (Celia Sanderson), Scott Holroyd (Grant L'Entrance), Lisa Long (Nasty Nancy), Linda Miller (Frankie), Elizabeth Gudenrath (Bartender), Tanya Little-Palmer (Foxy), Georgia Ragsdale (Duffy Brennan). **Credits:** *Producer:* Paige Bernhardt, Nancylee Myatt, Maeve Quinlan, Maile Flanagan, Joey Scott. *Director:* Courtney Rowe. *Writer:* Paige Bernhardt, Maile Flanagan, Nancylee Myatt, Georgia Ragsdale. **Comment:** Comedy mixes with light drama in a well-produced and acted series with kissing and G-rated sexual situations.

Episodes: 11 episodes have been produced but only the pilot film, which aired on the series *3 Way* remains on line.
1. Pilot. The four principal players are introduced with a particular focus on Geri.

121 *Front Seat Chronicles.* frontseatchron icles.com. 2012 (Anthology).

Light dramatic stories, typical of non-horror anthology programs of the 1950s that explore the conversations people engage in regarding who they are, where they are now situated and what the future possibly holds. Casts are listed with the individual episodes.

Comment: Short, right to the point stories that are all well-acted and produced.

Episodes:
1. I Didn't Get It. Elle Travis and Joshua Feinman as a married couple attempting to work out their problems before seeking a divorce.
2. The Story of My Life. A young woman (Veronica Sophia Rocha), feeling she has become involved in an unfulfilling relationship, seeks the advice of her best friend (Jessica Tome).
3 I'll Talk About You. A young boy (Esequiel Osaze Sowelle) tries to understand what is happening to his grandmother (Cassandra Braden) when she becomes very sick.
4. Every Other Weekend. A boy (Manny Hernandez) must adjust to living with his recently divorced parents on an every other weekend arrangement.
5. Do You Remember? A father (Edward Stiner) faces tough questions from his daughter (Lisamarie Harrison) when she asks why he was absent during her childhood.
6. Salvation Released. A young woman (Brandice Brenning), believing she is haunted by ghosts, fears losing her boyfriend (Stefan Rollins) if he should find out.
7. What Am I Supposed to Do? A woman's (Lony'e Perrine) fears when she discovers that her

boyfriend (Eduardo Ortiz), an unemployed Iraq War veteran, plans to leave her and return to the Middle East.

8. What Now? Two brothers (Tony Collins, Ivan Basso) struggle over finances when their funds for caring for their ailing father have run out.

9. Don't Go. A young woman (Yi Tian) plans to leave her American husband (Eddie Lee) and return to her home in China.

10. What Are You Going to Tell Them? Jillian Easton, Mimi Fuenzalida and Aleida Torrent star. A woman seeks a way to tell her children that she and their abusive father are divorcing and they will not be seeing him again.

11. Homecoming. A sister (Katherine Barcsay) tries to help her brother (Michael Robert Kelly) overcome his addiction to pain killers.

12. Everybody Knew. A couple (Lara Butler, Gabriel Rissa) discover, as they are about to divorce that their daughter has been diagnosed as autistic.

13. If I Tell You. A couple (Walter Fauntleroy, Patrice Fisher) must adjust to tragic circumstances when a medical exam reveals unpleasant news.

14. The "L" Word. A young girl (Evelyn Kang) struggles to accept the fact that she has been diagnosed with Lupus and that she may not have long to live.

15. Don't Mean Nothin'. A young man (Demetrius Butler) recounts a war experience after visiting with his father and half-siblings.

16. I Got In. Gabriela Banus and Karla Zamudio in a story about an immigrant mother's feelings when her daughter is accepted into college.

17. Try Again. A husband and wife (Brien Perry, Monique Carmona) discuss the alternatives to having children when it is learned the wife cannot conceive.

18. The Beer Run. A story about cyber-bullying as discussed between two friends (Austin Fryberger, Dallas Gart).

19. Back to the Front. An Afghan war vet (Michael Woolston) finds help from a friend (Granison Crawford) in dealing with his violent temper toward his wife.

20. The Yard Sale. A daughter (Mary Harris) learns about racial bigotry from her father (Kevin Bailey).

21. Bottom of the Rock. A young mother seeks to overcome her bout with alcoholism. Adriane McLean and Camille Wyatt star.

22. Not a Mistake. A single mother (Lavetta Cannon) attempts to have "the sex talk" with her son (Rorrie Travis).

23. The Traditionalist. A wedding discussion between two women (lesbians) who want to marry—one (Elvina Beck) fears her father will object while the other (Joni Colburn) seeks a grand affair.

24. K-i-s-s-i-n-g. While not related to the above episode, a father (Howard Dell) confronts his daughter (Jenai Beal-Permal) about gay marriages.

25. Differences. A third story about same sex marriage as explored through a young couple (Mia Eden, Kinyumba Mutakabbir).

26. 'Bout This Life. A youth learns more than he bargained for when he buys a gun and seeks revenge. Marcuis Harris and Damien D. Smith star.

27. She Looked Nice. How a death in the family affects individual members. Robin Dionne and Gregor Manns star.

28. Welcome to the Gun Show. Fearful about the violence that surrounds her, a young mother (Donna Rush) weighs the possibility of buying a gun.

29. It's All Fun and Games. Two sisters (Sarah Kay Jolly, Karli Kaiser) attempt to come together after a family tragedy.

30. See You in Court. Denisha Hardeman, Paul Jai Parker, Onderful Martin and Forrest Martin in a story about a same sex couple who are served with child custody papers on the eve of their wedding.

31. First Grade Picture. A mother (Ginger Marin) struggles to come to terms with the loss of her son (Brandon Espy).

32. Love U, Mean It. Maxfield Lund and Sarah Schreiber as a married couple reflecting on the trying times they've had over the years.

33. Meet the Parents. A young African-American woman (Jessica Obilom) tries to understand why her boyfriend's (Dylan Saccoccio) white parents object to her.

122 *The Further Adventures of Cupid and Eros.* cupidanderos.com. 2010–2011 (Comedy-Drama).

Although Cupid, the God of Love, is believed to be one god, it is actually two beings—Cupid and Eros, each of whom makes love happen, but in different ways. Cupid, considered "the original nice guy," is sweet, charming and "a mortal's best friend." Eros is just the opposite, a sex-crazed goddess who believes she is irresistible to any god, mortal or anything in between. Cupid is thus the ultimate romantic while Eros, as beautiful as she is, is thus the ultimate personification of sexuality. While their main goal is to perform matches and stem the tide of divorce and infidelity, they are also confused about what they create. Stories follow their efforts to really understand what they do and what happens when their matches are not always "made in heaven."

Cast: Jo Bozarth (Eros), Josh Heine (Cupid), Aliza Pearl (Isis), Kiera Anderson (Jo), Bradford Anderson (Achilles), Sheila Thiele (Lacey), Jeffrey Cannata (Apollo), Kaathleen Curran (Psyche), Dexx Hillman-Sneed (Thoth), Taryn O'Neill (Athena), Courtney Richards (Shango), Nikki Storm (Earth Goddess). **Credits:** *Producer:* Avi Glijanksy, Andy Wells. *Writer-Director:* Avi Glijansky. **Comment:** Amusing series with good acting and production values. Taking ancient gods and placing them in modern times is not new, but the way it is presented here

The Further Adventures of Cupid and Eros. **The cast in a posed scene (photograph by Carole Lowe; copyright Avi Glijansky, 2011).**

is different and well thought out. If it was meant to show that gods are people too—and have the same problems as mortals, then it was achieved.

Episodes:

1. I'm Fine. Introduces Cupid and Eros as modern day match makers—not the Greek gods they once were. Cupid, depressed since his love, Psyche, abandoned him, longs for someone to accompany him to a social gathering. To help him, Eros takes Cupid to a bar to find a mortal female companion.

2. Two Gods Walk into a Bar... At a bar, Eros finds Cupid a woman, then begins a search for a mortal man for herself.

3. Hopeless Romantics. Just as Cupid attempts to seduce the woman Eros has chosen, he learns that the woman is destined for someone else and must give her up.

4. Good Idea/Bad Idea. Again heartbroken, Cupid fiddles with the idea of terminating his job if he cannot find love.

5. Hello, My Pantheon Is. Eros hatches a plan to get Cupid and Psyche back together at the upcoming Inter-Pantheon Mixer. Unfortunately, the god Apollo is also seeking a girl and sets his sights on Psyche.

6. Dueling and Diapers. Eros seeks a way to orchestrate a happy outcome for all concerned when Apollo challenges Eros to a fight for Psyche's love.

7. Will You Be My... Explores how Valentine's Day began and how Cupid feels about it. In the three-part episode, Cupid laments that he hates the holiday and how commercial it has become; Eros, on the other hand, sees it as a day off when she can become a part of earth life and have some unsupervised fun. However, when Cupid decides he has had enough with Valentine's Day, Eros must somehow convince him otherwise or his decision will mark the end Valentine's Day and Eros and Cupid's matchmaking career.

123 The Fuzz. yahooscreen.com. 2013 (Crime Drama).

In a time that appears to be the present, New York City has an alternate race of people—puppets that perform duties the same as ordinary human beings. Puppets, however, are regulated to an area of Manhattan called P-Town (for Puppet Town) and crime among the puppet race has caused a serious problem for the N.Y.P.D. (as seen on police cars). To solve the problem, the police department has incorporated a puppet squad (The Puppet Task Force) to work alongside human police officers. One such puppet officer is Herbie, who has been teamed with the human Officer Sanchez. The program relates their efforts to foil crime, which is becoming increasing

troublesome as humans and puppets have banded together to create havoc on both factions of the city.

Cast: David Fino (Off. Herbie), Jon Garbus (Off.
Sanchez), Dorothi Fox (Chief McNair), Peter
Bradley (Rainbow Brown), Joseph R. Dannascoli
(Sonny), Rachel Bloom (Roxy), Haley Jenkins (Abigail), Nate Lang (Jake), Wayne Chang (McNair's
aide), Curtis Shumaker (Off. Doyle). **Credits:** *Producer:* Dave Becky, Kristin Jones, Tom Lassally. *Director:* Duncan Skiles. *Writer:* Jon Watts, Christopher D. Ford. **Comment:** Although not an original
idea (the Fox TV series *Greg the Bunny* used the same
human-puppet format) the idea is still fresh and
amusing and very well presented here. The acting
(human and puppet) and all production values are
also very good. Comedy mixes with crime drama
(and bleeped foul language) and additional episodes
are planned (as the concluding episode leaves the
Jellybean caper unresolved).

Episodes:

1. Gangs of Puppet Town (a.k.a., Welcome to
Puppet Town; 4 min., 34 sec.). A sudden crime wave
has Officer Herbie assigned to track down Jake
(human) and his puppet lackey Rainbow Brown as
they are the leading Jellybean distributors and ad-
dicting children to sugar. The case causes Herbie to
suffer a serious injury while chasing Rainbow that
requires his pregnant wife (Abigail) to mend his torn
arm.

2. Rainbow's Big Break (6 min.). Rainbow, set up
by Jake to take the fall as the notorious Jellybean distributor, makes news headlines (on "The Snooper's
Report" evening news broadcast) after shooting a
prostitute and three strung-out puppets during a police pursuit.

3. Rainbow's New Friends (7 min., 12 sec.). As
Jake faces harsh words from mob boss Sonny for the
puppet massacre he initiated, Herbie is teamed with
Sanchez to stop the Jellybean Trade. Meanwhile,
Rainbow makes peace with Sonny when he tells him
he's had it with Jake.

4. The Best Friends Detective Task Force (5 min.,
24 sec.). Sonny assigns Rainbow as the new Jellybean
distributor while a police department public service
announcement insures citizens that puppet and
human police officers are working together for the
greater good.

5. Getting Loco with the Banana Brothers (5
min., 56 sec.). Hoping to prove his abilities as a Jellybean distributor, Rainbow sets up a deal with the notorious Banana Brothers.

6. Old and New Pals (7 min., 51 sec.). Just as
Rainbow appears to be moving up the mob ladder,
he incurs Sonny's hostility when he begins making
eyes at Sonny's girl, Roxy. Meanwhile, the police
chief demotes Herbie and Sanchez to ammo locker
duty for their failed efforts to bring down the Jellybean Trade.

124 The Gallery. thegallerywebseries.tv.
2013–2014 (Drama).

Intrigue set against the background of a Los Angeles art gallery (Conway Place Gallery, owned by
Thomas Tally) as seen through the eyes of the trans-
planted New York woman who runs it (Alexandra)
and the clients she handles—people involved in the
international world of art treasures and not always
the most upstanding or law abiding people in the
world—a world where art riches are sought and
money corrupts.

Cast: Christina Lee (Alexandra Song), Cynthia
Sosa (Ruth Colon), Jay Renshaw (Robert Owens),
Mykee Selkin (Eli Turner), Jodi Taffel (Rachel
"Rachelle" Rose-Bloom), Chris Gustin (Sean Clark),
Milan Kelley (Olivia Tally), David Mingrino (Thomas
Tally), Lane Carlson (Miles Samualson), Harmoni
Everett (Trista), Jodi Taffel (Jess), Chris Gustin
(Sean). **Credits:** *Producer:* Carla Nassy. *Writer-Di-
rector:* Eric Scot. **Comment:** In the early days of tel-
evision and on the long forgotten DuMont network
Anna May Wong starred in a program called *The
Gallery of Mme. Lui Tsong. The Gallery* is, in part, a
modern retelling as both dealt with the world of fine
art objects. While no known copies of that DuMont
series exist *The Gallery* does and is well done, both
for its acting and production values. It is something
different (for its subject matter) in Internet series.

Episodes:

1. Pilot. Alexandra Song, recently moving to Los
Angeles from New York, acquires her position with
the Conway Place Gallery.

2. Don't Mix Company Business with Pleasure.
As Alexandra plans for the upcoming Billy Joyce ex-
hibition, she finds herself also involved with a staff
that is anything but responsive to what she requires.

3. Where Is Crystal Lake? Alexandra finds that,
as she finalizes the exhibit, her client (Billy) has become severely intoxicated after a night of partying
and that Ruth (a gallery employee) is becoming "too
friendly" with clients.

4. Where Is Billy? It is the night of the Gallery
opening and Alexandra finds herself not only dealing
with patrons, but Billy, who has failed to appear.

5. Why Are the Police Here? Tragedy strikes the
opening when Billy is found dead in the back of the
gallery and the police are called in to investigate.

6. Stay with Me. The concluding episode wherein
a drug deal gone bad is suspected of leading to Billy's
death; Sean, Alexandra's co-worker, breaks up with
his girlfriend Trista; and Alexandra, learning that
Sean has no place to stay, offers to let him stay at her
apartment. Ends unresolved.

125 The Gap. webserieschannel.com.
(Drama).

Matt and Rachel are a married couple with a
young daughter. Matt works in a frozen yogurt shop
and believes his daughter sees him as an alien. Rachel

and Matt attended high school together and, even though Rachel claims that "she would never have dated someone like him," they did marry seven years ago. Their lives are not sugar-coated and they have apparently been growing apart as "The Gap" has entered their lives, that space that is created when each partner begins to wonder what they are now and what they could have been. The program charts the problems that enter Matt and Rachel's lives and their efforts to deal with a widening gap that could spell the end of their marriage (as Matt says, "I can't remember the reason why I fell in love with the woman I am now married to").

Cast: Nick Diaz (Matt), Adrienne Hartvigsen (Rachel), Chris Henderson (Jack), Chantel Flanders (Nicole), Joshua Cameron (Steven), Jessica Pearce (Heather), Jesse Peery (Todd), Maryn Taylor (Shayla), Greg Barnett (Tommy), Spencer Belnap (Andrew), Jeff Dickamore (Rick). **Credits:** *Producer:* Chris Henderson, Jessica Pearce. *Director:* Antonio Lexerot, Chris Henderson, Aline Andrade, Adrienne Hartvigsen, Hunter Rose. *Writer:* Chris Henderson. **Comment:** Seemingly a well acted and produced drama based on the teaser.

Episodes: All episodes, with the exception of a teaser that runs 2 min. and 6 sec., have been taken off-line. Following is an episode listing: *1.* You Wear Contacts Now. *2.* What Came Before? *3.* You Two Keep Your Little Secret. *4.* You're Gonna Love Your Frame. *5.* Two Pink Lines. *6.* Patrick Was the Really Weird One. *7.* There Was No Tongue. *8.* Purple Cow. *9.* You Can and I Will. *10.* I'll Take Someday. *11.* Of Course He Brought You a Stuffed Hippopotamus. *12.* Out of Order. *13.* Fate of the Universe.

126 Girl/Girl Scene. webserieschannel. com. 2010 (Drama).

Kentucky provides the backdrop for a look at the lives of five beautiful women who are also lesbians: Evan, a "serial womanizer" (the equivalent of a male ladies' man); Jessie, a 16-year-old girl who has just come to terms with the fact that she is attracted to other girls; Zoe, Evan's slightly neurotic friend, a woman who is still struggling to overcome a breakup with a woman she truly loved; Maxine, a girl who can attract other women, but is unable to maintain a steady relationship; and Trista, an aggressive woman whose attitude makes it difficult to find someone she feels is her equal. Incorporating tenderness with drama and light comedy, the program explores their lives as each seeks to fulfill her life with another woman.

Cast: Tucky Williams (Evan), Joe Elswick (Jessie), Kate Moody (Zoe), Katie Stewart (Maxine), Roni Jonah (Trista), Lauren Virginia Albert (Ling), Kayden Kross (Avery), Cyndy Allen (Susan), Abisha Uhl (Bender), David Henry (Dan), Santana Berry (Tyler), Eric Butts (Thomas). **Credits:** *Producer:* Tucky Williams, Bill Bassert, Nic Brown, Bill Span-

ler. *Writer-Director:* Tucky Williams. **Comment:** Although comparisons can be made with the TV series *The L-Word*, *Girl/Girl Scene* is a much more dramatic approach to detailing the lives of a group of lesbians. There is some foul language, numerous kissing scenes, moments of tenderness and genuinely convincing performances by a well-chosen cast. The acting is above par for a web series and the production values can compare with *The L-Word*. While not the first (or only such) web series dealing with lesbians, it is at the top of the ladder and well worth watching.

Episodes:

1. Lovers' Split. Evan, Maxine, Zoe and Jessie are introduced as the four principal characters with Susan, Jessie's mother and Elliott, Jessie's (a man) best friend.

2. A Case of You. As Jessie attempts to tell her mother that she is a lesbian, Zoe seeks to begin a relationship with Maxine.

3. Tired of Sex. A birthday celebration for Jessie becomes a night of tenderness for the girl-hungry Maxine. It is also revealed that Zoe has a younger sister (17-year-old Tyler) and that Zoe suffers from bipolar depression (and isn't regimental when it comes to taking her medication).

4. Chinese Burn. When Susan, Tyler's mother, discovers that Evan is having an affair with Tyler, she informs authorities, hoping to have Evan arrested for seducing a minor. The tables are turned when Susan is informed that in Kentucky 16 is the age of consent and repressed feelings that she too may be gay are brought to the surface.

5. Help I'm Alive. Although she loves women, Jessie also likes men and feels she and Elliott need time apart when she realizes that Elliott is only interested in her for sex. Meanwhile, Susan comes to the realization that she is attracted to women but finds it difficult to accept that realization.

6. The Flower of Carnage. Evan, concerned over her friend Trista's continual use of drugs, decides to confront her while Susan, building up the needed courage, ventures into a lesbian bar "to check out the dating scene."

7. Psycho Suicidal Girl. As Jessie prepares to attend her high school prom—with three suitors (Evan, Tyler and Elliott), Susan begins to find an attraction to some of the gorgeous women frequenting the bar.

8. Episode 8. Recaps the prior 7 episodes with a dramatic climax: At Evan's home, she and Tyler are kissing when an intruder enters, knocks Evan unconscious and whisks Tyler off to a bedroom. As Evan gains consciousness, she takes a gun from a drawer, enters the bedroom and kills the intruder, saving Tyler's life.

9. Season 2, Ep. 1. As Evan is arrested and questioned by police over the shooting incident, several new women are introduced: Avery, the seductive call girl; Bender, a lesbian addicted to drugs; and Ling, a mysterious Oriental girl.

10. Season 2, Ep. 2. The sexual tensions that exist between Evan, Avery and Maxine are explored.

11. Season 2, Ep. 3. As Bender, infatuated with Ling, makes her move to seduce her, Maxine and Avery begin an intensive relationship.

12. Season 2, Ep. 4. Continues to explore the relationship between the characters from the prior episode while Evan, found not guilty of a crime, faces a civil lawsuit from the mother of the teenager she shot.

13. Season 2, Ep. 5. Maxine's world begins to take a turn for the worse when she turns to Bender for drugs.

14. Season 2, Ep. 6. Ling's relationship with Bender appears to be over when Ling meets a new girl (Finn) and becomes attracted to her.

15. Season 2, Ep. 7. The concluding episode wherein Ling begins a new relationship, Avery encounters "a quarter-life crisis" and Evan's life takes a new turn when her estranged father re-enters her life and offers her a proposition that will erase the lawsuit and make it appear like it never happened.

127 *The Girl with the Tattoo.* youtube. com. 2011 (Drama).

Carmen Lewis is a young woman who seemed to have it all: college honor student, ability to sing and dance, beauty and a pending scholarship. Following an accident in which her younger sister (Camil) succumbs to a coma, Carmen's life takes a turn for the worse when she drops out of school and becomes a stripper. The program follows what happens in Carmen's life as she struggles to cope with the situations that surround her, all of which are made more difficult when her secret is discovered and it begins to affect the lives of the people around her.

Cast: Tebby Burrows (Carmen Lewis), Damali George (Janet Lewis), Joelle Davis (Robyn Cole), Jay Wiles (Jordan Channing), Samone Davis (Nina Pierre), Stephanie St.-Fleur (Dr. Frasier), Chloe Westrich (Nurse Holly), Akemi Lopez Carter (Camil Lewis), Rashida Robinson (Ebony Cox). **Credits:** *Producer-Writer-Director:* Joey Ashley. **Comment:** Touching at times story about a lost girl who is just trying to find herself. The acting and production values are good although dialogue is a bit hard to understand at times. The program's episodes are not in the proper aspect ratio (stretched to fill the screen) although the trailers are. To some this is distracting because performers appear unflattering and it could prevent people from watching (all sharing websites have the same aspect ratio problem).

Episodes:

1. Her Hidden Mark (12 min., 17 sec.). Carmen is introduced as she struggles to not only cope with what happened to her sister (Camil) but with her ex-boyfriend's (Jordan) attempts to rekindle their lost love.

2. Episode 2 (12 min., 33 sec.). Carmen's attempt to visit Camil in the hospital becomes intolerable when her older sister (Janet) lashes out at her for what she has done with her life. Meanwhile, Carmen's friend, Robin, has problems of her own as she faces a custody battle with her ex-husband for her son.

3. Episode 3 (11 min., 38 sec.). As Camil's condition worsens, Jordan tries to cheer up Carmen while Robin's situation appears even worse as she fears her ex will gain custody for being the better parent.

4. Episode 4 (11 min., 11 sec.). As Carmen and Jordan appear to be getting close again, Carmen faces her worst fear: Janet has decided that Camil will never awaken and started procedures to have her life support removed.

5. Episode 5 (15 min., 29 sec.). The concluding episode wherein Carmen, learning that Jordan has a chance to further his art career in Europe, feels she should not stand in his way and convinces him that he should pursue that path. With thoughts of Camil on her mind, Carmen meets Janet at the hospital and reluctantly accepts Janet's decision and whatever happens.

128 *Girls Don't Fight: The Series.* you tube.com. 2012 (Drama).

The Taymoore School for the Performing Arts is outwardly a prestigious educational institution devoted to ballet. But beneath its hallowed halls lies a secret student organization called PTA (Post Totem Anthem), a student-led society that maintains order through fear, intimidation and manipulation (sort of psychological warfare). The PTA Raffle, wherein two randomly selected students (one male, one female) face each other in a no rules bout called Fight Night is the main "entertainment" function of the PTA. Students at the school include Starlaina, Angel, Siobhan, Brenda, Jessica and Devin. Starlaina and Angel are lesbians and life changes drastically for Starlaina when Angel commits suicide and Starlaina feels she no longer belongs in a world she once loved. Seeing that Starlaina is vulnerable, Jessica manipulates her (as well as Siobhan, Jessica and Brenda) into joining the PTA. Still depressed over Angel's death, Starlaina is now faced with the school's dark side and stories follow Starlaina as she and her friends become a part of the fist-fighting world of the PTA.

Jessica actually lives two different lives—the manipulative leader of the PTA and to teachers and parents, the personification of morality and perfection. Jessica feels she is unique and must control the humanity of others and destroy everything that makes a person different from her.

Brenda, in love with Siobhan, is the cute, perky girl everyone loves and adores. She was raised by her brother Mitch and his then girlfriend (now wife) Digna since she was five years old (at which time her mother abandoned the family).

Siobhan, the school beauty, is an unapologetic

lesbian who does as she pleases without regard to anyone else's feelings. She is the "school bitch" and the dream girl of every guy—and girl—at the school. Despite her attitude, she is a loyal friend, especially to Starlaina, whom she has known since kindergarten.

Devin is Starlaina's best male friend, the guy who holds the group together and fixes their problems.

Other Characters: Samuel is the dreamboat of the straight girls at the school (and accustomed to girls "throwing themselves at him"); Sebastian is Siobhan's older brother, a senior at the school and somewhat angry with Siobhan as his girlfriend's always become attracted to his sister; Jason is the school genius (IQ of 178) and hates women (stems from his hate of his twin sister, Jessica, whom he feels is hollow inside, exploits men and is the reason why men fail); Benjamin, a guy's man (he is gay), excels in school and does what he wants to do; Lucy, the only girl not in love with Jessica, is the PTA's main fighter, but she is also a girl who is angry at the world and into self-mutilation; Sara, the girl with no respect for authority, feels that the only way she can connect to boys is through sex; Miriam is the school's gossip queen; Mitch is Brenda's older brother.

Cast: Brittany Michelle (Starlaina Hallows), Jacklyn Lisi (Jessica Mooney), Gwyneth Jonnes (Brenda Lively), Mia Topalian (Siobhan Whitney), Mikey Costa-Brown (Devin Mitchell), Jaffrey Amador (Samuel Kilden), Matt Watson (Sebastian Whitney), Kyle Hoy (Jason Mooney), Ryan Foster Casey (Benjamin Abbitt), Naomi Pandolfi (Lucy Cruz), Crystal Yau (Sarah Kaddin), Sarah McAvoy (Miriam Finke), Jeremy Uliss (Mitch Lively). **Credits:** *Producer-Writer-Director:* Mia Kiddo. **Comment:** With only the "Minisodes" trailer to judge by, the program looked well-acted and produced. Only a glimpse of the fighting sequences is seen and it is not really possible to provide any further comment.

Episodes: All episodes have been taken off-line with the exception of two short videos: "Girls Don't Fight Minisodes" and "Girls Don't Fight Cast Interviews."

129 The Girls Guide. youtube.com. 2013 (Drama).

Lucy, Victoria and Shaun, friends since high school and now college graduates, are also roommates as they pursue their life's goals. Lucy and Victoria are lesbians (although not dating each other) while Shaun is a straight "dude"—and interested in girls, but not Lucy and Victoria. Victoria is a flirtatious girl and plays the field while Lucy feels more comfortable in a steady relationship. Shaun, like Lucy and Victoria, is seeking a girl and stories follow the three friends as they navigate "the oft tricky road to female affection."

Cast: Christa Anderson (Lucy), Briana Rayner (Victoria), Lucas Blaney (Shaun), Laura Geluch (Jessica), Chelsey Moore (Sarah), Natasha Alexander (Christina), Sean Hewlett (AJ). **Credits:** *Producer:* Tess Calder. *Writer-Director:* Justine Stevens. **Comment:** So well acted and produced that you feel as if you actually watching episodes of a network television series. There are some mild sexual situations and girl-girl kissing scenes but nothing is objectionable and the program is well worth watching.

Episodes:

1. Episode 1 (7 min., 6 sec.). The main characters are introduced in the series pilot film.

2. Episode 2 (9 min., 22 sec.). Lucy, a waitress at Porter's Coffee and Tea House, becomes attracted to a female customer that she later discovers is straight; AJ, Shaun's friend, warns Lucy and Victoria to stay away from his friend, Christina; Shaun fantasizes about meeting the right girl.

3. Episode 3 (6 min., 52 sec.). Lucy, Victoria and Shaun agree that the common areas of their apartment will not be used for romantic encounters while Victoria becomes attracted to a girl named Jessica.

4. Episode 4 (6 min., 20 sec.). As Victoria takes Shaun to a bar in an effort to meet girls, Lucy becomes attracted to a girl named Sarah—while still seeing Jessica.

5. Episode 5 (8 min., 30 sec.). Lucy, believing Sarah is the girl of her dreams, breaks up with Jessica only to later discover that Sarah has a boyfriend and apparently would rather be with him.

6. Episode 6 (5 min., 54 sec.). A party, arranged by Victoria and Shaun to celebrate Lucy's birthday, becomes a rather sad occasion for Lucy when she retreats to her room, lamenting over the fact that she has broken up with Jessica.

7. Episode 7 (8 min., 21 sec.). Realizing that she really loves Lucy, Sarah attempts to see Lucy on the night of her party but is turned away by Shaun; meanwhile, at the party, Victoria becomes attracted to the girl she was told to stay away from—Christina.

8. Episode 8 (7 min., 38 sec.). The concluding episode wherein Sarah, realizing her breakup with Lucy was a mistake, seeks a way to reconnect with her.

130 The Girls on Film. thegirlsonfilm. com. 2010–2011 (Anthology).

Role reversal project wherein women perform the roles originally enacted by men in major Hollywood motion pictures (and men in the roles originally performed by women).

Cast: Ashleigh Harrington, Cat McCormick, Jeff Hammond, Laura Miyata, Jenna Scott, Katerina Taxia. **Credits:** *Producer:* Jeff Hammond, Ashleigh Harrington. *Director:* Jeff Hammond. *Writer:* Jeff Hammond, Ashleigh Harrington, Cat McCormick. **Comment:** Canadian produced program that presents a unique idea and will intrigue those familiar with the movies that are parodied. The acting and production values are excellent and, although not

Girls on Film. Left to right: Laura Miyata, Jeff Hammond and Ashleigh Harrington on the set of the "No Country for Old Men" episode (copyright Hammond Cheeze Films).

full-length adaptations, a program well worth watching to see what could happen if roles were reversed.

Episodes:

1. The Town. *Cast:* Ashleigh Harrington (James Coughlin), Laura Miyata (Brendan Leahy), Cat McCormick (Doug McCray), Jeff Hammond (Claire Keesey).

2. Fight Club. *Cast:* Ashleigh Harrington (Tyler Durden), Cat McCormick (The Narrator).

3. Star Trek. *Cast:* Ashleigh Harrington (Capt. James T. Kirk), Katerina Taxia (Capt. Christopher Pike).

4. No Country for Old Men. *Cast:* Ashleigh Harrington (Carson Wells), Laura Miyata (Anton Chigurh).

5. The Twilight Saga. *Cast:* Ashleigh Harrington (Edward Cullen), Jenna Scott (Jacob Black), Jeff Hammond (Bella Swan).

6. Drive. *Cast:* Ashleigh Harrington (The Driver).

131 *Girltrash.* ovguide.com. 2007–2009 (Crime Drama).

Tyler Murphy and Daisy Robson are beautiful lesbians and lovers who live on the edge. They reside in Los Angeles and make ends meet through petty crimes (although it is mentioned that Tyler, the tougher of the two, has committed murder). LouAnne Dubois, a flirtatious lesbian who will seduce any woman she admires, is also a criminal and thrives on her talent as a con artist. LouAnne, however, is tired of petty crimes and sets her sights on something bigger—two million dollars, which she steals from Monique Jones, an out-of-control, extremely violent woman who wants her money back—at any cost, no matter who gets hurt (or killed) in the process.

Having known LouAnne from past encounters, Tyler and Daisy again find themselves involved with her when they discover what she has done—not only steal the money but put the blame on them and now Monique is seeking to not only kill her but them as well. Complications set in when Monique, in a plan to bring Tyler, Daisy and LouAnne in the open, kidnaps Daisy's sister, Colby (a lesbian) and her girlfriend (Misty) and threatens to kill them if the money is not returned to her. The program follows what happens as Tyler and Daisy not only attempt to avoid Monique but free Colby and Misty as well.

Cast: Michelle Lombardo (Tyler Murphy), Lisa Rieffel (Daisy Robson), Riki Lindhome (LouAnne Dubois), Margaret Cho (Min Suk), Rose Rollins (Monique Jones), Amber Benson (Svetlana "Lana" Dragovich), Gabrielle Christian (Colby Robson), Mandy Musgrave (Misty Monroe), Maeve Quinlan (Judge Cragen), Jimmi Simpson (Valentine), Joel Michaely (Dryer Guy). **Credits:** *Producer:* Angela Robinson, Alexandra Kondracke, Josh Polon, Rebecca Sekulich. *Writer-Director:* Angela Robinson. **Comment:** The women, including the teenage Misty and Colby, are all very attractive and perform their roles well. The program is filmed in black and white which makes for a different feel as opposed to it being done in color. There is an abundant use of vulgar language and numerous kissing scenes (but no nudity and nothing that borders on pornography) and the program, although tailored to a lesbian audience, can be enjoyed by anyone (just be prepared for the trashy language). The program originally aired on www.outchart.com.

Episodes:

1. Episode 1 (3 min., 40 sec.). Introduces Tyler and Daisy as they contemplate matters they are facing.

2. Episode 2 (1 min., 38 sec.). LouAnne is introduced as she meets with Tyler and Daisy.

3. Episode 3 (3 min., 43 sec.). Tyler and Daisy discover what LouAnne has done and now all three are on the run for their lives.

4. Episode 4 (3 min., 53 sec.). A flashback to the time Tyler and Daisy first met LouAnne.

5. Episode 5 (3 min., 10 sec.). With no other choice, Daisy and Tyler join with LouAnne to defeat Monique.

6. Episode 6 (2 min., 44 sec.). LouAnne's heist has so angered Monique, a woman called "The Widow Maker" that she connects with a criminal gang to do her dirty work.

7. Episode 7 (2 min., 26 sec.). Unable to find her targets, Monique devises another way to get them: she kidnaps Daisy's younger sister Colby and her girlfriend Misty.

8. Episode 8. When word reaches Tyler and Daisy about the kidnapping, Daisy turns to Tyler for her help in freeing Colby. A plan to use LouAnne as bait to draw out Monique fails and the girls are back to square one.

9. Episode 9 (2 min., 57 sec.). With no other choice, Tyler and Daisy seek the help of Lana, a deadly assassin.

10. Episode 10 (4 min.). As Misty and Colby attempt to escape from their locked room, Lana begins preparations to get Monique and free Misty and Colby.

11. The Lost Misty Scenes. In 2007, after filming *Girltrash* for 12 days, funds ran out and the series was never completed. This episode consists of unedited and not used footage that focuses on Misty and Colby who, after untying themselves but are unable to escape, turn to each other for comfort (in a sensual kissing scene that is interrupted when they hear someone at the door and prepare to defend themselves. The program ends at this point).

132 *Girltrash: All Night Long.* girltrashall nightlong.com. 2013 (Musical).

Characters from the series *Girltrash* appear in a feature-film length version of the above title wherein one night in the lives of the principal characters, from love making to cat fighting, is charted through a series of lively musical numbers.

Cast: Lisa Rieffel (Daisy Robson), Michelle Lombardo (Tyler Murphy), Gabrielle Christian (Colby Robson), Mandy Musgrave (Misty Monroe), Kate French (Sid), Clementine Ford (Xan), Kelly Ogden (Herself), Rose Rollins (Monique Jones), Megan Cavanagh (Officer Margie), Jessica Chaffin (Officer Jackie), Mike O'Connell (Valentine), Malaya Rivera Drew (Lauren), Joanna Canton (Mitchele), Theron Cook (Crisp), Heather Thomas (Nadine). **Credits:** *Producer:* Stacy Codikow, Lisa Rieffel, Angela Robinson, Lisa Thrasher. *Director:* Alexandra Kondracke. *Writer:* Angela Robinson. *Music and Songs:* Killola. **Comment:** Filmed in color and a surprisingly well done program. Lisa Rieffel, a member of the real life group Killola, and the rest of the cast all handle their acting/singing roles well and the movie makes for a pleasant diversion on the comedy and drama series devoted to lesbians.

133 *Give Me Grace.* givemegracetheseires. com. 2010 (Drama).

Grace, a young woman in a relationship with another woman (Jolie), leads a somewhat mysterious life. She appears to be a martial arts instructor but is actually part of "The Family," a candle-stein group of women led by Marah, that appears to fulfill contracts of unethical means for clients (exactly what "The Family" is or what they actually do is not clearly stated). The program follows events in Grace's life beginning when she receives a text message ("You Fail, She Dies") indicating that Jolie's life is in danger if Grace fails to accomplish an assignment and her efforts to not only protect Jolie, but uncover the unknown sender's identity.

Cast: Raelaine San Buenaventura (Grace), Jessica Etheridge (Jolie), Rinabeth Apostol (Ari), Khary Moye (Red), Tiana Salim (Marah), Dana Soliman (Nikki). **Credits:** *Producer-Writer-Director:* Jorna Tolosa-Chung. **Comment:** The program captures your attention from the very beginning (with the text message) and flows into a smooth running, well-acted and produced thriller. It is also a mystery in a way as the released episodes do not fully explain who Grace really is (and how and why she is presumably an assassin) and what "The Family" is all about.

Episodes:

1. Episode 1 (6 min., 10 sec.). Begins the mystery—not only of what "The Family" is but who is threatening Jolie's life.

2. Episode 2 (11 min., 5 sec.). Nikki, Marah's ruthless daughter, feels that her mother's leadership is below par and that she should be running the organization in the treacherous manner of her late father, bringing her in conflict with Grace, who, though fearful of Marah, respects what Marah is accomplishing.

3. Episode 3 (13 min., 10 sec.). Another text message ("Play Nice") is sent to Grace while a sudden

death in "The Family" (Marah) by an unknown assassin brings Nikki into power—to run the organization as she sees fit—and find her mother's killer at any cost. The program's concluding unresolved episode.

134 *Going Our Way.* goingourwayweb series.com. 2012 (Drama).

Caz, an unemployed screenwriter, hopes to further her career by acquiring a writer's internship on *Next Door*, Australia's top-rated television soap opera. Her life changes for the better when she applies, but finds competition from Ralph, her life-long nemesis, who is also seeking the same position and who has a much better chance as he already works on the show. The program not only follows the events that spark Caz's life as she and Ralph clash, but her involvement with Matt Doyle, an actor on the show who has fallen for her.

Other Characters: Saj is Caz's gay friend, who is jealous that his dream guy—Matt—is seeing Caz; Rhiannon, a 25-year-old who hopes to change laws, especially traffic, for the safety of the public; and Tobi, a six-year-old, extremely bright child, whose parents are not seen but who lives in the same building with Caz, Saj and Rhiannon in Melbourne, Australia.

Caz is a very gifted girl but not highly motivated and thus not always being able to achieve what she is capable of (especially when she always loses out to Ralph). Following her graduation from college, Caz struck out on her own and moved in with her friends Saj and Rhiannon, but she still remains unmotivated and would rather just watch TV than write it. Her motivation rises when she learns Ralph is applying for an internship and she feels it is now time for her to beat him.

Saj was born in Sri Lanka and moved to Australia when he was a teenager. Although he studied marketing in college, he was interested in filmmaking and met Caz after sneaking into one of her film classes. With no interest in marketing or acquiring a job, he watches films and TV shows and spends his time blogging about them.

Rhiannon, a law student, was raised in a rather unusual environment. After her brother was killed in a car accident, her parents wandered into a world of drinking and drugs and it did change the course of Rhiannon's life as she switched her major from Arts to Law to become a politician and change traffic laws for the better. Her relationship to Caz is closer now than it was when Caz's brother and her brother were friends.

Ralph and Caz have been friendly enemies since grade school and he has made it a goal to be the best at everything, especially when it comes to Caz. While Caz has the same goals as Ralph, he is far more motivated and Caz always comes in second. He works as a runner (gopher) on the show and secretly runs the show's fan forum.

Matt, the principal star of the show, is a simple guy who finds himself competing for Caz against a different kind of competition: Ralph, but not in the normal sense as Caz is now totally focused on getting the internship and finally beating Ralph at something. Information on Tobi, "child genius," is marked "Classified" and nothing is revealed.

Cast: Donna Pope (Caz), Matt Young (Matt Doyle), Sajeeva Sinniah (Saj), Tobi Johnson (Tobi), Gordon Boyd (Ralph), Thomas Bulle (Jay), Don Bridges (Al), Clara Pagone (Liz), Chris Chalmers (Eddie). **Credits:** *Producer:* Jessica Brajoux, Fiona Eloise Bulle. *Director:* Jessica Brajoux, John Erasmus. *Writer:* Fiona Eloise Bulle, Thomas Bulle, Dean Watson. **Comment:** An amazingly well produced and acted program that was, according to the producer, made for $18 ("We entered a competition to create our own web series and win $50,000 ... but we were unsuccessful. We didn't take this as a setback, rather a challenge ... we tried to make one for as little money as possible. By gathering a talented group of people and finding a few friends with equipment, we managed to make this web series for $18"). Maybe the networks could take a lesson and see that enormous amounts of money are not needed to produce an enjoyable program.

Episodes:

1. Episode 1. Saj and Rhiannon talk Caz into "stalking" the stars of their favorite soap opera.

2. Episode 2. While seated in a bar waiting for the cast to appear, Caz learns of an internship position on the show.

3. Episode 3. As Caz ponders over a decision as whether or not apply for the internship, the roommates prepare for a visit from Rhiannon's hippie parents.

4. Episode 4. Caz decides to apply for the internship—only to discover that Ralph has applied for the same position.

5. Episode 5. Saj becomes jealous when he learns that his heart throb, Matt, has asked Caz out on a date.

6. Episode 6. Caz and Matt's date is anything but common when Caz's clumsiness makes it appear that the two can never be an item—which delights Saj as he now feels he may still have a chance with the show's star.

7. Episode 7. Caz finds herself in a compromising situation when she attempts to sabotage Ralph's efforts—and gets caught by Matt.

8. Episode 8. Caz receives the news she has been hoping for (the internship) and she and her friends celebrate at the Felix Bar, where it all began. The first season concludes.

9. Episode 9. The second season opens with Caz, now with a new job and a new home, still wondering if she can get out from under Ralph's shadow, now that he too has been offered the internship.

10. Episode 10. Eddie, Caz's brother arrives unannounced, putting a damper on her fresh start as he

appears to be looking for a place to stay while he works out his personal problems.

11. Episode 11. Saj's inability to accept Caz and Matt as a couple, has him acting strangely and Eddie wondering what kind of men his sister is dating.

12. Halloween Special, Part 1. Caz, Saj and Rhiannon decide to celebrate Halloween with a spooky party.

13. Halloween Special, Part 2. As the party gets underway, Caz feels all is not right when strange things begin to happen.

14. Episode 14. As Caz begins to help write *Next Door* Matt finds Rhiannon becoming attracted to him.

15. Episode 15. At a *Next Door* staff party, Caz finds herself caught in the middle between Saj and Matt when Saj makes a play for him.

16. Episode 16. The concluding episode wherein Ralph realizes that what he has been doing to Caz over the years was wrong and attempts to apologize and make friends; Caz responds with "Let's just say friendly" leaving the doorway open for additional episodes.

135 *Good Lovin'.* webserieschannel.com. 2013 (Drama).

Trina Bailey and Lonnie Goodman are young peo-ple in love—or at least Trina believes so. Their relationship is a bit strained as she works days and he works nights, leaving them little time together, but in that time together Trina believes Lonnie only sees her as a sex object. After six months of a mismatched relationship, Trina realizes that she is settling into a situation where sleeping with Lonnie is becoming increasingly frustrating. Hoping to find out if Lonnie sees her as a person, Trina confronts him and finds that he can not even answer the simplest questions about her (like what color are her eyes and when she was born). His inability to answer any of her questions correctly has Trina believing she and Lonnie are like strangers and only hooking up for one night stands. The program follows what happens when Lonnie learns how Trina feels and Trina attempts to change their relationship to a point where they can get to know each other and become a normal couple.

Cast: Blair Sharne (Trina Bailey), David Hunter, Jr. (Lonnie Goodman). **Credits:** *Producer:* Rhonda Kennedy, Denise Kennedy, John Hermann. *Director:* John Hermann. *Writer:* Rhonda Kennedy.

Comment: Based on the only episode that has been released, the program is well produced and shows potential for a number of situations wherein each tries to please the other in a non-sexual manner.

Episodes:

Good Lovin'. **Left to right: Rhonda Kennedy (writer-producer), John Hermann (director), David Hunter, Jr. (plays Lonnie), Blaire Sharne (plays Jina) (photograph copyright Rhonda Kennedy, 2013).**

1. Pilot. It has been six months since Trina and Lonnie hooked up and Trina's growing frustration with Lonnie's lack of interest in her other than for sex, prompts her to confront him.

136 *Good People in Love.* wardpicture company.com. 2011 (Drama).

Carolyn and Max, a couple about to be married, plan to celebrate the occasion by inviting their best friends, Sarah and Scott and Beth and Anna to an engagement party. Sarah and Scott have differing views on marriage, especially those involving gay and lesbian couples. It is a time in New York City when the equal rights marriage bill has been passed and Scott and Sarah set out to explore their points on love and marriage by using the party's other two couples as guinea pigs in their little experiment. The program charts what happens when Scott and Sarah's manipulative actions cause more concern than just acquiring answers.

Cast: Rachael Hip-Flores (Sarah), Heather Leonard (Carolyn), Steven Alexander (Max), Megan Melnyk (Anna), Renee Olbert (Beth), Jesse Wakeman (Scott). **Credits:** *Producer-Writer-Director:* Tina Cesa Ward. **Comment:** Network TV-like drama with good acting and production qualities. There is some vulgar language and girl/girl kissing scenes, but nothing objectionable and the program flows smoothly from beginning to end.

Episodes:

1. Setting the Table (6 min., 4 sec.). Sets the scene as the party guests arrive and Scott and Sarah begin preparations to manipulate their friends.

2. A Drink Before Dinner (6 min., 44 sec.). Beth and Anna's attempts to make love are not so secretive when Sarah realizes what they are up to.

3. Main Course (7 min., 38 sec.). At dinner, the conversation turns a bit ugly when hidden feelings are revealed.

4. Left Over (6 min., 42 sec.). Continues from where the prior episode left off with Beth and Anna relating their feelings about each other—and now not so sure they are the perfect couple.

5. Call It a Night (9 min., 51 sec.). While Anna and Beth seek to resolve their differences, Carolyn and Max have a confrontation when Max reveals that, although he loves Carolyn, she is very manipulative and it could be impairment to their future happiness together. The program's concluding episode.

137 *Goth Girl.* watchgothgirl.com. 2009–2012 (Comedy-Drama).

Susan "Suzie" Anderson is a pretty teenage girl who feels that her parents hate her—"They just had me so they could come home and make someone as miserable as they are." She also feels she has only one true friend—Asteroth—"His parents hate him too which is why we get along so well." Suzie also has anger management issues (she is seeing a shrink, as she calls her), has encompassed the Goth world and has changed her name to Selena Ravenvox—"and I'm

Good People in Love. From center then clockwise: Steven Alexander, Rachael Hip-Flores, Megan Melnyk, Heather Leonard, Renee Olbert, Jesse Wakeman (copyright Ward Pictures Company).

an Internet blogging Gothic Goddess" (and, to avoid her anger issues, never, ever call her Suzie).

Selena's world totally revolves around being Goth—but not just a member, but its Queen—"It's a Goth turf war out there and nobody's taking over—not on my watch. I'm Selena Ravenvox—and I'm Goth Girl!" Selena would also like to find someone who would come along "and take me from this hellish existence ... a dashing gentleman who will sweep me off my feet—a vampire. We would sleep all day and go out at night and feed upon all the cheerleaders at my school."

Selena believes her parents and sisters do not understand her; her teachers are amazed at her personality change and she has encompassed friends who are only Goth—"Welcome to my world—Biatches!" Stories relate events in the life of a Goth Girl—a girl who wants things done her way, but also a girl desperately trying to discover who she is in a world she feels she does not truly belong.

Cast: Vera VanGuard (Selena Ravenvox), Joel Reed (Asteroth), Emily Yetter (Taylor), Darth Schuhe (Sadisto Ameroth), Mister Marco (Dad), Laura Renee James (Mom), Marcus Langston (Bobby), Jacelyn Schutte (Desiree Angelripper), Hana Lash (Wynter), Lauren Bennett (Erica), Cara Manuele (Trinity Divinity), Scott Blugrind (Uncle Charlie), Cosmoe Tayson (Mortalis), Joe Filippone (Quill Cadaver), Mariah Pasos (Aluna), Kristal Luna (Vulvet), Dave Max (Dan the Man), Alex Cartana (Malicia), Audrey Cain (Tormentra), Anne Arreguin (Devianna), Elspeth Weingarten (Rosey Hips), Nathan Pata (Vlad), Ellen Clifford (Lustina), Valerie Cavero (Amanda), Melida Lee (Selena's Shrink), Darth Schuhe (Sadisto), Sphinxie Bites (Aluna), Colette Brown (Killary). **Credits:** *Producer:* Nick Griffo, Vera VanGuard. *Writer-Director:* Nick Griffo. **Comment:** Billed as both a comedy and a drama, with the program leaning more toward comedy, it is nonethe-less, an enjoyable, well-acted program. Vera VanGuard as Selena is a delight and really captures the feel of a Goth Girl (not only in appearance but in performance). The other performers play their roles just as well and the only negative aspect about the program is its occasional use of vulgar language.

Episodes:

1. The Dream Killers. Introduces the pretty—but scary Selena as she tells her Internet viewers exactly who she is—and what her life is all about.

2. Half-Ass Pool Party. A normal pool party becomes anything but when Selena and Asteroth become invited guests.

3. Sisters, Neighbors and Twilight. Selena reflects on her desire to be swept off her feet by a vampire—and also reflects on her younger sister, Taylor and older sister Erica.

4. Meltdown in the Bedroom. Sadisto, Asteroth's cousin, and Desiree, Sadisto's controlling and psychopathic girlfriend, visit Selena (in her bedroom) for a social call that is anything but social when De-

siree believes Sadisto is eyeing Selena's cleavage and trying to look up her dress and goes berserk, practically killing him for even looking at another girl.

5. Get Out of My Face, Freak Show! Selena's anger issues come into play when she confronts an annoying guy whose car's blasting horn is disturbing her.

6. The Lecture. Just before Dad (Eric) decides to have a father-daughter lecture with Susan (his "Little Pumpkin") about her outrageous behavior, Selena reflects on how delightful it would be if she were a vampire and could drain her annoying family dry.

7. I Have a Dream. At a party being given by Asteroth, Selena's jealousy rears its ugly head when her sister, Erica, shows interest in Zachary (Asteroth to Selena) and she and Selena come to blows—in a fist fight wherein both girls take a beating.

8. Are You a Vampire? As the party continues, Selena's vampire dream may become a reality when she meets a party guest (Vlad) who insists he is a real vampire.

9. Apologies = Enslavement. Continues from the prior episode with Asteroth attempting to make amends with Selena for the fight he caused between her and Erica over his affections.

10. Avenge My Nuts. A dark cloud descends on Selena when her arch nemesis, Malicia, threatens her Goth Girl standing.

11. Pubic Pizza. Selena is still searching for the vampire of her dreams—"I work hard for this body. I stay out of the sun so my skin stays silky smooth for my vampire king to sink his teeth into." Her dream is interrupted by Dad when he decides to give Selena another boring lecture about her behavior.

12. Operation Erica. Believing that maybe Asteroth and Erica are meant to be together, Selena puts him to the test by forcing him to confront Erica and ask her for a date (a situation that does not go well when Asteroth fumbles, believing Erica is too much for him to handle).

13. Who's Shrinking Who? In an effort to control Selena's anger issues, Mom and Dad feel a house visit by her psychiatrist may be the right therapy.

14. Sibling Promiscuity. Selena's young sister, 12-year-old Taylor, has a boyfriend and a desire—to have sex. Selena is overly concerned that Taylor is only 12, but also by the fact that, at 17, she is a virgin.

15. Be Edward for Me. Selena's plan for Asteroth to seduce Erica backfires when a rival for Erica's affections (Sadisto) appears (although he fears Desiree if she should find out).

16. The Night Ends Prematurely. Continuing from episode 14, Selena feels that Taylor "cannot get deflowered before me" and goes on the prowl seeking a victim for sex. Her choice just adds to her misery when she finds a guy with more issues than she does and must accept the fact that she will remain a virgin.

17. Stockings Stomp Down. While Sadisto apparently showed interest in Erica, it was Selena with whom he developed an obsession—so much so that he stole a pair of her stockings. Discovering that her stockings are missing and deducting that Sadisto is the culprit, Selena calls Desiree—and all hell breaks loose when Desiree beats Sadisto into a pulp for what he did.

18. Halloween Magic. It's Halloween and Selena's trick-or-treating adventures are explored.

19. Gothic Smack Down. Malicia, Selena's nemesis for Goth Queen, crashes Asteroth's Halloween party only to encounter Selena's wrath—and a cat fight wherein Selena emerges as the winner and still Goth Queen.

20. Twilight by Selena. Selena presents her own version of the movie *Twilight* via Barbie-like dolls as the characters.

21. Selena's Fan Mail. At a house her mother (a real estate agent) is trying to sell, Selena and her friends hope to find something creepy—"like a body buried in the walls."

22. Know Your Place, Biatch! Selena seeks a way to deal with Necrole, the Goth Girl who now poses a threat to her standing as the Goth Queen.

23. The Joke's on You. The results of Selena's anger issues come to light when it is revealed that her mother "was thrown" into a mental institution; her sister Taylor "moved to Europe with my creepy Uncle Charlie; and poor Erica, I tortured her so much she abandoned her family."

24. Handle My Light Work. Trinity Divinity, Selena's childhood friend, seeks to get even with Selena for not being included in her circle of friends. As kids, Trinity felt Selena always had the best (like real Barbie dolls; not the Chinese knock-offs she got) and now, as a Goth Girl, plans to dethrone Selena.

25. Taking Out the Trash. Believing that Trinity is now a threat, Selena feels she must devise a sneaky plan to discredit Trinity unaware that Trinity is plotting to steal Asteroth from her.

26. I Know You're Not Back-Talking Me, Monkey Bitch! Asteroth's decision to be with Trinity devastates Selena, who is now feeling abandoned and will never have a boyfriend, not even her vampire dream lover.

27. Just When You Thought It Couldn't Get Any Creepier... Uncle Charlie returns from Europe—and immediately shows his creepy side by hitting on Selena's underage friends.

28. Asteroth Fail. After Asteroth believes it is best for him and Selena to spend time apart (as he is now with Trinity), Selena's friends attempt to cheer her up by introducing her to Goth guys.

29. Shrinks, Strippers, and One, Big, Happy Family. After scolding Uncle Charlie for his inappropriate behavior (hitting on underage girls), Selena finds her father has found a new girlfriend—a stripper (Rosey Hips) and a new shrink to deal with.

30. Selena's Relationship Device. Selena returns to her Internet blog and attempts to answer some fan mail—and giving advice that has earned her the nickname "The Mistress of Mayhem."

31. Dad's Internet Victory. When Selena finds that her father is getting more on-line attention than she is, she plots a way to reverse the situation.

32. Asteroth Moves On. In a plan to outdo Selena, Trinity begins her own video blog—and angers Selena even more than she already has when she invites Asteroth to be her guest.

33. 70s Martial Arts Cinema Duel. Trinity's taunting of Selena comes to final blows when they face each other in a showdown for the top honors in the Goth world.

34. Uncle Charlie's Fantasy. Feeling that creepy Uncle Charlie is just too creepy to have around, Selena plots a way to make him leave.

35. Dad vs. the Po-Po. Although she never expects much from her father, Dad intervenes and together they devise a plan to rid their lives of Uncle Charlie (but Selena also considers her father's relationship with Rosey also a bit creepy).

36. This Is Burbank. Wanting to once and for all declare herself as the Goth Queen, Trinity approaches Selena for a final confrontation. Trinity is defeated—and the confrontation is witnessed by someone who may change Selena's life forever.

37. Selena's Big Break. A television producer who witnessed the battle between Selena and Trinity approaches Selena and tells her that he has been following her video blogs and she is the girl he has been seeking for a TV series. Selena agrees on condition that "We do it in Europe and I go to Vampire Fest."

38. Epic Goth Brawl. Selena, saddened that she has lost Asteroth to Trinity, but enthusiastic about meeting a real vampire in Europe, finds that her Goth Goddess standing is still threatened by Trinity. In the concluding episode, Selena faces Trinity's wrath as she plans to take over as the town's premiere Goth Goddess and displace Selena.

138 Gotham. gothamtheseires.com. 2009 (Drama).

Following a devastating divorce from her irresponsible husband, Jon (an unemployed Wall Street day trader), in 2008, Catherine Prescott gained sole custody of their daughter (Ava) and set out to make a new life for herself and Ava. By 2009, she had become a successful sales executive for Nicole Miller and stories relate events in her life and the people she interacts with: Richard Manning, a broker called "The Crown Prince of Wall Street" and her new romantic interest; Claire Ryan, Catherine's older sister; Elizabeth Manning, Richard's mother, the president of Manning and Associates Investments on Wall Street; Tina Havens, Catherine's best friend; Liam, Elizabeth's business partner (runs the accounting division); Ava, Catherine's daughter, a talented singer and dancer who yearns for an acting career; Veronica,

Richard's "soon-to-be" ex-wife, and the mother of his two children, Rachel and Nicholas; and Rachel Manning, Richard's daughter.

Cast: Martha Byrne (Catherine Prescott), Michael Park (Richard Manning), Kin Shriner (Jon Prescott), Anne Sayre (Tina Havens), Jessica Griffin (Ava Prescott), Melanie Smith (Claire Ryan), Anna Stuart (Elizabeth Manning), Margaret Reed (Sheila Stevens), Caroline Byrne (Rachel Manning), Kurt McKinney (Liam Kelly), Suzan Perry (Doris Curvan), Maeve Kinkead (Dinah Cummings), Brianne Moncrief (Samantha), Lisa Peluso (Veronica Manning), Lamont Craig (Jayqui Knowles), Paolo Seganti (Dominic Siliceo), Matthew Crane (Perry Baxter). **Credits:** *Producer:* Martha Byrne, Jodi Redmond, David Wenzel. *Director:* Lisa Brown. *Writer:* Martha Byrne, Alexandra Roalsvig. **Comment:** Based on the trailer, the program is well acted and produced and follows the typical formula set by daytime TV soap operas like *Days of Our Lives* and *The Young and the Restless*. Whether to purchase or rent is based solely on what one derives from watching the preview episode.

Episodes: Episodes are only available through purchase ($1.99) or rental ($.99 for 24 hours) agreement. Only a free trailer remains on line that previews the series and what to expect.

139 Gray Matters. graymatterstheseries. com. 2010 (Comedy-Drama).

Leonarda Whilaminski is a young architect, employed by the New York–based firm of Henderson and Hawkes who suffers from an extreme form of Obsessive-Compulsive Disorder. The disorder has Leonarda so paranoid that to deal with life and its germs, she has created an illusion that the world is gray and thus she can function as a normal person. But, as the situation grows worse and her fear of touching people begins to excel, she must face a realization that to enjoy her life and function in today's world, she must overcome her affliction.

Cast: Alexis Fedor (Leonarda Whilaminski), Richard Alleman (Daniel Hawkes), Saidah Arrika Ekulona (Elaine Paige), John Anthony (Jonathan), Robert Funaro (Travius Cavos), Jaiden Kaine (Mark Leonard), Craig Zisel (Bradley Hawkes). **Credits:** *Director:* Kevin T. Collins. *Writer:* Kevin T. Collins, Alexis Fedor. **Comment:** Immediately the television series *Monk* will come to mind. While Leonarda's condition is not as serious as those experienced by Adrian Monk (who was not only afraid of germs, but virtually everything else) Leonarda seems to have a better handle on things and can function on her own. The series is well produced and acted and the doorway is left open to further explore Leonarda's mind and learn what caused her disorder, but most importantly, can it be cured.

Episodes:

1. A Gray in the Life (9 min., 25 sec.). Leonarda is introduced as she struggles to deal with her disorder.

2. The Thin Gary Line (9 min., 18 sec.). Leonarda finds herself in danger of losing her job when her late boss's son, Bradley Hawkes, takes over and becomes attracted to her.

3. The Little Gray Things (7 min., 55 sec.). Leonarda ponders the decision to seek help from a therapist or deal with her disease on her own.

4. Menage-a-Gray (11 min., 5 sec.). Realizing there is hope Leonarda makes a life-changing decision and finds a therapist (Elaine).

5. A Hard Gray's Night (11 min., 46 sec.). The concluding episode wherein Leonarda's first session with her therapist begins to uncover the hidden feelings that may have led to her disorder.

140 The Grove. thegrovetheseries.com. 2013 (Drama).

The Grove is a town on the Central Coast of California. It was founded in the early 19th century by members of the Moynihan family, Irish settlers who planted almond trees on the hundreds of acres of baron land that would eventually become known as The Grove. Over time other families had settled there, including the Kincaids, who acquired land from the Moynihan's but eventually sold portions off to develop new ventures. Once friends, the families are now in a battle to acquire as much land as possible to plant almond trees. A look at the differences and similarities of both families are seen in a rather unusual way: through flashbacks that begin when two beautiful lesbians marry: Cordelia Nicolette "Nico" Moynihan, an auto mechanic, and the daughter of Doyle Moynihan (owner of the Grove Tavern and Inn) and Ivy Rose Rodriquez, a baker she met in East Los Angeles (where Nico purchased Ivy's famous sweet bread; Ivy later works as head baker at Doyle's tavern).

Lauren is Doyle's daughter, an entertainment lawyer and Nico's half-sister; Sean is Lauren's brother and now head of the Moynihan family almond business. Patrick "Paddy" Kincaid is the man responsible for destroying almond groves to develop an office park and his mini-mansion. Gloria is Patrick's spoiled socialite wife; Maximus, called Max, is Patrick's homophobic son, "the bad boy about town." Marigold is Patrick's selfish, spoiled rotten daughter; Prissy is Patrick's mistress (and proud of it); Katherine, called Kitty, is Patrick's niece, an activist and political fund raiser; Jonny Chavas is the foreman of Doyle's almond groves.

Cast: Christine Chappell (Nico Moynihan), Jessica Leccia (Ivy Rodriquez), Jordan Clarke (Patrick Moynihan), Beth Maitland (Gloria Moynihan), Christian LeBlanc (Max Moynihan), Nadia Bjorlin (Marigold), Bobbie Eakes (Katherine), Peter Reckell (Jonny), Linsey Godfrey (Poppy), Judi Evans (Prissy), Harrison White (Bobby). **Credits:** *Producer:* Crystal

The Grove
THE SERIES

The Grove. Scene from "The Wedding" episode (used by permission of Open Book Productions and Crystal Chappell).

Chappell, Christina Morris, Michael Sabatino, Hillary B. Smith, Paul Barber, Karen Wilkens, Susan Flannery. *Director:* Karen Wilkens, Susan Flannery. *Writer:* Crystal Chappell, Michael Sabatino, Paul Barber. **Comment:** Although only a pilot has thus far been produced it sets the stage for a serial-like presentation that will show the intrigues that exist between the two families. There are sexual situations (especially between Nico and Ivy) and the sexual chemistry between Crystal and Jessica is the highlight of the program.

Episodes:

1. The Grove Pilot (1 hr., 9 min., 36 sec.). The saga of the Moynihan and Kincaid families begins as the weeding between Nico and Ivy becomes the catalyst that will bring to light (via flashbacks) the past indiscretions that haunt both families.

141 H2O Magic. youtubecom. 2012 (Comedy-Drama).

Two young girls, Macy and Isabella, discover a strange cave near a river. While exploring it, they are exposed to strange moon-like beams they later discover have endowed them with Mermaid abilities (or as they call themselves, "Merfreaks"). Now, when they make contact with water, they are transformed into Mermaids and must learn to live a normal life while accepting the fact that they are also creatures of the ocean.

Cast (as credited): Emmie (Isabella), Emme (Macy). **Credits** are not given. **Comment:** An obvious inspiration based on the TV series *H20: Just Add Water* that has poor sound, capable acting and acceptable photography.

Episode List: *1.* Merfreaks. *2.* Power Surge. *3.* Sea Jewelry. *4.* Shaking the Truth. *5.* A New Fin. *6.* Bella's Dying of Boredom.

142 Halo 4: Forward Unto Dawn. web serieschannel.com. 2012 (Adventure).

It is the year 2526 and the UNSC (United Nations Space Command) Military Academy (on the planet Cirnicus IV) trains cadets as soldiers to protect the world from the Covenant, alien insurrectionists in the outer colonial planets (they are religiously offended by Humanity and seek to destroy it). (In the 22nd century the United Nations established the UNSC as a means to relieve the severe overpopulation problem by colonizing other planets. It was not until the late 24th century that the Covenant became a threat and the UNSC found it necessary to establish its own defense force to protect its united planets.) Thomas Lasky is one such cadet at the Corbulo Academy of Military Science, who is following in the footsteps of his parents and older brother. But unlike those who preceded him, Thomas has his doubts about war and struggles with the expectations that have been set for him as a potential military leader. The program charts what happens when the Covenant attacks and Thomas, guided by John-117 (the Master Chief) must do what it takes to save his fellow cadets and defeat the enemy. It is actually presented as a flashback with Thomas in the year 2557 (when he had risen to the rank of Captain and commander of the vessel *Infinity*) recalling the year 2526 when he was a cadet at the Corbulo Academy (a training facility for the children of high-ranking UNSC officers) and the devastating war with the Covenant.

Cast: Tom Green (Cadet Thomas Lasky), Ty Olsson (Adult Thomas Lasky), Anna Popplewell (Cadet Chyler Silva), Enisha Brewster (Cadet April Orenski), Osric Chau (Cadet Junjie Chen), Kat DeLieva (Cadet Dimah Tchakova), Iain Belcher (Cadet Walter Vickers), Masam Holden (Cadet Michael Sullivan), Jill Tweed (Col. Lasky), Avelet Zurer (Col. K.L. Mehaffey), Daniel Cudmore (John-117). **Credits:** *Producer-Director:* Stewart Hendler. *Writer:* Aaron Helbing, Todd Helbing. **Comment:** Visually impressive, well acted and produced program for fans of the Halo Universe. However, people not familiar with the Halo Universe may find it rather slow moving and confusing as there are no real storylines, characters are vague and nothing is really done to explain things. Unfortunately, all the action is thrown at the viewer at once with the Covenant attacking and the Master Chief attempting to save what cadets he is able (his top priority being Thomas Lasky). The title refers to a ship called *Forward Unto Dawn* that is seen drifting through space (in the opening sequences) and triggers Captain Lasky's war flashback when its artificial intelligence Cortana, dispenses a distress call. The special effects are very good but there is a lot of violence (killing in the last two episodes) and it is difficult to watch (with kids being blown up and subject to bleeding and gory injuries).

Note: The Halo Universe is a fictional world of the 26th century wherein mankind has colonized the galaxy but has yet to conquer the numerous hostile aliens drawn together by a religious alliance (the Covenant) and motivated by the writings of the Prophets and its philosophy of a paradise after death—which can only be achieved with the destruction of humanity. In essence, *Halo* "is an epic journey to save humanity from a terrible menace." Prior to the above Internet series, there have been numerous video games, comic books, short films and even an anime (Japanese) video series.

Episodes:

1. Part 1 (18 min., 50 sec.). Introduces the newest freshman recruits (the Hastai Squad) at the UNSC's Corbulo Academy of Military Science.

2. Part 2 (16 min., 43 sec.). As Thomas Lasky struggles to find his place within the academy, Michael Sullivan attempts to break a hidden combat video code.

3. Part 3 (16 min., 45 sec.). The code is broken, telling of an invasion, but it appears to be too late as the enemy's super soldiers begin an attack on Corbulo Academy.

4. Part 4 (15 min., 59 sec.). The invading Covenant Army appears to have the upper hand as cadets are killed and the academy is on the verge of destruction.

5. Part 5 (17 min., 11 sec.). The concluding episode depicts that the only hope for the surviving cadets is Thomas Lasky, who has conspired with the Master Chief to outwit the enemy.

143 *Hand of Glory.* webserieschannel.com. 2013 (Thriller).

A lonely delivery man (Joseph) becomes attracted to Karen, a prostitute addicted to alcohol who frequents one of the stops along his route. Joseph works up the courage to approach Karen and soon the two become friends. But Karen's strange behavior makes it impossible for Joseph to really get to know her and, in a desperate attempt to win her affections, seeks a supernatural means by which to accomplish his goal, a mystical relic called The Hand of Glory. The program follows Joseph as he incorporates the abilities of the relic, which purports to have the abilities to unlock any door, to discover who Karen really is, not realizing that the relic has its own requirements for granting desires.

Cast: Darren Marlar (Joseph), Heather Dorff (Karen), Ann Marie Boska (Young Karen), Richard Bunch (Hank), Joe DeBartolo (Victor), Berdella Endress (Cassie), Brian Kramer (Nick), Justin R. Romine (Pimp), Michael Schmid (Eddie), Stuart Wahlin (Barfly). **Credits:** *Producer-Writer-Director:* Stuart Wahlin. **Comment:** Two episodes were produced but have been taken off line ("Sorry, This Video No Longer Exists" will appear). Based on what is available, the program does appear interesting and what the relic requires for its use would be an interesting concept to discover as the story plays out.

144 *Hard Drive 13.* webserieschannel.com. 2010 (Action).

While searching the Internet for his father, who mysteriously disappeared, a corporate spy and computer hacker (Nomad) stumbles across what appears to be a vast and lethal conspiracy ("When you dig up research for a living, anything can happen. Knowledge is power and their secrets are weapons"). Nomad's findings bring him in contact with Dee, a beautiful government agent who has joined him to stop the conspiracy. The program charts their attempts to unravel the conspiracy and avoid their pursuers—assassins of a rogue agency, the Interplanetary Security Department, who have orders to stop them at any cost.

Cast: C.B. Shaw (Nomad), Denyc (Dee), Terry Levergood (Lifer), M. E. Lewis (Agent 01), Matthew Thiessen (Agent 02). **Credits:** *Producer:* Stephen H. Plitt, M. E. Lewis, S. Preston Chuhon, Michael Chmara. *Writer-Director:* Stephen H. Plitt. **Comment:** Based on the trailers, the program appears to be well produced and acted and has an intriguing premise as two fugitives try to stop a great catastrophe from occurring (not explained what it is in the trailers or on its website).

Episodes: Three episodes were produced but have since been taken off line. Three trailers (running 21 sec., 53 sec. and 1 min., 12 sec.) can still be viewed.

145 Heathens. blip.tv. 2007 (Western).

Freedom, Texas, in the year 1846 provides the setting. It is here that being a fast draw, a marshal or sheriff, gambler or outlaw has no real meaning; men inflating their egos and proving their manhood (by indulging in carnal pleasures) is what makes a man a man—not his ability to uphold the law or break it. The adult-themed western, with its tag line, "Stripping away the layers of society," explores such men—men who possess ivory (not gold, silver or paper money) to indulge in pleasure (especially with the mysterious Savage Woman).

Cast: Jana Lee Brockman, Jay Jennings, Paris Patrick, Lloyd Harris, Christopher Rocha, Paul Erwin, Troy Dillinger, Patrick Crowley, Jason Newman, Andrew Maguire, Charles Ney, Shannon Riggs Erwin (there are no character/cast match-ups on the screen or its website). **Credits:** *Producer-Director:* Jesse Patrick. *Writer:* Rachel Ney, Jesse Patrick **Comment:** Do not expect a take-off on such TV series as *Maverick, Cheyenne* or *Gunsmoke* as none of these programs dared venture into the territory covered by *Heathens.* While well-acted and photographed, it plays more like an X-rated adult film (minus the nudity and hard-core sex) and is not, for the most part, a conventional western. It is a different take and a curiosity to check out.

Episodes:

1. Meet the Savage. While there is no real introduction to any of the town regulars, the beautiful but mysterious (and rather cave girl-like dressed) temptress, the Savage Woman, is seen for the first time.

2. Meet the Writer. Hearing stories about the un-usual occurrences in Freedom, Boston writer Andrew Crawley sets out on a journey to uncover the true story.

3. Meet the Heathens. Rather than celebrate the arrest of a captured outlaw, the men of the town indulge in drinking at the saloon to celebrate a citizen's (Charlie) night of sexual pleasure.

4. Seeking Shelter. Andrew arrives in Freedom and immediately sees that the town is unlike any town he has read about, especially when he learns about the Savage Woman.

5. Research Begins. To begin his story, the unwelcome Andrew decides to do a background search on the local townspeople.

6. Character Study. While the local sheriff (Lathem) contends with a domestic dispute, Andrew falls prey to the carnal pleasures of Freedom.

7. Coming of Age. Another temptress, Daisy, is introduced; it is also revealed that in one week Texas will be joining the Union.

8. A Building Curiosity. Figuring Daisy is a likely subject to interview, Andrew begins questioning her, hoping to uncover the secret behind the town's strange addiction.

9. Reflections. Flashbacks are used to reveal incidents in town life before Andrew's arrival.

10. Walk the Walk. As Andrew continues his research, he arranges an encounter with the Savage Woman (who takes teeth from her "lovers" as souvenirs).

11. True Inspiration. Sheriff Lathem and a woman (Clara) indulge in a new "game" in town—voyeurism, rather than worry about a drought that plagues the town and a conflict that has arisen over dry water pumps.

12. Walk of Shame. Unknown to Andrew, his meeting with the Savage Woman has stirred a betting frenzy on how many teeth she will take.

13. Conflicted. Andrew's night with the Savage Woman has corrupted his thinking and attempts to write a letter to his fiancé in Boston and break up with her never happen (crucial to the last episode).

14. Rite of Passage. A confrontation arises between the Savage Woman and the Old Native American (her guardian) while Jonathan, the young man eager to prove his manhood, seeks to do just that with the Savage Woman.

15. Abandoned. As the drought situation worsens, Daisy seeks a way to stop Jonathan from succumbing to the desires of the Savage Woman.

16. Dark Quandary. With the drought situation worsening, irrational behavior is erupting in town just a few days away from Texas joining the Union.

17. Transcended. Andrew's quest for a story has him wondering what has been happening to him after his encounter with the Savage Woman appears to have changed his perspective on life.

18. Fear-Ridden Shame. As time for joining the Union nears, a dark cloud suddenly appears over Freedom with its citizens now laden with shame and

fear if what has been happening here becomes known elsewhere.

19. Manifest Destiny. Andrew's decision about his story (actually his book, *Manifest Destiny*) could either condemn the town if he publishes it or spare its dark secret if he elects not to submit it.

20. Manipulation. In an attempt to make his story sensational, Andrew feels that manipulating the townspeople will give him what he requires; he begins by abducting the Savage Woman then letting it be known she has been kidnapped and may be dead.

21. Making Martyrs. News of the Savage Woman's disappearance has the citizens upset, sending them on a frenzy to find her. Their encounter with the Old Native American Woman (the Savage Woman's guardian) becomes violent when they believe she is a witch and kill her, sending a dark cloud over Freedom.

22. Freedom's Demise. As Andrew completes his story (for a book) the town suddenly becomes like other towns and succumbs to lawlessness.

23. Undone. Freedom continues to fall into ruin with Andrew thinking of only the grandeur and wealth his book will bring him when he returns to Boston.

24. Release. Texas is literally only hours away from joining the Union and its economy is now suffering as the strong Union dollar has collapsed its local Confederate-based economy; thinking it is best to move on, the Sheriff and Clara part for greener pastures, leaving Freedom without any protection.

25. Decimation. The law is gone; several townspeople have died and, amidst the still on-going carnal pleasures, the drought ends with a storm erupting—a supply of water but not a washing away of the unsavory life that is now Freedom.

26. Narrative Legend. Andrew's manipulation backfires when the Savage Woman escapes, and seeking revenge, abducts him. Andrew, tied to a tree watches as the Savage Woman takes his book, looks at it then throws it into a fire she has started.

27. A New Zeal. Despite what is happening, the thought of joining the Union appears to be the only hope for Freedom and an end to its sexually-depraved society.

28. Retribution. Inaugural day has arrived and does appear to be the hope for a new and brighter future for Freedom. It has also been three months since Andrew left Boston. He returns to find that his neglect in contacting anyone to let them know he arrived safely in Freedom, has led to his fiancé marrying his best friend and his dreams of wealth are now shattered without his book.

146 *Hero Treatment.* blip.tv. 2011 (Drama).

The Department of Meda-Human Affairs, a segment of The Hall of Justice, is a training ground for super heroes. It is run by Alice Glass and its newest inductee is a young man who calls himself Deluxo. Deluxo expressed super hero tendencies and was forcibly invited to join the organization (agents simply appeared at his apartment and escorted him to The Hall of Justice). Deluxo, however is not exactly what the agency is seeking as he failed (miserably) every test a super hero must pass: luck, endurance, strength, perception, charisma, agility, intelligence and physique. But potential is seen and Deluxo (who now wants to call himself Super Boy) is prohibited from leaving the center. He possesses a special gene (presumably a super hero gene) and it needs to be found and activated—no matter how long it takes. The program charts, in the only episode that was produced, his induction into the center and how he must train to become the hero he is meant to be.

Cast: Brett DelBuono (Deluxo), Stacey Ann Shevlin (Gail), Jamaal Murray (Lifesaver), Michael Caruso (Roger), Traycee King (Plus One), Beau Ryan (The Docent), Dot-Marie Jones (Alice Glass), Jillian Clare (Cyberella), Kristyn Burtt (Herself) **Credits:** *Producer-Writer-Director:* JD Piche. **Comment:** It is doubtful any additional episodes will air as the pilot was produced in 2011. The program does show potential for something different when it comes to super heroes (training) with good acting and production values.

Episodes:

1. Pilot: The Potential for Potential (4 min., 30 sec.). The story line is established with an ending tagline "Next time on *Hero Treatment* and a brief teaser as what to except.

2. Hero Treatment Teaser. Brief scenes from the pilot are showcased.

3. Hero Treatment Elevator Outtakes. A behind-the-scenes look at the filming of a scene from the series.

147 *Hidden by Scales.* youtube.com. 2012 (Comedy-Drama).

Friends Alyssa and Tori are hanging out together when Alyssa receives a text message: "If you do not forward this to 100 people in the next 10 hours you will become a part of the ocean." Alyssa ignores it. Later, in her backyard, Alyssa and Tori discover the results of not forwarding that text: spilled bottled water transforms them into Mermaids. Now, with new identities, Alyssa and Tori must lead dual lives—publicly as ordinary school girls and secretly as Mermaids.

Cast (as credited): Madisyn (Alyssa), Lindsey (Tori). **Credits** are not given. **Comment:** A slightly different twist on Mermaid mythology but the program suffers from poor sound.

Episodes:

1. The Forward (7 min., 34 sec.). Establishes the story line as Alyssa gets a text message but suffers the consequences for not responding.

148 *Hitman 101.* badguyfilms.com. 2012 (Thriller).

John Smith, as he is known, is a hitman. Once given an assignment, the hit is accomplished without difficulty. The client gets what he wants and John what he wants—satisfaction (although he says the situation often sickens him). The program charts a series of hits John must accomplish during one week. Each envelope he receives contains the name of a victim and how John goes about sizing up, then completing each assignment is detailed. For the initial presentation, John learns that the hits were contracted by a crime lord (Terry Harrow) seeking revenge on the jurors who voted not guilty in a case wherein a mobster (Nikolai Korsoff) raped and killed his daughter but, even with overwhelming incriminating evidence gathered by the police, was freed by the jurors who were bought.

Cast: Georgie Daburas (John Smith), Laura Adkin (Eva), Timothy Lyle (Det. Madsen), Jackie Froese (Det. Cole), Nathan Durec (Staal), Momona Komagata (Mace), Denton Winn (Carnahan), Darren Andrichuk (Capt. Hollis), Kerrie Gee (Ginger), Gabrielle Giraud (Tina), Dominika Zybko (Nikki). **Credits:** *Producer:* Paige Heuser. *Writer-Director:* Scott Staven. **Comment:** Violence, sexual situations and vulgar language are all present in a well-produced and acted program that holds your interest from the very beginning. The concluding episode leaves the possibility open for more stories but thus far this has not happened.

Episodes:

1. Always the Hardest (8 min., 48 sec.). John Smith is introduced as he begins his first assignment.

2. Along Came Eva (7 min.). At a diner John meets—and becomes captivated by a woman named Eva.

3. Mouse Meet Cat (6 min., 51 sec.). During a hit, John is spotted by a man John must now silence. But before he can do so, the witness is killed by someone else (not revealed).

4. Caught (6 min., 47 sec.). The police arrive at the scene and take John in as suspect (although he clears himself by saying that he just happened to be there).

5. Devil's in the Details (6 min., 24 sec.). After being released, John is kidnapped by goons of the man who hired him and learns that he is not the only player in the game; that others have also received the letters to ensure the targets are disposed of.

6. Enemies Close (8 min., 38 sec.). Now that he is a player John feels he needs to sharpen his skills to win—and collect the money.

7. Trust (6 min., 1 sec.). John discovers that the girl he met at the diner, Eva, is a hit man also (her real name is Lorraine).

8. Unhappy Ending (5 min., 57 sec.). John learns that Eva poses as a prostitute to seduce her targets before she kills them.

9. No Rest for the Wicked (5 min., 43 sec.). A third killing has the police baffled, but determined to uncover the culprit.

10. Our Fallen Brothers (6 min., 46 sec.). John contacts a friend (Pierce), a former FBI agent and learns more about the hits (explained in the story line above).

11. Payment Upon Delivery (7 min., 52 sec.). John's investigation leads him to the crime lord in charge—Harrow.

12. The Fifth (12 min.). The concluding episode wherein John goes on a killing rampage, taking out Harrow and his mobsters, but is himself shot with his fate unknown as the series ends.

149 *Hollywood East.* hulu.com. 2010 (Drama).

A story of adjustment as an intertwined group of young people (an up-coming rock band and fashion models) struggle to cope with and make it in the difficult world of professional entertainment. Episodes chart their beginnings to their achieving celebrity status—and attempts to achieve even greater heights at the risk of also losing it all as they seek the top rung on the entertainment ladder. Scott, Ashton, Lee, Taylor and Bobby are the musicians; Arial, Chloe, Cindy, Eve and Paige are the stylish models.

Cast: Timothy Woodward, Jr. (Scott), Lindsay Brown (Arial), James Forgey (Ashton), Scarlett Futch (Cindy), Jaime Moffett (Eve), Brandon Luck (Lee), Nate Panning (Taylor), Summer Rahn (Chloe), Patrick Priestley (Bobby), Regan Lee (Paige), Madison Moss (Sara), Christopher Ryan Church (Benny), Kelsey Keeler (Closet Girl), Jodie Sweetin (Herself). **Credits:** *Producer:* Tyler Skipper, Paul Voelker, Brent Biles, Kent Fields. *Director:* Charles Stewart, Jr., Matthew K. Hacker. *Writer:* Matthew K. Hacker, Stephen Ruiz, Charles Stewart, Jr. **Comment:** Only 1 episode remains on line and judging by it, the program is well acted and produced. Actress Jodie Sweetin (from TV's *Full House*) appears and adds a bit of nostalgia to the program for those who remember her as sweet young Stephanie Tanner (a role so different as to her role here, in episodes 3 and 4, as the sexual object of affection for the guys in the band).

Episode List: *1.* The Pilot. *2.* Looks Can Be Deceiving. *3.* Operation Hero. *4.* Give Me a Break. *5.* Gone in 60 Seconds. *6.* Hung Over & Out. *7.* Hook, Line and Singer. *8.* Cause and Effect. *9.* Behind the Scenes.

150 *Homicide: Second Shift.* ovguide.com. 1997 (Crime Drama).

The first web series to encompass aspects of a broadcast television series (*Homicide: Life on the Street*). Using a static comic book format, the program delves into the lives of the second shift of detectives of the Homicide Squad (those that report for duty when the TV regulars quit for the day).

Voice Cast: Joe Grifasi (Lt. Walter F. Neal), Allison Janney (Det. Raymonda "Ray" Cutler), Ray Anthony Thomas (Det. Layton "Lee" Johnson), Michael Ornstein (Det. Tony Bonaventura), Josh Pais (Det. Joe Landau), Murphy Guyer (Det. L.Z. Austin). **Comment:** With nothing on line to view visually, it is not possible to present an assessment on this particular series.

Episodes: All episodes, including titles, have been taken off line.

151 *House of Cards.* netflix.com. 2013–2014 (Drama).

Washington, D.C. provides the backdrop for a political drama focusing on Francis "Frank" Underwood, a South Carolina Democrat (5th Congressional District) and the intrigue that develops when he sets out to gain a position of power through deceit and manipulation (and not caring who gets hurt as he pursues his own political agenda). As the series progresses, he becomes House Majority Whip, the U.S. Vice President and finally the 46th President of the United States.

Claire Underwood, Frank's wife, originally oversaw the Clean Water Initiative before abandoning her position to become Second Lady of the U.S. Her appearance as a loving wife is deceiving as she is just as devious and manipulative as Frank as his goals are also her chance to become a woman of power.

Zoe Barnes and Janine Skorsky are first newspaper reporters (*The Washington Herald*) then on-line reporters (for Slugline); Lucas Goodwin is an editor for the *Herald*; Remy Danton is a lawyer and lobbyist employed by a gas company (SanCorp); Rachel Posner is the prostitute caught up in Frank's plans; Christina Gallagher, is a congressional staffer who later becomes Frank's personal assistant; Edward Meechum, a U.S. Capitol Police Officer, is Frank's bodyguard (later a Secret Service agent); Garrett Walker, is the former U.S. President; Patricia Walker is Garrett's wife; Linda Vasquez is Pres. Garrett's Chief of Staff; Douglas Stamper is Frank's Chief of Staff; Raymond Tusk is the billionaire businessman and Frank's close friend; Jacqueline Sharp is the Congresswoman who succeeds Frank as Majority Whip when he becomes Vice President; Peter Russo is a U.S. Representative from Pennsylvania hooked on drugs and alcohol; Catherine Durant, a Missouri Senator who, through Frank's manipulation, becomes Secretary of State; Freddy Hayes owns Frank's favorite eatery, Freddy's BBQ; Seth Garrison is Frank's Press Secretary; Margaret Tilden is the owner of *The Washington Herald;* Xander Feng is the corrupt Chinese businessman; Terry Womack is the House Majority Leader; Gillian Cole is head of the grass-roots organization World Well.

Cast: Kevin Spacey (Francis J. Underwood), Robin Wright (Claire Underwood), Mahershala Ali (Remy Danton), Sebastian Arcelus (Lucas Goodwin), Rachel Brosnahan (Rachel Posner), Kristen Connolly (Christina Gallagher), Nathan Darrow (Edward Meechum), Michel Gill (Garrett Walker), Sakina Jaffrey (Linda Vasquez), Michael Kelly (Douglas Stamper), Kate Mara (Zoe Barnes), Constance Zimmer (Janine Skorsky), Jayne Atkinson (Catherine Durant), Gerald McRaney (Raymond Tusk), Molly Parker (Jacqueline Sharp), Corey Stoll (Peter Russo), Derek Cecil (Seth Grayson), Reg E. Cathey (Freddy Hayes), Ben Daniels (Adam Galloway), Terry Chen (Xander Feng), Joanna Going (Patricia Walker), Jeremy Holm (Nathan Green), Sandrine Holt (Gillian Cole), Lance E. Nichols (Gene Clancy), Benito Martinez (Hector Mendoza), Mozhan Marno (Ayla Sayyad), Boris McGiver (Tom Hammerschmidt), Jimmi Simpson (Gavin Orsay), Larry Pine (Bob Birch). **Credits:** *Producer:* Dana Brunetti, David Fincher, Eric Roth, Kevin Spacey, Beau Willimon, John P. Melfi, David Manson. *Director:* James Foley, Carl Franklin, Robin Wright, Jodie Foster, Joel Schumacher, David Fincher, Charles McDougall. *Writer:* Beau Willimon, Sarah Treem, Laura Eason, Sam Forman, Bill Kennedy, David Manson, Gina Gionfriddo, Keith Huff, Bill Kennedy, Kenneth Lin, John Mankiewicz, Kate Barnow, Michael Dobbs, Andrew Davies, Rick Cleveland, Bill Cain. **Comment:** Adapted not only from the novel by Michael Dobbs, but a BBC (British Broadcasting Corporation) television miniseries that captures the political flavor of the book and series. Television veterans Kevin Spacey, Constance Zimmer, Gerald McRaney and Kate Mara are well cast and the story flows smoothly from beginning to end. Although shades of the NBC series *The West Wing* may come to mind, the production values are excellent and overall, if political intrigue interests you, *House of Cards* will fascinate you.

Episodes: Two 13 episode seasons have thus far aired with a third season projected for 2015. To encompass all three seasons, a summary of each season is presented below.

Season 1 (2013): Chapters 1–13: Introduces Frank Underwood, the Democratic Congressman, his wife, Claire, the political reporter (Zoe) and the Chief of Staff (Linda) and how each becomes a part of Frank's plan to become Secretary of State. Zoe is also seen as an ambitious young reporter who will apparently stop at nothing to achieve greater heights.

Season 2 (2014): Chapters 14–26: Frank's manipulating has earned him the rank of Vice President of the U.S. but he must now sever all the unethical ties that lead to that position. Janine and Zoe, reporters for the *Herald*, leave their newspaper positions for reporters on Slugline, an on-line service that has a far greater reach than the printed word. Zoe's death (by Frank to silence her as she was a part of his scheme) sends Janine back home (where she becomes a teacher) and Frank back on the political trail to achieve his ultimate goal—President of the United States.

Season 3 (2015): Information based on a Netflix press release of February 4, 2014. Appears to be a prequel to what happened in the prior two seasons with Frank, a House Majority Whip, beginning his devious plan by first extracting revenge on those he feels who have wronged him—from his own Cabinet members to the current 45th President (Garrett) then beginning the climb to the top of the political ladder—all of which is sanctioned by Claire, his ambitious wife, who has also begun her own vicious plans to become the top lady in Washington.

152 *The Hunted.* thehunted.tv. 2001–2014 (Anthology).

Varying stories and casts that delve into the world of the supernatural, specifically humans that have been bitten by vampires but who have yet to turn. Creating their own little society to protect themselves, they (called The Hunted) have curtailed their thirst for human blood and have vowed to help others who become victims of actual vampires. While still being sought (considered meals for vampires) they also face a new challenge as vampires have developed immunity to the traditional methods of disposal (holy water, the cross, sunlight, a stake through the heart) and can now only be killed by beheading by sword.

Cast: Robert Chapin (Bob), Kendall Wells (Kendall), Elisha Patterson III (Eli), Audrey Wells (Audrey), Ned Donovan (Ned), Jochen Repolust, Mary De Longis (Mikey), Derek Conley (Derek), Charlie Forray (Charlie), Mitchell Murdock (Mitchell), Anthony DeLongis (Vincent), Patti Pelton (Wren), Andrew Helm (Evil Kevin), Morgan Lee (Morgan), Max Lorn-Krause (Max), Graham Drake-Maurer (Graham), Devala Rees (Vlad Bloodhound), Kit Davlin (Kit), Genevieve Andersen (Shadow Agent), Amanda Andersen (Vamp), Brett D. Jones (Leroy), Will Boyajian (Will), Justin Colombo (Justin), Charlotte Brooks (Charlotte), Kimberly Fox, Chelsea Povall (Booth Babe). **Credits:** *Producer:* Kendall Wells, Derek Conley, Chris Fields, Robert Chapin, Brett D. Jones. *Director:* Robert Chapin, Kendall Wells, Ned Donovan, Derek Conley, Chris Fields, Kevin Inouye, Kirsten Foe, David Kessler. *Writer:* Robert Chapin, Kendall Wells, Devala Rees, Ned Donovan, Derek Conley, Chris Fields, Andrew Helm, Mark Bedell. **Comment:** The program is actually a combination of the TV series *The Twilight Zone, Tales from the Darkside, Buffy the Vampire Slayer* and *Tales from the Crypt* as it combines elements of mystery, the supernatural and humor. Stories are relatively short (4–6 minutes) thus making several characters appear in arc-like episodes as opposed to telling a complete story in one segment.

Episodes: Of the 50 episodes produced only the following titles remain on line: *1.* Breaking Up (Parts 1 and 2). *2.* Two for One. *3.* Tough Love. *4.* Blade in Training. *5.* Dance of the Undead. *6.* The Stalker. *7.* That's Showbiz. *8.* Class Ritual. *9.* Rendezvous. *10.* Con Job. *11.* Faire Warning. *13.* Return of the Stalker. *14.* Film at 11. *12.* Among Us. *14.* Star Power. *15.* Slay Me in St, Louis. *16.* Generations. *17.* Vampires, Drugs and New Friends.

153 *Hunter.* webserieschannel.com. 2012 (Adventure).

Hunter Logan is a young man who, after the mysterious death of his mother begins his own investigation when authorities fail to apprehend the killer. His trail leads him to discover that the simple break-in at his home that claimed his mother's life was more than it appeared and that something unnatural is at large. The two bite marks on her neck lead him to believe a vampire is responsible and his suspicions are confirmed when he saves his girlfriend, Emily, from such an attack. The program follows Logan as he turns hunter, operating above the law to find and destroy the creature that killed his mother.

Cast: Lee-loi Chieng (Hunter Logan), Sophie Petticrew (Emily), Dafe Orugbo, Ben Davis. **Credits:** *Producer-Writer-Director:* Lee-loi Chieng. **Comment:** After watching the only episode produced your reaction will most likely be "What?" A foggy story line coupled with bad sound makes it difficult to figure out what is going on. Add to this vulgar language, mediocre acting and less-than-desirable photography and one may well be turned off before the end is reached (which is unresolved and leaves the doorway open for further episodes).

Episodes:
1. The Investigation Begins (7 min., 19 sec.), Establishes the series story line as Logan turns vampire hunter.

154 *Hunter's Moon.* youtube.com. 2012–2013 (Drama).

The Society is an organization that battles the evils of the world in particular The 8 Sides of the Black Lotus, a society that is the personification of evil. Jacob Chapel, one of the founders of The Society, and his wife, Victoria Rayne-Chapel (a high-ranking Society member) are the parents of Joseph. It is also a society to which Joseph becomes a member, first fighting the unseen supernatural forces to the demons that are in plain sight (like vampires), then switching sides to battle the human offenders; it is also a look at how The Society was formed and how it safeguards civilization from the unknown.

Cast: J. Benedict Larmore (Jacob Chapel, Sr.), Janelle Graham (Victoria Chapel), Kelly Weaver (Joseph Chapel), Julie Gottfried (Gabriella Chapel), Anja Akstin (Jennifer Morgan), Alayna Akutagawa (Mary Beth Dunham), Ashley Alford (Tabby), Holie Anderson (Cervantes), Joe Arcaro (Zain), Lisa Arcaro

(Lilith), Jessica Baier (Dawn), Kelly Balagurchik (Maria Rosario), Anthony Belevtsov (Baltazar), Lianne Beth (Donella), Cameron Bigelow (Donovan Chapel), Brittany Blades (Young Jade), Marion Blount (Brian Williams), Sheryl Carbonell (Madison Rayne), Amanda-Ashley Carrigan (Raina Torres), Bonnie Cobb (Mandy), Dena Cordell (Chastity Andrews), Emily Cutting (Morrigana), Laura D'Anieri (Heather Chapel), Keith Froling (Young Jacob), Aaron Quick Nelson (Jonathan Dunham), Sheree Shearey (Angelina Delfino), Jackie Dozier (Helena Wilkens), Ally Marcus (Allyson Wilkens). Allie Hendron (Amber Hood), Sandra Lee (Ann-Marie Torres). **Credits:** *Producer:* Kelly Weaver, Amy Rinaldo. *Writer-Director:* Kelly Weaver. **Comment:** Talkative good vs. evil saga with good acting and production values. The cast is rather large for an Internet series and there are many more plot-lines than have been outlined below (only the basic presented).

Episodes:

1. The Awakening. Introduces the main characters and establishes that a secret society battles evil throughout the world.

2. Destiny. Explores the chance meeting Jacob Chapel has with Victoria Rayne and how it would set Jacob on the path to establishing The Society.

3. A Change of Heart. Further explores the conflict that exists between The Society and The 8 Sides of the Black Lotus.

4. Board Meeting. Jacob's decision to leave The 8 Sides of the Black Lotus and join The Society has The Society unsure if his intentions are actually for good or something more devious.

5. First Assignment. Now, as members of The Society, Jacob and Victoria, assisted by Mary Beth and Jonathan, receive their first assignment: break up a coven of vampires that are threatening the lives of innocent people.

6. Rebirth. Jacob and Victoria celebrate a special anniversary: their first meeting and the events that changed the course of Victoria's life forever.

7. 8 Sides of the Black Lotus. A flashback that explores the life of Jacob's younger sister, Jade, as she turns 16 years of age.

8. The Academy. A flashback with Victoria seen as a teacher at The Society coupled with aspects of training young recruits to become Hunters (its soldiers).

9. New Recruits. Establishes the two main Hunter Divisions, Section 25 and Section 52 and how, after taking The Hunter's Oath, the recruits are assigned their first mission: save the daughter (Angelina Delfino) of a Society member from a gang of demons.

10. Chance Meeting. Season 1 concludes with Sections 25 and 52 enacting their plan to rescue Angelina.

11. Revelations. Season 2 begins with Joseph questioning the death and destruction that brought about Angelina's rescue and his doubts about remaining with The Society.

12. The Reason. Realizing that battling demons is not the right choice for him, Joseph elects to quit and instead deal with human cases as a police officer.

13. Forsaken. Explores the fate of two women, Kristy and Chastity, who awaken in a mysterious room with no recollection as to how they got there. The episode is flawed by an over-powering background noise during the crucial explanation of what happened that could not be deciphered to explain things.

14. My Sister's Keeper. Two sisters (Allyson and Helena) are seen following in their parents' footsteps and training to become Hunters.

15. Betrayed, Part 1. As Jade celebrates the birth of her child and Joseph discovers he has a daughter he never knew he had, two covens of vampires are plotting to overtake The Society.

16. Betrayed, Part 2. Joseph, now a detective, tries to help a fellow officer (Madeline Torres) deal with her sister's (Raina) involvement with her new friend (Tabby) and her dangerous circle of friends.

17. To the Pot with You. A young woman's (Anne-Marie) ability to use witchcraft for good comes under the scrutiny of her father, who, not understanding it, forbids her to use it.

18. The Deal, Part 1. The Society's Section 8 team investigates a killing in which two demons took the lives of five people.

19. The Deal, Part 2. It is revealed that Jade has sided with The 8 Sides of Black and has devised a way to stop Section 8. Meanwhile, members of the Hunter's Circle seek to help a fellow member (Amber) who has been scratched by a werewolf.

20. Finale. The concluding episode wherein Jacob, Victoria and Joseph must stand together and battle Jade before she and The 8 Sides of Black destroy them.

155 *Hustling.* hustling.tv. 2011–2013 (Drama).

Ryan Crosby, a successful adult film star and male escort (working under the name Rod Driver) had it all—when he was in his twenties and thirties. Now, at 40, clients are few, adult film roles are just as few and the thrill of pornography has lost its appeal. Realizing that he has reached a turning point in his life, Ryan suddenly sees life in a different light and begins to wonder what he has accomplished and what lies ahead. With dwindling resources and no job prospects, Ryan consults a career counselor for help. Although Ryan is an excellent cook he fails to see this as an alternative; instead, lacking the self-confidence and self-worth to believe in himself, he ventures back into the world in which he feels safe—sex. During one such film Ryan meets a makeup artist (Liv) who changes the course of his life and makes him see what he is actually capable of achieving. The program charts Ryan's regression than transformation as he learns that being middle age doesn't mean you can not move on and accept other challenges.

Cast: Sebastian La Cause (Ryan Crosby), Jessica Press (Liv), Daphne Rubin-Vega (Rosa Juarez), Andrew Glaszek (Jay), Mara Davi (Charlie), Sharon Washington (Lena), Gary Cowling (Mitchell Getz), Gerald McCullouch (Geoffrey), Kevin Spirtas (Joel), Wilson Cruz (Dr. Gabe Bermudex), Gail Herendeen (Lorraine Munson), Brian Keane (Franco La Rock), Facundo Rodriquez (Julien Massi). **Credits:** *Producer-Writer-Director:* Sebastian La Cause. **Comment:** Intended for mature audiences with sexual (gay) situations and vulgar language. The acting and production values are excellent and a parental warning is stated before each episode begins.

Episodes:

1. Pilot: Let's See How You Like It. Ryan, realizing that he needs a change in his life, visits a career counselor (Mitchell Getz), but becomes somewhat evasive when he asks about his job history.

2. Deep End. Finding little help from the counselor, Ryan, assisted by his friend Jay, attempts to do an on-line job search.

3. New Information. Ryan's decision to work on a film for Franco La Rock brings him in contact with Liv, a sexy makeup artist who will soon change his life.

4. Dead. As Ryan prepares himself for a scene, he and Liv start to become friends.

5. Now or Never. Having found inspiration from Liv, Ryan returns to his counselor while also taking advice from Jay.

6. Ibitha. As Ryan and Liv become closer, Ryan begins thinking about using his cooking skills and getting out of the porn industry.

7. A Hard Bargain. Ryan takes the first step and acquires a job as an apprentice to an established personal chef (Geoffrey).

8. The Flow. As Ryan and Liv's relationship grows closer, Ryan reveals incidents about his past life.

9. Old Habits. As his old habits begin to manifest themselves, Ryan has difficulty focusing on his new job.

10. After Taste. As Ryan tries to reconnect with his estranged mother (Lena), Geoffrey becomes increasingly attracted to Ryan.

11. Chairo Pacea "O." Ryan's landlady, Rosa, offers him some cooking advice while Lena tries to understand where Ryan's love of cooking came from.

12. Open Door. Ryan continues his escort activities with Gabe (his psychiatrist) and begins to wonder if he is bi-sexual now that he and Liv are close.

13. Hunger Pangs. As Liv and Ryan deal with relationship issues, Ryan finds himself getting close to his film co-star (Julien).

14. G and T. Now that he and Liv are close, Ryan tries to tell Jay about it (as it will affect their relationship).

15. Laundry. Ryan meets with his mother's psychiatrist after he learns that she attempted suicide and gets more than he bargained for when she makes

him see more clearly where his life is headed when he reveals that his mother never approved of his porn star life.

16. Chateau Margaux, Part Uno. As Rosa continues to show Ryan cooking techniques, Ryan considers opening his own restaurant.

17. Chateau Margaux, Part Deux. Ryan continues his efforts to open his own restaurant while at the job with Geoffrey, Ryan meets his new assistants Olivia and Cherry. Meanwhile Ryan discovers that Liv has a secret life—in love with another man (Joel) and yearns to become his trophy wife.

156 *I Can Still Tell Your Wife Bill.* blip.tv. 2002 (Drama).

In 2001, a young woman (Hartley) acquired stolen sex tapes, photos and hidden camera videos and posted them on-line via a reveal-all website called ICanStillTellYourWifeBill.com. The site generated over four million views during its first week, but as mysteriously as they were posted, they were abruptly removed (apparently hacked) and the videos, along with Hartley, vanished. Hartley's disappearance still remains a mystery and all videos were thought lost until a back-up server used to upload Hartley's videos was found and its contents allowed partial reconstruction of the videos. While what happened to Hartley is not disclosed, the videos are shown to give the viewer an insight to what Hartley originally posted (although the sexual aspects have been edited; for example, in the episode "Who Is She," a very pretty girl is seen putting on her makeup then dressing; the scene where her breasts were exposed has been noticeably edited).

Cast: Deborah Makahra (Hartley), Roy Werner (Bill), Irene Warner (Patsy), Ian Dewberry (Tray), Mandy Fisher (Lilly), Katherine Randolph (Tanya), Ted Shilowitz (Creepy John), Janet Tracy Keijser (Delores), Michael May (Ted). **Credits:** *Producer-Director:* Tim Street. **Comment:** The on-line series is produced as a tie-in with the mystery-thriller books by Tim Street (as the website says: "To get the entire story of what happened to this beautiful intelligent woman, buy the enhanced Mystery Thriller eBook Vids on the iBookstore"). How some scenes were allegedly filmed using hidden cameras may peak your curiosity but having to endure a 30 second commercial before each episode begins (running longer than some of the episodes) is the program's only drawback.

Episode List: Although all episodes are on line, they are very short and only present a very brief glimpse into the filmed subject.

1. You Have One Week (Sept. 12, 2011; 1 min., 22 sec.).

2. Six Days (Sept. 12, 2011; 6 sec.).

3. Leather Lover (Sept. 12, 2011; 1 min., 33 sec.).

4. William (Sept. 12, 2011; 45 sec.).

5. Don't Call Me (Sept. 12, 2011; 44 sec.).

6. Repo Man (Sept. 13, 2011; 20 sec.).
7. Study Hard (Sept. 13, 2011; 59 sec.).
8. Washington Monument (Sept. 13, 2011; 57 sec.).
9. Try to Stop, but You May Continue (Sept. 13, 2011; 1 min., 30 sec.).
10. I Know About Lilly (Nov. 1, 2011; 36 sec.).
11. Need More Convincing? (Nov. 2, 2011; 9 sec.).
12. Sticks and Stones (Nov. 2, 2013; 31 sec.).
13. Oriental Friends (Nov. 13, 2011; 31 sec.).
14. Who Is She (Nov. 13, 2011; 58 sec.).
15. Xmas Shopping (Nov. 14, 2011; 32 sec.).
16. Lil Boy (Nov. 17, 2011; 37 sec.).

157 *I Hate Tommy Finch.* onemorelesbian.com. 2012 (Drama).

A look at the lives of life-long friends (and lesbians), Stephanie and Alyssa, from ages 8 to 35 as they contemplate the events of their lives—from their first meeting to coming to terms with their sexuality. The program is actually a play that, during a Chicago performance, was filmed and reedited into an Internet series.

Cast: Nicole Pacent (Stephanie), Shannan Leigh Reeve (Alyssa). **Credits:** *Director:* Jessica King, Christin Mell. *Writer:* Julie Keck, Jessica King, Christin Mell. **Comment:** Five episodes were produced that basically break the play down into five acts of discussion. It is well acted with sometimes touching insights given as the women look back on their lives. There are minimal sets (as it is a filmed stage play) and the intimacy of a play is captured—even over the Internet.

Episodes: Available only through a paid subscription service. On-line, free episodes are as follows: *1.* Bosom Buddies. *2.* Birthday Wish. *3.* Teaser: Lip Gloss. *4.* Teaser: Sleepover Sneaks. *5.* Sneak Peak: Age 21 (from episode 23). *6.* A Sneak Peak of *I Hate Tommy Finch*. *7. I Hate Tommy Finch* Trailer.

158 *I Kill Monsters.* ikillmonsters.com. 2011 (Thriller).

The G&B Monster Hunting Agency is a bottom-end business run by a dysfunctional family (considered frauds by some, legitimate to others and social outcasts by a combination of both). Go, the team leader, is a seeker of fame who uses his supposedly real tales of monster slaying to build an international reputation; Emmett, is his partner, a man who speaks through a voice box (but is most often "his silent partner"); Piper is a young (20-year-old) college intern and technical wizard; and Luke is an embittered 25-year-old who joined the group to avenge the death of his father, the victim of a monster. The team operates out of the seemingly monster-ridden town of Bith County, a community that is protected by Frank Sargeant, a police chief who has set his goal to discredit Go and his misfit team (for all the chaos they cause) and return his town to normal. The team is hindered by back luck, but there are monsters to fight and the program relates their efforts to incorporate whatever is at their disposal "to save the world one monster at a time."

Cast: Alan Catlin (Go), Jenny Raven (Piper), Andre Sills (Emmett), Kyle Buchanan (Luke), Randy Thomas (Frank Sargeant), Kassandra Santos (Medusa), Terri Catlin (Raggedy Hag), Ariyena Sorani (Little Girl). **Credits:** *Producer:* Allan Magee, Neil Huber, Desmond Sargeant. *Director:* Neil Huber. *Writer:* Desmond Sargeant.

Comment: A mix of comedy, horror and thrills that has good special effects, capable acting and good production values. Some scenes are a bit dark and difficult to see and, based on the pilot it has potential for some creepy future stories.

Episodes:
1. The Pilot (11 min., 51 sec.). Establishes what the series will entail, beginning with the team's efforts to stop an old witch, posing as a beautiful Raggedy Ann doll, from luring children to her home on Halloween, their meeting Luke, who wants revenge, and their attempts to battle a snake woman (Medusa) whose look can turn people into stone.

159 *iBanker.* webserieschannel.com. 2011 (Drama).

Wall Street in New York City provides the backdrop for a look at the lives of a group of iBankers, the newly minted term for young men and women in their twenties and possessing their MBA degrees, who have called the stock market home (here as employees of the firm of Beckman-Colliers).

Cast: Anthony Gaudioso (Michael Baci), Louis Vanaria (Benny), Jo Newman (Julia Beard), Arthur Gerunda (Joseph Beckman), Giselle Rodriquez (Lina), Sterling Sulieman (Reed Armstead), Richard Koyasu Park (Darren Cho). **Credits:** *Producer:* Mark Petruzzi, Richard Scalea, Mario Dell'anno, Richard Dell'anno. *Director:* Stephen Franciosa, Jr. *Writer:* Tom Lavagnino, Mark Petruzzi. **Comment:** Wall Street has been tackled numerous times, both in comedy and drama on television and in the movies. *iBanker* updates the premise a bit by focusing on a new breed of investors with good acting and production values. The doorway is left open to provide more episodes should the producers continue with the project.

Episodes:
1. The Letter (3 min., 53 sec.). The principal characters (Michael, Julia, Lina, Benny and Darren) are introduced as each receives a letter of acceptance at Beckman-Colliers.
2. The New Arrivals (3 min., 59 sec.). The first day on the job is explored as the iBankers begin their duties.
3. The Boss (5 min., 29 sec.). A fancy dinner at

his mansion allows the head of the firm to acquaint himself with his new employees.

4. The Flip (8 min., 36 sec.). Employees Michael and Darren are profiled as they get their first taste of big business.

5. The Mole (1 min., 43 sec.). As Michael and Benny clash over their differing opinions about investments, they are unknowingly being watched by their boss.

160 *Idle Times.* idletimes.com. 2012 (Drama).

"A new-age crime drama told in a way that you have not seen before." With shades of the TV series *Dallas, Knots Landing* and more so with the daytime soap opera *The Young and the Restless, Idle Times* is actually a serial-like saga of the powerful Adonis family and the problems they face as they seek to increase that power, using sometimes questionable methods to acquire whatever they need to defeat their enemies (business rivals) and remain at the top of the business world.

Cast: J. Scott (Michael Adonis, Sr.), Omatayo Marshall (Adrian Adonis), Tavares Wilson (Michael Adonis, Jr.), David Alexander (Capt. John Ellis), Amber DeVos (Erin Page), McCartney Forde (Terry Matthews), Cory Jaccino (Vincent Moretti), Bee Moe Slim (Det. Ryan Turner), Christopher Jones (Cable), Scott McDonald (Agent Paul Reeves), Karissa Parran (Camille), Sy Sayonara (Savannah), Brett Tolliver (Paulie), Glenn Turner (Mayor William Contee), Susan D'Angelo (Sarah Cates), Marlo Gardner (Tami), Bill Pacer (Bruno Moretti), Tevon Plunkett (Tank), Ashley Wells (Kelly), Erika Weathers (Brooke Houston), Teresa Britton (Angela). **Credits:** *Producer:* Marquitta Baines, Marlo Gardner. *Writer-Director:* Tavares M. Wilson. **Comment:** The program, based on the first episode that is on line, is well written (although vulgar language is used), directed and acted. While descriptions are on line for the episodes, they are rather vague and do not give the information that is needed to present comprehensible descriptions as has been done with other programs in this book. The first episode establishes the fact that Michael Adonis, Sr. has just become a widower and that, while he mourns the loss of his wife, he and is sons, Michael, Jr. and Adrian, must put their grief aside and manipulate the acquisition of a city contract that will shift a balance of power to them.

Episode List: *1.* Destiny, Part 1. *2.* Destiny, Part 2. *3.* Motives. *4.* Chaos, Part 1. *5* Chaos, Part 2. *6.* Caution, Part 1. *7.* Caution, Part 2.

161 *If I Was Your Girl: The Web Series.* girlcrushtv.com. 2012 (Drama).

Adaptation of the feature film of the same title that focuses on the relationship between two lesbian

If I Was Your Girl: The Web Series. **Left to right: Marquita "Temper" Brooks, Toy McNeely, Alana Mike, Rondala Kelly, Dana Guest (copyright and photo by Melvin Adams, 2013).**

couples: Lynn and Stacia and Rhonda and Toi. Lynn is a successful corporate executive who sees Stacia as a sexual plaything (her "girl toy") while Stacia, fifteen years younger than Lynn, is hopelessly in love with Lynn and remains with her hoping to change the way Lynn sees and treats her. Rhonda and Stacia became friends while serving time in prison and have remained so. Rhonda is the typical butch lesbian who needs to control her lover, as she does with Toi, who to keep Rhonda as her lover, accepts the consequences. The program explores each of the women— the domineering Lynn and Rhonda and the complacent Stacia and Toi and how their lives intertwine and how, despite their differences, they are there for each other in times of need.

Cast: Dana Guest (Lynn), Marquita Temper Brooks (Stacia), Rondala Kelly (Rhonda), Alana Mike (Toi), Toy McNeely (Neena). **Credits:** *Producer:* Coquie Hughes, Jeremy Jones. *Writer-Director:* Coquie Hughes. **Comment:** The program is tailored to African-American audiences. It is one of the very best of such programs and worth watching to see how time and care can accomplish a realistic program that does not delve into depravity. There is partial nudity, sexual situations and foul language and the four leads do a good job in representing their characters.

Episodes: Only four of 10 episodes were produced. According to the producer "Production has been cancelled indefinitely for the *If I Was Your Girl* project. I apologize to our fans that we were unable to present episodes 4–9 which explains what led to the bizarre yet international presentation of episode 10. Never-the-less, thank you for your support." Episodes 1, 2 and 3 have been edited to form an 87 minute movie while the concluding episode just continues to follow incidents in the lives of the women.

162 *iKILL*. webserieschannel.com. 2012 (Thriller).

Clyde Harris is a man, falsely accused of a robbery charge, who finds an alternative to prison when he is approached by a government agent and asked to participate in a new drug experiment. If he agrees, the charges will be dropped. Clyde agrees and the program follows Clyde as the drug creates new problems and Clyde must navigate the effects the drug causes on his mind as he attempts to put his past behind him.

Cast: Chioke Jelani Clanton, Ron Kaell, Andre Matthieu, Chyenne Costanza, Mitch Costanza, Jessica Sonneborn, Phillip Jeanmarie, Jessica Roth, Dane

Welsh, Michael Coons. **Credits:** *Producer:* Nate Golon. *Writer-Director:* Andre Welsh. **Comment:** There appears to be only one episode, which has been taken off line. It is not possible to make a judgment for this program as only printed information remains.

Episodes:
1. Episode Zero: Answers Are Prison (10 min., 12 sec.). A man, framed for robbery, is offered a chance to avoid prison by participating in a governmental drug experiment.

163 *Imaginary Bitches*. imaginarybitches. com. 2008–2009 (Comedy-Drama).

Catherine is a rather mean young woman, very greedy and selfish and very demanding. Heather, called "an anxiety whore" by Catherine, is perky, rather nice but too promiscuous (she also yearns to have sex with TV's *Hannah Montana*; a.k.a. Miley Cyrus). Jennifer is as beautiful as Catherine and Heather but more of a down-to-earth girl. She is a lesbian and in love with her creator, Eden. Catherine, Heather and Jennifer all have one thing in common—they are girls created in the mind of (and can only be seen by) Eden, a beautiful, slightly self-conscious young woman who feels neglected as all her friends are in a relationship. When loneliness got the better of her, she created Catherine, Heather and Jennifer as companions, someone to talk to—but the "girls" evolved into "Imaginary Bitches" and cause Eden more problems than she had before she created them. The program relates the situations that occur—and how Eden handles them as Catherine, Heather and Jennifer become more real than imaginary to her.

Lizzie, Brooke and Connie are Eden's closest friends while Jessalyn, a friend to Eden at first, becomes more of her nemesis as stories progress (especially when it is revealed that she is a lesbian).

Imaginary Bitches. **Eden Riegel (left) and Jessalyn Gilsig (photograph by Quyen Tran; used by permission).**

Cast: Eden Riegel (Eden), Brooke Nevin (Brooke), Elizabeth Hendrickson (Lizzie), Connie Fletcher (Connie), Jessalyn Gilsig (Jessalyn), Angela Trimbur (Angela), Michael Daniel (Cassady), Megan Hollingshead (Shannon), Brittany Ishibashi (Brittany), Sam Page (Riley). **Credits:** *Director:* Andrew Miller. *Writer:* Andrew Miller, Nichole Millard, Jeffrey Poliquin, Bo Price, Kathryn Price, Sam Riegel. **Comment:** In a single word, Enjoyable. The acting, writing and production values are top rate and Eden Riegel as Eden is so natural that she makes you believe she is really talking and reacting with someone as opposed to speaking into thin air (the "bitches"). As it stands now, it would make a good transformation to a network (or cable) television series as all aspects are already in place for one to start.

Episodes:

1. It's Not Easy Making Imaginary New Friends. Following a date that Eden is anxious to tell her girlfriend about but finds no one will listen, she creates Catherine as a means by which to relate her daily happenings.

2. The Dirtier Isn't Always Better. When Eden's friend, Lizzie, doesn't invite her to a couples' party, Catherine voices her objections, calling Lizzie a terrible friend. Unable to deal with Catherine's accusations, Eden creates Heather as a means to defend Lizzie.

3. Where Were You When Eden Got Drunk and Puked All Over Me and Lizze. When Brooke, Eden's friend, discovers Eden's "friends," and fears losing her to them, she confronts them to win Eden back.

4. A New Leper in the Colony. Eden's life appears to be improving when she is invited to a single's party but encounters a real bitch—Jessalyn, her nemesis, who could put a damper on her happiness.

5. It's Totally What You Think. Eden discovers she is not the only one living with imaginary friends when Eden meets a man (Mark) with his own imaginary life.

6. Help Dr. James Help You. On Brooke's advice, Eden visits her psychiatrist, Dr. Kee (James Kee) only to discover he is more out of touch with reality than she is.

7. A Spiritual Bitch Bath. Catherine and Heather step in to help Eden see that Brittany, a spiritual guru she and Brooke trust, is a fraud.

8. Sexy Secret Santa. Catherine, Heather and Jennifer seek a way to get rid of Connie, Lizzie and Brooke when they crash their Secret Santa Party with Eden.

9. Porn Star Priest. Catherine, Jennifer and Heather find their existence threatened when Connie convinces Eden to have a priest (Charlie Kiznik) exorcise them.

10. Imaginary Bridezilla. Eden's "bitches" are delighted when Lizzie, breaking up with her boyfriend, has too much to drink and has a dream wherein she marries but sees herself as a "bridezilla."

11. Only Crazy Girls Quife. The "bitches" come to Eden's rescue when she falls for a man that just doesn't seem right for her.

12. Three Bitches Is an Imaginary Crowd, Part 1. Jennifer helps Eden create an on-line dating profile that, like Jennifer, has Eden seen as a lesbian.

13. Three Bitches Is an Imaginary Crowd, Part 2. The program concludes with Eden encountering Jessalyn's hostility when Eden meets a girl on-line and arouses Jessalyn's jealous streak.

164 Intersection. intersectionseries.com. 2009 (Drama).

Time passes quickly and a group of friends, no longer the dreamers they once were, have reached a new stage in their lives—the realization that what they hoped for 10 years ago has not happened and they must now accept who they are and what they did achieve. The program relates the incidents that affect each of the friends (listed below) and how what they hoped to achieve and what has actually become of them.

Casey, named by his parents after their favorite poem about baseball ("Casey at the Bat") is a graduate of Farmingdale State College (on Long Island in New York) and played baseball on the school's team, but never pursued that goal any further. Instead, he headed to Manhattan, acquired a job as bartender, married (and divorced) shortly after and is currently happy as he is, tending bar.

Darlene is a talented actress with the uncanny ability to empathize (step into someone else's shoes and feel what they are feeling). Unfortunately, for Darlene, her gift leaves her with emotional problems that she has not yet fully figured out how to handle. Darlene attended college in New York and appeared in a number of regional plays based on the works of such playwrights as Shakespeare, Chekov and Ibsen but never anything that is comparable to a Broadway production. Although frustrated, Darlene has vowed to remain in New York to reach the heights she knows she is capable of despite the fact that producers are not breaking down her door. She also feels, that being a lesbian, she can never find satisfaction in a relationship as her empathetic abilities make it difficult for her to be herself (she instinctively becomes involved with the emotions of whom she dates and herself becomes vulnerable).

Denton, a few years older than Cindy, teamed with her to form the underground's first music scene couple. It was the early 2000's and they appeared to be made for each other. He was quite talented and provided the support and encouragement that Cindy needed at that point in her life. But Denton felt it was time for him to start a family but knew Cindy would not give up her career to do so. After expressing his feelings to Cindy, they agreed to amicably break up. Cindy sought her own goal while Denton would later marry and begin a family. Neither regrets what happened and are still close friends.

Hal, born in the Midwest, worked as a software developer in Manhattan for 10 years before quitting what he considered a boring, dead-end job to get in on the ground floor of a start-up company.

Iris, born on Long Island, majored in psychology in college and later acquired a teaching certificate (she is now a high school history instructor). She dated Hal and has dreams of beginning a family.

Karen, a former actress and theater school graduate had a few off–Broadway roles but after 1,001 auditions Karen realized it was fruitless to continue and quit acting to acquire a non-theatrical job. She is dating an actor (Vince) and hopes to one day settle down, marry and raise a family. Although it appears, at times, that Karen regrets the decision she has made, it seems she enjoys reliving her acting career through Vince.

Lynda is a yoga instructor whose dreams of becoming a professional dancer were cut short by a debilitating injury. When her dream was shattered Lynda was at a loss as what to do next. She tried everything from waitress to cosplay (dressing up as cartoon characters at trade shows) but nothing appealed to her until she found a love of yoga—first as a student, then instructor and finally the owner of her own studio. Dating at the present is not on her agenda as she is still trying to adjust to her new life.

Megan is Cindy's older sister, a girl who, during grade school knew what was expected of her—good grades to lead to college and a good job. Megan's enthusiasm never influenced Cindy and Megan realized as they both grew up that Cindy, although talented, would never achieve the same success as her. Megan cares for Cindy and still tries to instill her values in her and knows she will succeed in convincing Cindy that life can be better (a corporate job, a family and life in suburbia) than chasing pipe dreams.

Nathaniel, born in New Hampshire, believes music is the most important thing is his life and everything else including relationships, take a back seat. Nathaniel began writing his own songs in middle school but never considered it a paying career until 10 years after working for a Wall Street firm when he realized the wheeling and dealing didn't give him the satisfaction he received from song writing. He quit his job and has now put all his energies into a music career.

Vince, a graduate of the American Academy of Dramatic Arts, is steadily employed as a commercials actor although he is also in demand as a stand-in for feature films and TV programs. Vince lives for the moment and is not ready to settle down, a life-style that cost him a three-year relationship with Karen, who wanted to begin a family and settle down.

Cast: Becca Ayers (Cindy), Cotton Wright (Darlene), Merritt Minnemeyer (Karen), Gabe Silva (Hal), Jessica Stone (Lynda), Jeffrey Lamar (Nathaniel), Jessica Henson (Iris), Joe Mihalchick (Vince), Stephen Ott (Jeff). **Credits:** *Producer:* Jonathan Betzler, Nicolas Bernardine. *Director:* Jonathan Betzler, James Minihan, Minnie Tran, Ricard Atkinson. *Writer:* Kelly Jean Fitzsimmons, Jim Cairl. **Comment:** A like-able cast in a light drama with good acting and production values. While the idea is not new (the TV series *Friends* will come to mind) *Intersection* is different in that it looks at what was hoped for as opposed to what was been achieved and how hope for something swiftly fades as one grows older.

Episodes:

1. March 4, 2009 (10 min., 45 sec.). The various cast members are introduced to viewers.

2. March 5, 2009 (12 min., 28 sec.). Explores the career choices the friends have made, including Karen and Nathaniel, who have made the most dramatic changes.

3. Thursday, March 5, 2008 (13 min., 13 sec.). Stories of past incidents are revealed as the friends meet at a bar for a get-together.

4. March 6, 2009 (12 min., 18 sec.). As Karen begins her new job, Darlene's audition doesn't quite go as well as she had hoped.

5. Monday, March 16, 2009 (12 min., 55 sec.). Darlene, as she takes a temp job, and Lynda, as she begins a new business are profiled.

6. Friday, March 27, 2009 (9 min., 19 sec.). Jeff becomes increasingly obnoxious as he and the girls accompany Cindy on an outing to meet a musician.

7. Thursday, April 2, 2009 (9 min., 27 sec.). Hal is the center of attention as he institutes some rules in his company.

8. Thursday, April 2, 2009 (11 min., 12 sec.). Cindy's life becomes a bit more complex when her sister (Megan) comes to visit.

9. Friday, April 3, 2009 (8 min., 31 sec.). Cindy and Megan's efforts to reacquaint themselves have them experiencing some mishaps when they have a bit much to drink.

10. Friday, April 3, 2009 (9 min., 44 sec.). Megan decides to return home while Jeff, seeking an apartment, finds help from Hal in looking for one.

11. Friday, April 10, 2009 (10 min., 48 sec.). Cindy finds her career on the rise when she collaborates with a fellow musician.

12. Friday, April 10, 2009 (9 min., 1 sec.). Lynda's date is explored as Jeff continued his search for an apartment.

13. Saturday, April 11, 2009 (13 min., 19 sec.). The program concludes by presenting a series of events in the lives of the friends.

165 *Into Dust.* intodust.com. 2010 (Adventure).

Janey Santiago is a teenage girl living in a small U.S. border town in West Texas. She attends Elmore High School, has a best friend (Pilar) and extraordinary abilities, powers (strength and energy discharges) she acquires by crossing her hands across her neck and concentrating on the mysterious necklace and bracelet she wears. Janey is not sure how she acquired her abilities but believes it may have been inherited from her grandfather, a shaman. The program follows Janey as she and her sidekick (as Pilar considers herself) battle evil with Janey seeking to learn the secret of her supernatural abilities.

Cast: Erin Taylor (Janey Santiago), Marie Du-Pont (Pilar Luviano), Aaron Reyes (AugustoTrueno), Kole Collins (Carlitos Santiago), Mike Vera (Oscar Martinez), Vernon Tuck (Eddie Romero), Geoff Ingram (Len Hawkins). **Credits:** *Producer:* Amy Quick Parrish, Mark Parrish. *Writer-Director:* Amy Quick Parrish. **Comment:** Intriguing program that is handled quite well. The leads (Erin Taylor and Marie DuPont) are well chosen, and form the perfect friendship between a Latina hero and her American sidekick. The production values are very good and Janey's search for her mystical roots is fascinating and leaves the program open for additional episodes to follow.

Episodes:

1. The Pilot (5 min., 51 sec.). Establishes the story line as Janey befriends Pilar at school and discovers she has special abilities.

2. Into the Desert (7 min., 39 sec.). As Pilar learns about Janey's secret abilities, Janey seeks to find a man (Augusto) who may be able to explain what has happened to her.

3. Crossing Over (7 min., 2 sec.). Janey attempts to protect her friend, Carlitos, from thugs (Oscar, Eddie, Len) who want him to join their gang.

166 *Into Girls.* intogirlswebseries.com. 2013 (Anthology).

Vignettes that depict brief incidents in the lives of women who are also lesbians.

Cast: Melanie Rothman (Alice), Christine Lee (Sam), Krystine Summers (Kayla), Emerald Sullivan (Jasmine), Nelcie Souffrant (Stephanie), Sarah Miller (Morgan), Annalisa Chamberlin (Chelsea), Sam Glovin (Alex), Jin Kim (Herself), Mackenzie Wyatt (Herself). **Credits:** *Producer:* The Fourth Wave. *Writer:* Jin Kim. **Comment:** Enjoyable, non-offensive series (for its lesbian themes) that is well acted and produced. Topics range from meeting over the Internet through Skype ("Skype Sex"), a girl revealing to her parents that she is a lesbian ("Meet the Bockers") and sex toy shopping ("Babeland").

Episodes:

1. Is This a Date? Although Sam and Tess appear to like each other, Sam begins to wonder when they go out on a date and Tess is anything but romantic.

2. The Purchase. Alex and Chelsea find that, after purchasing a sex toy, it is not right for them and must now try to figure out how to return it.

3. The Naked Roommate. Episode removed from the Internet.

4. Girlfriends. Although they have been friends for some time, Alice cannot hold back any longer and attempts to seduce her straight best girlfriend Morgan.

5. Butthole. Episode removed from the Internet.

6. Danielle. A young woman (Danielle), whose mother is not aware of her sexuality or her lesbian-themed poetry, ponders whether or not to recite one of her poems at her mother's upcoming wedding when she is asked to do so.

7. Dick. An obnoxious young man, who cannot accept lesbians, brings out the worst in Laura when she faces him and defends her sexuality.

8. Ready, Set, Go. Continues from episode four with Alice now even more determined to have Morgan as her lover.

9. Meet the Bockers. An awkward situation arises when Chelsea brings her girlfriend (Alex) home to meet her parents.

10. This Is a Date? Sam and Alice embark on their first date—then ponder what they should do.

11. Morning After. A date shared by Sam and Alice is explored.

12. Snapback. Feeling that her appearance is preventing her from finding the perfect girl, a young lesbian (Jasmine) goes a bit overboard in a make-over to increase her chances.

13. Grool. Sam and Alice embark on a second date in a sequel to episode 11.

14. Skype Sex. A text-messaging hookup unites Alice with Kayla.

15. Navigate. A recent high school graduate (Jasmine) begins questioning her sexuality and whether she still likes girls when she feels attracted to men and begins dressing more like them.

16. Babeland. Alex and Chelsea attempt to buy a sex toy at an adult store (Babeland).

17. Coming Out. Alice faces her biggest challenge—telling her parents she is a lesbian.

18. Separate Paths, Part 1. Chelsea and Alice's relationship suddenly changes when Chelsea returns from a trip to California (to New York) and tells Alice that she has been offered a good job but may reject it to be with her.

19. Separate Paths, Part 2. Chelsea and Alice ponder their future together following Chelsea's announcement.

20. Dear Alice. Explores what could be the end of Morgan and Alice's relationship when Morgan announces she is moving to L.A.

167 *Investments: The Series.* investments theseries.com. 2014 (Drama).

Jaliyah and Jay, young teen siblings orphaned after the death of their parents, find their lives changing for the worse when they are sent to a foster home. Not wanting to get stuck in the foster care system, and believing they can take care of themselves, they run away only to encounter a powerful and dangerous politician (Mr. Robby) who promises to invest in their lives if they will, in turn help him: prevent a scandal by killing his pregnant mistress, who refuses to have an abortion. With no money and no place to live, they complete the task and, as promised are cared for by Mr. Robby. As time passes, life for Jaliyah and Jay improves greatly but soon becomes a nightmare when Jay, after having too much to drink, reveals his secret past to his girlfriend Sasha and sets in motion a series of events wherein Jaliyah and Jay now fear Mr. Robby as Sasha's efforts to blackmail them will bring to light their past and expose Mr. Robby. The program relates what happens as Jaliyah and Jay are faced with a dangerous situation: what to do about Sasha (kill her?) and how to protect the life they now lead and have invested so much into.

Jaliyah, street and book smart, is a survivor but stubborn and always puts her needs second. Jay is intelligent, possesses leadership qualities but acts on impulse and is still trying to define himself. Sasha, a persistent girl, is fearless and selfish, suffers from trust issues and is an expert manipulator. Stephanie, loyal and compassionate, has an explosive temper and is always seeking acceptance by others.

Cast: Shashone Lambert (Jaliyah), Daniela Libertini (Teresa), Kaetlin Perna (Stephanie), Jarred Solomon (Jay), Anastacia Tucker (Sasha), Diquan Brown (Russell), Jenelle Valle (Mother's voice). **Credits:** *Director:* Steven Strickland. *Producer-Writer:* Shashone Lambert. **Comment:** Unusual story to say the least but well acted and produced. One of the better African-American produced programs that stray from violence and the overly abun-

dant use of vulgar language. Although the hit aspect is established (killing Sasha), the program ends unresolved at the time (July 2014).

Episodes:
1. Episode 1 (5 min., 59 sec.). Introduces Jaliyah and Jay and reveals that Jaliyah has been taking care of her brother (Jay) since the death of their parents. It is also hinted, because they live well but have no jobs, that something is not right.
2. Episode 2 (6 min., 8 sec.). Delves into the dark lives Jaliyah and Jay lead as they are revealed to be hired assassins (killing for a Mr. Robby—a man who came to their aid when their parents died).
3. Episode 3 (6 min., 21 sec.). Weary about what they are doing—but needing to protect their investments, Jaliyah and Jay ponder just how far they should go for Mr. Robby.
4. (4 min., 55 sec.). Unknown to Jaliyah and Jay, Mr. Robby is already aware of Sasha's blackmail plan and has his own agenda as what to do.

168 The Invited. vimeo.com. 2014 (Drama).

It has been five years since her mother's passing and Katie Morris has set her goal to visit the gravesite. But before she leaves, her best friend, Luke, makes a bet that she will be too frightened to call on the spirits of the cemetery to follow her home. In a surprise move, Katie takes the bet and finds her life changing when she asks—and they accept. Katie is now haunted (somewhat like Melinda Gordon on TV's *Ghost Whisperer*) wherein spirits appear to her to ask for her help in seeing the light and moving on. The program follows Katie as she finds she cannot reverse the invitation and must now become a detective of sorts to help troubled spirits move on.

Cast: Jackey Hall (Katie Morris), Justin Gardner (Luke Daniels), Tori Lee Teller (Young Katie), Paul Sieber (Terry Morris). **Credits:** *Producer:* Jackey Hall, Jonathan Moody, Nick Lakey. *Director:* Jackey Hall, Matthew Ewald, Jonathan Moody. *Writer:* Lewis Leslie, Jonathan Moody. **Comment:** Based on text and the short teaser (which only consists of text) it appears the program will be quite interesting, perhaps a combination of CBS's *Ghost Whisperer* and NBC's *Profiler* as the episodes could encompass anything from playful ghosts to vicious spirits.

Episodes: Episodes have not yet been released (as of July 2014) and only a short teaser appears.

Investments: The Series. Poster art from the series (used by permission of Shashone Lambert).

169 It's Just Business. webserieschannel.com. 2013 (Crime Drama).

Big Leo is a Mafia Boss who, to conceal his illegal activities, hits on a plan to use a funeral home as his base of operations. To make the business look legitimate, Big Leo hires a manager (Sam Magee), incorporates two gangsters (Rizzo and Billy) as workers and incorporates the services of a celebrity make-up artist (Katrina) known for her "make-overs of the deceased." To make sure everything runs smoothly, Big Leo assigns his number one man, Marcelo, to oversee operations for him. All is progressing well until a newspaper reporter (Andy) notices an excessive amount of activity at the funeral parlor. The program follows Andy as he begins an investigation to uncover what is happening, a situation that becomes complicated when he befriends and falls in love with Katrina.

Cast: Richie Noodles (Sam Magee), Tina Costello (Katrina), Joseph Scarpino (Andy), Randy Barrett (Ralph), David Bezyak (Rizzo), Damien Alaric (Marcelo), Randy Barrett (Ralph), Kyle Davis (Billy), Bob Rogers (Charlie), Tony Bunton (Antonio), Daniel Smith (Bryon Davis). **Credits:** *Producer:* Carlos Garcia Ibarra, Debra Johnson, Richie Noodles. *Director:* Carlos Garcia Ibarra. *Writer:* Debra Johnson.

Comment: Based on the four episodes that have thus far been produced, the program does show potential for intrigue as Marcelo attempts to ensure the home's secret is kept. Dialogue is a bit hard to understand at times (like the microphone is too far away) and the acting forced at times (just not realistic).

Episodes:

1. The Pilot (7 min., 21 sec.). Establishes the storyline as Sam becomes the manager of a front for illegal Mafia activities.

2. Farmers Hope Inn (8 min., 41 sec.). Billy and Rizzo meet with Marcelo at Farmers Hope Inn to do a little dirty work for Big Leo.

3. The Assignment (13 min., 51 sec.). Billy and Rizzo are on another assignment, this time on behalf of Sam, while Andy feels he may just be unto something big.

4. Diamonds (14 min., 7 sec.). A diamond transaction falls apart when the shipment is ripped off. The concluding unresolved episode.

170 Jamie's Way. jamiesway.com. 1998–2001 (Drama).

Pioneering Internet drama about a group of teenagers that attend The Greenfield School in Baltimore, Maryland. Jamie Watts, the principal student, is the daughter of Mark and Lauren, has a younger brother (Mark) and has been a student at Greenfield (a private school) for six years (she previously attended Guilford Elementary School). She and Mark are the children of divorce and live with their mother (the owner of a clothing store in Fells Point) in a row home owned by the family (their father lives in a condo about 15 minutes away).

Jamie, five feet, six inches tall with hazel eyes and brown hair, is 17 years old. English, computer science and math are her favorite subjects while singing, dancing and arm wrestling are her favorite sports (as she calls them). She considers film, fashion and web design her hobbies. Her favorite colors are baby blue and purple and she prefers Golden Grahams cereal for breakfast. Daisies are her favorite flower and she loves Chocolate Brownie Fudge ice cream (as well as Blow Pops, Snickers candy bars and Winter Fresh gum). Jamie loves the beach, "chillin' with my friends," shopping (she tends to wear Capri pants and glittery tank tops) and "chatting on the net." When it comes to movies, *Pretty Woman* is her favorite while on TV she watches *Gilmore Girls* and *The Real World*. Jamie, like most teenage girls enjoys music and has a famous Uncle—Asher Daniels, lead singer of the rock band 13-13.

Samantha Jenkins, Jamie's friend, practically grew up at the Greenfield School having attended it since nursery school. She is 16 years old and, since the seventh grade, has been a member of the Upper School Cheerleading Squad (she is now head cheerleader; her father is also the cheerleading squad coach and the Principal, Mr. Craft, is her godfather). Samantha, with her blue eyes and dark blonde hair, stands five feet, six inches tall. She likes Lucky Charms and Special K cereal, Vanilla ice cream "with lots of toppings," pink roses and Trident gum. Cheerleading, gym and lunch are her favorite subjects while dance, acting, flirting and chatting on the net are her hobbies. Samantha prefers wearing sportswear during the day "and sexy little dresses at night." *Dark Angel*, *Charmed*, *Roswell* and *Popular* are her favorite TV shows. If Samantha were to have a catch phrase, it would be "You Go, Girl!"

April Karlow previously lived in Chicago before moving to Baltimore in 1997 and has been a student at Greenfield for two years. She and Jamie became friends when they first met in class and, because each had been wearing the same outfit and looked like sisters they were called "The Twins." April has a younger sister, Kerri (age 11), a stay-at-home mother and a father (Hal) who is a computer salesman. April (born in April), is five feet, four inches tall, has brown eyes and medium brown hair. She likes roses (her favorite flower), peppermint and dark chocolate candy, Bubble Yum gum, basketball "and anything with water." Pink is her favorite color, Lucky Charms her favorite cereal and reading poetry, roller-skating and making jewelry are her hobbies. *Dawson's Creek* is her favorite TV show and *Pretty Woman* and *The Wizard of Oz* are her favorite movies. April prefers sun dresses, sandals "and anything silk" and e-mail ("Luv it! It's like getting a gift!").

Max Sweeney, a bit younger than April and Jamie, has, at 14 years of age, developed a crush on April. He is a freshman at Greenfield and is working on creating his own on-line site. He loves soccer and English and art are his favorite subjects in school.

Tyler Hanson stands six feet one inch tall has hazel eyes and light brown hair. He loves boxing and basketball and English, history, philosophy and architecture are his favorite subjects. He also has a crush on April ("But don't tell").

Toby Jones is 16 years old, loves photography and claims that he "is such a busy guy" that he has two e-mail addresses (cutetobyjones@hotmail.com and greenfieldhunk@excite.com).

Cast: Kristen Keswick (Jessie Watts), Jessica Morton (Samantha Jenkins), Danielle Faurot (April Karlow), Ezra Moses Galston (Tyler Hanson), Shepherd Stede (Max Sweeney), Matthew McClain (Toby Jones). **Credits:** *Producer-Writer-Director:* Elena Moscatt. **Comment:** Producer Elena Moscatt conceived of the idea in 1985 at a time when network television had only presented sitcom-based high school programs like *Welcome Back, Kotter* and comical dramas like *Room 222. Jamie's Way* could be considered a mix of the two with more of a dramatic focus and in the making four years before *Saved by the Bell* hit the airwaves on Saturday mornings. *Jamie's Way* is unique because it tries to present characters as real people experiencing real problems (like Jamie's parents divorcing and teenage crushes—two of the elements also covered on *Saved by the Bell*). Unfortunately for fans of *Jamie's Way* it was made for the Internet at a time when such concepts were actually experiments (like with television in the 1930s) and little was produced. Pioneers like Ms. Moscatt set the pace for what was to follow and what is now flourishing on the Internet. Based on the videos that appear on YouTube, it appears the programs were shot on VHS as the quality is not comparable to digitally-produced programs (a situation that can also be seen in the early *Star Trek* Internet TV shows as well as some of the early lesbian-themed horror programs). Ms. Moscatt has also produced *Life After Lisa* (see entry) and, although not covered here, the Internet comedy series *Chasing Brianna*.

Episodes:

1. The King of Yang. As life changes for Jamie when her mother receives the divorce papers, (destroying her hope that their parents would reconcile), she finds comfort from her instant message friend, "The King of Yang" (who has concealed his true identity from her).

2. The Autograph. Jamie receives a visit from her Aunt Emmie (the wife of rock star Asher Daniels) and Cousin Zack and finds herself seeking to impress Toby (her secret crush) by acquiring autographs of Asher and his band. Meanwhile, April tries to figure out who sent her a mysterious Valentine card—and it's not even Valentine's Day.

3. Tyler's Way. Tyler, the school prankster, seeks to ask April for a date (to the school's Spring Fling Dance) before Max beats him to the punch.

4. The Spring Fling. Focuses on the principal characters at the dance with Tyler trying to convince Jamie to get on the dance floor (while at the same time keeping on eye on April—who is dancing, well attempting to dance with the two left feet Max).

5. Aunt Victoria's Secret. A rehearsed but not produced episode that was to air in December of 2002 and bring Jamie and her friends up-to-date from the prior 2001 episode with Jamie most likely encountering new adventures as she graduates from high school. It also revolves around Toby, who is depressed (possibly losing April to Max) and her Aunt, Victoria, who has come to visit and the phone call she receives that has adverse affects when Jamie discovers who made the call and the secret her aunt has been keeping.

Note: The four produced episodes require Windows Media Player to watch. There are also two videos on YouTube:

1. Jamie's Way Ep. 4 Preview (1 min., 51 sec.).

2. Behind the Scenes of Web Drama Jamie's Way (4 min., 54 sec.).

171 John Woo Presents 7 Brothers. you tube.com. 2011 (Animated Adventure).

In 1423, before the explorations of such men as Christopher Columbus, Magellan, Cortez and Cooke, the Chinese had reached the shores of America and circum-navigated the earth. Two years prior, in 1421, the Chinese Emperor's dean sent four great treasure fleets to every country in the world. More than 800 vessels traveled for two years, mapping every mission of the treasure fleets in the cause of peace and discovery. The sailors, however, were denied their legacy when the ships returned and its crews found their homeland ravaged by pestilence and open to revolt. The situation grew from bad to worse when Chinese merchants, attempting to conduct business on foreign lands, were considered pirates and put to death. The maps and journals that had been compiled from the voyages were burned— and what treasure remained was destroyed. Ships used by the sailors were destroyed and virtually all evidence of their existence was written out of the annals of history, as if it had never taken place.

It is modern-day Los Angeles when the story begins and a mysterious woman (Rachel) has gathered seven men, each from a different ethnic background (Ronald, Daniel, Robert, Jagdish, Gabriel, Jenkins and Jack) for a special mission: recover the lost treasure of the Chinese and defeat the Son of Hell, a demon who, having failed in his quest to rule the world 600 years ago, has returned to fulfill that goal. The program charts Rachel's warriors, the 7 Brothers, as they begin a quest that could cost them their lives.

Voice Cast: Janet Caine (Rachel), Sam Brice (Ronald/Robert/Skull), Pete Daoust (Jack/Son of Hell), Michael Pearson (Baz), Eric Guman (Jagdish/Gabriel/Fong/Jenkins), Dave Simmons (Narrator), Jack Porter (Daniel/Muhammed/Xia). **Credits:** *Producer:* John Woo, Terence Chang, Lori Tilkin.

Animation Producer-Director: Jeremiah Strackbein. *Writer:* Desiree Akhavan, Ingrid Jungermann, Tavet Gillson. **Comment:** An animated project, created by filmmaker John Woo that is fast-moving and well written. The voice actors are perfect for their roles but there is an extraordinary amount of vulgar language, something that was really not needed to present the story. There are no parental warnings and the program is well worth watching for a unique good vs. evil overtones.

Episodes:

1. That's What's Gonna Save the World (6 min., 4 sec.). Explores the world of China 600 years ago and presents a look at some of the future Brothers.

2. And Then There Were 7 (6 min., 24 sec.). Rachel unites the 7 Brothers for a special mission as past incidents in the lives of the men are seen.

3. Enter the Son of Hell (6 min., 55 sec.). Rachel, who has promised each of the Brothers $100,000, explains her reasons for hiring them and that their enemy is an evil sorcerer who chose the name the Son of Hell.

4. Believes and Badass MF'ers (6 min., 36 sec.). With their mission established, the Brothers prepare to uncover the clues necessary to find the treasure and defeat the Son of Hell.

5. Chopsticks (6 min., 35 sec.). As the Brothers begin their uncertain quest by entering a strange cave, the Son of Hell incorporates an ancient assassin known as Zheng to stop them.

6. Hell Is Cold (6 min., 36 sec.). While exploring the cave, the Brothers encounter the Son of Hell.

7. You Almost Killed a Ninja for Me (6 min., 33 sec.). The Brothers face not only the wrath of the Son of Hell, but Zheng.

8. Dragon Lines (6 min., 58 sec.). It is learned that the Son of Hell needs to connect ancient dragon lines around the world to uncover the lost gold and achieve his goal.

9. Seven Coffins (6 min., 43 sec.). A battle to defeat Zheng fails as the Brothers are killed and sent to Hell.

10. Face Off (6 min., 42 sec.). Ronald sees the ghost of an ancient ancestor (Fong) who assisted the Son of Hell 600 years ago and explains that the Son of Hell can be defeated.

11. The Dead Must Rise (6 min., 42 sec.). With Fong's help, the Brothers are returned to life on Earth to complete their mission.

12. Hell on Earth (6 min., 47 sec.). Now, back in the cave, the Brothers must join forces and use their abilities to defeat the Son of Hell.

13. Dragonfire (6 min., 59 sec.). The concluding episode finds the Brothers facing the Son of Hell in a final battle to determine the fate of the world.

172 *Johnny Dynamo.* johnnydynamo.com. 2013 (Drama).

In the world of 1980s television there was a series far superior to *Mike Hammer* and *Magnum, P.I.* called *Johnny Dynamo.* Johnny, played by Robert Pierce Mitchell, was a tough, dedicated New York police department detective whose portrayal of a cop was so realistic that it earned him many awards until a failed publicity stunt ruined his career and soon afterward led to the show's cancellation and *Johnny Dynamo* and its star quickly became a thing of the past. It is now 25 years later and Robert has been living a rather unassuming, quiet life in Nashville with his wife (Sandy) and daughter (Hailee). He has been out of the spotlight and away from television until a tabloid TV series (*Hollywood Hotline*) puts him in the spotlight on a "Where Are They Now" segment. While thinking nothing of it, other than letting his fans know that he is still alive, it brings unsuspected results when three entertainment upstarts (Ira Stein, Jack Meredith and Hannah Motlow) persuade him to do a movie (*Dead No More*) and re-ignite his career. The program charts Robert's experiences as he attempts to make a comeback.

Cast: Rick Wells (Robert Pierce Mitchell), Sarah Shoemaker (Hannah Motlow), Jennifer Shelton (Sandy Mitchell), Hailee Ricci (Hailee Mitchell), Jonathan Everett (Jack Meredith), Danil Mark Collins (Ira Stein), Bethany Sharp (Carol Adams), Dennis Mareno (George Laksey), Buddy Farler (Mayor Stone). **Credits:** *Producer-Director:* Joe Thomas. *Writer:* Joe Thomas, Dennis Mareno. **Comment:** Plays like a regular TV series with good acting and production values.

Episodes:

1. Happy Anniversary. *Hollywood Hotline*'s story on Robert brings him into the spotlight once again.

2. Say Goodbye to RPM. Robert meets with the three producers whose plan is to get his name back in the press via a "hot, new film" (unfortunately, they haven't figured out what the movie is).

3. Ok, I'm Back. The producers come up with a part of a plan: get newspapers to print photos of Robert attending a cocktail party hosted by Mayor Buddy Stone.

4. Laskey, Cometh. At the party, Robert confronts producer George Laskey, the man he claims stole his career.

5. Dead No More. A well-placed newspaper article appears to be putting Robert's career back on track ("George Laskey in talks with Johnny Dynamo about a new movie").

6. The Empty Café. As Robert begins to gain recognition, George is rather upset about the newspaper article and plans to swiftly squash Robert's career.

7. Johnny, We Have a Problem. The producers find they have a problem: they must tell Robert that the movie rumors about *Dead No More* are false.

8. Bring a Muffin to Work Day. Having encountered the wrath of Laskey, the producers must either deny the story or state that it is fact.

9. Just Say Yes. The season finale wherein Robert

admits there is no movie deal and Robert's future uncertain.

173 *Just Us Guys.* webserieschannel.com. 2013 (Comedy-Drama).

Explores the sometimes difficult relationship between a gay father (Scott) and his straight, 15-year-old son (Max) and how they try to maintain a best friend relationship.

Cast: Daniel Marks, Jr. (Scott), Matthew Boehm (Max), Claudia Dibbs (Amy), Phylicia Goings (Elsie), Charlie Smith (Sean), Todd Carlton Lanker (Gary), Daniel MK Cohen (Gary), Ryan Stout (Himself). **Credits:** *Producer-Writer:* Chris Lilly. *Director:* Tony Oliver. **Comment:** Although billed as a drama, it has moments of comedy and is well acted and produced. The series could be considered complete as is but because of the premise additional episodes could continue to relate the mishaps encountered by Scott and Max.

Episodes:

1. Call Me, Maybe (5 min., 35 sec.). Scott, who owns a comic book store, and Max, who works for him, try to bond their relationship by attending a Comic-Con convention.

2. The New Girl (5 min., 8 sec.). Scott finds he has a new worker when a former customer, Elsie, returns as an employee. She was nasty and obnoxious as a customer and hasn't changed.

3. Are You a Geek or a Nerd? (4 min., 19 sec.). Viewers are enlightened to the difference between a geek and a nerd during a conversation between Max and Scott.

4. Where the Bartender Knows Your Name (3 min., 57 sec.). Dylan, Scott's friend, the owner of Dylan's Bar, surprises Scott by booking his favorite comedian, Ryan Stout.

Note: There is also a two-part episode (labeled 5 and 6 and titled "The Panel, Part 1" [14 min., 19 sec.] and "The Panel, Part 2" [14 min., 57 sec.]) that presents interviews and a question-and-answer session with the cast and crew that was filmed at the Los Angeles Premiere Screening on February 26, 2013. J.P. Karliak moderates.

174 *Justice: The Series.* webserieschannel.com. 2012 (Crime Drama).

Marc Justice is a detective with the N.Y.P.D. He is happily married (to Candice) and enjoys his job—especially when he can collar criminals, even when he is off duty. Some criminals, however, find Justice a threat and seek to get even. One apparently does by killing Candice in her home—but was it a felon out for revenge or was it someone she knew as there was no indication of forced entry and there were signs that she put up a struggle. Marc, now bitter and out for revenge, begins a quest to find those responsible. He turns in his badge (feeling he cannot "go by the rules") and the program charts Marc's investigation—as he turns to his partner (Rosa) for comfort and becomes involved with drugs and the music industry (which may hold the key he is seeking).

Cast: Damian Bailey (Marc Justice), Ellen Domingos (Rosa), Krystal Farris (Candice Justice), Dayla Perkins, Okema Moore (Jade), Thyais Walsh (Lt. Calabrese), Dayla Perkins (Kara), Toni Robinson-May (Alicia). **Credits:** *Producer:* Craig T. Williams. *Director:* Rosalyn Coleman Williams. *Writer:* Damian Bailey. **Comment:** African-American themed cop drama that is well acted and produced. While the revenge aspect has been done countless times before, it plays well here with likeable leads. The first scene with Ellen Domingos as Rosa was most likely designed to capture attention—attired in a slinky red dress (with her badge pinned to her dress) as she covers the murder scene.

Episodes:

1. Desire Brings Ruin (8 min., 7 sec.). Establishes the premise as Marc seeks to avenge the death of his wife.

2. Do Justice No Harm (6 min., 3 sec.). Marc begins his investigation with clues indicating that the killers are linked to the Manhattan record industry.

3. Justice Mourning (5 min., 6 sec.). Although he has suffered a great loss, Marc finds comfort from Rosa, his partner.

175 *Justin America.* youtube.com. 2013 (Western).

Shades of the ABC TV series *Alias Smith and Jones* as a wanted outlaw (Justin) seeks to give up his life of crime, go straight "and earn an honest dollar." Trouble is, his gang (Audry [a girl], Max and Tanner) do not want that to happen and hope he will return to his nefarious ways once he sees that right is not right for him. It appears to be working for Justin. Although he is stripped of all his belongings, including his guns and boots, and set to go his own way, Audry shoots Justin as he walks away. She convinces Max and Tanner to leave. As they ride off, Justin is seen getting to his feet. Did Audry miss him on purpose to save him from Max and Tanner and allow him a chance to become honest? As the pilot film ends, Justin begins his trek to an unknown destination.

Cast: Myko Oliver (Justin), Samantha Colburn (Audry), Mark Jeffrey Miller (Max), Aaron Lyons (Tanner). **Credits:** *Producer:* Jared Isham, John Schimke, Paul Kraf, Preston Zietewey. *Writer-Director:* Jared Isham, John Schimke. **Comment:** Internet Westerns are rare (see also: *Heathens, Sundown* and *Thurston*) and the few that are produced are well done. Although the going straight aspect has been done before (also on TV series like *Johnny Ringo, Have Gun—Will Travel* and *Hotel DeParee*), *Justin America* is the first Internet series to tackle the subject. It is well acted and produced.

Episodes:

1. Parting Ways (6 min., 10 sec.). Establishes the series premise as described above.

176 *Kate Modern.* youtube.com. 2007–2008 (Drama).

A sister series to *Lonely Girl 15* that is set in East London, England, and tells the story of Genevieve Strathcorran, called Kate, a young artist and video blogger who, like Bree from the original series, possesses the abnormal blood type Trait Positive and is being sought by The Order, a mysterious, world-wide cult that requires such blood for its sacrifices (they are opposed by an organization called the Hymn of None). Unlike Bree, who resisted The Order, Kate is drawn in and eventually loses her life when she tries to escape but fails.

Other Characters: Charlie, Kate's best friend, a girl from Australia; Gavin, Charlie's romantic interest; Tariq, Kate's ex-boyfriend (he and Gavin own GT&T, a software company) is a member of the Hymn of None who realizes The Order exists after Kate's death; Julia, a high-ranking Hymn of None member; Lee, the intern at GT&T who joins the effort to find Kate's killers; Matthew, a vicious member of The Order; and Lauren, a girl who joins the K-Team to avenge the death of her sister (who was Trait Positive). *Season 1* (2007) establishes the premise and follows Kate as she blogs about her life and what has been happening since it was learned she possesses the rare blood type. The concluding episode of the season finds Kate being killed and opens the doorway for a second season. *Season 2* (2008). Kate's friends are now seeking to find her killers (as the K-Team) and save other girls who possess the same blood type. See also *Lonely Girl 15*, *Lonely Girl 15: The Last*, *Lonely Girl 15: Outbreak*, *Lonely Girl 15: The Resistance* and *NIckola*.

Cast: Alexandra Weaver (Genevieve "Kate" Strathcorran), Tara Rushton (Charlie), Ralf Little (Gavin Taylore), Jai Rajani (Tariq Bhartti), Giles Alderson (Steve Roberts), Lucinda Rhodes Flaherty (Julie Cowan), Sam Donovan (Lee Phillips), Matthew Gammie (Terrence), Emma Pollard (Lauren). **Credits:** *Producer:* Miles Beckett, Greg Goodfried, Joanna Shields, Amanda Goodfried, Kelly Brett, Pete Gibbons. *Director:* Miles Beckett, Gavin Rowe, Luke Taylor. **Comment:** Well done program, produced in England that captures the ambiance of the original series as it establishes its own battle against The Order. The title is a pun based on "Tate Modern," the famous London art museum.

Episodes: (a title and time listing of remaining on-line episodes as of July 2014).

1. Fight and Flight (37 sec.).
2. I Like Pigeons (1 min., 11 sec.).
3. A Room with a View (39 sec.).
4. A Friendly Lie (2 min., 25 sec.).
5. Spiders (1 min., 56 sec.).
6. Who Would Live in a Room Like This? (2 min., 42 sec.).
7. Welcome to the Roof (1 min., 47 sec.).
8. Derrida (2 min., 21 sec.).
9. Awful Dream (56 sec.).
10. Coming Up Roses (2 min., 19 sec.).
11. Money in the Bank (1 min., 48 sec.).
12. Sangas (1 min., 32 sec.).
13. Lovers Quarrel (1 min., 43 sec.).
14. I Can't Remember Anything (51 sec.).
15. A New Friend (43 sec.).
16. Charlie's Workout (1 min., 41 sec.).
17. A Friend Indeed (1 min., 20 sec.).
18. Office Space (2 min., 16 sec.).
19. Charlie's Party (3 min., 31 sec.).
20. Tariq Attack (2 min., 6 sec.).
21. Free Will (2 min., 14 sec.).
22. Walk of Shame (2 min., 16 sec.).
23. A Message from Me (31 sec.).
24. Bird Watching (2 min., 19 sec.).
25. Trait Positive (2 min., 40 sec.).
26. I Have to Go (49 sec.).
27. Salty or Sweet (1 min., 27 sec.).
28. Dizzy Rascals (35 sec.).
29. Creep or Unique (1 min., 2 sec.).
30. Carnaby Street, Saturday 18 August, 10 A.M. (4 min., 26 sec.).
31. Office Romance (1 min., 3 sec.).
32. Once Upon a Time (2 min., 4 sec.).
33. Hero for Hire (2 min., 15 sec.).
34. I Know Hallam Foe! (1 min., 17 sec.).
35. Ding Dong (1 min., 56 sec.).
36. The Prisoner (2 min., 32 sec.).
37. Explain Yourself (3 min., 21 sec.).
38. Forgiveness Prevails? (53 sec.).
39. The Rescue (31 sec.).
40. The Story So Far... (2 min., 11 sec.).
41. Gavin Steps Up (3 min., 30 sec.).
42. Ultimatum (3 min., 19 sec.).
43. A Day in the Life (2 min., 58 sec.).
44. Disturbia (2 min., 30 sec.).
45. False Alarm (1 min., 23 sec.)
46. Dot, Dot, Dot (30 sec.).
47. There Goes the Neighborhood (1 min., 46 sec.)
48. Girls Are from Venus (58 sec.).
49. Keep Your Socks On (2 min., 32 sec.).
50. Who Watches the Watcher? (2 min., 20 sec.).
51. Girl Power (1 min., 33 sec.).
52. The End (1 min., 35 sec.).
53. Tell Kim I Love Her (3 min., 25 sec.).
54. Dr. Weirdo (3 min., 43 sec.).
55. Super Kate (1 min., 30 sec.).
56. Desperately Seeking Shia (1 min., 20 sec.).
57. Somebody Do Something (2 min., 26 sec.).
58. Saved By LaBeouf (3 min., 15 sec.).
59. Pest Control (2 min., 41 sec.).
60. The Bald Guy (2 min., 41 sec.).
61. A Close Shave (2 min., 6 sec.).
62. Dream Lover (1 min., 34 sec.).

63. Dudley Did It (1 min., 25 sec.).
64. The Gallery—6 P.M., 22 September 2007 (4 min., 3 sec.).
65. Pack Up Your Troubles (2 min., 12 sec.).
66. Devon Days (2 min., 44 sec.).
67. Orange Wednesday (2 min., 59 sec.).
68. The Days—Evil Girls (1 min., 43 sec.).
69. Moving On (2 min., 17 sec.).
70. Goodbye Devon (2 min., 54 sec.).
71. Why? (3 min., 41 sec.).
72. A Quiet Night Out (1 min., 30 sec.).
73. Hymn of None (2 min., 27 sec.).
74. Somewhere Only We Know (1 min., 59 sec.).
75. Cooking with Tariq (3 min., 25 sec.).
76. Enter the Order (2 min., 52 sec.).
77. Fever Pitch (2 min., 50 sec.).
78. Bless You (4 min., 5 sec.).
79. Hear My Song (2 min., 20 sec.).
80. Escapism (1 min., 56 sec.).
81. Starry, Starry Night (2 min., 30 sec.).
82. No Turning Back (3 min., 30 sec.).
83. Van Sandwich (2 min., 30 sec.).
84. Sabotage (1 min., 49 sec.).
85. What the Hell?! (1 min., 45 sec.).
86. My Last Report (1 min., 31 sec.).
87. Out of the Frying Pan (2 min., 13 sec.).
88. The Message (2 min., 13 sec.).
89. Kate Returns (2 min., 30 sec.).
90. Birthday Surprise (4 min., 8 sec.).
91. Trait Negative (1 min., 37 sec.).
92. Act Positive (2 min., 49 sec.).
93. Genevieve (1 min., 50 sec.).
94. Creepy (4 min., 11 sec.).
95. Losing My Religion (2 min., 3 sec.).
96. Anything Can Happen on Halloween! (2 min., 8 sec.).
97. The Last Chance (1 min., 8 sec.).
98. The Viral (3 min., 7 sec.).
99. Abstract Heart (2 min.).
100. Flat Mate (3 min., 28 sec.).
101. Big Boys (2 min., 24 sec.).
102. The Big Day (2 min., 35 sec.).
103. Subservient Lee (2 min., 40 sec.).
104. The Leak (3 min.).
105. Pissed (1 min., 49 sec.).
106. Hung Over (1 min., 45 sec.).
107. The One That Got Away (3 min., 4 sec.).
108. Terrence (2 min., 35 sec.).
109. Let the Games Begin (1 min., 15 sec.).
110. Pass the Port (2 min., 15 sec.).
111. Return of the Days (1 min., 41 sec.).
112. Before the Clock Strikes Six. (53 sec.).
113. Parliament Square—6 P.M., 19 November 2007 (2 min., 20 sec.).
114. Thirteen and a Half (1 min., 32 sec.).
115. Waterloo Station—6 P.M., 20 November 2007 (5 min.).
116. All the World's a Stage (51 sec.).
117. Waterloo Station—6 P.M. 21 November 2007 (3 min., 49 sec.).
118. You're Almost There! (1 min., 14 sec.).
119. St. Paul's Cathedral—6 P.M. 22 November 2007 (4 min., 11 sec.).
120. One More Chance (1 min., 8 sec.).
121. Seven Dials—5 P.M. 23 November 2007 (4 min., 49 sec.).
122. Sinking In (2 min., 49 sec.).
123. Commitment (2 min., 32 sec.).
124. The List (3 min., 18 sec.).
125. Overtime (1 min., 26 sec.).
126. Operation Doorstep (3 min., 7 sec.).
127. The Confession (5 min., 19 sec.).
128. The Trains (1 min., 45 sec.).
129. From Above (2 min., 22 sec.).
130. I'm Not a Lonely Girl ... Am I? (2 min., 52 sec.).
131. Janet (2 min., 4 sec.)
132. Charlie and the Seven Snorks (1 min., 48 sec.).
133. Deal with the Devil (4 min., 1 sec.).
134. You Stink (44 sec.).
135. Smells Like Xmas Spirit (3 min., 15 sec.).
136. Help Me Get Charlie (3 min., 41 sec.).
137. The Last Time (1 min., 10 sec.).
138. The Sleepover (1 min., 53 sec.).
139. Grabbed by the Bells (3 min., 45 sec.).
140. The Mystery Texter (2 min., 2 sec.).
141. Coming Home for Xmas (4 min., 32 sec.).
142. The Ice Man (2 min., 48 sec.).
143. War Is Over (6 min., 9 sec.).
144. Frozen Friendship (4 min., 20 sec.).
145. Kate Come Home (1 min., 34 sec.).
146. Homeless (4 min., 20 sec.).
147. Kate Positive (1 min., 25 sec.).
148. Good Grief Charlie (2 min., 27 sec.).
149. I Did It! (1 min., 40 sec.).
150. St. Kilda Beach (4 min., 4 sec.).
151. Happy New Year? (2 min.).
152. Down Under (1 min., 32 sec.).
153. Resolution (3 min., 11 sec.).
154. Kate Modern Season One Recap (2 min., 10 sec.).
155. Back to Brick Lane (2 min., 3 sec.).
156. Trouble on Brick Lane (1 min., 48 sec.).
157. I Miss You (2 min., 54 sec.).
158. HoO, What, When, Where How? (3 min., 41 sec.).
159. Prime Suspect (1 min., 28 sec.).
160. East London (4 min., 17 sec.).
161. 33 Days Till Launch!! (3 min., 2 sec.).
162. It's Hymn! (2 min., 50 sec.).
163. Internet Celebrity Revealed (1 min., 26 sec.).
164. Flowers (3 min., 48 sec.).
165. Kate's Memorial Service (7 min., 7 sec.).
166. Help, I Need Somebody (3 min., 35 sec.).
167. Man on a Mission (2 min., 8 sec.).
168. What Does Patricia Know? (1 min., 34 sec.).
169. Don't Bring the Goos (2 min., 24 sec.).
170. Enter the FTO (3 min., 21 sec.).

171. Back to Business (4 min., 20 sec.).
172. Self-Help Section (2 min., 20 sec.).
173. Mates (2 min., 59 sec.).
174. Julia Incredible (1 min., 45 sec.).
175. Drive Goo (1 min., 19 sec.).
176. Arma-goo-den (3 min., 57 sec.).
177. 2008 Will Not Suck (4 min., 25 sec.).
178. On the Job (1 min., 49 sec.).
179. Here Aygo! (2 min., 41 sec.).
180. Boobcast (2 min., 37 sec.).
181. Rupert (4 min., 45 sec.).
182. Sausage Sangas (2 min., 33 sec.).
183. Group Hug (2 min., 32 sec.).
184. Scene of the Crime (2 min., 9 sec.).
185. Stiff Upper Lip (4 min., 39 sec.).
186. Who Are the FTO? (5 min., 48 sec.).
187. The Road to Manchester (3 min., 28 sec.).
188. Mini Bah (2 min., 48 sec.)
189. Nuts and Needles (4 min., 4 sec.).
190. Night Terrors (1 min., 38 sec.).
191. Touch the Toyota (2 min., 10 sec.).
192. Her Alibi (5 min., 22 sec.).
193. You Gotta Go (3 min., 39 sec.).
194. Terry (3 min., 35 sec.).
195. WC One (4 min., 23 sec.).
196. Temper, Temper (2 min., 39 sec.).
197. Scouting for Boys (9 min., 35 sec.).
198. The Ex-Factor (2 min., 39 sec.).
199. Credible (2 min., 29 sec.).
200. Office Chaos (3 min., 10 sec.).
201. Brighton Beach (6 min., 52 sec.).
202. Season 2 Week 9 Recap (6 min., 52 sec.).
203. Who Killed? (9 min., 58 sec.).
204. Can You Keep a Secret? (4 min., 49 sec.).
205. Merry-Go-Round (59 sec.).
206. Half the Week Away (2 min., 1 sec.).
207. The Easter Party (2 min., 26 sec.).
208. Lauren (5 min., 6 sec.).
209. Season 2 Week 10 Recap (3 min., 13 sec.).
210. Door Stepping (9 min., 55 sec.).
211. Batwoman (3 min., 57 sec.).
212. Bust Incredible (2 min., 28 sec.).
213. The Weekend Starts Here? (6 min., 37 sec.).
214. Season 2 Week 11 Recap (4 min., 13 sec.).
215. Let My Sister Go (9 min., 59 sec.).
216. Message to Lauren (1 min., 17 sec.).
217. A Call from Kate (1 min., 3 sec.).
218. The Killer Is Dead (21 sec.).
219. Season 2 Week 12 Recap (3 min., 14 sec.).
220. Precious Blood: 11:00 A.M. (6 min., 25 sec.).
221. Precious Blood: 12:00 P.M. (4 min., 8 sec.).
222. Precious Blood: 1:00 P.M. (2 min., 3 sec.).
223. Precious Blood: 2:00 P.M. (3 min., 18 sec.).
224. Precious Blood: 3:00 P.M. (3 min., 12 sec.).
225. Precious Blood: 4:00 P.M. (3 min., 18 sec.).
226. Precious Blood: 5:00 P.M. (6 min., 53 sec.).
227. Precious Blood: 7:00 P.M. (7 min., 14 sec.).
228. Precious Blood: 8:00 P.M. (3 min., 32 sec.).
229. Precious Blood: 9:00 P.M. (3 min., 17 sec.).
230. Precious Blood: 10:00 P.M. (2 min., 14 sec.).
231. Precious Blood: 10:30 P.M. (6 min., 11 sec.).
232. The Day of the Eternal Song (29 sec.).
233. The Drugs Do Work (6 min., 32 sec.).
234. Happy Food (3 min., 24 sec.).
235. Infested (5 min., 6 sec.).
236. Mrs. Van Helden? (3 min., 57 sec.).
237. Voicemail (3 min., 19 sec.).
238. Bang Out Order (2 min., 42 sec.).
239. Call to Arms (2 min., 17 sec.).
240. Lord Carruthers (2 min., 7 sec.).
241. My Couch, My Rules (1 min., 13 sec.).
242. L.A. to London (2 min., 15 sec.).
243. Hunting the Elder (6 min., 19 sec.).
244. Special Relationship (1 min., 39 sec.).
245. Raise the Roof (6 min., 16 sec.).
246. What Is She Saying? (5 min., 42 sec.).
247. Outta Here (3 min., 28 sec.).
248. Season 2 Week 15 Recap (4 min., 49 sec.).
249. Crazy Border Crossing!! (9 min., 55 sec.).
250. Hot Tacos (2 min., 26 sec.).
251. Computer Penetration (3 min., 48 sec.).
252. Politics Gone Wild! (3 min., 40 sec.).
253. Alone in the Woods (7 min., 12 sec.).
254. Season 2 Week 16 Recap (3 min., 41 sec.).
255. The Celestial Network (9 min., 52 sec.).
256. Connect with This! (3 min., 51 sec.).
257. Primrose Hill (2 min., 16 sec.).
258. Lee for Hire (2 min., 34 sec.).
259. Hey Jerk, You Work (2 min., 15 sec.).
260. The Dinner Party (3 min., 2 sec.).
261. Very Important Lee (5 min., 27 sec.).
262. Season 2 Week 17 Recap (7 min., 39 sec.).
263. The Invitation (10 min.).
264. The Wedding Video (3 min., 22 sec.).
265. Peace of Work (1 min., 18 sec.).
266. Sex, Drugs and on the Dole (1 min., 14 sec.).
267. The Hen Night (1 min., 57 sec.).
268. Julia & Rupert (9 min., 51 sec.).
269. Season 2 Week 18 Recap (11 min., 37 sec.).
270. I Know (9 min., 47 sec.).
271. Fictionality (1 min., 41 sec.).
272. Straight to the Top (4 min., 58 sec.).
273. The Naked Truth (5 min., 1 sec.).
274. Back on Brick Lane (5 min., 57 sec.)
275. Season 2 Week 19 Recap (2 min., 57 sec.).
276. Skittle Yourself (10 min., 3 sec.).
277. Bump in the Night (3 min., 11 sec.).
278. Five's a Crowd (5 min., 25 sec.).
279. Didn't They Do Well! (3 min., 21 sec.).
280. Honeymoon Blues (1 min., 57 sec.).
281. Season 2 Week 20 Recap (1 min., 24 sec.).
282. Speaker's Corner (9 min., 9 sec.).
283. Coconuts (5 min., 51 sec.).
284. Celestial Not-work (1 min., 10 sec.).
285. Golf Day Out (2 min., 57 sec.).
286. The Day She Died (8 min., 16 sec.).
287. Season 2 Week 21 Recap (4 min., 4 sec.).
288. Phillips (2 min., 50 sec.).
289. Answers (2 min., 21 sec.).

290. Much, Much Worse (2 min., 21 sec.).
291. Season 2 Week 22 Recap (6 min., 12 sec.).
292. Orivwa (10 min., 57 sec.).
293. Her Indoors (56 sec.).
294. Rupert's Dead (4 min., 59 sec.).
295. Disconnect with Me (2 min., 12 sec.).
296. Love on the 436 (4 min., 38 sec.).
297. Season 2 Week 23 Recap (4 min., 3 sec.).
298. Tour de France (12 min., 33 sec.).
299. Operation: Rescue Jools (5 min., 49 sec.).
300. The Morning After (8 min., 41 sec.).
301. Ga Ga (3 min., 50 sec.).
302. Charlie Is Innocent (2 min., 6 sec.).
303. You've Been Framed (1 min., 37 sec.).
304. Pointing Fingers (1 min., 46 sec.).
305. Whodunit? (2 min., 31 sec.).
306. Name the Traitor (6 min., 20 sec.).
307. The Traitor Revealed (3 min., 50 sec.).
308. Season 2 Week 24 Recap (2 min., 59 sec.).
309. Message from Grinstead (Extended Episode: 28 min., 26 sec.).
310. The Last Work: 12:00 P.M. (45 sec.).
311. The Last Work: 1:00 P.M. (9 min., 22 sec.).
312. The Last Work: 2:00 P.M. (2 min., 47 sec.).
313. Live Chat: 2:00 P.M. (1 min., 21 sec.).
314. The Last Work: 3:00 P.M. (6 min., 49 sec.).
315. The Last Work: 4:00 P.M. (3 min., 47 sec.).
316. Live Chat: 4:00 P.M. (4 min., 59 sec.).
317. The Last Work: 5:00 P.M. (2 min., 39 sec.).
318. The Last Work: 6:00 P.M. (1 min., 58 sec.).
319. The Last Work: 7:00 P.M. (3 min., 32 sec.).
320. The Last Work: 8:00 P.M. (1 min., 10 sec.).
321. Live Chat: 8:00 P.M. (10 min., 34 sec.).
322. Live Chat: 9:00 P.M. (9 min., 3 sec.).
323. The Last Work: 10:00 P.M. (2 min., 17 sec.).
324. The Last Work: 11:00 P.M. (7 min., 57 sec.).
325. Live Chat: 11:00 P.M. (3 min., 33 sec.).
326. The Last Work: 12:00 A.M. (6 min., 27 sec.).

177 Kelsey. *blip.tv.* 2013 (Comedy-Drama).

Kelsey is a young woman looking for romance with another woman. She is pretty although she has a tendency to point out her faults (like her weird sense of humor) and feels, that after her current breakup, there is no way she can feel whole again—that is, until she hits on the notion of making herself whole again by forgetting the past and dating new prospects. Being a lesbian and being a bit off-the-wall does make for a challenging situation but Kelsey, who is also quite talkative, finds help from her friends Samantha, Tyrone and Rowan and stories relate the drama, chaos and mishaps that occur as Kelsey seeks the right woman for herself.

Cast: Nichole Yannetty (Kelsey Steeler), Sharina Martin (Samantha), Lauren A. Kennedy (Joanne), Brennan Taylor (Rowan), Daniel K. Issac (Tyrone), Richard Bird (Leroy), Christian Cartell (Kate). **Credits:** *Producer:* Christina Raia, Kelsey Rauber.

Director: Christina Raia. *Writer:* Kelsey Rauber. **Comment:** Subtle drama mixes with comedy to detail the efforts of a slightly awkward woman as she seeks romance. Nicely acted and well produced and worth checking out for a different approach in a lesbian-themed web series.
Episodes:
1. Palette Cleanser. The bubbly Kelsey is introduced in a rather unflattering manner: seen with a bruised lip after being dumped not so tenderly by an ex-girlfriend (Shane).
2. Don't Hit Send. Feeling that the Internet may be the place to find a mate, Kelsey also finds that she is rather uninformed when it comes to computer dating.
3. www.dating? Kelsey faces a drawback when she learns that Shane has moved on and is now seeking romance with another woman.
4. Shopping in Groups. Kelsey seeks the help of a friend (Joanne) to help her write an on-line dating profile.
5. A Best Friend's Birthday. Kelsey's habit of relentlessly rambling is explored after she acquires a computer date.
6. U-Haul-er. Kelsey confides in her friend (Tyrone) about her computer date and how it never turned into a one-night stand.
7. Hanging Out Without. Kelsey discovers that her best friends are having a secret affair.
8. Bluffing. A poker party thrown by Kelsey reveals incidents in the lives of Kelsey and her friends.
9. Drive Through. A ride in Tyrone's new car turns out to be anything but pleasurable when Kelsey and her friends become cramped for space.
10. Making Things Work. The concluding episode finds Kelsey, now in a relationship with Joanne, discussing events of the past few months.

178 Kiss Her I'm Famous. kissherimfamous.com. 2013–2014 (Comedy-Drama).

A sex tape involving a married senator and his mistress is uncovered by the tabloid television program *Now* and exposed on the air. As Mandy and Jen, two best friends watch the program, they see that the mistress (Sophie Benoit) has become famous, rich and given her own reality television series. Hoping to change their dreary lives, Jen hits on a plan to become rich and famous by creating their own fake sex tape and leaking it to the media. The program relates their efforts to create a sex tape and become famous.
Cast: Tracy Ryerson (Mandy), Ilea Matthews (Jen), Ellyn Daniels (Irene Wasserman), Fawzia Mirza (Kam Kardashian), Omar Elba (Santa), Kevin Kieta (Tom), Ashley Mitchell (Sophie Benoit), Noureen DeWulf (Hannah), Corey Jackson (Joe). **Credits:** *Producer:* Rolla Selbak, Reena Dutt, Whit Spurgeon, Richard Martinez. *Writer-Director:* Rolla Selbak. **Comment:** Enjoyable program with two very attractive and like-able leads. The acting is very

good and the production values comparable to most TV series. While there are brief sexual situations in the free episodes, sharing site YouTube has restricted episode 4 ("The Audition") to persons over 18 years of age (e-mail address needed to watch). The episode is actually quite tame as it just details the behind-the-scenes activities before shooting begins.

Episodes:

1. The Crush (7 min., 5 sec.). After seeing a TV report on a sex tape scandal, Jen hatches a plan to create one of her own and become rich.

2. The News (5 min., 28 sec.). Jen's enthusiasm has Mandy a bit worried when she learns Jen will direct and she will be the star—something she is not willing to do (as she doesn't relish having sex on camera).

3. The Plan (7 min., 23 sec.). Realizing that her plan may now never get off the ground, Jen changes the direction of the tape to make Mandy feel more comfortable by having her making love to another woman rather than a man.

4. The Audition (8 min., 3 sec.). Jen begins gathering actors (by posting flyers around town and advertising on Craigslist).

5. The Tape (8 min., 39 sec.). With the cast and crew assembled, and rehearsals about to begin, Jen finds resistance form Mandy when Mandy learns Jen changed direction and she must now perform on camera with a male.

Note: The above episodes, which are available to view for free, conclude without resolution. The following seven episodes (listed by title only) are only available through a pay subscription service: *6.* The Break. *7.* The Leak. *8.* The Agent. *9.* The Show. *10.* The Bar. *11.* The Ex. *12.* The Love.

179 *Kung Fu Jonny.* youtube.com. 2013 (Action).

Kiss Her I'm Famous. Tracy Ryerson (left) and Ilea Matthews (copyright Rolla Selbak Pix, 2014).

The Shade is a mysterious organization that recruits men and women with advanced fighting and survival skills to become assassins and fulfill contracts. When Jonny, an ex-con now working as a restaurant dish washer and only seeking to turn his life around, is approached by The Shade and refuses to join, he becomes their enemy and soon learns that he is marked for assassination. The program follows Jonny, possessed of unique martial arts skills, as he battles his own demons, and, while attempting to avoid the masked villain seeking to kill him, helps people in trouble. **Cast:** Jon Rodriquez (Jonny), Ashley Turkowski (Emily), Tommy Else (George), Professor Kliq (Simon Syringe), Kevin Czarnecki, Andrew Hempfling, Dana Dajani. **Credits:** *Producer:* Kevin Czarnecki, Jon Rodeiquez. *Writer-Director:* Andrew Hempfling. **Comment:** The program was made by a group of Columbia University college students over a three year period. Although a bit violent, is well acted and produced.

Episodes:

1. Pilot (8 min., 51 sec.). Jonny risks his life under the radar when he helps a girl (Emily) being threatened by three thugs seeking to collect money from her.

2. Where's Rodney? (5 min., 32 sec.). Jonny finds repercussions after helping Emily when he encounters Rodney, a high-end drug dealer who is not pleased by what he did (as Emily owes him money).

3. Failure to Comply (10 min., 2 sec.). Jonny, taught a lesson for interfering by Rodney (beaten to a pulp) attempts to drown his sorrows at a bar when he is approached by a member of The Shade to join their organization.

4. Doctor's Orders (12 min., 57 sec.). Jonny's refusal to join The Shade places him in extreme danger when Simon Syringe, a cold-blooded killer, is ordered to eliminate him.

5. Temptation Incarnate (11 min., 41 sec.). Knowing that he doesn't stand a chance against The Shade, Jonny begins a regime of training his mind and body for what lies ahead.

6. It's a Cold World (13 min., 54 sec.). Jonny, captured and tortured by Simon, manages to escape and is being nursed back to health by Emily, unaware that The Shade has dispatched Aurora, a beautiful and deadly assassin to do what Simon could not.

7. The Hunt (13 min., 54 sec.). With Emily's

help, Jonny manages to avoid Aurora, further irritating The Shade (an organization of ruthless killers).

8. The Shadows (9 min., 42 sec.). With orders to kill dropped, The Shade has now assigned its top agents to bring Jonny in alive.

9. Taking the Sword (9 min., 4 sec.). Jonny's lone battle against The Shade begins when he encounters Red Shadow, a retired assassin who believes capturing Jonny will be his greatest achievement.

10. All Hail the Shade (15 min., 21 sec.). The concluding episode finds Jonny escaping Red Shadow but facing a final showdown with The Shade.

180 Lady Cops (2008). youtube.com. 2008 (Comical Crime Drama).

Roxie DeJour and Margo Kildare are Special Police (as their badges read) with The Lady Cop Precinct of an unidentified city. They are very pretty, a bit off-the-wall and take orders from a photograph (with a voice over) of Reginald Vel Johnson (in police uniform from his role on the TV series *Family Matters*). Roxie and Margo half-heartedly follow his instructions and the program charts their efforts to solve crimes as best they can, which is not saying much as they approach everything as if it were a joke (as the program states: "Meet Roxie and Margo.... They're lady cops.... They're good-for-nothing, but they sure are pretty"). If pretty can solve a crime, then Margo and Roxie are the best weapons against crime the precinct has. **Cast:** Amy Harper (Off. Roxie DeJour). A girl, credited only as Erin, plays Officer Margo Kildare and an actor, credited only as Reuben provides the voice of their superior (the photograph). **Credits** are not given. **Comment:** The program has numerous possibilities and with such attractive leads and improbable stories, it is one of the best cop spoofs produced. Unfortunately, only two short episodes were made and it appears unlikely any additional episodes will follow. The acting, meant to be corny, is very good and the production values just standard for an Internet program. Virtually all information regarding the program has been taken off line. There are no credits listed on the screen or in text information. **Episodes:**

1. At the Office (3 min., 37 sec.). It's just one of those days. Roxie and Margo are not too thrilled about patrolling the streets so they decide to solve crimes from their desks—and over the telephone. As anyone can guess, it won't work—especially when they attempt to talk a gun-wielding caller into putting down his gun. Gun shots heard over the phone indicates they failed.

2. Undercover Crack Whores (4 min., 2 sec.). Being as pretty as they are comes into play when Margo and Roxie decide to pose as hookers to bust a drug lord. Unfortunately, their information is not too reliable, as they target a parish priest by mistake.

181 Lady Cops (2009). afterellen.com. 2009 (Drama).

Mikki Majors and Lara Lancaster are actresses who star as Jo and Sienna on the television series *Lady Cops*. In real life they are straight and despise each other, but on their series they are lesbians and secretly in love with each other (having to keep their affair a secret fearing dismissal). The program explores incidents in their off-screen and on-screen lives with the intent to not only spoof the numerous crime dramas on TV but poke fun at the lesbian community as well. **Cast:** Liz Vassey (Mikki Majors/Sienna), Christina Cox (Lara Lancaster/Jo), Donna Scott (Winter Kole), Rob Moran (Brick Schlouse) **Credits:** *Producer:* Maeve Quinlan, Nancylee Myatt. **Comment:** Nicely presented program with more of a focus on their on-screen characters and how they work together as police officers. The program is a spin off from episode six (*Lady Cops*) that aired on the anthology series *3Way*. **Episodes:**

1. Lady Cops: Brotherly Love (15 min., 36 sec.). Jo and Sienna investigate a case involving the murder of a young woman, who died from booze, pills and a blow to the head.

182 The Lake. webserieschannel.com. 2009 (Drama).

Lake Eleanor, a fictional resort, provides the backdrop for a look at the lives of a group of close-knit friends who gather there each summer. In fashion typical of teen programs that aired on the now-defunct WB broadcast channel, *The Lake* follows an established format as romance, scandal, betrayal and heartbreak also become a part of their time together. **Cast:** Elisa Donovan (Leslie), Sarah Jessica Parker (Mimi), Samantha Cope (Alexis), Devin Crittenden (Drew), Heather Ann Davis (Olivia), Drew Van Acker (Ryan), Erica Dasher (Madison), Nick Thurston (Luke), Robb Derringer (Jack), Meredith Dilg (Shelby), Mim Drew (Claire), Amy Stewart (Sondra), Mark Totty (Dennis). **Credits:** *Producer:* Jason Priestley, Jordan Levin. *Director:* Jordan Levin. **Comment:** With Jason Priestley (from *Beverly Hills, 90210*) as its director; established stars (Elisa Donovan [from the TV series *Clueless*] and Sarah Jessica Parker [*Sex and the City*]) and the WB behind it, it is an above average Internet series with excellent acting and production values. But, like the WB (and even the current CW broadcast network) the program is a serial and geared to a teen audience. **Episodes:**

1. Summer Begins (11 min., 25 sec.). The story begins with Olivia, a first-time visitor to the lake, moving in with her aunt, Leslie.

2. Summer Solstice (9 min., 19 sec.). As Olivia mingles she meets those with whom she will spend

the summer (Madison, Drew, Alexis, Ryan and Luke) and partakes in the annual summer kick-off, The Cove BBQ.

3. Summer Sparks (8 min., 57 sec.). While the BBQ was a success, Alexis, drawn to Ryan, plots to get closer to him through sex.

4. Summer Secrets (9 min., 31 sec.). With the summer just beginning, Claire and Dennis, Alexis's parents, feel that Alexis and the other girls should be "given the talk" about sex.

5. Summer Revelations (11 min., 1 sec.). As the teens gather to celebrate Drew's 16th birthday, Claire approaches Leslie (a widow) to tell her that she should get back into the dating scene.

6. Summer Opportunities (11 min., 48 sec.). The "Talk" has Alexis and Ryan discussing their future together while Olivia, drawn to Drew, have their first date (which has Leslie, Olivia's aunt concerned as Luke is not what he pretends to be).

7. Summer Changes (9 min., 38 sec.). As Ryan tells Luke about a wild spring break party he had (but kept from his parents), Olivia feels that, even though she dates, that she will never have her first kiss.

8. Summer Decisions (6 min., 59 sec.). The upcoming Summer Dance, the event of the season, has the teens each seeking a date (but who will ask who first appears to be the problem).

9. Summer Kisses (11 min., 8 sec.). Madison and Drew are left out in the cold (no dates) while Olivia feels slighted when Luke shows up with Alexis at the dance.

10. Summer Confessions (7 min., 59 sec.). As Olivia confides in Madison about her "boy dilemma" (never getting kissed), Aunt Leslie confronts Alexis about her habit of using boys to get attention.

11. Summer Questions (10 min., 18 sec.). As the summer draws to an end, the teens gather for the annual "Final Picnic" before leaving to go their separate ways.

12. Summer Ends (11 min., 23 sec.). The concluding episode wherein the picnic concludes, truths are revealed and a doorway is left open for a second season of episodes that could reunite the teens a year later—but a year wiser?

183 *The League of Extraordinary Dancers.* thelxd.com. 2010–2011 (Drama).

The LXD (The League of Extraordinary Dancers) are a group of heroes, based in the town of Pleasanton, whose dancing skills present them with abilities called "The Ra" to defeat evil, specifically The Alliance of the Dark, rival dancers who also acquire power through their dancing acumen. The battle of good vs. evil, however, is also further enhanced by its time coverage—from the 1920s through the year 3000 and its incorporation of many different dance skills—from ballet to hip hop. Season 1 is basically an introduction to the LXD and its amazing dancers. As Season 2 begins, the conflicts between the LXD

and its enemies, the Umbras and Organization X (called the Ox) heats up and comes to final blows in the final third season with information on how the LXD was formed and how the Umbras and the Ox united to form the Alliance of the Dark.

Cast: Roger Aaron Brown (Narrator), Chadd Smith (Sp3cimen), Terence Dickson (Minijack), Aja George (Stereo), Straphanio Solomon (Phono), Luis Rosado (Trevor Drift), Harry Shum, Jr. (Elliot Hoo), Carey Ysais (Karey), John Nelson (Dark Doctor), Marie Medina (Autumn), Christopher Scott (Copeland), Wilbur Urbina (Joe Drift), Richard Vasquez (Spexor D), Ivan Velez, Joshua Lee Ayres, Jaime Burgos III (Observer), Jesse Brown (Peetie), Galen Hooks (Ninjato), Aaron Cooke (Dante), Shelby Rabara (Dark Nurse), William Wingfield (Katana), Daniel Campos (Illister), Christopher Toler (Z), Travis Wong (Christopher Angel), Charlie E. Schmidt (Ringmaster), Josue Anthony (Stakka), Nicholas Braum (Cole Waters), Anis Cheurfa (Achilles), Carly Lang (Alice Wondershaw), Ricardo Rodriquez (The Wave), Tony Styles (Waru), Nancy Yu (Countess), Oscar Orisco (Tendo), Diva Zappa (Ruth), Robert Rich (Gus), Brandon Philips, Bryan Tanaka, Dondraico Johnson, Giobanni Watson, Cassidy Noblett, JD McElroy, Mykal Bean (Umbra), Tara Mackin, Luke Broadlick, Beau Smart (Ox). **Credits:** *Producer:* Jon M. Chu, Zev Suissa, Larry Tanz, Hieu Ho. *Director:* Jon M. Chu, Charles Oliver, Ryan Landels, Scott Speer, Christopher Scott. *Writer:* Jon M. Chu, Ryan Landels, Charles Oliver, Charlie E. Schmidt. Harry Shum, Jr. **Comment:** Needless to say, somewhat of an unusual take on the super hero craze as these heroes need to dance to acquire their powers (possibly an attempt to cash in on super hero theatrical films and TV shows like *Glee* and *Dancing with the Stars*). Ridiculous as the concept sounds, it does have its shining moments: the choreography and dancing are spectacular and it dominates much of the series story lines as good attempts to defeat evil and vice versa. Even if one is not a fan of dance, the choreography is so well done that it can captivate you and keep you tuned from beginning to end.

Episodes:

1. The Tale of Trevor Drift (13 min., 40 sec.). A teenager, Trevor, discovers his powers at the senior prom.

2. Anti-Gravity Heroes (8 min., 51 sec.). While exploring a warehouse, two friends acquire amazing dancing skills when they find a magic package of packing Styrofoam peanuts.

3. Robot Love Story (10 min., 59 sec.). A man, waking up in a hospital with no memory and suffering from convulsions is introduced.

4. The Uprising Begins (7 min., 16 sec.). A dance showdown between rivals Tendo and Spex is showcased.

5. The Letter Makers (3 min., 54 sec.). As the uprising begins, the Letter Makers begin recruiting an LXD army.

6. Duet (5 min., 26 sec.). Former members of the LXD come forward to join the new team.

7. The Dark Doctor Deal (4 min., 45 sec.). A rogue LXD dancer (Autumn) finds her life changing when she finds herself being reprogrammed by the Dark Doctor.

8. Elliot's Shoes (7 min., 29 sec.). Magic shoes give Elliot the ability to dance.

9. Fanboyz (9 min., 32 sec.). Stereo, Phono, and Minijack, obsessed with the LXD, dream of becoming a part of the team.

10. I Seen a Man (12 min., 35 sec.). Copeland, a man with great potential, struggles to cope with his personal demons as Season 1 concludes.

11. Origins (6 min., 24 sec.). The second season begins with an exploration of the origins of the dance rivals.

12. Experiments (6 min., 10 sec.). To wreck-havoc within the LXD, the psychopathic Dark Doctor seeks "the perfect specimen" to do his bidding.

13. The Legion (10 min., 26 sec.). The underground headquarters of the LXD is explored.

14. Lessons (11 min., 5 sec.). As the members of the LXD train, secrets of the Ra begin to surface.

15. Rising (10 min., 8 sec.). As the LXD organizes, an unsuspecting evil (Organization Ox) is gearing up to attack.

16. Mark of the Ox (10 min., 40 sec.). Organization Ox's harsh recruiting program is explored.

17. The Good, the Bad and the Ra, Part 1 (14 min., 35 sec.). A premiere mission for the newly formed LXD: rescue people from a remote town.

18. Tails of War (11 min., 3 sec.). To achieve their means, Ox schemes to encompass deadly creatures to bait and kill off the LXD.

19. The Greatest of Two Evils (9 min., 20 sec.). The Ox battles the Dark Doctor and his Umbras Army.

20. The Good, the Bad and the Ra, Part 2 (10 min., 12 sec.). The mission begun in episode 17 finds the LXD in a showdown with villains as Season 2 concludes.

21. Extraordinary (11 min., 28 sec.). Season 3 opens with an exploration of the LXD and its enemies.

22. Ashes (7 min., 52 sec.). Karey and the Ringmaster face off in a confrontation.

23. Forbidden (7 min., 32 sec.). A temptress (in dance) attempts to seduce the Extraordinary 7, once evil and having given up their powers, to return to their former ways.

24. Can't Dance (9 min., 19 sec.). LXD member Fanboyz attempts to help Elliot repair his magical shoes by taking them to an eccentric seamstress.

25. Salvage (8 min., 22 sec.). The Doctor's Sp3cimen and Autumn are reunited after a long absence.

26. Reprogram (6 min., 35 sec.). With changes now affecting their lives, Autumn and Sp3cimen reevaluate their relationship.

27. RA Games (7 min., 38 sec.). New recruits to the LXD are taught how to harness the power of the Ra.

28. Mess in Aisle 7 (9 min., 38 sec.). The LXD embarks on a mission to find the evil Dark Doctor.

29. Alliance of the Dark (6 min., 26 sec.). In a sinister move, the Dark Doctor forms an uneasy alliance with Karey to destroy the LXD.

30. Rise of the Drifts (11 min., 45 sec.). The battle that began years ago intensifies into war "and just the beginning" as the series concludes.

184 The Legend of Detective Harris. web serieschannel.com. 2013 (Drama).

Bill Harris is a police detective. He is single although he lives with his partner's (John) ex-wife (Kate). What will happen? Will he wear the blue shirt? Will he have a case? Does he like the life he leads? In the episodes presented, each is a brief look at incidents that befall Bill at home.

Cast: Roger Pfeiffer (Bill Harris), Isobel Arnberg (Kate), Chris McFarland (John), Leroy Verdin (Police Chief), Ronnie Hooks (Janet), Johnny Rock (Ted). **Credits:** *Producer-Writer-Director:* Dorian Dardar. **Comment:** Unusual to say the least. There is no action; there are no case investigations; no car chases, gun battles or interrogations. Some will find it intriguing while others will become turned off after the first episode (as the title is quite deceiving, leading one to believe it will be an action-adventure series). The acting and production values are adequate although Bill's attitude can become quite annoying as he just doesn't seem believable at times.

Episodes:

1. Suit Up (3 min., 21 sec.). Bill awakens and must now get ready for work.

2. The Kate Predicament (4 min., 25 sec.). Bill faces "the wrath" of Kate's ex-husband, who wants his red shirt back.

3. On the Job (5 min., 7 sec.). Bill receives an assignment from the police chief.

4. With the Fam (6 min., 41 sec.). Bill pays a visit to his sister (Janet).

5. Living the Dream (1 min., 45 sec.). Bill fantasizes about a life of luxury.

185 Lenox Avenue. lenoxavenueseries.com. 2012 (Drama).

Set against the background of Lenox Avenue in Harlem (New York), the program charts the experiences of four close friends (Owen, Sellars, Vaughn and Ebony) and the decisions they make that not only affect them, but those that are around them.

Cast: Al Thompson (Owen), Dorian Missick (Sellars), Ryan Vigilant (Vaughn), Althena Colon (Jeanette), Almeria Campbell (Dr. Kim), La Rivers (Ebony), Carmen Hooper (Gina), Christina Marcelle (Francesca). **Credits:** *Producer:* Al Thompson,

Zeke Dunn, Regina Scott. *Director:* Al Thompson. *Writer:* Al Thompson, La Monte Edwards. **Comment:** One of the better African-American produced programs that is filmed in Harlem and presents a realistic look at life in Harlem with capable acting and production values. Contains brief nudity and sexual situations.

Episodes:

1. Pillow Talk (7 min., 12 sec.). Introduces the principal players as Vaughn, friends with Francesca since the tenth grade, learns that she is moving to San Francisco; and Sellars finding that his love-making sessions with Ebony are not to her pleasing as he falls asleep during sex.

2. Friends with Benefits (7 min., 27 sec.). As Vaughn ponders his relationship with Francesca, Owen begins to make plans for Sellars up-coming wedding.

3. Groceries (5 min., 14 sec.). As the guys engage in some grocery shopping, Owen meets a woman who captures his fancy.

4. Booty Call (6 min., 55 sec.). A night out partying has Vaughn realizing that the single life, especially without Francesca, is not the dream life he envisioned.

5. Ebony (8 min., 1 sec.). As Owen impresses a girl with his knowledge of dry cleaning silk, Vaughn, a tutor, is introduced to a girl (Jeanette) who requires help in math to pass a college exam.

6. Girls Basketball (4 min., 10 sec.). Owen and Sellars attend a girls' basketball game while Vaughn and Jeanette appear to be becoming closer.

7. Cheating (11 min., 31 sec.). Owen's encounter with an old friend (Dr. Kim) finds him cheating on Ebony while Sellars becomes uneasy about an upcoming job interview at Lexington Capital.

8. Dream (6 min., 38 sec.). The concluding episode wherein Vaughn discovers that Jeanette is not the type of girl he thought (she is more of a party girl); Owen's affair has him wondering if Ebony is the right girl for him; and Sellars prepares for the job interview.

186 *Lesbian Cops.* blip.tv. 2011 (Crime Drama).

Tori Jones is a beautiful police detective with a penchant for losing her partners through tragic circumstances during case investigations. She is also a lesbian and must endure the flack she receives from fellow officers (including the police chief). Although Tori is a top notch detective when it comes to solving crimes, paring her with someone appears to be a matter of who is expendable (whether it is a seasoned professional or rookie, their chances for survival with Tori have the odds stacked up against them). To solve the problem, Chief Wilson assigns Tori a female partner, Rashida Thompson, a butch-type lesbian he feels will make Tori more responsive to protecting her partner and vice versa. In the presented story

Tori and Rashida attempt to solve the drug-related murder of a teacher at Hamilton Elementary School.

Lesbian Cops is a rather unusual Internet series in that the episodes are actually scenes from a feature film that was then in production and used to interest investors to help writer-director Firouz Farhang finish the film ("In honor of his grandmother who just came out of the closet on her 80th birthday").

Cast: Gena Shaw (Det. Tori Jones), Krystal Marshall (Det. Rashida Thompson), Thomas Jones (Chief Wilson), Dane Reade (Det. Frank Martin), Casey Nelson (Off. Casey), Suzanne Quast (Virginia Cunderson), Shawn G. Smith (Dustin Brown). **Credits:** *Producer:* Firouz Farhang, Jessica Matthews, David Aslan, Aaron Burnett. *Writer-Director:* Firouz Farhang. **Comment:** An extremely vulgar program that uses an over-abundance of foul language. The acting and production values are good, but the attempt to mix crime drama with comedy falls flat; obscene words simply do not turn drama into comedy. The lesbian match-up is also hard to fathom (the women are just not compatible) and having a superior (Wilson) belittle a subordinate (Tori) for her sexual preference is a poor stab at comedy (as it too does not work—even if Tori lashes back with her dose of foul language). The concept is said to be "an action-packed cop drama inspired by movies like *Death Wish, Lethal Weapon, Bad Boys* ... and anything else that kicks ass!" It fails to meet those standards and there is no nudity, kissing or scenes of affection between Tori and Rashida in the episodes. There is also no parental warning (the episodes can also be viewed on sharing sites like YouTube) although two versions of the episodes have been released: "Uncensored" and "Censored" (which contains bleeped foul language). *Lesbian Cops: The Movie* was made and has also been released on DVD.

Episodes:

1. I Hate Drugs, Part 1 (3 min., 50 sec.). Tori is teamed with Rashida after her prior partner, a recent rookie school graduate, is shot.

2. I Hate Drugs, Part 2 (5 min., 18 sec.). The investigation begins as Tori and Rashida investigate the death of a school teacher.

3. We've Got Solid Evidence (5 min., 56 sec.). The suspects in the case are questioned.

4. Not Again (7 min., 13 sec.). Tori and Rashida become close for the first time when Rashida tries to help Tori overcome her feelings that she has hit rock bottom.

5. I Heard Crazy (4 min., 57 sec.). Tori, back on her feet aggressively pursues clues to find the killer.

6. Why's He Beeping (7 min., 6 sec.). Tori and Rashida continue their investigation as the series concludes.

187 *LESlieVILLE.* llvseries.com. 2013 (Drama).

Sera, a young woman recovering from a broken

relationship with her former girlfriend (Gwen), becomes attracted to Ona, a lesbian who, unknown to her, is involved in a relationship with another woman (Laura). As Sera takes the first steps to meet Ona her life is thrown into a whirlwind of uncertainty when Gwen returns to her and she again finds herself being drawn to her. Ona, who has fallen for Sera, has concerns of her own as she loves Laura, but is also attracted to Sera. The program follows the decisions each woman must make as their romance blossoms but at what cost to the women who really love them.

Cast: Samantha Wan (Sera), Tiffany Claire-Martin (Ona), Jenna Harder (Gwen), J.M. Frey (Casey), Sarah Grace (Jeri), Meghan Campbell (Laura). **Credits:** *Producer:* Nadine Bell, Stephen Leck, Russell Winkelaar. **Comment:** Tenderly portrayed saga of women in love and what happens when uncontrollable events enter the picture to change the bliss each hopes to find. Nicely acted and well produced, the program is an insightful look at women navigating the world between lust and true desire.

Episodes:

1. Sight. Sera, a single girl becomes attracted to the mysterious Ona, a young woman already involved with another woman (Laura).

2. Getting to Know You. Unaware that Ona has been dating another woman, Sera attempts to get to know Ona by asking her out on a lunch date.

3. The Great Debate. Gwen, Sera's former lover, re-enters her life while Ona arouses Laura's jealous streak when she tells her about Sera.

4. Shoes, Shoes, Shoes. With eyes only for each other, Sera and Ona continue their blossoming romance—and embark on a shoe shopping spree.

5. Birds of a Feather. While helping her friends, Jeri and Casey with their wedding plans, Sera fantasizes about her own wedding to Ona.

6. The Great Debate Redux. With Gwen back in her life, Sera is now torn between Gwen and Ona.

7. Close Quarters. As Sera and Ona spend more alone time together, Sera finds herself becoming deeply attracted to Ona and finding it difficult to keep their relationship platonic.

8. Jill and Jill Went Up a Hill. At a party given for Jeri and Casey, Ona becomes jealous when she sees Sera and Gwen together.

9. The Morning After. The party winds down—with Sera and Gwen reliving old times by having a romantic encounter.

10. A Few. Although it appears that Sera and Gwen will reconnect, Ona confronts Laura about her feelings for Sera.

188 Less Than Heroes. webserieschannel. com. 2011 (Action Comedy).

Frosty, J.D. and Andy are friends with super powers who rather play video games than save the world (or even help someone in trouble). Their less than heroic adventures are charted as they seek to enjoy the simple life they have chosen for themselves.

Cast: Ben Parks (Frosty), J.R. Raines (J.D.), Micah Jones (Andy), Frances D'Imperio (Jayme). **Credits:** *Producer:* Diane Baldwin, J.R. Raines. *Director:* Richard Whiteside. Writer: J.R. Raines, Randall Self. **Comment:** While nothing spectacular happens and the fantasy element is virtually lost in the comedy presentation, there is the potential for follow-up episodes wherein the guys actually use their powers to not only impress a girl (Jayme)—but help some poor soul who is crying out for help but can't be heard.

Episodes:

1. Like a Lot Strong (9 min., 17 sec.). Introduces the heroes as their powers begin to increase but who see it as an annoyance because it interferes with their video game playing.

2. Desperation & Delivery (5 min., 1 sec.). A delivery girl (Jayme) enters the guys' lives and threatens to change them forever.

3. Screwing Andy (6 min.). The guys find Jayme not only a threat to their video game addiction, but their manhood as well.

4. Plus a Good Tip (7 min., 17 sec.). The guys suddenly realize that Jayme is much hipper and cooler than they are. But will they change and use their powers to impress her (and actually help people threatened by evil)? The program's concluding episode.

189 Libelle the Series. libelletheseries.com. 2012 (Thriller).

Sonia Engelhardt is a young scientist working on a revolutionary process to bring trees to full maturity in a relatively short period of time as opposed to the normal decade's process. She is working for Eddy McIntyre, the impatient head of a logging company that hired her believing that he could make huge profits from her discovery. However, with backers demanding money, McIntyre stops Sonia's funding, bringing her project to a state of crises. Sonia believes that trees are connected. There are the large trees (Mother Trees) that care for the smaller trees (seedlings) and without additional funds Sonia cannot finalize her process and her Mother Trees will be harvested for lumber. McIntyre's indifference infuriates Sonia who vows to find a way to stop McIntyre and continue her research. Sonia's actions bring her in contact with two ex-cops (Ann and Bill), members of an organization called Libelle, which is dedicated to stopping crime. The program charts what happens when Sonia defies McIntyre and continues her forest research, becomes involved in a murder (of McIntyre) and must escape (with Ann's help) the assassins hired by persons unknown to stop her and her research as something unnatural has apparently resulted (not revealed).

Cast: Julia Dordel (Sonia Engelhard), Anita

Libelle: The Series. Eric Breker (left) and Julia Dordel (photograph by Mike Mander, copyright 2010; program copyright by Dorcon Film UG).

Reimer (Analena "Ann" Tempest), Olivia Cheng (Jasmin Lu), Douglas Roy Dack (Eddy McIntyre), Eric Breker (Bill Jones), Bernadeta Wrobel (Stephanie Nowak), Michael Teigen (Det. Michaels), Adrian Holmes (Inspector Zet). **Credits:** *Producer:* Julia Dordel, Anita Reimer. *Director:* Neil Every, Brent Crowell, Guido Toeike, Kryshan Randel. *Writer:* Julia Dordel, Neil Every. **Comment:** A well-produced and acted eco-thriller with many more twists and turns than presented in the episode descriptions. The outdoor locations are well chosen and the accompanying photography steady (no shaky camera), adding to the overall suspense the program offers. The program does end in a cliffhanger but is still enjoyable and well worth watching. A sequel (feature film) has been developed under the title *Mission Ninety-Two* and was released in 2014. The series was originally titled *Dragonfly* but due to several projects under that title, the German language word for dragonfly, Libelle, was used instead.

Episodes:

1. Chapter 1 (10 min., 48 sec.). Establishes the story line as Sonia believes she is nearing a breakthrough but finds her dreams shattered when her boss (McIntyre) cuts off her funding.

2. Chapter 2 (7 min., 20 sec.). Police detectives (Ann and Bill) begin an investigation of McIntyre, believing he is involved in contraband operations.

3. Chapter 3 (9 min., 35 sec.). After failing in an effort to convince McIntyre of the importance of her research, Sonia devises her own method to finish her research.

4. Chapter 4 (9 min., 18 sec.). Sonia retreats to the forest to continue her project while Ann and Bill continue to observe McIntyre.

5. Chapter 5 (10 min., 30 sec.). When Ann and Bill's efforts to nab McIntyre continually fail and frustrate their superior (Inspector Zet), they are suspended—but are recruited by Libelle to bring down the corrupt logging operations overseen by McIntyre.

6. Chapter 6 (7 min., 38 sec.). As Ann and Bill begin their undercover assignment for Libelle, Sonia is unknowingly being watched by a hired assassin (Jasmine).

7. Chapter 7 (5 min., 29 sec.). McIntyre, head of the logging society (The Midnighters) begins a search for Sonia, seeking to stop her in her tracks. Ann and Bill have also begun a search for Sonia as she may be the key to solving their case.

8. Chapter 8 (6 min., 50 sec.). McIntyre, believing he is alone, suddenly realizes he is being stalked—and is killed by someone (assumed to be Jasmine) wielding a chain saw.

9. Chapter 9 (5 min., 56 sec.). Ann finds Sonia, but their meeting turns deadly when Jasmine closes in on them.

10. Chapter 10 (6 min., 39 sec.). A confrontation ensues, with Ann, using her martial arts abilities, defeating Jasmine, and allowing her and Sonia to escape deeper into the forest.

11. Chapter 11 (5 min., 37 sec.). Inspector Zet learns of McIntyre's death and begins his investigation in the forest's crime scene. Unknowingly they are being observed by Jasmine.

12. Chapter 12 (8 min., 1 sec.). Ann and Sonia believe something other than blue plants has resulted from her discovery when they spot men in Hazmet suits (but why?) probing her research area. Meanwhile, as the episode concludes, Jasmine has her gun sights set on killing, but whom?

13. Chapter 13 (7 min., 53 sec.). Ann and Sonia, wanted for murder, seek a way out of the forest. Adding to the mystery is a discovery of dead fish on the lake—an effect of Sonia's research?

Life After Lisa. Left to right: **Bridgetta Tomarchio (left) and Crystal Milano (used by permission of Elena Moscatt).**

190 *Life After Lisa.* lifeafterlisa.net. 2010 (Mystery).

It is 1987 and Jessica "Jessie" Beaumont is a new student at Baltimore's Brighton College. She is a film major and has been assigned a room in Adele Hall—a room (301) that was previously occupied by a girl named Lisa Marie Shatner, a very sexy co-ed who died in a (mysterious?) car accident while in her junior year. As Jessie begins to settle in she finds her room is not normal as she feels there is a presence that does not want her there. Although a bit unnerved, Jessie soon becomes intrigued about Lisa: who was she and what really happened to her. As Jessie begins to associate with Lisa's friends and discovers more about her, she hits on an idea to make a documentary about Lisa for her Film 101 class. Jessie begins by interviewing Lisa's friends but encounters a stumbling block when she meets Kapria Coswell, Lisa's best friend, who appears to be opposed to what she is doing. As Jessie continues her filming, she becomes so obsessed with Lisa that she not only begins to wear her clothes (left in the dorm room) but acting and looking like her (upsetting Kapria even more than she already is). The program follows Jessie as she produces her documentary and her struggle with what to do: show Lisa as the beautiful fun-loving girl everyone liked or expose the truth about Lisa and the dark, unflattering life she really lived.

Tammy Tyrell is the house president of Adele Hall; Vera Michaels, an art student, was a friend of Lisa's; Lido, a student, dated Tammy but secretly loved Lisa; Sheila Hawn is Jessie's roommate; Kay, a music major, lives down the hall from Jessie; Mimi, considered Lisa's "little sister," was the freshman Lisa befriended; Toejo (apparently in love with Lisa), Greg and Robby are frat brothers and part of Lisa's group of friends.

Cast: Stephanie Danielson (Jessie Beaumont), Bridgetta Tomarchio (Lisa Marie Shatner), Johnny Alonso (Steven Shatner), Zoe Sloane (Kapria Coswell), Crystal Milano (Sheila Hawn), Cory Parker Robinson (Greg Watkins), Lauren Lewis (Alice Leery), Aaron Mathias (Toejo Warner), Tracie Jules (Jessie's mother), Tiffany Ariany (Mimi Dimaio), Megan Therese Rippey (Tammy Tyrell), Elena Moscatt (Abby Coswell), Marlena Neal (Jazzman Summers), Sabrina Taylor-Smith (Kay Willis), Michael Finnegan (Frank Coswell), Jon Klipa (Brad Beaumont), Michael Tecce (Robby Sandler). **Credits:** *Producer:* Elena Moscatt, Paul A. Moscatt, Chris Montgomery-Bender. *Director:* Palmer Enfield. *Writer:* Elena Moscatt. **Comment:** Intriguing program that captures your attention as soon as Jessie arrives and establishes that something is not right when a girl (Kapria) appears to be spying on her and Jessie envisions seeing the car accident that took Lisa's life. The program is true to its late 1980s setting and the acting and production values very good. Stephanie Danielson also plays Lisa in flashback sequences, and Kapria realizing that Jessie resembles Lisa adds to the intrigue.

Episodes:

1. Jessie Moves in (6 min., 47 sec.). It is January 27, 1987 and Jessie, just arriving on campus, has a vision of seeing a girl (Lisa) being hit by a car then experiences her first taste of dorm life when she is shown to her room and sees a message written on the door—"Stay Out." "Goodbye Mom and Dad," she says, "Hello college hell."

2. Café Brighton (9 min., 23 sec.). As Jessie walks across the campus she encounters two girls (friends

of Lisa) and learns a bit more about her. Intrigued, Jessie sets her goal to learn all she can about Lisa and what happened to her.

Note: In addition to the two episodes listed above, there are also the following video segments:

1. Life After Lisa: Episodes One and Two (15 min., 34 sec.). An edited version of the story.

2. Moments with Lisa—Life After Lisa: The Web Series (2 min., 5 sec.).

3. Tammy's Profile Video 1(1 min., 47 sec.).

4. Life After Lisa Preview: Ep. 3—Across Campus (1 min., 49 sec.).

5. Lifer After Lisa: It's All About Kay! (4 min., 51 sec.).

6. For Mimi's Profile Page (6 min., 35 sec.).

7. 80's Dancing with Marlena (1 min., 51 sec.).

8. To Our Twitter Followers (1 min., 34 sec.).

9. Life After Lisa's Dance Competition (55 sec.).

10. Life After Lisa Teaser (4 min., 11 sec.).

11. Who Is Lisa? A Montage and Preview (1 min., 14 sec.).

12. Zoe Sloane Introduces Life After Lisa (1 min., 14 sec.).

13. Life After Lisa: Raw Footage: A Scene from Webisode 2 (4 min., 17 sec.).

14. The Jessie Cam One: First Moments in College (3 min., 57 sec.).

15. The Stephanie and Zoe Show—Part 1 (4 min., 41 sec.).

16. The Stephanie and Zoe Show—Part 2 (8 min., 55 sec.).

17. Intro to Life After Lisa Site (29 sec.).

18. Obama Forever (18 sec.).

19. Life After Lisa Audition: Jessie Improv 2 (1 min., 14 sec.).

20. Jessie Beaumont Improv by Zoe (1 min., 44 sec.).

21. Life After Lisa Intro by Zoe, 1 (15 sec.).

22. Life After Lisa Intro by Zoe, 2 (10 sec.).

23. Jessie's 80's Fashion Segment 1 (1 min., 3 sec.).

191 _Lilyhammer_. lillyhammer.com. 2012 (Crime Drama).

Frank Tagliano, called "The Fixer," is a member of the American Mafia who, after turning state's evidence (testifying against New York mobster boss Aldo Delucci) was placed in the FBI's Witness Protection Program and relocated to the small Norwegian town of Lilliehammer under the assumed name Giovanni "Johnny" Henriksen (Frank chose the town after seeing images of it from the 1994 Winter Olympics). Johnny adjusts quickly and soon afterward opens his own nightclub (the Flamingo) but complications arise when a police officer (Geir) uncovers a photo of Johnny that bears a striking resemblance to a New York gangster (Frank Tagliano) who mysteriously disappeared. Curious, Geir probes further and Johnny is revealed as Frank with stories fol-

lowing Johnny as he finds he must resort to his old ways to begin his new life—by first overcoming the obstacles that stand in his way—eliminating the hit men from New York who are out to get him for what he did. The series title changes the spelling of the town to reflect the name of Frank's dog, Lily.

Cast: Steven Van Zandt (Frank Tagliano), Trond Fausa (Torgeir Lien), Steinar Sagen (Roar Lien), Marian Saastad Ottesen (Sigrid Haugli), Tommy Karlsen (Arne), Fridtjov Saheim (Jan Johansen), Robert Skjaerstad (Roy Aass), Anne Krigsvoll (Laila Hovland), Mikael Aksnes-Pehrson (Jonas Haugli), Henriette Steenstrup (Randi), Nils Jorgen Kaalstad (Dag Solstad), Kamal Mustaffai (Hassan), Richard Skog (Oddjob), Tom Ahern (Robert Grasso), Sven Nordin (Julius Backe), Kyrre Hellum (Geir "Elvis" Tvedt), Momobou Lamin Touray (Balotelli), Kyrre Haugen Sydness (Thomas Aune), Greg Canestrari (Jerry Delucci), Nasrin Khusrawi (Aisha), Hamid Karmi (Yusuf), Silje Torp (Mette Hansen), Valentina Alexeeva (Jelena), Erik Madsen (Cookie), Jon Oigarden (Bjorn Hansen), Jakob Oftebro (Chris), Oystein Roger (Richard Nilsen). **Credits:** _Producer:_ Steven Van Zandt, Lasse Hallberg. _Director:_ Geir Henning-Hopland, Lisa Marie Gamlem, Simen Alsvik, Ole Endresen. _Writer:_ Anne Bjornstad, Jadranko Mehic, Helena J. Nielsen, Eilif Skodvin, Tomas Solli. **Comment:** A Norwegian produced program that became the first series to be presented on Netflix. Although well produced and acted, it contains very little English and relies heavily on subtitles, which distracts from the story.

Episodes: Season 1 episodes (described below) remain on line. Season 2 episodes (not available) are listed by title only.

1. Reality Check. Establishes the story line as Frank is given a new identity after testifying against a Mafia boss.

2. The Flamingo. Shortly after opening his night club, Johnny finds his first taste of trouble when a contraband shipment of liquor is delivered to the Flamingo.

3. Guantanamo Blues. With the Flamingo established, Johnny looks into investing money in an apartment complex that sounds too good to be true.

4. The Midwife. Sigrid, a girl with whom Johnny had an affair is about to give birth while a police officer uncovers a photo of Frank that looks just like Johnny.

5. My Kind of Town. As the police officer (Geir) heads to New York for information, Johnny attempts to launder money through an art deal scheme.

6. Pack Your Lederhosen. Geir's probe alerts the Mafia to Frank's new identity and location; meanwhile the housing development project falls through for Johnny when he learns it will be for families, not singles.

7. The Babysitter. Sigrid and Johnny are now parents; Geir is killed by the mob and hit men are now in Norway seeking Johnny.

8. Trolls. Johnny's situation suddenly takes a turn for the worse when he realizes that his identity is in danger of being exposed.

Season 2 Episode List (episodes off-line):
1. Millwall Brick. Oct. 16, 2013.
2. Out of Africa. Oct. 23, 2013.
3. Fiddler's Green. Oct. 30, 2013.
4. The Black Toe. Nov. 13, 2013.
5. The Island. Nov. 20, 2013.
6. Special Education. Nov. 27, 2013.
7. The Freezer. Dec. 4, 2013.
8. Ghosts. Dec. 11, 2013.

192 *The Lines.* allstate.com/teen/the-lines-web-series.aspx. 2011 (Drama).

Teen-themed drama about six high school students and how they deal with the issues that affect them: Ashley, the most popular girl in school; Rick, the basketball team's star player; Brooke, Ashley's best friend (until she started hanging out with "the cool Kids" and began ignoring her); Fiona, the wild, unpredictable girl that attracts trouble; Derek, the loner; and Luke, the rich kid. **Cast:** Teresa Cesario (Ashley Ferguson), Bridgette Pechman (Brooke), Kyle Sandgate-Blix (Ricky), Jackson Schultz (Derek), Chase Maser (Luke), Corey Doyle (Fiona), Paige Collins (Mary), Dominick Coviello (Charlie). **Credits:** *Producer:* Charlie Breit, Peter B. Williams. *Director:* K.C. Norman, Kipp Norman. *Writer:* Charlie Breit, Nathan Lackie, K.C. Norman, Kipp Norman. **Comment:** The program, also known as *Allstate: The Lines* for its production in association with Allstate Insurance, is well acted and produced. Although most teen-centered programs lean more toward comedy, *The Lines* chose the dramatic angle as teens also face problems other than figuring out the cafeteria food and which girl to take to the dance.

Episodes:
1. Episode 1 (6 min., 28 sec.). Introduces the six main students and the situation each faces.
2. Episode 2 (6 min., 17 sec.). As Ashley and Brooke begin to grow further apart as friends, Rick contemplates dropping out of the basketball team to pursue a law internship.
3. Episode 3 (6 min., 32 sec.). Ashley, as well as the team coach, is not happy with Rick's decision while Brooke becomes closer to the troublesome Fiona.
4. Episode 4 (5 min., 57 sec.). Now that he has quit the team, Ricky seeks to make it on his own without any help from his father.
5. Episode 5 (6 min., 22 sec.). Brooke's association with Fiona is beginning to have repercussions as Brooke's mother does not want her to associate with Fiona.
6. Episode 6 (7 min., 11 sec.). Ricky feels his decision may have been made in haste as he is now facing a barrage of difficult choices; meanwhile, Brooke

is continuing to see Fiona despite what her mother told her.
7. Episode 7 (9 min., 30 sec.). Brooke's defiance finds her and Fiona stuck in the city when her car malfunctions; Ashley and Luke appear to be getting close now that Ricky has changed the direction of his life.
8. Episode 8 (7 min., 31 sec.). Brooke, safely at home, finds herself being grounded; Ricky prepares for his internship meeting; and Ashley seeks to redirect her life in the concluding episode.

193 *LIPS.* flovinger.com. 2012–2013 (Comedy-Drama).

LIPS is a British lesbian rock band organized by London (lead singer) and Didi (London's mate "and the real talent behind the band"). "If you have never heard of us," says London, "then you must not live on the planet Earth." The band, however, has not made it (yet) and stories relate their dreams and attempts to make the big time by performing (and achieving fame) at the Dinah Shore (1940s singer) Weekend Main Stage in Hollywood. **Cast:** Florence Vinger (London), Vivi Rama (Didi), Marlyse Londe (Tangent Queen, Helen), Elaine Hendrix (Herself), Ashley St. Pierre (Tangent Queen, Doris), Hana Mae Lee (Endora), Christine Lakin (Rocker Chick), Sheetal Sheth (Rousaura), Debra Wilson (X-Girlfiend), Brian Jay Ecker (Bubba), Lita Lopez (Barista), Bernardo Verdugo (Armondo), Catherine Waller (Snaps), Amber Tisue (Amber), Michael Comacchia (Amber). **Credits:** *Producer:* Florence Vinger, Brian Jay Ecker, Kate Tobia. *Director:* Florence Vinger, Chad Callner. *Writer:* Florence Vinger, Brian Jay Ecker. **Comment:** Although the program ends unresolved, it is well acted and produced and a slightly different approach to series encompassing lesbian characters. There is plenty of eye candy and kissing and comical mishaps as the band struggles to achieve their dream.

Episodes:
1. Chicks with Licks (4 min., 57 sec.). Bubba, LIPS' biggest fan and mediocre film maker, begins an assignment making a rockumentary of the band as they seek stardom.
2. Dinah or Bust (4 min., 48 sec.). Helen and Doris sign on as Tangent Queens (backup lesbian eye candy as LIPS has a lesbian following) while Didi hires a manager (Fiona) with a gambling problem (in high school she was known as "Sticky Fingers Fiona").
3. The Love Itch (5 min., 22 sec.). As it is revealed that Bubba has deep feelings for London, a ghost from Didi's past—Armondo, enters her life.
4. Trickery (5 min., 40 sec.). It is revealed that Didi ruined Armondo's life by sleeping with his fiancé and now he seeks revenge—by getting her deported.
5. Working for Tips (5 min., 54 sec.). Fiona's

bookings are anything but typical as she has LIPS' performing first at a Brisk then a funeral.

   6. Audition This! (3 min., 55 sec.). The second season begins with the group preparing to perform at Coacehlla.

   7. Lips or Bust (4 min., 1 sec.). LIPS performs the song "If You Were a Booger" for potential band mates at an audition.

   8. Elaine Hendrix Won't Take No for an Answer (3 min., 22 sec.). As film and television actress Elaine Hendrix displays her musical abilities for the band, London and Didi show they are more interested in her breasts than her lack of musical talent.

   9. Debra Wilson Faces Off with London (4 min., 43 sec.). London and her ex-girlfriend (Debra Wilson) cross paths again but neither is happy to see the other.

   10. Snaps and Gino (5 min., 12 sec.). As two young women, Snaps and Amber audition for the band, London hires Gino, a would-be Mafia gangster, as their manager.

   11. Swept Off Her Combat Boots (5 min., 8 sec.). As Helen fantasizes about having London, Rousaura is the one who sweeps London off her feet. Meanwhile Gino takes over the band.

   12. Rousaura Rocks London's World (5 min., 3 sec.). It is a love at first sight for London when she sees Rousaura, a sexy dancer.

   13. Lip Locked (4 min., 22 sec.). As London and Rousaura become closer, Helen is tricked into making out on camera.

   14. Dreadlock Lap Dance (3 min., 1 sec.). London's relationship with Rousaura intensifies after Rousaura gives London a sensual lap dance.

   15. Ur the Opposite of That (4 min., 35 sec.). Now inspired by her infatuation with Rousaura, London writes her first love song—"Ur the Opposite of That."

   16. Love Hurts (2 min., 53 sec.). Bubba's love for London angers his girlfriend, Endora, a woman involved in voodoo and black magic, who is determined to change Bubba's outlook.

   17. You're in My Personal Space (6 min., 45 sec.). London's fascination with Rousaura takes her into a world of lust and love that she has never before experienced.

   18. Barbie's a Lesbian (7 min., 29 sec.). As Endora continues to test Bubba's love for her, a girl (Doris) sets her sights on Helen.

   19. R.I.P. Fiona (6 min., 41 sec.). Although London is unsure of her love for Rousaura, Rousaura continues pursuing her. Meanwhile, Endora attempts to use her voodoo powers to destroy London.

   20. The Ultimate Kiss (5 min., 2 sec.). With London still being pursued by Bubba, London herself is unsure of her feelings until Rousaura pins London in a closet and gives her "the kiss of her life."

   21. Here Today, Gone ... Today (6 min., 33 sec.). When Snaps makes a move on Doris and she is exposed as being a lesbian, Doris tries to come to terms

with her once hidden sexuality; meanwhile, as the second season ends, London finds a note that reveals Rousaura has left the country, making Bubba believe that he now has a chance to be with London (forgetting that Endora is still seeking to "hang London by her toenails and staple her legs together").

194 The Listless. blip.tv. 2013 (Drama).

   It could be now; it could be the future; it is a time when a plague has virtually destroyed the world through addiction to a devastating, mind-destroying drug called Blue. While it is addictive and virtually impossible to resist, it can be overcome if its symptoms can be detected before it is too late. For those who have overcome the addiction, it has become a world where survival is now a daily struggle—seeking not only food but avoiding the affected, who have become zombie-like and have no regard for anyone or anything. One such survivor is Lily, a young woman who must not only battle her addiction, but the chaos that surrounds her. Lily was once a normal person, a woman with a purpose. Now her days are spent in solitaire, hiding and reliving memories of a time that was. She is one of The Listless, people who live day-by-day in a non-accomplishing life hoping society will once again return to the way it was before drugs destroyed it. **Cast:** Heather Headrick (Lily), Anna Maria Bryant (Daisy), Brandon Kreuger (Stranger). **Credits:** *Producer:* Cameron Smith. **Comment:** Exceptionally well done program that combines black and white with color scenes to give it a sense of authenticity as Lily faces life. By what little has been produced, it appears that the program will be an eerie and fascinating look into a world destroyed by a plague that is literally already with us—drugs.

   Episodes:

   1. Dirt in the Ground. Introduces Lily and the world in which she now lives.

   2. Goin' Out West. Lily ventures outside her deplorable sanctuary in an effort to find food.

   3. Don't Go Into the Barn. Lily is taken captive by a strange man and brought to his barn as night falls (for safety?). The program ends unresolved.

195 Literally Dysfunctional. literallydysfunctional.com. 2013 (Comedy-Drama).

   It appears that since fictional stories have been written (including fairy tales) the intentions set forth by authors regarding their characters have changed over time. It could be perceived as people interpreting what is written differently or that filmmakers have expanded on an original creation to suit their own particular needs. Even though they are fictional characters "they have real needs." There is an unseen world wherein Guardians perform the services of therapists to maintain the integrity and longevity of the characters as they were originally written. Dr.

Lynn Chaucer is one such therapist and the program follows her efforts to council various literally figures whose characters have evolved beyond their original creation and return them to their origins before their stories become unknown to future generations. It is also hinted that if they are not made whole, it could mean the destruction of the world.

Cast: Susan Papa (Lynn Chaucer), Darby McCullough (Little Red Riding Hood), John C. Crow (Jay Gatsby), Emily Peck (Catherine Earnshaw), Alex Santori (Scarlett O'Hara), Alice Sherman (Kate Minola), Leah Steiner (Stella Kowalski), Daved Wilkins (Arthur Dent), Aubrey Wakeling (Declan Chaucer). **Credits:** *Producer:* Christopher Gallego, Amber Shaw. *Diretcor:* Christopher Gallego. *Writer:* Amber Shaw. **Comment:** There are numerous story line possibilities in an intriguing series that presents a totally new look at literary characters. The casting is well done, especially for Little Red Riding Hood as she develops anger issues over her loss of innocence. The program does explore some character problems but ends unresolved.

Episodes:

1. The Id, the Ego and the Fictitious (6 min., 1 sec.). The concept is introduced as Lynn meets with her newest patients, Scarlett O'Hara, Little Red Riding Hood and Kate Minola.

2. Never Can Tell What Lies Ahead (6 min., 7 sec.). Little Red believes she has been stripped of her innocence and her fairy tale can no longer be lived. Meanwhile Catherine Earnshaw is lamenting over the fact that she may never see her world in England as it was written for her.

3. The Mouth of the Wolf, or the End of the World (6 min., 16 sec.). In an effort to help Little Red, Lynn takes her into the real world to show her she has nothing to fear, especially the big bad wolf.

196 *Little Horribles.* littlehorribles.com. 2013 (Comedy-Drama).

Amy is a 27-year-old lesbian living in Los Angeles. She is pretty, a bit overweight and appears to envy the more glamorous and seductive lesbians she encounters. She is looking for a relationship with another woman but finding that special person presents its own share of problems. She is not seductive, she does not pretend to be something she is not and she is a bit shy when it comes to approaching beautiful women. With those strikes already against her, Amy tries to navigate the lesbian scene and find the romance she is seeking.

Cast: Amy York Rubin (Amy), Ann Carr, Leslie Korein (Emily), Ilana Glazer (Lindsey), Echo Kellum (Paul), Ana Cristina Mayer (Herself), Misty Monroe (Girl), Sophia Mayer Pliner (Herself), Hannah Victoria Stock (Hannah), Cynthia Stevenson (Amy's mother), Tom Virtue (Amy's father). **Credits:** *Producer:* Amy York Rubin, Issa Rae. *Director:* Amy York Rubin, Bridget Palardy. *Writer:* Amy York

Rubin. **Comment:** There are a few kissing scenes, but no nudity or intense sexual situations. The program is well acted and produced and the episodes are just the right length so as not to stretch out a situation and make it boring. The concluding episode leaves open the doorway for future encounters for Amy as she seeks that one special mate.

Episodes:

1. Sexual Activity (4 min., 34 sec.). Amy's hopeful romance with a new girlfriend goes from good to bad when the girl breaks up with her.

2. LMFAO (4 min., 1 sec.). At work, Amy begins a computer chat with a fellow worker (Lindsey) that looks promising but later fizzles out.

3. Date (4 min., 31 sec.). Amy secures a date with an attractive girl whose sole ambition in life is to become a florist.

4. Road Rage (4 min., 41 sec.). Explores the problems Amy encounters when she becomes stuck in a traffic jam.

5. Stunning (2 min., 35 sec.). Amy becomes depressed when see sees a girl she likes being seduced by a gorgeous lesbian.

6. Member (6 min., 40 sec.). A look at Amy's family—from a mother who isn't quite sure if Amy is a lesbian or bi-sexual; a father who doesn't seem to care and a kid sister who knows exactly who Amy is.

7. Bathroom Mirror (5 min., 21 sec.). In the ladies room at a local bar, Amy encounters two lesbians who give her advice on how to attract a woman.

8. Armrest (7 min., 49 sec.). On a plane flight, Amy finds herself dealing with a crying baby, an annoying little boy and a gorgeous mother that arouses feelings within her.

9. Basketball (10 min., 11 sec.). Since all the conventional ways to meet a girl appear to be failing, Amy joins an all-girl basketball team hoping for something more than just shooting baskets.

10. Oldies (6 min., 4 sec.). Amy finds that even as she tries to enjoy her favorite pastime, watching movies at the Silent Movie Theater, she encounters sympathy from the elder patrons who wonder why she is at the theatre alone.

11. Spinning (5 min., 15 sec.). Amy's decision to not purchase fast food at a drive through causes problems when she begins arguing with two female customers over the fatty content and high calorie count such foods contain.

12. Two Parties (9 min., 28 sec.). Amy's luck may have changed when she attends two parties on the same night as the program concludes.

197 *Living It Up.* webserieschannel.com. 2012 (Comedy-Drama).

Bianca Hicks is a young woman, interested in becoming a model, who is currently a college student (majoring in psychology). Her life, however, revolves around the models and actors who are her friends and the program follows the incidents that affect Bianca as she faces deception, arrogance and competition in her attempt to become a top fashion model.

Cast: Tandreka Keaton (Bianca Hicks), Da'Ron Mitchell (Christopher Jackson), Sherri Nelson-Jones (Carla Daniels), Jeanette Drake (Raquell Moore), Jevin Hartzman (Jason Alexander), Grant Hagene (John Matthews), Michael W. Campbell, Jr. (Darrius Jones), Dennis Doyle, Jr. (Gordon). **Credits:** *Producer-Writer-Director:* Malcolm Roberson. **Comment:** All episodes have been taken off line. Even though episode descriptions remain, they are very vague and a judgment cannot be made from them (especially when characters are mentioned with no clues to who they are or what relationship they have to Bianca).

Episode List: *1.* Welcome Home. *2.* Truth Be Told. *3.* Brand New. *4.* Mid-Terms. *5.* Me, Myself and the Note. *6.* One Step Forward and Two Steps Back. *7.* Drama Free. *8.* Down Hill Spiral. *9.* The Heat of the Moment. *10.* Awkward Moments. *11.* The Calm Before the Storm. *12.* Too Much to Bare, Part 1. *13.* Too Much to Bare, Part 2.

198 The Lizzie Bennet Diaries. lizziebennet.com. 2012–2013 (Drama).

Elizabeth Bennet, called Lizzie, is 24 years old and a graduate student in mass communications. When Charlotte, her best friend and hopeful film maker, convinces Lizzie to create a vlog series for her senior class thesis, Lizzie aggress and begins a series of short videos wherein she relates aspects of her life—from her relationship with her family and friends, the situations that affect her in her daily life to her thoughts on life after graduation and the problems and fears she faces. The program conveys each story (set primarily in Lizzie's bedroom) through vlogs (her speaking directly to the camera with characters related to the story also appearing with her, but to relate a different perspective on what happened). As the series progressed, other settings were encompassed to bring on characters apart from Lizzie: her sisters (Lydia and Jane) and her friend Charlotte. "My name is Lizzie Bennet and this is my life." The program is a modern adaptation of the novel *Pride and Prejudice* by Jane Austen.

Jane, Lizzie's older sister, works as a Merchandise Coordinator in the fashion industry. Lydia, Lizzie's younger sister is a bit more energetic than Lizzie, attends college and has a cat named "Kitty Bennet." Mary Bennet is Lizzie's cousin, a down-to-earth girl who enjoys reading and keeping to herself. Charlotte is Lizzie's best friend (they attend grad school together and have been friends since childhood). Maria is Charlotte's sister, a girl with an uncanny interest in science fiction movies and TV series.

Bing Lee is Lizzie's neighbor, a medical student; William Darcy is Bing's friend (heir to the company, Pemberley Digital; where Lizzie temporarily works); Ricky Collins is Lizzie and Charlotte's childhood friend (now the owner of the media company Collins and Collins; Charlotte later works for him); George

***The Lizzie Bennet Diaries.* Left to right: Julia Cho, Ashley Clements, Mary Kate Wiles, Laura Spencer (used by permission of Pemberley Digital).**

Wickman is the swimming coach; Gigi is Darcy's younger sister (a graphic designer at Pemberley Digital).

Cast: Ashley Clements (Lizzie Bennet), Julia Cho (Charlotte Lu), Mary Kate Wiles (Lydia Bennet), Laura Spencer (Jane Bennet), Briana Cuoco (Mary Bennet), Ricky Collins (Maxwell Glick), Wes Aderhold (George Wickham), Daniel Vincent Gordh (William Darcy), Janice Lee (Maria Lu), Craig Frank (Fitz Williams), Allison Paige (Georgiana "Gigi" Darcy), Jessica Jade Andres (Caroline Lee), Christopher Sean (Bing Lee). **Credits:** *Producer:* Bernie Su, Hank Green, Jenni Powell. *Director:* Bernie Su. *Writer:* Bernie Su, Margaret Dunlap. **Comment:** Exceptional video quality coupled with very good acting in a program that retains aspects of the original characters as they are transported from the 18th to 21st centuries. The writing and directing is also very good and the program is captivating from start to finish.

Episodes (Lizzie's Video Diaries):
1. My Name Is Lizzie Bennett. April 9, 2012.
2. My Sisters—Problematic to Practically Perfect. April 12, 2012.
3. My Parents: Imposingly Supportive. April 16, 2012.
4. Bing Lee and His 500 Teenage Prostitutes. April 19, 2012.
5. After the Wedding: The Real Bing Lee. April 24, 2012.
6. The Snobby Mr. Douchey. April 27, 2012.
7. The Most Awkward Dance Ever. April 30, 2012.
8. Charlotte Is Back. May 4, 2012.
9. Single and Happyish. May 7, 2012.
10. Cats and Chinchillas. May 10, 2012.
11. Charming Mr. Lee. May 14, 2012.
12. Jane Chimes in May. May 17, 2012.
13. Bing! It's Time for Dinner. May 21, 2012.
14. I Suck at Video Games. May 24, 2012.
15. Lizzie Bennet Is in Denial. May 28, 2012.
16. Happiness in the Pursuit of Life. May 31, 2012.
17. Swimming with Scissors. June 4, 2012.
18. Douchebags and Gentlemen. June 7, 2012.
19. The Green Bean Gelatin Plan. June 11, 2012.
20. Enjoy the Adorbs Jane. June 14, 2012.
21. The Semester Is Over. June 18, 2012.
22. The Unavoidable Invitation. June 21, 2012.
23. One Sister Behind June. June 25, 2012.
24. Jane Is Back and Mom Isn't Happy. June 28, 2012.
25. Vidcon Interruption. July 2, 2012.
26. Mom's Convoluted Plan. July 5, 2012.
27. Welcome to Netherfield. July 8, 2012.
28. Meeting Bing Lee. July 12, 2012.
29. Ethics of Seeing Bing. July 17, 2012.
30. Ticking Clock. July 19, 2012.
31. Convertible Carpool. July 23, 2012.
32. Turn About the Room. July 26, 2012.
33. Nope, He Doesn't Like Me. July 30, 2012.
34. Lizzie Come Home. Aug. 2, 2012.
35. Home Sweet Home. Aug. 6, 2012.
36. Mr. Collins Returns. Aug. 9, 2012.
37. Lydia vs. Mr. Collins. Aug. 13, 2012.
38. Tale of Two Gents. Aug. 16, 2012.
39. The Insistent Proposal. Aug. 20, 2012.
40. The Proposal Fallout. Aug. 23, 2012.
41. Your Pitch Needs Work. Aug. 27, 2012.
42. Friends Forever. Aug. 3, 2012.
43. Missing Charlotte. Sept. 3, 2012.
44. Darcy Wickham Drama. Sept. 6, 2012.
45. Wickham Story Time. Sept. 10, 2012.
46. Birthday Party Battle Plan. Sept. 13, 2012.
47. It's About Communicating. Sept. 17, 2012.
48. Snickerdoodles. Sept. 20, 2012.
49. Not Paranoid. Sept. 24, 2012.
50. Moving On. Sept. 27, 2012.
51. Together Again. Oct. 1, 2012.
52. Better Living. Oct. 4, 2012.
53. Royal Dining. Oct. 8, 2012.
54. Annie Kins. Oct. 11, 2012.
55. Robot Surprise. Oct. 15, 2012.
56. A New Buddy. Oct. 18, 2012.
57. Weirded Out. Oct. 22, 2012.
58. Care Packages. Oct. 25, 2012.
59. Staff Spirit. Oct. 29, 2012.
60. Are You Kidding Me! Nov. 1, 2012.
61. Yeah, I Know. Nov. 5, 2011.
62. Letter Analysis. Nov. 8, 2012.
63. Unexpected Returns. Nov. 12, 2012.
64. C vs. C. Nov. 15, 2012.
65. Turkey Days. Nov. 19, 2012.
66. Giving Thanks. Nov. 22, 2012.
67. Back Home Again. Nov. 26, 2012.
68. Leftovers. Nov. 29, 2012.
69. Summer Friends. Dec. 3, 2012.
70. New Jane. Dec. 6, 2012.
71. Mr. Bennet's Christmas Train Extravaganza. Dec. 10, 2012.
72. Party Time. Dec. 13, 2012.
73. 2 +1. Dec. 17, 2012.
74. How to Hold a Grudge. Dec. 20, 2012.
75. Merry Christmas. Dec. 24, 2012.
76. Wishing Something Universal. Dec. 27, 2012.
77. Tour Leader. Jan. 7, 2013.
78. The Lizzie Trap. Jan. 10, 2013.
79. The Unavoidable Mr. Lee. Jan. 14, 2013.
80. Hyper-Meditation in New Media. Jan. 17, 2013.
81. Awkward. Jan. 21, 2013.
82. Checks and Balances. Jan. 24, 2013.
83. Corporate Interview. Jan. 28, 2013.
84. Ugh. Jan. 31, 2013.
85. Consequences. Feb. 4, 2013.
86. Sisterly Support. Feb. 7, 2013.
87. An Understanding. Feb. 11, 2013.
88. Okay. Feb. 14, 2013.
89. Insomnia. Feb. 18, 2013.
90. Something Lighter ... Please. Feb. 21, 2013.

91. How About That. Feb. 25, 2013.
92. Goodbye Jane. Feb. 28, 2013.
93. Look Who's Back. Mar. 4, 2013.
94. Revelations. Mar. 7, 2013.
95. End of the Line. Mar. 11, 2013.
96. Talking to Myself. Mar. 14, 2013.
97. Special Delivery. Mar. 18, 2013.
98. Gratitude. Mar. 21, 2013.
99. Future Talk. Mar. 25, 2013.
100. The End. Mar. 28, 2013.

Episodes (Lizzie's Q & A). Lizzie responds to and chats with viewers.

1. Lizzie's First Q &A. May 5, 2012.
2. Lizzie's Second Q & A: Lizzie Answers Questions. June 23, 2012.
3. Lizzie's Third Q & A: Lizzie and George Answer Questions. Sept. 15, 2012.
4. Lizzie's Fourth Q & A: Lizzie and Fitz. Oct. 20, 2012.
5. Lizzie's Fifth Q & A: Lizzie and Ricky. Nov. 10, 2012.
6. Lizzie's Sixth Q & A: Lizzie and Gigi. Jan. 19, 2013.
7. Lizzie's Seventh Q & A: Feb. 8, 2013.
8. Lizzie's Eighth Q & A: Lizzie and Darcy: Mar. 23, 2013.

Episodes (Lydia's Videos). To present a different aspect on what happens, Lydia creates her own series of vlogs ("The Lydia Bennet") that are seen when she and Lizzie are apart (for example, when Lizzie is away from home seeking job opportunities). Lydia's vlogs are also different in that they are set in the locals in which she appears (for example, in Los Angeles to visit Jane).

1. Lydia Bennet Episode 1: Boredom. July 13, 2012.
2. Lydia Bennet Episode 2: About a Boy. July 17, 2012.
3. Lydia Bennet Episode 3: The Lodger. July 20, 2012.
4. Lydia Bennet Episode 4: Peer Pressure. July 24, 2012.
5. Lydia Bennet Episode 5: Baby Sitting. July 27, 2012.
6. Lydia Bennet Episode 6: Kitty Bennet. July 31, 2012.
7. Lydia Bennet Episode 7: Going Home. Aug. 3, 2012.
8. Lydia Bennet Episode 8: Miss Me Yet? Oct. 12, 2012.
9. Lydia Bennet Episode 9: Study Break. Oct. 16, 2012.
10. Lydia Bennet Episode 10: Ditching. Oct. 19, 2012.
11. Lydia Bennet Episode 11: Girl Talk. Oct. 23, 2012.
12. Lydia Bennet Episode 12: Life of the Party. Oct. 26, 2012.
13. Lydia Bennet Episode 13: Runaway. Oct. 30, 2012.

14. Lydia Bennet Episode 14: Halloween, Holla!! Oct. 31, 2012.
15. Lydia Bennet Episode 15: The High Life. Nov. 2, 2012.
16. Lydia Bennet Episode 16: Sister, Sister. Nov. 6, 2012.
17. Lydia Bennet Episode 17: The "D" Word. Nov. 9, 2012.
18. Lydia Bennet Episode 18: There's Something About Mary. Nov. 13, 2012.
19. Lydia Bennet Episode 19: Friction. Nov. 16, 2012.
20. Lydia Bennet Episode 20: Friends. Nov. 20, 2012.
21. Lydia Bennet Totes Thanksgiving. Nov. 23, 2012.
22. Lydia Bennet Episode 22: Dear Lizzie. Dec. 19, 2012.
23. Lydia Bennet Episode 23: Vegas, Bitches! Dec. 28, 2012.
24. Lydia Bennet Episode 24: Midnight. Jan. 1, 2013.
25. Lydia Bennet Episode 25: Midnight. Jan. 1, 2013.
26. Lydia Bennet Episode 26: Surprise. Jan. 4, 2013.
27. Lydia Bennet Episode 27: Mistakes, Jan. 8, 2013.
28. Lydia Bennet Episode 28: Strangers. Jan. 11, 2013.
29. Lydia Bennet Episode 29: Dreams. Jan. 18, 2013.
30. Lydia Bennet Episode 30: Heartbreaker. Jan. 22, 2013.
31. Lydia Bennet Episode 31: Special Two. Jan. 25, 2013.
32. Lydia Bennet Episode 32: Good Enough. Jan. 29, 2013.

199 *LOL (Teen Web Series).* blip.tv. 2008 (Drama).

London, England provides the backdrop for a look at the lives of a particular group of teenagers (Keely, Jaz, Cam, Skellhorn, Dawber and Mase) and the world in which they have chosen to live—a world filled with drugs, sex and alcohol. Through the use of flash forwards, incidents that have occurred are seen first with a flashback showing how those incidents not only affected the teenagers, but their friends and families as well.

Cast: Nicola Mahoney (Keely Cooper), Bryony Seth (Jaz Nerini), Joe Hughes (Tom "Mase" Mason), Michael Lawrence (Oliver Skellhorn), Nico Mirallegro (Cam Spencer), Dan Pye (Scott Dawber), Toni Cummings (Helen Cooper), Andrew Sykes (James Garner), Eliza Kempson (Jo Nerini), Chris Holding (Milo Peet), Victoria Hammett (Beth Thompson), Mark Fenton (Marshy), Dane Brooks (P.C. Kane), Bernadette Nuttall (D.C. Wells), Kathryn Maye-

David (Ms. Stanton), Roni Ellis (Di Spencer), Sharma Walfall (Nina), Mark Horrobin (Dean).
Credits: *Producer-Writer-Director:* Ric Forster. **Comment:** Although there is a viewer advisory for sexual situations and vulgar language, the program is very disturbing for its extremely realistic presentation. It's just something that an American network or basic cable TV station would not broadcast. The program involves the viewer in the teen's lives, especially Keely and Jaz, from the very beginning and keeps you hooked to see how (or if) they will overcome their addictions. Being produced in England (and not for American audiences) it is also very difficult to understand at times due to thick British accents. It does takes some rewinding to understand what was said, but still worth watching for something totally different (perhaps shocking at times).

Episodes:
1. Webisode 1 (4 min., 37 sec.). The program begins with an introduction to 15-year-old Keely, the daughter of a single mother (Helen); Jaz, her best mate; Dawber, Jaz's boyfriend, a high school dropout; and Cam, a schoolmate.

2. Webisode 2 (3 min., 58 sec.). When Helen discovers Keely's activates (pictures of her drunk and having "fun") on her web page, she alerts other parents, leading to a showdown between the two generations.

3. Webisode 3 (3 min., 29 sec.). At a party, an intoxicated Keely becomes too close to Dawber, causing Jaz to confront her and accuse her of trying to steal her boyfriend.

4. Webisode 4 (5 min., 11 sec.). Hoping to make amends for what happened, Keely takes Jaz out "for a night of boozing."

5. Webisode 5 (4 min., 44 sec.). When their attempt to buy alcohol fails, Keely and Jaz accept an invitation to drink from Skellhorn and Mase—a situation that soon gets out of hand when the guys try to take advantage of them.

6. Webisode 6 (3 min., 42 sec.). Managing to fend off the guys, the girls return home with Keely not only trying to hide the fact that she has a hangover, but facing the wrath of her mother who demands to know where she was all night.

7. Webisode 7 (3 min., 5 sec.). Keely's night out also has adverse effects on Cam, who is angry at Keely for the chances she took just to get drunk.

8. Webisode 8 (3 min., 6 sec.). At a party being thrown by Marshy, tensions between Cam and Keely appear to be easing as Cam is seeking to apologize for his actions.

9. Webisode 9 (2 min., 47 sec.). As the party continues and Jaz slowly becomes intoxicated, she indulges in sex with a boy.

10. Webisode 10 (4 min., 30 sec.). Although drunk, Keely realizes she still has feelings for Cam and attempts to make amends with him.

11. Webisode 11 (3 min., 45 sec.). Several days have passed and the consequences of her actions become apparent when Jaz discovers she is pregnant.

12. Webisode 12 (4 min.). Scared and not knowing what to do, Jaz attempts to come to terms with what has happened to her.

13. Webisode 13 (3 min., 33 sec.). With courage she didn't know she had, Jaz tells her mother that she is pregnant but fears telling the baby's father.

14. Webisode 14 (2 min., 56 sec.). Realizing that her intoxication is alienating her from her friends, Keely tries to mend her friendship with Mase.

15. Webisode 15 (3 min., 5 sec.). As Keely celebrates her 16th birthday, she and Mase appear to be growing closer together.

16. Webisode 16 (4 min., 35 sec.). Keely befriends a new girl (Beth) and immediately finds they have a connection—alcohol and head out for some drinking fun.

17. Webisode 17 (2 min., 32 sec.). Unable to put up with Keely's irresponsibility, Helen (Keely's mother) grounds her in an effort to get her to see what she is doing.

18. Webisode 18 (3 min., 55 sec.). Bitterly objecting to what her mother has done, Keely decides she needs to get out and runs away.

19. Webisode 19 (4 min., 17 sec.). Although Keely is safe (with Jaz, the one person she can trust), a police search is begun to find her as Helen fears the worst has happened to her.

20. Webisode 20 (8 min., 27 sec.). The program concludes with Keely coming to terms with all that she has done wrong and Jaz giving birth to a daughter (Isabella Brooke).

200 *Lonely Girl 15.* youtube.com. 2006–2008 (Drama).

Bree Avery is a 16-year-old girl who, under the user name lonelygirl15, presents a series of Internet video blogs wherein she not only comments on everyday issues (as any teenage girl would) but on her observations about secret occult practices and how, after she refused to participate in a cult gathering prescribed by "The Family," her parents mysteriously disappeared. As the vlogs continued, Bree revealed she possessed a rare blood type (Trait Positive) and she, as well as other girls possessing the same blood, are being sought by The Order, a strange cult that requires such blood for their sacrifices (with Bree as their main objective). (The vlogs were presented so realistically that it was believed that what Bree was relating was actually happening and not just fantasized for a series.)

Season 1: Establishes that Bee, a Los Angeles–based teenager, possesses a rare blood type and that she, along with other innocent girls who possesses the same Trait Positive Blood are being sought for sacrifices ("The Ceremony") for a cult called The Order. Daniel, Jonas, Spencer, Sarah and Becki, Bree's friends become involved in her plight and become saviors of sorts as they now seek to protect those threatened by The Order.

Season 2: Sarah, Daniel and Jonas, now joined by Emma and Jennie, continue to battle The Order with Jonah looking back to his past and Daniel looking to the future for answers.

Season 3: Continues the story line as the battle against The Order continues.

Other Characters: Daniel, user name Danielbeast, is Bree's best friend, a romantic who risks his life to protect Bree from The Order.

Jonas Wharton (user name jonastko) is the on-line boy Bree befriends whose family has ties to The Order.

Sarah Genatiempo (user name theskyisempty99) is the 19-year-old girl who becomes romantically involved with Daniel.

Becki (username soccerstar4ever) is Sarah's younger sister, an expert computer hacker (and devoted soccer player).

Spencer Gilman (user name LAlabrat) works at Nutrogena and has connections with the science division of The Order (he is seeking to develop a Trait Negative Serum).

Emma Wharton is Jonas's sister, a girl with Trait Positive Blood who is constantly battling The Order's efforts to acquire her blood.

Jennie, Sarah's friend, is romantically involved with Jonas and has knowledge on how The Order functions.

Gina Hart is Bree's older sister, a girl who spent most of her early life as a test subject for Trait Positive Blood.

Sonja is a member of the Hymn of None, the organization battling The Order.

Cast: Jessica Lee Rose (Bree Avery), Yousef Abu-Taleb (Daniel), Jonas Wharton (Jackson Davis), Alexandra Dreyfus (Sarah Genatiempo), Becki Kregoski (Taylor Genatiempo), Maxwell Glick (Spencer Gilman), Katherine Pawlak (Emma Wharton), Melanie Merkosky (Jennie), Crystal Young (Gina Hart), Raegan Payne (Sonja). **Comment:** Concern over what was being broadcast raised suspicions among alert YouTube viewers who discovered that Bree, as lonelygirl15, was not real but 19-year-old American–New Zealand actress Jessica Lee Rose playing a role so convincingly that she convinced viewers her life was in jeopardy. Efforts to make lonelygirl15 appear real were supplemented by Bree dropping names of real YouTube users as well as giving her a My Space page wherein she chatted with users. It was then publicly revealed that the show's creators, Ramesh Flinders, Miles Beckett and Greg Goodfried were the principal people responsible for creating a false impression among YouTube followers. Although many of the episodes are off-line, the essence of the program can still be felt through what remains. The program is, in a way, like the Halloween of 1938 radio broadcast of *The War of the Worlds* wherein star Orson Welles presented a program so convinc-ingly real that many listeners believed the world was being attacked by Martians and a panic resulted.

Episode List: The following episodes, of the 547 that were produced, remain on line:

1. Lonelybeast and Danielbeast (1 min., 37 sec.).
2. My Lazy Eye (and P. Monkey Gets Funky) (1 min., 53 sec.).
3. He Said, She Said (47 sec.).
4. Boy Problems (2 min., 12 sec.).
5. My Parents ... Let Us Go Hiking! (1 min., 49 sec.).
6. Proving Science Wrong (1 min., 37 sec.).
7. Daniel Returns—and More Interesting Fac-toids (3 min., 28 sec.).
8. My Parents Suck (1 min., 2 sec.).
9. Grillzfeat and Danielbeast (2 min., 55 sec.).
10. My Comments Were Deleted (26 sec.).
11. The Danielbeast (1 min., 54 sec.).
12. School Work in Summer ... BLECHH!! (2 min., 24 sec.).
13. Purple Monkey (1 min., 24 sec.).
14. First Blog/Dorkiness Prevails (1 min., 36 sec.)
15. YouTubers Secret Language (57 sec.).
16. Payotheorderoffofof vs. Dinosaur (42 sec.).
17. The Equinox (1 min., 15 sec.).
18. Learning to Drive (1 min., 48 sec.).
19. My First Kiss (3 min., 3 sec.).
20. In the Park (1 min., 37 sec.).
21. House Arrest (2 min., 19 sec.).
22. I'm Going to the Party (1 min., 24 sec.),
23. Should I or Shouldn't I? (2 min., 10 sec.).
24. Poor Pluto (1 min., 56 sec.).
25. A Change in My Life (1 min., 8 sec.).
26. Bree the Cookie Monster (1 min., 44 sec.).
27. Swimming (3 min., 4 sec.).
28. I'm Really, Really, Really Excited! (1 min., 39 sec.).
29. A Peace Offering (and P. Monkey Boogies) (2 min., 17 sec.).
30. Mysteries of My Past ... Revealed! (2 min., 29 sec.).
31. I Probably Shouldn't Post This... (1 min., 32 sec.).
32. Me, Religion and Daniel (1 min., 26 sec.).
33. What Did Daniel and Dad Talk About? (3 min., 30 sec.).
34. Daniel the Neanderthal (1 min., 55 sec.).
35. The Tolstoy Principle (2 min., 3 sec.).
36. On the Run (4 min., 12 sec.).
37. Where Are My Parents? (32 sec.).
38. Still at Daniel's (1 min., 16 sec.).
39. Life's Not Fair (1 min., 31 sec.).
40. What Makes Us Sad? (2 min., 26 sec.).
41. Thanks Gemma... (1 min., 26 sec.).
42. Proving Longitude Wrong (2 min., 18 sec.).
43. I Talked to My Parents (1 min., 26 sec.).
44. Hi Gemma! (1 min., 30 sec.).
45. I Listened to Daniel (2 min., 4 sec.).
46. I Lied to Daniel (1 min., 35 sec.).

47. Where's Daniel? (1 min., 1 sec.).
48. Daniel, Be Careful (1 min., 24 sec.).
49. I Completed the Ceremony! (1 min., 28 sec.).
50. The Ceremony Is Tomorrow (2 min., 52 sec.).
51. Zodiac of Denderah (2 min., 39 sec.).
52. Daniel Crossed the Line (1 min., 19 sec.).
53. How My Parents Met (2 min., 3 sec.).
54. My Helper (1 min., 57 sec.).
55. My Difficult Decision (1 min., 42 sec.).
56. Daniel's Missing (1 min., 38 sec.).
57. Time to Grow Up (2 min., 19 sec.).
58. Truth or Dare (3 min., 59 sec.).
59. Hiding in the Bathroom (2 min., 4 sec.).
60. My Dad Said... (3 min., 52 sec.).
61. The Unthinkable Happened (2 min., 54 sec.).
62. Mystery Movies (2 min., 26 sec.).
63. Skateboarding (2 min., 29 sec.).
64. Bree Phone Home (3 min., 27 sec.).
65. Cheer Me Up (1 min., 56 sec.).
66. War Walking (2 min., 39 sec.).
67. Ransacked (2 min., 22 sec.).
68. Thanksgiving (2 min., 54 sec.).
69. Date with P. Monkey (1 min., 18 sec.).
70. Survival Skills (2 min., 42 sec.).
71. Fleeing the Watcher (1 min., 47 sec.).
72. Man in the Suit (2 min., 43 sec.).
73. Exploring the Motel (2 min., 16 sec.).
74. Motel Pool (1 min., 49 sec.).
75. Aunt Alex (2 min., 57 sec.).
76. My Hand Hurts (2 min., 25 sec.)
77. Flesh Wound (2 min., 5 sec.).
78. Beach Bum (2 min., 32 sec.).
79. Sorry Jonas (3 min., 5 sec.).
80. On the Road Again (2 min., 14 sec.).
81. Proving Bree Wrong (1 min., 54 sec.).
82. Is He Out There? (1 min., 3 sec.).
83. What the Hell (1 min., 40 sec.).
84. How Dumb Am I? (2 min., 29 sec.).
85. Men Are from Mars (2 min., 52 sec.).
86. Snow Angels (2 min., 14 sec.).
87. Yellow Snow (2 min., 26 sec.).
88. Watch This! (56 sec.).
89. Rescuing Daniel (2 min., 21 sec.).
90. The Human Ransom (2 min., 21 sec.).
91. Me for Daniel (2 min., 18 sec.).
92. The Cowboy (2 min., 30 sec.).
93. Sleepover (2 min., 12 sec.).
94. Looking for Daniel (1 min., 25 sec.).
95. The Perfect Beach (2 min., 42 sec.).
96. Spanglish (4 min., 7 sec.).
97. Apology Accepted? (3 min., 6 sec.).
98. Hug It Out (2 min., 57 sec.).
99. Confrontation (2 min., 26 sec.).
100. Spring Break Sucks (4 min., 21 sec.).
101. Lying Bastards (2 min., 42 sec.).
102. Losing My Religion (2 min., 35 sec.).
103. Missing My Religion (2 min., 35 sec.).

104. Missing Days (3 min., 30 sec.).
105. Communication Terminated (1 min., 51 sec.).
106. Psychological Torture (3 min., 24 sec.).
107. Subjects Apprehended (1 min., 38 sec.).
108. Vegas, Baby! (3 min., 32 sec.).
109. Co-Ed Foosball (3 min., 28 sec.).
110. Truck Stop Reunion (4 min., 18 sec.).
111. Alex Is... (2 min., 54 sec.).
112. Lucky!?!? (50 sec.).
113. Uncle Dan (5 min., 2 sec.).
114. On the Hot Seat (2 min., 30 sec.).
115. Training Hard (2 min., 26 sec.).
116. The Mistress (3 min., 55 sec.).
117. Follow Your Happiness (3 min., 55 sec.).
118. Going Home (1 min., 54 sec.).
119. IhATE tHeSe PeOple (46 sec.).
120. Getting Her Back (3 min., 12 sec.).
121. Be Part of Something (1 min., 40 sec.).
122. Sing with Me (1 min., 9 sec.).
123. Let's Play Doctor (2 min., 52 sec.).
124. What the F*@K??? (1 min., 29 sec.).
125. She's Missing (2 min., 40 sec.).
126. Naïve Girl (52 sec.).
127. It's Not Kidnapping (1 min., 41 sec.).
128. We Found Julia (1 min., 40 sec.).
129. No Trespassing (2 min., 24 sc.).
130. Crazy Emo Chick (1 min., 30 sec.).
131. Out of the Bunker!! (2 min., 35 sec.).
132. A Solid Lead (2 min., 32 sec.).
133. Blog Girl (2 min., 52 sec.).
134. Sloppy Drunk (2 min., 10 sec.).
135. New Girl (2 min., 54 sec.).
136. Lonely Girl 15 Season Finale 12 of 12—7 p.m. (4 min., 45 sec.).
137. Lonely Girl 15 Season Finale 11 of 12—6 p.m. (6 min., 9 sec.).
138. Lonely Girl 15 Season Finale 10 of 12—5 p.m. (2 min., 39 sec.).
139. Lonely Girl 15 Season Finale 9 of 12—4 p.m. (2 min., 39 sec.).
140. Lonely Girl 15 Season Finale 8 of 12—3 p.m. (2 min., 31 sec.).
141. Lonely Girl 15 Season Finale 7 of 12—2 p.m. (2 min., 48 sec.).
142. Lonely Girl 15 Season Finale 6 of 12—1 p.m. (2 min., 30 sec.).
143. Lonely Girl 15 Season Finale 5 of 12—12 p.m. (3 min., 25 sec.).
144. Lonely Girl 15 Season Finale 4 of 12—11 a.m. (1 min., 34 sec.).
145. Lonely Girl 15 Season Finale 3 of 12—10 a.m. (3 min., 17 sec.).
146. Lonely Girl 15 Season Finale 2 of 12—9 a.m. (2 min., 21 sec.).
147. Lonely Girl 15 Season Finale 1 of 12—8 a.m. (2 min., 33 sec.).
148. They Broke In!! (1 min., 14 sec.).
149. Proceed with Caution (2 min., 32 sec.).
150. Mission Gemma (2 min., 2 sec.)

151. Deep Throat (2 min., 2 sec.).
152. All Wet (2 min., 55 sec.).
153. Rockin' the Boat (2 min., 26 sec.).
154. Revealing My Secret (1 min., 52 sec.).
155. School's In (47 sec.).
156. School's Out (1 min., 49 sec.).
157. Around the World (2 min., 20 sec.).
158. What Happened? (6 min., 11 sec.).
159. Is This the End? (7 min., 43 sec.).
160. Lonelygirl15 Season 2 ... So Far (5 min., 3 sec.).
161. What's Going On? (3 min., 56 sec.).
162. A Woman's Touch (5 min., 55 sec.).
163. They Beat Her!!! (4 min., 40 sec.).
164. They'll Do Anything (2 min., 22 sec.).
165. We All Make Mistakes (3 min., 19 sec.).
166. Ninja Video—by ELizKM86 (4 min., 57 sec.).
167. Tailgating (4 min., 13 sec.).
168. Secrets Revealed (3 min., 11 sec.).
169. Robbing the Cradle (3 min., 32 sec.).
170. I Like Being Me (2 min., 23 sec.).
171. Decision Time (2 min., 26 sec.).
172. Go for It (5 min., 50 sec.).
173. What Happened (1 min., 29 sec.).
174. Shadow of Death (2 min., 50 sec.).
175. OMG! You Have to Save Her (46 sec.).
176. Shocking Discovery (1 min., 29 sec.).
177. Eat Pie (3 min.).
178. Doctor Visit (2 min., 53 sec.).
179. Drunk by Bedtime (1 min., 57 sec.).
180. Who's That Girl? (1 min., 35 sec.).
181. Would You Pick Me Up? (1 min., 21 sec.).
182. Dangerous Desert (2 min., 27 sec.).
183. Intense/In Tennis (2 min., 11 sec.).
184. Rescued?! (58 sec.).
185. Groping in the Dark (2 min., 53 sec.).
186. They're Gone (2 min., 7 sec.).
187. Lonelygirl15 Week 14 Recap (7 min., 39 sec.).
188. Abducted? (1 min., 20 sec.).
189. Gay or Not? (1 min., 13 sec.).
190. Sick Dreams (2 min., 35 sec.).
191. The Ladies Room (2 min., 23 sec.).
192. Connections (2 min., 1 sec.).
193. Sarah and the City (2 min., 57 sec.).
194. A Girl Alone (3 min., 17 sec.).
195. Am I a Murderer? (2 min., 43 sec.).
196. Tired of B*tches (2 min., 19 sec.).
197. Procreating on Peyote (3 min., 2 sec.).
198. Corporate Thugs Are Stalking Us (2 min., 31 sec.).
199. Free Love (3 min., 38 sec.).
200. Rebound Action (1 min., 47 sec.).
201. I'll Do Whatever It Takes (3 min., 48 sec.).
202. Get Your Freak On (2 min., 37 sec.).
203. Germ Warfare Attack (2 min., 28 sec.).
204. Hot for Teacher (2 min., 15 sc.).
205. Conjugal Visit (1 min., 8 sec.).
206. Jennie Bares All (2 min., 46 sec.).
207. Playing Doctor (2 min., 48 sec.).
208. Killers at the Door?! (1 min., 15 sec.).
209. Missing Girl Found (2 min., 24 sec.).
210. Evil Drug Company Exposed (2 min., 47 sec.).
211. xxKissKissxx (1 min., 32 sec.).
212. Can't Sleep. Wanna Char? (2 min., 46 sec.).
213. Ambushed in a Tent (1 min., 7 sec.).
214. Am I a Criminal? (4 min., 39 sec.).
215. Beer Bath (7 min., 56 sec.).
216. Girl Tied Up (2 min., 13 sec.).
217. Dangerous Territory (1 min., 11 sec.).
218. Stay Strong (2 min., 22 sec.).
219. Long Drive Home (2 min., 34 sec.).
220. Watch Me Balance (2 min., 21 sec.).
221. Kidnapped! (2 min., 41 sec.).
222. Looking for a Date (3 min., 22 sec.).
223. Cream or Sugar? (2 min., 1 sec.).
224. Can't Sleep ... with Me (1 min., 38 sec.).
225. Bus-ted (1 min., 53 sec.).
226. Splitting Up (1 min., 22 sec.).
227. Party Chasers (2 min., 5 sec.).
228. Being Stalked (2 min., 20 sec.).
229. Party of One (3 min., 6 sec.).
230. Help Me Save Them (2 min., 6 sec.).
231. Share My Sleeping Bag (2 min., 6 sec.).
232. Killed By Big Pharma (2 min., 1 sec.).
233. Hot Tubbing (4 min., 16 sec.).
234. I've Never Done This Before (2 min., 34 sec.).
235. Cat Fight! (2 min., 32 sec.).
236. I Lost It (3 min., 17 sec.).
237. Things Fall Apart (1 min., 28 sec.).
238. I Love You All (5 min., 8 sec.).
239. A Woman's World (2 min., 8 sec.).
240. Playing with Wood (4 min., 6 sec.).
241. 4 Girls, 2 Guys (2 min., 19 sec.).
242. She Lost a Lot of Blood (1 min., 43 sec.).
243. Stock Options (3 min., 27 sec.).
244. Hostage Crisis (2 min., 55 sec.).
245. It's the Doing That Matters (2 min., 25 sec.).
246. Mexican Mating Machine (2 min., 39 sec.).
247. Coffee and Donuts (3 min., 45 sec.).
248. Spanish Princess (3 min., 8 sec.).
249. Tangled Web (3 min., 16 sec.).
250. At the beach (4 min., 39 sec.).
251. In the Bedroom (2 min., 53 sec.).
252. What Have I Done? (1 min., 54 sec.).
253. Prey (1 min., 10 sec.).
254. She's Ready (2 min., 57 sec.).
255. Out of Control (3 min., 12 sec.).
256. Looking for Gina (3 min.).
257. Spicing Things Up (1 min., 47 sec.).
258. Coming for You (1 min., 21 sec.).
259. Drawing in Bed (1 min., 54 sec.).
260. Born to Run (1 min., 59 sec.).
261. Babe in the Woods (2 min., 13 sec.).
262. Hangover Hell (2 min., 32 sec.).
263. Mmm Beer! (1 min., 53 sec.).
264. Adios Amigos (1 min., 49 sec.).

265. Final Appeal (1 min., 20 sec.).
266. Shop of Horrors!!! (2 min., 58 sec.).
267. Bathroom Talk (2 min., 8 sec.).
268. Crusin' with the Ladies (2 min., 43 sec.).
269. I Miss Her (2 min., 12 sec.).
270. Morning Glory (2 min., 19 sec.).
271. Hook Up at the Park (2 min., 25 sec.).
272. Varsity Blues (1 min., 39 sec.).
273. A Stranger Calls (2 min., 20 sec.).
274. Fried and a Shakedown (2 min., 11 sec.).
275. I'm on Fire (1 min., 6 sec.).
276. The Devil Speaks (3 min., 3 sec.).
277. All I Ever Wanted (1 min., 7 sec.).
278. Recovered Memory (3 min., 2 sec.).
279. Kick His A$$ (1 min., 51 sec.).
280. Girl, Returned (3 min., 10 sec.).
281. Bree's Mom (2 min., 17 sec.).
282. Through My Eyes (1 min., 20 sec.).
283. Stiff (5 min., 56 sec.).
284. Booby Trap (2 min., 42 sec.).
285. Backseat Shocker (3 min., 19 sec.).
286. Sneak Attack (4 min., 5 sec.).
287. Satan's HQ (3 min., 32 sec.).
288. Casting Couch (4 min., 19 sec.).
289. Corn Nuts (4 min., 55 sec.).
290. We Will Fight (2 min., 56 sec.).
291. Alone in the Woods (3 min., 41 sec.).
292. Politics Gone Wild (7 min., 12 sec.).
293. Computer Penetration (3 min., 40 sec.).
294. Hot Tacos (3 min., 48 sec.).
295. Crazy Border Crossing! (2 min., 26 sec.).
296. Outta Here (4 min., 40 sec.).
297. What Is She Saying? (3 min., 28 sec.).
298. Raise the Roof (5 min., 42 sec.).
299. Hunting the Elder (6 min., 16 sec.).
300. LA to LDN (6 min., 19 sec.).
301. Escape to London (1 min., 8 sec.).
302. Beach Party (2 min., 55 sec.).
303. Hangman's Noose (2 min., 5 sec.).
304. Evergreen Saves the Day (1 min., 46 sec.).
305. Undercover Lovers (2 min., 46 sec.).
306. A Woman Scorned (3 min., 49 sec.).
307. No More Fear (6 min.).
308. Prom—It's to Die For, Part 4 (6 min., 35 sec.).
309. Prom It's to Die For, Part 3 (4 min., 6 sec.).
310. Prom, It's to Die For, Part 2 (5 min., 17 sec.).
311. Prom, It's to Die For, Part 1 (6 min., 23 sec.).
312. Partner Swap (7 min., 28 sec.).
313. Dressing Room Hi-Jinks (5 min., 30 sec.).
314. Cabin Fever (3 min., 30 sec.).
315. Sticks and Stones (2 min., 46 sec.).
316. British Invasion (4 min., 49 sec.).
317. Goodbye ... for Now (39 sec.).
318. Doing It Myself (5 min., 37 sec.).
319. Tick, Tick Boom (2 min., 42 sec.).
320. Backyard Bikini Patrol (4 min., 31 sec.).
321. Girl Grown Up (5 min., 30 sec.).
322. Operation Emma (2 min., 45 sec.).
323. Dangerous Injection! (4 min., 10 sec.).
324. Blood Will Flow (4 min., 43 sec.).
325. Reclaim My Identity? (5 min., 9 sec.).
326. Cooling Off (3 min., 19 sec.).
327. Eclipse of the Heart (2 min., 16 sec.).
328. A New Direction (3 min., 27 sec.).
329. Going Down (6 min., 42 sec.).
330. Awkward Threesome (3 min., 10 sec.).
331. Born Free (3 min., 53 sec.).
332. Breaking Up? (4 min., 43 sec.).
333. I Have a Confession (3 min., 41 sec.).
334. Playing with Fire (2 min., 29 sec.).
335. Words of Wisdom (3 min., 47 sec.).
336. Nasty Bite (5 min., 11 sec.).
337. Secrets in the Closet (2 min., 37 sec.).
338. Cold War Revisited (3 min., 9 sec.).
339. Bullet to the Head (3 min., 22 sec.).
340. Getting Wet (3 min., 41 sec.).
341. Boy Tied Up (2 min., 9 sec.).
342. 2:00 P.M. (1 min., 26 sec.).
343. 1:00 P.M. (1 min., 34 sec.).
344. 12:00 P.M. (34 sec.).
345. 11:00 A.M. (1 min., 30 sec.).
346. 10:00 A.M. (1 min., 32 sec.).
347. 9:00 A.M. (1 min., 16 sec.).
348. 8:00 A.M. (1 min., 12 sec.).
349. 2:00 A.M. (2 min., 2 sec.).
350. Proof of Life (16 sec.).
351. Lonelygirl15 Season 3 Recap (2 min., 31 sec.).
352. Basement Captive (2 min., 33 sec.).
353. Sing Before the Sun Fades (59 sec.).
354. We're Screwed! (3 min., 33 sec.).
355. Grave Drawings (1 min., 51 sec.).
356. In the Closet (3 min., 13 sec.).
357. Shaken Up (2 min., 4 sec.).
358. I'm Back!!! (2 min., 14 sec.).
359. Hidden Treasures (3 min., 41 sec.).
360. Handcuffed (3 min., 59 sec.).
361. Rooftop Brawl (1 min., 59 sec.).
362. In My Sights (1 min., 12 sec.).
363. 7:00 P.M. (2 min., 38 sec.).
364. 6:00 P.M. (1 min., 27 sec.).
365. 5:00 P.M. (1 min., 53 sec.).
366. 4:00 P.M. (2 min., 35 sec.).
367. 3:00 P.M. (1 min., 2 sec.).

Note: See also *Lonely Girl 15: Outbreak*, *Lonely Girl 15: The Last*, *Lonely Girl 15: The Resistance*, *Kate Modern* and *NIckola*.

201 *Lonely Girl 15: Outbreak.* youtube. com. 2010 (Drama).

Lonely Girl 15 spin off that begins a new chapter in the saga of the resistance group, the Hymn of None and their efforts to defeat the mysterious cult The Order (seeking to acquire girls that contain the rare Trait Positive blood gene) and how a brother and sister (Gregory, a member of the resistance; and Crystal, a college drop out who was abandoned by Gregory as a child) become involved with (and attempt to battle) a new faction of The Order called SheNtek (which is specifically designed to extract the Trait Blood from its female carriers). See also *Lonely Girl 15*, *Lonely Girl 15: The Last*, *Lonely Girl 15: The Resistance*, *Kate Modern* and *NIckola*.

Cast: Gregory Austin McConnell (Gregory "Mason" Almeida), Dani Martin (Crystal O'Brien), Lance Little (William Powers). **Credits:** *Producer:* Gregory Austin McConnell, Lance Little, Vincent Rouse. **Comment:** An interesting continuation in the *Lonely Girl* saga. Although the resistance group is seen on screen as The Hymn of None, virtually all printed matter refers to it as The Hymn of One. The acting and production values are good and the program intriguing.

Episodes: (a title and time listing of remaining on-line episodes as of July 2014).

1. New Town, New Story (3 min., 34 sec.).
2. What's a Vlog? (2 min., 5 sec.).
3. Forgotten (2 min., 8 sec.).
4. I Got Jacked (2 min., 8 sec.).
5. Objective Assigned (1 min., 51 sec.).
6. Welcome to SheNtek (4 min., 7 sec.).
7. Point Insertion (3 min., 55 sec.).
8. Boredom: Cured (2 min., 43 sec.).
9. Um, a Problem (1 min., 51 sec.).
10. Catching Up, Closing Out (5 min., 14 sec.).
11. Happy Birthday Crystal (7 min., 59 sec.).
12. Until Next Time (2 min., 12 sec.).
13. Wishful Thinking (2 min., 23 sec.).
14. Vlogging: A definitive Guide (6 min., 55 sec.).
15. The Date (3 min., 39 sec.).
16. Finding Help (4 min., 2 sec.).
17. Because I Left (5 min., 58 sec.).
18. You Thought It Was Over (2 min., 36 sec.).
19. Roadblock (4 min., 13 sec.).
20. Please Select Alternate Route (3 min., 32 sec.).
21. Training Day for Will (5 min., 12 sec.).
22. At the Docks (3 min., 1 sec.).
23. At the Apartment (2 min., 44 sec.).
24. It's Like There's Blood on My Hands (2 min., 14 sec.).
25. What Is Kavion? (5 min., 22 sec.).
26. Let's Get This Party Started (2 min., 30 sec.).
27. The Rescue (4 min.).
28. Up to You Now (5 min., 13 sec.).
29. Nothing Left (3 min., 35 sec.).
30. Helping Hand (2 min., 45 sec.).
31. Power Down (2 min., 18 sec.).
32. Touchdown (2 min., 21 sec.).
33. Takeoff (2 min., 44 sec.).
34. Knight Vision (3 min., 21 sec.).
35. Our Mutual Goal (2 min., 11 sec.).
36. Revelations (3 min., 31 sec.).
37. Singing Off (2 min., 23 sec.).
38. The Betrayal (2 min., 33 sec.).
39. Security Feeds Cracked (1 min., 39 sec.).
40. Co-Ed Billiards (1 min., 54 sec.).
41. In Danger (3 min., 2 sec.).

202 *Lonely Girl 15: The Last.* youtube. com. 2009 (Drama).

A spin off from *Lonely Girl 15* that continues the overall theme of the series: girls, possessing Trait Positive Blood being sought by The Order, a mysterious, world-wide cult that requires the blood of such girls for their sacrifices. Antonia, Chasina, Leigh, and Jayde are four such girls, each with Trait Positive Blood, and each now in danger as The Order has discovered who they are and where they live (Australia). Chasina, through an e-mail from Jonas Wharton (from the parent series) informs her that she and three other girls possess a rare blood type and that their lives are in danger. The program follows what happens as Chasina, Antonia, Jayde and Leigh begin a desperate battle to defeat the cult members who are seeking them. They are aided by Mitch (Chasina's boyfriend), Bray (a bartender friend) and Sibylla and her twin brother Xavier, who pretend to help but are actually working to tear the group apart for The Order. See also *Lonely Girl 15*, *Lonely Girl 15: Outbreak*, *Lonely Girl 15: The Resistance*, *Kate Modern* and *NIckola*.

Cast: Catherine Williams (Chasina "Chas" Wilson), Jessica Shipley (Leigh Taylor), Emily Rose Robinson (Jayde Cooper), Samantha Carr (Antonia Moore), Tom Mesker (Mitch Evans), James Olds (Bray Johnson), Anthony Strouthos (Xavier Weave). *Note:* The actress playing Sibylla is not credited (on screen or on site). **Credits:** *Producer:* Samantha Carr, Emily Rose Robinson, Catherine Williams, Andrew Strouthos. **Comment:** Well done and acted and, being considerably shorter than its parent series, presents the same intrigue as The Order seeks girls with special blood.

Episodes: (a title and time listing of remaining on-line episodes as of July 2014).

1. Alone (8 min., 10 sec.).
2. Only a Life Lived for Others (9 min., 7 sec.).
3. Betrayal Is the Willful Slaughter (2 min., 41 sec.).
4. Backfire (2 min., 2 sec.).
5. It's Not What It Seems (4 min., 47 sec.).
6. New Agendas (4 min., 13 sec.).
7. Lost and Found (9 min., 22 sec.).
8. End of the Line (4 min., 23 sec.).
9. The Spider and Its Venom (5 min., 7 sec.).
10. Cum Tacent, Clamant (4 min., 2 sec.).
11. 2 A.M. (2 min., 35 sec.).
12. Take Charge (7 min., 28 sec.).
13. The Disturbing Truth (5 min., 10 sec.).
14. For the Love of Paranoia (4 min., 49 sec.).
15. Dying Flames (4 min., 49 sec.).
16. On the Run (4 min., 37 sec.).
17. Destroying the View (4 min., 2 sec.).
18. Don't Assume Anything (3 min., 55 sec.).
19. Sounds of Silence (1 min., 42 sec.).
20. Stop the Celebration (5 min., 41 sec.).

21. The Present (3 min., 33 sec.).
22. They Must Be Stopped (1 min., 55 sec.).
23. Confessions (3 min., 25 sec.).
24. Girl Talk (3 min., 1 sec.).
25. Getting Wet (6 min., 30 sec.).
26. Boiling Point (2 min., 3 sec.).
27. Up Close and Personal (1 min., 55 sec.).
28. Mornings with Jayde (5 min., 50 sec.).
29. Beneath the Surface (1 min., 42 sec.).
30. Siege and Conquer (2 min., 8 sec.).
31. One Happy Family (4 min., 6 sec.).
32. Q&A (4 min., 19 sec.).
33. Welcome Back (4 min., 28 sec.).
34. This Is What I Know (3 min., 1 sec.).
35. Close Call (3 min., 36 sec.).
36. Shot Down (1 min., 41 sec.).
37. You've Gotta Be Kidding (2 min., 17 sec.).
38. The Gold Coast (2 min., 43 sec.).
39. Paranoid Past (2 min., 19 sec.).
40. Urgency (2 min., 20 sec.).
41. Call Me Toni (2 min., 16 sec.).
42. If You're Out There (2 min., 11 sec.).
43. The Show Is Yours (1 min., 11 sec.).
44. Virgil Knocks Up Lucy??!! (6 min., 34 sec.).
45. Tales of a Watcher (3 min.).

203 *Lonely Girl 15: The Resistance.* you tube.com. 2008 (Drama).

A spin off from the series *Lonely Girl 15* that focuses in particular on Jonas and Sarah, principal characters on the parent series. As the story begins the Hymn of None, the organization resisting The Order, has posted a series of videos and blogs hoping to get Jonas (Bree's friend from the original series) to join them and help put an end to The Order. Jonas however, refuses, as he fears putting his or anyone else's life in danger. Sarah (Bree's friend also) is a member of the Hymn of None and has been assigned the task of changing Jonas's mind and become a part of the resistance. As more information is revealed about the Trait Positive gene (a rare blood disease) and Jonas eventually decides to join Sarah, the program charts their adventures as they not only battle agents of The Order, but seek to shut down Lifes-Blood Labs, a company seeking to acquire the blood of Trait Positive girls for their own experimentation. See also *Lonely Girl 15*, *Lonely Girl 15: Outbreak*, *Lonely Girl 15: The Last*, *Kate Modern* and *NIckola*. **Cast:** Jackson Davis (Jonas Wharton), Alexandra Dreyfus (Sarah Genatiempo), Marnette Patterson (Maggie Schaeffer), Brett Ryback (Reed Barnes). **Comment:** Only one episode remains on line and judging by it, it follows the documentary-like format of its sister series with good acting and production values. It also encompasses the talents of Marnette Patterson, a well-know TV series actress of the early 2000s.
Episodes:
1. A Call to Arms (12 min., 14 sec.). Partially

establishes the story line as the resistance movement begins to grow.

204 *Looking for Grace.* lookingforgrace. com. 2008–2009 (Mystery).

For reasons that he cannot explain, a young man (Harold) finds that his memories have been replaced by those of a mysterious woman named Grace. As Harold struggles to recall events from his past life but is only able to recall those of Grace, he sets out on a quest to discover who Grace is and why she has stolen his life. The program follows Harold as he begins a quest where he soon discovers a strange world in which nothing appears as it should and that there are others who are also "Looking for Grace."
Cast: Nathaniel Halpern (Harold), Mary Kate Wiles (Mystery Girl), Teresa Noreen (Dolores), Diane Van Patten (Martha), Edward L. Green (Higgins), Robin Martell (Beauty Pageant Host), Aletta Manniz (Lonely Dancer), Alex Sell (Spangler), Jennifer Faulkner (Secretary), Josh Wingate (The Stranger), Mike Zehr (Mr. Stinchfield), Jennipfer Foster (Miss Sleepy Eye), Evelyn B. Danford (Edith), Maria Aceves (Rita), Joey Kern (Billy), Joyce Liu (The Widow Sunday). **Credits:** *Producer:* Nathaniel Halpern, Aaron Rubin, Chris Palsho. *Writer-Director:* Nathaniel Halpern. **Comment:** Intriguing drama that plays well from beginning to end. The acting and production values are first rate and the concept very well thought out and presented.
Episodes:
1. Dynamite Dream Girl (7 min., 42 sec.). Begins the story as Harold realizes that his memories are virtually gone and have been replaced by Grace—a woman, apparently from a past time (looks to be the 1940s) whom he is now determined to find.
2. Red Letter Day (10 min., 30 sec.). After meeting with a man (Higgins), Harold learns that there are others who are experiencing the same unexplainable nightmare.
3. Sleepy Eye (11 min., 38 sec.). As Harold's visions of Grace continue (seen in brief antiquated-like scenes) the viewer is drawn further into his plight as his sanity now at stake.
4. The Dead End Kid. Episode taken off-line with no description listed. What happens is unknown.
5. To Truly Be Together (9 min., 8 sec.). Without the prior episode as a lead-in, it appears that Harold's visions are becoming more frequent and he is now more determined than ever to unravel the mystery.
6. X Marks the Spot (13 min., 25 sec.). Harold's search leads him to a wooded area alongside a river. There he discovers a weathered cross with the name "Grace" on it.
7. The Widow of the Web (8 min., 58 sec.). As Harold realizes that Grace is dead, he is confronted by the eerie spirit of a woman (apparently jilted) who appears to want to kill him (he is saved by Higgins).

8. The Gates to Elsewhere (10 min., 15 sec.). After encountering the spirit, Harold seeks out a psychiatrist and learns that his visions and memories of Grace (and her of him) make it possible for him to return to the past as they are connected. However, to accomplish this, he must acquire the key—which is worn by the spirit he encountered.

9. When World's Collide (13 min., 11 sec.). Seeking to complete her task, the spirit reappears but is tricked when Harold rips the key (worn as a necklace) from her neck. As the spirit vanishes, Harold is transported back in time (looks to be the 1940s) where he sees himself as a husband and father.

10. Grace (16 min., 13 sec.). Harold enters the house in which he saw the vision and meets Grace (somewhat older than him). He learns that he is in a past life and must let his memories of her go so that he may live his new life in the future. Only then will he be free of her memories and his memories of his new life will return. As Grace and Harold embrace, Harold is magically transferred to his present life.

205 Love Bytes. lovebytestheseries.com. 2013 (Comedy-Drama).

Jade, a vegetarian and a passionate advocate for animal rights, is looking to have as much fun as possible before seeking the woman of her dreams. She is 26 years old, a Virgo and works as a videographer. Jade, attracted to girls for as long as she can remember, is a bit picky when it comes to dating and prefers women who are more eccentric than normal. Michael, a strong believer that money can often spoil relationships, is gay and looking to become a trophy husband by finding a man who is rich and will spoil him rotten. Until that time comes he avoids dating men who are poor fearing he may fall in love and ruin his dream. He is 27 years old, has the astrological sing of Leo and works as a receptionist. Stacey, 28 years old and single, is straight and dreams of settling down, having a family and living in a cottage in the country. She is a Pisces, works as an artists' representative and finding the man of her dreams is much more difficult than she imagined as she has a tendency to meet men who are anything like what she pictures. Jade, Michael and Stacey all have one thing in common—they are friends and share an apartment together. The program follows their mishaps as each ventures into the world of dating with each seeking that special someone that neither seems able to find.

Cast: Emily Rose Brennan (Stacey), Billie Rose Pritchard (Jade), Adriano Cappelletta (Michael), Bec Irwin (Samantha Fox), Dave Halalilo (Adam). **Credits:** *Producer:* Tonnette Stanford, Emma McKenna. *Writer-Director:* Tonnette Stanford. **Com-**

Love Bytes. **Left to right: Emily Rose Brenna, Adriana Capelletta and Billie Rose Prichard (used by permission of Tonnette Stanford).**

ment: British produced, delightful lesbian-gay mix series. The characters are very well executed and likeable with excellent writing and directing. There are sexual situations, kissing (mostly girl/girl) and a well thought out and executed program.

Episodes:

1. Herpes of the Lips. Jade believes she is in seventh heaven when she begins dating Samantha Fox, a sexy lesbian D.J. while Michael finds his life turned upside down when he responds to an on-line dating opportunity and finds the man faked his profile and is actually a despicable dud.

2. Justin Beaver. Hoping to glamorize herself for a night out on the town with Samantha, Jade borrows Stacey's valuable ring and later, while making love to Samantha, manages to lose it "in the most unusual (and intimate) of places." With Stacey demanding her ring back and Samantha in a panic, Michael steps in to resolve the situation by performing an emergency ring extraction. Due to its mature subject matter, the episode is restricted on YouTube and requires proof of age to watch (using an e-mail account).

206 *Love Just Is—Emma.* blip.tv. 2010 (Drama).

Emma and Kevin are a young couple who have had a steady romance for seven years. When Emma feels that she needs to move their relationship forward but finds Kevin reluctant to make a commitment, she believes it is time for her to move on and leaves him. The program follows Emma, without a relationship for the first time since graduating college, as she tries to reconstruct her life and find the one man with whom she can marry and start a family.

Cast: Dawn Moeller (Emma), Angie Dick (Janet), Patrick Roe (Kevin), Jon Gormley (Jack), Joe David (Keith), Casey Fitzgerald (April), Tiffany Pulvino (Kate), Kelly Polk (Riley). **Credits:** *Producer:* Jeff Gottlieb, Joe David, Dawn Moeller. *Director:* Jeff Gottlieb. *Writer:* Jeff Gottlieb, Dawn Moeller. **Comment:** Judging by the pilot (the episodes have been reedited and released on DVD) it is well written, directed and acted.

Episodes: 12 episodes were produced but only 1 episode remains on line.

1. Pilot (5 min.). Emma is introduced as she and Kevin discuss their relationship and their close friends, Janet and Jack, who are also seeking lasting relationships.

207 *Love on the Line.* youtube.com. 2013 (Comedy-Drama).

Holly Landers is a young woman with a serious problem: she is unable to find the perfect man. She has tried the traditional methods of dating and has ventured into on-line match-making but nothing has paid off as the men she meets are all losers. After 10

years (she is now 30 years old) of "projecting my magical abilities and getting nothing in return," Holly believes there is a better way and decides to use the Internet as a dating site that will introduce women to men through a series of tiers, allowing each individual to choose the man she feels is best suited for her. With what she believes is a great idea, but unable to establish the site by herself, Holly, based in Los Angeles, posts help on the Internet and acquires two associates: Suzy Goldberg and Michael Dumphrey (Suzy, age unknown, is a bit off-the-wall and becomes instantly attracted to Holly while Michael, a 30-year-old computer wizard, can't find a job and has little motivation to advance his position in life). Within days Holly accomplishes her goal and establishes her site—I'mTheOne.com wherein men purchase one of three tier levels and women can choose a date from either tier (Tier 1 is reserved for men of wealth and status; Tier 2 is middle class and Tier 3 for the desperate, broke and unattractive). For Holly the site has the added advantage that she can choose any man before anyone else. The program follows Holly as she seeks that man of her dreams unaware that he may be a she as Suzy has fallen in love with her.

Cast: Fiona Bates (Holly Landers), Bryn Woznicki (Suzy Goldberg), Danny Jordan (Michael Dumphrey), Chelsea Morgan (Debby Langford). **Credits:** *Producer:* Fiona Bates, Luce Woods, Bryn Woznicki. *Director:* Bryn Woznicki. *Writer:* Fiona Bates, Chelsea Morgan, Bryn Woznicki. **Comment:** Enjoyable, well-acted program with a few twists and turns as one girl (Suzy) sets her sights on another girl (Holly) who has no idea that she is a sex object to women. Although tagged as both a comedy and a drama, light comedy prevails and Holly addressing the audience adds to the program's charm.

Episodes:

0. Hi, My Name Is Holly (5 min., 3 sec.). An introduction to Holly and the mishaps she encountered trying to meet the perfect man.

1. Increasing the Odds (6 min., 22 sec.). Holly's continual frustration leads her to develop a specialized web site for women to find the perfect man.

2. The Dream Team (6 min., 31 sec.). Realizing that she cannot create the site alone, Holly seeks the perfect team to see her dream become a reality.

3. Tiers on the Line (6 min., 1 sec.). Feeling that she has the key to success, Holly explains the tier theory she developed.

4. The Tier That Got Away (6 min., 15 sec.). Seeing that she is already acquiring clients, Holly decides that she will pick the best of the best in hopes of finding the perfect mate.

5. Best Friends Forever (5 min., 40 sec.). Realizing that she needs publicity, Holly hires her best friend, Debbie Langford as her PR lady.

6. It's Raining (5 min., 50 sec.). Holly accomplishes her next step—producing an infomercial to lure clients over the airwaves (1-900-IAM THE1).

7. Practice, Practice, Practice (6 min., 40 sec.). Holly, attracted to a Tier 1 client, chooses to date him herself.

8. The Meet Chute, Part 1 (5 min., 22 sec,). Holly's date is anything but pleasing when she finds her Tier 1 is gay.

9. The Meet Chute, Part 2 (5 min., 40 sec.). While Holly turns to drinking to overcome her date, Debbie reveals that Michael is in love with Holly and sets her sights on helping him get her, unaware that Suzy also fancies her.

10. In Your Dreams (6 min., 40 sec.). Holly, somewhat intoxicated, is taken home by Suzy who |is struggling to control her urges to take advantage of the situation and make love to Holly. As Holly awakens the following morning she sees that she is naked and Suzy sleeping next to her. Did Suzy take advantage? The program's concluding unresolved episode.

208 *Love Struck.* webserieschannel.com. 2013 (Drama).

In a world where Cupid would find it difficult to make a love match (present-day Los Angeles), a group of young people are not only navigating life but love and relationships as well. The program follows four such couples (Meagan and Zeke; Courtney and Greg; Cassandra and Todd and Liz and Ken) and the not-so-wise choices they make. **Cast:** Darrell Lake (Zeke Radford), Bambadjan Bamba, (Todd Washington), Hilary Wagner (Courtney Hawkins), Ryan Caltagirone (Kenneth Conway), Sarah Fontenot (Cassandra Sparks), Carl Peterson (Greg Burton), Lauren Elaine (Lizabeth Holland), Mara Lane (Meagan Takahashi). **Credits:** *Producer:* Darrell Lake, Bambadjan Bamba. *Director-Writer:* Darrell Lake. **Comment:** Enjoyable mix of humor and light drama with good acting, writing and directing. Although the program ends unresolved, the doorway is left open for additional incidents in the lives of the characters.

Episodes:

1. The Odds Are Already Against You (9 min., 2 sec.). Meagan fears Zeke wants to take their relationship to the next level; Liz, a musician, attempts to deal with a cancelled gig while Ken hopes for a promotion at work; Cassandra and Todd make preparations to move into a new apartment and Greg begins to feel uncomfortable about Courtney's business trip to Las Vegas.

2. Roses Are Red, Violets Are ... WTF (6 min., 37 sec.). As Cassandra and Todd relish in their new home, Zeke prepares to meet Meagan's family for the first time while Ken must face Liz and tell her that he lost his job (their only source of income).

3. Love Is Not for the Faint of Heart (5 min., 19 sec.). Another out-of-town business trip has Greg wondering about Cassandra's faithfulness while Zeke contends with Meagan's sister, who appears to mak-

ing a play for him; Ken uncovers Liz's secret (uses drugs).

4. The Consequences of Love (8 min., 27 sec.). Ken confronts Liz about her drug use, offering her an ultimatum that could cost them their relationship; Gregg seeks Todd's advice regarding Courtney's business trips. The program's concluding episode.

209 *Luck and the Virgin: A 60 Second Soap Opera.* blip.tv. 2010 (Comedy-Drama).

Valentina is a mysterious young woman from Texas who possess money stolen from her drug-selling boyfriend (Carlos); Ricardo is a burned-out hit man working for a U.S. drug cartel who decides to vacation in the small Mexican city of San Miguel de Allende. By chance the two meet when their bags are accidentally switched and the program relates the problems that occur when they become friends—but Ricardo is ordered to kill Valentina and retrieve the stolen drug money.

Cast: Whitney Moore (Valentina), Carlos Sanagustin (Ricardo), Juan Carlos Vinacourt (Mario), Jeronimo Cadena (Carlos), Mauricio Diaz (Juan), Roderick Reinhart (Doug), Tess Quintana (Antonia), India Bastien (Angela). **Credits:** *Producer:* Adam J. Cohen, Jaime Byrd. *Writer-Director:* Jaime Byrd. **Comment:** Each episode is only 60 seconds long (including the theme) which presents a fast-paced story that is not only missing episodes (8–11 and 20–23) but has no conclusion. The acting and production values are good and the program was shot on location in Mexico.

Episodes:

1. Leaving Carlos. Establishes the story as Valentina steals the drug money.

2. Where's My F***ing Bag? Valentina and Ricardo's bags are accidentally switched.

3. Spanish—The Language of Spain. Valentina, seeking to find her bag, encounters difficulty communicating as she doesn't speak Spanish.

4. He's Looking for Bush. Valentina continues to search for her bag of stolen money.

5. Threesome. Valentina finds her bag—but involves Ricardo in her plight.

6. How Do You Curse in Spanish? The situation becomes intense as Valentina becomes Ricardo's next hit.

7. You Smell Balls. Unable to kill Valentina, Ricardo tries to figure out his next move.

Note: From this point on, only the following episodes (of 23 that were produced) are on line:

12. I Don't Have a Wife, I Have Juan. *13.* This Is My Juan. *14.* The Proposition. *15.* Some Sort of Saint. *16.* Coming to San Miguel. *17.* Primos. *18.* Shake the World Hard Enough. *19.* Angela.

210 *Luke 11:17.* webserieschannel.com. 2010 (Drama).

Luke Vincent seems to have it all—outwardly. He is a successful, sought-after celebrity lecturer who is known for his work in helping recovering addicts. Inwardly, however, he is a different man, suffering from personal demons he must hide from his adoring fans or suffer the consequences of being exposed as a fraud. The program follows Luke as he attempts to deal with his personal problems while at the same time presenting himself as the man who can help anyone overcome an addiction. **Cast:** Ryan V. Cafeo (Luke Vincent), Chrishell Stause, Karen Maruyama, Sarah Butler, Christina Carlisi. **Credits:** *Producer:* Christopher Sherman, Michael Caissie, Ryan V. Cafeo. *Writer:* Michael Caissie. **Comment:** Luke is not the most like-able of characters and the program is rather harsh in its presentation (you get the feeling you are intruding on something you should not). The acting and production values however are good. There is foul language but no parental warning is issued.

Episodes:

1. Crucified Between Two Thieves (11 min., 48 sec.). As Luke completes one of his stage lectures, a young woman (Sandy) has double-crossed her drug dealing boss (Eddie) and is now seeking the money she needs to square herself with him.

2. Don't Invade Other's Space (9 min., 4 sec.). Hoping to get the money she needs, Sandy breaks into Luke's home and encounters Sarah, Luke's mentally unstable sister.

3. We Are What We Think About All Day Long (9 min., 1 sec.). Instead of calling the police, Luke offers to help Sandy; meanwhile, Luke is struggling to compose his next lecture and deal with his manager (Debra).

4. The Elephant in the Room (7 min., 25 sec.). Luke seeks a way to overcome his writer's block and compose his next lecture.

5. Poor Foundations (9 min., 51 sec.). After Luke meets a girl on the beach (Madison), but fails to impress her, it is learned that Luke is also in therapy—but not a model patient.

6. Brand Recognition (11 min., 4 sec.). Luke is surprised to meet Madison again when he arrives at Debra's home for a dinner party and learns that Madison is her niece. This time, however, Luke is able to talk to and befriend Madison.

7. I Think We Are Out of Time (11 min., 31 sec.). While his relationship with Madison seems to be progressing well, Luke confessions to his therapist that he fears Sarah is a thorn in his side and needs to know how to deal with her.

8. Be Kind Rewind (9 min., 34 sec.). The concluding episode wherein Luke seeks a way to deal with his problems, especially Madison (whom he can't seem to seduce) and Sarah, whom he feels should be put in an institution.

211 *Lyle.* lylemovie.com. 2013 (Thriller).

Leah and June, a lesbian couple and the parents of a child (Lyle) given birth to by Leah, have just moved into a new apartment. Leah, pregnant with a second child (a daughter) appears to be happy until uneasiness comes over her. Lyle, though a toddler, appears to be talking to someone Leah cannot see and a young woman, pregnant and new to the building, has Leah feeling something is not right about her. The program, billed as a lesbian version of the film *Rosemary's Baby*, establishes, by the two released episodes, that something evil is lurking but exactly what is not revealed (site information states that the remaining seven episodes will disclose that Leah will discover that her fears are real as she will encounter a satanic cult seeking her child).

Cast: Gaby Hoffmann (Leah), Ingrid Jungermann (June), Rebecca Street (Karen), Michael Che (Threes), Kim Allen (Taylor), Eleanor Hopkins (Lyle), Christaine McCloskey (Diane), Margaux Whitney (Marhaux), Charly Esterly (Charly). **Credits:** *Producer:* Alex Scharfman. *Writer-Director:* Stewart Thorndike. **Comment:** Former child actress Gaby Hoffmann (from the TV series *Someone Like Me*) stars in a well produced and acted program that, judging by the first two episodes, will be not only a suspenseful series but one that will well be worth watching. A mystery is established almost immediately and draws the viewer right in. The shortness of the episodes allows for situations to unfold swiftly and keep your attention, thus avoiding all the unnecessary filler material needed to stretch scenes if they were produced for broadcast TV or cable.

Episodes:

1. Episode 1 (4 min., 13 sec.). As Leah and June settle into their new apartment, Leah discovers that one of the rooms had been previously used as a nursery but all such evidence had been sealed over with new wallpaper.

2. Episode 2 (4 min., 11 sec.). Leah and June's first night together is a restful one but Lyle's strange behavior the following morning and Leah's seeing that a new tenant (the pregnant girl) has become her neighbor, has her believing something is just not right.

212 *The Lyons Den.* webserieschannel.com. 2012–2013 (Drama).

The sudden death (a murder is hinted) of William Lyons, the head of a seemingly typical, middle-class family, unites his children and their offspring for the first time in a number of years. The family, some of whom are at odds with each other, must now come to terms with what has happened and what they each mean to each other. The program profiles the individual family members as they deal with the pressures and realities of life while at the same time learning a difficult lesson on what it means to be a family.

Cast: Shantelle Wheeler (Keysha Lyons Monroe), Reishal Monique (Sherri Covington Lyons), Victoria Wilson (Raven Lyons), Sam Evans (Jarvis Clifford

"J.C." Lyons), JaPrince Briggs (Lucas Lyons), D.J. Jackson (Ryan Lyons), Noah Quarles (Noah Lyons), Jonah Quarles (Jonah Lyons), Antrinese Snell (Aisha Lyons), Natalya Johnson (Delila Lyons), Aulysiana Manor (Leesy Lyons), Gabriella Wilson (Gabby Lyons), Angela Griffin (Melissa Lyons), Kendra Clay (Shayquan Turner), Torrence White (Desmond Jenkins), Altina Menefee (Tammi Sanders), Matt Calcutt (Charles Sanders), Shatareia Stokes (Bobbi Ward), Courtney Dionne (Angel Jackson), Shantay Evans (Jasmine Harris), Stacy Camille (Ashley Murphy). Karlton T. Clay (Desmond Jenkins), Jaye Starkes (Alexander "A.J." Wilkerson, Jr.). **Credits:** *Producer-Writer-Director:* Karlton T. Clay. **Comment:** Episodes that are still on line are rather long (most over 30 minutes) and, while well acted, lack good production values (rather poorly lit, not well edited and at times loud dialogue). The intent is good and tightening the episodes to a shorter length would have made for a more intense look at a troubled family.

Episodes:

1. Dawn of a New Day (31 min., 15 sec.). The death of William Lyons, possibly murdered, brings the Lyons family together.

2. Saturday (28 min., 13 sec.). The family introductions continue as the funeral is planned.

3. Back, Back, Forth and Forth (34 min., 39 sec.). At a therapy session, to hopefully find closure, events from the past of certain family members are brought into the open.

4. So Gone (26 min., 45 sec.). A.J., an old family friend comes to visit—with intentions that also appear to seduce Keysha.

5. Kissing You Is All I've Been Thinking Of (31 min., 16 sec.). A criminal investigation is begun to probe the circumstances surrounding William's death; meanwhile, Keysha has become attracted to A.J. and fears giving into temptation.

6. Daddy Dearest (39 min., 51 sec.). To hopefully bring the family closer together, a party is thrown to celebrate what would have been William's next birthday.

7. Coming Home (30 min., 13 sec.). The party has adverse effects as memories of their pasts are brought to light.

8. No B.S. (48 min., 25 sec.). As the police investigation continues, information is revealed that could change the lives of the family members forever. Concludes the first season.

Note: The following episodes, all of which begin with "Victory Productions Presents The Lyons Den" (followed by the actual episode title) have been taken off line.

9. Do I Ever Cross Your Mind ... Anytime? Sept. 7, 2012. Begins the second season.

10. New Faces, New Places. Sept. 21, 2012.

11. Back to Life, Back to Reality. Oct. 5, 2012.

12. Got an Icebox Where My Heart Is a Stereo. Oct. 19, 2012.

13. 4 A.M. to 5 O'clock in the Morning. Nov. 2, 2012.

14. Torn in Between the Two. Nov. 16, 2012.

15. Tell Me How I'm Supposed to Breathe with No Air. Nov. 30, 2012.

16. Fallin'. Dec. 7, 2012. Concludes Season 2.

17. Apologize, It's Too Late. Mar. 8, 2013. Begins Season 3.

16. Rolling in the Deep. Mar. 15, 2013.

19. Watch Me, Watch You, Watch Him. Mar. 29, 2013.

20. Soul Mate. April 12, 2013.

21. Eat, Pray ... and Pray Some More. April. 26, 2013.

22. Ready or Not (Part 1). May 10, 2013.

23. Here I Come (Part 2). May 24, 2013.

24. We Found Love in Hopeless Places. June 7, 2013.

25. Papa Was a Rolling Stone. Jun. 14, 2013. Concludes Season 3.

26. Sweet Dream, Beautiful Nightmare. Sept. 20, 2013. Begins Season 4.

27. L-O-V-E and Affection. Sept. 27, 2013.

28. We Can't Be Friends. Oct. 4, 2013.

29. Got a Secret, Can You Keep It? Oct., 11, 2013.

30. The Other Side of Me. Oct., 18, 2013.

31. Game, Set, Match. Oct. 25, 2013.

32. He's My Brother, and I Love Him Like Myself. Nov. 1, 2013.

33. A Thin Line Between Love and Hate. Nov. 8, 2013.

34. Tide Is High ... but I'm Holding On. Nov. 15, 2013.

35. Poor Up (Drink) Headshot (Drink) Faded ... Faded... Nov. 22, 2013.

36. Save Me. Nov. 29, 2013.

37. Love and War. Dec. 6, 2013. Concludes the series.

213 *The Magic of Mermaids.* youtube.com. 2012 (Comedy-Drama).

While in the backyard of her home with her dog, a teenage girl (Caroline) finds a bottle with a light blue liquid in it and an inscription on the bottom of the bottle that reads "For Ice Cream." Curious, Caroline takes the bottle into the kitchen and begins wondering about it—"Could it be a Mermaid potion? Could it be poisonous?" When her curiosity gets the best of her, she opens the bottle and pours its contents into a glass and sips it. When she discards what remains in the glass, a bracelet appears. After taking the bracelet, Ashley accidentally spills water on herself and magically transforms into a Mermaid. She is not startled, however, and after drying her purple tail (to return her legs) she finds that she also has the power to make wishes come true. Her adventures as she adjusts to her Mermaid life are chronicled. Also known as *Mermaid Magic.*

Cast (as credited): Pianopup210 (Caroline and

Serena). **Credits** are not given. **Comment:** As the first episode plays, the following message will appear over the picture: "This is my first episode and is very bad quality. Like really, really bad quality. I promise it gets better eventually and the plot gets more interesting. Please excuse this horrible episode" (to delete the message, click on the text image, then click the "x" in the upper right corner). Caroline is a very pretty girl and she acts naturally. Simple plot, pretty girl and the episode does not play as bad as indicated. The sound is poor (camera microphone used) and does require an extra effort to hopefully understand. But the production values do improve in succeeding episodes.

Episodes:

1. Magic Potion (8 min., 45 sec.). Establishes the story line as Caroline's dog uncovers a Mermaid potion.

2. Powers and Disasters (8 min., 53 sec.). Although it appears the Mermaid potion is gone, having been consumed by Caroline, it reappears under the full moon and is found by Caroline's younger brother, David.

3. Troubled Waters (5 min., 6 sec.). Trouble brews for Caroline when the potion transforms David into a Merboy and she is unsure how to reverse the process.

4. Full Moon (2 min., 49 sec.). Caroline's inability to turn David back finds her facing the wrath of the Mermaid Government, who have threatened to "take away her tail" if she does not turn him back by the next full moon.

5. Random Potion (8 min., 33 sec.). Caroline discovers that if David will eat a special fruit the transformation will be reversed. All is going well until Caroline's mother returns home and Caroline desperately seeks a way to conceal what happened from her.

6. Discovered (5 min., 17 sec.). While Caroline believes she has changed David back into a boy she is unaware that she is being watched by the evil Siren Selena (Sirens, creatures of the sea hate Mermaids and seek only to destroy them as they are all good).

7. Season Finale (4 min., 27 sec.). Selena strikes and captures Caroline; David, cured of being a Merboy has transformed into a Siren and rescues his sister.

8. Crisis (3 min., 8 sec.). Season 2 begins with Caroline facing another crisis: her powers have gone haywire and she can no longer control her transformations from girl to Mermaid and vice versa.

9. Return of the Sirens (5 min., 42 sec.). In an attempt to stop what is happening, Caroline mixes a Mermaid potion with a Siren potion and incurs the wrath of the Mermaid Government when it is learned the end result could destroy all Mermaids and bring victory to the Sirens.

10. Consequences (4 min., 1 sec.). As a result of what she did, Caroline is brought to the Mermaid Court where she is tried, found guilty, stripped of her tail and expelled from the Mermaid society.

11. Reactions (4 min., 35 sec.). Caroline's expulsion, however, does not change what is happening as Mermaids and Sirens have engaged in a war for supremacy.

12. Siren Rebellion (5 min., 1 sec.). To hopefully right what she has done, Caroline sets out to confront the Siren that first captured her (Selena) and use the power of her magic gemstone to stop the war.

13. Season Finale, Part 1 (5 min., 23 sec.). While in the woods Caroline discovers a cave and uncovers the magic Athena Shell. It can grant her powers (like creating fire then rain to douse it) but it is also a symbol for good that was stolen by a Siren and used for evil.

14. Season Finale, Part 2 (4 min., 54 sec.). When Caroline discovers that the shell is being sought by Selena (as possessing it will make her Queen of the Mermaids), she attempts to destroy it but finds it appears to be indestructible. As the program concludes, Caroline attempts to bury the shell and hide it from Selena but is unaware that Selena is watching her every move.

214 The Magic Shell Mermaids. youtube.com. 2011–2013 (Comedy-Drama).

After returning from the beach with sea shells they found, two young girls (Sofia and Lexi) discover that their contact with the shells have caused a metamorphous: when they touch water they become Mermaids. As the story progressed, Lexi and Sofia encounter the rage of an evil Siren and must also decide whether or not to join King Neptune in the undersea kingdom and assist him in keeping the oceans safe.

Cast (as credited): Taylor (Sofia), Bella (Lexi). **Credits** are not given. **Comment:** One of the longer-running Mermaid series that, despite its sometimes poor sound and questionable photography, does present an intriguing story as the girls adjust to becoming Mermaids.

Episode List: *1.* The Magic Shell. *2.* A Fishy Secret. *3.* Investigation and Teleportation. *4.* Power Showers. *5.* Lake Date. *6.* Bubbles Bring Best Friends. *7.* Siren's Tale. *8.* A Mermaid's Gift. *9.* Neptune's Honor. *10.* Treasure Hunt. *11.* Mermaid's Necklace. *12.* More Powers. *13.* Potion Commotion. *14.* Mysterious Voice. *15.* Cave Conniption. *16.* River's Tail. *17.* Kidnapped. *18.* Found. *19.* Half-Scaled. *20.* Dream Chased. *21.* Moon Stones. *22.* Best Friend For-Never. *23.* Dayna's Secret. *24.* Frenemies? *25.* Siren's Trinkit. *26.* Rained Out. *27.* Which Witch Is Which? *28.* Amethyst's Voice. *29.* Intruder. *30.* Taken. *31.* Moon Blinded. *32.* Message in a Bottle. *33.* Siren Sofia. *34.* New Mermaid?!?! *35.* Time Travel Tails. *36.* Hurricane of MerPowers. *37.* Concluding Episode.

215 Magic Tails (2012). youtube.com. 2011 (Comedy-Drama).

A young girl (Lela) walking along the beach shore finds a dolphin necklace and a mysterious liquid (Magic Mio) that she is compelled to drink (possibly from possession of the necklace). The liquid not only transforms her into a Mermaid, but her friends Taylor and May, when they become jealous and yearn to become Mermaids. The girls must now learn to control their transformations and still appear as normal girls.

Cast (as credited): Ellie L., Katie T., Gracie W. **Credits** are not given. **Comment:** Good idea, pretty girls, capable acting but the production suffers from poor sound.

Episode List: *1.* Wonderstruck. *2.* Amazement. *3.* The Crazy Side of Taylor. *4* Control May. *5.* We're More Powerful Then We Think. *6.* Watch Out. *7.* Halloween House of Horror. *8.* Who's Future? *9.* Kidnapped. *10.* Give Us Answers. *11.* Sneaking In. *12.* Saved at Last. *13.* Leila, Taylor and Taylor. *14.* The Mermaid Christmas, Part 1. *15.* The Mermaid Christmas, Part 2. *16.* A Witch or a Mermaid. *17.* The Time Is Limited.

216 Magic Tails (2014). youtube.com. 2014 (Comedy-Drama).

While walking on the beach, a young girl (Sydney) finds a magic ring that when placed on her finger transforms her into a Mermaid. While she could keep it a secret, she doesn't and tells her friends (Maggie, Cassie, Emma, Lily, Zoe and Samantha) about it. Excited, and wanting to also become Mermaids, the girls head to the beach, where they each find a ring—and are granted their wishes. Seven girls, seven Mermaids and how each adjusts to her new life is the focal point of stories.

Cast (as credited): Maggie, Cassie, Emma, Lily Zoe, Samantha, Zac, Ryan. **Credits** are not given.

Comment: While the program does encompass a large cast (including a rarity in Mermaid series—boys) it suffers from poor sound and sometimes poor camera angles.

Episode List: *1.* Mermaid Magic. *2.* Zac and Cam. *3.* Merman. *4.* Friends. *5.* Party Tails. *6.* Mermaid vs. Mermen. *7.* Missing Tails. *8.* New Mermaid and New Merman. *9.* Paranormal Mertivity. *10.* Bath Bomb. *11.* New Story. *12.* New Life. *13.* New Water Hits. *14.* New Tails. *15.* Magic Tails. *16.* Magic Hits. *17.* Happy Times. *18.* Rick's Return. *19.* Frozen. *20.* Sad Times. *21.* New Times.

217 Mantecoza. mantecoza.com. 2011 (Comical Adventure).

Sebastian King is a man just struggling to keep his head above water and his life together. He has a boring job as an accountant, a delinquent sister (Raven) he is trying to keep out of jail, a mother (Judy) who suffers from Alzheimer's and needs to be put into a group home, and a magic ring with mystic powers.

Sebastian didn't ask for and does not want the ring as it means accepting a life of challenge that he is not prepared to tackle. For Sebastian, it began one night when he came to the aid of a woman being attacked and saved her from a mugger. The woman handed Sebastian the ring (with the words "Don't let them get it"), which he thought nothing of at first until it (the ring) revealed to him that he has been declared as the Ring Wizard and has been assigned the task of defending the magical kingdom of Mantecoza from the evil Lord Barr and his minions, the Goons, who seeks to control it. Although reluctant, Sebastian must accept what fate has bestowed upon him and, with the guidance of the beautiful Lady Chenna Danbeau (liaison between the Ring Wizard and Mantecoza) and the help of his sister Raven (a kleptomaniac) and his friend Joe (a slacker), Sebastian becomes the defender of Mantecoza as stories relate his battle against Lord Barr.

Lady Chenna, who wields a magic sword, is the Minister of the Wizard (the daughter of the Wizard of Mantecoza, the man who created the ring) and has been assigned the task of training wizards in combat and teaching them to encompass the powers of the ring.

Joe Jayze is Sebastian's childhood friend who looks upon Sebastian and his family as his surrogate family and Sebastian (whom he calls "Baz") as his brother. Although he is a slacker, Joe always manages to come up with the right plan to help Baz in his battle against Lord Barr.

Joanne King, called Raven, is Joe's younger sister, who became his responsibility when she was eight years old (when their father died). Raven has an obsession for other people's possessions and her compulsion to have them made her a thief (as she would sneak into people's homes when they were out, look over their items and take something as a memento). Her larcenous ways now help Sebastian as he deals with Lord Barr.

Lord Barr is a bit unbalanced and seeks to rule Mantecoza and recreate it in his own image. He is greatly feared and his trickery always defeats the wizards who have been sent to stop him. Sebastian has presented a new challenge and Lord Barr is determined to defeat him and acquire his Magic Ring.

Durrus, Lord Barr's right-hand man, is the "Chief Goon Wrangler" (specifically over Goon #1 and Goon #2). He is cold and calculating and virtually nothing is known about his past.

Cast: Tony Ambrose (Sebastian King), Katherine Stewart (Lady Chenna Danbeau), Tommy Schaeffer (Joe Kayze), Mallory Adams (Raven King), Vincent Maeder (Lord Barr), Marshall Glass (Durrus), Chris Michael Dennis (Goon #1), Will Leon (Goon #2). **Credits:** *Producer:* Susan Kaff, Lon Muckey, Katherine Stewart, James Leatherman. *Director:* Susan Kaff, Kevin R. Phillips. **Comment:** The teaser shows great promise for what appeared to be a fun series. The acting and production values are very good, the characters like-able and background locations very well chosen to represent a medieval setting.

Episodes: All episodes have been taken off line with the exception of the following (view-able on YouTube.com): A teaser (or trailer) that combines a brief introduction to the series with a fund-raising pitch; and four question-and-answer videos conducted by the stars of the program.

218 *Masters of the Universe.* blip.tv. 2012–2013 (Adventure).

A trilogy based on the comic book *He Man and the Masters of the Universe* (which relates the heroics of He-Man, the protector of the Castle Greyskull. In actuality He-Man is Prince Adam, the son of King Randor and Queen Marlena, the rulers of the planet Eternia. The Sorceress of the Castle Greyskull has given Adam special powers and his weapon, the Sword of Greyskull, to defend the castle from Skeletor—an evil sorcerer "from another dimension" with a skull for a head who operates from Snake Mountain and seeks the powers of the Castle Greyskull).

Trilogy Main Cast: David McCullars (He-Man), John F. Carroll (Malik), Bridget Farias (Kareen), Chris Romani (Evil-Lyn), Bethany Harbaugh (Teela), Russell Minton (Kothos), Andrew Brett (Skeletor), Elisabeth Raine (Rayna), Lee Wilson (King Greyskull), Bjorn Korthof (Prince Adam), Juli Dearrington (Sorceress), Javier Smith (Keldor/Zodac), John Athin (General Blade), Darwin Miller (Eldor), Emily Hampton (Princess Adora/She-Ra), Joseph Fontinos (King Randor), Joseph Gouldthrope (Stratos), LeRoy Beck (Melaktha).

***Wizard of Stone Mountain* Additional Cast:** Tyler J. Belcik (Tri-Klops), Braden Hunt (Count Marzo), Terri Lynne Hudson (Artana Gossip), Wes Hampton (Caligar Ambassador), James Ireland (Artana Merchant), Javier Smith (Chief Carnivus), Jacqueline Lies (Royal Healer Kesara), Joshua Marriott (Master of Evil), Angela Pierce (Deirdra), Candice Roma (Royal Healer Endymia), Allison Wood (Royal Healer Brina).

***Fountain of Life* Additional Cast:** John F. Carroll (General Tataran/The Faceless One/Hordak), Jennifer Goeller (Catra), Jack Giminiani, Laurie Kail, Eric Schott, Briony Zakes, Jeffrey Miller (Goblin Mercenary), Justin Hampton (Temple Guard), Peter Olemann (Temple Currier), Matt Dysart (Evil Guardian), Jared Minton (Greyskull Guard).

***Trials of Darksmoke* Additional Cast:** Alice Ndirangu (Guardian of Darksmoke), Peggy Scott (Queen Angela), Terri Lynne Hudson, Jenni Bauer (Guardian of Darksmoke), Rigel Smith (Young Malik), John F. Carroll (Hordak), Kenneth C. Liverman (King Randor), Bob Swaffar (King Miro), Patti Neff-Tiven (The Enchantress), Briony Zakes (Frosta), Greg De-Blieux (Horde Wraith). **Series Credits:** *Producer-Writer:* John F. Carroll. *Director:* John F. Carroll, Russell Minton. **Comment:** Could be considered a live-action version of the animated TV series *He-Man and the Masters of the Universe* with good acting and production values.

Episodes:

1. Wizard of Stone Mountain. Malik, the Wizard of Stone Mountain, seeks to win the love of his life (Teela) by impressing her with great powers. To do so, he makes a bargain with a demon but finds it was a mistake when the demon seeks to gain control of his soul. Malik's efforts to overcome the demon's power over him and regain the life he once lived are the focal point of the story.

2. The Fountain of Life. Knowing that controlling Malik will help him achieve his goal of conquest, Skeletor devises a plan to use Evil Lyn and an equally evil wizard, Kothos, to attack the Fountain of Life and bring Malik to him.

3. The Trials of Darksmoke. Skeletor's failed attempt from the prior episode has him devising a new one: attack Castle Greyskull and for once and all defeat He-Man.

219 *Measures.* blip.tv. 2013 (Drama).

Cay and Alvis are friends without jobs and desperately in need of money. They are rather uncouth, use drugs and survive by committing varying degrees of criminal acts to acquire cash. They literally live by chance (hoping not to get caught) and the program relates the incidents that occur in their lives, the choices they make ("the measures we act upon in life") and the consequences they must face.

Cast: Colin Chick (Alvis Allister), John-Paul Pace (Cay), James Adam (Penklis), Jake Lyall (Shane), Brendan Byrne (Joe), Steve Maresca (Ben), Amara Picke (Alex). **Credits:** *Producer:* Jilvan M. Simatos, John Simatos. *Writer-Director:* Jilvan M. Simatos. **Comment:** Australian produced program that is quite gritty with vulgar language rampant throughout. The acting and production values are acceptable but the characters are so despicable (no redeeming qualities) that they could be more of a turnoff than a draw.

Episodes:

1. Introductions, Part 1. Rather unsavory start to the program as Alvis and Cay are seen doing drugs.

2. Introductions, Part 2. As they continue to use drugs, Alvis and Cay comment on their lives and the situation they currently face.

3. Limbo. Alvis and Cay plot to rip off a drug dealer in an attempt to acquire money and drugs.

4. Lost & Found. The theft becomes a serious problem when they become sought by pushers who want their stash back.

5. A Case of Bad Luck. Feeling that drugs are ruining his life, Alvis attempts to turn over a new leaf by eliminating them.

6. No Direction Home. The fate of Alvis and Cay is left unresolved after a violent confrontation with drug dealers in the concluding episode.

220 *Meet Me in the Graveyard.* blip.tv. 2008 (Drama).

Viola is a very pretty single young woman confined to a mental institution in Georgia. The death of her mother consumed her and it was determined that it was best for her if she were under supervised care (as she apparently lacks the ability to cry or feel sadness). Ace, a recovering alcoholic who resides in a half-way house in California, bides his time by posting videos on the Internet under the user name "Rosehill Cemetery." One day, while surfing the web, Viola comes across one of Ace's videos with a graveyard photo background and becomes intrigued when she sees her mother's headstone in the picture. Viola contacts Ace, the two become friends and the "love letters" each sends to the other become the basis of each episode.

Cast: Milly Sanders (Viola), Adam Sanders (Ace), Onyay Pheori (Angeline). **Credits:** *Producer-Writer* Milly Sanders. *Director:* Benjamin Epps, Matt Thiesen. **Comment:** Producer Milly Sanders has created a web series that can easily trick people into believing Viola and Ace are real people posting their "love" letters to each other, while in reality they are actors pretending to be real people. The production values (as well as the acting) are very good and, to give a different perspective on each of the characters, two directors were encompassed—Benjamin Epps to shoot Ace's sequences and Matt Thiesen to tape Viola's segments. The program is sort of a "Beauty and the Beast" analogy with Viola, pretty, sweet and innocent falling for a degenerate (Ace) with no apparent morals. Overall, an exceptionally well done series that appears more realistic especially through Viola, than fictional.

Episodes:

1. Episode 1. The correspondence begins with Viola responding to a video "Respect the Graveyard" when she notices her mother's headstone in the background.

2. Episode 2. The video's sender (Ace) replies and he and Viola begin corresponding.

3. Episode 3. Viola explains to Ace that she is in a mental institution due to her inability to accept what happened, feel sadness or even cry.

4. Episode 4. Ace, rather uncouth and with a vulgar mouth, reveals that he is in a half-way house and was once addicted to alcohol.

5. Episode 5. Viola and Ace make a promise to video chat once a week.

6. Episode 6. Ace fulfills an unusual request by Viola—to send her mother's grave stone size so she can determine if she is ascending toward Heaven.

7. Episode 7. Viola expresses her feelings that her doctor is acting strange and not letting her participate in certain activities.

8. Episode 8. Ace makes the first step and asks Viola to be his video girlfriend.

9. Episode 9. Delighted that she and Ace are boyfriend/girlfriend, Viola draws up a "boyfriend contract" for them.

10. Episode 10. Ace creates a silent film to relay a past incident in his life—he was responsible for the death of a family, but found insane at the time (due to alcohol) and sent to the half-way house.

11. Episode 11. Ace returns the signed contract Viola created but is disturbed to learn that on April 22 at 5:14 p.m., when Viola turns 27, if he doesn't visit her she will kill herself.

12. Episode 12. Viola sends Ace her mother's locket to pay for his trip to see her, but begins to panic when he fails to respond to the message.

13. Episode 13. Ace attempts to visit Viola but is turned away by the guards at the front door of St. Vincent's (the institution in which Viola resides).

14. Episode 14. Viola expresses her feelings (but not crying) that Ace could not see her.

15. Episode 15. In a new video, Ace explains that if he takes another chance and is caught, he will be

Meet Me in the Graveyard. **Milly Sanders in a scene from the program (used by permission of Milly Sanders).**

sent to jail for leaving the center. Thus he will not be coming to see her.

16. Episode 16. After receiving Ace's message, Viola tells Ace goodbye, indicating that she may do something desperate.

17. Episode 17. Ace reveals that Viola lied to him—St. Vincent's is a voluntary mental institution, not the confined institution she told him. He feels her lie could destroy their relationship (as she was free to leave at anytime and he took a needless risk to see her).

18. Episode 18. In an effort to teach Viola a lesson, Ace sends her a video that shows him kissing the mute girl (Angeline) who resides at the half-way house but also a disturbing message that he will commit suicide.

19. Episode 19. As Viola's birth date time approaches, it is revealed that her doctor had been trying to make her cry (by doing everything possible to make her experience sadness) but failed. But it is Ace's video that brings a tear to her eye and makes her feel sadness—and realize that life has a lot to offer and that she now needs to live. But did Ace really commit suicide?

221 *Mermaid at Heart.* youtube.com. 2013–2014 (Comedy-Drama).

When a 10-year-old girl (Riki) begins exploring a cave she discovers on the beach, magically enhanced water splashes on her and its powers transform her into a Mermaid. Now, with newly acquired abilities, Riki must learn to keep a secret while attempting to live a normal life and fulfill a destiny that could affect the oceans of the world (as her developing powers will enable her to defeat The Evil Ones who are seeking to destroy Mermaids and their goodness).

Cast (as credited): Emily (Riki and Amber). **Credits** are not given. **Comment:** Emily is a pretty girl and handles her roles well although the production has poor sound and only acceptable photography.

Episodes:

1. Shoreline, Part 1 (5 min., 31 sec.). Establishes the story line as Riki discovers a strange cave on the beach.

2. Shoreline, Part 2 (5 min., 10 sec.). Riki's first experiences as a Mermaid (with a yellow tail) as she attempts to understand what has happened to her.

3. Exposed (12 min., 53 sec.). A newspaper reporter (Amber) becomes suspicious of Riki's actions and decides to investigate.

4. The Journey Begins (12 min., 57 sec.). Just as Riki is adjusting to what she has become, a magic box mysteriously appears to her. Inside is a bottle with a note attached: "Drink Me." Thinking the blue liquid is safe, Riki drinks it and transforms into a Mermaid with a blue tail and hair. Suddenly a voice is heard that tells Riki she is a force for good and must fear The Evil Ones, creatures who hate Mer-

maids and seek only to destroy them. The liquid changed her colors to prevent The Evil Ones from tracking her and stopping her from fulfilling her destiny to protect the ocean.

5. She's Back (8 min., 56 sec.). As Riki realizes that she is more than just an ordinary Mermaid, Amber's investigation is close to uncovering Riki's secret. The concluding, unresolved episode.

222 *Mermaid at Midnight.* youtube.com. 2012 (Comedy-Drama).

While swimming at the beach, a young girl (Brinn), stumbles across a secret cave, enters it and apparently blacks out. She awakens in her home, but is unaware as to how she got there. Passing it off as just a weird dream, Brinn becomes thirsty and, after taking a drink of water, magically transforms into a Mermaid. She must now learn how to control her Mermaid abilities and also live her life as a normal school girl.

Cast (as credited): Weibits (Brinn). **Credits** are not given. **Comment:** The sequence with Brinn "swimming in the ocean" can clearly be seen as being shot in a swimming pool and "the cave" [with tile walls], is apparently her home's bathroom. Weibits is the only performer and the overall production is acceptable although it does suffer from poor sound at times.

Episodes:

1. The Moon Shell (8 min., 49 sec.). As Brinn attempts to adjust to the fact that she is now a Mermaid, she learns that she also possesses magical abilities (like freezing and heating water).

2. Weird Waves (6 min., 13 sec.). As Brinn examines the unusual necklace she found in the cave, she places it around her neck and immediately creates a duplicate image of herself (by removing the necklace, her duplicate vanishes).

3. An Evil Presence (5 min., 30 sec.). Brinn is dreading another boring day until she spies a mysterious box in her backyard with her name on it. Upon opening it, she finds a necklace—but one that, when worn, brings out the evil in a person.

4. Just the Beginning (4 min., 2 sec.). Brinn, placed in a trance by the necklace, is seen in a sinister state until she removes it and is returned to normal. Brinn has no memory as to what happened when she wore the necklace and the program ends unresolved with the possibility of Brinn becoming a pawn in a good vs. evil situation.

223 *Mermaid Miracles.* youtube.com. 2013 (Drama).

During the early 18th century a young couple walking along the beach finds a nest and what appears to be an abandoned baby Mermaid. With no one else in sight they take the baby and decide to raise her as their own child (whom they name Ana).

Unknown to the couple, fate had intended for them to find Ana and thus create a legacy that would carry Ana's mission of protecting the oceans for the future through her children and her children's children.

It is the year 2013 and sisters Inga and Ilsa, the great, great grandchildren of Ana, have also been endowed with Mermaid abilities, but have kept it secret from their children, Maya (Inga's 13-year-old daughter) and Ashley (Ilsa's daughter). While Inga appears to be living a normal life with Maya, Ashley's life is quite different as her mother mysteriously disappeared several years ago but she has hope that her mother will return to her. One day, while on the beach Maya finds a bottle that apparently washed upon shore and opens it. Inside is a note, somewhat aged over time, that reads, "You are at the age when your powers come. Don't be alarmed. Don't run." Maya and Ashley are unable to make sense of it and ignore it, although Maya elects to keep the note. Suddenly, an unexpected wave washes upon the shore and splashes Maya and Ashley with water. Immediately, they are transformed into Mermaids. Although a bit shocked, they are quite rational and when their mermaid tails dry, they return to normal.

Ashley is a bit reluctant to accept what has happened and wonders why while Maya is eager to embrace her metamorphosis. Their questions are answered by Inga, when she tells them that she too is a Mermaid and they have reached the age when they too must embrace their heritage. They also learn why: to love, respect and protect the oceans at all times. It is also learned through Inga that "when the tide is high be open to help others; when the tide is low, be open to receiving help from others." She concludes with, "Be careful to whom you give your heart" (as a Mermaid has only one chance to truly fall in love). As Maya and Ashley begin to embrace what they have become, they also learn that Isla was kidnapped by Sirens, evil sea creatures who are seeking the Tempest, a mysterious object that can destroy mankind, and must keep them from ever finding it. The program follows teenagers Maya and Ashley as they attempt to embrace their abilities and live the lives of normal teenage girls.

Cast: Maya Tritt (Maya), Ashley Harmon (Ashley), Inga Tritt (Inga), David Tritt (David, Maya's father), Chad Rush (Chad), Hanna Formica (Roxy), James Cooney (Ricky), Abby Oliver (Isla), Chloe Hightower (Chloe), Kias Porter (Kias). **Credits:** *Producer:* David Tritt, Maya Tritt. *Director:* Brett Mazurek. *Writer:* Maya Tritt. **Comment:** Charming Mermaid tale with good acting and production qualities. The underwater sequences are well done and comedy (with the Mermaid hunters) mixes with light drama. The series, written by star Maya Tritt when she was 12 years old, has a very large world-wide following (over 3 million views on YouTube alone) and is really unique when one so young not only encompasses Mermaid mythology but respect for the oceans and ecology as well. While it is aimed at chil-dren and teens, it is easily enjoyed by any age group. If you have seen the movie *Aquamarine* and/or the TV series *H2O, Just Add Water* you will also enjoy *Mermaid Miracles.*

Episodes:

1. Pilot (6 min., 58 sec.). Establishes the story line as Maya finds a mysterious bottle that has washed up on the beach.

2. True Self (7 min., 2 sec.). Maya and Ashley attempt to adjust to what has happened with Maya seeking more information about Mermaids.

3. Shiny Things (5 min., 18 sec.). The disorganized Mermaid hunters, Ricky and Kias are introduced as they believe mermaids exist in California.

4. The Golden Rules (4 min., 31 sec.). Maya and Ashley learn of their heritage from Inga and of Isla's mysterious disappearance.

5. The Chase (8 min., 37 sec.). Maya and Ashley learn their secret identities are being threatened by the arrival of the Mermaid hunters.

6. Mermaid Party (8 min., 44 sec.). What starts out to be a normal party reveals that Maya and Ashley's friend, Roxy, is also a Mermaid—and that their friend, Chad is aware of her secret.

7. I Dream of Mermaids (3 min., 55 sec.). At his birthday party, Chad also learns that Maya and Ashley are Mermaids and vows to keep their secret (as he did with Roxy).

8. The Siren's Song (9 min.). In addition to the Mermaid hunters, the girls now have to fear the Sirens, three beautiful sea witches who have come ashore seeking the Tempest. Concludes Season 1.

9. Heart's Desire (17 min., 16 sec.). The second season begins with Inga being captured by the Sirens.

10. Sirens vs. Mermaids (4 min., 44 sec.). Maya, Ashley, Roxy and Chad devise a plan to find Inga and defeat the Sirens. Armed with a magic compass Maya finds in an old trunk and information about help from something called the Oracle, the group sets out on an unknown path to find it.

11. Follow Your Heart (22 min., 5 sec.). At the beach Maya finds the Oracle, a woman who has always been with her (in spirit watching over her) while Inga, reunited with Isla in a cave, learns that Isla was abducted in an effort to acquire the Tempest (apparently in her and Inga's possession). Now, with Inga as a prisoner, the Sirens believe they can use Isla as a bargaining chip for Inga to reveal the location of the Tempest. Meanwhile, with the help of the Oracle, Maya, Ashley, Roxy and Chad have learned the whereabouts of Inga and Isla but how to rescue them? They also have to fear the Mermaid hunters who are becoming increasingly close to discovering that Mermaids do exist. The program concludes unresolved.

224 Mermaids. youtube.com. 2012 (Comedy-Drama).

Liz, a girl recently relocating to Texas with her

family, befriends a girl named Kenna and becomes fascinated with a stone pendant she possesses. Kenna sells Liz the pendant and, upon purchasing it, acquires the abilities of a Mermaid. Now, with both Liz and Kenna possessing the same attributes, they must learn to embrace their Mermaid heritage while at the same time live life as ordinary young girls.

Cast: A cast and **credits** are not given. **Comment:** Even crediting the girls with first names (as has been done on other Mermaid series) should have been done as the program is a bit better than others like it. The girls are good although the sound is poor at times.

Episode List: *1.* Mermaids. *2.* Power Surge. *3.* Tail of Halloween. *4.* The Deep End. *5.* Dreams (Power Hour). *6.* Unknown (removed for unexplained reasons). *7.* Stone Trouble. *8.* Season Finale. *9.* The Uninvited Guest (Begins Season 2). *10.* Two of the Same. *11.* Bubbly Message. *12.* A Splashtastic Problem. *13.* The Siren's Tower. *14.* Season 2 Finale. *15.* MER (Begins and ends the Third Season).

225 *Mermaids 4 Life.* youtube.com. 2013 (Comedy-Drama).

After enjoying the day swimming at the local pool, friends Taylor and Erica find a mysterious rock with a ring and necklace that are beside it. Rather than just pass it by, they decide to take them. Later, when they go swimming, the water transforms them into Mermaids—a result of acquiring the ring and necklace. Now, faced with new challenges, Taylor and Erica must keep secret their abilities while at the same time lead normal lives.

Cast (as credited): Mariella (Taylor Brooke), Charlie (Erica Wilson). **Credits** are not given. **Comment:** Acceptable production (although the sound is poor at times). The girls are pretty and handle their roles well.

Episode List: *1.* Pilot. *2.* Jellyfish and Swimming the Ring Is Lost. *3.* New Tail Way. *4.* Sico. *5.* Hard Tails, Parts 1 and 2. *6.* Serious People. *7.* Episode 7. *8.* Episode 8. *9.* School Episode. *10.* Season Finale.

226 *A Mermaid's World.* youtube.com. 2012 (Comedy-Drama).

While at a lake, two girls (Dylan and Sadie) each find a star-shaped necklace which they each place around their neck. The following day, when the girls use the local swimming pool, everything is normal. However, when they return home and shower, the necklaces transform them into Mermaids—secrets they must keep while leading ordinary lives.

Cast: Micah Cornor (Dylan King), Kinley Miller (Sadie Collins), Mikayla Welsh (Paige). **Credits** are not given. **Comment:** Poor sound quality (like wind blowing into the camera microphone) hampers an interesting production based on Mermaid mythology.

Episodes:
1. A Whole New World (5 min., 41 sec.). The discovery of two necklaces changes the lives of two young girls (Dylan and Sadie) forever.
2. Power Practice (7 min., 55 sec.). After discovering they are Mermaids, Dylan and Sadie find a journal, written in 1924 by a girl named Alyssa, that contains her personal experiences as a Mermaid and that she was the one who hid the necklaces at the lake.
3. Sick Days (4 min., 43 sec.). The girls soon discover that catching a cold can wreck havoc with their powers when Sadie comes down with one and transforms into a Mermaid without touching water.
4. The Eclipse (9 min., 10 sec.). An upcoming eclipse is anything but enjoyable for Dylan and Sadie when they are transformed into Mermaids and Sadie is attacked by what she calls "a water tentacle."
5. Three's a Crowd (6 min., 4 sec.). As a new girl (Paige) moves into the neighborhood and introduces herself to Dylan and Sadie, she takes a particular liking to Dylan, making Sadie feel jealous.
6. Season Finale (6 min., 7 sec.). Realizing that she is ignoring Sadie to be with Paige, Dylan makes an effort for Paige and Sadie to become friends. It seems to work until Paige splashes them with water and takes a picture of them as Mermaids. Paige had suspected something was different about Dylan, and now with proof, she plans to expose them at Science Headquarters. The episode concludes with Dylan and Sadie saving Paige's life when, during a chase she falls into lake and in gratitude gives Dylan the camera.

227 *The Midnight Room.* webserieschannel.com. 2013 (Anthology).

A room, occupied by different people at different times, is the setting for unusual stories that have a *Twilight Zone*–like feeling but an *Alfred Hitchcock Presents*–like conclusion (leaves it up to the viewer to determine).

Cast: John Harn, Zack Elledge, Daniel Silver, Dawn Jeffers, Jonathan Hart. **Credits:** *Producer:* John Harn, Zack Elledge, Jonathan Hart. **Comment:** The episodes may sound interesting but they are badly presented. The acting is below par, the direction is very bad and photography not only relies on the nauseating shaky camera but some frames are out of focus. Overall it is difficult to figure out what is going on and after a few minutes you simply don't care as the presentation is simply unappealing.

Episodes:
1. The Visitor (2 min., 47 sec.). An alien (or so it appears) is inspecting the room when he finds a picture—of his parents (?).
2. The Artist (3 min., 12 sec.). A struggling artist, using the room as his galley, finds a small sketch book of drawings that inspires him to create a great work of art.
3. The Button (4 min., 14 sec.). It is the future

and a man, who drinks, is supposedly responsible for the lives of millions of people as he is the only one who can press a button and destroy countries. When a phone call from the President (of the U.S.?) orders him to destroy New Korea, he ponders what to do.

4. The Funny Man (4 min.). A stand-up comedian performs to an empty house (in the room!) and suddenly finds himself being stalked by someone who presented him with a photograph, cut into a puzzle, of his performance. Who? Why?

5. Escape One (3 min., 38 sec.). A sequel to the first episode where the alien (?) apparently trapped in the room is seeking a way to escape.

6. The Operative (4 min., 31 sec.). Talkative episode about two agents assigned to uncover an operative known as Agent Zero.

228 Milk + Honey. milkandhoneyseries.com. 2011 (Comedy-Drama).

Nia, Samirah, Harper and Farrah are young African-American women living in Los Angeles and hoping to take the world by storm. Their dreams, their struggles and their relationships are explored as each tries to become the person she has dreamed of becoming.

Nia, described as "the beautiful girl next door," is charming, fun to be with and a loyal friend. She is a rising actress but has yet to land a role that will make her a household name.

Samirah, a free spirit, is a photographer who has been called "a blipster" (half hipster, half nerd). She is an Ivy League school graduate and also works as a DJ.

Harper, a hopeless romantic, is driven, well educated (attended Spellman and Harvard) and aspires to become a top notch entertainment agent. She is also considered a "Black American Princess" as she apparently gets what she wants and, according to some, "needs to get more "no's' in life."

Farrah, the "fashionista" of the group, was raised by a well-to-do family, and never experienced the harsher side of life as a child. Called a "stunning wild child siren," she is a college dropout and constantly searching for love.

Will, Nia's life-long love, is an investment banking consultant who moonlights as a music producer.

Eva Monroe, a legendary, award-winning actress, is Nia's acting instructor, a woman who hopes to realize her career through Nia.

Cast: Asha Kamali (Nia), Yanni King (Samirah), Shauntay Hinton (Harper), Faune Chambers (Farrah), Lance Gross (Will), Debbie Allen (Eva Monroe), Bryce Wilson (Jonathan), Charles Divins (Jace), Rob Smith (Isaac). **Credits:** *Producer:* Idris Elba. *Director:* Jeanette McDuffie. *Writer:* Jeanette McDuffie, Asha Kamali May. **Comment:** Many African-American web series are rather gritty (vulgar language, violence and strong sexual situations) and not well acted or produced. *Milk + Honey* rises above

the others as being well acted, written and directed. It is a well-paced drama that presents the characters as actual people, facing the normal problems of life without stretching ideas to a point where they become boring or hard to accept as actually happening.

Episodes:

1. Episode 1 (11 min., 6 sec.). The principal women are introduced as they continue their efforts to achieve their goals.

2. Episode 2 (8 min., 10 sec.). Focuses mainly on Harper as she meets with a potential client and, despite her illustrious educational background and perky attitude, is rejected, being told not only is she not right, but needs a life lesson in being told "no."

229 Millennium Apocalypse. blip.tv. 2004–2011 (Drama).

Season 1 Premise: Jordan Black is a young woman with the ability to see the future through visions she apparently inherited from her father. Her father, however, mysteriously disappeared 12 years ago and left Jordan and the government agency for which he worked baffled as to what could have happened. When it is discovered that a great catastrophe will soon occur that could destroy the planet, Jordan is recruited by the same agency for which her father worked to encompass her visions to stop the Apocalypse before it happens. The program follows Jordan as she becomes involved in a web of intrigue—struggling to prevent impending doom but also encountering conspiracies while seeking to once and for all solve the mystery of her father's disappearance.

Season 2 Premise: It has been six months since the events of the prior series and Jordan is now living in San Francisco and attempting to help children understand and accept the same abilities she possesses. The story itself follows Jordan as she attempts to solve a string of mysterious murders that appear to be linked to some of her students.

Season 1 Cast: Shoni Alysse Cook (Jordan Black), Jacqueline Goehner (Taylor), Johnny Gilligan (Riley), Valerie Gutierrez (Amanda), Jeff Allen (Andrew), Doc Divecchio (The Old Man), Douglas Olsson (Avatar), Rob Tillitz (Peter), West Ramsey (The Elder), Jessica Buchleitner (Agent Malcolm), Florentino Gonzales (Agent Daniels).

Season 2 Cast: Shoni Alysse Cook (Jordan Black), Valerie Gutierrez (Amanda Diaz), Jacqueline Goehner (Taylor Watts), Johnny Gilligan (Marcus Riley), Douglas Olsson (Serial Killer), Doc Divecchio (The Old Man), Jeff Allen (Andrew Bishop), Florentino Gonzales (Agent Daniels), Jessica Buchleitner (Agent Malcolm), Judy Cerda (Patricia Roebuck), James Brewer (Mr. Roebuck), Cynthia Gatlin (Mrs. Franks), Amelia Avila (Maria Diaz), West Ramsey (Group Leader).

Season 1 Credits: *Producer-Director:* Jason D.

Morris. *Writer:* Michael B. Martin, Erin McRaven, Jason D. Morris.

Season 2 Credits: *Producer:* Jason D. Morris, Shoni Alysse Cook, Colby Heyes. *Director:* Jason D. Morris. *Writer:* Jason D. Morris, Colby Heyes, Rob Carrera.

Comment:

Season 1: An apparent spin off from the Chris Carter TV series *Millennium*. Although ambitious, it is also very low budget and can become confusing if your full attention is not given to the plot. The production qualities are standard for an Internet series and Shoni Alysse Cook (as Jordan) is very believable and the highlight of the program. The program was edited and released on DVD (thus first season episodes are no longer on line) but apparently crucial scenes were deleted and reviews have been very harsh (stating "very bad acting" and "an end result that is basically a confusing mess"). The program also hints of borrowing aspects from TV series like *Dark Angel* and *The X-Files* as they also used the end-of-the-world scenario.

Season 2: Episodes are an improvement with better acting and production values and a far-less confusing story.

Episode List (Season 2): *1.* The Future. *2.* A Murder of Crows. *3.* My God, It's Full of Stars. *4.* The Future and Its Enemies. *5.* Pains. *6.* Points of Darkness.*7.* Something Old Is New Again. *8.* The Devil You Know. *9.* Daimonzimanis. *10.* Non Omnis Moriar.

230 *Miss Behave.* missbehave.tv. 2010 (Drama).

Victoria Anne Archer, called Tori, is a pretty teenage girl living in Malibu, California. She is the daughter of a Hollywood publicist (Elizabeth) and a famous writer (William) and was raised without the proper parental guidance (as her mother and father were too busy pursuing their careers). Her life has progressed from good girl to wild girl and she is actually leading two lives: good girl high school student and wild girl dealing with adult responsibilities and sexual identity issues. The program follows the events that spark Tori's life as she struggles to avoid letting her worlds collide.

Other Characters: Dylan, Tori's friend since grade school, has always had a crush on her and is now determined to win her heart. He tends to see the good in everyone and suspects there is something different about Tori, but can't figure it out (her double life).

Danielle, Tori's best friend since kindergarten, suspects Tori is lying about her actions to cover up something. Unknown to Dylan, Danielle has a crush on him and hopes he will realize it and like her instead of Tori.

Billy, Tori's older brother, lacks motivation, discipline and self-control and has recently been expelled from college. His mother, called "The Queen" (re-

ferring to her publicity status) has set high expectations for him, but his inability to live up to them is apparently the cause of his problems.

Tasha, a party girl who loves to live on the edge, is Tori's friend and the bad influence in her life. Tasha is always on the lookout for a new boyfriend and has influenced Tori to lead that secret life.

Christian, Danielle's bad-boy romantic interest, has a secret crush on Tori and has plans to approach Tori and begin a relationship with her.

Alex, Tori's cousin, is a world traveler who is there for Tori when she needs help.

Noah is the Australian actor promoting his film in the U.S. whom Tori meets through Alex and who becomes infatuated with Tori.

Riley, Tasha's step-brother, is a ladies' man who has just dropped out of college. He is not ambitious and appears to just hang out with his friends and party.

Cast: Jillian Clare (Tori), Brett DelBuono (Dylan), Jenna Stone (Danielle), Trevor Doyle Nelson (Billy), Bianca Magick (Tasha), Jamison Tate (Christian), James Rustin (Alex), Michael Bolten (Noah), Terri Garber (Elizabeth Archer), Patrika Darbo (Dr. Freed), Jacee Jule (Kristina), Eric Martsolf (Marcus Dunne). **Credits:** *Producer:* Susan Bernhardt, Jillian Clare, Bernadette Olivares. *Director:* Jon Zimmerman, Sarah Smith, Patrika Darbo. *Writer:* Frances Gilbert. **Comment:** Fast moving teen drama with good acting, writing and directing. Patterned after network soaps like *Beverly Hills, 90210* and *Dawson's Creek* it plays well on the Internet as the episodes are straight forward and not dragged out to fill a specific time limit.

Episodes:

1. Liar, Liar, Pants on Fire, Part 1 (8 min., 24 sec.). Tori and her brother Billy are introduced.

2. Liar, Liar, Pants on Fire, Part 2 (8 min., 25 sec.). Continues the introduction with viewers seeing that Tori is not the sweet, heart of gold girl she appears to be and Billy attempting to deal with the demons in his life.

3. All the World's a Stage, Part 1 (6 min., 49 sec.). An upcoming school production of *Romeo and Juliet* has Tori setting her sights on acquiring the lead role.

4. All the World's a Stage, Part 2 (5 min., 54 sec.). As Tori acquires the role of Juliet to Dylan's lead as Romeo, Billy finds himself questioning his sexuality (gay?) after meeting the aggressive Tasha for the first time.

5. Bring the House Down, Part 1 (6 min., 17 sec.). As Tori attempts to cope with unexpected guests when her friends show up at her house, Billy and Tasha hook up at Tasha's home.

6. Bring the House Down, Part 2 (6 min., 30 sec.). Continues the story with a focus on how Tori and Billy handle their respective situations.

7. Point of No Return, Part 1 (7 min., 30 sec.). Tori's decision to live a *Ferris Bueller's Day Off* type of life, causes her to miss the first day of rehearsal.

8. Point of No Return, Part 2 (6 min., 16 sec.). Tori's day of leisure raises suspicions among her friends and has her now fearing that she may have exposed her secret life.

9. Teacher Knows Best, Part 1 (6 min., 20 sec.). Billy's encounter with Tasha makes him believe that he may not be gay.

10. Teacher Knows Best, Part 2 (6 min., 3 sec.). As Billy comes to terms with his sexuality, Tori seeks a way to remain in the play after missing the first day of rehearsal.

11. Much Ado About Nothing, Part 1 (6 min., 55 sec.). In an attempt to double date "for therapeutic reasons," Billy talks Tori into accepting a date with Riley so he and Tasha can connect.

12. Much Ado About Nothing, Part 2 (7 min., 28 sec.). Concludes the prior episode with Tori realizing Riley may not be right for her.

13. Parting Is Such Sweet Sorrow (6 min., 36 sec.). Elizabeth, Tori's mother is introduced as she attends the school's wrap party for the final performance of *Romeo and Juliet*.

14. A Dream Is a Wish (7 min., 43 sec.). Alex comes to Tori's aide and introduces her to a therapist (Dr. Freed) after Tori's fears about getting caught with Riley begin to overpower her.

15. Water Under the Bridge (9 min., 53 sec.). Tori's therapy session with Dr. Freed is explored.

16. It's My Party and I'll Cry If I Want To (8 min., 51 sec.). Tori's 17th birthday party turns out to be a depressing occasion for Tori; meanwhile, Dylan hooks up with a new girl (Samantha).

17. The Calm Before the Storm (7 min., 45 sec.). Trouble brews at the party when Danielle confronts Tori about her feelings for Christian—and Christian, tired of Danielle's immature outlook on life, sees a possible way to become closer to Tori.

18. You Can't Always Get What You Want (6 min., 42 sec.). Alex returns to town and, at the birthday party, introduces Tori to Noah, squashing her daydreams about Riley.

19. The Icing on the Cake (8 min., 28 sec.). As Tori's friends become more concerned about her unusual behavior, Tori becomes attracted to Noah.

20. 17 Candles (6 min., 56 sec.). Tori's party goes from sad to a fun time for her as Noah also seems to be infatuated with her.

21. The Last Straw (6 min., 10 sec.). Although she has feelings for Noah, Tori cannot get Riley out of her system and prepares to tell Noah about him.

22. Over My Dead Body (14 min., 1 sec.). Alex, realizing that Tori is now more troubled than ever, persuades her to return to therapy and hopefully come to terms with her own fears and move on. The concluding episode.

231 *Mob on the Run.* mobontherun.com. 2013 (Comedy-Drama).

Michael "Mickey" Costavento (also called "Mick the Quick") is a small-time mobster arrested for book making and sentenced to five years in the Lewisburg Federal Penitentiary in Philadelphia. Mickey has several unethical business operations and, before beginning his prison term, stashed a considerable amount of money, which he planned to use

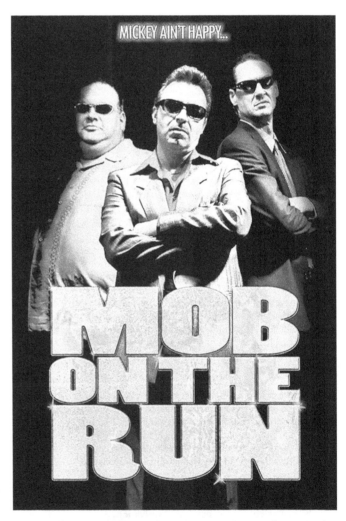

Mob on the Run. **Poster art from the series (copyright Michael Belveduto).**

to restart operations once he was released. Unknown to Mickey, his two less-than-intelligent associates, Dominic "Dom the Bomb" Delegino and Tony (Anthony "Two Ton Tony" Martin), have squandered that money and now, as Mickey is nearing his release, are fearful for their lives. To hopefully recoup the money they spent they establish On the Run, a travel agency front for a book-making operation. Mickey, released from prison, returns to his base of operations but instead of being angry or vengeful, accepts what Dominic and Tony (with the assist of Mickey's girlfriend Vivienne) have done and plans to actually make On the Run legitimate to further conceal its true nature. The program follows Mickey as he attempts to run a book-making business, keep the Feds from discovering the true nature of his operations and please "The Family," the New York City–based head of the organization who often worry that Mickey's activities could expose them.

Cast: Michael Belveduto (Mickey Costavento), Barry Tangert (Dominic Delegino), Rob Misko (Tony Martin), Carrie Leigh Snodgrass (Vivienne Longetti), Joseph D'Onofrio (Sonny Falco), David Giordano (Lorenzo Locatelli), Analise Traficante (Angelica "Angel" Mistro), Albert Gomez (Nico "Steady Nick" Luchessi), Mark "Madcat" Capone (James "Crowbar" D'Angelo), Paul Dudrich (Patrick "Paddy" McGonegal), Mike Adler (Frankie Santori), Anthony Romano, Jr. (Vito "Big Man" Toscano), Michael Shands (FBI Agent Gerry Jackson), Matt Duffin (FBI Agent Michael Sandusky), Antonia Menta (Geanna Russo), Rick Romano (Vincent "Iceman" Moretti), Joe Gawalis (Nino "Babyface" Scalini), Carlo Bellario (Carmine "The Jaw" De-Rossi), Eddy Privitzer (Franco "Double D" DeLuca), Steven Bongiovanni (Bobby "Loops" Victorio), Johnny G. Lee (Alexi Azajov), Chris Sloane (Agent Jack Grady), Karl Barbee (Johnny "Knock Your Rocks Off" Kyro), Dan Eash (Gene Boner), Christopher Waite (The Squealer), Andrew Rodes (Kitty Pitty). **Credits:** *Producer:* Michael Belveduto, Barry Tangert, W. Jeff Crawford, Andrew Rodes. *Director:* Michael Belveduto, W. Jeff Crawford, Andrew Rodes, Barry Tangert. *Writer:* Michael Belveduto. *Location Manager:* Amber Escott. *Production Manager:* Giulio Marchi. *Photography:* Johnny Gee. **Comment:** Smartly acted, written and directed spoof of the hardcore gangster sagas. Once the initial shock of the vulgar language passes, the program becomes enjoyable with a smooth-flowing story that captures your attention from the very beginning. The characters are well depicted and so gangster-like that the Marlon Brando (*Godfather*)–like image soon becomes passé. There is a unique viewer discretion (one of the best for such programs) that appears before each episode begins, stating that it has an equivalent (to a feature film) "R" rating "for situations that may contain a Whole Lotta Ass-Kicking, Friggin' F-Bombs, Nice and Sexy Situations and Stuff that Will Jail Ya." There is also the possibility of additional episodes as the program leaves the doorway open to continue the story.

Episodes:

1. Mickey Ain't Happy. Mickey, still in prison, contemplates his release and return to his book-making business.

2. Mickey Gets Out. Mickey, picked up by his driver (Vito) relishes his first day of freedom, unaware of what his associates have done.

3. So Why Here and Why Me? Mickey's discovery of what has been done initially fosters an angry response until he rationalizes that On the Run may be just what he is looking for.

4. Here Comes Trouble. As Mickey plans to legitimize On the Run, "The Family" questions his motives as being too risky and will bring too much attention to the business.

5. Caught in the Act. Mickey's concern about his mob is explored, especially about Knuckles, who has mysteriously disappeared.

6. Nothing but a "G" Thing. As Mickey's business begins to take shape, he learns that he must accept Lorenzo "The Lip" Locatelli, a funny-talking New York associate—good at collecting, but a screw-up—when orders come directly from his superior.

7. Mickey Approves Some Action. When Mickey discovers that "his boys" are not collecting money as they should, he decides to take matters in his own hands to show them how it is done.

8. The Angel and the Devils. A bit of Mickey's back story is told as a new girl, Angelica (called Angel) begins working for On the Run.

9. It's Sonny in Pennsylvania. After his release from Sing Sing Prison in Upstate New York, Mickey's cousin, Sonny, feels the need to stretch his wings and heads to Carbondale (Mickey's headquarters) to pay a not-so-friendly visit.

10. Sonny ... with a Chance of Dead. The concluding episode as Mickey's problems continue to grow—this time from Sonny who, defying "The Family" and the Feds, elects to muscle in on Sonny's operations.

232 *Mob South.* webserieschannel.com. 2011 (Crime Drama).

The Milano Vineyards and a night club, Wild Rose, are fronts for Cameron David Milano, the head of the Georgia-based Milano Family crime organization. Cameron is ruthless and will stop at nothing, including murder, to exert his influence and ensure that his business enterprises are profitable. The program explores the inner workings of organized crime as seen through the individual members of the Milano family.

Cameron has named the club after his mother, an elder woman, once as ruthless and deceiving as he is, who now resides in a nursing home—but whom Cameron often seeks advice from when family members need a lesson.

Mary, called "Big Mama," is Cameron's wife, a woman who is not as sweet as she looks; she is deadly and handles the family books, making sure their illegal business dealings all appear on the up and up.

Dominic Michael Gardella, Cameron's nephew, is the "Under-Boss" and nicknamed "Capo Bastone." As the second-in-command, he is responsible for selecting the people to do "the dirty work" and ensure that the profits flow into the family's accounts.

Michael Palermo, called "Mikey" is Cameron's Consigliore (right-hand man and advisor) and the third highest ranking member in the family organization. **Cast:** Michael A. Burger, Jr. (Cameron Milano), Kristie Leigh Burger (Mary Milano), Jason Coggins (Mikey Palmero), David Michael Burger (Dominic Gardella), Amy Aguirre (Sarah Lucia), Danielle Dickinson (Samantha Smith), Tristan Michael Burger (Tony Lucia), Jimmy Griffin (Jimmy Wayne), Chris Knox (Jessie James). **Credits:** *Producer-Writer-Director:* Michael A. Burger, Jr. **Comment:** Only a short teaser (1 min., 15 sec.) remains on line that very briefly gives an insight into the program. It is not possible to make a fair assessment based on so little footage and thus an opinion is not expressed.

Episodes: All episodes have been withdrawn. While episode descriptions appear on-line, they are very vague and it is not possible to provide an informative episode description from them. The episodes are: *1.* Coming to Georgia. *2.* Hello Jimmy Wayne. *3.* Will Jimmy Help Jessie? *4.* I Must Get Milano! *5.* Don't Be Looking Over Here! *6.* He's a Ghost I'm Going to Catch! *7.* Watch Dominic Closely. *8.* Poor, Poor Jimmy Wayne. *9.* Can I Get a Ride? *10.* The Game. *11.* Interrogation. *12.* We Have Too Much to Discuss. *13.* Help Me, Dr. Gallo! *14.* Sounds Like Post Traumatic Stress.

233 *The Mole.* webserieschannel.com. 2012 (Action).

Following a breach of the CIA's security system, wherein the true identities of agents have been revealed, a search is begun to fix the problem by finding and eliminating the person responsible—the mole. The program focuses in particular on two CIA agents, Johnny, the suspected mole, and his friend and fellow agent, Dan, who has been assigned the unpleasant task of finding him. Complicating the situation is Jenna, once Johnny's lover who has now become involved with Dan. **Cast:** Keir Yhirus (Dan), Kristy Rose (Jenna), Nick Casucci (Johnny), Nikhil Vallabh (Hazeed). **Credits:** *Producer:* Nick Casucci, Keir Thirus. *Director:* Nick Casucci. *Writer:* Nick Casucci, Mike Casucci.

Comment: Episodes have been taken off line thus providing an analysis is not possible.

234 *Montez.* vimeo.com. 2013 (Action).

Robert Montez is a man falsely imprisoned for a crime (murder) he did not commit. Someone had framed him but he could not prove his innocence. After two years evidence was found that cleared Montez of the charge and he was set free. But his time in prison embittered him and he is now a changed man. The program follows Montez as he begins his self-proclaimed mission to find the man who framed him and see that real justice is done. **Cast:** Dawid Paszkiewicz (Robert Montez), Monika Dudycz (Sabina), Michal Picz (Det. Thomasz Wladko), Maciej Maciejewski (Mr. Montez). **Credits:** *Producer-Writer-Director:* Dawid Czupryniak. **Comment:** Thus far only a pilot film has been produced and, judging by it, the program has the potential to be an interesting take on the revenge theme. The acting and production qualities are good and it is unknown if additional episodes will be produced.

Episodes:
1. Fresh Start (5 min., 22 sec.). The pilot film that finds Robert Montez released from prison and swearing his oath to seek justice.

235 *Moon Mermaids.* youtube.com. 2013 (Comedy Drama).

While swimming in what appears to be a manmade lake, a young girl (Aqua) finds a necklace that she later shows to her friend Angel. The necklace apparently has no effect on Aqua, but it does transform Angel into a Mermaid when she comes in contact with water. Problems arise when Aqua's brother, Noah, becomes suspicious of his sister and sets his goal to find out what she is hiding. Stories follow Aqua as she attempts to help Angel adjust to her Mermaid abilities while at the same time protect her from her brother whose discovery could reveal to the world what she has become.

Cast (as credited): Jenna (Angel), Kenzi (Aqua), Maddie (Crystal), Noah (Noah). **Credits (as listed):** *Writer:* Kenzi. *Director:* Maddie. **Comment:** While the girls are cute, the sound is poor and the picture suffers from unsteady movement.

Episodes: Episode 1. Aqua finds a magic necklace that affects only her girlfriend Angel. 2. Episode 2. An accidental splash of water transforms Angel into a Mermaid and arouses the suspicions of Noah, Aqua's younger brother, when he hears them talking "about a secret." 3. Episode 3. With Aqua attempting to help Angel adjust to her Mermaid abilities, Noah schemes to learn more about what is happening. 4. Episode 4. Hoping to find some answers, Aqua and Angel return to the pond where the original necklace was found only to find, hidden under some rocks, another necklace. Will it transform Aqua? The concluding episode.

236 Mortal Kombat: Legacy. youtube.
com. 2011–2013 (Action).

An adaptation of the "Mortal Kombat" video
game franchise. Mortal Kombat is a tournament
wherein participants duel to the death. Three syndicated televisions series have been produced (*Mortal Kombat* [1995], *Mortal Kombat: Defenders of the
Realm* [1996] and *Mortal Kombat: Conquest* [1998])
and the web version follows in the same tradition
with warriors, both human and alien, battling to the
death for reign over the various realms (such as the
Earth Realm) that occupy the universe. Season 1
episodes are a character profile rather than the actual
tournament bouts while Season 2 focus on the actual
battles for control of the realms.

Shang Tsung is the devious sorcerer who serves
Shao Kahn and hosts the Mortal Kombat tourna-
ments (he also leads the warriors in their battle
against the warriors of the Earth-Realm). Shao Kahn
is the Emperor of the Outworld and the adoptive father to Kitana and Mileena (see below).

Sonia Blade, a Lieutenant, and Jax, a Captain are
with the Outworld Investigation Agency. Johnny
Cage is a noted TV actor who is struggling to maintain his fame—and fortune.

Baraka is the General under Shao Kahn of the
Outworld Tarkatan Warriors. Cyrax is a ninja assassin working for Lin Kuei. Ermac is a fighter who encompasses the souls of deceased warriors.

Kano is head of the Black Dragon crime organization. Kenshi is a sightless swordsman with the
power of telekinesis.

King Jerrod is the former ruler of Edenia. Queen
Sindel is Jerrod's wife, the former Queen of Edenia
and the mother of Kitana. Kitana, the former
Princess of Edenia, battles alongside Shang Tsung.

Kurtis is a Deacon City Police Department Lieutenant. Kung Lao is a Shaoin monk that sides with
the Earth Defenders. Mileena, half Tarkatan and half
Edenian, is Kitana's clone and an assassin.

Quan Chi is a sorcerer and loyal to Shang Tsung
(fights on the side of the Nether-Realm). Raiden,
leader of the Earth Forces against Shang Tsung, is
the God of Thunder and Protector of the Earth-
Realm.

Hanzo is the General of the Japanese Shirai Ryu,
a Ninja clan. Sektor is a cybernetic warrior and assassin for Lin Kuei.

Shao Kahn is the Emperor of the Outworld and
the adoptive father to Kitana and Mileena. Bin-Han,
an Earth Defender, was previously an assassin for the
Lin Kuei clan. Kuai Liang is a warlord advisor and
the younger brother of Bin Han.

Cast: Johnson Phan, Cary-Hiroyuki Tagawa
(Shang Tsung), Aleks Paunovic (Shao Kahn), Jeri
Ryan (Sonya Blade), Fraser Aitcheson (Baraka),
Shane Warren Jones (Cyrax), Kim Do Nguyen
(Ermac), Michael Jai White (Jackson "Jaxx" Briggs),
Matt Mullins, Casper Van Dien (Johnny Cage), Dar-

ren Shahlavi (Kano), Daniel Southworth (Kenshi),
Kirby Morrow (King Jerrod), Samantha Tjhia (Ki-
tana), Tahmoh Penikett, Eric Jacobus (Kurtis
Stryker), Mark Dacascos (Kung Lao), Brian Tee (Liu
Kang), Jolene Tran, Michelle Lee (Mileena), Michael
Rogers (Quan Chi), Beatrice Ilg (Queen Sindel),
Ryan Robbins, David Lee McInnis (Raiden), Ian An-
thony Dale (Hanzo Hasashi), Peter Shinkoda
(Sekor), Kevan Ohtsji, Eric Steinberg (Bi-Han),
Harry Shum, Jr. (Kuai Liang). **Credits:** *Producer:*
Tim Carter, Aaron Helbing, Todd Helbing, Lance
Sloane, Kevin Tancharoen. *Director:* Kevin Tan-
charoen. *Writer:* Kevin Tancharoen, Aaron Helbing,
Todd Helbing. **Comment:** Fast-moving, action-
packed program that, although it will be more ap-
pealing to people familiar with the game, has taken
the time to explain things to make watching easier
(as opposed to assuming the viewer knows the characters and format of the Mortal Kombat Universe.).
The acting and production values are good and the
program quite captivating (it also encompasses Jeri
Ryan, the sexy 7 of 9 from the TV series *Star Trek
Voyager*).

Episodes:
1. Jax, Sonya and Kano, Part 1 (12 min., 25 sec.).
Jax and Sonya attempt to retrieve a shipment of Ro-
botic Defense Program materials that were stolen by
the Black Dragon criminal organization (led by
Kano).

2. Jax, Sonya and Kano, Part 2 (8 min., 49 sec.).
Concludes the above story with Jax risking his life
to not only battle Kano, but save Sonya from imminent death at the hands of the Black Dragons.

3. Johnny Cage (11 min., 49 sec.). Finding that
his TV career as an American action super hero is
going nowhere, Johnny falls prey to Shang Tung and
becomes a warrior in the Mortal Kombat tourna-
ments.

4. Kitana & Mileena, Part 1 (9 min., 10 sec.). Introduces the beautiful skilled assassins Kitana and
Mileena and how Shao Kahn tricks Shang Tsung into
making him clone Mileena from Kitana.

5. Kitana & Mileena, Part 2 (8 min., 30 sec.).
Continues the story with Shao Kahn using both Kitana and Mileena to destroy his adversaries with
more background information given on Kitana and
Mileena as they realize what has happened and they
are not real sisters (Mileena being Katina's clone) and
plot revenge against Shao Kahn.

6. Raiden (12 min., 58 sec.). A change of pace
episode wherein Raiden, the God of Thunder, finds
himself in the earth year 2011 and confined to a mental institution (being confined for his "delusions" of
an alternate universe). His efforts to escape and return to Outworld and defend the Earth-Realm from
Shao Khan are depicted.

7. Scorpion and Sub-Zero, Part 1 (10 min., 51
sec.). Hanzo, the warrior known as Scorpion, and his
mortal enemy, Sub-Zero, meet at a time when Hanzo
must return to his clan (the Shirai Ryu) when they

are threatened by an enemy they cannot defeat by themselves.

8. Scorpion and Sub-Zero, Part 2 (10 min., 51 sec.). Hano's encounter with Sub-Zero prevents him from saving his people, thus sending his soul to the depths of Hell. He finds a reprieve when he is visited by a sorcerer who restores his essence when he agrees to enter the Mortal Kombat tournament.

9. Cyrax and Sektor (10 min., 27 sec.). The concluding episode that focuses on Cyrax as he ponders his fate when he is chosen by the Grand Master to be the future of the Lin Kuei by becoming a cyborg to destroy the evil Hydro and protect the future of his people.

237 *Move Along.* youtube.com. 2012 (Mystery).

Jenna is a very pretty young woman who appears to be working at an office job she not only hates but in which there appears to be no chance for advancement. One day, following work, she decides to relax by a nearside lake and is startled to find a duffel bag filled with money. Composing herself, Jenna nonchalantly walks off with the bag while unknowingly being watched by someone who has recorded her every move. The program presents an intriguing mystery that, unfortunately, is not resolved. **Cast:** Celia Duport (Jenna), Clementine Bouzidi, Cedric Cruchon, Tony Berraud. **Credits:** *Producer-Writer-Director:* Tony Berraud. **Comment:** A unique program that is told like a music video (there is no dialogue and the music sets the scene for Jenna's actions). It is well acted and produced and leaves the doorway open for more episodes to relate what Jenna will do with the money but most importantly who is watching her and why (was the money planted to see what someone would do if it was found)? **Episodes:**

1. Realist Alive (3 min., 21 sec.). The story line is established as Jenna finds the bag of money.

238 *Multiuniverse War.* multiuniverse.com. 2013 (Action Adventure).

In a future era of a quantum mechanical universe time traveling technology has been developed but it has not been perfected. Travelers in time are subjected to excessive levels of energy and its resulting powerful magnetic field. The end result finds the traveler's body is scarred with disabilities of a damaged brain and Central Nervous System. Since many possible futures exist (the Quantum Mechanics interpretation of "Many Worlds") there is also a need for time travelers (soldiers) to go back in time to protect the people and events that lead to their timeline while destroying the timelines that could change their history (the enemy timelines). One such time traveler is Aidric, a soldier dedicated to serving and protecting the people of his time line. Karl is a so-

phisticated computer hacker living in the present. While hacking into a Department of Defense computer, Karl uncovers evidence of time travel, but most importantly, Aidric. When Aidric discovers that Karl has tapped into his time line, he sets out to assassinate him to maintain operational security only to learn that Karl is an important part of his time line. The program follows Aidric and Karl (in the year 2013) as they seek to learn how their fates are connected and defeat their enemies—the time traveling assassins who could change the course of Aidric's future if Karl were to be eliminated (as the future has already been written with Karl a part of it). **Cast:** Reid Morgan (Aidric), Henry Sansom (Karl). **Comment:** Only a 45 second trailer has been released that briefly highlights what the program is about. A fair assessment is not possible based on so little footage.

239 *My Best Friend Is a Mermaid.* youtube.com. 2012 (Comedy-Drama).

Hoping to be like her slightly older friend, Kristina, a young girl (Emma) begins by trying to emulate her. One day, when Kristina stumbles across a gate that leads to a lake, she becomes compelled to go swimming; unknown to Kristina she has been followed by Emma. Although it appears that Kristina has been unaffected by the water, she later discovers that when she comes in contact with water, she transforms into a Mermaid. Emma, drawn to the magical lake, also swims in it, and she too becomes a Mermaid when water touches her skin. Now, with Mermaid abilities in common, Kristina and Emma must conceal their secret and try to live normal lives. **Cast (as credited):** Brianna (Kristina), Elizabeth (Emma), Sky (Sophie), Bree (Jordan). **Credits** are not given. **Comment:** The girls handle their roles quite well and overall a good production although some scenes are a bit blurry and jumpy. **Episode List:** *1.* The Fall That Changed Everything. *2.* True Friends. *3.* Secret Revealed ... Again. *4.* Fish'd. *5.* Power Point. *6.* Cursed Shell. *7.* Season 1 Finale. *8.* Promises (Season 2 Begins). *9.* Untrusted. *10.* Moonlight Dreams. *11.* The Potion. *12.* Transformed. *13.* The Sleepover. *14.* Season 2 Finale. *15.* The New Beginning (Season 3 Begins). *16.* New Moon. *17.* Wet Works. *18.* The Missing. *19.* Closed Doors. *20.* Bucket List.

240 *My Bitchy Witchy Paris Vacation.* bitchywitcythefilm.com. 2010 (Comedy-Drama).

Diane is a middle-aged woman and the mother of 24-year-old Ashley and 15-year-old Miranda. Diane is menopausal and has just separated from her husband; Ashley is pregnant; and Miranda, not quite 15 when the series begins ("14 and 363 days old") is "desperate for her first period to come while she is on vacation." The vacation is in Paris and the program follows their efforts to cope with everything that surrounds them—from their relationships with each other, to Ashley and Miranda bonding to all the anxiety they encounter as they deal with their own personal issues.

Cast: Kate Michaels (Diane), Esmee Buchet-Deak (Miranda), Pelham Spong (Ashley), Alyssa Landry (Belle), Sebastian Galluci (Ferdinand). **Credits:** *Producer-Writer:* Alexis Niki. *Director:* Katrik Singh. **Comment:** Nicely paced, enjoyable program that is well acted and produced. It was filmed on location in Paris and presents both a comical and moving look at the lives of three women who have grown apart but try to come together during a vacation that is anything but typical.

Episodes:
1. It'll Never Be Over (5 min., 53 sec.). Establishes the story as the family begins their Paris vacation. Diane is experiencing hot flashes; Ashley has just realized all the problems motherhood will bring; and Miranda is angry that she is the only girl in her class that has "not become a woman."
2. A Deal with Santa (5 min., 32 sec.). It is Miranda's 15th birthday and what she had hoped for has not happened. Now, feeling she cannot return home without having her first period, Miranda prays to St. Nicholas when she visits the Notre Dame Cathedral to get her wish.
3. Baby Pictures (6 min., 5 sec.). To celebrate Miranda's birthday, Diane presents her with an album of photos of her as a little girl. Miranda, however, is not concerned about the past—just the future as she approaches puberty.

241 My Life as a Video Game. mylifeasavideogame.com. 2013 (Adventure).

Princess Kera of the House of Althorn is the only child of the rulers of The Great Interstellar Althorn Empire. She is next in line to inherit the throne but the brutal General, Atticus Dynas, sees things differently. When a military coupe erupts and Kera's family is overthrown and killed, she is captured and placed in prison. Believing he has achieved his goal, Atticus assumes control, unaware, at first, that Kera has escaped from her cell and has stolen not only an old ambassadorial ship called *The Fortress* but her family's personal M.E.N.U., a super computer. As a child Kera heard legends of a Grand Champion, a hero of video games who united video game heroes to battle a common threat. Believing that the Champion is more than just a legend, Kera sets out on a mission to find such a person and seek his help in regaining her throne.

Don DeWitt is a young man overly addicted to video games. He has great potential to become anything he wants, but has zero ambition. One day he finds a magical disk that when placed in his gamming

system, transports him into an alternate reality where video games are real life. Don and Kera are not known to each other, but Don had experienced a fate similar to Kera: When he was a child his peaceful life in the Cyprus town of Famagusta was abruptly ended when his home was invaded by a group of militants. He and his parents survived and it was perhaps that action that set him on the road to becoming the video game champion Kera is seeking. Fate unites Kera with Don with Don becoming a First Person Shooter and joining Kera in her quest. The program charts their adventures as they battle numerous video game foes with Don not only seeking to defeat Atticus but find a way to return to his own world.

M.E.N.U (Multi Electrical Networked User System) is the sarcastic super computer that accompanies Kera and stores all knowledge related to the Althorn Empire. He appears as a floating head on a screen (mostly on Kera and Don's wrist-mounted portable system).

Sarge, a super soldier and a member of the United Freedom of Alliance, is always eager to "kill the bad guys" and is the first aide Kera and Don acquire. He is an expert on explosives, a suburb marksman and a Champion of the First Person Shooter world (inspired by video games like *Battlefield*, *Call of Duty* and *Doom*).

Johnny and Bobby, born of 1980s style video games but live in that time's imagined future (1998) in the City of Neo Dystopia, a "post-apocalyptic Kung Fu nightmare city." Dumb as they are, they are literally the only hope the people have against the gangs run by the evil Big Adam.

The Smoker, as he is known, is the Lieutenant of General Dynas, the man who killed Kera's father in the take-over of her world. He is also a man who helps defeated villains from various video games achieve the goals they could not accomplish on their own.

Christy is the girlfriend of brothers Johnny and Bobby (she is not really sure which one as both claim the same thing). Christy is the damsel who is always in distress (placed in precarious situations by Big Adam's goons) and constantly needs rescuing. Believing that Christy is his girl, Johnny (and Bobby, believing Christy is his girl) risk their lives to save her—but why Big Adam places Christy in extreme danger is a mystery. To have fun watching the brothers attempt to save her, for some unknown sinister purpose, to make Christy fend for herself as the brothers may not always be there to help her?

Big Adam, the gang leader of the City of Neo Dystopia, achieves his evil goals through fear and intimidation. Unlike other members of his gang, who are armed only with a whip or lead pipe, Big Adam carries an assault rifle and is known as "The Man with the Only Gun."

Grunt is Big Adam's dim-witted "six-foot monstrosity." He is armed with giant red barrels that he can hurl at fantastic speeds and cause considerable damage. Grunt is also the one to be feared for his "insta-KO punch," which can place one in a state of unconsciousness for hours after a single smash to the face.

Cast: Petros L. Ioannou (Don DeWitt), Jennifer Polansky (Kera Althorn), Brent Black (M.E.N.U.), Katie Massey (Christy), Xander Farrell (The Smoker), Cody Griffis (Johnny), Andrew Gelles (Bobby), Ian Roberts (Sarge), Andrew Hawthorne (Big Adam), Verrett Harper (Grunt). **Credits:** *Producer:* Petros L. Ioannou, Brian Dickson, April Joy Haddad. *Writer:* Petros L. Ioannou. *Director:* Brian Dickson. **Comment:** Intriguing concept that is well acted and produced.

Episodes:

1. Loading (7 min., 3 sec.) Don inserts a magical disk into his gamming system and is transported to an alternate reality.

2. Duty Calls (7 min., 50 sec.). Don and Kera unite—but face The Sarge, a hulking super soldier on one side and Nazi's, Terrorists and Communists on the other.

3. No. "I" In the Team Deathmatch (10 min., 30 sec.). With Sarge now a part of the team, Don and Kera face a sniper warlord called "The Noob Killer."

4. Kill Streaking (9 min., 14 sec.). Don faces "The Knoob Killer" in a final showdown that concludes the first season.

5. Righteous & Radical (8 min., 57 sec.). Season two begins with a trip back to 1980s–styled video games wherein Don and Kera come face to face with Kung Fu assassins.

6. Beaten Up (13 min., 10 sec.). With shades of the video games *Double Dragon*, *Streets of Rage* and *Final Flight*, Don and Kera continue their fight against the game's Kung Fu assassins.

7. My Body Is Ready (10 min., 37 sec.). Hoping to defeat the assassins, Don plunges into full throttle and later crosses the path of someone who may hold the key for the return to his world.

8. The Man with the Only Gun (10 min., 20 sec.). Having won the battle, Don and Kera, with the assist of the Brothers (Johnny and Bobby) and their mutual girlfriend, Christy, now face the menacing Big Adam in the season finale.

242 *My Magical Mermaid Life.* youtube.com. 2012 (Comedy-Drama).

During their swim in a public pool, two girls (Jessie and Emma) find ankle bracelets on the pool floor. The girls exit the pool, place the bracelets on their ankles and return to the water. Magically they are transformed into Mermaids (by coincidence, there are no other swimmers and their secret is not exposed). Later, the girls each discover they have a power: Jessie can freeze water, Emma can heat it. The program follows Emma and Jessie as they must learn to accept what they have become.

Cast (as credited): Emma (Herself), Jessie (Herself). **Credits** are not given. **Comment:** Pretty girls but a very badly presented pilot with an unsteady camera and a splashed water drop on the camera lens that blurs images.

Episodes:

1. The Pilot. The potential series story line is established as described above.

243 *My Magical Secret Mermaid Life.* youtube.com. 2013 (Comedy-Drama).

Jessica is a teenage girl who returns from school to find a bracelet in a cup of water in her room. Why is it in water? Who put it there and why? Not having the answer to any of the questions, Jessica places the bracelet on her wrist and is suddenly endowed with dual abilities: those of a Mermaid and those of a wizard. In a twist on normal Mermaid stories, Jessica must now learn to not only control her transformations into a Mermaid but also adapt to her life as a magical wizard.

Cast (as credited): Sarah (Jessica, Brenna, Mom and Brittany). **Comment:** Sarah plays all the roles (even sings the theme) but all hope for the series is lost with bad filming and equally bad sound. While used, special effects are very poorly done. Sarah appears to be having a good time, but her enthusiasm does not spill over to attract viewers. If some care had been taken to script the program and incorporate one or two other girls to play roles, it might have come off better than it now plays.

Episode List: *1.* Bracelet in Water. *2.* Tail Wizard and Friend. *3.* Enemy Plus Powers. *4.* Pool Party Mayhem. *5.* The Rock. *6.* Scavenger Hunt to Save a Secret. *7.* The Cave. *8.* Brittany's Heroes Are Not Heroes.

244 *My Secret Mermaid Life (2012).* youtube.com. 2012 (Comedy-Drama).

While swimming a young girl (Samantha) discovers a magic fountain that sprays her with water, but soon becomes frightened and swims away. Exiting the pool, Samantha dries herself off and returns home. The following day, however, when Samantha returns to the pool, the effects of the fountain become effective when she transforms into a Mermaid (with a pink tail). Realizing that it was her encounter with the fountain that caused the metamorphosis, Samantha finds that she must now encompass her Mermaid abilities while at the same time, conceal her secret and resume her life as an ordinary school girl.

Cast: Samantha Pape (Samantha). **Credits** are not given.

Comment: Capable acting by Samantha but the program is flawed by poor sound (resulting from only using the camera microphone) and a very unsteady picture at times.

Episode List: (Episodes have since been taken off line). *1.* Metamorphosis. *2.* Surprise Tail. *3.* The Weird Change. *4.* Splash of Legs and Tail. *5.* Bath Tail. *6.* Finding 2 Powers. *7.* Finding Another Power and Tail. *8.* Tail Trouble. *9.* The Crescent Moon Light. *10.* Washing and Water Tail. *11.* Powers, Water, Tail. *12.* Tail and Powers. *13.* Beach Tail. *14.* Tail, Powers, Water and Natalie—What Next? *15.* Treadmill Tail + Drawing Tail. *16.* Tail and Searching. *17.* Pool, One Wish Plus Magic Bath, *18.* Ring and Strange Water Craving. *19.* Full Moon, Magic Fountains and Spilling Water. *20.* Grandma and Trouble. *21.* Powers, Natalie's Tail. *22.* Uh-Oh. *23.* My Secret Slipped. *25.* Dream, Pass Out, Shower.

245 My Secret Mermaid Life (2013). youtube.com. 2013 (Comedy-Drama).

As a young girl (Ashley) begins swimming her eye catches a shiny object that draws her to it and magically transports her into a cave (The Moon Cave). At that exact moment, the water, affected by the moon's rays, begins to bubble and appears to trap Ashley. Ashley, keeping a cool head, manages to find her way back to the ocean and safety. Although unnerved, she appears to be unharmed. The following day, however, when Ashley comes in contact with water, she transforms into a Mermaid and must now navigate life as a creature of the sea and a normal young girl.

Cast (as credited): Ashley (Herself). **Credits** are not given. **Comment:** Underwater scenes are well done, Ashley is good but the program, although only a pilot has thus far been produced, suffers from poor sound.

Episodes:
1. The Pilot. Ashley is introduced as she encounters The Moon Cave.

246 Mystery Mermaids. youtube.com. 2013 (Comedy-Drama).

While on the beach, a teenage girl (Fay) sees a young girl lying on the sand (a Mermaid washed up from the sea and with her human legs). The girl (Willow) is struggling to adjust to her "land legs" (after spending much time as a Mermaid) and is wearing a strange bracelet—a bracelet that is identical to the one Fay is wearing. The program ends here and it can be assumed that the bracelets are linked to each other and Fay is also a Mermaid.

Cast (as credited): Maija (Willow), Laura (Fay). **Credits** are not given. **Comment:** *Mystery Mermaids* could be considered one the worst of the Mermaid series as Fay is not very like-able and a bit overweight to become an attractive Mermaid. She is also very unsympathetic—as Willow struggles to get to her feet and is asking for help, Fay just stands there and watches. It is only when Willow does manage to get

to her feet that Fay shows any signs of compassion when she notices the bracelet.

Episodes:
1. The Pilot. Fay and Willow meet for the first time as the story begins.

247 The Mystic Tails. youtube.com. 2012 (Comedy-Drama).

While walking through the woods, two girls, Izzy and Maya, are attracted to a river's memorizing waterfall and find two necklaces sparkling in the water. The girls place the jewelry around their necks and everything appears to be normal. That night, when the girls come in contact with water, they transform into Mermaids—a secret they soon discover is also possessed by a school mate (Kylie) who also found a necklace in that river. Three girls drawn together by a secret and their abilities to guard that secret form the bases of the series.

Cast (as credited): Hannah H. (Izzy), Kaylan Y. (Maya), Kaylynn K. (Kylie), Candice R. (Morgan), Becky K. (Kahea). **Credits** are not given. **Comment:** Acceptable Mermaid series although using camera microphones presents sound that is quite poor at times.

Episode List: *1.* Beginning Through Trouble Waters, Parts 1 and 2. *2.* And Then There Were 3. *3.* A Book Can Say a Thousand Words. *4.* Frozen in Fear. *5.* The Acceptance of Something Great. *5.* Unraveled Mysteries. *6.* The Bigger Picture. *7.* Decisions, Decisions. *7.* Dreams of Danger. *8.* Abducted. *9.* Game On.

248 Mythos. mythosseries.com. 2012–2014 (Drama).

"Sometimes I wonder what things could be like if I stayed and done what everyone expected me to. If I had done what I always had most days, I am fully convinced that I made the right decision—most days." These words, spoken by a young woman named Morgan, is a housewife and mother who is secretly the ancient warrior goddess Athena. Athena the child of the All-Father, and others like her abandoned their mythological heritage to live among humans when cosmic conflicts between the ancient gods caused the children of the All-Father to seek alternative lives. The world has suffered since, being without its heroes to protect it, but the All-Father feels that, as his powers are becoming weaker, he needs to reunite his children and once again protect humans from the forces that threaten their lives. The program follows Morgan's journey as she helps reunite her family and decide if returning to what she once was is the path she must now take.

Cast: Miriam Pultro (Morgan), Tyler Herwick (Pan), Mark Banik (Lee), Adam Henry Garcia (Aaron), Torri Yates-Orr (Selena), Drew Moore (Carl), Jael Golad (Nadia), Gary-Kayi Fletcher

(Mark), Ava Idelchik (Sophia), Erik Parillo (Anu), David Michael Kirby (Luke), Laurel Lockhart (Nyx), Alexa Swinton (Ellie), Chen Tang (Shiva), Jessica Mazo (Delia), Grace Gray (Docen), Drew Moore (All-Father). **Credits:** *Producer:* Miriam Pultro, Tom O'Brien, Richard Cline, Adam Henry Garcia. *Writer-Director:* Miriam Pultro. **Comment:** Miriam Pultro is so believable as Morgan that one would never suspect that she was actually Athena. The fast-paced, well written and directed program holds your attention from the beginning with excellent acting and production values. Although the story may appear a bit complex as a lot happens in a relatively short period of time, it is easy to follow and well worth watching as one of the better web series playing on the Internet.

Episodes:

1. Episode 1 (9 min., 14 sec.). Morgan's life appears to be that of a simple housewife until one of her brothers, Lee, appears at her home to seek her help on behalf of the All-Father.

2. Episode 2 (8 min., 20 sec.). To help Lee, Morgan, who works for a publisher, tells her husband (Aaron) that she needs to leave town on a business trip.

3. Episode 3 (7 min., 41 sec.). As Morgan and Lee begin their quest, they find Carl but Morgan has growing concerns that her family may be in danger, especially after she encounters the evil Pan, an adversary from her past.

4. Episode 4 (9 min., 44 sec.). As Lee and Carl continue their quest, seeking Nadia and Mark, Morgan, now back home, receives a visit from All-Father in a dream with advice to seek the goddess Nyx, who may be able to help her make a decision.

5. Episode 5 (8 min., 30 sec.). Morgan's fears continue to grow after another encounter with Pan who appears to have something in store for her.

6. Episode 6 (6 min., 15 sec.). Morgan, like her brothers and sisters, have been reunited by the All-Father to attend a council meeting—something she must do and again must abandon her family.

7. Episode 7 (6 min., 15 sec.). At the council meeting the All-Father explains that his powers are weakening and that his children must resume their old lives to save mankind. Meanwhile, an uninvited guest, the Trickster appears and voices his objections to what is happening.

8. Episode 9 (3 min., 54 sec.). Morgan, still undecided about what to do, returns home to find that Aaron has been killed (not shown by whom) and that her children are safe (but where is not stated).

9. Episode 9 (6 min., 46 sec.). Bitter over what has happened Morgan realizes that her choice to live as a mortal may not have been the right one and needs to once again resume her life as a goddess.

Note: There is a second season two-part preview episode called "Sea and Sky" that explores Morgan in her new life as Athena and sets up the story for future episodes.

249 Neptune's Mermaid. youtube.com. 2013 (Comedy-Drama).

A young girl (Kristie) wishing that she could be like her late mother (a Mermaid) finds that forces beyond her control have granted her wish: when she touches water she transforms into a Mermaid and must now encompass the abilities of a Mermaid while attempting to lead an ordinary life.

Cast (as credited): Brianna (Kristie and Alyssa). **Credits** are not given. **Comment:** Acceptable photography but the production suffers at times by poor sound.

Episode List: *1.* Changes. *2.* Adjustments. *3.* New Girl. *4.* A Fishy Birthday. *5.* Ashley. *6.* The Abduction. *7.* Phase 2 of the Mermaids. *8.* Season 1 Finale. *9.* Caves and Sirens (Start of Season 2). *10.* Mer-Hunt. *11.* Tied Up and Everything. *12.* The Siren's Realm (series finale).

250 The Newtown Girls. thenewtown girls.com. 2012 (Comedy-Drama).

Scarlet is a young woman living in Newtown, Sydney, Australia. She is very pretty and a lesbian and hoping to find the girl of her dreams. Although Scarlet has dated several women, finding her soul mate has not happened. The program explores the obstacles Scarlet faces—from ex-girlfriends, complicated relationships, her relationship with her best friend, Alex and virtually anything else that can complicate her life as she turns to pretending she is someone she really isn't to find the right girl.

Cast: Debra Ades (Scarlet), Renee Lim (Alex), Kylie Watson (Veronica), Kate Austin (Kym), Elizabeth Gibney (Lexie), Sontaan Hopson (Nicki) Shalane Connors (Rachel). **Credits:** *Producer:* Natalie Krikowa, Ann Pilichowski. *Director:* Julie Kalceff, Emma Kelite, Imogen Dall, Spencer Harvey. *Writer:* Julie Kalceff, Natalie Krikowa. **Comment:** Australian produced program that combines elements of drama and comedy in an enjoyable program that is nicely acted and produced. There are girl-girl kissing scenes but nothing objectionable.

Episodes:

1. I'm Home. Introduces Scarlet as she returns to Newtown from a year-long trip in South East Asia (to get over a breakup with Kym) and begins preparations to re-enter the dating scene.

2. Dress Up. Feeling that she needs some help getting back in the game, Scarlet seeks the advice of her friend Alex.

3. The Justin Bieber Look. After becoming intoxicated during a date and losing a potential lover, Scarlet realizes that she must change her ways if she is ever going to find her dream girl; she begins by acquiring a new wardrobe.

4. The Puppy Episode. Scarlet turns to Internet dating but finds she too is unlucky there when her inbox remains empty. She then hits on the idea to get a puppy "because lesbians love puppies."

The Newtown Girls. **Left to right: Kylie Watson, Renee Lim, Kate Austin and Debra Ades (photograph by Sharna Turner © Zenowa Films, 2011).**

5. Juicy. After failing with the puppy trick, Scarlet joins the Newtown Lesbian Book club (run from Veronica's bookstore, where Scarlet is also employed)—but has trouble trying to read the required book in time for the weekly discussion.

6. Balls. Scarlet manages to bluff her way at the book club gathering, meets some girls and even encounters hits on the Internet. She also learns that lesbians like sports and figures to become a sports enthusiast to attract one.

7. It's a Date. Scarlet secures a date for the first time in a year with "a hot chick" (Lexie).

8. Super Green. As Scarlet seeks a way to impress Lexie, Alex tries to convince her that she should be herself and not put on airs to impress her.

9. At the Vanishing Point, Part 1. Scarlet believes she has found the perfect mate in Lexie until doubts are raised when her ex-girlfriend (Kym) returns.

10. At the Vanishing Point, Part 2. Scarlet's feelings for Kym are rekindled when they meet and now Scarlet must choose between a new love (Lexie) and an old love (Kym) in the concluding episode.

251 *The Next Shot?* webserieschannel. com. 2013 (Thriller).

An interactive program that involves the viewer who can choose how scenes unfold thus making the outcome a bit different for each episode. The overall program depicts a control for territory and the two rival gangs seeking it. Because the program does not follow the normal conventions of story-telling, further and only overall story line information is presented through the episodes listed below.

Cast: Rebecca Reyes (Angela), J.G. Blodgett (Jagga), David Stout (Dave), Tony Mendoza (Tony), Jared Smith (Aldo) **Credits:** *Producer-Director:* Tony Mendoza. *Writer:* J.G. Blodgett. **Comment:** At first glance the program is an immediate turn off: truly annoying close-ups (just too close), vulgar language and scenes that are not in the proper aspect ratio (stretched to fill the screen). However, sticking with the mostly black and white production will render a nicely done (although a bit violent) conflict between rival motorcycle gangs. Color bursts are incorporated for brief images of the character Angela and of bullets being fired during a shootout. Effectively enhances the program's overall production as something different.

Episodes:

1. The Funds (4 min.). Cyclist Jagga, desperate for money, plays the wrong hand when he steals money from gang leader Tony.

2. Hello Beautiful (4 min., 55 sec.). Tony's thugs first kidnap Jagga then his girlfriend, Angela.

3. Waiting (4 min., 54 sec,). Both Jagga and Angela are being held captive in a warehouse; their fate to be determined by Tony.

4. Yellow Carnations (6 min., 26 sec.). Tony has decided his captives' fate: Angela is forced to shoot Jagga; Tony then kills Angela.

5. Redemption (7 min., 59 sec.). Dave, Tony's right-hand man, rebels against what Tony has done, vowing to get even.

6. Blood Ties, Part 1 (5 min., 56 sec.). Dave and Tony face off against each other for control.

7. Blood Ties, Part 2 (9 min., 53 sec.). In the face-off Tony is wounded and his blood-thirsty son, Aldo, is now seeking to take Dave down in the concluding episode.

252 N1ckola. N1ckola.pl. 2009 (Drama).

A Polish-produced spin off from the American series *Lonely Girl 15* that continues to follow the original series story line about young girls being sought by a mysterious organization called The Order for their Trait Positive blood. Ola Polak, a Trait Positive girl, is the focal point of the program as it charts her experiences when, after returning to her home in Poland for a vacation (having moved to London to escape her over-protective parents) she discovers unsettling information not only about herself (the blood she possesses) but her family's link to The Order.

Other Characters: Ursyn, a reporter attempting to expose the Hymn of None (the resistance group of the Order and later becomes involved in the battle to stop The Order); Bartek, an agent for The Order assigned to keep track of Ola; Ewa, Ursyn's assistant is a member of the Hymn of None and in battle against The Order; Pyton, the paparazzi photographer who assists Ewa and Ursyn in their battle against The Order; Karolina, an audio-visual expert and lip-reader who helps Pyton battle The Order.

Cast: Ania Narloch (Ola Poltak), Bartek Picher (Bartek Sfinks), Konrad Marszalek (Ursyn Wysocki), Julia Trebacz (Ewa), Jakub Krawczyk (Pyton), Anna Kordus (Karolina). **Credits:** *Producer:* Marcin Meczkowski, Miles Beckett, Greg Goodfried, Amanda Goodfried, Kamil Przlecki, James R. Sterling. *Writer:* Jakub Kossakowskim Maura Ladosz, Zdzislaw Miskiewicz. **Comment:** All 101 episodes, including titles, descriptions and trailers (teasers) have been taken off line thus not making an assessment or title listing possible.

253 Night Walkers. youtube.com. 2010 (Anthology).

Varying stories about people, who live, play and encounter the unknown at night.

Cast: Travis Quentin Young, Richard Penn, Beni Mabhena, Lauren Martin, Doug Burch, Katherine Everett, Toby Meuli, Caitlin Moreland, R.D. Call,

Jesse Bean. **Credits:** *Director:* Jon D. Wagner. *Writer:* Sam Ingraffia. **Comment:** Elements of *The Twilight Zone* and *Alfred Hitchcock Presents* can be seen in stories that explore normal topics but with unpredictable outcomes. The acting and production value are good and each story is complete in itself.

Episodes:

1. Act Like Men. A young man learns the meaning of respect when he tries to muscle in on someone else's territory.

2. Jazz Man. A down-on-his-luck jazz musician finds his life changing when a mysterious woman enters a bar and he is irresistibly drawn to her.

3. Heads of Tails. A compulsive gambler makes an unusual bet to get even: his life against the stakes on the table.

4. A Valuable Lesson. A pool hustler finds he is in for the game of his life when a curvy blonde in a blood-red dress challenges him to a game and his concentration is on something other than pool.

5. A New Arrival. A young couple believes they have found the apartment of their dreams—until they move in and find it is anything but.

6. Solace. A disturbing May–December romance is explored by two people that are seemingly meant for each other.

254 Nikki and Nora. onemorelesbian.com. 2013 (Crime Drama).

At 213 Toulouise Street in New Orleans, Louisiana, reside two beautiful women—Nikki Beaumont and Nora Delaney, lovers and former detectives with the N.O.P.D. (New Orleans Police Department) who now work as private detectives. Nikki and Nora were born in New Orleans and have a unique perspective about the town in which they live, especially the French Quarter, which (for the series) is laden with crime and secret identities that require "the touch of the velvet hammer" (seductive women) to solve and uncover. Being lovers appears to have been the main reason why Nikki and Nora resigned from the police department (just not acceptable to some). Becoming private detectives is their way of "solving your problems" and "fixing what is broken." The program follows their efforts to solve crimes while at the same time dealing with the personal issues their relationship creates in a time when such relationships are still not accepted.

Cast: Liz Vassey (Nikki Beaumont), Christina Cox (Nora Delaney), Armin Shimerman (J. Hewitt Kemp), Jim Beaver (Arliss Fontenot), Janina Gavankar (Lea Sadina), Kitty Swink (Dottie Reid), Ian Castleberry (Ace), Holis Hannah (Celia South), Tess Harper (Mary Delaney), Charlie Hoffacker (Det. Mugammed Al-Sidr), Thayer Abigail Lund (Abby), Candice L. Preston (Det. Kendall Clark), Shannan Leigh Reeve (Det. Riley Morgan), Aasha Davis (Violet Craig), Wallace Langham (Carl Mottenberg). **Credits:** *Producer:* Paige Bernhardt, Christin Mell,

Nancylee Myatt, Liz Vassey, Christina Cox. *Writer-Director:* Nancylee Myatt.

Comment: *Nikki and Nora* is a well-produced, well-acted program that has its roots in an unaired 2004 network TV pilot film called *Nikki and Nora: Lady Cops.* The pilot was pitched to the now defunct UPN network but was rejected for its lesbian theme. It was leaked to the Internet and received numerous hits on YouTube suggesting to producer-creator Nancylee Myatt that such a series could be produced but in a different medium. A trailer was produced followed by four episodes and an open doorway for more stories to follow. The actual pilot storyline (a murder investigation) was recreated for the web series (the exception being that Nikki and Nora were police officers with the Special Crimes Unit of the N.O.P.D. and that their relationship was not actually stated but obvious they were lovers. Even though lesbians have been featured on broadcast TV—and in more suggestive scenes than presented in *Nikki and Nora* it can only be assumed UPN executives were reluctant to showcase women as lovers at the time). Had the pilot sold, it would have been the first crime drama with lesbian protagonists as lead characters. Liz Vassey and Christina Cox are expertly cast as the lovers and one may find that some scenes are very dark and difficult to determine what is happening. There are scenes of affection between Nikki and Nora as well as brief kissing sequences but nothing as compared to girl/girl scenes on such TV shows as *The L-Word.*

Episodes:

1. Episode 1 (7 min., 58 sec.). Nikki and Nora investigate the death of a young woman (Elizabeth Turner) who was apparently killed by someone she knew.

2. Episode 2 (10 min., 15 sec.). Nikki and Nora question Elizabeth's brother, Peter, learning that she had dated several men, including a wealthy man who began stalking her after their breakup.

3. Episode 3 (8 min., 40 sec.). A coroner's report reveals that skin fragments had been found under Elizabeth's fingernails. To add to the tragedy, she was also beaten but did put up a struggle as her left shoulder was dislocated and her lung punctured. It is also revealed that she had been raped.

4. Episode 4 (9 min., 42 sec.). Clues lead Nikki and Nora to suspect that a police officer (Codell) is the culprit as he has a violent temper and was dumped by Elizabeth. But to prove it becomes the problem as the series concludes.

255 *Not So Super.* webserieschannel.com. 2012 (Action Comedy).

Vince Ible, married to Genevieve and the father of Hannah, is a middle-aged super hero living in a decent environment called Prime City. Fifteen years ago, however, Prime City, overrun with criminal activity, was called Crime City. It took the heroics of

one man (Vince, called Hero) seeking a decent place to settle down to change all that and return Prime City to its once illustrious glory. Being a super hero has its benefits (fame) and its downfall (he is now struggling to make ends meet and he feels he has lost his purpose in life as Prime City no longer needs his services). As life for Vince further spirals downward, a glimmer of hope appears when criminal activity again surfaces but does Vince have the ambition to once again become a hero? The program follows Vince as he contemplates what to do—sit back and do nothing and complain about the misery that surrounds him or get back in shape and save Prime City from the dark forces that will soon destroy it.

Cast: Christophor Rick (Vince Ible/Hero), Rob Mass (Ben/Scandal), Trish Hundhausen (Genevieve Ible), Hannah Schmidt (Hannah Ible), Taylor Klaustermeier (Odile), Tommy Balistreri (Archon Anders). **Credits:** *Producer:* Christophor Rick, Jeff Garbarck. *Writer-Director:* Christophor Rick. **Comment:** A nice twist on the super hero genre focusing instead on what happens to a super hero when he has done his duty and feels he is no longer useful.

Episodes:

1. Pilot (12 min., 41 sec.). Sets up the series story line with a brooding Vince not sure as to what he should do now that he is facing a mid-life crisis.

256 *The NX Files.* webcast.com. 2005 (Action).

An ability called the NX Secret allows people who can encompass it to acquire super abilities, including strength, agility and speed. Seven young martial arts black-belt champions have encompassed such powers and have created Team Xtreme, an organization that dedicates them to battling evil wherever it may exist. Such evil is Lord Tragos, a megalomaniac who controls an evil band of ninjas (the Kurai Kai) and is seeking to acquire the NX Secret for his own diabolical means. In season one episodes Team Xtreme battles to keep Lord Trajos from accomplishing his goal. Season two places Team Xtreme in battle against advanced, super intelligent (but evil) beings called The Archons (led by Mr. Black) as well as deadly hybrid creatures called Hybrids (led by Golock).

Team Xtreme Members: Spike, co-owner of NX Martial Arts and Fitness, is a black belt in the art of Mugen Budi Jiu-Jitsu. It was he, along with Rex and Tornado that formed Team Xtreme. He has the ability to create duplicates of himself through Phantom Budo.

Rio, a thrill-seeker, possesses a black belt in Mugen Budi and has the ability to defy the laws of gravity.

Ronin, a clone of Spike, is identical in appearance to Spike, but possesses a greater fighting ability.

Rex, a third degree black belt and weapons master, is co-owner (with Spike) of NX Martial Arts. He possesses Super Budo, the ability to move at super accelerated speeds.

Sniper, a second degree black belt, is the group's technology expert and is responsible for creating NXISS (NX Intelligence Security System). He also possesses Accu Budo (enhanced vision and reflexes). Katana, a first degree black belt (Mugen Budo Jiu-Jitsi), is a telepathic and versed in weapons and various styles of fighting.

Sabre, a second degree black belt, is highly intelligent, an exceptional fighter and possesses a knack for talking himself out of any situation. He has an ability called Cogno Budo, which allows him to see clearly what others see as a puzzle.

Krush, a Mugen Budo second degree black belt, possesses the ability of Iron Budo (incredible strength).

Tornado, a third degree black belt, possesses the power of Mystic Budo (highly developed telekinetic abilities).

Mr. Black and Mr. Brown are Archons (pure energy), members of a secret society that maintain the balance throughout the physical universe.

Kruz, a second degree black belt, is responsible (with Sniper) for creating the systems contained with the NX Chambers.

Villains: Lord Tragos, leader of the Kurai Kai, possesses numerous abilities that he uses to acquire the power of the NX Secret. He was once known as Team Xtreme member Tornado but became evil when the Mugen Kurai corrupted him and created the Tragos personality (Tornado found a book called *The Book of Mugen Kurai* that endowed him with a thirst for power. To seize that power he recruited gang members and created the Kurai Kai).

Akuma is an evil demon spirit that must inhabit a body to interact in the physical world. He is recognized by a dark red mask which, when coming in contact with an individual's face, allows him to possesses that person.

Malak, Lord Tragos's right-hand man, was the first gang member recruited and now serves Tragos by recruiting members and carrying out all the dirty work that needs to be done.

Saris, recruited by Malak, is a top-level Ninja and literal killing machine. Although graceful and elegant in her moves, her actions are deadly.

Rico, trained by both Lord Tragos and Malak, is a Ninja possessed of incredible strength.

Cast: Alain Moussi (Spike/Ronin), Stephen Roy (Rex), Patrick Beriault (Rio), Robert Baldwin (Krush), Emilie Lavoie (Katana), Jean-Francois Lachapelle (Tornado), John Purchase (Mr. Black/Mr. Brown), Matthew Danielson, Eric Robert (Lord Tragos), Jeff Burgess (Rico), Peter Moscone, Marc Knowles, Alain Moussi, Eric Gratton (Akuma), Christine Picknell (Saris), Marc-Andre Terriault (Malak), Marc-Andre Gautheir (Kruz), Sylvie Genest (The Prefect). **Credits:** *Director:* Robert Baldwin. *Producer-Writer:* Robert Baldwin, Alain Moussi, John Purchase. **Comment:** Although actual episodes are not available, it appears to be very action-oriented and the fighting scenes well-choreo-

graphed. The story line is a good variation on what has been done numerous times before and the acting and production values also look good.

Episodes: 17 episodes (two of which never aired) were produced but all have been taken off-line. Two videos, however still exist:

1. NX Files Lost Episode #1 (2 min., 2 sec.). Team Xtreme is explored as they engage in a battle against the ninjas.

2. The NX Files Production Video (5 min., 12 sec.). Looks at the methods used to produce the series.

257 *Oblivion.* webserieschannel.com. 2009–2011 (Darma).

Holwenstall, a fictional city where a counter-culture lifestyle reigns supreme, provides the backdrop for a look at a group of rockers, punks and mods as they begin to come of age and attempt to deal with the problems of real life.

Cast: Julie Pepin (Blair Kerrigan), Mike Cuenca (Ziggy Romero), Kimberly Higgins (Darla Dagger), Chad Post (Frankie Robinson), Max Jones (Cliff Montelle), Kirk Podell (Dexter Gordon), Jeff Rice (Vince Arthur), E.D. Augustine (Billy "Rat" Laverne), Rachel Castillo (Joy Santiago), Dylan Chavles (Penelope Undai), Josh Hicks (Pox), Jennifer Higgins (Louise Martin), Kenny Zardenetta (Vinnie Arsenic), Jason Lawless (Jake Weavers), Sara Camille Rivello (Fay Darrow). **Credits:** *Producer-Writer-Director:* Mike Cuenca. **Comment:** Adapted from film maker Mike Cuenca's feature film *Welcome to Oblivion* wherein the main players were first introduced. The program is well done, but rather harsh for its violence, nudity and vulgar language.

Episodes: All episodes have been taken off-line, making a descriptive listing, based on the vague information that does exist, impractical. The episodes are: *1.* Blueprint for Joy. *2.* When the Sh*t Hits the Fan. *3.* Revenge. *4.* Johnny, Remember Me. *5.* How Low Can a Punk Get. *6* The Phone Call. *7.* Punish or Be Damned: The Oblivion Halloween Special, Part 1. *8.* Die, Die My Darling: The Oblivion Halloween Special, Part 2. *9.* Sanctum Sanctorum: The Oblivion Halloween Special, Part 3. *10.* I Heard a Rumor. *11.* What Love Is. *12.* Madcap Laughs. *13.* Goo. *14.* Accidents Never Happen. *15.* Crazy Rhythms.

258 *Ocean Heart.* youtube.com. 2009–2013 (Comedy-Drama).

While alone at home, a young girl (Rizu) hears a knock at her front door. Opening the door, she sees there is no one in sight—but she does find a strange heart-shaped stone on the front porch. Picking it up, she takes it with her and closes the door. Later, when she washes her hands, the water transforms her into a Mermaid; when she dries herself off, she regains her human legs. Rizu theorizes that the stone is magic and she must now encompass the life of a Mermaid (a member of the Sisterhood of Mermaids) while also trying to keep her secret and retain her identity as a normal school girl.

Cast (as credited): Lizzie (Rizu), Abby (Michi, Rizu's sister). **Comment:** One of the longer Internet Mermaid series that has good underwater photography but suffers at times from poor sound (resulting from using camera microphones).

Episode List: *1.* The Stone. *2.* And Then There Were Two. *3.* Testing the Waters. *4.* Christmas Special. *5.* Visiting Yia Yia. *6.* The Musical. *7.* Hurricane Brittani. *8.* Virtual Reality. *9.* Our Fishy Cousin. *10.* Hector the Pest. *11.* Disturbance in the Air. *12.* Interesting Neighbors. *13.* Getting Mono. *14.* The Return of Cousin Waldorf. *15.* The Merman. *16.* Dancing on Water. *17.* The Discovery. *18.* Powers. *19.* The Dangerous Boyfriend. *20.* Mysteries Abound. *21.* Deep Freeze. *22.* Season Finale. *23.* Rizu Come Home. *24.* Got Hunger. *25.* Mermaid Dungeon. *26.* Christmas Special. *25.* Clarence the Tutor. *26.* Alter Egos. *27.* Halloween Special. *28.* Shellfish Secret. *29.* Fat Camp. *30.* She's a Robin Egg.

259 *The Oligarch Duplicity.* theoligarchduplicity.com. 2010 (Drama).

Kathryn Bale, a reporter for the *Metro City Times* is also a most unusual newspaper reporter in that her twin sister, Kerry, secretly tackles the sometimes dangerous assignments while Kathryn takes the glory (writing them). Life changes drastically for the sisters when Kerry is abducted in Rome while covering a story about a villain called The Oligarch and Kathryn must now become the reporter her sister was and not only find her, but uncover the identity of and bring The Oligarch to justice.

Cast: Kathryn Fumie (Kathryn Bale), Jeremy Funke, John Pyron, Vic Terenzio, Andrew Gullans, Joel Vetsch, Anna Hayes, Maureen Kelley, Tracy James, Jeffrey Sherman, Alexandra McDougall, Sara Alvarez, Mike Chaiken, Camisha Farquharson, Tobe Johnson, Wendy Olafson, Karen Connelly, Tucker Chase, Gregiore Mouning, Dave Fuller, Jaspar Law, Joseph Mallon. Cast and character match-ups are not given on screen or on its website. **Credits:** *Producer:* J. Sibley Law, Jeremy Funke, Patti Law, Nathan Wrann. **Comment:** Well combined stock footage of Italy and Russia that actually gives the impression that action takes place overseas (while the actual program was produced in Connecticut). The acting and production values are very good and the program moves swiftly along keeping interest from the very first episode.

Episodes:

1. Where's Kathryn? When Kathryn learns that her sister Kerry has disappeared while researching a story in Rome she immediately leaves for Italy to search for her.

2. Where's Your Star Reporter? Kathryn's search for Kerry has repercussions back home when the paper's warehouse is destroyed in an explosion.

3. The Printing Press. As the explosion becomes big news, a TV anchor (Cheryce) and her crew arrive at the paper's office to cover the story. Cheryce then learns that Kathryn is also missing. Unknown to all, Kathryn has been abducted and is being held prisoner in a cell.

4. Toilette. As Kathryn meets her captor, the Italian-speaking Captain Hook, Jack, the newspaper publisher, learns that a woman (Aisha Washington) was at the warehouse at the time of the explosion and may have valuable information.

5. Secrets. As Kathryn escapes from her cell, she learns about The Oligarch and his illegal business operations. Meanwhile Cheryce seeks to learn more about Kathryn's sudden trip overseas.

6. Who Do We Know in Minsk? Kathryn's information leads her to Russia, where she hopes to find The Oligarch; meanwhile, Jack tries to find her help through the paper's contacts.

7. Someone's on to Me. As Kathryn continues her search for both Kerry and The Oligarch, she realizes that she is being watched as someone is always one step ahead of her.

8. Already in Play. Kathryn's infiltration of The Oligarch headquarters reveals a startling find: her name is on a kidnap list and not Kerry's. Meanwhile, the situation regarding the newspaper bombing takes a turn for the better when a witness is found.

9. Identification. As Kathryn returns home from Minsk, Jack learns that the witness can identify the bomber.

10. The Puppet House. With information gathered in Minsk, Kathryn sets a meeting up with a contact at a theater (The Puppet House). In a twist, Kerry appears with The Oligarch and Kathryn learns that her sister is the enemy—and the one she needs to fear (in a rather vague explanation, Kerry states that two years ago she acquired "a job for a government something" while at the same time doing the reporting for Kathryn). Her dual life apparently led her to The Oligarch and she joined him. The episode ends unresolved.

260 *One Different Secret.* youtube.com. 2012 (Comedy-Drama).

While swimming in the ocean two young girls (Aly and Serena) see a mysterious white rock (which they touch), hear hypnotic-like music and see the splash of what appears to be the tail of a fish (actually the tail of a Mermaid). It is the following morning and the girls, at Serena's home, have no idea as to how they got there or whether what they saw in the ocean was real or just a dream. Their mystery is solved when Serena accidentally spills a glass of water on herself and she transforms into a Mermaid (with a gold tail). Aly is unbelieving until Serena throws water on her and she too transforms into a Mermaid (with a blue tail). Minutes later they transform back into normal girls when the water evaporates and their legs reappear. Aly and Serena, however, are no longer normal girls; they have been endowed with Mermaid abilities through contact with the white rock and must now learn to encompass their abilities as Mermaids to protect the oceans while at the same time resume their lives as average American girls. The plot also has the girls using their powers to stop an evil Shape Shifter (Talie).

Cast (as credited): Claire (Aly Fisher), Avery (Serena Watchmen), Sophie (Talie Kresh), Olivia (Marlowe Kresh), Laura (Laura Star). **Credits:** *Producer-Writer-Director:* Avery (as credited). **Comment:** For a program that is apparently run by a young girl (Avery) it is a remarkable achievement. While not as professional as other such programs about Mermaids (but on the level with *A Splashy Tale*, which is also done by a young girl) it does show that with a good idea a program can be developed— and turn out better than you would think being done by someone so young (and obviously talented).

Episodes:

1. Ocean Swim. Aly and Serena find a mysterious white rock while swimming that transforms them into Mermaids.

2. Element Change. The girls each learn they have a power: Serena has the ability to freeze water while Aly can heat it.

3. Shape Shifter's Trick. After finding a bracelet, apparently from a Shape Shifter, Serena and Aly find themselves transported to an island in the middle of nowhere.

4. Bad News. Serena and Aly discover that they were seen as Mermaids and to make matters worse, their images appeared on TV.

5. The Unexpected. While in the park, a book of Mermaid spells falls from a tree and into the path of Aly and Serena; later, they find a Mermaid amulet, which when picked up by Aly, causes her to vanish.

6. The Missing Mermaid. A dream by Serena wherein Aly warns her about approaching danger in the form of an invisible Shape Shifter may be more than just a dream.

7. Forgotten Memories. Aly battles a case of amnesia when the evil Shape Shifter, Talie places a curse on her wherein she no longer recognizes Serena as someone she knows.

8. Answers Lead to Questions. A piece of paper, found by Serena, leads her to Marlowe, a good Shape Shifter—and Talie's sister (as kids they found a black and white rock in their backyard and touched it. Marlowe, touching the white side, became good [life and air] and Talie, touching the black side became evil [death and Earth]). Aly (the sun) and Serena (the moon) also have elements but are unable to defend themselves when Talie appears and kills Serena.

9. A Half for a Whole. After Marlowe uses her powers to restore Serena's life, Marlowe loses her Shape Shifter powers and transforms into a Mermaid.

10. Old Age Magic. Crystals, found by Aly, Marlowe and Serena, may be the weapon the girls need to battle the evils of Talie, who seeks their powers.

11. How About an Upgrade. As Talie steals Marlowe's powers, Serena and Aly decide on a plan of action to defeat her; all does not go well when Talie teleports herself into Aly and steals her powers.

12. Call of the Sirens. Complex episode: Siren sisters Amber and Topaz attempt to possess Aly and Serena; Laura, a good Shape Shifter, helps Marlowe escape Talie's clutches; Amber and Topaz blackmail Laura: do what they command or they will reveal to Talie that she has turned to the side of good.

13. Laura's Potion. Aly and Serena regain control of their bodies when Amber and Topaz abandon them but a potion causes problems for Laura when it erases her memories of mythical creatures and turns her against Aly and Serena.

14. The Beginning of Something New. Talie, now in possession of the powers once possessed by Aly, Serena and Marlowe, begins using Laura to do her bidding.

15. Life with Talie. On Talie's orders, evil Laura begins her quest to capture Aly, Serena and Marlowe's lives in a cursed conch. Aly and Serena escape the first attempt but Marlowe is captured and brought to Talie. In a strange twist, Talie kills Marlowe and Laura and sets out to finish the job by destroying Aly and Serena. The program's concluding episode.

261 *One Life to Live.* hulu.com. 2013 (Drama).

A revised version of the canceled ABC daytime serial that continues to relate events in the lives of the residents of Llanview.

Cast: Erika Slezak (Victoria Lord), Melissa Archer (Natalie Buchanan), Kassie DePaiva (Blair Cramer), Michael Easton (John McBain), Shenell Edmonds (Destiny Evans), Josh Kelly (Cutter Wentworth), Ted King (Tomás Delgado), Florencia Lozano (Tea Delgado), Kelley Missal (Danielle Manning), Sean Ringgold (Shaun Evans), Andrew Trischitta (Jack Manning), Jerry Ver Dorn (Clint Buchanan), Tuc Watkins (David Vickers), Sean Ringgold (Shaun Evans), Shenaz Treasury (Rama Patel), Nick Choksi (Vimal Patel). **Credits:** *Producer:* Jennifer Pepperman. **Comment:** Aired on an alternating basis with *All My Children* with a recap episode called *More One Life to Live* airing on Fridays. The program continues in the tradition set by the ABC series with excellent acting and production values.

Episode List:

1. Brand New Start. April 29, 2013.
2. Back from the Dead. April 30, 2013.
3. Who Are You? May 1, 2013.
4. The Giraffe. May 2, 2013.
5. The Real Husbands of Llanview. May 6, 2013.

6. I Got You Babe. May 7, 2013.
7. Good Intentions? May 8, 2013.
8. Poison and Pellegrino. May 9, 2013.
9. Leaving Llanview. May 13, 2013.
10. Cain and Abel. May 14, 2013.
11. Bag the Decanter. May 15, 2013.
12. Who's Watching? May 16, 2013.
13. Finish What You Started. May 21, 2013.
14. Families Take Care of Each Other. May 23, 2013.
15. Snoop Don't Lie. May 28, 2013.
16. No Regrets. May 30, 2013.
17. Nail Salon. June 4, 2013.
18. Snoop Lion Is in Da House. June 6, 2013.
19. Shots Fired. June 11, 2013.
20. The Night Bird. June 13, 2013.
21. Catfish. June 18, 2013.
22. The Truth About Michelle. June 2, 2013.
23. Call off the Dogs. June 25, 2013.
24. In Memory of Briana Marland. June 27, 2013.
25. Hot Teacher. July 1, 2013.
26. Not Really a Date. July 1, 2013.
27. She's Got It Maid. July 8, 2013.
28. Back Off Bitch! Now! July 8, 2013.
29. The Snooze Test. July 15, 2013.
30. Love Is in the Air. July 15, 2013.
31. Who the Hell Are You? July 22, 2013.
32. Anatomy of a Divorce. July 22, 2013.
33. Everything's Changed. July 29, 2013.
34. Clint Just Wants to Dance. July 29, 2013.
35. I'm Gonna Miss You. August 5, 2013.
36. It's Your Tell. August 5, 2013.
37. Phase Two. August 12, 2013.
38. This Ain't Over. August 12, 2013.
39. Ready or Not, Here I Come. August 19, 2013.
40. Payback's a Bitch. August 19, 2013.

262 The One Percent. theonepercentweb series.com. 2011–2012 (Drama).

Arianna, Camille and Vanity are three young actresses with only one goal: reach the top level (the One Percent) in the entertainment industry. Each of the women is ambitious and devious and will use or do whatever it takes to become A-List celebrities. But each also has self-doubts. Camille feels she is overweight (or, as she says, "I'm fat") and feels this will hinder her chances even though she diets. Vanity is a seductive woman who seduces men and uses her assets ("You've got to use what you got to get what you want") to acquire acting jobs. Arianna is obsessed with breasts and feels her small ("My medium size") breasts are her downfall. She wants implants but her boyfriend, James is opposed, feeling she is too focused on her figure and not her career. The program charts their individual attempts to pursue their dreams of fame and fortune.

Cast: Vanessa Giordano (Camille Guilino), Marcie Scott (Arianna Bradley), Daffany McGaray Clark (Maria Diaz/Vanity), Brandon Heitkamp (Daniel), Michael Cory Davis (James), Leon Walker (Tony), Jay Brothers (Davis Arrington). **Credits:** *Producer:* Vanessa Giordano, Marcie Scott, Daffany McGaray Clark. *Director:* Choice Skinner. *Writer:* Benjamin C. Jones. **Comment:** Very well acted, written and directed program that, although it ends unresolved, is well worth watching. The leads are very appealing and the story moves right along, capturing your interest from the very beginning.

Episodes:
1. Episode 1 (7 min., 10 sec.). With the encouragement of their acting teacher (Davis) Camille, Arianna and Vanity begin their quest to become the One Percent.
2. Episode 2 (6 min., 38 sec.). Camille, Arianna and Vanity reveal their inner feelings about themselves (Camille, her weight problem; Arianna, her breasts; and Vanity, her seduction methods).
3. The Audition (9 min., 9 sec.). Not being a member of SAG (Screen Actors Guild) begins to take its toll on Camille when she is ignored—but when called for an audition, she gives an incredible performance.
4. Boomerang (4 min., 45 sec.). Vanity's effort to seduce a producer (Tony) into giving her a role on a TV show backfires when he realizes what she is doing.
5. The Make-Up (3 min., 37 sec.). Arianna's thrilling news that she landed a TV series role has her excited—until she tells James it will mean working six months in Canada and their romance will have to be put on hold.
6. The Turning Point (7 min., 56 sec.). James and Arianna's argument continues with James putting the damper on her acting opportunity but it appears he is starting to accept what has happened.
7. The Call (4 min., 20 sec.). Although Camille feels her weight is preventing her from reaching the One Percent, she falls prey to a womanizing producer (Daniel) who begins playing on her insecurities.
8. The Anniversary (5 min., 59 sec.). As Arianna and James celebrate their anniversary, the question of Arianna's "boob job" comes up with James becoming annoyed that since she set her new goal, she has changed into a person he no longer recognizes. The concluding episode.

263 One Warm Night. onewarmnight. com. 2012–2013 (Mystery).

Julie is a beautiful young woman who has been scorned too many times. She has had enough and believes it is time to get even with the men who have made her life miserable. Julie begins her quest by contacting The Ninja Killer ("Hello Mr. Ninja. I need your help killing a bunch of men and maybe some others depending on how the night goes. Can you help? Signed Scorned"). The Ninja Killer accepts and Julie sets up a party wherein she invites her 12 former suitors (who believe they will get a second shot at dating her) with a plan to kill each one of them. She begins by making the situation uncomfortable by raising the heat so the room they occupy becomes increasingly warm. The program then follows Julie—and her Ninja Killer as she extracts her sweet revenge.

Cast: Julie Manriquez (Julie), Sean Michael Afable (Sean), Justin Lee (Jonathan), Jared Hernandez (Jared), Koko Laimana (Koko), Anthony Kongphan (Killer Ninja), Joe Salling (Joe), Laura Meadows (Laura), Brandon Thomas (Brandon), Ryan Tsang (Matt), Janessa Beth (Janessa), Yasmeen Yamak (Yasmeen), Mac Chapel (Mac), Frances Tang (Frances), Matt Lunn (Billy). **Credits:** *Producer-Writer-Director:* Steven G. Lowe. **Comment:** Light comedy mixes with drama, mystery and suspense in an enjoyable but highly impractical murder mystery based somewhat on Agatha Christie's *Ten Little Indians*. The acting and production values are good although the presentation of some of Julie's former lovers leaves the viewer to wonder why she dated such morons, wimps and losers in the first place and not realizing that even before a first date only heartbreak would result in the end.

Episodes:

1. The Reason We're All Here Is... The stage is set as Julie's ex-boyfriends arrive, each of whom believe he has a chance of rekindling their romance.

2. And Then There Were 12. The Ninja Killer also arrives and becomes a part of the mix.

3. Lights On, Still in the Dark. For reasons that the guys can't comprehend, the room is becoming increasingly warmer and one guest in particular, Jared, begins to lose his grip on reality.

4. Brandon's Last Stand. As the heat continues to rise, ex-boyfriend Brandon begins to lose control.

5. Shot Heard Round the Room. Ex-boyfriend Sean is reminded of what he did to Julie while the heat continues to rise and the Ninja starts to take action.

6. He Has a Condition. Brandon becomes the first victim (shot) while Julie reminds Jared of his past with her.

7. The Plot Thickens. The increasing heat causes Jared to have a meltdown while Matt and Jonathan (brothers who dated Julie) recall their association with her.

8. It's a Killer Barbecue. It is revealed that the Killer Ninja has accomplices (Janessa and Koko), that Laura is an FBI agent (but is helpless to save anyone) and that Jared has lost his grip on reality. Meanwhile, no one appears to be able to help the wounded Brandon while Julie's actual plan is re-vealed—to turn the room into "a red-hot barbecue" and smother her guests with extreme heat.

264 Or So the Story Goes. orsothestory goes.com. 2014 (Anthology).

Modern adaptations of classic fairy tales are presented in multi-part episodes on *Or So the Story Goes* while condensed versions are presented on the spin off series *Or So the Story Goes: One Shots*. Both versions present a darker retelling of each fable. At the time of publication only one story, "Little Rosemary" had been produced for the parent series (in three parts) while a one episode production, "The Box," had been created for the spin off.

Cast (*Little Rosemary*): Rainni Moran (Hazel), Rayna Loos (Lilah), Lilla Cabrera (Rosemary), Blake Weissman (Matty), Christopher Michael Christiana (Simon), Noah Dunton (Rich), Penelope Hinds (Seana), Melissa Malone (Rachel), Diann Gogerty (Lexi), Anais Fifer (Charlene), Edward Nolan (John). **Cast** (*The Box*): Rainni Moran (Lauren), Melissa Malone, Diann Gogerty. **Series Credits:** *Producer:* Melissa Malone, Jackie Moran. *Director:* Melissa Malone, Theresa Lobreglio. *Writer-Creator:* Melissa Malone. **Comment:** Based on "Little Rosemary" the program shows promise of being a bright spot in the field of Internet television. Rainni Moran is especially engaging as the program's heroine and she, and the other children in the cast all perform their roles quite well. The production values are very good and it appears the parent program will build suspense in small doses (multiple episodes) while the spin off, to achieve an end result, will present everything in one suspense-filled episode. There are numerous fairy tales from which to adapt material and encompassing the same child performers in various roles could make the program more kid friendly as

Or So the Story Goes. **Rainni Moran as Hazel from the story "Little Rosemary" (copyright Melissa Malone, 2014).**

certain performers will become favorites to viewers. Although comparisons could be made to the television series *Goosebumps*, *Nightmare Room* and even *Shelley Duvall's Faerie Tale Theater*, *Or So the Story Goes* is a totally different take on what has been done before and will hopefully follow in the tradition that has already been set.

Episodes (*Or So the Story Goes*):

1. Little Rosemary, Part 1 (8 min., 41 sec.). A retelling of *Little Red Riding Hood* that begins when a 10-year-old girl (Rosemary Hooper) mysteriously vanishes and her friend, 12-year-old Hazel Leonard sets out to discover what happened to her.

2. Little Rosemary, Part 2 (6 min., 21 sec.). Canisville, the small town in which Hazel lives, appears to be just that—a typical small town until Hazel's investigation reveals that dark forces could be responsible for Rosemary's disappearance. Hazel is also unaware that she is being observed and that her friends may not be as innocent as they appear to be.

3. Little Rosemary, Part 3 (7 min., 28 sec.). Hazel uncovers evidence that ancient wolf tribes (creatures capable of assuming human form) still inhabit the town and that Rosemary's abduction could be their first step in reclaiming the land that once belonged to them.

Note: A second, multi-part episode titled "Happy Thoughts" was released in the fall of 2014 and told of a family's efforts to destroy the ghost of a charming but homicidal teenage boy that is haunting their new home.

Episodes (*Or So the Story Goes: One Shots*):

1. The Box. Following the death of her mother, a 14-year-old girl (Lauren) receives a box as an inheritance from her mother with a stipulation that she never open it. The story focuses on Lauren as her curiosity grows and temptation beckons her to open the box.

265 *Orange Is the New Black.* netflix.com. 2013–2014 (Drama).

Piper Chapman is a young woman, sentenced to 15 months in Litchfield Prison, for her involvement in drug trafficking. Piper was raised in an upper middle class family, graduated from college but made a wrong decision in life when she met a woman at a bar (Alex) and began a romantic and adventurous relationship with her (Alex is a lesbian; Piper bi-sexual). Piper was soon reeled into Alex's world of trafficking for an international drug cartel. But it was not the life for Piper and she and Alex parted ways—but not before Piper had come under the radar of authorities. As Piper changed her life for the better and began a promising relationship (with Larry), her past comes back to haunt her and she is charged as an accomplice to money laundering and drug smuggling. Piper accepts her punishment, hoping to pick up her life with Larry after her release, and begins her new life as an inmate (coincidentally, in the same prison where Alex is also serving time). The program charts Piper's life in prison with flashbacks detailing the lives of the inmates and personnel (some of whom are exploitative and corrupt) who also reside within the penitentiary.

Cast: Taylor Schilling (Piper Chapman), Danielle Brooks (Tasha "Taystee" Jefferson), Taryn Manning (Tiffany "Pennastucky" Doggett), Laura Prepon (Alex Vause), Emma Myles (Leanne Taylor), Jessica Pimentel (Maria Ruiz), Diane Guerrero (Maritza), Abigail Savage (Gina Murphy), Lolita Foster (Eliqua Maxwell), Alysia Reiner (Natalie Figueroa), Michael Harney (Sam Healy), Kate Mulgrew (Galina "Red" Reznikov), Michelle Hurst (Miss Claudette Pelage), Jason Biggs (Larry Bloom), Pablo Schreiber (George Mendez), Nick Sandow (Joe Caputo), Natasha Lyonne (Nicky Nichols), Dascha Polanco (Dayanara Diaz), Lauren Lapkus (Susan Fischer), Lea DeLaria (Big Boo), Matt McGorry (John Bennett), Yael Stone (Lorna Morello), Catherine Curtin (Wanda Bell), Uzo Aduba (Suzanne "Crazy Eyes" Warren), Laverne Cox (Sophie Burset), Robert Stanton (Murray Kind), Madeline Brewer (Tricia Miller), Lorraine Toussaint (Vee), Beth Fowler (Sister Ingalls), Tracee Chimo (Neri Feldman), James McDaniel (Jean Baptiste), Deborah Rush (Carol Chapman), Todd Susman (Howard Bloom). **Credits:** *Producer:* Jenji Kohan, Sara Hess, Liz Friedman, Lisa Vinnecour, Michael Trim, Gary Lennon. *Director:* Michael Trim, Andrew McCarthy, Phil Abraham, Uta Briesewitz, Jodie Foster, Constantine Makris, Matthew Penn. *Writer:* Piper Kerman, Jenji Kohan, Sian Heder, Sara Hess, Nick Jones, Lauren Morelli, Marco Ramirez, Liz Friedman, Tara Herrmann, Gary Lennon. **Comment:** Very harsh program that portrays life in a women's prison with a particular focus on Piper and how she must learn to accept and become a part of a strict system. The acting and production values are top notch and the characters convincing in their roles. There are sexual situations, nudity and vulgar language and the hope of one woman as she waits for the day she will be released and returned to the outside world. The program, based on the novel *Orange Is the New Black: My Year in Prison* by Piper Kerman, is also the first such program to feature a real trans-gender woman, Laverne Cox, as a transgender character (Sophie).

Episodes:

1. I Wasn't Ready. Piper begins her prison sentence with a flashback sequence depicting her life before prison when she discovers that Alex is also an inmate.

2. Tit Punch. Although Piper and Alex are no longer lovers, Piper finds herself being hit upon by a lesbian inmate known as "Crazy Eyes."

3. Lesbian Request Denied. Piper, aware of Crazy Eyes' intentions, rejects her and moves in with another cellmate (Claudette); a flashback sequence explores Sophie's world and how she committed credit card fraud to finance her sex-change operation. This episode is directed by actress Jodie Foster.

4. Imaginary Enemies. Piper's relationship with Claudette is explored as she is assigned to work with her in the electrical shop. A flashback sequence depicts how Claudette came to be imprisoned: by killing a man who abused one of her employees in her housekeeping business.

5. The Chickening. It is revealed that an inmate (Alex) informed authorities about Piper; Claudette applies for an appeal to her case; Red, the kitchen cook, offers a gift to the inmate who can capture a stray chicken that had wandered into the compound.

6. WAC Pack. As Piper has a confrontation with her mother (Carol), Larry believes there is a story here and sets out to write about Piper's incarceration. Piper, asked to run in an election for head of WAC (Women's Advisory Council) refuses—but is placed on the ballet by a prison staffer (Sam).

7. Blood Donut. As Piper tries to again get closer to Alex, she finds that her appointment to WAC has infuriated another inmate (Tiffany) who had wanted the position. Meanwhile, Red is propositioned by a guard (Mendez) to help smuggle drugs into the prison.

8. Moscow Mule. A flashback depicts Red's involvement with the Russian mafia, while Piper, again becoming close to Alex, feels slighted that Larry's published article is full of inaccuracies.

9. F**ksgiving. Thanksgiving at the prison finds Mendez using Red's connections to smuggle drugs into the prison and threatening her life if she doesn't cooperate. A flashback sequence to Alex's past shows that she was raised in a lower economic environment (than Piper) and how she became involved with the drug cartel. Alex and Piper continue to become close, especially after they perform a sexually arousing dance during a show.

10. Bora, Bora, Bora. A look at how the program "Scared Straight" works when juveniles arrive at the prison to get a dose of what lies ahead for them if they do not straighten up. One juvenile in particular, Dina, is profiled as Piper tells her that the most frightening part of incarceration is not the walls that confine you but having to come face-to-face with who you are. Meanwhile, Mendez's drugs cause the death of an inmate (Tricia), threatening an investigation that could expose him.

11. Tall Men with Feelings. Fearing a federal investigation, prison authorities cover up Tricia's death and make it appear she committed suicide. Meanwhile, Larry's appearance on a radio program angers inmates, especially Crazy Eyes and Claudette, when he negatively speaks about them, but praises others (like Red) for the good job they are doing. Later, when Piper admits to Larry that she loves Alex, Larry tells her that it was Alex who turned her over to authorities.

12. Fool Me Once. Larry's radio interview causes unforeseen problems when a journalist inquires about sudden spending cuts when the prison had just received increased funding. Meanwhile, Piper con-

fronts Alex and learns that she was hurt and turned her in when Piper dumped her. Hoping they are still lovers, Alex confronts Piper: "Nest with Larry or travel with me and be prepared for anything."

13. Can't Fix Crazy. The concluding first season episode wherein it is revealed that Piper has chosen Larry over Alex; however, when Larry visits Alex, hoping to tell her to stay out of Piper's life, he learns that it was Piper who rekindled their relationship and that his inability to make a serious commitment is responsible for Piper's actions. After reflecting, Larry ends his relationship with Piper and Piper attempts to return to Alex.

266 *Orange Juice in Bishop's Garden.* orangejuiceinbishopsgraden.com. 2006– 2012 (Drama).

To most students, The Bishop's Garden is a family where a majority of the students have known each other since middle school. It is a place where friends are made for life and it is a place where it is hard for students to fathom a school other than Bishop for the bonds that have been created between them. It is the 1990s when the students are first seen and episodes detail the events that spark their lives and on the fashion, culture and lore of the series setting, Washington, D.C.

The Students: Sarah, 15, was born on March 9th; she is a Pisces, loves the colors maroon and green and Coffee is her favorite flavor of ice cream.

Alex, the newest arrival (from Rhode Island) hopes to become a journalist. Mango Sorbet is her preferred ice cream choice; she loves cooking, the color aqua blue and was born on July 1st (making her a Cancer).

Ryan, born April 6th (Aries) is fond of the color red, loves Vanilla ice cream and considers himself the life of any party.

Gwen, a Capricorn (born January 1st), goes crazy over Bubble Gum flavor ice cream and lavender is her favorite color (she claims her talent is touching her tongue to her nose).

Chloe, born November 15th (Scorpio), loves Rum raisin ice cream but has no favorite color. She is a ballet school drop-out and has a knack at carpentry ("I have made Adirondack chairs").

Tamsin, favorite colors green and black, is a Gemini (born May 21st) and Dark Chocolate is her preferred ice cream flavor. Being the undefeated video game champion of Teenage Mutant Ninja Turtles is her claim to fame. She likes horror movies and if she can't be a rock star, she will settle for a career as a writer.

Libby is an independent girl who says, "Please don't call me Liberty. My mom only uses my 'government name' when I am about to be grounded." She was born on February 3rd ("Which means I am an Aquarius baby!"), loves the color purple ("Not the movie, but the actual color"), keeping the peace, concerts "and all the other stuff hippies partake in." As she says, "Love, Peace and Chicken Grease."

Drew, born July 8th (Cancer) loves Strawberry ice cream and the color Navy blue.

Rob (real name Robin), is a Sagittarius (born December 10th) and red is his favorite color. He has his own band (The Skullions) and loves to play at wild parties.

Remi (real name Remington) is a health nut (prefers frozen yogurt over ice cream) and is an Aquarius (born February 4th). Silver and Chrome are his favorite colors. He says "Some people call me Tinkerbell" and he is into "the new stuff like raves."

Maggie, an Aries (born April 18th) loves Chocolate Chip Cookie Dough ice cream and the color Magenta ("Oh and mustard yellow too"). "Here's the scoop," she says, "I love Bishop's Garden and my gal pals. Sarah is my best friend in the whole wide world!" She likes long walks in the park, a good book and a night out on the beach with that special someone. She also says, "Maggie, Mags ... even the dreaded Margaret are what I go by, but YOU can, and will call me Maggie!"

Strawberry Shortcake, born in July (Cancer) is fond of the colors pink, rose and magenta and says," Your Majesty, Her Royalty, Your Highness, or just Queen. Whatever it is you feel like calling me ... I AM the Queen of the rave scene."

Cassandra, a Tarsus (born May 8th) likes the color Sunset orange and says, "My parental units are still stuck in the 60's and don't believe in the formal educational system, so I'm home-schooled." She is living a Spice Girls wannabe world after having performed in a band and will take risks and try things she does not feel comfortable with. "When it comes to people, I'm outgoing and protective of my friends. When they get hurt, I arm myself with some truth, major mojo and tarot cards."

Davis, born July 5th (Cancer), loves Neapolitan ice cream and the color neon orange. He claims he can build anything out of Legos.

Colin, born September 13th (Virgo) likes the color orange and Chocolate Chip ice cream.

Yasmine, a Pisces, was born on March 7th and Tin Roof Banana Splits is her desert choice (she also likes the color—not the movie—purple). She considers herself the most popular girl in school ("I mean everybody wishes they were me. I have the cutest clothes, the cutest hairstyles, the cutest accessories, the nicest house. Who could ask for more?").

Kristina, a Taurus (born April 26th) loves Rocky Road ice cream, the color yellow and says, "I'm pretty quiet and shy around people I don't know very well; so making friends isn't always easy for me. Once you get to know me, I'm super friendly and a completely loyal and devoted friend."

Brianna, who loves Peach ice cream and bright colors, is an Aquarius (born February 17th) and has set her sights on becoming a rapper.

Slake, a Gemini (born in June) is a ladies man (his favorite color is whatever a girl's eyes are) and Mint Choco Chip is his favorite flavor of ice cream.

Travis, favorite color red, is a Sagittarius (born December 20th). He likes Chocolate ice cream and "When I'm around, you can be absolutely sure that you're gonna have a story to tell tomorrow, guaranteed or your money back!"

Laura, born November 2nd (Scorpio) loves the color black and Dark Chocolate Chunk ice cream. She is a Goth girl, can play bass and is considered "the scary but cool girl in black."

Roxanne, a Virgo (born September 19th) loves the color Pastel pink and Orange Sherbet ice cream. She can knit and is loyal to her friends, charming and a free-spirit.

Fumkie, born May 6 (Taurus) is fond of the color green and Peanut Butter Cup ice cream. As she says, "Hey what's up you guys, this is Fumike. I'm an 18 year old, fun loving individual. I love eclectic vintage clothes and take a lot of pride in my style. I love music! Hanging out with my friends and such. My friends are like my life. They are basically the coolest people I know."

Adrian, a 22-year-old bike messenger hangs out with the teenage students. He is a Libra (born October 5th), likes Vanilla ice cream and the color burnt amber.

Cast: Ellen Winter (Sarah Roberts), Rachel Peters (Alex Anders), George Ross (Ryan Whistler), Katie Foster (Gwen Ennis), Nick Libowitz (Adrian Johnson), Storm Garner (Chloe Bastion), Kristin Rogers (Tamsin English), Donnis Collins (Liberty "Libby"), DeAndre Baker (Drew Wilson), Albert Tholen (Rob), Orla Conway (Remington "Remi" Davis), Aleca Piper (Maggie Frederick), Desirae Zentz (Strawberry Shortcake), Sarah Hirsch (Cassandra), Roberto Carmona (Sam), Clayton Pelham (Colin Mitchell), Le'Asha Julius (Yasmine Barhum), Verity Allen (Kristina Mitchell), Billie Krishawn (Brianna Lewis), Jesse Swire (Slake Ostler), Andrew Cohen (Travis Kauffman), Hannah Goldman (Laura Mortison), Laura Long (Roxanne Grey), Antonio Tillman (Fumike Okoye). **Credits:** *Producer-Writer-Director:* Otessa Ghadar. **Comment:** With many episodes off-line one can only get a feel for the series. The acting and production values are good although the stories seem to focus more on the party life than the academic life, especially in season one.

Episodes: 98 Episodes were produced. Following is a season-by-season listing of episode titles. All of Season 1 episodes have been taken off-line with the exception of a 2 minute and 38 second recap.

Season 1 Episodes: *1.* Orange Crush. *2.* Will You Be There Tonight? *3.* Boys Night Out. *4.* Yasmine's House. *5.* Misery in McMansions. *6, 7, 8.* Midnight, Hunter's Moon (Parts 1, 2 and 3). *9.* Fleshy Ears. *10.* Operator. *11.* Whisper Down the Lane. *12.* Brutus and Caesar Will Have Their Revenge on DC. *13.* The Secret Halloween Easter Egg.

Season 2 Episodes: *1.* Have a Good Summer. *2.*

Hearsay, Rumor & Scuttlebutt. *3.* Carly's Birthday. *4.* L+T & S+G. *5.* Do You Like Me? *6.* Yes or No. *7.* Not Your Training Bra. *8.* You're My Needle and I Found You. *9.* Poor Cinderella. *10.* Trouble in Paradise. *11.* The Lunar Landing.

Season 3 Episodes: *1.* The Friend Percent. *2.* Escape to Candyland. *3.* Cavort in the Borg. *4.* Doors of Perception. *5.* Worst Day Ever. *6.* Best Served Cold. *7.* Something to Put in Your Hat. *8.* A Simple Answer. *9.* Ding Dong Ditch.

Season 4 Episodes: *1.* Sarah Live! At Comet Ping Pong Tonight. *2.* C Is for Clandestine. *3.* Ask Me Anything. *4.* Paradise Found. *5.* Break Up or Stay Together. *6.* The Recruit. *7.* Freshman at Beach Week Music Video.

Season 5 Episodes: *1.* Summer of '97. *2.* The Audition. *3.* What the Cards Hold. *4.* Signed, Sealed & Delivered. *5.* Trial Expired. *6.* Go Fish. *7.* Fairytale in the Supermarket.

Season 6 Episodes: *1.* Summer of '97 Continues. *2.* Brought to You By the Letters DXM. *3.* Have You Seen My Friends? *4.* Berries, Cream and Untold Dreams. *5.* Taking Out the Trash. *6.* Table for Two.

267 *Our Mermaid Adventure.* youtube.com. 2012 (Comedy-Drama).

One day two sisters (Saraphina and Lizzie) find a strange note that tells them they are about to embark on an adventure: "On a day of the month when the moon is visible during the day, take a bath as if you were dry." Saraphina and Lizzie follow the instructions but shrug it off as nonsense when nothing happens. Later that day, however, when the girls come in contact with water, they transform into Mermaids—and must now guard their secret while also pretending to be normal girls.

Cast (as credited): Saraphina, Lizzie, Alyssa. **Credits** are not given. **Comment:** Enjoyable Mermaid adventure with good acting and underwater photography but the use of camera microphones makes it difficult to understand the dialogue at times.

Episode List: *1.* The Book. *2.* The Secret. *3.* Do the Mermaid. *4.* We'll That Didn't Last Long. *5.* Cousin Alyssa. *6.* Being a Mermaid Is Not Always Easy. *7.* Shopping Weekend.

268 *Out of the Blue.* web9pearl.wix. 2013 (Comedy-Drama).

Are incidents that occur out of the blue predestined by fate? Are they coincidences? Or are they things that just happen? The program explores a series of such incidents and their effect on a divorcee (Nadia), her son (Dominique), daughter (Steffanni), her ex-husband (Kennedy) and Nadia's friend (Harmony).

Cast: Sharon Elliot (Nadia Jackson), Erynn MacKenzie (Harmony), Kyla Collins (Steffanni Jackson), Troy Pryor (Jacque), K.C. Lee (Kennedy Jackson), Darrell Galloway, Jr. (Dominique Jackson), Sherrice Eaglin (Mommy), Eugene Parker (Daddy). **Credits:** *Producer-Writer-Director:* Annette Galloway. **Comment:** Well-acted program with standard production values (although some scenes are dark and dialogue is a bit hard to understand at times). There is some vulgar language but the story progresses well from beginning to end.

Episodes:

1. Sisterly Advice (14 min., 14 sec.). Nadia ponders an out-of-the-blue situation when her cheating ex-husband (Kennedy) suddenly reappears in her life, hoping to make amends.

2. Mommy Still Got It (10 min., 5 sec.). Nadia's mother dispenses advice about relationships.

3. Let's Get It On (12 min., 13 sec.). Kennedy's sudden return has Nadia perplexed when he vows to remain faithful to her.

4. Love in Perfect Harmony (13 min., 41 sec.). As Harmony plots to win the man of her dreams (Antonio), Kennedy plots to win Nadia back.

5. You Celibate, I'll Buy a Bit (9 min., 1 sec.). Nadia and Antonio meet to discuss their relationship while Nadia feels she cannot trust Kennedy enough to return to him.

6. That Line Crossed (11 min., 30 sec.). Steffanni, Nadia's daughter, begins to suspect that her mother, a teacher, is getting much too close to one of her students (Jacque) when she goes to his apartment to help him with a class project.

7. Good Morning Heartache (9 min., 39 sec.). Nadia ponders another out of the blue situation when her son's (Dominique) teacher calls to report that he is acting up, his grades are falling and he may be expelled from the school basketball team. To further complicate the situation, if Dominique doesn't straighten up he will lose a chance at a college scholarship.

8. It Ain't Over Until It's Over (13 min., 23 sec.). The concluding episode wherein all chances Kennedy had to make amends appears doomed as he becomes intoxicated and no one can seem to get through to him.

269 *Out with Dad.* outwithdad.com. 2010–2014 (Drama).

Rose Miller is a 15-year-old girl living in Toronto, Canada. She is the daughter of Nathan, a widower (of Sarah) who works as a freelance graphic designer. Rose has two best friends, Vanessa and Kenny and is seemingly a typical girl until she finds that she has become attracted to Vanessa (and Vanessa to her) and they share a first kiss together. The program explores what happens to Rose when she comes to realize she is drawn to girls and how the situation affects all the people who are close to her.

Claire is the lesbian who later becomes close to Rose; Alicia is Kenny's girlfriend; Angela is Nathan's romantic interest, a realtor; Johnny is Nathan's gay friend and advisor; Dave is an architect and Nathan's work partner; Theresa is Vanessa's mother; Steven is Vanessa's father; Jacob is Vanessa's younger brother; Marion is Claire's mother.

Cast: Kate Conway (Rose Miller), Will Conlon, Jonathan Robbins (Nathan Miller), Lindsey Middleton (Vanessa LeMay), Catherine Medrek (Claire Daniels), Corey Lof (Kenny), Laura Jabalee (Alicia Van Haren), Kelly-Marie Murtha (Angela), Darryl Dinn (Johnny), Ashton Catherwood (Dave), Wendy Glazier (Theresa Le May), Robert Nolan (Steven LeMay), Jennifer Kenneally (Marion), Dan Beausoleil (Ethan). **Credits:** *Producer:* Jason Leaver, Eric Taylor, Kara Dymond, Rebecca Rynsoever. *Writer-Director:* Jason Leaver. **Comment:** Well-acted, written, directed and produced program that honestly deals with a sensitive topic and how it affects teenage girls. While there are girl/girl kissing scenes, they are tastefully done and the situations encountered by Rose are also handled with care. Additional episodes are planned and will no doubt follow in the tradition set by the prior episodes.

Episodes:

1. Rose with Vanessa (5 min., 38 sec.). Introduces Rose as she shares her first kiss with Vanessa then becomes a bit confused as to what has just happened.

2. Out to Lunch (10 min., 1 sec.). When Rose's father (Nathan) suspects that Rose may be a lesbian, he seeks advice from Johnny, his gay friend, on how to deal with the situation.

3. Movie Night with Dad (10 min., 12 sec.). As Rose begins to realize what is happening and that she prefers girls, Nathan attempts to bond with Rose in an attempt to open up about her sexuality.

4. Party Out (5 min., 54 sec.). At a party Rose believes her secret may be revealed when a friend notices she is dancing with Vanessa rather than a boy.

5. Blind Date with Nathan (7 min., 26 sec.). As Rose's party continues, Nathan meets Angela on a blind date set up by Johnny for him. Hoping to get some advice, Nathan reveals his beliefs about Rose to Angela.

6. Tea with Dad (3 min., 9 sec.). The party ends, Nathan's date ends and Rose and Nathan conclude the day by discussing their night out over a cup of tea.

7. Chemistry with Vanessa (6 min., 43 sec.). As Rose and Vanessa study for a chemistry exam, they each find they are sexually attracted to the other.

8. Out with Kenny (6 min., 55 sec.). In an attempt to build up the courage to tell her father about her liking girls, Rose practices first by revealing her secret to best friend Kenny. Season one concludes.

9. Out with Dad (14 min., 13 sec.). As season two opens, Rose builds up the courage and reveals her sexual preferences to her father.

10. Asking Out Alicia (4 min., 50 sec.). When Rose notices that Kenny has become attracted to Alicia (their schoolmate) she helps Kenny work up the courage to ask her for a date.

11. Having It Out (12 min., 43 sec.). Theresa, Vanessa's closed-minded mother, fears for Vanessa when she discovers that Rose is a lesbian and, hoping to protect her from the "evil" that Rose has become, forbids her to hang out with Rose.

12. With Jacob and Vanessa (3 min., 35 sec.). The situation between Vanessa and Rose has Vanessa's parents arguing while Jacob, Vanessa's younger brother, fears losing her like their older brother (who was "pushed away" for being gay).

13. Striking Out (12 min., 18 sec.). As Vanessa tries to come to terms with her mother's demands, Alicia begins to fear Rose (not knowing she is a lesbian) and her continual involvement with Kenny (as they are just best friends).

14 Working It Out (14 min., 29 sec.). With the situation between Rose and Vanessa becoming increasingly troublesome for all concerned, Nathan again seeks Johnny's help, this time being advised to attend a PFLAG meeting.

15. Out with PFLAG, Part 1 (12 min., 12 sec.). Rose, believing PFLAG could help, joins with Nathan and Johnny and attends a meeting.

16. Out with PFLAG, Part 2 (14 min., 42 sec.). At the meeting, Rose befriends a woman (Claire) facing the same challenges.

17. Chatting with Claire (7 min., 36 sec.). Rose and Claire's attraction to each other appears to be drawing them closer together.

18. The Museum Outing (14 min., 13 sec.). Rose, excited about her new friendship with Claire, invites Kenny to meet her at work (at the Scarborough Historical Museum in Toronto).

19. Out with Doubts (13 min., 55 sec.). An uncomfortable situation arises for Rose when, at a café with Claire, she meets Vanessa and her suppressed feelings for her begin to surface again.

20. Out of Mind (10 min., 1 sec.). Realizing that seeing Vanessa has changed Rose, Claire attempts to help by getting Rose to open up about her. Season two concludes.

21. Starting Out (9 min., 53 sec.). The chance meeting at the café has also affected Vanessa, who is now finding it difficult to keep away from Rose. Meanwhile Rose has accepted an invitation from Claire for dinner at her house. Season 3 begins.

22. Dining In & Out (11 min., 16 sec.). As Rose meets Claire's family and prepares for dinner, Nathan finds that Angela is upset that he has not told Rose about his relationship with her.

23. Storming In & Out (6 min., 3 sec.). Although Claire is older than Rose, they are sexually drawn to each other and begin kissing—only to be caught by Claire's father and ostracized.

24. Swashbuckling Adventures of Making Out (7 min., 52 sec.). A date at the movies for Rose and Claire becomes more than just watching a film when they begin kissing. Unknown to Rose, a classmate is spying on her.

25. Outed (11 min., 29 sec.). The following day

at school Rose faces the unkind consequences of her movie night with Claire when word starts spreading about what happened and what Rose is.

26. Out with Song and Dance (9 min., 14 sec.). The concluding episode wherein Claire tries to help Rose deal with the situation at school and Vanessa, desperate to be with Rose, runs away from home.

270 *Oz Girl.* vimeo.com. 2009 (Comedy-Drama).

Sadie Brown, born and raised on a farm in rural Australia, finds that the simple life she has been living is not what she desires and, after making arrangements with her cousin Megan to share her apartment, moves to the city (Melbourne). With ambitions to become a photographer, but taking a waitress job to make ends meet until that time comes, Sadie becomes a part of a life she has never experienced before and stories chart her experiences as she deals with living on her own for the first time.

Cast: Sophie Tilson (Sadie Brown), Shanrah Wakefield (Megan Brown), Nicola Collie (Lisa Williams), Joel Famularo (Tony), Janet Watson Kruse (Robyn Brown). **Credits:** *Producer:* Sophie Tilson, Darryl Carlton, Nicholas Carlton, Shanrah Wakefield. *Director:* Nicholas Carlton. *Writer:* Sophie Tilson, Nicholas Carlton, Lisa Bedwell. **Comment:** A unique presentation that is well acted and produced. It is unique because while it follows the style of a TV comedy-drama, it deviates from the set standards to focus on the main characters as if they were your friends, addressing the camera and speaking directly to you (sort of a scene setter for what has or what will take place).

Episodes:

1. A New Life (6 min., 4 sec.). The story line is established as Sadie moves in with her cousin Megan.

2. Party Girls (5 min., 24 sec.). To introduce Sadie to life in the city, Megan takes her on a tour of Melbourne.

3. Job Hunting (4 min., 53 sec.). While Megan works as an actress, Sadie has no special skills and is seeking anything she can find to support herself.

4. City Days (4 min., 6 sec.). Against her better judgment, Sadie decides to tour the city alone—and becomes lost in the process.

5. The New Sadie (4 min., 37 sec.). Sadie gets her first makeover when she and Megan visit a beauty salon.

6. The Café (3 min., 14 sec.). With Megan's help, Sadie acquires a job as a waitress at George's Café.

7. House Party (5 min., 5 sec.). Sadie, accompanied by Megan, attends her first house party.

8. Wicked (3 min., 50 sec.). Megan has her first city date when her boss (George) asks her to attend a musical play.

9. Dragging Sex into It (5 min., 32 sec.). Sadie accepts a date (against her better judgment) with a guy she meets at the café (whose later attempts to rape her leaves Sadie emotionally shattered).

10. The Return of Sadie (4 min., 59 sec.). Sadie, recovering from the attack, is back to her normal self and ready to face life again.

11. City Girl, Country Girl (3 min., 57 sec.). To help Sadie, Megan and George plan a camping trip together.

12. The Bathrobe Showdown (5 min., 32 sec.). With Megan falling in love with George, and believing Sadie is also interested in him, Megan accuses Sadie of trying to steal him (this leading to their "fight" wearing only their bathrobes).

13. The Best Friend (6 min.). The fight has an unforeseen result—Megan kicks Sadie out, leaving her with no place to go. While wandering, she meets an old friend (Lisa) she hasn't seen in over a year and is later invited by George to share his apartment.

14. Three's a Party (3 min., 2 sec.). Megan's jealously grows intense when she learns that Sadie is now living with George.

15. Girl Power (4 min., 39 sec.). George finds his life a *Three's Company* (TV series) situation when Lisa is invited to stay with them and he has no personal time.

16. Boys and Toys (4 min., 52 sec.). Finding that they are ruining George's life, Sadie and Lisa move into their own apartment.

17. The Incredible George (3 min., 30 sec.). Sadie helps George celebrate his birthday.

18. First Date (3 min., 47 sec.). As George and Sadie appear to be growing closer, they embark on a date.

19. Even Animals Have Rights (4 min., 1 sec.). When Lisa discovers that the makeup she buys uses animals for testing, she vows to protest by finding another brand that is animal free.

20. The Bitch Is Back (5 min., 59 sec.). In an unexpected moment, Megan appears at Sadie and Lisa's doorstep, asking for help (acting jobs have been scarce and she is broke).

21. Family Ties (7 min., 20 sec.). As Megan and Sadie forgive each other, Megan finds her life drastically changed when, at an art exhibit, she sees Robyn, her mother, who abandoned her and her family when she was a child.

22. The Brown Family (5 min., 27 sec.). At an outdoor restaurant where Megan and Robyn have agreed to meet, Megan learns why Robyn left her and how her life has progressed over the years (she is now an artist).

23. Oz Girl Season Finale (9 min., 34 sec.). In the concluding episode, Megan's life changes when she accepts an invitation to live with Robyn in Spain, ending her relationship with both Sadie and George.

271 *Palisades Pool Party.* webserieschannel.com. 2009 (Comedy-Drama).

It is the summer and Cassidy Flowers, a popular Pacific Palisades High School girl, has plans: throw the biggest summer bash imaginable. With her parent's permission and the help of her close-knit friends (Bianca, Tori and Mischa), arrangements are being made and all is progressing well until Cassidy succumbs to temptation and sleeps with Josh, an unpopular student (and her next-door neighbor). As word leaks out, the backlash threatens to ruin Cassidy's party and the program follows what happens to Cassidy and her friends when she tries to make up for what she did and continue with her party plans.

Cast: Ashley Schneider (Cassidy), Karen Austin (Desiree), Katie Seeley (Bianca), Mary Kasnias (Tori), Francesca Fauci (Tiffani), Ronnie Alvarez (Mario), Joseph Lee Fields (Antwon), Philip Marlatt (Chad), Andrew Pandaleon (Scott), Whitmer Thomas (Josh), Danny Zaccagnino (Mischa). **Credits:** *Producer:* Tai Fauci. *Director:* Jack Monroe. *Writer:* Jack Monroe, Tai Fauci. **Comment:** Ashley Schneider shines as Cassidy as she struggles to overcome the numerous obstacles that threaten her party. The acting and production values are overall very good and the story flows smoothly from beginning to end.

Episodes:

1. Sex with Neighbor Boy (10 min., 24 sec.). Cassidy finds that the party of the year may be ruined when her friends discover that she slept with the unpopular Josh.

2. I'm Out of Her Top 8 (10 min., 33 sec.). The fallout continues as Bianca tries to sabotage Cassidy and Josh's relationship. Meanwhile, Mario finds himself becoming a third wheel when Scott attempts to seduce Tori.

3. Heroine Kills People (10 min., 1 sec.). Angered by what Bianca is doing, Josh plots revenge by hacking into her e-mail and inviting the people she and Cassidy blacklisted to the party.

4. The Dirty Little Secrets Girls Keep in Their Makeup Bags (8 min., 56 sec.). As the party preparations continue, Josh (as Captain Josh42) begins an on-line romance with a girl (SOpHia08) whom he invites to the party in an attempt to get even with Bianca.

Note: There are also two teasers: "Trailer 01" (27 seconds) and "Oh, Cassidy' (1 min., 37 sec.) that gives a brief overview of the series.

272 *Past Meets the Future.* webserieschannel.com. 2013 (Mystery).

One hundred years ago a man uncovered a strange treasure (not stated what) that he buried hoping to keep others from finding it. The man and his teenage daughter, Victoria, lived in a shack in the woods and felt they were safe until rival treasure hunters tracked him down. Victoria, alone in the shack, is accosted by the treasure hunters and killed when she refuses to betray her father and reveal the location of the treasure.

It is the present when a teenage girl (Bonnie) stumbles onto that shack in the woods (in the middle of nowhere) and brings her friend Eliza to search it with her. While doing so, Bonnie knocks a candle off a table and both she and Eliza are startled to see the ghost of a girl—Victoria—appear before them. Victoria tells them that she needs their help to move on but the only way that can happen is if they uncover the treasure that was stolen by her father. Victoria is unable to tell them where the treasure is buried, but she can provide the clues she composed 100 years ago to help them. She also tells them that others (Scarlet and Clare) have become aware of the treasure and are also seeking it. Before disappearing, Victoria gives Bonnie an Eliza their first clue: "On the opposite side of an artist's expression you will find the key." Feeling that she needs help, Bonnie asks her friend Daniel to assist her. He deciphers the clue to mean the back of a painting. As Bonnie looks around the shack, she sees a painting, checks the back and finds the key of which Victoria spoke. But what does it open? The program charts Bonnie, Eliza and Daniel's search to unravel clues and find the treasure so Victoria can move on.

Cast: Sarah Peterson (Eliza), Tunji Wolfe (Bonnie), Rhett Davis (Daniel), Isabella Minter (Scarlet), Abby Miller (Clare), Elinor Hudson (Victoria). **Credits:** *Producer-Writer-Director:* Rhett Davis **Comment:** An all teenage cast and a surprisingly well produced and acted series. Story line wise, there are some problems (which are easily overlooked to enjoy the program). These include Victoria's history (which is not really explained) and the treasure (it is unknown how her father acquired it and what it is). The shack, for being in the woods for 100 years is in remarkable condition (with all its furnishings still intact) and for some unknown reason, never before discovered. Scarlet and Clare, the rival treasure hunters, are nasty and get away with everything they do, even kidnapping Bonnie, Eliza and Daniel (who, for unknown reasons, do not seek help from the police or anyone else). *Past Meets the Future* is the type of web series that would make a good transformation to cable TV on either Nickelodeon's Teen Nick or its regular NIK channel.

Episodes:

1. The Mysterious Shack (7 min., 48 sec.). Bonnie and Eliza investigate the shack that Bonnie accidentally stumbled upon.

2. Trapped in Confrontation (5 min., 20 sec.). Bonnie encounters Scarlet, a girl who has also found the shack and seeking the treasure (how she learned about the treasure is later mentioned as by doing research).

3. The Secret Revealed (5 min., 16 sec.). Bonnie and Eliza encounter Victoria for the first time when Bonnie knocks a candle to the floor.

4. Help Wanted (4 min., 41 sec.). Feeling they need help, Bonnie recruits her friend Daniel.

5. Double-Cross (5 min., 52 sec.). Bonnie summons Victoria (by lighting the candle) and learns that she and Eliza have only 37 hours left to find

the treasure or Victoria will be trapped on earth forever.

6. The Meeting (3 min., 37 sec.). Scarlet and her partner, Clare, approach Bonnie seeking what information she has uncovered.

7. Breaking and Entering (6 min., 11 sec.). By the strangest of coincidences, a chest in Eliza's room (that once belonged to Victoria) is what the first clue piece will unlock. Upon opening it, a medallion is found, the second clue.

8. Coming Clean (5 min., 54 sec.). Scarlet and Clare abduct Eliza and Daniel (placing them in a barn) while Bonnie, also kidnapped, is questioned about the medallion by Scarlet.

9. Kidnapped (5 min., 39 sec.). Eliza and Daniel escape but Bonnie, tied to a chair in the shack, faces more questioning from Clare.

10. Pure Hearts (12 min., 12 sec.). The concluding episode wherein Scarlet believes Bonnie knows what the medallion means and appears to be resorting to desperate measures to get that information when the program ends.

273 Persephone. webserieschanel.com. 2013 (Animated Comedy-Drama).

In the underworld of Greek mythology there exists the goddess Persephone. Zeus, King of the Gods, and Demeter, the Goddess of the Harvest (also Queen of the Underworld), are her parents. Persephone, blessed with extraordinary beauty, became the object of desire, especially to Hades, ruler of the underworld, who yearned for her love. One day, while collecting flowers on the plain of Enna, Hades abducted Persephone and took her to his world beneath the earth. The abduction, however, was only witnessed by Zeus and the all-seeing sun, Helios. Demeter, learning of her daughter's mysterious disappearance, began wandering the earth looking for her and found the answer she was seeking when Helios revealed what happened. Bitterly angered and unable to rescue Persephone, Demeter succumbed to a state of deep depression wherein the earth ceased to be fertile (thus winter was created and vegetation non-existent). The legend continues to state that Zeus, unable to let Demeter suffer, intervened and ordered Hermes to rescue Persephone. Before giving up his beloved Persephone, Hades gave her a pomegranate, which, upon eating bound Persephone to the underworld for one-third of each year (the time of winter) and the remaining time with her mother (when the earth would become fertile again). Adapting the basic myth with other myths surrounding the Greek goddess, the program explores Persephone's cycle of life and death and of the struggle between Demeter and Hades for the love of Persephone and how each must rule the world they have created. In Roman mythology, Persephone is called Proserpina, and her mother Ceres.

Voice Cast: Carrie Anne Hunt (Persephone), Sketch MacQunior (Hades), Linda Donnell (Demeter), Carrie Johnson (Althea), Josie Lawson (Enchantress). **Credits:** *Producer-Writer-Director:* Lisa Stock. **Comment:** Striking animation, especially with the characters (whose eyes appear in white). The characters are not as fluid as seen on television series but their lack of total movement just heightens the effect to present something that captures your attention and makes you curious to see more of the presentation.

Episodes: Only two episodes remain on line: The Abduction and a 90 second teaser. Following is a title listing: *1.* The Abduction. *2.* The Descent. *3.* The Tales of the Deer Queen. *4.* The Tower of Hades. *5.* The Enchantress. *6.* The Fight. *7.* The Deer Queen Ascends, *8.* The Return.

274 Pink. youtube.com. 2007–2009 (Crime Drama).

Natalie Cross is young, beautiful and employed in a most unusual occupation: assassin for a mysterious woman known only as Wilson. For Natalie it began when she was just seven years old. Her mother had abandoned the family when she discovered that her husband was a hit man. It was also at this time that Natalie was taught by her father how to handle guns, a rifle in particular, and how to become a deadly shot. Although she would not see a friend of her father's (Beeson) until she entered college, it is learned that Beeson contracted her father's services for specific hits. As Natalie grew she became an expert sharpshooter and eventually followed in her father's footsteps. One hit, however, went wrong and Natalie was arrested, charged with attempted murder and sentenced to prison.

At first Natalie felt safe ("I never want to leave this place") but as time passed she realized her biological clock was ticking and her dream of having children could not come true. Prior to her sentencing Natalie was approached by an ex-government agent (Wilson) and offered a choice: work for her as a mercenary or spend time in prison. Natalie refused her offer and accepted her punishment. But circumstances have changed and Natalie now finds that time is running out and that to achieve her goal, she must kill. The program encompasses numerous flashbacks coupled with present-day activities to tell the story of Natalie Cross—from her formative childhood years, her time in college and the contracts she must fulfill in order to gain a pardon and hopefully begin her family. Natalie is teamed with a young assassin named Bunny and it is revealed that her college roommate, Rhonda, nicknamed her "Pink" after her predominately pink wardrobe.

Cast: Natalie Raitano (Natalie Cross), Sheree J. Wilson (Wilson), Matthew Tompkins (Natalie's father), Cameron Ten Napel (Pre-teen Natalie), Kim Matula, Sarah Zuck (Teenage Natalie), Katy Rowe (Bunny), Brad Hawkins (Dante), Vikas Adam

(Ahmed), Curt Mega (Noah), Brittany Joyner (Hannah), Shauna McLean (Honey Weathers), Nicole Leigh (Rhonda), Lawrence Varnado (Beeson). **Credits:** *Producer:* Natalie Raitano, Mehrdad Moayedi, Ken Crain, Blake Calhoun. *Director:* Blake Calhoun. *Writer:* Mike Maden, Blake Calhoun. **Comment:** Natalie Raitano (from the syndicated TV series *V.I.P.*) and Sherrie J. Wilson (from the CBS series *Walker, Texas Ranger*) star in a well-produced series that holds viewer attention from the very beginning. Rather than present Natalie's history in a single episode, a wise choice was made to use flashbacks as it slowly establishes Natalie's character from an early age to her first year in college when her life would change forever. The supporting characters handle their roles well and the overall production is well worth watching. One of the problems with older Internet series (and 2007 is old as it is one of the earlier crime dramas) is that printed information differs from video information. The episode titles and times presented here are based on viewing the episodes, not the text information that appears. Although it is a crime drama, it has very little violence, minimal sexual situations and no nudity; the perfect candidate for a network pickup.

Episodes:

1. Let's Get Started (3 min., 5 sec.). Although Natalie feels secure in prison, she realizes that she must make a deal with Wilson if she is to begin a family.

2. Daddy's Little Girl (2 min., 52 sec.). In a flashback Natalie is seen being taught how to use a rifle by her father.

3. It's Hard to Be a Pimp in Here (2 min., 50 sec.). Natalie looks back at prison for the last time as she accepts Wilson's offer to gain a pardon.

4. Meet the Parents (2 min., 57 sec.). Young Natalie learns that her father is a hired killer and meets Beeson for the first time.

5. The Wedding Crasher (4 min., 23 sec.). Natalie learns that Wilson possesses "The List," a folder of people that need to be silenced and receives her first assignment.

6. First Things First (4 min., 23 sec.). Before she stalks her target, Natalie does something unusual (for her): gets a tattoo.

7. Feels Like the First Time (4 min., 33 sec.). As Natalie begins tracking her target (Marcos) she recalls her first hit.

8. The Big Date (3 min., 45 sec.). Natalie gets a bit too close to Marcos and begins to develop feelings for him.

9. Father Knows Best (3 min., 20 sec.). As Marcos becomes suspicious of Natalie and manages to elude her, Natalie asks her father for help.

10. Like Riding a Bike (3 min., 29 sec.). Acting on her father's advice, Natalie sets a trap to silence Marcos.

11. No Good Dead (4 min., 26 sec.). Natalie, seen in a prison flashback, considers accepting Wilson's offer. In the present, Bunny is assigned as Natalie's partner by Wilson.

12. Screwed on Straight (4 min., 46 sec.). As Natalie plans her future (a family) a flashback reveals the time her mother abandoned her and her father.

13. Viva Las Vegas (3 min., 35 sec.). Natalie receives her next assignment: silence "a big mouth that needs to be shot."

14. Speed Dating (4 min., 31 sec.). Natalie closes in her target when she joins a speed dating service.

15. Duck Duck Goose (4 min., 7 sec.). Natalie, in another flashback, is seen as a teenager beginning college and meeting her Goth girl roommate, Rhonda.

16. Rebel Without Ecru (4 min., 37 sec.). Natalie, as a college student, becomes attracted to her poetry instructor (Prof. Malle); in the present, Natalie and Bunny accept an assignment that will net Wilson triple the normal fee.

17. Educating Rita (3 min., 23 sec.). Feeling that Bunny is still a little wet behind the ears, Natalie introduces her to her routine: working out before a hit.

18. Knocking on Heaven's Door (3 min., 55 sec.). A college flashback with Natalie and her professor becoming increasingly close.

19. The Professional (3 min., 55 sec.). Natalie's first date with the professor is overshadowed by a man from her past—Beeson, who has kept track of her and wants her to work for him as a contract killer.

20. The Harder They Fall (3 min., 59 sec.). Natalie, in a flashback to her college days, displays her expertise at dueling.

21. Speed Dating Kills 2 (3 min., 47 sec.). While in a hot tub, Natalie has visions of her past killings.

22. The Laws of Attraction (4 min., 14 sec.). A flashback to college wherein Natalie meets a charming artist (paralleling her life in the present, where she has fallen for an artist named Dante).

23. Tonight's the Night (4 min., 27 sec.). Natalie conducts an Internet search and discovers Dante has an arrest record—but it doesn't appear to faze her.

24. Someone to Watch Over Me (4 min., 21 sec.). In a college flashback, Natalie is drugged and about to be raped at a frat party when she is saved by Beeson—but for his sinister reasons (to convince Natalie to work for him).

25. Think Different (4 min., 10 sec.). In the present, Natalie begins a relationship with Dante.

26. The Pickup Artist (3 min., 16 sec.). College is revisited through a flashback to explore Natalie's infatuation with an artist.

27. In the Paint (4 min., 54 sec.). To accommodate her new found love, Natalie agrees to have her body painted.

28. No Country for You (4 min., 48 sec.). Natalie and Bunny tackle an assignment overseas that has them treading on dangerous ground and possible incarceration if caught.

29. About a Boy (3 min., 48 sec.). A flashback that traces Natalie's first hit as a coed.

30. All Ye Know on Earth (4 min., 37 sec.). A look at Bunny's past—wherein she killed her mother for having an affair with a married man.

31. Sunshine of Your Life (4 min.). As Natalie becomes close to Dante, she is being observed by persons unknown.

32. DZP 214 (3 min., 22 sec.). A crucial glimpse into Natalie's past that sets her on her path as killer. A driver (hired by Beeson) runs down Natalie's friend Noah and leaves the scene of the crime. Natalie, however, caught the license plate—DZP 214.

33. Love and a .45 (4 min., 24 sec.). Tracking the owner of the car, Natalie also finds a "gift" from Beeson—a .45.

34. Klaati Barada Nikto (3 min., 18 sec.). Natalie kills the driver and must now lead a life under the radar.

35. First and Last (4 min., 10 sec.). An unknown assailant takes out Wilson and, as the unresolved series concludes, has Natalie in his gun sight.

275 *Pledge.* vimeo.com. 2013 (Thriller).

A young man (Christian) has been asked to pledge a college fraternity. He accepts the invitation and shortly afterward begins to feel uneasy about accepting, especially when he has a dream wherein he is brutally killed by someone wielding a fraternity initiation paddle. The program follows Christian as he becomes a pledge but is continually plagued as aspects of his nightmare slowly become reality.

Cast: Miles Pisani (Christian), Lexi Lapp (Megan), Leah Voysey (Tiff), Joey Chase D'Allesando (Dom). **Credits:** *Producer-Director:* John Addington. *Writer:* Chelsey Neders. **Comment:** A nicely produced and acted mystery that needlessly incorporates foul language. The characters are well depicted but the story, while not resolved, does not appear to have much left to explore once Christian's fate is revealed.

Episodes:

1. The Dream (5 min., 36 sec.). Establishes the story line as Christian awakens from his nightmare just as he is being attacked.

2. Baptism (7 min., 22 sec.). As Christian becomes more involved with the fraternity, he discovers the paddle that he saw in his dream.

3. The Party (6 min., 54 sec.). Christian attends a party being held to honor the new inductees as his fears about the fraternity become more prominent.

4. Scavengers (8 min., 25 sec.). Christian confides in his friend, Megan, about his dream and how it is beginning to surface as becoming real.

5. Look Out (9 min., 19 sec.). The concluding, unresolved episode wherein Christian's dream appears to become a reality when Megan, wielding the paddle, strikes him and says, "I thought you were my friend."

276 *Poker Girls.* webserieschannel.com. 2010–2012 (Drama).

In an attempt to crack down on crime, a police detective (Summer) and her team (Kathryn, Marcy, Vicki and Teresa) begin a rather unusual undercover assignment—posing as poker players to get close to unsuspecting criminals, beat them at their own game and eventually arrest them. The intent sounds good and begins well but it does not always play well and the program charts what happens when Summer's undercover assignments become anything than typical.

Cast: Jewelle Colwell (Summer), Toni Lynne (Kathryn), Lara Taillon (Vicki), Dawn Harvey (Teresa), Marie Muncaster (Rose), Rae Farrer (Marcy), Leanne Khol Young (Sara), Teddy G. Alexander (Brad). **Credits:** *Producer:* Rob Colwell, Jewelle Colwell. *Director:* Neshe Delici, Neil Schell, Jewelle Colwell. *Writer:* Jewelle Colwell. **Comment:** A difficult series to judge as only a teaser that runs one minute and 56 seconds remains on line. Based on what is available, there are hints of comedy mixed in with the poker scenes as Summer's efforts do not always go as planned. The acting and the production values both appear to be good.

Episodes: All episodes have been taken off-line; following is a title listing: *1.* Winner Takes All. *2.* The Announcement. *3.* The Reaction. *4.* Episode 1.4. *5.* Fresh Out of Losers. *6.* Who's There to Like? *7.* Changes. *8.* Christmas Special. *9.* Intruder Alert. *10.* Life Is Slippery ... Here, Take My Hand. *11.* The Darkest Night. *12.* If You Would Lift Me Up.

277 *Port City P.D.* elevenbravoproductions.com. 2009 (Crime Drama).

Detectives attached to the Port City Police Department run the gambit from the top notch investigators to those who have seemingly mundane responsibilities (such as solving petty crimes). Dekker, A.J. and Williams are three of the detectives who comprise that "dead-end" unit. Each has his or her own personal demons and each must work to prove they are more than just a dumping ground for cases nobody else seems to want (or particularly care about). Stories follow the detectives as they struggle to prove their worth by solving the cases that are given to them—cases that are often more involved than originally thought.

Cast: Shaun O'Rourke (Alex Dekker), Raymond Shepard (Det. Williams), Sheila Brothers (Det. A.J.), Rachel Lewis (Dr. Miller), Brandon Luck (Det. Mitchell), Christopher Brockmeyer (Malcolm Bryce), Cari Moskow (Sarah Dekker), Langley McArol (Det. Langley), Barrett Stevens (Capt. Riley), Christopher L. Haywood (Det. Haywood), Leah Marie Parker (Dana Chase), Zach Hanner (Chief), Quentin Kerr (Frank Reuter). **Credits:** *Producer:* Susan B. Flanagan, Bidwell C. Tyler II, Sheila Brothers.

Director: Charles Stewart, Jr., Kelly Neilon, Richard Gehron, Billy Lewis. *Writer:* Sheila Brothers, Roxanne Marchand, D.J. Naylorm Kelly Neilon, Shaun O'Rourke, Raymond Shepard, Charles Stewart, Jr. **Comment:** The program has been reviewed as "a character-driven study" of the detectives featured, but this is really not new as programs such as *Dragnet, N.Y.P.D. Blue* and *Blue Bloods* have also tackled that aspect. It is a rarity in that it has been re-edited and syndicated (where it ran on the broadcast channel Tuff TV).

Episodes: All nine episodes have been taken off line due to its re-edited release as a syndicated television series. Following is an episode listing.

1. Port City P.D. Pilot. *2.* I Scream, You Scream. *3.* Getting to Know You. *4.* Cursed. *5.* Get Over It. *6.* Nothing's as It Seems. *7.* The Final Countdown. *8.* Closed Mouths. *9.* Triple Threat.

278 *Precinct 757.* precinct757.com. 2013–2014 (Crime Drama).

Hampton Roads is a city like many others—plagued with crime and corruption and seeking a way to deal with such problems. A police precinct, the 757, and the men and women who serve it are the city's best defense against the growing crime rate. While its Captain, Eric Baxter, claims "The only thing that matters is protecting the 757 and that's all that matters," the program charts the precinct's elite team of detectives and select street cops as they attempt to bring down the city's most notorious criminals.

Cast: Frances Owens (Det. Helen Weaver), John Bargeman (Det. James Bennett), Carrie Lynn King (Off. Nikki Marquez), Jaye Taylor (Patricia Miles), Tierre Arrington (Shyne), Robert Milton (Bitmo), Ahmad Resean (Chaney), Fo'ree Shalom (Big Dose), Marx G. Sims (Achilles), Anthony Barker (Eddie Navarro), Lanza Williams (Lanza Turner), Patricia Gee (Martina Goldman), N.R. Hunt (Judge Dex Dexter), Tony Wade (Agent Len Vance), Chris Lythgoe (Det. Frank Goldman), Lamonte Mills (Sgt. William "Squeeze" Boston), Rosalind Russell (Lt. Deanna "Spyder" Webb), Robert Shepherd (Capt. Eric Baxter). **Credits:** *Producer:* Ron Campbell, Russ Fulmore, Myron Campbell. *Director:* Russ Fulmore, Chris Abaya. *Writer:* Charles Farmer, Russ Fulmore, Shiree Hayden. **Comment:** It is not really possible to judge the program by the video information that remains on line as it does not truly represent the series. The program does sound interesting in that it takes big city crime and transports it to a small town but how the procedural is presented (along with the acting and production values) is not known.

Episodes: All actual episodes have been taken offline. Following is a listing: *1.* In the Beginning. *2.* Circles. *3.* Boxed In. *4.* Out of the Box.

The following non-episode videos remain on line:

1. Precinct 757 Promo Reel (3 min., 57 sec.).
2. Precinct 757 Music Video (2 min., 58 sec.).
3. Precinct 757: Training Part 3 (1 min., 54 sec.).
4. Precinct 757: Dark Figure Teaser (1 min., 54 sec.).

279 *Pretty Dirty Secrets.* abcfamily.com. 2012 (Mystery).

A spin off from the ABC Family series *Pretty Little Liars* that is set in Rosewood, Pennsylvania and follows a group of teenagers who are somehow involved in the mysterious death of one of their friends (Allison) and, while none are charged with the crime, they are haunted by an unknown cell phone stalker they call "A" (after their friend) who appears to know their secrets and threatens to expose them for what they really are ("Pretty Little Liars"). The web series aired between the conclusion of the third season and the start of the fourth season of *Pretty Little Liars* and is set in Rosewood during the days leading up to Halloween and an upcoming Halloween bash. "A" is again on the prowl, this time stalking a group of people not directly associated with the TV series storyline, but people with "Dirty Little Secrets" that someone ("A") feels the need to expose.

Cast: Aeriel Miranda (Shana), Vanessa Ray (CeCe Drake), Yani Gellman (Garret Reynols), Brant Daugherty (Noel Kahn), Brendan Robinson (Lucas Gottesman), Drew Van Acker (Jason DiLaurentis), Jennifer Cain (Voicemail Message voice). **Credits:** *Writer:* Kyle Bown, Kim Turrisi. *Director:* Arthur Anderson. **Comment:** Well-acted and produced companion series to *Pretty Little Liars.* While none of the series regulars appear, the spin off holds its own and does set up the story to continue, although this has not happened.

Episodes: (all titles revolve around the mysterious "A" and are thus made to represent the letter A).

1. *A* Reserv*A*tion. A mystery begins when "A" believes someone associated with the Rosewood Halloween Spectacular Store is evil and needs to be exposed.

2. *A* Reunion. Shana is made to look suspicious when she eavesdrops on CeCe and Jason at the Halloween Store.

3. *A* Voicem*A*il. Through a voicemail message left by "A" it is learned that two residents, Garrett and Mrs. Reynolds are suddenly planning to leave town.

4. I'm *A* Free M*A*n. As Noel and Garrett confront each other about Jeanna choosing Noel over Garrett, Shana is again seen eavesdropping on their conversation.

5. Tr*A*de-off. At the store, Shana, reading a comic book spies a costumed person approaching her friend, Lucas, and whispering something in his ear. As Shana watches, Lucas follows the figure into a dressing room where he is handed a note. Lucas then gives the costumed figure an envelope, arousing Shana's suspicions.

6. *Associ*A*tion*. As Shana checks her cell phone, numerous blocked messages from "A" are seen. However, when the blocked ID calls Shana, it appears she knows more about "A" than she is revealing.

7. *C*A*ll Security*. "A" hacks into the store's surveillance video to pause at a scene where a person wearing a red coat is seen. After a few seconds, "A" deletes the footage leaving no trace that the red-coated person entered the store.

8. *The* A *Tr*A*in*. The concluding, unresolved episode (leading into the TV series) where "A" is seen looking over plans for the town's annual Ghost Train Party.

280 *Pretty Tough*. webserieschannel.com. 2011 (Drama).

Charlene, called Charlie, and Krista are sisters who attend the same high school (Beachwood Acad-emy). Krista is the more outgoing popular girl (the second most popular girl in school) while Charlie is just the opposite: laid back and not as actively involved in school activities, especially sports as Krista. Life changes for both girls when Charlie is recruited to become a member of the soccer team and must play alongside Krista, the team's top player. The program follows the events that spark the sister's lives as they learn life's lessons—on and off the playing field.

Cast: Adelaide Kane (Charlene "Charlie" Brown), Crystal Young (Krista Brown), Matthew Florida (Noah), Jess Adams (Brooks), Guy Wilson (Cam), Beth Behrs (Regen), Elvina Beck (Darcy), Dalila Ali Rajah (Martie), Casey Fitzgerald (Buffi), Brandi Chastain (Herself), Vincent Duvall (Bradley), Alli Kinzel (Jamie), Shanica Knowles (Pickle), Sherri Parker Lee (Sarah), Jenny Sauer (Rachel), Corey Saunders (Mark), Allison Weissman (Tiffany). **Credits:** *Producer:* Tim Williams. *Director:* Stewart Hendler. *Writer:* Marguerite MacIntyre. **Comment:** While the episodes are quite long, they do progress rapidly although one must endure a series of commercials during each episode. The acting and production values are very good and the doorway is left open for more incidents in the lives of Charlie and Krista as they enter college. For some, shades of the TV series *Sweet Valley High* can be seen as it too dealt with sisters who were also in high school.

Episodes:
1. Episode 1 (22 min., 6 sec.). Krista and Charlie are introduced as the new school year begins with Charlie being recruited to join the soccer team by Martie.

2. Episode 2 (22 min., 15 sec.). As Charlie begins to come out of her shell and make new friends, Krista encounters difficulty preparing her college entrance essay (for Denver University)—as what comes easily to Charlie is not easy for Krista.

3. Episode 3 (23 min., 44 sec.). Adjustments are made to the soccer team when Martie reverses Charlie and Krista's positions and disappointment confronts Krista when she is not made team captain.

4. Episode 4 (20 min., 43 sec.). As the homecoming dance begins, Noah expresses his feelings for Krista while Krista finds herself faced with an angry boyfriend (Cam) when she refuses to sleep with him.

5. Episode 5 (23 min., 32 sec.). The concluding episode wherein Krista and Charlie clash at the soccer

Pretty Tough. **Poster art from the series (copyright Vuguru, LLC, 2010. All rights reserved).**

championship game while Cam rejects Brooks (the most popular girl in school) advances to remain with Krista.

281 *Private.* alloyentertainment.com. 2009 (Drama).

Easton Academy is a prestigious, private boarding school in New England that is steeped in the tradition of honor and excellence. Its students are from the finest families but Easton is also an institution with dark, hidden secrets. As Reed Brennan enrolls at the school she quickly learns that the school is not what it appears and episodes trace her experiences as she becomes involved in a series of strange incidents that could mean her life. **Cast:** Kelsey Sanders (Reed Brennan), Natalie Floyd (Ariana Osgood), Samantha Cope (Noelle Lange), Sanna Haynes (Kiran Hayes), Tristin Mays (Taylor Bell), Chord Overstreet (Josh Hollis), Brant Daugherty (Thomas Pearson). **Credits:** *Director:* Dennie Gordon. **Comment:** Although the series is based on the books of the same name by Kate Brian, the series plays a bit like the TV series *Strange Days at Blake Hosley High* that also presented a newly enrolled teenager encountering unusual happenings at a private boarding school. Differences aside, it is well acted and produced and holds your attention from the first scene when Reed arrives at the school.

Episodes:

1. Episode 1. Introduces Reed as she arrives at the school and quickly learns all is not what it appears.

2. Episode 2. After settling in, Reed befriends Ariana and is warned to avoid a fellow student (Thomas Pearson) who will cause her nothing but trouble.

3. Episode 3. Eleanor Billings, head of the prestigious Billings Girls' clique, approaches Reed as a possible candidate.

4. Episode 4. Reed, ignoring Ariana's warnings, has befriended Thomas, so much so that they share a kiss—which is secretly recorded by a cell phone camera.

5. Episode 5. Reed is put to the test of becoming a Billings Girl when Noelle instructs her to steal a physics test and present it to Ariana.

6. Episode 6. Reed, accomplishing her goal, is awarded by joining Eleanor and Noelle at a bonfire. However, all is not gayety when a seemingly upset Thomas arrives, demanding that Reed come with him. Reed refuses and elects to stay with her friends.

7. Episode 7. The following day, as Reed tries to call Thomas and apologize for not going with him, Reed learns from her friend Josh that Thomas never returned home from the party.

8. Episode 8. Eleanor, seeing that Reed is worried, tries to convince her that Thomas is okay. Shortly after, Ariana tells Reed Thomas did her a favor by leaving her. The situation changes when Reed returns to her room and a police detective is waiting to see her.

9. Episode 9. After being questioned about Thomas's disappearance, Reed joins Noelle, Kiran and Ariana at the Billings Girls Legacy party. Here, after having a bit too much to drink, Reed believes she sees Thomas outside.

10. Episode 10. Reed, gaining her mobility, rushes outside only to discover Thomas to be her friend Blake. As Reed rejoins the party, still worried about Thomas, Taylor reveals to her that Thomas has been killed.

11. Episode 11. Reed and her friends are questioned by the police as all being suspect in Thomas's killing.

12. Episode 12. Each of the students is questioned separately by detectives with Reed, who had the last contact with Thomas, being the prime suspect.

13. Episode 13. The students, including Reed, are released. Although it is a sad time Reed is inducted as an official Billings Girl.

14. Episode 14. As it is revealed that Thomas dealt drugs, Reed overhears Noelle and Ariana trying to quiet Taylor, who had feelings for Thomas. Meanwhile, the baseball bat that was used to kill Thomas is traced to its owner—Josh.

15. Episode 15. Shortly after Josh is arrested for murder, Reed visits him and learns that the baseball bat was his but that it was stolen several weeks prior to the murder, but no one will believe him. Josh then tells Reed that on the night of the party he and Thomas fought, and the only witness was Blake, Thomas's brother.

16. Episode 16. Believing that Josh was framed, Reed seeks and finds Blake and convinces him to help free Josh.

17. Episode 17. Blake's story frees Josh but the killer is still at large—presumably a female as a mysterious figure is seen with Thomas's cell phone and jacket.

18. Episode 18. Complications arise when Reed finds a note in her purse telling her not to trust the Billings Girls.

19. Episode 19. As Reed leaves her room she notices Ariana taking pictures of Noelle and Kiran and follows Ariana to the cloakroom were, when Ariana is not watching, sees a video phone clip of Thomas and Ariana kissing.

20. Episode 20. Reed discovers that Ariana is the killer—but whose life is now in danger as Ariana plans to kill her. The program's concluding episode.

282 *Producing Juliet.* producingjuliet.com. 2013–2014 (Drama).

Rebecca Welles, a corporate executive, and Laura Gordon, an actress, are in love but also in an open relationship with a third girl (Michelle). Rebecca and Laura's relationship appears to be a happy one although Rebecca feels somewhat neglected as Laura is more focused on her acting career than on her. One night, after attending Laura's performance in a play called *Comforts of Home* at The Secret Theater, Rebecca meets Juliet Bello, the play's struggling author. As Rebecca becomes friendly with Juliet, she believes she has found a new focus in life and impulsively decides to resign from her job to produce Juliet's second play (*When I Imagined You with Me*). As Rebecca comes to know Juliet, she learns that Juliet has feelings for, but has never become romantically involved with Evan, her gay friend (currently in a relationship with a man named Henry). Evan has feelings for Juliet but is unable to accept the thought of becoming her lover. Rebecca, although in

Producing Juliet. **Poster art from the series (copyright 2013 Ward Picture Company, Inc.).**

an open relationship, desires more attention from Laura; Juliet must come to terms with her feelings for and relationship with Evan; and Evan must choose between Juliet and Henry. The program relates the choices each must make to achieve the happiness each desires.

Cast: Alisha Spielmann (Rebecca Welles), Rachael Hip-Flores (Juliet Bello), Jenny Grace (Laura Gordon), Andy Phelan (Evan), Betty Kaplan (Andrea), Stacey Raymond (Michelle), David Drake (Henry), Chinaza Uche (Jacob Aarons), Kevin Sebastian (Richard Nichols). **Credits:** *Producer:* Tina Cesa Ward, Rochelle Dancel, Allison Vanore. *Writer-Director:* Tina Cesa Ward. **Comment:** Exceptionally well acted and produced drama with a story line that flows smoothly from beginning to end. There are girl/girl kissing scenes, but nothing objectionable. If anthology series (such as *Ford Television Theater* and *Playhouse 90*) were still being produced by network TV, *Producing Juliet* would make an excellent addition to anyone of them.

Episodes:

1. Pilot (12 min., 18 sec.). Establishes the story line as Rebecca meets Juliet outside The Secret Theater.

2. Necessary Condition (10 min., 46 sec.). As Rebecca makes a life-changing decision to resign from her job and produce Juliet's second play, an intimate look at her and Laura's relationship is also seen.

3. The Play's the Thing, Part 1 (7 min., 1 sec.). Rebecca's new venture has Laura wondering how this will affect their relationship while Evan fears he will lose Juliet forever.

4. The Play's the Thing, Part 2 (12 min., 31 sec.). As Evan confronts Juliet about her play he learns that it is literally about her and how she is desperately struggling to find a way to move on without him (as he can't have her and his boyfriend, Henry); meanwhile as Rebecca commits herself to producing Juliet's play (and acquires the help of Andrea, the theater producer), Laura begins the first move to rekindle her romance with Rebecca.

283 Progress. progresstheseries.com. 2013 (Mystery).

England, in the late 19th century, is perhaps most famous for the prostitute killings attributed to the notorious Jack the Ripper. Many television programs (and movies) have been devoted to the subject, but none have ever been able to positively solve the mystery surrounding Jack the Ripper's true identity. In a twist, bringing modern technology (computers and the Internet) to Victorian England, one man, Oscar Lerwill, a computer hacker, believes he can solve the mystery. Through the use of steam power, an Internet has been created (Virtual Whitechapel). Jack the Ripper is the first to take advantage of the new technology by posting encrypted files of his foul deeds on WikiPunch (the 19th century version of WikiLeaks). When Oscar accidentally discovers one of Jack's files, he becomes intrigued and sets out to break the code and reveal Jack's true identity. Complicating his efforts are Jack himself, who has become aware of Oscar, and has set his sights on Oscar's beloved Lila DeClide (who could become the next victim as her life depends on Oscar's ability to decipher the codes) and Adam Rhett, "The Mad Troll of WikiPunch," who delights in taunting Oscar.

Cast: Ben Whalen (Oscar Lerwill), Rebecca Lynch (Lila DeClide), Derek Houck (Adam Rhett), Anna Mountford (Voice of Oscar's Computer), Andy Pandini (Mr. Humbbaugh), Kai Cofer (Constable Alben Scot). **Credits:** *Producer:* Nicole Wright, Armando Saldanamora. *Director:* Nicole Wright. *Writer:* Armando Saldanamora.

Comment: Although 10 episodes are mentioned as being produced, only three episodes are on line (in production at the time of book publication). While the subject matter is not new, its presentation is unique (especially how steam power can run computers and the Internet; a typewriter has been encompassed to act as the keyboard). Whether interested in Jack the Ripper or not, a worthy series to check out for something really different.

Episodes:

1. iAm Involved in a Mystery. Oscar's hacking abilities bring him to a posting by Jack the Ripper.

2. iFall Into Captivity. With the onslaught of "filth" on the Internet, Oscar finds that the government is beginning a campaign to filter it.

3. Mischief. A war brews (with casualties) as Oscar and other Internet users battle the government's intrusion on what they can and cannot see on line.

Progress. **Poster art from the series (art work by Andrea Garduno; copyright Flawless Victory Media, 2014).**

284 *Project Schoolies.* webserieschannel. com. 2012 (Drama).

Australian-produced program that follows a group of high school graduates (called here "school leavers") as they celebrate the end of their senior year and head to Surfers Paradise to experience beach parties, hooking up and paying the consequences of their sometimes foolish actions.

Cast: Celeste Cotton (Lara), Leigh Scott (George), Adrian Giribon (Hamish), Tahlia Ponting (Jem), Alexander Fechine (Dane), Natalie Mitchell (Gabriella), Tamaha Carroll (Zak), Jade Prechelt (Leonie). **Credits:** *Producer:* Zoltan Deak. *Writer-Director:* Ric Forster. **Comment:** Filmed in Queensland, Australia, with good acting and production values. Interesting to see how, when school ends in another country, students react—although not much different from the U.S. tradition of Spring Break for college students.

Episodes:

1. The Guys Hit Surfers. The 2012 school year has ended and a group of friends head for Surfers Paradise.

2. The Morning After. A night of partying not only has George getting intoxicated, but wondering, when he wakes up the following morning, how he wound up in the same bed with Gabriella.

3. Episode 3. Gabriella's encounter with Jay from *Geordie Shore* (the UK version of America's reality series *Jersey Shore*) is explored.

4. Episode 4. As George meets a girl who shares his interest in science, Dane and Lara appear to be having problems that could end their relationship.

5. Episode 5. Unable to resolve their differences, Dane and Lara break up. Both appear to be fine with what happened until Dane sees Lara with another guy and realizes he still loves her.

6. Episode 6. The concluding episode wherein the teens must end their week of freedom and return to face what the future holds for them.

285 *Project Z: History of a Zombie Apocalypse.* savage lightstudios.com. 2012–2013 (Comedy-Drama).

It could be at any time when scientists, experimenting with genetically modified organisms (Project Z), go beyond what is known and create a deadly virus that escapes into the atmosphere and brings the dead back to an "un-life" (zombies). The dead are now roaming the planet seeking human nourishment and mankind has become the hunted. Stories follow various survivors of the Z-Day catastrophe as they seek to destroy a new menace and return the world to the way it once was.

Cast: Harrold Gene Franques (Matt), Ken Halhober (Greg), Allyson Leigh Jordan (Allyson), Karla Belile (Dr. Hope), Lisa Wilde (Maria), Jack Buttitta (Jack), Keegan Macy (Tyler), Sylvia Grace Crim (Leona), Tim Wright (Lt.), Max Jay-Dixon (Jake), John Swider (Kriss), Tom Bubrig (Dr. Potts), Kristina Kingston (Sally), Gideon Hodge (Daryl), Daylon Micah Othello (Jeff). **Credits:** *Producer:* Harrold Gene Franques, Kristopher Hoffman, Allyson Leigh Jordan, Kerri LuLie, M. Jearl Vinot. *Director:* Kristopher Hoffman, M. Jearl Vinot. *Writer:* Kristopher Hoffman, Trey Wickwire, Laurie Notch, M. Jearl Vinot. **Comment:** The program could have been produced several different ways: horror, thriller, drama or comedy. The producers chose to combine all genres in a rather amusing effort that is well acted and produced.

Episodes: Initially only seven of 10 produced episodes remained on line. These have also been removed as of April 2014.

1. Pilot. One group of survivors is introduced and the initial problems that are facing mankind.

2. Legend of the Zombie Queen. Maria, a group member who practices modern-day Voodoo, believes that magic is responsible for raising the dead and magic can also control them.

3. Doctor, Doctor. Daryl, an assistant to Dr. Hope, becomes a valuable tool when he is infected with the Z-Strain and studying his progression could lead to a cure.

4. Antigen. Camp Defiance, a secure, zombie-free area in Louisiana, becomes the center of attention when a man (Tyler), bitten by a zombie but immune to the Z-Strain, seeks refuge and has doctors eager to figure what caused his immunity.

5. Just the Two of Us. A married couple (Sally and Jack) seek a way to escape (or at least survive) when their home becomes surrounded by zombies.

6. Snack Time. Two roommates become the center of attention when they seek a way to replenish their food supply when they are totally surrounded by zombies.

7. Ku Klux Zombies. Two dimwits (Greg and Matt) capture a female zombie with an inane plan to poison her, let her go and kill the other zombies who will eat her.

Note: The remaining three episodes, which had been removed prior to compiling the entry are: *8.* No Such Thing. *9.* Voodoo Zombie. *10.* Two Hits.

286 Prom Queen. promqueen.tv. 2007–2012 (Drama).

It is several months before graduation at Edward Adams High School (also called East Adams High School) and the senior class is eagerly awaiting their prom. The students appear to be just like any other high school teenagers but at Adams High it is what lies beneath the surface—deception, betrayal, gossip and sex—that will slowly surface to literally damper preparations for prom night and the crowning of Prom Queen from the five not-so-innocent girls who are seeking the lustrous title. The program charts what happens as the prom nears—and secrets are revealed that could expose all that is not right at Adams High School and its students.

The Students: Sadie, a writer for the school newspaper, appears to despise the idea of a prom (but secretly wants to attend). Ben is Sadie's brother through whom the mystery begins when he receives a cryptic message ("U R going to kill the prom queen").

Nikki is one of the girls seeking the coveted title of Prom Queen. Chad, the school's star athlete, is Nikki's boyfriend. Lauren, the second girl seeking the crown, has serious issue problems with her mother, Jill (who was Queen at her prom).

Danica, a Prom Queen candidate, is a British exchange student living with Lauren and her family. Courtney, another candidate, likes Ben and is the school's top theater arts star. Curtis is Sadie's bit-off-the-wall friend and Josh is Ben's friend, who prefers to keep to himself. See also *Prom Queen: Homecoming* and *Prom Queen: Summer Heat.*

Cast: Katy Stoll (Sadie Simmons), Sean Hankinson (Ben Simmons), Alexandra French (Nikki), Laura Howard (Danica), Haley Mancini (Lauren), Sheila Vand (Courtney), Kateland Carr (Michelle), Amy Kay Raymond (Jill), Jake Shideler (Josh), David Loreb (Chad), John Shires (Nolan), Mills Allison (Curtis), Andre Boyer (Brett), Dani Owen (Ms. DeWitt), David Storrs (Coach Zumwalt), Stephanie Furr (Mandy), Kristi Engleman (Vera), Angela Arimento (Marisol). **Credits:** *Producer:* Chris Hampel, Douglas Cheney, Chris McCaleb, Ray Wise, Laura Boersma, Michael Eisner. *Writer-Director:* Chris Hampel, Douglas Cheney, Chris McCaleb, Ray Wise. **Comment:** Each episode runs 90 seconds and presents an overall mystery surrounding the prom, the text message sent to Ben and why someone wants to destroy the happiest night for the graduating class. Despite the fact that websites for episode airings can be found, none of the episodes will play (messages like "This Video Does Not Exist," "Sorry About That" and "We Can No Longer Play This" will appear). It would seem that since Michael Eisner, the former head of the Disney Company is one of the producers, the program was well produced (TV quality) and well-acted.

Episodes: All episodes have been taken off-line. Following is a title and date listing.

1. The Long Walk. April 2, 2007.
2. Teenage Wasteland: The Video Yearbook. April 3, 2007.
3. Winning Streak. April 4, 2007.
4. Game Day Ritual. April 5, 2007.
5. Home Sweet Home. April 6, 2007.
6. Pool Party. April 7, 2007.
7. Sleepless. April 8, 2007.
8. The Committee. April 9, 2007.
9. Six. April 10, 2007.
10. Josh's Place. April 11, 2007.
11. Two Loners. April 12, 2007.
12. Mother of the Year. April 13, 2007.
13. Sex on the Beach. April 14, 2007.
14. Daddy Iraq. April 15, 2007.
15. Mr. DeWitt Threatens Nikki. April 16, 2007.
16. Play with Me. April 17, 2007.
17. U Should Come. April 18, 2007.
18. Take Off Your Shirt. April 19, 2007.
19. Kiss Her. April 20, 2007.
20. Off Like a Prom Dress. April 21, 2007.
21. Flashing Fancy. April 22, 2007.
22. In Josh's Case. April 23, 2007.
23. 2 Shades of Pink. April 24, 2007.
24. Hoplessful. April 25, 2007.
25. NSFW. April 26, 2007.
26. The Breaking Point. April 27, 2007.
27. You Can't Hurt Me. April 28, 2007.
28. Sadie's Little Secret. April 29, 2007.
29. Best Friends for Never. April 30, 2007.
30. Forget Lauren. May 1, 2007.
31. Sleeping with Danica. May 2, 2007.
32. Hard to Believe. May 3, 2007.
33. Learning Swerve. May 4, 2007.
34. Mi Amor No More. May 5, 2007.
35. This Is How I Cry. May 6, 2007.
36. Prank Day. May 7, 2007.
37. Going Deeper. May 8, 2007.
38. Back Seat Heat. May 9, 2007.
39. Sweet Dreams. May 10, 2007.
40. Sexy Teen Jenna. May 11, 2007.
41. Courtney's Secret. May 12, 2007.
42. Mother's Day. May 13, 2007.
43. You Screwed Me. May 14, 2007.
44. Sea Biscuit. May 15, 2007.
45. The Big Game. May 16, 2007.
46. The Big Loss. May 17, 2007.
47. Something's Going Down. May 18, 2007.
48. A Date with Fate. May 19, 2007.
49. Kiss and Tell All. May 20, 2007.
50. More Than Willing. May 21, 2007.
51. The Royal Court. May 22, 2007.
52. How Does It Feel? May 23, 2007.
53. The Truth About Josh. May 24, 2007.
54. School Spirit. May 25, 2007.
55. The First Time. May 26, 2007.
56. High Hopes. May 27, 2007.
57. Queen 4 a Day. May 28, 2007.
58. The Anti-Promise. May 29, 2007.
59. Webgirl. May 30, 2007.
60. Test Me. May 31, 2007.
61. Out of Control. June 1, 2007.
62. Take It and Go. June 2, 2007.
63. Sister Ally. June 3, 2007.
64. In Trouble. June 4, 2007.
65. My Fair Sadie. June 5, 2007.
66. Judgment Day. June 6, 2007.
67. Naked in the Rain, June 7, 2007.
68. Skin Deep. June 8, 2007.
69. The Prom, Part 1. June 9, 2007.
70. The Prom, Part 2. June 10, 2007.
71. The Prom, Part 3. June 11, 2007.
72. The Prom, Part 4. June 12, 2007.
73. The Prom, Part 5. June 13, 2007.
74. The Prom, Part 6. June 14, 2007.
75. The Prom, Part 7. June 16, 2007.
76. The Prom, Part 8. June 16, 2007.
77. The Prom, Part 9. June 17, 2007.
78. Green with Envy. June 18, 2007.
79. Ashes to Ashes. June 19, 2007.
80. Bad Girl. June 10, 2007. Concludes Season 1.
81. Lost and Bound. Aug. 27, 2007. Season 2 Begins.
82. Forced Entry. Aug. 28, 2007.
83. Mystery Girl. Aug. 29, 2007.
84. Sexy Bikini. Aug. 30, 2007.
85. Blindfold. Aug. 31, 2007.
86. Put Your Hands on Me. Sept. 3, 2007.
87. Bedroom Eyes. Sept. 4, 2007.
88. Episode #2.8. Sept. 5, 2007.
89. Episode #2.9. Sept. 6, 2007.
90. Episode #2.10. Sept. 7, 2007.
91. The Tooth Fairy. Sept. 10, 2007.
92. Ruse Awakening. Sept. 12, 2007.
93. Broken. Sept. 13, 2007.
94. Letting Go. Sept. 14, 2007.
95. Nevermore. Sept. 14, 2007. Concludes Season 2.
96. Destiny. Oct. 12, 2012. Begins Season 3.
97. Take Off My Shirt. Oct. 12, 2012.
98. #1 Girl. Oct. 12, 2012.
99. Knockout. Oct. 21, 2012.
100. Satellite of Lust. Oct. 21, 2012.
101. Let Me In. Oct. 21, 2012.
102. Naked in the Sun. Oct. 28, 2012.
103. Stripped. Oct. 28, 2012.
104. Far and Few Between. Oct. 28, 2012.
105. Reality Bites. Nov. 4, 2012.
106. Cry Some More. Nov. 4, 2012.
107. Starting Over. Nov. 4, 2012.
108. Poker Face. Nov. 11, 2012.
109. Close Encounters. Nov. 11, 2012.
110. Sexy Models. Nov. 11, 2012. Concludes the series.

287 *Prom Queen: Summer Heat.* youtube. com. 2007 (Drama).

The first spin off from *Prom Queen* (see also *Prom*

Queen: The Homecoming) wherein the graduating class of East Adams High School (also known as Edward Adams High School) retreat to the south of Mexico to find relaxation and escape the tragic consequences of the Prom Queen murder that occurred on the night of the senior prom.

Cast: Katy Stoll (Sadie Simmons), Laura Howard (Danica), Sean Hankinson (Ben Simmons), David Loren (Chad), Alexandra French (Nikki), Jake Shideler (Josh), Angela Arimento (Marisol). **Credits:** *Producer:* Chris Hampel, Douglas Cheney, Chris McCaleb, Ray Wise, Laura Boersma, Michael Eisner. *Writer-Director:* Chris Hampel, Douglas Cheney, Chris McCaleb, Ray Wise. **Comment:** Based on the prior *Prom Queen* programs, this too was no doubt interesting, well-produced and well-acted.

Episodes: All 15, two minute episodes, including descriptions, have been taken off line.

288 *Prom Queen: The Homecoming.* you tube.com. (2012) Drama.

It has been two years since Sadie Simmons graduated from East Adams High School (also known as Edward Adams High School) and in that time, two Prom Queen's have been murdered on the night of the senior prom. Sadie, having fled from Los Angeles after the first murder, has returned to discover what is happening and who is responsible for the Prom Queen murders. The story follows Sadie as she uncovers the clues she hopes will lead her to solving the mysterious deaths. See also *Prom Queen* and *Prom Queen: Summer Heat.*

Cast: Katy Stoll (Sadie Simmons), Laura Howard (Danica), Sean Hankinson (Ben Simmons), David Loren (Chad), Alexandra French (Nikki), Jake Shideler (Josh), Angela Arimento (Marisol). **Credits:** *Producer:* Chris Hampel, Douglas Cheney, Chris McCaleb, Ray Wise, Laura Boersma, Michael Eisner. *Writer-Director:* Chris Hampel, Douglas Cheney, Chris McCaleb, Ray Wise. **Comment:** The final spin off from *Prom Queen* that incorporates the same qualities (good production values and acting) but is difficult to follow as most episodes have been withdrawn.

Episodes: A listing of the episodes that remain on line.

1. Number One Girl (3 min., 28 sec.).
2. Knockout (3 min., 58 sec.).
3. Satellite of Lust (4 min., 3 sec.).
4. Let Me In (5 min., 22 sec.).
5. Naked in the Sun (3 min., 42 sec.).
6. Poker Face (5 min., 54 sec.).
7. Close Encounters (4 min., 52 sec.).
8. Sexy Models (5 min., 28 sec.).
9. In Too Deep (4 min., 52 sec.).
10. Zero Sum Game (5 min., 34 sec.).
11. Lap Dance (4 min., 42 sec.).
12. Breaking Free (5 min., 24 sec.).
13. The Dress (5 min., 41 sec.).
14. Captive Audience (7 min., 1 sec.).
15. Good Girls Go Bad (6 min., 26 sec.).
16. Stripped (4 min., 24 sec.).
17. Far and Few Between (6 min., 2 sec.).
18. Reality Bites (6 min., 48 sec.).
19. Cry Some More (5 min., 21 sec.).
20. Starting Over (5 min., 40 sec.).

289 *Proper Manners.* propermanners.tv. 2012–2014 (Drama).

Life in the fictional American town of Proper, U.S.A., with a focus on a group of teenagers who have just graduated from high school and facing the difficult times that lie ahead. Season 1 episodes focus on how Proper is run and how those in charge manipulate its citizens, especially teenagers. Season 2 changes the pace a bit to focus on scandals and the search for a mysterious killer that is preying on teenagers.

Cast: Hunter Gomez (Joey Sorrento), Beau Stein, Nathan Day (Jef Knights), Walter Platz (Alessandro Sorrento), Anne Sward (Blanche Crawford Sorrento), Victoria Lynn (Trinity Rose), Orion Hansen (Terence Dalton), Aaliyah Lightfoot (Breanna Summerfield), Victor Medina (Nico Lopez), Guy Nardulli (Antonio Sorrento), Rebecca Peterson (Chrissy Robinson), Tristan L. Phillips (Cody Trapnell), C.J. Prather (Zach Tever), Amy Savannah (Shila Hicks), Mia Tate (Fancy Collier Hicks), Nichele Swertfeger (Hope Rogers), Antonio Louis Gallegos (Roger Soto), Carolyn Koskan (Margot Langley), Jake Taylor (Luis Ricardo), Mark Toth (Donnie Knights), Jenny Martin (Lizzy Hinsdale), Leenie McDonough (Erin Bodell), Flo Donelli (Mari Lopez), Terry D. Gibson (Dr. Douglas Summerfield), Zach Hursh (Rock Marshall), Morgan Mabey (Nicki Griffin), Monica Mounts (Maria Sorrento), Anna Warner (Reese Polk), Emily Arnold (Trina Trapnell), Corinne Broskette (Mildred Dean Crawford), Keen Cooper (Maggie Fletcher), Amy Lia (Claire Walden), Michael Solarez (Guy Walden), Melinda Chilton (Crazy Jane), Augusto Cruz (Corey Langley), Carly Reiche (Shelly Balducci), Shawn Reiche (Sheldon Balducci), Mattea Denney (Michelina Sorrento), Terayha Anderson (Reba Collier), Jonathan Malaer (Chance Sylvan), Jon Muench (Clancey Mahue). **Credits:** *Producer:* Jef Phillips, Peter D'Lession, Brandyn Cross, Tina Rayley, Travis Victor Webb, Nichele Swertfeger, Mimi Peyregne, Gordon Joksimovich, Mattea Denney, Michelle Christensen, Theo Caesar, Valerie Burnett, Hazel Burnett, Ryan McDonald, Colby Deaton, Christine Taylor, Ernest Macias, Elizabeth Macias, Mark Loren Fletcher, Janis Race-Bigelow, Elizabeth Cobb, Paul G. Smith, Ben Sant, Ashley Eliza Parker, Jaison H. Costley, Andrew Jackson, Robin Westover, Theo Ceaser, Marc Anthony, Stephanie Kellum, Jennifer Griendal, Debbie Starr Jackson, Tracy Townsend, Mary Alice Nelson. *Director:* Jaison H. Costley, Matt Johnson, Shannon Reiche, Kelly Adolphson, Nick Burke, Robin Westover, Cate Allen, Terayha Anderson, Ean Bigelow, Hazel Burnett, Mattea Denney, Boni Loving, Alan Meyer, Jon Muench, Mary Alice Nelson, Mimi Peyregne, Janis Race-Bigelow, Nichele Swertfeger.

Writer: Peter D'Alessio, Jef Phillips, Brandyn Cross, Brian Pickard, Michael Berry, Shila Marie McLemore, Carolyn Russell, Jason White, Michelle Wilson, Kelly Adolphson, Mande Opheikens, Shannon Reiche, Robin Westover, Nancey Ahlstromer, Emilyne Guglietti, Grant Morgan, Cassidy Ward, Nick Burke, Cate Allen, Terayha Anderson, Ean Bigelow, Hazel Burnett, Alan Meyer, Mattea Denney, Jon Muench, Mimi Peyregne, Walter Platz, Ira Popper, Janis Race-Bigelow, Shawn Reiche, Carly Reiche, Nichele Swertfeger, Travis Victor Webb.

Comment: Most television series cannot compare to the amount of people needed to produce, direct and write this series. It is an extraordinary amount of talent devoted to one project (in many cases, one or two people handle such jobs on virtually all Internet series). Even with the very long cast the program is not extraordinary. It is well acted and produced and compares with many other Internet series with far less cast and credits.

Episode List:
1. Pilot. May 31, 2012.
2. You've Been Warned. June 7, 2012.
3. Fancy Meeting You Here. June 14, 2012.
4. Mommie Dearest, Part 1. July 19, 2013.
5. Mommie Dearest, Part 2. Aug. 1, 2013.
6. Meet Magnolia. Jan. 24, 2014.
7. Caught on Camera: Detective Sanford. Jan. 27, 2014.
8. Meet Sandra Sylvan. Jan. 28, 2014.
9. Caught on Camera: Morris Finkleman. Jan. 29, 2014.
10. Caught on Camera: Susan Black. Jan. 30, 2014.
11. Meet Hope Rogers. Jan. 30, 2014.
12. Mommie Dearest, Part 3. Jan. 30, 2014.
13. Meet Sheldon and Shelley. Jan. 31, 2014.
14. Frank's True Colors. Feb. 1, 2014.
15. Meet Miles Barnes. Feb. 2, 2014.
16. Caught on Camera: Alessandro Sorrento. Feb. 7, 2014.
17. Meet Michelina. Feb. 22, 2014.
18. The Mayor. Mar. 14, 2014.
19. Meet Olive Tever. April 23, 2014.
20. Inferno, Part 1. April 24, 2014.
21. Meet Sherrie Simmons. April 29, 2014.
22. Magnolia Hears an Explosion. April 30, 2014.
23. Meet Reba Collier. May 3, 2014.
24. Meet Michael Knights. May 5, 2014.
25. Clancey and Alvin. May 8, 2014.
26. Hope and Erin. May 8, 2014.
27. Meet Lizzy Hinsdale. May 8, 2014.
28. Inferno, Part 2. May 8, 2014.

290 Proxy Influence. blip.tv. 2012 (Drama).

For untold centuries a war has been fought between two groups of immortals who, to tip the scales in their favor, have each spread chaos throughout the world. Soldiers from both factions are present and each seeks to defeat the other to insure that their faction rules. The program was set to follow two groups of immortal agents, in particular Livius and Unruh (apparently representing the good faction) as they unite with other agents to defeat the dark element and ensure that the good rule.

Cast: Janden Hale (Livius), Josh Jameson (Unruh), Melody Esler (Sloan), Sephen Van Doren (Iain), Sam Kerber (Nova). **Credits:** *Producer:* Dustin Carpenter, Rose Quinn, Daniel Culp. *Director:* Dustin Carpenter, Janden Hale. *Writer:* Ascher Halden, Janden Hale.

Comment: Rather confusing program as it begins without explaining anything and the viewer is immediately lost as to what is going on and who is who. The special effects (agents disappearing in a burst of energy) are good and the acting acceptable. There is some foul language and use of the annoying shaky (unsteady) camera is not needed, especially on long shots (where you do not need to see the picture bobbing up and down).

Episodes:
1. Pilot (11 min., 12 sec.). A man (later revealed to be Livius) is seen being held hostage, driven to a desolate location and killed. From out of nowhere, agents (the good) resurrect him to join their side (as he has abilities and must train to develop them in a forthcoming battle). The episode concludes at this point.

291 Pur Aqua Mermaids. youtube.com. 2013 (Comedy Drama).

After returning home from vacation, a young girl (Siara) comes in contact with water and is magically transformed into a Mermaid. While unsure at first as to what happened she removes a stone from her pants pocket and theorizes that the stone is magical (found while swimming in a place called Pur Aqua) and caused her to become a Mermaid when she touched water. Now, accepting what she has become, Siara must learn to live two lives—ordinary girl and Mermaid.

Cast (as credited): Sydney Peterson (Siara), Aimee (Ariana). **Credits** are not given. **Comment:** Sydney is charming as is Ariana (the Mermaid she later befriends). The underwater photography is good but the program suffers from poor sound at times as well as sometimes unsteady images.

Episode List: *1.* A Mermaid!? *2.* My Tail Is Not for Show. *3.* An Un-Forgotten Place. *4.* The Call. *5.* Ariana. *6.* Episode Taken Off Line. *7.* Cursed Island. *8.* Home Again. *9.* A Full Moon. There is also an introduction video called "One Strange Vacation."

292 *The Puzzle Maker's Son.* webseries channel.com. 2010 (Mystery).

Several days after the death of his father (Garrison) in a suspicious car accident, David Harding receives a package in the mail (clues sent by his father before his death). Unknown to David, a stranger (the Suited Man) is observing him. As David unravels the clues (a series of wooden puzzle pieces) the program charts his efforts to learn why his father sent him the package and whether his father's death was accidental or premeditated—all the time being observed by the mysterious Suited Man. **Cast:** Michael Field (David Harding), Barbara S. Brown (Audrey Harding), Michael Butler (Benji), Elizabeth DeSantis (Cynthia), David F. Savo (Suited Man). **Credits:** *Producer-Writer-Director:* Michael Field. **Comment:** Even reading the episode descriptions peaks your curiosity—and the episodes, just long enough to sustain suspense accomplish the same objective. The acting, writing and directing are good and the program well worth watching.

Episodes:

1. Just Like Him (3 min., 19 sec.). The mystery begins as David receives the package in the mail.

2. Two Violets (2 min., 23 sec.). As David opens the package he finds an address (123 Ocean Avenue) and learns that his co-worker and friend, Benji has also received a package from his father (both of which were sent from Los Angeles).

3. A Message (3 min., 28 sec.). At the address, David and Benji find several landscape paintings that, when placed together, form a map of a local park. Following the map they uncover a buried briefcase.

4. Chunks of Wood (2 min., 36 sec.). Opening the briefcase, David finds two wooden puzzle pieces (that he recognizes as a childhood puzzle he had). Meanwhile, his actions are being observed—and reported to someone who apparently hired the Suited Man.

5. It's Done (5 min., 45 sec.). A flashback (to a week prior) shows that Garrison (David's father) was killed by the Suited Man—but not before he mailed the packages.

6. A Riddle (2 min., 32 sec.). As they examine the briefcase, David and Benji uncover a clue (a riddle) that reveals the location of the next two (of 6) puzzle pieces.

7. Someone Else Is Interested (3 min.). The riddle leads David and Benji to the beach where they find a brick marked with David's initials—and two puzzle pieces under it.

8. Edward von Fluffington (1 min., 58 sec.). Feeling that his apartment is no longer safe, David seeks the help of his estranged sister (Cynthia)—and learns that she also received a package from their father in the mail—and another clue.

9. The Puzzle Cube (3 min., 40 sec.). As Cynthia solves the clue (the backyard of their childhood home) David and Benji find the last two remaining puzzle pieces. With Cynthia's help, they piece the puzzle together and find that it conceals a key in a hidden compartment.

10. Peter (4 min., 26 sec.). David believes all the clues are related to his family, including his deceased brother Peter. As he looks at the key he deduces that it is from a locker and possibly located at the resort where the family spent their final vacation together. In the locker David finds a sealed thermos and returns home. As he opens the thermos and takes out a mysterious object, he is blinded by a light and shot with a tranquilizer dart. As he begins to lose consciousness, he sees a woman pick up the contents of the thermos. The screen turns to black as the episode ends.

293 *Quarterlife.* quarterlife.com. 2007–2008 (Drama).

Quaterlife.com is a social networking Internet site hosted by Dylan Kreiger, an associate editor for *Attitude* magazine who reveals incidents in the lives of herself and friends (Lisa, Debra, Danny and Jed), all of whom are in their early twenties. The program follows incidents in the lives of each of the young adults as reported by Dylan.

Dylan feels she is cursed—"I can see what people are thinking, what they want to say but can't." These thoughts are seen by the viewer as her blog's.

Debra, Dylan's best friend and roommate, works in her father's appliance store and suffers from anxiety problems.

Lisa, a bartender, "has party girl syndrome," says Dylan. Lisa is also hoping to become an actress but her acting instructor feels she lacks talent (or, as he says, "She thinks her beauty can get her anything").

Jed, Dylan's next-door neighbor, is a commercials filmmaker and shares a business with Danny.

Andy, who considers himself a "sidekick," assists Jed and Danny in producing videos.

Eric, an environmental activist, is Debra's friend, who is seeking to pursue a romantic relationship with her.

Vanessa is a rather unusual girl who is unable to make up her mind about who to date as a steady but dates Jed, Danny and Andy. Brittany is Dylan's boss; John is the musician who talks Lisa into becoming a singer in his band; Mindy is Dylan's mother. **Cast:** Bitsie Tulloch (Dylan Kreiger), Maite Schwartz (Lisa Herford), David Walton (Danny Franklin), Michelle Lombardo (Debra Locatelli), Scott Michael Foster (Jed Berland), Kevin Christy (Andy Melman), Lolita Davidovich (Mindy Kreiger), Barret Swatek (Brittany), Barnara Williams (Maggie), Jill E. Alexander (Mary), Bree Turner (Carly), Mike Faiola (Eric Greensohn), Majandra Delfino (Vanessa), O.T. Fagbenle (John). **Credits:** *Producer:* Marshall Herskovitz, Edward Zwick, Joshua Gummersall. *Director:* Marshall Herskovitz,

Eric Stoltz. *Writer:* Edward Zwick, Devon Gummersall, Marshall Herskovitz, Lucy Teitler. **Comment:** Well-acted and produced program that was adapted to NBC in 2008, but cancelled the same night it premiered (Feb. 26, 2008) due to poor ratings (the unaired network episodes aired on the cable network Bravo).

Episodes: All episodes have been taken off-line. A title listing follows.

1. Pilot. Aired in six parts, Nov. 11–Nov. 25, 2007.
2. Compromise. Six parts, Nov., 29–Dec. 16, 2007.
3. Anxiety, Six parts, Dec. 20, 2007–Jan. 6, 2008.
4. Goodbyes. Six parts, Jan. 10–Jan. 27, 2008.
5. Finding a Voice. Six parts, Jan. 31–Feb. 17, 2008.
6. Home Sweet Home. Six parts, Feb. 21–Mar. 9, 2008.

294 *The Quest.* webserieschannel.com. 2012 (Adventure).

In a futuristic time an experimental program was designed to enhance ordinary humans to enable them to protect the Earth from its alien enemies. One test subject, a boy, given the special serum, grew to acquire extreme speed, an ability he encompasses as The Crimson Blur. The program, unfortunately, has not been very successful as it has also produced "Volvers," renegade test subjects that developed a warped sense of morality and have turned to evil. The program charts the efforts of The Crimson Blur to track down the defective Volvers and return them to the test center for rehabilitation. **Cast:** Colin Bass (Crimson Blur), Randy Ralston (Jade Sorcerer), Brett Mason (Diesel), Sean Swanson (Bruce Balnowski). **Credits:** *Producer-Writer:* Colin Bass. *Director:* Sean Swanson. **Comment:** In writing, the program appears to have an intriguing premise (although it appears to be a take-off on the super hero The Flash). Unfortunately, all episodes have been taken off line and a comparison or further comments are not possible.

295 *Ragged Isle.* raggedisle.com. 2011–2013 (Mystery).

Ragged Isle, a small lobster community off the coast of Maine, provides the setting. Its seemingly quiet existence has been shattered by a series of recent deaths wherein victims supposedly drowned— but their bodies were found in areas where no water exists. When Vicki Burke, a young university journalism graduate acquires her first job (as a photographer) for Van Trundle, editor of the local newspaper (*The Ragged Isle Star*), she becomes curious about the mystery surrounding the deaths and begins her own investigation. The program follows the intrigue that follows as Vicki attempts to uncover a puzzle and piece it together to uncover a killer.

Other residents of Ragged Isle include: Rick Dalton, the local sheriff; Gus Hendershot, the local gossip, the owner of the center of activity, the Island Grocer.

Paul Soucey, captain of the principal lobster ship; Sea Bass, a clerk at the Island Grocer; Madame Clelia, a psychic called "The Island Witch"; Gail Monroe, the island's lone physician; Harrison Shaw, the seafood distributor; Colleen Drake, the local librarian; Julie Katsarakis, the chairwoman of the Island Council; Dan Therrien, Rick's deputy; Allison Thorne, an agent with the Department of Homeland Security; Rachel Moody, owner of the island bar, The Glass Jaw; Eric Burke, Vicki's twin brother, a lobster-man.

Cast: Rick Dalton (Sheriff Dalton), Meghan Benton (Vicki Burke), Ian Carlsen (Paul Soucey), Adam Cogswell (Louis Gilbert), Erik Moody (Deputy Dan Therrien), Michael Dix Thomas (Eric Burke), Kathryn Morrison (Madame Clelia), Denis Fontaine (Van Trundle), Christine Louise Marshall (Colleen Drake), Amie Marzen (Julie Katsarakis), Beth Saufler (Rose Fuller), Brent Askari (Gus Hendershot), Cathy Counts (Dr. Gail Monroe), Kathryn Perry (Agent Allison Thorne), Benjamin Row (Agent Murphy), Greg Tulonen (Dr. Brian Hoffman), April Joy Purninton (Rachel Moody), Sebastan Carlsen (Sea Bass). **Credits:** *Producer:* Karen L. Dodd, Rick Dalton, David Dodd, Greg Tulonen. *Director:* Barry A. Dodd. *Writer:* Rick Dalton, Barry A. Dodd, Karen L. Dodd, Jacob Lear, Greg Tulonen. **Comment:** Gorgeous scenery, good acting, a well-developed and suspenseful story make for a web series that is worthy of network TV. The mystery pulls you in from the beginning and keeps you not only guessing and trying to figure out who the killer is, but how the victims drowned in the absence of water.

Episodes:

1. Stranger in a Strange Land. Introduces Vicki Burke as she returns to Ragged Isle after graduating and acquires a job on the local newspaper.
2. 11 O'clock Tick Tock. A recent murder not only has locals worried but arouses Vicki's curiosity about how someone drowned when not near water.
3. Shadows and Tall Trees. As Vicki begins her job as a photographer, the Sheriff starts questioning people about the murder.
4. No Line on the Horizon. While preparations are being finalized for the annual lobster festival, Vicki begins her own investigation into the murder.
5. I Will Follow. With no solid clues as to who the culprit could be Sheriff Dalton discovers that the elusive killer has claimed another victim.
6. Running to Stand Still. As Sheriff Dalton and Deputy Dan intensify their search for clues, Vicki, assisted by Paul, seeks a different route in the investigation.
7. The Unforgettable Fire. The story behind the woman seen in the photograph that hangs on the wall in The Glass Jaw is explained by Rachel as Dan begins questioning suspects.

8. One Step Closer. Madame Clelia, called "The Island Witch" by residents, attempts to help Sheriff Dalton by explaining that she had visions of a woman (Rose Fuller) being in danger.

9. Last Night on Earth. The Ragged Isle Talent Show is showcased with performances by local talent.

10. Love Comes Tumbling. As the celebration continues and the annual Lobster Festival is about to begin, a stranger, dressed in white, appears. Tragedy strikes when his touch can kill people and a panic ensues.

11. A Sort of Homecoming. As authorities begin investigating the Lobster Festival incident, Vicki and Paul follow a different path when Vicki begins to realize that events of the present are linked to something from the towns past.

12. I Still Haven't Found What I'm Looking For. Facts about the town's mysterious secret has Vicki probing deeper and, although the clues are right in front of her (newspaper clippings on the wall), she is unable to make the connection.

13. Drowning Man. Another vision brings Madame Clelia to the Sheriff—this time to present him with a knife—the reason is unknown, "but the lives of people on the island" depend on his having it.

14. Sometimes You Can't Make It on Your Own. Another glance at the newspaper clippings (which tell of ships sinking and crews drowning) connects the puzzle pieces and Vicki believes that the mysterious deaths are linked to sunken lobster ships from the past.

15. Moment of Surrender. Shades of the movie *The Fog* as Vicki's discovery also reveals that supernatural forces may be controlling good people and making them kill.

16. Where Did It All Go Wrong? Paul believes that the only way he and Vicki can be safe is to leave the island; Vicki, however, feels they need to go back to where it all began—along the docks that are scarred by the remains of sunken ships.

17. Speed of Life. As Vicki and Paul continue their probe, they discover that the mysterious North Shore of Ragged Isle, which is considered off limits, holds the secret to a 40 year mystery.

18. Gone. Flashbacks to the island 40 years earlier reveal that something apparently came from the waters and possessed fishermen to do its bidding.

19. 40. The concluding, unresolved episode wherein it is learned that certain people living on the island are not human in the true sense as they were born in the waters off the island, can breathe underwater and have a link to what happened 40 years ago (but exactly what? Additional episodes are planned).

296 *Ravenswood.* webserieschannel.com. 2013 (Mystery).

Ravenswood is a small town in North Carolina that is home to Damon Alexander, a supernatural hunter, and his daughter Renee. While Damon has been successful in his quest to rid the world of demons, he does not have all that is required. Legend states that there is a mysterious book that holds the secrets of the supernatural. Damon requires that book and the program was to relate his search, helped and hindered by Renee, who wants to be like her father, and demons that are also seeking the book—as its possession by mortals could mean their demise.

Cast: Adrian Dent (Damon Alexander), Wendy Conway (Renee Alexander), Joshua Conway (Marcus Hamilton), Lola Sonona (Elsie Hamilton), Curtis Dublin (Kendall), Jonathan Dino (Eric Cortez), Amos Anderson (Sheriff Billy). **Credits:** *Producer-Director:* Adrian Dent. *Writer:* Victor Chaney. **Comment:** Demon hunters are not new to TV, movies or even the Internet but presenting one that is a mystery (the search for the book) is a bit different. Based on the brief teaser, the program does appear interesting and well worth watching when episodes are released.

Episodes: Only a 27 second trailer has been released that barely highlights the program's potential.

297 *Red Circles.* redcircles.ws. 2011–2013 (Mystery).

Twenty years ago, in 1990, in the O'Brien house, a woman and her brother were found murdered, but the case was never solved. The lead detective on the case, J. Arlington, eventually committed suicide (presumably over his inability to bring the culprit to justice) and left behind a daughter, Sophie Arlington, who would eventually become a police officer. It is 2011 when in the O'Brien house, the body of a young woman (Samantha) is found in the shower, covered in blood, and her brother (Matthew), found murdered in the backyard shed. Sophie, now a detective, and her partner, Jane, are assigned to the case and Sophie soon realizes that the current crime has similarities to the one her father investigated. The program follows Sophie as she sets out to solve a case that may date back 20 years and caused the death of her father. The title refers to a repetitive murderous cycle wherein the same events will occur over and over again unless someone (here Sophie) can figure out how to stop it.

Cast: Corey Arruda (Det. Sophie Arlington), Sophie Kreyssig (Agent Tiffany Simmons), Eva Davenport (Dr. Hayley Warren), Susan T. Travers (Det. Hannah Jones), Matthew Lacombe (Chief Burt Kane), Krystal Hall (Det. Allison Erics), Paul Kandarian (Hunter Jackson), Jennifer Walsh (Agent Jillian White), Theresa Chiasson (Sarah Waters), Julian Trilling (Agent Erica Thomas), Willow Jayne Anderson (Det. Jane Roberts), Kathy Sullivan (Emma Waters), Kathy Bebeau (Kelsey Harolds), Mary Paolino (Miriam Arlington), Mary C. Ferrara (Gloria Jackson), Danya Martin (Elizabeth Wood),

Evan Konstantine (Det. Eric Goyle), Samantha Gabrielsen (Catherine O'Brien), Daniel Lee White (Agent James Henderson), Timothy Bonavita (Det. Adam Hartt), Bailey Arruda (Young Sophie), Cody Flynn (Matthew O'Brien). **Credits:** *Producer-Writer:* Seth Chitwod, January Adams. *Director:* Seth Chitwood. **Comment:** The program begins as a seemingly normal crime drama to find a killer but progresses into a complex situation involving spirits, plot twists, flashbacks and flash forwards. The acting and production values are good but holding the viewer's interest is the test as such programs work better on broadcast or cable TV where there are far less distractions.

Episodes:

1. The Beginning. The body of a woman covered in blood is discovered the O'Brien home.

2. No Answers. It is revealed that the case has similarities to a murder that occurred 20 years ago.

3. Arlington's File. As the FBI becomes involved in the investigation, Agent Erica Thomas consults with Detective Sophie Arlington about the past crime, which involved her father.

4. I Never Loved Her. Facts about the 1990 case are revealed.

5. Moments in Minutes. As the case investigation intensifies, the police chief (Burt Kane) learns from his wife (Sandra) that their son (Ben) is missing.

6. Not Human. Sophie encounters what appears to be the ghost of Emma Waters (the first victim in the house) and mystically sees what occurred in 1990.

7. Knowing Nothing. As the search for Ben Kane continues, a suspect in the murder (Hunter Jackson) is revealed. It is also learned that the blood found in the shower with Elizabeth's body was not hers, but the killer's.

8. Do You Get It? As the 1990 case is reopened, Sophie learns that her father worked with and was having an affair with a fellow detective (Kelsey Harolds) while her current case has been compromised by a reporter (Tiffany) who has set her sights on digging up dirt on the case.

9. Behind Closed Doors. Tiffany begins by interviewing Hunter Jackson, the man who lived on the same block when Emma was killed in 1990. Meanwhile, Emma's sister (Sarah) is found and questioned about the night of Emma's murder.

10. Red Circles. It is revealed that Tiffany is actually an FBI undercover agent and that she has suspicions that Hunter may be hiding something. Sophie's visions of the past continue, this time revealing that Hunter Jackson is the killer but also receiving a warning from the ghosts of Emma and Catherine— "Stop the Red Circles." The first season concludes.

11. The Middle. It has been six months since the murder and the case still remains unsolved. As the second season opens, Sophie has teamed with Kelsey while the search continues for Ben and also for Hunter, who fled in the prior episode.

12. Beyond the Pond. As a new police chief (Donna) arrives to replace Kane (who has resigned to search for Ben), it is learned that Hunter is a serial killer when another victim (Mary) is found dead in her shower.

13. Elizabeth's Story. FBI Agents Thomas and Simmons join the new case investigation while Sophie visits her mother, hoping to learn something about her father's case at the time.

14. Confrontation and Altercations. Burt Kane's self-imposed investigation reveals that he has tracked down Hunter's half-sister (Gloria) and finds that she believes Hunter is responsible for the killings (started when he killed their abusive mother).

15. A Family Secret. As Burt heads back to Newport, Tiffany begins questioning Mary's neighbor (Mrs. Jones) who reveals she saw Mary talking with someone on the night of her murder.

16. Recorded Confession. Sophie learns from her mother, who is confined to a mental institution (resulting from her husband's suicide) that information about the case is contained in a safe.

17. What Tomorrow Brings. As a video tape is recovered from the safe, Mrs. Jones is found stabbed but before dying she gives police a message left by the killer: "He said to leave Hunter Jackson alone."

18. Facing the Truth. The tape reveals incidents in the final days of Sophie's father's life but complications arise when Kelsey Harolds is found dead.

19. Revelations. A flashback reveals the circumstances that led to Emma's death in 1990 (Hunter seeing her as a negligent mother, devoting more time to work than caring for her son), while Burt finds himself coming face to face with Hunter.

20. Call Me Emma. Burt, overcome by Hunter and tied to a chair, finds Hunter is furious at him for neglecting his family; meanwhile, a flashback reveals that after Emma's husband, Tom was killed in a car accident and Emma was awarded $250,000 in a settlement, she began devoting more time to her son, Bobby.

21. No Forgiveness. Sophie learns, while visiting her mother (Miriam), that before he committed suicide, her father received a series of strange phone calls that totally unnerved him. The second season concludes.

22. The End. As Sophie and Agent Thomas work on tracing the phone calls, an FBI agent (Davis) discovers Ben, Burt's son, locked in a room at the Waters house. The start of season 3 also reveals that Ben's mother, Sandra, has been murdered.

23. Bloody Paths. With Ben wanting to help the police bring Hunter to justice, he and Sophie head to Hunter's apartment. While Ben waits in the car Sophie enters—to see Burt tied to a chair, but herself caught off guard and held captive by Hunter.

24. Letting Him Go. The story starts to become complex when Hunter forces Sophie to kill Burt and Sophie learns, from a ghostly vision, that Hunter

Jackson is really Tom Waters, Emma's husband, who found a way to resurrect himself as Hunter Jackson.

25. Scary People. As a new agent (Tiffany Simmons) takes over the case and secures the help of James Henderson, a notorious criminal analyst, another blood-covered shower is discovered in a home belonging to Penny Jones.

26. A Child's Game. As the search for Penny continues, it is learned that Hunter only kills on nights of a full moon.

27. The Devil's Deal. Sadie Watson, a woman who has the ability to talk to the dead, is consulted and shown pictures of the crime scene.

28. Not My Body. Sophie's involvement in the case becomes increasingly mysterious when she receives a knock on her door and encounters a police officer dying of stab wounds with a note attached to his chest—"Trust No One."

29. Spiritual Advisors. Feeling that Emma's body may hold clues that were overlooked, Sophie has it exhumed—but the unforeseen happens when she receives ghostly images that the key evidence lies in the Waters home.

30. A Heart for a Heart. It is revealed that in 1990 Hunter had kidnapped Elizabeth, raped her and she had a daughter named Penny. Elizabeth's ghost reveals that Penny, kidnapped by Hunter, is locked in a warehouse.

31. Open Eyes, Open Minds. Penny is found by the police but the situation becomes complex when it is discovered that she is locked in a booby-trapped closet and Hunter's half-sister, Gloria, holds a remote control switch that can activate a bomb. As Gloria is subdued and Penny is rescued, a message from Sadie from the world beyond instructs detectives to search the Waters home for new evidence.

32. Awake. At the Waters home, Hunter is found dead, but the culprit is not known.

33. The Second Beginning. The third season concludes and sets in motion a plan to change the past and stop the Red Circles from occurring.

298 *The Red Project.* webserieschannel. com. 2012 (Thriller).

Jane is a pretty teenager who believes she can see people and things that cannot be seen by others. She also has issues about talking to people and discussing her feelings. Jane is also under a psychiatrist's care and has been told to create a video blog as a means of relieving her inner inhibitions. Although Jane is reluctant, she agrees and the viewer becomes a part of her life. All is apparently progressing well. Jane is loosening up (although about herself she says "I'm Jane, and that's all you need to know about me") but her claim of seeing what others cannot brings her in contact with a mysterious blogger (PiaPhasma), who has uncovered the mysterious Red Eye Project, a secretive psychological study that was conducted on select young people with special abilities—like Jane (and apparently PiaPhasma). As Jane continues her blogging, the program explores the mystery surrounding the Red Eye Project—and PiaPhasma. **Cast** and **Credits** are not given. **Comment:** Although the program ends unresolved, the warning could be a message from PiaPhasma regarding the Red Eye Project. The program is well done, although it is mostly Jane relating her vlogs with PiaPhasma seen in continually interrupted videos (like someone was trying to block him from sending them). Unfortunately, the program has no cast or credits listing (other than "Jane" and "PiaPhasma" as they are listed on the official website).

Episodes:

1. Hi (1 min., 58 sec.). Jane is introduced as she makes her first video blog.

2. Round Two (1 min., 36 sec.). Although reluctant to make further videos, Jane forces herself to continue her therapy.

3. Jane (38 sec.). The mysterious PiaPhasma connects with Jane.

4. Weird Dream (3 min., 15 sec.). Unable to rid her mind of a dream, Jane decides to document it (about her entering a diner alone and ordering a table for six).

5. Bored? (2 min., 25 sec.). Jane's inability to determine what PiaPhasma wants has her seeking a way to find him.

6. So You Think You Can Edit? (1 min., 33 sec.). Although Jane is unable to connect with PiaPhasma, he is able to contact her with warnings about the Red Eye Project.

7. Speak (25 sec.). Jane receives a message from PiaPhasma: "You don't know me. I know you. I see everything you do." Jane decides to ignore it.

8. Waiting (31 sec.). A second message arrives from PiaPhasma: "Jane, where have you been? I am waiting patiently."

9. Thank You (38 seconds). Jane responds to PiaPhasma: "I read your creepy videos."

10. Truth (1 min., 16 sec.). Jane continues to receive a series of videos from PiaPhasma.

11. Buzz Off, Fat Guy (1 min., 56 sec.). Jane again responds to PiaPhasma, this time telling him that he is budding into her business.

12. Warning! (1 min., 9 sec.). PiaPhasma warns Jane that she is in danger as her abilities have made her special.

13. Taking Some Advice (2 min., 52 sec.). Feeling that her psychiatrist may have something to do with what is happening, Jane takes her camera with her to an appointment.

14. Mission Accomplished? (2 min., 41 sec.). Jane hatches a plan to steal her file from her psychiatrist's office.

15. We Saw You (40 sec.). Jane's caper doesn't go as planned. She is caught on surveillance cameras. A message then appears on the screen: "You've gotten yourself into something way beyond your under-

standing. This is a warning. Stay Out." This is the program's concluding episode.

299 *Red Rover.* blip.tv. 2012 (Drama).

A young woman, alone in her apartment, is attacked by an intruder and killed. The killer strips her (the girl is seen only from the shoulders up) and, as he drags her body to the bathroom he is overcome by a female voice that is apparently haunting him. The voice appears to have a momentary effect on him as he stops what he is doing but once the sensation is gone, he proceeds to stab her (he is seen covered in blood). Before he leaves he uses the girl's blood to inscribe a message on the wall: "Red Rover, Red Rover, Let Mary Come Over." The message becomes the first clue the police have and the story follows the investigations of the two Austin, Texas, homicide detectives assigned to the case—Jesse and Travis and their efforts to capture him, made more disturbing when it is realized that he may be one of their own.

Cast: Danny Trevino (Det. Jesse Guerrero), Eric Robbins (Det. Travis Greene), Ryan Wickerman (Jacob Sawyer), Shayla Bagir (Elizabeth Guerrero), Michael Fensterbush (James Kelly), Jennifer Cundiff (Linda Greene), Lizabeth Waters (Emily Sawyer), Mallory Culbert (Mary Kelly), Kelly Dealyn (Voice of Jennifer Green). **Credits:** *Producer:* Edward St. Joseph, Eric Robbins. *Director-Writer:* Edward St. Joseph. **Comment:** Although only a pilot film has been produced, it is well done and acted. It could have taken a dark turn and focused on the more gory aspects of the killings but it instead chose to be a bit more discreet and, while there is blood, it is not upsetting to watch (at least not in the pilot).

Episodes:
1. Pilot, Part 1 (7 min.). The killing as described above is established.
2. Pilot, Part 2 (7 min., 38 sec.). The detectives try to figure out the clue and who Mary is.

300 *Redemption's End.* youtube.com. 2013 (Thriller).

Michael, his girlfriend, Mia, and his two best friends, Samuel and Aiden are desperate individuals who have embarked on a most unusual (if not bizarre) endeavor to earn money: robbing the graves of freshly buried bodies then selling them on the black market. With Mia's brother, Dean, and Samuel's friend, Cory, also involved in their business, the program relates the dilemma that befalls the group as they are now criminals and can they come to terms with what they are doing (does the end justify the means and can they seek redemption after crossing the line).

Cast: James Wardell (Aiden), Claudius Peters (Michael), Rowan Clift (Samuel), Daniel Ahmadi (Corey), Belinda Fenty (Mia), Gershwyn Eustache,

Jr. (Dean). **Credits:** *Producer:* Claudius Peters, Daniel Rusteau. *Writer-Director:* Daniel Rusteau. **Comment:** British produced program that presents an intriguing concept but is rather talkative and a bit hard to understand at times due to the British accents. The characters are not very like-able and are more of a turn-off than an invitation to watch. The program also incorporates an abundance of vulgar language.

Episodes:
1. Episode 1 (10 min., 22 sec.). The story line is introduced as the body snatching begins.
2. Episode 2 (9 min., 21 sec.). A friend, Cory, becomes part of the group.
3. Episode 3 (7 min., 37 sec.). The friends have begun arguing over their business, so much so, that the driver of their van becomes distracted and strikes and kills a young woman.
4. Episode 4 (14 min., 49). The girl's death threatens to expose their unsavory activities in the concluding episode.

301 *Regulators.* blip.tv. 2013 (Western).

In what is called "a steam punk future" an Old West–like city called Capitol has been threatened with a takeover by the Cardinal, the leader of a vicious religious cult group. To overthrow the Cardinal, a revolt group called the Regulators is formed and a battle to defeat the Cardinal begins. Also involved in the conflict are the city heroines, the Battle Maidens, the Outlaws (who seize upon every opportunity to steal from both sides) and the Bounty Hunters, who seek the riches offered by the Cardinal on captured Regulators.

Cast: Steven McQueen (Oliver), Aliza Schneider (D'Art), Doug Life (Isaac), Nathan McCandless (Rochelle), Rob Helms (Biff), Gregg Gansworth (Peter), Loraine O'Donnell (The Queen), Nicole Skelly (Stiletto), Patrick "Gus" Posey (Cardinal Bishop), Jimmie Byrd (Clayton), Kay Kerimian (Constance), Leanne Troutman (Florida), Elliot Fox (Dirty), Josh Dillon (Smudge). **Credits:** *Producer-Writer-Director:* Billy Horn. **Comment:** Unusual program to say the least. Aspects of the Old West (guns, attire) are combined with modern-day dress, technology (even motorcycles) and a religious-like wardrobe for the cult leaders. The acting is good and the program moves right along with acceptable choreography for the fight scenes (it can be seen that it has been staged, but is still effective). Production suffers at times from unsteady scenes (shaky camera method) to blurry images due to camera lens adjustment during shooting. Aliza Schneider, as the innocent and vulnerable D'Art, is delightful and enhances the production.

Episodes:
1. Episode 1. The story line is established as Regulators face a problem of their own—warding off bounty hunters seeking the cash offered for their hides by the Cardinal.

2. Episode 2. A young girl (D'Art) unwittingly becomes a part of the battle when she stumbles upon a group of the Cardinal's men mercilessly killing outlaws.

3. Episode 3. The religious leaders, the Cardinal, the Queen and Claymore devise plans for their conquest of Capitol. Meanwhile, the mysterious D'Art (pronounced Dart) continues her journey.

4. Episode 4. The purpose of D'Art's journey is revealed at Regulators headquarters when she asks to join (as her late father was a member) and receives a cold reception—until she proves she is worthy and is accepted.

5. Episode 5. Claymore, a Regulator, is revealed as traitor (loyal to the Queen) at the same time a Regulator member's (Peter) attempt to flirt with a Battle Maiden backfires and he is captured and arrested by Bounty Hunters.

6. Episode 6. Problems continue to plague the Regulators as Claymore, head of the Cardinal's Guard, continues to hunt them down while Peter's capture has the Regulators plotting to set him free.

7. Episode 7. As D'art becomes a part of the Regulators and demonstrates her ability to profile, an attempt to break Peter out of jail fails when it appears his arrest was a trap to lure other Regulators to him.

8. Episode 8. In the ensuing battle to rescue Peter, a Regulator (Rochelle) is wounded while the Queen learns from Claymore that an assassination attempt on her life has been discovered.

9. Episode 9. Constance, a Battle Maiden, reveals that the Cardinal "is mad" and has issued orders that all Regulator leaders (including those no longer in active duty) be killed (as traitors to the Crown).

10. Episode 10. On orders by the Queen, Claymore and his guards begin an assault to wipe out the Regulators and those close to them.

11. Episode 11. As the assault continues, the Cardinal begins his take-over of Capitol.

12. Episode 12. The history of Constance and Stiletto (who are sisters) are explored in a flashback.

13. Episode 13. In an unusual move, the Regulators, Outlaws and Battle Maidens join forces in a last ditch effort to stop the Cardinal.

14. Episode 14. The concluding episode wherein the result of the Regulator uprising is seen and the Crown is defeated—but not after many casualties on all sides.

302 *The Resolve.* webserieschannel.com. 2010 (Thriller).

Mike Patterson may appear like an ordinary individual but he suffers from a severe case of O.C.D. which causes him to have issues with humanity and constantly clash with others. He is seeing a therapist (Sean Miller) but has also found a way to deal with his disorder—eliminate those he feels are responsible for the misalignment in humanity. The program fol-

lows Mike as he begins a killing spree, disposing of those he perceives as a menace.

Cast: Russ Cootey (Mike Patterson), Alex Ballar (Sean Miller), Ellen Dubin (Megan Frost), Kristina Hughes (Alison Miller), Zachary Selber (Chad Breutenbach). **Credits:** *Producer:* Russ Cootey. *Director:* Alex Ballar. *Writer:* Alex Ballar, Russ Cootey. **Comment:** Based on the two remaining episodes, the program, although laced with vulgar language, is intriguing with good acting and production values.

Episodes: Five episodes have been produced, but only two remain on line: "First Kill" (episode 1) and "Something Came Up" (episode 2). The withdrawn episodes are "Do I Know You," "Group Therapy" and "Danny Lives Here."

303 *Rest for the Wicked.* blip.tv. 2013 (Action).

James Cathcart is a man seeking revenge for a crime he didn't commit against the criminal organization that framed him and sent him to prison. James, however, is not a man to just sit back and let what happened to him go unpunished. If the law will not help, he believes in taking the law into his own hands. His time in prison is well spent, calculating exactly what to do to achieve his revenge when released. When the program begins James has already been released and he is seen sitting opposite a young woman, whom he has tied to a chair. As he begins questioning her, it is learned he is seeking the name of a contact who apparently had something to do with his frame. As the girl refuses to answer his questions, James becomes increasingly irritated and begins torturing her, first by jabbing a knife into her leg. The pain forces the girl (Alice Alcott) to reveal what she knows—but James feels she is now a witness and kills her. When the police begin an investigation of the murder, it is learned that Alice was a police woman and the partner of Los Angeles Homicide Detective Dinah Horn. Dinah, now bitter, has set her goal to find Alice's killer and the program not only follows her efforts, but those of James, as he seeks to avoid the police and do whatever it takes to achieve his revenge.

Cast: Jose Prendes (James Cathcart), Sara Fletcher (Dinah Horn), Stephanie Greco (Sabrina Lazlo), Jonathan Nation (Captain Brody), Brent Lydic (Carl Reyes), Giselle Marie (Waitress), Steve Hanks (Gregory Lazlo). **Credits:** *Producer:* Jessica Prendes, Jose Prendes. *Director:* Josh Garrell, James Kondelik, Jon Kondelik, J.D. Koumendakis, Bobby K. Richardson, Graham Denman. *Writer:* Jose Prendes. **Comment:** There is a third episode, "Partner," that has not been released at the time of publication. Based on the two available episodes, the program is quite gritty and action-packed. The acting and production values are very good and the program holds your interest from the very beginning.

Episodes:

1. L.A. Weirdoes. Begins James's apparent crime spree to seek revenge by killing Alice then following up on the lead she gave him.

2. Blow Your Horn. James's next victim is Carl Reyes, the criminal organization errand boy, who can lead him to Gregory Lazlo, the crime boss. Unknown to James (and Dinah), Lazlo has become aware of James and has set his own plan in motion to stop him.

304 *The Riveter.* webserieschannel.com. 2014 (Drama).

England, at the start of World War II is the setting. It is at this time (1939) that Victoria and Michael Walbrook have been married for one year. When Michael is called into active duty by the Crown, Victoria, 25 years of age, and needing work, finds employment at Motor Works, a company run by Mr. Cartwright, a veteran of the First World War who was refused for service in the current conflict. "I was there fixing motors. At first I hated it; after a few months I got use to it; after a year I loved it." Victoria felt she had become set "Until I met him (George Thompson)," an RAF (Royal Air Force) pilot. The time is 1941 and a relationship between a woman like Victoria (white) and a man like George (black) was uncommon. During the time between Michael's departure (1939) to her first meeting George (1941) Victoria had written letters and sent parcels to Michael but he never responded. Had he been killed in action? Where was he? As the days passed, "It soon became about him (George)," Victoria says, "and our passion-filled moments together." Then, like a bolt from out-of-the-blue, Michael returns (wounded in action) as George returns to the war front. Not wanting Michael to learn about her affair with George from someone else, she elects to tell him herself. Michael is silent; "he showed no emotion. As the days passed we drifted apart and that is when I realized I was never really in love with him (Michael)." Victoria's thoughts are now about George and, as the pilot film ends, Victoria has returned to her job, doing what she can to help in the war effort. Additional episodes have not been released, but, according to available information, they would concentrate on Victoria and Michael's now troubled marriage, her strained relationship with George and how the on-going war will affect their lives. **Cast:** Emma Lowe (Victoria Walbrook), Jimmy Guy (Michael Walbrook), Abu Zayd DeGale (George Thompson), Donna Preston (Narrator), Lee Forrest (Mr. Cartwright). **Credits:** *Producer-Writer-Director:* Nehir Glean.
Episodes:
1. The Riveter Pilot (20 min.). The story line as described above is established.
Comment: Absolutely captivating and nostalgic. The acting and production values are suburb and the

program is so well coordinated that it is worthy of a network or cable presentation. The sentimental music coupled with outstanding cinematography and well-chosen background locales is so well blended together that the program is like a time capsule back to a time that history recorded as World War II—without the bloody battlefields.

305 *Rochelle.* webserieschannel.com. 2010 (Drama).

Rochelle, an attractive housewife and mother, has had her life shattered when her husband (Charlie) left her for a younger, sexier woman. Rochelle, married to Charlie for 26 years, struggled to put Charlie through business school and truly loved him. She received a generous divorce settlement but for Rochelle that was not enough. She wants revenge—but a strange one and the only way she can seem to acquire it is through the services of a prostitute. At a restaurant Rochelle is seen for the first time seated across a table from a gorgeous woman named Panna. Rochelle has hired Panna, a prostitute to seduce her ex-husband, make him fall in love with her, and in the end break his heart by leaving him. The program follows what happens as Rochelle seeks her revenge. **Cast:** Rosanna Arquette (Rochelle), Nazanin Boniadi (Panna). **Credits:** *Producer:* Jon Avnet, Rodrigo Garcia, Jake Avent, Marsha Oglesby. *Director:* Rose Troche. *Writer:* Scott Turow. **Comment:** A two character play that is expertly acted, written and directed. TV veteran Rosanna Arquette shines as the distraught victim with newcomer Nazanin Boniadi providing her perfect compliment. The program flows smoothly from beginning to end although some may find the use of split screens (seeing the same character in two different aspect ratios) a bit unusual.
Episodes:
1. Episode 1 (8 min., 52 sec.). Rochelle, who acquired Panna through a connection with her brother, Rod, sets the stage for her plan by hiring Panna to seduce her ex-husband.
2. Episode 2 (10 min., 23 sec.). Several weeks have passed since their initial meeting and it is learned that Panna, hired as a secretary in Charlie's company, has gotten to know her boss.
3. Episode 3 (11 min., 15 sec.). It is six weeks later and the moment Rochelle has been waiting for has occurred—but not as she hoped (Panna did break Charlie's heart—but he cried for Rochelle, not Panna; the program concludes with tears filling Rochelle's eyes).

306 *Rockville, Ca.* webserieschannel.com. 2010 (Musical Drama).

Club Rockville, a fictional somewhat grungy Los Angeles rock venue provides the backdrop for performances by guest rock bands coupled with incidents in the lives of a group of people who regularly frequent the club: Deb, Syd, Shawn, Callie and Chambers.

Cast: Alexandra Chando (Deb), Jelly Howie (Callie), Bonnie Burroughs (Shawn), Andrew West (Hunter), Ryan Hansen (Chambers), Matt Cohen (Syd). **Credits:** *Producer:* Josh Schwartz, Alexandra Patsavas. **Comment:** Although there are 20 episodes, they are short and flow smoothly from beginning to end. The acting, directing and writing are good and each episode features a band's performance that fits well into each story as situations unfold.

Episodes:

1. Solo Acts (6 min., 25 sec.). The band NICO STAI performs as the club regulars are seen for the first time.

2. The Douche (6 min., 13 sec.). While the guest band, The Kooks perform, Chambers, also known as "The Douche," tries to impress Deb and Hunter by extolling the virtues of his band, Pretty Committee.

3. Into Me (4 min., 26 sec.). Callie, a cocktail waitress at the club, gives Chambers the wrong impression when she touches his arm and he believes she is into him. Meanwhile, as the band The Broken West performs, Deb sees Callie doing the same thing with another customer.

4. Shoegazed (5 min., 25 sec.). The band The Duke Spirit performs as Deb's friend, Isabel (guest Natalie Morris), appears at the club, dressed in six-inch stripper heels, hoping to hook up with a band member.

5. D-List (4 min., 53 sec.). Explores the Douche's "D-List" guests through Jackie (Mandy Musgrave) and Nikki (Melinda Sward) as they arrive at the club to hear the band Passion Pit perform.

6. A Tale of Two Bathrooms (4 min., 54 sec.). The band Kaiser Chiefs performs as Deb, talking with Callie, expresses her dismay that she cannot get a date while Hunter reveals to Syd that he has a crush on Callie.

7. Sound Check (4 min., 4 sec.). Hoping to hook up with Callie, Hunter approaches her only to find her suggesting he ask Deb for a date. Meanwhile, as the band Oppenheimer performs, it is revealed that Deb and Hunter have a strong dislike of each other.

8. Don't Get It (4 min., 56 sec.). Shawn, the club owner, becomes annoyed with Chambers, her partner, when Chambers spends a small fortune on Air Jordans and leaves Shawn strapped for cash and unable to pay the bills. The band, Travis performs.

9. Backstage (3 min., 44 sec.). Although the band, The Little Ones perform, confusion reigns at the club when the band leaves for another gig, leaving Shawn and Chambers in a bind as what to do for the rest of the evening's entertainment.

10. Codpiece (4 min., 36 sec.). Eagles of Death Metal perform as Hunter tries to determine if Deb is coming on to him or just being playful and teasing him.

11. Brett (4 min., 25 sec.). As Chambers fails in an effort to get Callie and Deb to join him at a party in Malibu, Hunter's friend Brett (guest Michael McMillian) becomes friendly with Deb. The band Bishop Allen performs.

12. Are You Single? (4 min., 9 sec.). It is revealed that Deb and Brett are old friends while he and Hunter play a game of guessing which band member will go home with which groupie. The band LYKKE LI performs.

13. Lost in the Supermarket (6 min., 39 sec.). Callie has a meltdown, questioning what she is doing with her life, while Hunter tries to accept the fact that Brett and Deb kissed and are now going out on a date. The band Frightened Rabbit performs.

14. Fine? (5 min., 53 sec.). Deb's response ("Fine") to Hunter's question about how her date went has Hunter wondering just what happened. Meanwhile, Shawn finds that Dax (guest Michael Cassidy) is interested in becoming a financial backer—if she will do away with live bands. The band Cass McCombs performs as Hunter asks Callie out on a date.

15. Non Sparks (5 min., 6 sec.). Shawn learns from Hunter that his date with Callie was less than promising (no spark between them). As the band LIGHTS performs, Deb reveals to Shawn that she believes Hunter and Callie's date went well, but her attitude is not all that happy.

16. Yes ... Yes ... No ... No (4 min., 33 sec.). After Brett leaves Deb, realizing he has no chance with her, Deb approaches Hunter and confronts him about his date with Callie. The band Phantom Planet performs.

17. About Last Night (5 min., 21 sec.). The confrontation clarifies Deb's misconception and she and Hunter go out on a date. The following day at the club Shawn asks Deb about her date with Hunter (which she says didn't go well as she got drunk) while Hunter, talking with Callie and Syd claims the date was fun. The band Anya Marina performs.

18. Aggressive (4 min., 35 sec.). The Republic Tigers perform in a episode that finds Deb, an A&R executive with Stax Records, accepting an invitation by Syd to meet a drummer she hopes to sign, making Hunter jealous.

19. Beatles and Stones (6 min., 1 sec.). Deb's so-called date with Syd finds her hung over and being approached by Chambers, who wants her to represent his band. The band Earlimart performs as Hunter discovers that Deb and Syd made out.

20. Rock & Roll Fantasy (5 min., 51 sec.). The concluding episode, featuring the band White Lies, wherein Deb and Hunter revisit their first meeting—but not before imaginations run wild at the bar with Deb "seeing" Hunter making out with Callie; Hunter "seeing" Syd kissing Deb; and Shawn smashing a beer bottle over Chambers head when she is forced to sell her share of the bar to him.

307 *Ruby Skye, P.I.* rubyskyepi.com. 2013 (Mystery).

"There are a few things that every detective needs: sharp senses, intuition, curiosity, determination, an understanding of human nature and the ability to put the clues together to tell a story. There are millions of mysteries in the big city—and I'm gonna solve all of them" says Ruby Skye, a modern-day, teenage Nancy Drew. Ruby has a knack for stumbling upon mysteries and is blessed with an insatiable curiosity to solve them. Ruby is stubborn, smart and determined. Once she feels something is not right she will pursue it until she uncovers what is troubling her. The program follows Ruby as she solves mysteries—most often finding mishap as she rarely has a plan and plunges head first into a situation. Assisting Ruby is her younger sister Hailey, a girl who is not as outgoing as Ruby but apparently joins her for the adventure she encounters; foiling Ruby is Diana Noughton, a girl who for "highly mysterious reasons," dislikes Ruby and does everything in her power to annoy her. "And there is this other thing that every detective needs," says Ruby, "and that is my sidekick, Griffin" (who is also her best friend).

Cast: Madison Cheeatow (Ruby Skye), Marlee Maslove (Hailey Skye), Elena Gorgevska (Diana Noughton), Kevin Gutierrez (Griffin Lane), Ali Adatia (Vinnie), Scott Beaudin (Edmund O'Fyne), Nawa Nicole Simon (Ms. Springer), Kirklynne Garrett (Mrs. Gooje), Rodrigo Fernandez-Stoll (Griffin's father), Rosemary Dunsmore (Ava O'Deary), Samantha Wan (Ophelia Bedelia), Laura Decarteret (Lillian O'Shyte), Jordan Prentice (Henry O'Henry), Shaun Shetty (Finch). **Credits:** *Producer:* Jill Golick, Steve Golick. *Director:* Kelly Harms. *Writer:* Jill Golick, Julie Strassman. **Comment:** Madison Cheeatow is delightful as Ruby in a fast-moving, enjoyable series. The production values are excellent with good writing and story direction. The mysteries presented are well paced and allow the viewer to follow the clues and uncover the culprit at the same time or perhaps even before Ruby.

Episodes:
1. Animal Farm. The mystery of "The Spam Scam" begins when Ruby discovers that her neighbor, Mrs. Gooje, has been scammed out of a great deal of money.
2. Kay Eye Ess Ess. Ruby discovers that an e-mail sent to Mrs. Gooje originated from a computer at her school, the Dragon Academy.
3. Break-In. Ruby and Hailey uncover evidence that Griffin may be the culprit (the Spam Scammer).
4. A Real Green Dress. While shopping, Diana plants a scarf on Ruby, who is caught with stolen property and taken to police headquarters.
5. Caught Ruby Red Handed. Things go from bad to worse when the police check Ruby's backpack and find the evidence Ruby uncovered about Griffin.
6. Sister Act. Unable to accept the fact that Grif-

fin is the thief, Ruby attempts to figure out what the spam victims have in common and clear Griffin.

7. Stalled. Ruby's findings show that a number of people had access to the victim's e-mail accounts, including Hailey (who is an excellent hacker), her teacher (Ms. Springer), Flint, Ms. Springer's fiancé, who is lacking financial resources and Vinnie, the school janitor, who has stolen Ruby's book on detective work.

8. Scissor Sandwich. Diana attempts to make peace with Ruby for planting the scarf on her while Ruby tries to win back the trust of Griffin and Hailey (whom she considered a suspect).

9. Tossed. Ruby uncovers evidence that Vinnie and Flint are the people responsible for the money scam.

10. Seven Minutes in Heaven. As Ruby and Griffin make up, Ruby realizes that they are now in danger as Vinnie has learned that he has been exposed.

11. Best Served Cold. A chase and some trickery by Ruby lead to the capture of the culprits.

12. Dunh Dunh Dunh. With her first case resolved, Ruby sets her attention on the case of a haunted library.

13. A Well-Read Poltergeist. Ruby begins her next case, "The Haunted Library," when she hears that strange happenings have been occurring at the O'Deary Library.

14. Ava's Last Puzzle. Shortly after visiting the library, Ruby learns of the mysterious death of the library owner, Ava O'Deary and that the fate of the library is at stake.

15. Where There's No Will, There's a Way. Ruby learns that Ava apparently did not leave a will and that a relative, Lillian O'Shyte, will inherit the library (and turn it into a condo).

16. Creepy. Ruby discovers that Ava did leave a will (Ava's Last Puzzle) and the relative that solves it first will inherit the library.

17. Edmund. As Ruby joins in the search for clues, she becomes involved with the various family members who are anything but loyal to each other. Ruby teams with Ava's relative (Edmund) in an attempt to find the mysterious will.

18. A Regular Sherlock. Ruby and Hailey find that after using Ava's e-mail address, Ava's ghost has responded to them and has brought them several steps closer to finding the will.

19. On the Trail of a Thief. With her mind on locating the will, Ruby suddenly finds herself on the trail of a thief when money raised by Hailey (selling lemonade) for the "Because I'm a Girl" campaign is stolen.

20. The Final Clue. Ruby reveals Diana as the thief (taking the money to prevent Hailey from winning tickets to a Mint Chip Girls Concert). She then returns to the library with all the clues needed to uncover the will.

21. Apparently the Heir. With relatives Henry, Edmund and Lillian all seeking the library, Ruby

presents the clues to Edmund, the deserving heir (who will keep the library going).

308 *Runaways.* webserieschannel.com. 2012 (Mystery).

Danbury Prep is a prestigious private school with a good reputation—until one night, after a house party, two of its most prominent students, Kalee and Mason are reported missing. Are they dead? Have they run away? The program charts the police investigation into what happened, and if it is murder, who is the culprit.

Cast: Stevie Lynn Jones (Anne), Lesli Kay (Olivia), Alexi Torres (Trevor Anthony), Noell Coet (Keesha Washington), Kelcie Stranahan (Lily Mars), Pierson Fode (Jared), Sideara St. Claire (Glinda Adams), Karalynn Dunton (Kalee), Grant Harvey (Mason), Michael Swan (Dean Van De Sant), David Stanford (Mike). **Credits:** *Producer:* Brian Robbins, Joe Dayola, Clark Mathis, Beth Szymkowski. **Comment:** Although the format has been done countless times before (differing stories relating to a case) the program is well produced and acted and keeps you interested. Additional episodes are planned to continue the story.

Episodes:

1. Episode 1 (5 min., 42 sec.). Students Lily, Jared, Keesha, Trevor, Glinda and Anne become involved in the police investigation.

2. Episode 2 (3 min., 39 sec.). Each of the students continues to relate their version of what happened on the night of the party.

3. Episode 3 (3 min., 38 sec.). The Dean (Van De Sant) is also questioned by the police about the couple.

4. Episode 4 (2 min., 27 sec.). Rumors begin to spread that the couple has been murdered.

5. Episode 5 (3 min., 9 sec.). Anne, the missing Kalee's younger sister, begins to fear more than ever that something sinister has happened to her sister.

6. Episode 6 (2 min., 24 sec.). Stories told by the students differ, leading police to believe that not everyone is telling the truth.

7. Episode 7 (4 min., 31 sec.). The concluding episode that raises the questions, Were they killed? Did they flee? Have they been kidnapped?

309 *The Runner.* therunnerseries.com. 2012 (Drama).

Josh Rundell, a political major college student who runs a campus social vlog, suddenly finds his life changing for the worse when a professor (Ben Vale) is found murdered and Josh is arrested for the crime (based on surveillance video footage showing him arguing with Vale); further evidence appears to be that Josh was also in Vale's class and worked as his research assistant, giving him a motive to commit the crime. Although Josh maintains his innocence,

he is convicted by a jury during a court trial and sentenced to 25 years in prison. Fate intervenes and Josh, being escorted to jail, escapes when the car in which he is traveling crashes and knocks out the guard. Now, as a fugitive (but called a runner), Josh seeks to find the real killer and clear his name.

Cast: Brendan Penny (Josh Rundell), Elfina Luk (Jin Choi), Craig Veroni (Det. Lopez), Patrick Sabongui (Det. Horowitz), Alison Wandzura (Det. Jansen), Will Erichson (Kevin), Donovan Kuhl (Ryan). **Credits:** *Producer-Writer-Director:* Liz Scully. **Comment:** While not an original idea, having been done on TV in series such as *The Fugitive* and in feature films (such as *I Am a Fugitive from a Chain Gang*), the idea is still fresh as varying the situation can and does present new twists and turns to the original idea. The acting and production values are good and, no matter how many similar shows you have seen, *The Runner* presents an intriguing variation.

Episodes:

1. Things Got Outta Hand, Right? (6 min., 29 sec.). While filming his vlog, Josh is approached by Detective Lopez and questioned about a murder.

2. I'm Innocent (4 min., 5 sec.). Circumstantial evidence appears to be virtually all that is needed to accuse Josh of murder and bring him to trial.

3. Three Boys Got a Lot to Say (5 min., 32 sec.). A car crash enables Josh to escape and sets the motion for him to prove his innocence—but Det. Lopez has formed a team to recapture him.

4. Anything You Want to Tell Me? (4 min., 44 sec.) Josh seeks the help of a friend (Jin) but must avoid Lopez, who is determined to capture his escaped prisoner.

5. You Know This Guy in the Suit (5 min., 37 sec.). The stress of running begins to take its toll on Josh as finding the killer has become more difficult than he assumed.

6. You Call This a Security System? (5 min., 19 sec.). As Josh tries to remain under the radar, Jin uses her hacking skills to uncover the actual surveillance film footage recorded on the night of the murder.

7. Lopez Hell (4 min., 28 sec.). With the video footage recovered, Josh and Jin examine the film, hoping to uncover the clues they need to find the real killer.

8. We've Got Action (5 min., 53 sec.). Angie, Josh's girlfriend, becomes involved in his plight, but Josh fears she may not be safe if she continues to see him.

9. 7 Days and Counting (4 min., 42 sec.). As Josh suspected, Det. Lopez confronts Angie, determined to break her down to learn of Josh's whereabouts.

10. The Bees Are Buzzing (5 min., 6 sec.). The concluding episode: Det. Lopez uncovers new evidence that could change the course of the case; Jin tries to help an increasingly depressed Josh cope with the situation that is surrounding him.

310 The Russian Spy. therussianspy.com. 2012 (Adventure).

The Organized is a group of international spies that has been formed to stop Global Warming by stopping those who oppose such actions. All information regarding Global Warming has been stored on a non-backed up hard drive and the disk is said to be worth millions of dollars on the open market. One Organized member, Marcus, believing there is a fortune to be made, steals the disk with a plan to sell it to the highest bidder. The program follows The Russian Spy, a beautiful The Organized member, as she sets out to find Marcus and retrieve the disk before it falls into the wrong hands.

The Russian Spy, as she is called, has a classified name. She has the ability to read minds (acquired after she was killed during an assignment and revived) and lets virtually everything get in the way of doing her job (she considers herself a bit flawed, but is earnest in her desire to do well for The Organized). Unfortunately, her mentor (and superior) Silas Chalk, is continually let down by her unpredictable antics. It was Silas that recruited her when he found her as a teenager, alone after her mother's death, and stealing to get by. But, when Silas saw her throw an empty can in a recycling bin, he knew she cared for the environment and would be a perfect agent. Perfect, no, but dedicated, yes. She is also opposed to

killing and will take an alternate path as a result of the loss of her mother (she knows "the bad guys" have mothers, kids and people who care about them and can't take that away from those people). The Organized has now become her family and she tries to do the right thing for them. She also has a dog named Pip that is constantly by her side.

Silas Chalk, the founder of The Organized, began gathering agents when he saw the world was heading for disaster with borders vanishing and countries dissolving. Seeing this as a fight for one cause—survival, he reached out to spies around the world, and regardless of race, religion or gender, formed his team. Silas began his career as a spy working for the Queen of England (gathering intelligence information from embassies all over the world in covert operations for her and the Prime Minister). His wife of three years (Joanna) left him for a billionaire (Hans) and, although he is a man of high standards, he will rarely give anyone a compliment.

Jerry "Badass" Tasini is a hit man who dreamed of becoming a bartender on a tropical island—until he learned he was allergic to shell fish and had no sense of conscience. With what he felt was no other choice, hiring out his services as a killer was the path to take. It didn't matter who if the price was right. It was he who killed The Russian Spy—or at least he thought he did, not knowing that she was revived.

Kristy Knowgood is The Russian Spy's best friend

The Russian Spy. Series poster art (copyright Hop Hop Productions).

(they met at a function celebrating Wave Energy and hit it off right away. Although Kristy was there to meet rich men and The Russian Spy was ordered to attend, they had drinks together and found they shared mutual interests—sex and men). Kristy suffers from a need for co-dependency and feels slighted when she is without it. While Kristy is normally a sensible girl, her sense of logic appears to be malfunctioning as she has become attracted to Jerry and a dark cloud now hangs over her as The Russian Spy detests him and their relationship could destroy her and Kristy's friendship.

Cast: Faleena Hopkins (The Russian Spy), Ray Trickitt (Silas Chalk), Timothy Davis (Jerry "Badass" Tasini), Cate Scott Campbell (Kristy Knowgood), Aisha Kabia (Bethany Lovelace), Danny Wildman (Marcus Black), Nick Caballero (Jameson), Sue Dion (Maggie Winters), Wayne Sousa (Baako), Asante Jones (Justin Bluth), John Alton (Bob Wells), Dan Pierson (Thomas Bukowski), Christian R. Pitts (Dylan Hepler), Kim Lazarus (Alala), Brittney Pitts (Kayla Barnes). **Credits:** *Producer-Writer:* Faleena Hopkins. *Director:* Faleena Hopkins, James Roddy, Justin Teixeira. **Comment:** Well-acted and produced spy adventure with comedy thrown into the mix. The program has all the elements for a successful program but being produced in 2012 it appears unlikely that additional episodes will be made.

Episodes:

1. Thwarted. As The Russian Spy attempts to breakup with her lover over a cell phone, technology (or the lack of) prevents it from happening with a continual loss of signal.

2. Ring Tone Meltdown. A connection is held long enough for The Russian Spy to learn her lover has already moved on. But technology hasn't as her phone continually acts up.

3. Death by Pool. Not a good day for The Russian Spy—she is killed by Jerry, who also abandons the dog (Pip) she will later adopt as her own after being brought back to life.

4. Marcus. Marcus Black steals the Global Warming disk and becomes the number one hunted man in the world. It is also at this time, after being revived, that The Russian Spy learns she has E.S.P.

5. I Heard That. Another bad day for The Russian Spy: a bit disheveled after an encounter with the bad guys she runs into her ex-boyfriend.

6. Fox Fire. Kristy's infatuation with Jerry has The Russian Spy angered as she can think of only one thing—getting even with Jerry for killing her.

7. Beauty and the Baako. A lead from Bethany has The Russian Spy hot on Marcus's trail.

8. I Love You. The concluding, unresolved episode wherein The Russian Spy feels she must stop the budding romance between Kristy and Jerry—not only for Kristy but herself as well.

311 Sam Has 7 Friends. samhas7friends. com. 2006 (Mystery).

Samantha Breslow, called Sam, is an aspiring actress. Patrick is her boyfriend; Willie, her former romantic interest; Dani, her best friend; Chivo, Dani's boyfriend; Scott, Sam's neighbor; Vera, Patrick's new girlfriend; and Roman, Sam's agent. The program relates incidents in the lives of each of the characters, with a particular focus on Sam (who is seeking a better life). As the episodes wind down, Sam is seen preparing to leave Los Angeles when, in the last episode she is murdered, presumably by one of her friends (but the killer is never revealed).

Cast: Stephanie Marquis (Samantha Breslow), Michael Finn (Patrick Ballard), Moneer Yaqubi (Willie Banner), Shantele Canzanese, Nelly Olmedo (Dolores), Keith E. Wright (Roman Reid), Kristi Engelmann (Vera), Tim Halling (Scott Nichols), Karen Kahler (Fran), Samantha Yonack (Mary Breslow), Mikaela Hoover (Cami), James Hart (James), Kimberly Trouville (Kim), Jan Anderson (Leena), Keith Wright (Roman Reid), Charles Pacello (Forrester), Caroline Kinsolving (Holly), Will Figueroa (Angelo). **Credits:** *Producer-Writer-Director:* Ryan Wise, Chris Hampel, Douglas Cheney, Chris McCaleb. **Comment:** While the 1998 web series *Jamie's Way* (see entry) holds the record for being one of the earliest of the dramatic web series, *Sam Has 7 Friends* is a pioneering series in that it was independently produced with television-like quality production values and, without a distribution deal, became the first scripted series to play on iTunes.

Episodes: All episodes have been taken off-line. Following is an episode and date listing.

1. Lust. Aug. 28. 2006.
2. A Brush with Death. Aug. 29, 2006.
3. Fine Wine, Bad Boys. Aug. 30, 2006.
4. Pink Panties. Aug. 31, 2006.
5. Touch Me. Sept. 1, 2006.
6. Catch and Release. Sept. 4, 2006.
7. You're Fat. Sept. 5, 2006.
8. Quiet. Sept. 6, 2006.
9. Touching Me. Sept. 7, 2006.
10. I Need You Back. Sept. 8, 2006.
11. My Angel? Sept. 11, 2006.
12. The New Black. Sept. 12, 2006.
13. CaliCutie. Sept. 13, 2006.
14. New Headshots. Sept. 14, 2006.
15. Mother Earth. Sept. 15, 2006.
16. Shoes United. Sept. 18, 2006.
17. Secrets and Lies. Sept. 19, 2006.
18. Secret Recipe. Sept. 20, 2006.
19. Liking Men. Sept. 21, 2006.
20. The Conversation. Sept. 22, 2006.
21. Weed Speed. Sept. 25, 2006.
22. 1000 Mile Smile. Sept. 26, 2006.
23. Real Beauty. Sept. 27, 2006.
24. Best Interests. Sept. 28, 2006.
25. Naked. Sept. 29, 2006.

26. Repose. Oct. 2, 2006.
27. Party Girl. Oct. 3, 2006.
28. Dani Loco. Oct. 4, 2006.
29. Big Ol' Jons. Oct. 5, 2006.
30. Spying on the Neighbor. Oct. 6, 2006.
31. Trifecta. Oct. 9, 2006.
32. Option 1. Oct. 10, 2006.
33. Emotional Masturbation. Oct. 11, 2006.
34. Glutton for Punishment. Oct. 12, 2006.
35. Creases. Oct. 13, 2006.
36. High Standards. Oct. 16, 2006.
37. Encouragement. Oct. 17, 2006.
38. Jail Bait. Oct. 18, 2006.
39. Scott's Friends. Oct. 19, 2006.
40. Sisters. Oct. 20, 2006.
41. Tell Me What I Want. Oct. 23, 2006.
42. Release. Oct. 14, 2006.
43. Super Mole. Oct. 24, 2006.
44. Train Tracks. Oct. 26, 2006.
45. Seduction. Oct. 27, 2006.
46. Happy Now? Oct. 30, 2006.
47. Halloween. Oct. 31, 2006.
48. Halloween Hangover. Nov. 1, 2006.
49. Kiss Me Like You Used To. Nov. 2, 2006.
50. Hollywood Game. Nov. 3, 2006.
51. Just a Friend. Nov. 6, 2006.
52. A Woman's Touch. Nov. 7, 2006.
53. Ultimatum. Nov. 8, 2006.
54. Cold Comfort. Nov. 9, 2006.
55. Home Alone. Nov. 10, 2006.
56. Lost. Nov. 13, 2006.
57. Beach Break-Up. Nov. 14, 2006.
58. The Pick-Up. Nov. 15, 2006.
59. Chips and Salsa. Nov. 16, 2006.
60. Time Lies. Nov. 17, 2006.
61. Rock Star Style. Nov. 20, 2006.
62. Leena's Secret. Nov. 21, 2006.
63. Dirty Work. Nov. 22, 2006.
64. No Thanks Giving. Nov. 23, 2006.
65. Sterility. Nov. 24, 2006.
66. Sex and Trust. Nov. 27, 2006.
67. Balls. Nov. 28, 2006.
68. Possession. Nov. 29, 2006.
69. The Symbol. Nov. 30, 2006.
70. The Monster. Dec. 1, 2006.
71. Green Light. Dec. 4, 2006.
72. Uni Mas. Dec. 5, 2006.
73. She's Not Real. Dec. 6, 2006.
74. Closing the Deal. Dec. 7, 2006.
75. Guardian Angel. Dec. 8, 2006.
76. Roman Empire. Dec. 11, 2006.
77. Cleaning House. Dec. 12, 2006.
78. Final Warning. Dec. 13, 2006.
79. Samantha's Eve. Dec. 14, 2006.
80. Requiem. Dec. 15, 2006.

312 Sands of Mexico. webserieschannel.com. 2011 (Drama).

The Villa Las Palmas, a Mediterranean-style villa in Manzanillo, Mexico, provides the backdrop for a story about four friends (Daniel, Kimberly, Alex and Lucy), just graduating from college, who gather at the villa to experience a summer of fun before beginning their individual careers.

Cast: Will Green (Daniel), Abica Dubay (Kimberly), Jennifer Rouleau (Lucy), John Beach (Alex). **Comment:** While the scenery is fabulous (filmed on location) the characters interesting and the program well written and directed, it is produced as a rather talkative program as strictly light drama and enjoyable as just that. The program is available only for viewing on the official website ("This Video No Longer Exists" or "This Video Is Private" will appear elsewhere).

Episodes: The series is one continuous look at the fun and slight problems the friends face. There is no action and no cliff-hanging stories. Hence, only titles are listed: *1.* Pilot (10 min., 26 sec.). *2.* Dissolved (11 min., 39 sec.). *3.* It's All Relative. *4.* Chasing Fiction (5 min., 20 sec.). *5.* Erase Me (9 min., 48 sec.). *6.* Re-solved (5 min., 53 sec.).

313 Scissr: A Lesbian Web Series. scissrwebseries.com. 2013 (Drama).

Aviva, Corey, Emily and Niamh are four women, strangers at first, who live in Brooklyn, New York, and meet, oddly enough through an iPhone app. The women are lesbians and, although they each hail from a different background, each is looking for that girl of her dreams. The women, in their early twenties, meet at their favorite bar, Scissr and the program charts their experiences as they each set out to accomplish their goals.

Aviva has just come to terms with her sexuality and "has come out of the closet." She lives in the East Village, is 22 years old and "seeking a serious relationship."

Niamh not only feels she is in a dead-end job but her love life is just as empty. She is 27 years old, lives in Williamsburg and is "seeking relationships."

Emily, 24 years old, lives in Bushwick and is, as she says, "seeking whatever." The "whatever" is an equally beautiful woman she hopes to impress and make a commitment with; not a woman only interested in one-night stands.

Corey, having just broken up with her lover (Caitlin), is 22 years old and looking for someone new.

Cast: Lauren Augarten (Aviva), Paulina Singer (Corey), Kelly Sebastian (Emily), Jamie Clayton (Niamh), Holly Curran (Eloise), Daniel Thompson (Mikey), Alisha B. Woods (Sam), Stephanie Begg (Caitlin), Taylor Blakin (Taylor). **Credits:** *Producer:* Lauren Augarten, Marshall Thompson, Teri Murphy Thompson, Stephanie Begg, Josh Mawer. *Director:* Josh Mawer, Stephanie Begg. *Writer:* Lauren Augarten. **Comment:** Well photographed (one can see care was taken), acted and produced program. While

Scissr: A Lesbian Web Series. The Ladies of Scissr (left to right) Kelly Sebastian, Lauren Augarten, Jamie Clayton, Paulina Singer (photograph copyright by Patrick James Miller [www.patrickjamesmiller.com]).

there is some vulgar language, the women are all very attractive and perform their roles well. It is a lesbian-themed show but deviates slightly from other such programs in that it attempts to profile such women in "a more realistic world, where gay women come in a multitude of colors, shapes, and sizes." And it achieves that goal.

Episodes:

1. Pilot (9 min., 40 sec.). The main characters are introduced as they meet and get to know each other.

2. Trailer (1 min., 3 sec.). Highlights from the first episode are presented with a sneak peak as what to expect in future episodes.

314 *Secret Diary of a Call Girl Webisodes.* sho.com. 2009 (Drama).

Secret Diary of a Call Girl is a Showtime TV series (2008–2011) about a gorgeous woman named Hannah Baxter (played by Billie Piper) who leads a double life—legal secretary by day and a prostitute named Belle by night. Hannah is obsessed with money and working as an escort assures her of a lucrative income. Bambi is a naïve escort, mentored by Belle, who yearns for that lucrative income. Bambi, however, has a shaky history with the men but finds the appeal of sex and money associated with being an escort as her way of making something out of her

life. Like the TV series, the program explores Bambi's experiences with her more distinctive clients and the sometimes unusual requests they make.

Cast: Ashley Madkwe (Bambi), Iddo Goldberg (Ben). **Credits:** *Producer:* Greg Berman, Michael Foster, Andrew Zien. **Comment:** With the intention being to relate the "journey of the transition from wide-eyed eager girl to seasoned pro," the program does achieve that goal in an adult-themed (sexual situations), well produced and acted program (and a good companion series to *Secret Diary of a Call Girl* that had the potential to become a Showtime series).

Episodes:

1. Five Year Plan. Bambi reveals her five year plan for success as the program beings.

2. There's Something About Belle. Bambi and her friend, Ben, reveal their feelings about Belle.

3. Low Fidelity. Shows that Bambi not only enjoys the money—but the gifts she receives from clients.

4. Ben's Cocktail Hour. Ben, in a change of pace episode, instructs viewers on how to make his favorite drinks.

5. Kiss and Tell. Bambi reveals some of her most unusual client encounters.

6. The Morning After. Ben is again showcased as he comments about cheating on his wife, Victoria.

7. A Little Treat. Through a telephone call, Bambi

seeks advice from Belle on how to end affairs with clients that are becoming too personal.

8. The Real Pro. Bambi talks to a journalist about her business.

315 Secret Diary of an American Cheerleader. cheerchannel.com. 2012 (Drama).

Season 1: Emma Franklin is a 17-year-old girl who looks at each day like there is something to cheer about; something to reach for. Her life changes drastically when her mother is killed in an automobile accident and her father loses his job. Having to move from their luxurious home and life style into a trailer and live on a tight budget, Emma feels embarrassed and falsifies her situation, claiming her mother is a famous author and her father a big time lawyer, when she enrolls in a new school. As Emma becomes accepted, she decides to join the school's cheerleading team, the Tornados and stories follow what happens when Emma's efforts to conceal her past fail and her former life is exposed.

Season 2: The characters from the first season are replaced by Courtney, Donna and Jessica, the principal cheerleaders of the Texas Twisters, two-time All-Star National Champions seeking to win the triple crown of cheerleading, the Three-Peat. As the team struggles to win that title they encounter The Fierce One, an unknown blogger who is posting videos in an effort to unravel the team and cost them the championship. The program charts Donna, Jessica and Courtney's efforts to uncover the identity of their unknown stalker and compete in the finals.

Season 1 Cast: Neva McIntosh (Emma Franklin), Bailey Noble (Mandy), Katie Gill (Stacy), Tianna Chanel Flynn (Teisha), Kyle Joseph (Cody), John Grady (Wes), Noah Swindle (Sam), Jonathan Dane (Coach Dan), Kyle Blitch (Coach Roger).

Season 2 Cast: Kylie Muczko (Courtney), Lauren Bray (Lorraine), Juliana DeStefano (Donna), Asjha Cooper (Jessica), Rosie Newell (Carrie), Cami Branson (Jill), Mason Dye (Brandon), Quetta Carpenter (Coach Tracy), Russell Miller (Coach Steve), Macie Dickey (Jenny), Rosie Newell (Carrie), Kyle Blitch (Cheer Channel Reporter). **Series Credits:** *Producer:* Lance Robbins, Cindy Villarreal, Jason Seltzer, Aaron Mendelsohn. *Director:* Jared Seltzer. *Writer:* Aaron Mendelsohn. **Comment:** Well-acted and written program that is executive produced by Lance Robbins and Cindy Villarreal, the team responsible for the successful teenage-themed school drama, the syndicated *Sweet Valley High* TV series. Both season stories are appealing and both well worth watching.

Season 1 Episodes:

1. A Girl's Gotta Cheer. Introduces Emma as she enrolls in a new school, pretending to be someone she is not to conceal her past.

2. Painting a Pretty Picture. Although Emma has been away from cheerleading for over a year, she con-

templates joining the school's team, the Tornados, especially when she becomes attracted to Cody, the team helper.

3. Little Brother's Are Good for Something. Emma's decision to bring her brother to practice angers the coach (Dan) and arouses suspicions in Mandy (who later discovers that Emma has lied about her mother).

4. Angels in the Area. As Emma shares some of the routines she performed with the Angels Cheerleading Team at her former school, she is surprised to get a visit from her former team.

5. Emma's Secret. Mandy, having found Emma's diary, uncovers and reveals the secret she has been hiding, exposing her as a liar to her teammates.

6. A Family Worth the Wait. The concluding episode wherein Emma must face up to the lies she has told and be the person she is, not the girl she once was.

Season 2 Episodes:

7. The Fierce One. Texas Twister cheerleaders Courtney, Donna and Jessica, hoping to compete in the Alamo Nationals, find someone called The Fierce One attempting to unravel them by posting non-flattering videos and pictures of them on The Cheer Board, the industry gossip board.

8. Nothing Is as It Appears. As a post exposing the team dropping their stunts (weaknesses) appears, it is revealed that Donna and her boyfriend, Brandon, are not on good terms; Jessica is somewhat of a careless party girl and Courtney is concerned about her family's financial resources.

9. Desperate Twisters of Texas. The team's spirit is slowly dwindling as the videos continue with someone desperately trying to ruin their chances at the finals.

10. Twisting the Truth. As Jessica tries to reinstate team spirit, the girls begin to piece together evidence to uncover The Fierce One and conclude that their rivals, the Shooting Stars are responsible.

11. Planting the Bait. Courtney, Donna and Jessica plot to expose the culprit by devising a plan to draw him into the open in the concluding episode.

316 Secret Life of a Mermaid. secretlifeofamermaid.com. 2009 (Comedy-Drama).

While swimming in the ocean, a young pre-teen girl (Amy) finds that she has ventured too far offshore and, as a thunderstorm approaches, seeks shelter in a cave that she spies on shore. Although the cave is half filled with water, Amy feels safe until she is suddenly engulfed in a mysterious water fall that douses her with its mystical drops of water. As the storm lets up, Amy thinks nothing about what just happened and returns home. The following morning she accidentally spills water on herself—and is magically transformed into a pretty Mermaid with a dark blue tail (when the water dries, her Mermaid tail vanishes and her legs return to normal). Although she is a bit shocked at first, she accepts what has happened (she later discovers that her friends Brenna and Kelsey are Mermaids, also having been engulfed by that mysterious water fall in the cave). Blaire, a young girl who later befriends Amy offers an explanation as to what has happened to them. Although Blaire is not a Mermaid (at first), her mother and grandmother are. She explains that certain females are descended from Mermaids and inherit a special gene that not only grants them power but the ability to transform from humans to Mermaids through contact with water. Each girl that transforms must protect her secret and use her abilities to protect the oceans from evil. For Blaire, it began before her birth when her mother (Terra) became fascinated by the ocean and would constantly spend time in the water. One day while swimming she met a fisherman and fell in love. They married, had a child (Blaire) and when Blaire turned 2, Terra returned to the sea to live her life as a Mermaid. Blaire has been raised by her father since (the past 10 years). Now, with magical abilities and power to control water, Amy, Kelsey and Brenna, with the assist of Blaire, struggle to keep their true nature a secret while attempting to live as normal pre-teen girls.

Amy Samuels, 10 years old, is the first of three girls to magically transform into a Mermaid (with a dark blue tail). She has brown eyes and brown hair and her powers include the ability to manipulate water and create rain.

Blaire Harris has blonde hair, blue eyes, a multicolored tail and the ability to breathe under water; she later develops telepathic powers. She is the only child of a fisherman (with whom she lived until she decided to fully encompass her powers and join her mother, Terra, a Mermaid, in the ocean world).

Kelsey Cork, with her brown hair and green eyes, has a green tail. She has the ability to freeze wind, rain and snow but is not as comfortable as Amy and Blaire being a Mermaid.

Brenna Edwards has green eyes, strawberry blonde hair and a yellow tail. She was the second girl to become a Mermaid and has the ability to heat water and create fire and lightning. Her powers can also place her in a trance-like state and turn her abilities into destructive forces.

Tess Samuels, Amy's older sister, has blue eyes and blonde hair. While not a Mermaid, she suspects Amy and her friends are Mermaids and have set her goal to expose their true nature.

Cast (as credited): Christine (Amy Samuels), Claire (Brenna Edwards), Emma (Kelsey Cork), Bridget (Tess Samuels), Tessa (Blaire). Christine has the on-screen credit of Teenie989. **Credits (as listed):** *Producer:* Teenie989. *Writer-Director:* Bridget. **Comment:** Nicely acted and produced Mermaid tale. The child actors handle their roles well and the underwater photography is quite good for a low budget production.

Episodes:

1. Flip Flop (1 min., 42 sec.). Establishes the story line as Amy finds a magical cave while swimming in the ocean.
2. Heat Wave (3 min., 2 sec.). As Amy slowly begins to adjust to what has happened, she discovers that she has the ability to control water.
3. Freezer Burn. As Amy continues to experiment, she finds she can create rain and heat water.
4. Tidal Wave (4 min., 50 sec.). Tess, Amy s older sister, begins to suspect something is different about Amy when their mother goes out of town and she is left in charge.
5. Breathless (4 min., 35 sec.). Amy s decision to experience her Mermaid abilities takes a turn for the worse when she transforms and finds herself trapped in the middle of a fishing tournament.
6. Fishy Trouble (5 min., 5 sec.). Amy meets her new neighbor (Brenna) unaware that she too is a Mermaid.
7. Sea Sick (4 min., 10 sec.). As Ashley decides to revisit the cave, she finds that wavy water can now make her sea sick.
8. Double Trouble (9 min., 59 sec.). Brenna begins to suspect something is different about Amy and begins collecting photographic evidence for a scrapbook.
9. Fish Out of Water (7 min., 24 sec.). Brenna's investigation arouses Amy's suspicions and leads her to discover that Brenna is actually a Mermaid.
10. Tail or Treat (7 min., 17 sec.). A Halloween party poses a threat when water is spilled on Amy and her secret could be exposed.
11. Whirl Pool (7 min., 30 sec.). Amy and Brenna find that spending too much time being Mermaids has put them behind in their school work and must now race against time to finish a science project.
12. Blue Moon (8 min., 24 sec.). Amy's pre-occupation with being a Mermaid strains her relationship with Brenna, who feels neglected and now not sure if Amy still wants to be her friend.
13. Wet Christmas (9 min., 59 sec.). Kelsey, not invited to Amy's annual Christmas party, decides to crash it which leads to a scuffle, Amy being splashed with water and her secret revealed.
14. Power Hour (7 min., 32 sec.). Kelsey's discovery has unnerved her, causing her to have nightmares—and a determination to find out more about Amy.
15. High Tide (8 min., 33 sec.). Kelsey's probe reveals to her that both Amy and Brenna are Mermaids and, jealous, now wants to become one herself.
16. The Scrapbook, Part 1 (8 min., 17 sec.). As a gesture of friendship, Kelsey makes a scrapbook for Amy—which, after soccer practice, Amy accidentally drops into the ocean.
17. The Scrapbook, Part 2 (4 min., 35 sec.). When she learns what has happened, Kelsey attempts to find the scrapbook for Amy.
18. Germany Journey, Part 1 (9 min., 49 sec.).

Amy and Tess are followed as they and their families begin a vacation in Germany.

19. Germany Journey, Part 2 (9 min., 11 sec.). The story continues as the girls further explore Germany.

20. Germany Journey, Part 3 (2 min., 56 sec.). Amy and Tess bond in the concluding arc of the German story line.

21. New Waters (9 min., 27 sec.). Kelsey, shown the magic waterfall by Amy, ventures into it and she too becomes a Mermaid. However, the water appears to have side effects—from Amy and Brenna's tails changing colors to their appearing and disappearing on their own.

22. Practice Makes Perfect (10 min., 1 sec.). A glass necklace found by Amy is more than just glass as it provides the girls with Mermaid powers, like freezing and heating water.

23. Splash of Knowledge (7 min., 36 sec.). While out for a swim, the girls encounter (in their Mermaid form) a girl named Blaire—who knows exactly what they are.

24. Birthday Splash (13 min., 49 sec.). Amy's celebration of her 11th birthday includes a mall scavenger hunt.

25. Scarce Scales (10 min., 29 sec.). Not realizing that revisiting the cave causes problems, Amy, Kelsey and Brenna again do so, this time temporarily losing their tails.

26. Answers Found (13 min., 23 sec.). While looking through her mother's "old stuff," Blaire finds information that her mother inherited a Mermaid gene from her mother and that Amy and Kelsey may also have the same gene.

27. Wild Fire (11 min., 49 sec.). A full moon causes problems for the girls when Brenna's heating powers appear to be getting out of control and Amy and Kelsey must find a way to help her.

28. Season Finale, Part 1 (12 min., 41 sec.). Two years have passed since Amy first became a Mermaid. She has managed to conceal her secret but it now may be exposed when the scrapbook that Amy dropped in the ocean washes ashore and is found by Tess (who is not aware that Amy is a Mermaid).

29. Season Finale, Part 2 (10 min., 5 sec.). Amy's efforts to convince Tess that the scrapbook is fake and that she is not a Mermaid appear to be failing as Tess can't be convinced otherwise.

30. Hooked (11 min., 28 sec.). Even though Kelsey warns Amy that revealing their secret is a bad move, Amy ignores her and tells Tess the truth. The second season begins.

31. Briny Dilemma (8 min., 31 sec.). With her secret revealed to Tess, Amy discovers that Tess has taken her information and sent it to a marine lab and now fears the world will know she, Brenna and Kelsey are Mermaids.

32. Cabin Fever (7 min., 31 sec.). Boredom rears its ugly head as Amy, Brenna and Kelsey, stuck in a cabin during a rainstorm, must wait it out before they can return home.

33. In Deep Water (12 min., 51 sec.). Blaire's investigation into what caused her mother to change into a Mermaid does relate to inherited genes and Amy, Brenna and Kelsey believe they must also have the same gene.

34. Fire & Ice (12 min., 11 sec.). Amy tries to settle an argument between Kelsey and Brenna while Blaire seeks to know more about her mother (Terra).

35. In the Wake (13 min., 8 sec.). A visit by Amy's aunt and cousin has the girls becoming extra cautious as any contact with water could reveal their secret.

36. The Siren's Song (12 min., 1 sec.). The girls discover that Blaire has a connection of another kind—to that of a Siren.

37. Season Finale (9 min., 59 sec.). When a Siren appears and threatens Blaire's life, Amy Kelsey and Brenna join forces to save her.

38. Season Finale, Part 2 (6 min., 52 sec.) With Blaire rescued and now reunited with her mother and desiring to become a Mermaid, Terra grants her wish. The episode concludes with Blaire returning to the ocean with her mother.

39 Landslide (17 min., 8 sec.). Blaire's decision to live with her mother arouses suspicions that something has happened to her and Amy, Brenna and Kelsey become the suspects in Blaire's mysterious disappearance. Begins the third season.

40. Splashin' Around the Christmas Tree (11 min., 29 sec.). Brenna, Kelsey and Amy celebrate Christmas in a holiday episode.

41. Man Overboard (14 min., 56 sec.). As Amy tries to become closer to her older sister (Tess), Blaire's upcoming birthday party may not be the happy occasion it should be with Blaire still ever present on her mind.

42. The Lonely Islander (17 min., 47 sec.). With her parents out of town and Kelsey and Brenna unable to keep her company, Amy seeks a way to entertain herself when she has to spend the day alone.

43. Red Tide (12 min., 31 sec.). Amy and Brenna face a new challenge when Kelsey, stricken with a strange sickness that makes her Mermaid powers unstable, try to figure out how to help her.

44. Changing Currents (8 min., 4 sec.). Someone—or something—appears to be out to expose Amy, Kelsey and Brenna—but who or what is not revealed to leave the doorway open for future episodes.

317 *Secret Life of 2 Mermaids.* youtube. com. 2013 (Comedy-Drama).

Rikki and Emma are strangers to each other until they meet at school and become instant friends. Each has a secret (they are a Mermaid) but they are not sure how they became one (both Emma and Rikki recall swimming in the ocean and entering a mysterious cave beneath the sea. The water engulfed them [at different times] and when they touched water they were transformed into a Mermaid). Shortly after befriending, the girls reveal their secret to each other—and must now safeguard their Mermaid lives while still living life as ordinary school girls.

Cast (as credited): Nicole (Rikki), McKenzie (Emma), Savannah (Melanie). **Credits** are not given. **Comment:** Pretty girls, good underwater photography but poor sound hampers the production.

Episode List: *1.* The Beginning of the Tails. *2.* A Fishy Sleepover. *3.* The Magic Necklace. *4.* Full Moon Madness. *5.* Power Storm. *6.* Tail Stories Told. *7.* Halloween Mermaids. *8.* Shell Crazy.

318 Secret of the Scales. youtube.com. 2012 (Comedy-Drama).

Returning home from school a young girl (Angela) finds a mysterious ring in her bathroom. Not knowing where it came from but becoming fascinated by it, she places it on her finger. Later, when she takes a drink of water, she is transformed into a Mermaid and must now learn to accept what she has become and conceal her secret from others.

Cast (as credited): Raphael Charles (Angela), Maeve (Alex). **Credits** are not given. **Comment:** The action centers around two girls and is interesting, but poor sound and sometimes equally poor photography (jumpy picture and blurry images) hampers the production.

Episodes:

1. The Ring. Establishes the story line as Angela finds the ring.

2. Powers and More. As Angela accepts what has happened, she begins to learn that she has powers.

3. More Powers and Teleportation. Angela discovers that she can not only control water, but can teleport herself from one place to another.

4. Slumber Party Antics. Angela's slumber party is anything but normal when splashed water could reveal her secret to her friend Alex.

5. Sleepover Switch. As Angela and Alex begin discussing matters, wishes to become someone else come true as they switch bodies and identities and must now find a way to reverse the process.

319 Secret Sea Life. youtube.com. 2012 (Comedy-Drama).

While on vacation in Hawaii, two young girls, Brooke and Destiny, enjoyed swimming in the ocean but, unknown to them at the time, the salt water had activated a recessed gene in their bodies. Shortly after, when returning home (to another state), they discover they are Mermaids when contact with water causes their legs to became tails. When drying off they return to normal and the program charts their adventures as they try to live life as ordinary girls.

Cast (as credited): Michelle (Brooke), Julie (Destiny), Natascha (Lauren). **Credits** are not given. **Comment:** The girls are pretty but the program has very poor sound and is difficult to understand.

Episode List: *1.* WTF?!!?. *2.* You're a What? *3.* Pretty Little Mermaid. *4.* Once Upon a Mermaid. *5.* Hurricane Mermaid. *6.* Tail Twister. *7.* Loss of Magic. *8.* A Change in the Past. *9.* Changes. *10.* Can You Keep a Secret? *11.* No Way Back!

320 Secretly Tailed. youtube.com. 2013 (Comedy-Drama).

Friends Jaylie and Amber are walking along the edge of a lagoon when they come across two strange-looking necklaces. The girls take the necklaces home and discover, that when worn and they come in contact with water, they are transformed into Mermaids. Now, with a secret they must keep, they struggle to encompass what they have become while continuing their lives as ordinary girls.

Cast (as credited): Jolie (Jaylie), Lily (Amber), Ginny B. (Julia). **Credits** are not given. **Comment:** Nicely photographed but like others of its type, the production suffers from poor sound quality.

Episodes:

1. A Fishy Secret. Jaylie and Amber's lives change forever when they each find a necklace.

2. Party Problems. As the girls prepare for Jaylie's upcoming birthday party, they find a strange book that contains Mermaid lore and secrets.

3. The North Star. Amber and Jaylie learn from the book that looking at the North Star can trigger an automatic transformation and reveal their secret to others.

4. Just a Little Walk. As Amber and Jaylie attempt to guard their secret, someone (not shown who) has been spying on them.

5. Splashy Secret. Amber and Jaylie find their secret in jeopardy when Amber invites her friend Julia over to her house and she and Jaylie unexpectedly transform into Mermaids. The program's concluding episode.

321 Seeking Simone. seekingsimone.com. 2009 (Drama).

Simone Selkin is an actress with a minor role on the television series *CSIS: Forensic SWAT*. She lives in Toronto, has a best friend, Audrey (an English teacher) and is looking for romance with another woman. Being attractive and a lesbian does not always mean she will attract the right girl as she has not yet found her ideal mate. To solve her dilemma, Simone permits Audrey to create an on-line profile for her (under the name "Spicy Lime") and stories relate Simone's encounters with a varied group of women—from one that could be her dream girl to those who could her worst nightmare.

Cast: Renee Olbert (Simone Selkin), Anna Chatterton (Audrey), Kiran Friesen (Caramel Kiss), Sara Gilchrist (Sylvia Grihm), Zoie Palmer (Rebecca), Michelle Girouard (Elisa), David Bronfman (Stone), Mike McPhaden (Leslie), Liz Pounsett (Gina), Evalyn

Parry (Betti). **Credits:** *Producer:* Renee Olbert, Rosemary Rowe. *Director:* Naomi Jaye. *Writer:* Rosemary Rowe. **Comment:** Charming series with acting and production values comparable to any television program in the same genre. There are scenes of intimacy between Simone and the women she encounters (kissing) but nothing objectionable as all are done within the realm of decency.

Episodes:

1. Single Lesbian Psychos. New to the world of Internet dating, Simone mistakenly allows her friend (Audrey) to create her profile, winding up with something that is not really her.

2. Please ... Please Stop. Simone's profile acquires her a first date—with a girl (Elisa) who appears normal—until her true nature (a crack-head) reveals itself.

3. Hammer Toes. Simone's profile brings her in contact with a lovely musician—a girl whose music is her life and with whom Simone finds nothing in common.

4. A League of Her Own. The passive Simone finds a challenge to her life style when she meets Caramel Kiss, an aggressive woman who immediately seduces Simone, causing Simone to realize such women are out of her league.

5. Dirty Birds. Simone's sexual encounter with Caramel Kiss has her rethinking her approach to women when she auditions for a role in the courtroom drama *The Albatross Appeal* and finds herself attracted to the show's gorgeous producer.

6. Free Tibette! When Simone learns that her character on *CSIS* is to be shot and she will be out of a job, Simone makes a play for the writer (Tibette) hoping to seduce her into keeping her job on the show.

7. Tippi Hedren's Slutty Daughter. In an attempt to find Simone the right woman, Audrey surprises her with a blind date—a girl (Sylvia) who immediately becomes attracted to Simone; so much so that Simone abandons her principals of not sleeping with a girl on a first date to make love to her. (Tippi Hedren is an actress best known for her role in the Alfred Hitchcock film *The Birds* although she has nothing to do with the episode).

8. Heat of Passion. Simone realizes that she should have remained true to her principals when she finds Sylvia wants to begin a steady relationship with her.

9. Dread Carpet. At an awards ceremony, Simone finds that her relationship with Sylvia is becoming a media issue.

10. Leslie. Feeling that it is best, Simone and Sylvia decide to breakup. The episode ends unresolved as a new woman enters Simone's life—an accountant named Leslie, a girl Simone chooses on her own.

322 *Shining City.* webserieschannel.com. 2012 (Drama).

Elias Porter is a young man who works for Bestway Auto. He is married and a father and normally doesn't involve himself in the problems of others. One day, however, he accidentally strikes a man with his delivery van when the man steps into the street and Elias cannot stop in time. Although the man is reluctant to receive help, Elias chooses to take him to the hospital. On the way, the man rambles about the city being under mind control and that all citizens are in danger. He claims that he was a former agent with the NSA and uncovered information that the government is the enemy and that he must let people know what is happening. Elias believes the ramblings are a result of the accident and shrugs them off. Shortly after, however, his world begins to change when he returns home and finds that his family is different and everything around him is now strange, like he is in another world. The program follows Elias as he seeks to uncover what happened, now believing that those ramblings he heard were actually the truth.

Cast: Spero Chumas (Elias), Kristy Hudson (Annie), Anna M. Ross (Della), Derwin Jordan (Jeremiah), Les Borsay (Nurse), Jansen Lashley-Haynes (Doctor). **Credits:** *Producer:* James Hereth, Sherri Stark, Jansen Lashley-Haynes. *Writer-Director:* Douglas Stark. **Comment:** Although similar ideas have been presented before, *Shining City* does manage to present a unique twist that is well produced and acted and opens the doorway for an intriguing concept if further episodes are produced.

Episodes:

1. Episode 1: Pilot (10 min., 50 sec.). Establishes the story line as Elias soon realizes that the world he once knew is no longer the way he remembers it.

323 *Simple Events.* simpleevents.tumblr.com. 2012 (Drama).

Leanne Wright is an 18-year-old bi-sexual teenager (although she leans more toward girls) who has just begun college in the city of Hamilton. She is pretty, energetic and following in the footsteps of her father (hoping to become a doctor). While she is taking pre-med courses she sometimes doubts she has chosen her career goal and feels it was thrust upon her. Attending classes and meeting new people is not a problem for her, but acquiring money is as she is living off what her scholarship pays and she soon finds that it is not enough (and, if she drops out or fails, she will have to immediately pay off the scholarship). On her first day in Hamilton, she meets Grace Burns, a political science major who offers to help her with her luggage and help her out financially—by offering her money if she will passionately kiss her in public. With only $20 to her name, Leanne agrees. She not only kissed a beautiful woman (as she exclaims) but has made a new friend and stories chart Leanne's experiences, more comical than dramatic, as she begins her first year of college at McMaster University.

Matt is Grace's 17-year-old boyfriend, a member of the school's hockey team; Joshua, 18 years old, is Matt's brother; Ravi is Grace's overprotective gay friend, a 19 year old who fears Leanne and Grace will become a couple and he will lose his best friend; Amanda is Leanne's roommate, a sexy girl with a knack for finding mishap. **Cast:** Kate Stephen (Leanne Wright), Katie Hill (Grace Burns), Michael Patricelli (Matthew Cote), Mike Desmond (Ravi Patel), Melissa Height (Amanda Sampson), Erich Szpytma (Joshua Cote). **Credits:** *Producer:* Linda Mitton. **Comment:** Smooth flowing story with enjoyable characters, some girl/girl kissing and a bit of comedy thrown into the mix. The acting and production values are good and a worthwhile program to watch.

Episodes:

1. Pilot (10 min., 32 sec.). Introduces Leanne as she meets Grace (wearing a rubber chicken hat) and is offered money if she will kiss her in public.

2. Jersey (2 min., 21 sec.). In a panic because he loaned his lucky jersey to Amanda, Matt seeks a way to recover it before hockey practice.

3. A Party (8 min., 8 sec.). Leanne attends her first party with Grace—only to see that things are getting out of hand when alcohol is introduced.

4. Charity (7 min., 4 sec.). As money problems still plague her, Leanne sets her sights on figuring ways to earn some without breaking the law.

324 *Sleepwalker.* webserieschannel.com. 2012 (Thriller).

John Marshall is a man who lives his nightmares. For reasons that he cannot explain, he falls asleep like any normal person but wakes up in strange places and experiences horrific situations. He always manages to return safely, but his wife (Dana) is concerned that his situation is something beyond normal—but what? At this point, there are no specific answers, only guesses as to what John is and why he is experiencing violent sleepwalking activities. The mystery deepens when a mysterious man (Agent Frost) is introduced and appears to be someone not of the present (judging by dialogue, Frost is a man from the future who has been sent back in time to monitor John, whom he calls a Sleepwalker and part of a future project that has an unspecified link to the evolution of the human race). As the series unfolds, more unresolved (not even explained) events occur, most notably, what (who) are the unknown beings with distorted faces that attack Frost and what is the Black Ash (apparently something from the future that has become prevalent now and can cause a disruption to the Sleepwalker Program).

Cast: Bryan Pecunia (John), LJ Grillo (Agent Frost), Katrice Galloway (Dana), Kristian Galloway (Michael), Jodue Young (Agent Blaze), Maria Young (Agent Jade), Jennifer Leonardo (Linda Frost), Ashley Lonardo (Emma Frost). **Credits:** *Producer-*

Writer-Director: Lee Thongkham. **Comment:** Despite all the problems with the script (that being, the situations are well presented but nothing is resolved) the program is well produced with very good special effects, especially with the unknown, distorted beings. The program is well worth watching as it draws you right into John's plight, but leaves you frustrated as you try to figure out what is happening and even more so when important aspects are not revealed.

Episodes:

1. John (7 min., 18 sec.). Establishes the story line as John returns home after a sleepwalking experience covered in blood.

2. Frost (7 min., 23 sec.). Agent Frost is revealed as a man taking orders from someone in a future time who must protect John at all costs—even if it means sacrificing his own life to do it.

325 *The Slope.* theslopeshow.com. 2011–2012 (Drama).

Park Slope in Brooklyn, New York, provides the backdrop for a story about Desiree and Ingrid, a real-life lesbian couple and the problems they face and attempt (but fail) to overcome to save their relationship. Desiree is more attractive and feminine (people say she looks like Sandra Bullock) while Ingrid, happy the way she is, appears a bit older and more masculine looking (as she wears little makeup and is not one for fancy clothes).

Cast: Desiree Akhavan (Desiree), Ingrid Jungermann (Ingrid). **Credits:** *Producer-Writer-Director:* Desiree Akhavan, Ingrid Jungermann. **Comment:** A true-to-life story of two women who were lovers but have since gone their separate ways. The women are instantly like-able and they encompass their roles well. There are no nude or kissing scenes and only one brief sexual situation. There is some offensive language (referring to street-slang for female body parts) and dialogue appears to be ad-libbed in some episodes (when the girls talk about their pasts). Overall the program is well done and a bit different than other lesbian-themed web series.

Episodes:

1. Miserable Animals (4 min., 20 sec.). Desiree and Ingrid are introduced for the first time as Ingrid adopts a stray dog (a Husky).

2. Pretty People (4 min., 1 sec.). Desiree and Ingrid in a discussion about their appearance and how other people see them.

3. Queer Programming (3 min., 25 sec.). While walking the dog, Ingrid runs into a bi-sexual friend and must endure her endless chatter about a TV soap opera called "The Real Albert" (about gays and lesbians).

4. Bottoms Up (3 min., 5 sec.). Desiree and Ingrid talk frankly about lesbian positions during sex.

5. It Gets Better (3 min., 3 sec.). The women relate incidents from their past lives.

6. Open Dialogue (3 min., 24 sec.). It is shown

that arguments between the two will eventually break them up. Here, Desiree tries to convince Ingrid to become intimate with a straight couple to experience something different.

7. Harnessing Jeff (2 min., 59 sec.). Ingrid's efforts to avoid a male friend while walking the dog fail and she is subjected to his endless chatter about going to the dentist.

8. Outtakes (29 sec.). An outtake from an episode is showcased as season one concludes.

9. Taking Spaces (4 min., 34 sec.). The start of season two begins with Ingrid finding herself being hit on by a man and Desiree talking about relationships with her friend Anna (Anna Rose).

10. Revolving Door (4 min., 41 sec.). A woman (Ann Carr) becomes attracted to Ingrid and attempts to seduce her, placing Ingrid in a difficult situation as she is dating Desiree.

11. Primary Care Giver (4 min., 12 sec.). To bond their relationship, an enthusiastic Desiree tries to convince a reluctant Ingrid that they should consider adopting a baby girl.

12. Pride and Prejudice (3 min., 26 sec.). Ingrid is shocked to discover that her gay friend Markus (Markus Kirschner) is opposed to lesbians and can't accept the fact that Ingrid is one when she reveals it to him.

13. The 5 Stages of Grief (2 min., 18 sec.). Desiree and Ingrid's continual disagreements cause them to call off their relationship after one year.

14. Conversation Theory (5 min., 37 sec.). As Desiree meets with her friend Kai (Beverly Whittemore), a lesbian gone straight, and her boyfriend, Mike (Pedro Gomez Milan) she continually talks about Kai's lesbian affairs in what appears to be an attempt by Desiree to win Kai's heart and turn Mike off to dating a former lesbian.

15. Fashion Forward (4 min., 54 sec.). Desiree's attempt to move on with her life is not as easy as she thought as she still pines for Ingrid.

16. Miserable Best Friends Who Used to Be Together (4 min., 57 sec.). Desiree and Ingrid meet to discuss their joint possessions—including the dog. It concludes with them unable to resolve their differences and agreeing not to see each other again (and the dog—both leave and the dog is torn with which one to follow home).

326 *So Awkward*. soawkwardseries.com. 2013 (Comedy-Drama).

Jeannie, young and pretty, is a bit awkward when it comes to the dating scene. Preston, a like-able young man, has nothing in common with Jeannie except that he too is awkward when it comes to dating. Each is seeking the perfect mate, unaware, even after dating each other, that fate had intended for them to be together. The program focuses mainly on Jeannie's life and dating experiences and what it takes for two people to realize that, despite all the awkwardness, they were meant for each other.

So Awkward. **Elliot Joseph (left) and Tarah Consoli (used by permission of Elliot Joseph and Tarah Consoli).**

Cast: Tarah Consoli (Jeannie), Elliot Joseph (Preston), Kate Spurgeon (Brenda), Emily Buck (Wendy), Paolo Mancini (Marco/Big Daddy), Erin Boyes, Heather Boothby, Susanna Herbert (Café patron). **Credits:** *Producer-Writer-Director:* Tarah Consoli, Elliot Joseph. **Comment:** Charming series with good acting and production values. Tarah Consoli and Elliot Joseph, the creators and stars, have managed to capture the awkwardness of dating in a manner that is amusing, yet sad in a way, as two people who are meant for each other, do not realize it until something is triggered to make them see the light. Well worth watching as it also has all the elements that would make a good transition to network or basic cable TV.

Episodes:

1. I Like Intelligent People (6 min., 50 sec.). Introduces Jeannie as she meets Preston—and each finds, that after talking with each other, that they have nothing in common.

2. Great Social Skills (4 min., 21 sec.). Jeannie, who dislikes blind dates, finds herself being set up by a friend (Brenda) on a blind date—with a man who also hates blind dates.

3. What's Your Mantra? (5 min., 6 sec.). Jeannie, parking her car in a no parking zone and later discovering that her car has been towed, encounters an awkward situation when Preston offers to drive her home.

4. One Coffee Bean at a Time (5 min., 6 sec.). Explores a meeting at Jeannie's job wherein the possibility of creating a coffee app is discussed.

5. Too Much Coffee? (5 min., 31 sec.). After admitting to a friend that she drinks 15–16 cups of coffee a day ("because I like the way it tastes") Jeannie decides to control her anxieties by joining a yoga class.

6. Dropping China in a Bullpen (6 min., 25 sec.). The concluding episode wherein, after numerous awkward dating situations, Jeannie discovers that what Preston is—trustful—is what she is looking for in a man.

327 *So Not Super.* day304.com. 2014 (Adventure).

"Do you possess a super power? Do you aspire to mingle with Captain Famous and other super heroes?" are the words spoken by a woman named Samantha, a therapist who mentors would-be super heroes who have not yet developed their powers but are eager to take their place in the world and, like Captain Famous, battle evil. The program appears to be both a presentation of the training aspects of soon-to-become super heroes and of their efforts to emulate their idol, Captain Famous, a super hero of unparalleled lengths.

Cast: Julie Wilhelm (Samantha), Libby Hunt (Elizabeth), Mason Hunt (Hiss), Mike Jordan (Bob), Peyton Mogley (Papercut), Kate Schaefer (Sheila Gibbs), Rich Burchett (Maurice Lock), Gary Lobstein (Captain Famous), Ben Watkins (Steam). **Credits:** *Producer-Director:* Gary Lobstein. *Writer:* Julie Wilhelm **Comment:** Thus far only a pilot film has been released and it appears future episodes will mix comedy with adventure as the heroes develop their powers and are mentored by Samantha. The acting and production values are good.

Episodes:

1. Pilot. Samantha and her group of future super heroes are introduced: Elizabeth, Hiss, Bob, Papercut, Steam and Maurice.

328 *Social Animals.* vimeo.com. 2011 (Comedy-Drama).

Three young women (Sarah, Riley and Kate), their male friend (Tom) and their efforts to overcome their seemingly directionless (and rather boring lives) as they try to help each other find the still unknown happiness they are seeking.

Riley is a glamorous girl who is drawn to other women but whom you would never suspect of being drawn to yard sales and involved in "dumpster diving" activities to acquire the "treasures" that someone else may have tossed away. She is also adventurous and always there for her friends in the time of need.

Thom had dated Kate, but when they realized they had nothing in common, they mutually agreed to break up but remain friends. Although Tom is straight, he contends that "dudes are boring" to hang out with and delights with his female "hangout friends."

Kate has not moved on and lives in the same neighborhood in which she grew up. She is an only child and "hates most people, including her friends" (a result of being secretly attention starved). Because her situation has not changed since she was a child, she has settled into her uninspired life and admits that she is just too lazy to meet new people.

Sarah, born in New England, is a flirtatious girl who grew up in a household with an abusive and alcoholic father. Although she hangs out with two women, she is straight but has a weakness for falling for older men in uniform. Her one principal fault could be considered her attempts to project her outlooks into the people who surround her—an effort to make up for the lack of affection at home from her father.

Cast: Riley Rose Critchlow (Riley), Kate Heckman (Kate), Sarah Erin Roach (Sarah), Thom Shelton (Tom). **Credits:** *Producer-Director:* Erin Weller. *Writer:* Kate Heckman, Erin Weller. **Comment:** Well-acted and produced and, although there is more comedy than drama, a enjoyable program to watch.

Episodes:

1. Perry's Party (7 min., 11 sec.). The friends discuss the prospect of attending a friend's birthday party—something they finally agree on despite the

fact that the girl, Perry (Allison Fields) is a flake and throws child-like parties.

2. Let's Get Physical (6 min., 8 sec.). When Riley feels that she may be putting on weight, Tom agrees, forcing Riley to seek an exercise program—until actually pursuing one takes more ambition than she has.

3. Adventures in Babysitting (6 min., 2 sec.). Sarah's job as a babysitter requires the help of her friends when she is left in charge of a wild child.

329 *Social Path.* webserieschannel.com. 2012 (Thriller).

Trevor and Kevin, members of an Army Special Forces unit called Team Monarch and an operation called Raven, are now the only two members of the unit still alive. Kevin believes that Operation Raven was a cover up for something sinister and the story relates a puzzle as Trevor and Kevin seek to put the pieces together and discover what Raven actually was.

Cast: JD Hart (Trevor Daniels), John Anthony Davis (Kevin Knight), Lauren York (Scarlett Cambridge), Tommy Barnes (Peter Lux), Drew Bourke (Damon Colton), Kathy Butler Sandvoss (Heather Trent), Erin Rose (Elisha), Sheyla Paz Hicks (Kathy), Lynn Bryan (Ton). **Credits:** *Producer:* JD Hart, John Anthony Davis. *Writer-Director:* John Anthony Davis **Comment:** Although the program is presented mainly through the use of web cams, it is well done and intriguing. The acting is good and the mystery is presented like a puzzle, allowing the viewer to try and piece it together as Trevor and Kevin uncover its many parts. The scenes with The Stranger are quite bad as it is very difficult to understand what he is saying—and he holds the key to what Raven is all about.

Episodes:

1. A Matter of Trust (7 min., 10 sec.). After having been missing for several weeks, Kevin contacts Trevor via an encrypted video link telling him that their experiences with Team Monarch go beyond what they knew.

2. What Was, What Is and What Will Be (12 min., 15 sec.). Kevin believes that because they are the only two members left, that their team has been marked for elimination.

3. The Return (10 min., 5 sec.). Trevor and Kevin find help from Sara Trent, a friend of Trevor's, who has been with the Company (the organization that oversaw Raven) for over 10 years and believes there was something sinister behind Operation Raven.

4. Folio Deux (7 min., 56 sec.). Although Kevin is using an encrypted video link, a man (The Stranger) breaks in and tells Kevin that he knows about Project Raven.

5. 'Twas Not a Dream (7 min., 18 sec.). Kevin informs Trevor about the Stranger while Sara begins her quest to uncover documents about Raven.

6. The Enemy Is Time (10 min., 5 sec.). The Stranger again contacts Kevin, this time telling him that his suspicions about Raven are right—that it was something sinister.

7. Absence of Malice (7 min., 18 sec.). The Stranger reveals that Operation Raven was a cover up for a genetics experiment that he created and that Monarch was actually a cover for mind control.

8. Placating the Mind (10 min., 52 sec.). Trevor and Kevin find that after talking with The Stranger, they are implicated in something, but still have more questions than answers.

9. Complacency (7 min., 17 sec.). The Stranger reveals that Trevor and Kevin's genetic structures were altered and a chip placed in their head.

10. Beguiled (9 min., 32 sec.). Scarlett Cambridge, a woman associated with The Stranger, tells Trevor and Kevin that the chip was meant to decipher specific information and control their actions.

11. Transverse (6 min., 37 sec.). Trevor learns that he and Kevin were given blood from a line that extends back many centuries and is rooted in evil.

12. Era-dict Reason (5 min., 18 sec.). The Stranger reveals that Raven was a project to take over the world and that he, Trevor and Kevin are the key elements in stopping it.

13. R:6:8 (6 min., 3 sec.). Peter Lux, a friend of The Stranger warns Trevor that the situation is becoming dangerous as Project Raven officials will kill anyone that starts digging into the project.

14. Unrecognizable Distraction (7 min., 39 sec.). Peter reveals that Project Raven was connected to a program wherein population control was the key factor in taking over the world.

15. What Was Is No More (7 min.). Trevor and Kevin learn that where Hitler failed in World War II to control the world, Project Raven is an extension of that goal.

16. The Dog Throw (8 min., 30 sec.). Heather, the sister of one of Raven's late team members (Blake), reveals to Trevor and Kevin that she noticed sudden changes in Blake's behavior before he was killed.

17. Liars and Magicians (9 min., 5 sec.). Kevin, who had taken to the road to seek out former contacts, returns empty handed as all traces of Project Raven have been covered up.

18. Rook to C2 (8 min., 36 sec.). After discussing recent developments, The Stranger tells Trevor and Kevin that they are chess pieces in a game—Check and Checkmate and the only ones who can expose Project Raven.

19. Machination (9 min., 46 sec.). A new player enters the picture—Damon Colton, a man who has been sent to fix what Trevor and Kevin have "dismantled, broken and set off course."

Note: 12 additional, second season episodes have been produced but only the first of these episodes ("Kubark: Dear Alice," which runs 9 min. and 28 sec.) has aired and picks up the story with The

Stranger continuing his quest to expose Project Raven and stop a world take over by persons unknown. The other episodes: *The Sabaean Tear, Powers and Dominions, V.M.A.2, The Mengele Manifesto, White Rabbit, A Traveling Man, Blood Dimmed Tide, Nocturnal Rapport, Sagacity in B-Minor, Nefarious Deluge* and *XII: Der Tod.*

330 *Sofia's Diary.* ovguide.com. 2008–2009 (Drama).

Sofia Taylor is a 17-year-old girl who lives with her stepmother and stepsister (Trisha) and stepbrother ("The Devil Child"). She lives in Stockport, England and posts her daily activities (her diary) on line for her friends (and viewers) to read. When her mother discovers ecstasy drugs in her bedroom and feels Sofia is heading down the wrong path, she sends her to live with her father (Simon) and his new wife (Emma) in London. It is here that Sofia acquires a job at *Wicked Magazine* and stories follow the incidents that affect her life and those of her friends through the videos she uploads on a daily basis.

Season 1: Episodes establish the format as Sophia makes the move from Stockport to London, enrolls in a new school, makes new friends and acquires a magazine job.

Season 2: As Sofia uploads her videos, she focuses particularly on her friend, Jill, and their struggles with the decisions they must make for their future happiness.

Season 3: Continues the thought presented in the prior season with Sofia and Jill hoping to accomplish what they set out to do, especially when *Wicked Magazine* folds and Sofia must re-direct her energies to acquire a new job, and Jill, struggling to become an established singer, finds interest from a record label.

Other Characters: Jill Johnson, Sophia's best friend, a hopeful singer; Alice Clayton Smith, Sophia's boss at *Wicked Magazine*; Sean Walker, Sofia and Jill's best friend, a musician; Rebecca Nixon, an employee at *Wicked* who taunts Sophia, hoping to get even for her dating the boy she liked (Josh Angelo, who also worked for *Wicked*); Simon Taylor, Sophia's father, now married to Emma.

Cast: Rachel Hyde Harvey (Sofia Taylor), Lauren Gordon (Jill Johnson), Heidi Monsen (Alice Clayton Smith), Junior Nunoo (Charles), Joseph Cappellazzi (Ioan), Georgina Leahy (Rebecca), Alex Rendell (Trellick), Raphael Peart (Scratch), James Nield (Josh Angelo), Lucia Giannecchini (Emma), David Avery (Flex), Ben Farrow (Tom), Adam Blake (Fin), David Avery (Flex), Billie Fulford-Brown (Summer), Isaac Olajun (Mikey), Andrea Coombs (Jackie). **Credits:** *Producer:* Debbie Nightingale, Triona Campbell, Nuno Bernardo, Serena Cullen, Antony Root, Trevor Curran. *Director:* Adam Linzey, Manny Bonnet. *Writer:* Pippa Hinchley, Melanie Martinez, Helen Bagnall, David Lemon, Nuno Bernardo, Marta Gomes, Danny Stack. **Comment:** The British-produced program does sound interesting to read, but what actually transpired by way of a video production is not possible to present as not even a trailer (or teaser) remains on line.

Episodes: 130 Episodes were produced, all of which have been taken off-line (including titles).

331 *Something Fishy.* youtube.com. 2011 (Comedy-Drama).

While studying (hoping to get better grades in Social Studies) a young girl (Alyssa) decides to take a break and goes to the kitchen for a drink. She removes what appears to be an ordinary pitcher of liquid but, upon drinking it, she transforms into a Mermaid. She is also perplexed—as to what happened (it is not explained what the liquid is or how it got into the refrigerator) but she soon exclaims "Totally Awesome!" Awesome or not, Alyssa must now learn to lead two lives—Mermaid and ordinary girl.

Cast (as credited): Ale Maria (Alyssa). **Credits** are not given. **Comment:** Ale Maria is pretty but the scenes are not well lit and her dog's barking overpowers some of her dialogue. It can also be heard that someone (possibly

Sofia's Diary. **Poster art from the series (copyright beActive Entertainment).**

her mother) is giving Ale verbal cues as what to do during certain scenes. Had any additional episodes been produced they would have no doubt explained the liquid Alyssa drank and how it turned her into a Mermaid.

Episodes:
1. Something Fishy Pilot. The story line is established as indicated above.

332 *Sorority Forever.* wb.com. 2008 (Comedy-Drama).

A college sorority (Phi Chi Kappa) provides the backdrop for a program that combines mystery, suspense and drama to focus on four new inductee freshmen, especially Julie Gold, as she slowly learns that all is not as innocent as it seems and that Phi Chi Kappa conceals many dark secrets of lies and deception.

Cast: Jessica Rose (Julie Gold), Anabella Cassanova (Bridget Reynolds), Mikaela Hoover (Madison Westerbrook), Taryn Southern (Taryn Monaghan), Angie Cole (Naomi King), Annemarie Pazmino (Rachel), Candice Patton (Mercedes Muna), Joaquin Pastor (Joaquin), David Loren (Matthew), Merc Boyan (Eric Blair), Cary Hungerford (Blake), Jessica Morris (Natalie Gold), Oriana Layendecker (Debra). **Credits:** *Producer:* Douglas Cheney, Chris Hampel, Chris McCaleb, Ryan Wise, McG. *Director:* Chris Hampel, Ryan Wise, Douglas Cheney, Chris McCaleb. *Writer:* Chris Hampel, Chris McCaleb, Ryan Wise, Douglas Cheney. **Comment:** Based on reviews that have appeared, reaction was both good (keeps your interest despite the short, 90 second episodes) and bad (no consistency to the story). Being that it was produced in part by McG (TV's *Supernatural*) and had the WB network behind it, acting and production values were no doubt very good.

Episodes: All episodes have been taken off-line. The following is a presentation of the weekly installments with the episodes that comprise that week's story line.

1. **Week 1.** The story line is established as four freshmen arrive at school and begin their tasks as pledges for Phi Chi Kappa Sorority. The episodes: *1.* Sisterhood. *2.* Terrible Mistake. *3.* Sexy Bra Shopping. *4.* Panty Pledge. *5.* Nobody Likes a Fat Girl.

2. **Week 2.** The pledges attend their first party at the Omega House Fraternity while Julie begins dating "The Forbidden Joaquin." Also adding to their misery is the "Weigh-In" for the annual Greek Week festivities. The episodes: *6.* Omega Party. *7.* Ribs. *8.* Sacrifice. *9.* Crush Party. *10.* Makin' Moves.

3. **Week 3.** A rivalry erupts between Madison and Taryn over a student (Matthew); Julie's curiosity about a mysterious Red Door in the sorority house is starting to get the best of her and she feels she needs to find out what's on the other side. The episodes: *11.* Control the Girls. *12.* Reputation. *13.*

I Kissed a Girl. *14.* Weigh-in Day. *15.* Sluts Will Be Pigs.

4. **Week 4.** As Julie suspects there is something more about Joaquin than he is revealing, the girls of Phi Chi Kappa compete against the girls of the Delta Delta Gamma Sorority in a muddy football game. The pledges attempt to raise money for charity by holding an all you can drink event. The episodes: *16.* Mud Bowl. *17.* Drunk Chicks. *18.* Beach Body. *19.* Lip Sync. *20.* Wanna Dance.

5. **Week 5.** Unable to control her curiosity, Julie makes preparations to discover what is behind the Red Door. Meanwhile Taryn is unaware that her life is in danger. The episodes: *21.* Hooknasty. *22.* The Omega Thing. *23.* Every Sister Has a Secret Bark at Her. *24.* Summer Love. *25.* Is This Really You?

6. **Week 6.** As the pledge week festivities begin tragedy strikes when one of the pledges (Taryn) is poisoned. The episodes: *26.* Girl on Girl. *27.* Return to Sender. *28.* They Can't Be Trusted. *29.* Deeper. *30.* Hard Pill to Swallow.

7. **Week 7.** As the school mourns the death of Taryn, Julie and Joaquin devise a plan that will allow them to open the Red Door. The episodes: *31.* Snuff Film. *32.* Bondage. *33.* Give It to Me. *34.* Slippery When Wet. *35.* Womanizer.

8. **Week 8.** The concluding five episodes that find Natalie, Julie's sister, pleading with her not to pledge Phi Chi Kappa and Julie determined to solve the mystery of what is behind the Red Door. The episodes: *36.* Womanizer. *37.* Is There Anything I Can Do to You? *38.* Lust and Sacrifice. *39.* The Red Door. *40.* Aurora.

333 *South Beach Undercover.* youtube.com. 2008 (Crime Drama).

Fabrizio Brienza is a former model who, though successful, yearned to become a police officer and gave up the runway for a badge—with the South Beach Police Department in Miami, Florida. Fabrizio is not the typical police detective as he thrives on breaking the rules and doing things his way. While Farbrizio works as a plainclothes detective (and sometimes undercover) he has made enemies of numerous people (including local mobsters) for his relentless pursuit of justice; but his lack of taking responsibility for the havoc he causes in that pursuit has also upset the Police Chief, who believes Fabrizio may be more of a liability than an asset. The program follows Fabrizio and his partner, Officer Martinez's case assignments—assignments that are anything but normal as Fabrizio has a knack for doing all the wrong things at the wrong time.

Cast: Fabrizio Brienza (Fabrizio), Lourdes Telena (Officer Martinez), Vincent D'Rosa (Don Vincento), Klodi Lemoine (The Bodyguard), Eduardo Kean (the Chief). **Credits:** *Producer-Director:* Luciano Alexandresco. *Writer:* Vincent DiRosa. **Comment:** Aspects of The TV series *Miami Vice* (costumes, music) and *Nash Bridges* (his car, a 1971 challenger) can be seen throughout the *South Beach Undercover* series. The program is fast-moving with acceptable acting and production values.

Episodes:

1. Meet the Bosses (2 min., 43 sec.). Mob boss Don Vincento is non-too happy with Fabrizio for interfering in his syndicated operations and plans to do something about it.

2. The Boss Story (2 min., 27 sec.). A criminal, with a passion for stealing first cars, then boats, then planes, meets a boss's wife. The wife, so taken by the crook, kills her husband, runs off with her new lover and sets Fabrizio on the path to find her.

3. The Tale of Two Bulls (2 min., 40 sec.). Fabrizio and Martinez are called into the Chief's office to explain recent happenings involving the death of a big boss (from the prior episode) and their inability to find the wife.

4. The Arrest (2 min., 39 sec.). A drug sting, set up by Fabrizio and Martinez goes wrong when Fabrizio and Martinez bust an undercover cop also working on the case.

5. The Punishment (2 min., 40 sec.). Fabrizio and Martinez, again called before the Chief, try to explain their way out of the drug bust blunder.

6. Finale (2 min., 40 sec.). Fabrizio's explanation was not his best doing as he and Martinez are busted to bicycle patrolling. The program's concluding episode.

334 *Spell Bound Tails.* youtube.com. 2012 (Comedy-Drama).

Hoping to discover more about her late mother, a young girl (Phoebe) finds a box that contains a false bottom. In it is a piece of paper (actually a spell) that, when Phoebe reads, transforms her into a Mermaid when she comes in contact with water. The program follows Phoebe as she navigates life as both girl and a Mermaid.

Cast (as credited): Raegan (Phoebe Wavly), Kaylyn (Alisandra Harris), Marlena (Violet Wavly). **Credits** are not given. **Comment:** Good underwater photography but poor sound quality hampers the production.

Episodes:

1. Pilot (14 min., 34 sec.). The story line is established when Phoebe finds the box.

2. Episode 2 (9 min., 34 sec.). As Phoebe reveals to her best friend (Alisandra, called Ali) that she is a Mermaid, Ali surprises her with the fact that she too is a Mermaid.

3. Episode 3 (12 min., 35 sec.). As the girls discuss what has happened to them they each learn they have powers that can control water.

4. Episode 4 (8 min., 46 sec.). Ali's attempts to play practical jokes on Phoebe backfires with Phoebe getting annoyed and leaves Ali.

5. Episode 5 (11 min., 28 sec.). After making up, Phoebe tries to help Ali, who appears to have a cold—but her efforts to help with a potion turn Ali into a boy.

6. Episode 6 (9 min., 31 sec.). With the spell reversed and Ali back to being a girl, Violet, Phoebe's younger sister, finds a book of spells and reads one from it. Shortly after, while taking a bath, Violet transforms into a Mermaid ("Wow, this is cool!"); the program ends with Violet exclaiming that she must keep secret what has happened from Phoebe (unaware that she too is a Mermaid).

335 *A Splashy Tale.* youtube.com. 2012– 2014 (Comedy-Drama).

Legend states that in the oceans of the world there exists Mermaids, creatures with the upper body of a woman and the lower portion of a fish. Fishermen and sailors on long journeys are said to be the only humans to have seen or come in contact with them. How such creatures came to be or how they have remained a mystery is one of the unsolved riddles of the sea. One such Mermaid is Summer, a once ordinary girl who, while walking along the beach, found a magic necklace and a sea shell that contained an enchanted potion (perhaps the answer to the mystery) that transformed her into a Mermaid. Summer, an apparently only child with few friends, accepted her transformation but longed for a friend who was also a Mermaid. Hoping to get her wish, Summer placed the potion in the bottom of a public swimming pool and hid the magic necklace a short distance away.

For three friends, Izzy, Razundull and Zalika, their day at that swimming pool would soon change their lives forever. While swimming, Izzy spies a strange object (the potion in a bottle) at the bottom of the pool and retrieves it. While showing it to Razundull and Zalika, the contents spill onto Izzy's hand (she is more concerned that her hand is stained rather than what the substance could be). Izzy appears to be fine but, after her friends leave to get a snack and Izzy returns to the water, she not only finds the necklace Summer hid, but discovers that her legs have become a tail and she is a Mermaid. While not shown, Izzy exited from the pool and when the water on her tail dried, her legs reappeared.

Although Izzy had apparently intended to keep secret what happened, Zalika and Razundull's return from the snack stand changes all that. Upset that Izzy chose not to join them (to get refreshments) a confrontation ensues followed by a shoving match that knocks the three girls into the water. Razundull and Zalika are shocked to see that Izzy has become a Mermaid. Now, with a secret first known only to Zalika and Razundull (later by Zannia, a girl at school, and Summer and Aqua, Mermaids Izzy later befriends), Izzy must face the challenges of not only being a pretty teenage girl—but a teenage girl who is also a Mermaid.

A Splashy Tale. **From left to right: Cierra Hutcheson, Charlee Witham, Dakota Hutcheson, Danika Green** (used by permission of Danika Green).

Cast: Danika Green (Izzy Sho), Kimberly Banks (Aqua Star), Cierra Hutcheson (Zalika "Zali" Collins), Dakota Hutcheson (Razundull "Razzy" Kin), Jessica (as credited; Summer), Charlee Witham (Zannia Zulie). **Credits:** *Producer:* Danika Green. *Director:* Danika Green, Charlee Witham, Cierra Hutcheson, Dakota Hutcheson, Kimberly Banks, Jessica, Jessica P. (both as credited). *Writer:* Danika Green, Charlee Witham, Cierra Hutcheson, Dakota Hutcheson, Kimberly Banks, Allison Akins, Jessica, Jessica P. (as credited). **Comment:** Although the entire production appears to be acted, produced, written and directed by teenage girls, it is quite an accomplishment. While there are some visual and audio flaws (remember, these are not professionals) it is a well-executed and entertaining. There are numerous Mermaid-themed series and *A Splashy Tale* is, with its attractive cast and well-constructed story line, one of the more enjoyable Mermaid fables.

Episodes:

1. Metamorphosis (3 min., 46 sec.). Establishes the story line as Izzy finds the magic potion at the bottom of a swimming pool.

2. The Fight (3 min., 13 sec.). A confrontation ensues when Zalika and Razundull return from the refreshment stand causing Izzy to reveal her secret when she is pushed into the pool.

3. The Power in Your Hand (5 min.). The pool also reveals another mystery when Izzy finds a strange box that contains a necklace and a note: "The power of your new life is contained in your hand, when you're a true Mermaid, in the water or on land."

4. A Fishy Surprise (5 min., 53 sec.). A slumber party, thrown by Izzy, nets an unwanted guest when a girl (Zannia), jealous she was not invited, crashes it—and uncovers Izzy's secret when she sprinkles her with bottled water.

5. Best Friends Fade Away, Parts 1 (3 min., 45 sec.) and 2 (3 min., 48 sec.). Zannia's discovery causes Izzy and Zalika to have an argument when Zalika cannot convince Izzy that she was careless and allowed an outsider to discover her secret. The following day at the beach Izzy befriends a girl (Summer)— the Mermaid who placed the enchanted potion at the bottom of the pool.

6. Christmas Fishes (4 min., 29 sec.). It is Christmas and Summer, invited to spend the day by Izzy at her home, reveals a startling fact about Izzy's necklace: that it can grant a wish—but she must think carefully before making that wish.

7. Strange Moon (7 min., 45 sec.). As Izzy and Summer speak, Izzy also learns she must be careful of the moon (if a Mermaid sees the moon on the six-month anniversary of her transformation, it can cause her to acquire peculiar traits and contact with water at such times can also cause her skin to become scale-like [reversed when the sun rises]).

8. Fishy Book (3 min., 43 sec.). Zannia, eager to learn more about Izzy, spies her and Summer at the beach and finds (and steals), hidden in the rocks, a Mermaid book owned by Summer.

9. Mermaid Journal (5 min., 12 sec.). At Izzy's home, Izzy shows Summer a journal she has been keeping about her Mermaid experiences. When Summer suggests they go swimming, the journal is left in plain sight on Izzy's bed. A brazen Zannia sneaks into Izzy's home, sees the journal and takes it.

10. Mermaid Proof (3 min.). After returning home from the beach Izzy realizes her journal is missing and suspects Zannia took it and now fears her secret could be exposed.

11. Dangerous Waters (14 min.). During a conversation with Summer, Izzy learns that it was Summer who placed the potion in the bottom of the pool that she eventually found.

12. Wish to Fish (9 min., 58 sec.). With Izzy's necklace able to grant a wish and with both Zalika and Razundull yearning to become Mermaids, Izzy, who is unable to make a choice, leaves it up to them. Zalika uses the wish to grant Razundull's desire.

13. Jealous of Fishes (6 min., 2 sec.). Zalika's unselfish wish has made her jealous as she is now the only one who is not a Mermaid. Summer, seeing that Izzy and Razundull are also upset by what has happened, attempts to intervene and keep everyone together. The episode, written by a Youtube subscriber (Allison Akins) through a contest held by the cast, earned her the honor of having her script produced as a story.

14. Only Magic (5 min., 27 sec.). Fate intervenes when Izzy finds another magic necklace and Razundull uses its powers to transform Zalika into a Mermaid.

15. Wings Between Us (5 min., 32 sec.). Summer's life again changes when she finds a strange necklace hanging from a tree branch and a dust contained within the necklace transforms her into a Fairy.

16. Wish for a Change, Part 1 (8 min., 43 sec.). Summer must decide which life to live: Mermaid or Fairy as she cannot possess the abilities of two beings.

Note: The following episode information, which has not aired at the time of publication, was supplied by the producer (Danika Green). It is also important to provide background for the character of Aqua for the episodes to make sense. In a flashback sequence, it is shown that Aqua was walking along the beach when she noticed a girl floating in the water. "I ran into the ocean to get her. She was so cold. I turned her over.... She was dead. So I pulled the body ashore and called the police." While waiting for the police to arrive, Aqua notices that the girl didn't drown; that she was murdered. "Scared that the police would think I was the murderer, I ran." Aqua, however, was not as free as she thought when her face appeared on the news as the prime suspect. "That's the day I left home. I didn't know where to go. All I could think of was the beach" (and what happened). Now, all alone and strolling along the beach, Aqua finds a strange bottle containing a liquid. As she poured the liquid on her hand, thinking it was perfume, water from the ocean washed it off but left a stinging sensation and a transformation occurred that changed her into a Mermaid. She began her new life as a creature of the sea and one year later would befriend Izzy.

17. Wish for a Change (8 min., 43 sec.). As Summer returns to the sea, preferring to remain a mermaid, she is killed in a shark attack, leaving Izzy, Zalika and Razundull stunned by what has happened. Meanwhile, as Zannia tells Izzy, Razundull and Zalika that she intends to prove Izzy is a Mermaid, Aqua breaks into Izzy's home, seeking items to steal. Her efforts fail when she is caught and Izzy, Razundull and Zalika learn that she is a Mermaid (Izzy later forgives her and the four become friends).

18. Christmas Police. Although meant to be a joyous season, Aqua's celebration with Izzy, Razundull and Zalika is anything but joyous when Aqua notices the police are in the neighborhood and, as Izzy soon notices, Aqua appears to be a bit frightened.

19. Fish Stuck. Zalika's efforts to buy cookies results in Zannia seeing that she is a Mermaid when Zalika slips on a wet floor and Zannia uncovers her secret (in a reverse situation, Zannia keeps her secret and soon befriends her, Izzy, Aqua and Razundull).

20. Fishy Troubles. Izzy, in a change of pace episode, visits her cousins Alex (played by Alli) and Caul (played by Ben) in Florida (Izzy lives in Virginia). Caul is, as can be expected, Alex's annoying little brother. When he pushes Izzy and Alex into the backyard swimming pool, Izzy's secret is revealed—as is Alex's—she too is a Mermaid. Caul is also shocked—but his cries, "You're a Mermaid," will apparently go unnoticed.

21. Lost Magic. While on the beach, Zalika finds what appears to be a magical Mermaid necklace. So she is able to go swimming with Aqua, Zalika buries the necklace in the sand. Following her swim, Zalika panics when she can't find the necklace (washed away by the incoming tide) and rushes to Izzy's house asking her, Razundull and Zannia's help in finding it. As the girls return to the beach, Zannia finds the necklace and conceals it from the others. It is also a time when Izzy has been having recurring nightmares about her, Razundull and Zalika being captured in their Mermaid forms and tied together on the beach.

22. Mermaid on the Run. Razundull leaves Virginia as she and her parents move to Paris—but Izzy

is still plagued by nightmares of now only her and Zalika being captured and tied together on the beach. Izzy can see a figure but cannot clearly make out her captor's face. Meanwhile, as Aqua's jittery behavior continues (fearing capture by the police), Izzy, Zalika and Zannia learn how she became a mermaid (the flashback sequence as described above). It is also revealed that the situation between Aqua and the police is resolved (she is not charged) and that the figure in Izzy's nightmares was Aqua.

23. The Ocean's Calling, Parts 1, 2, 3 and 4. An intriguing Season 2 finale that encompasses a principal story line wherein a trance transforms Aqua into an evil Siren and her efforts to live forever in the ocean by using the power of the Super Moon to strip Izzy and Zalika of their Mermaid abilities.

336 *Split.* splittheseries.com. 2013 (Drama).

Dana and James Lafferty are a seemingly happily couple (married 15 years) with two children, Katie and Brian. James is a doctor and they are living a comfortable life. One day an anonymous letter arrives for Dana stating that her husband has been having an affair with another woman for the past 13 years. When Dana confronts James and finds out that it is true, she files for a divorce. Katie and Brian are caught in the middle when they become the victims of a child custody suit. As the divorce proceedings continue, Dana learns that James, a doctor, is broke (victim of a Ponzie scheme) and he has lost his job at the hospital. To make matters worse, Katie has become rebellious (unable to accept what is happening to her parents) and Dana is informed by James's attorney that she will not be getting alimony due to James's financial situation. Dana, having devoted her life to raising her family and without any job experience or skills, must now find a way to make ends meet (as she has temporary custody of the children until the case is settled). Unknown to Dana, James has stashed away funds and has hired Michelle, their mediator for the child custody hearings to use her influence to make sure he receives custody of the children; and, unknown to James, Jennifer, his mistress, has stopped taking her medication (for a chemical imbalance) and is plotting to make sure Dana is out of the picture so she and James can be together. The story relates the twists and turns that occur as both James and Dana seek to get what they each want most—custody of their children.

Cast: Lisa Roumain (Dana Lafferty), Tim Lane (James Lafferty), Olivia Dunkley (Jennifer Hutchins), Chloe Golden (Katie Lafferty), Tammy Kaitz (Michelle), Logan Prince (Brian Lafferty), Sara J. Stuckey (Cheryl Whitfiord). **Credits:** *Producer-Writer:* Rebecca Norris, Gabrielle Glenn. **Comment:** Tightly woven program that is straight-to-the-point. Acting and production qualities are very good and the characters well written as deceiving (James), good (Dana) and unbalanced (Jennifer).

Episodes:

1. Episode 1 (7 min., 56 sec.). Begins the story as Dana receives the anonymous letter (was it sent by James, Michelle or Jennifer?) and the beginnings of the child custody hearing.

2. Episode 2 (5 min., 59 sec.). Without the funds needed to maintain their luxury home, Dana, Katie and Brian move into a small apartment. Later, in a parking lot, Dana is approached by a masked, knife-wielding woman. A scuffle ensues and the masked woman is stabbed in the stomach.

3. Episode 3 (7 min., 9 sec.). As Dana drives a block away and calls the police, the mystery woman appears to be okay and manages to flee the scene.

4. Episode 4 (5 min., 16 sec.). The mystery woman is revealed to be Jennifer. When James sees that she is upset, she shows him the knife wound and explains that she was attacked by a woman for no apparent reason. Her description of the woman has James thinking it may have been Dana.

5. Episode 5 (4 min., 16 sec.). At the custody hearing Dana learns that James is broke and she will receive no alimony. It is later shown that James has conspired with the mediator (Michelle) "to tighten the grip on Dana."

6. Episode 6 (5 min., 36 sec.). Dana must figure out a way to make money while Jennifer appears to be plotting a way to rid her life of Dana in the concluding episode.

337 *Starting from ... Now.* onemorelesbian.com. 2014 (Drama).

Stephanie Fraser, called Steph, is a somewhat naive young woman (also a lesbian) who relocates from the country to the city (Sydney, Australia) to begin her dream job as a graphic artist at a large company. Having previously made arrangements with her childhood friend, Kristen, Steph moves in with her and her long-time girlfriend, Darcy. The situation becomes a bit awkward when Steph and Darcy are drawn to each other and Steph is not only faced with problems at work (prove her abilities within three months or face termination) but at home where her attraction to Darcy could destroy her relationship with Kristen if she should pursue it.

Cast: Sarah de Possesse (Steph Fraser), Lauren Orrell (Kristen Sheridan), Rosie Lourde (Darcy Peters), Bianca Bradey (Emily Rochford), Linda Grasso (Trish Faulkner). **Credits:** *Producer-Writer-Director:* Julie Kalceff. **Comment:** An Australian serial that is well acted and produced. The story line is well presented and the women chosen for their roles are very appealing and can draw you right into the story (especially Steph, who is so sweet, but so naïve at times, that you feel for her as she faces life in the big city). Those not familiar with seeing Australian produced movies or TV shows may find the accents a bit hard to understand at times but do not let that deter you from seeing just how good foreign-produced programs can be.

Episodes:

1. Episode 1 (6 min., 29 sec.). Introduces Steph as she moves in with Kristen, meets a girl at a bar (Darcy) then discovers Darcy is Kristen's live-in girlfriend.

2. Episode 2 (7 min., 51 sec.). Steph's dream job turns out to be more of a bust when she reports to work and is told she has three months to prove herself or face termination. The good thing: she befriends Emily, the gorgeous office manager (who appears to have become instantly attracted to her).

3. Episode 3 (6 min., 49 sec.). At home, as Steph broods about her day at work, she not only finds a sympathetic ear in Darcy but sees that she and Darcy are becoming increasingly attracted to each other.

338 *Steffi*. webserieschannel.com. 2013 (Musical Drama).

Steffi McBride is a young woman, working as a dishwasher in a hotel, who dreams of becoming an actress. She is talented but her alcoholic (and cruel when he is drunk) father forbids it, believing it is not steady employment. Steffi, however, has her dream and is determined to pursue it. The program, adapted from the novel *The Overnight Fame of Steffi McBride* by Andrew Crofts and set in London, England, charts Steffi's efforts to follow her dreams and what happens when becomes an overnight sensation when she lands a role on the TV soap opera *The Talent*.

Cast: Jasmine Breinburg (Steffi), Jamal Edwards (Pete), Jade Ewen (Lara), Lee Boardman (Quentin), Tara Hodges (Kim), Emma Davies (Dora Stevens), Pooky Quesnel (Audrey), Sharon Duncan Brewster (Ella), Michael Nardone (Michael), Shannequa Duprey (Jenny), Kate Hollowood (Sarah), Robin Crouch (Stagsy), Arjun Coomaraswamy (Luke). **Credits:** *Writer-Producer:* Carol Ann Docherty, Aileen Docherty. *Director:* Richard Elson. **Comment:** The program is produced in England and Jasmine Breinburg is delightful as Steffi (she makes the whole program with her appealing personality and natural approach to acting). The writing and directing are very good and Steffi speaking directly to the camera to relate her feeling is a nice touch (makes Steffi seem more real). For unknown reasons, the concluding episode has been taken off-line ("This Video No Longer Exists" will appear) which, although the series is enjoyable to watch, leaves the viewer to wonder what happens.

Episodes:

1. My First Audition (7 min., 22 sec.). Steffi's first break comes when, during her acting class, she impresses a casting director (Audrey) for *The Talent* and is asked to audition for a role.

2. Taking It Back (4 min., 33 sec.). Introduces Steffi's boyfriend, Pete (who seems less than enthu-

siastic about Steffi's audition) and Lara and Kim, Steffi's friends who are not impressed by what has happened (especially Lara, who has eyes for Pete).

3. My Big Break (4 min., 23 sec.). With her agent, Dora by her side, Steffi auditions for *The Talent* but her anxiety gets the best of her and she runs off the stage when she sees that Lara also has an audition for the same role.

4. My X Factor Moment (4 min., 23 sec.). With Dora's help, Steffi composes herself and returns to the stage for her audition.

5. Can You Hear Me? (3 min., 24 sec.). Steffi's audition impresses the show's producer—but, upon returning home, she encounters her father's hostility when he learns she will be quitting her dish washing job (apparently the only income the family has as her father was fired for drinking on the job).

6. My Overnight Fame (3 min., 39 sec.). Steffi's dream becomes a reality when she acquires the role—but is it what she really thought it would is probed as the series concludes.

339 *The Steps*. blip.tv. 2010 (Thriller).

Charlie Madison is a Hollywood-based private detective who is good at his job, but he suffers from an addiction to alcohol. His addiction has caused him blackouts and may have also turned him into a killer (of his girlfriend). But Charlie has little recollection of what happened and he soon becomes a suspect in a police investigation. Charlie, however, believes he is innocent, and flees to Chattanooga, Tennessee to escape what may be a criminal past. The program follows Charlie's experiences in Tennessee and later in Los Angeles when he returns to prove he is innocent by finding the evidence he needs—evidence that is buried with the body of his girlfriend—a girl Charlie can't be sure he didn't actually kill.

Cast: Dylan Kussman (Charlie Madison), Kim Jackson (Tamara Jenkins), Dwayne Gordon (Det. Phipps), Joe McNutt (Simpson), Lisa Lynch (Anna), Leith Burke (Roderick), Allelon Ruggiero (Jonas), Adam Paul (Sydney), Maria Sanger (Doris), Becky Willard (Katie). **Credits:** *Producer:* Adam Paul, Tiffany J. Shuttleworth. *Writer-Director:* Dylan Kussman. **Comment:** Although the program ends unresolved, the first season is complete and presents a well-acted, fast-moving and intriguing story. The production values are good and the program is well worth watching despite the use of unsavory language.

Episodes:

1. In Hell (6 min., 56 sec.). Establishes the story line as Charlie flees to Tennessee, hoping to escape his past life in Los Angeles.

2. The Job (5 min., 39 sec.). Gary, a fellow alcoholic, hires Charlie to follow his fiancée, Tamara, believing she is being unfaithful to him.

3. The Body (6 min., 4 sec.). Charlie begins the case but feels something is just not right as he trails Tamara.

4. Holding On (6 min., 34 sec.). Circumstances are forcing Charlie to once again hit the bottle—until he seeks help from Doris, a friend who has been alcohol free for 21 years.

5. The Visit (7 min., 3 sec.). An anonymous tip to Timothy Simpson, the L.A. Assistant D.A. assigned to prosecute Charlie, causes problems for Charlie when Simpson meets with a local detective (Phipps) with information about his escaped fugitive.

6. Happy Birthday (6 min., 22 sec.). As Charlie celebrates one year of sobriety, he discovers that Tamara is a coke dealer.

7. Falling Further (5 min., 49 sec.). Phipps becomes interested in Simpson's story as Charlie discovers that a man he thought was his friend (Gary) is a drug dealer.

8. The Bartender (8 min., 32 sec.). Charlie becomes a suspect in a murder when Gary kills a bartender who tried to rip him off.

9. Ride Home (6 min., 51 sec.). Phipps confronts Charlie and is about to arrest him when Charlie tells him he has evidence that Gary is the killer.

10. Coming Clean, Part 1 (4 min., 57 sec.). Charlie, set free by Phipps, seeks to bring the real killer down.

11. Coming Clean, Part 2 (7 min., 1 sec.). Charlie resolves the case and considers returning to Los Angeles to find the person who framed him in the concluding season one episode.

12. The Pick-Up (7 min., 38 sec.). Charlie returns to Los Angeles to find the real killer of his girlfriend in the second season opening episode.

13. It's My Game (6 min., 52 sec.). In the concluding episode Charlie, with the help of his friend Anna (a prostitute) sets his plan in motion.

340 Stirred, Not Shaken. stirrednotshakentv.net. 2009 (Drama).

"Life's a trip. You're born, you work, you die. Hopefully you know a few people who can stir things up a bit like I do." Kim is a free-spirited young woman who opens the program with those words and whose experiences unfold in a series of events, told in serial-style, that affect her friends and family (basically, her friend Jackie [sensible] and Chris [playboy]).

Cast: Kysa Siovan (Kim Owens), Mary McCallum (Jackie Lewis), Cortez Lee (Chris Bennett), Diana Holland (Jeannette). **Credits:** *Producer-Writer-Director:* Kysa Siovan. **Comment:** The program, produced in Nashville, apparently aired on local cable TV before being placed on the Internet as episodes contain commercial pitches for local Nashville businesses. Overall through, it is well done and acted and interesting to see what localized producers and actors have made before their work is exposed to anyone on the Internet. It is also billed as "Nashville's first and only urban soap opera."

Episodes:

1. Pilot Episode, Part 1 (8 min., 35 sec.). Kim, Jackie and Chris are introduced in the program's pilot episode.

2. Pilot Episode, Part 2 (8 min., 54 sec.). The story continues with the three, employed at the same company, concerned about their jobs when word spreads about possible layoffs.

3. Chapter 2, Part 1 (7 min., 14 sec.). Jeannette, Chris's latest girlfriend, causes tension among the friends when Kim takes a dislike to her—something that could ruin her friendship with Chris.

4. Chapter 2, Part 2 (9 min., 13 sec.). Kim finds herself being confronted by Jeannette when Jeannette realizes she has issues about her.

5. Chapter 2, Part 3 (9 min., 50 sec.). The concluding episode wherein Chris, angered by Kim's confrontation with Jeannette, appears to be undecided as to whether forgive Kim or end their friendship to be with Jeannette.

341 The Story. The Song. story-song.com. 1996 (Anthology).

Each song that has ever been written has a story that inspired it to be created. How songs came to be written were to be showcased in with a performance of the song to open each episode and the dramatic details that led to the creation of that song.

Cast: Madison Gorman (Jane as a teenager), Nicole Galiardo (Jane as an adult), Vince Butler (Hoagy Carmichael), Andrew Stevens (Walter Winchell).

Comment: Just based on the only produced episode, this appeared to be not only one of the earliest Internet series in any genre, but one with a wealth of material from which to choose. It is unknown who produced, wrote or directed the program but it was well acted and produced. The information that appears was compiled prior to the program being taken off line.

Episodes:

1. I Get Along Without You Very Well. In 1928, a romantic teenage girl (Jane Brown) wrote a poem called "I Get Along Without You Very Well" for composer Hoagy Carmichael when he appeared at her school. Hoagy placed the poem in a folder and eventually forgot about it. Ten years later, when Hoagy was asked to write a song for radio's *The Dick Powell Show,* he found that poem and placed music to it. But in all consciousness, he could not place his name on it as the lyricist. With the help of radio newscaster Walter Winchell, Hoagy began a nationwide search to find that unknown teenage girl. The search found the girl, now Mrs. Jane Thompson. Jane, however, was in failing health but did hear her poem performed on the radio in the presence of Hoagy before she passed away.

342 *The Stranger.* whoisthestranger.net. 2013 (Mystery).

A young mother, returning home from an undisclosed location, enters her home and is unknowingly being watched by a mysterious figure in black and hiding in the shadows. As the mother checks to see that her child is okay, she finds, a short distance away, the body of her sister (Jessica Langley) lying on the floor and her head covered in blood. The intruder is scared off by the mother's screams and the town in which the crime occurred, Evergreen, Tennessee, becomes the focal point of an intense investigation when a police detective (Cal Hayes) joins with a private investigator (Nicole James) to solve a case where nothing seems to make sense.

Cal Hayes is a Lieutenant with the Evergreen P.D. and is a stickler for following the rules, hoping that the smallest piece of evidence will eventually lead him to the bigger ones needed to solve a crime.

Nicole James is a young woman who, although her marriage to Steven is facing troubled times, tries to put her personal issues aside to devote all her efforts to solving cases. She will take chances and knows she needs to dig deeper than what lies on the surface.

Jessica Langley, although a murder victim, is still very much alive within the memories of the townspeople. Now, everything that has been happening appears to trace back to Jessica's untimely death. Nicole's dreams are also haunted by Jessica's presence, possibly due to the fact that she could not foresee that Jessica's mother, Sheri, would also become a victim of an unsolved murder.

Other Town Residents: John Commons is the Evergreen Police Department's tech officer; Mena Covax, the woman seeking political victory; Liz Darden, a police sergeant; Preston Strong, the police captain (and Liz's lover); Katie Pratt, the daughter of an abusive father (Robert Pratt); Allison Bridges, the mysterious woman, secured in her new identity as a member of the Witness Protection Program; Rose Pennington, the Mayor's personal assistant; Melissa Travers, the town doctor; Barb Tanner, a woman of mystery who has put herself under suspicion for stealing evidence from a crime scene; Nick Daley, a former police officer who left the department after feeling threatened by the legalities of the system; Gordon Reese is the Mayor; Olivia Bestwick is the woman who has taken on the cause of caring for abused women and children and runs a violence center.

Cast: Austin Olive (Cal Hayes), Tanesha Franklin-White (Nicole James), Kacy Tiller (Jessica Langley), John L. Altom (Gabriel Tilson), Sabrina Kitto (Mena Covax), Hannah Faith Rader (Barb Tanner), Camielle Reed (Liz Darden), D.W. Reiser (Nick Daley), Mike Sant (Preston Strong), Toby Wilkins (Winston Tapp), Michelle Hachten (Allison Bridges), Dalton Stout (Michael Pratt), Eugene White (Steven James), Eric Doepel (John Commons), Callie Worley (Katie Pratt), Steve Crisp (Sam Langley), Robert McCrary (Robert Pratt), Jay D. Bowman (Gordon Reese), Laura Lakins (Olivia Bestwick), Lisa Howell (Sheri Langley), Amy N. Edwards (Joy Ratner), Rachel Lawson (Rose Pennington), Libby Tipton (Dr. Melissa Travers). **Credits:** *Producer:* Dustin Street, Drew Howell, Christian Cummins, Tanesha Franklin-White, Eric Doepel, John Altom, Hannah Faith Rader. *Director:* Dustin Street, Hannah Faith Rader, John Altom, Eric Doepel. *Writer:* Dustin Street, Hannah Faith Rader, Eric Doepel, Drew Howell, Christian Cummins. **Comment:** While the investigation proceeds, the Stranger is seen dressed in black and always in a situation where his (or her) features cannot be fully recognized—a nice twist to add more intrigue to an already intriguing story. The acting and production values are also good.

Episodes:

1. Cradle. The story line is established as the body of Jessica Langley is discovered.

2. Grave. The events that led up to Jessica's murder are revealed as Cal and Nicole team to solve the crime.

3. Breaking. As Cal and Nicole begin to question suspects, the Police Chief (Tilson) holds a press conference about the murder.

4. Entering. Cal begins to piece together aspects of Jessica's life before the murder while Nicole takes things one step further and ventures on her own to follow leads.

5. Catch. As the investigation continues, Tilson receives a tip that someone has tampered with the crime scene.

6. Release. Nicole, caught tampering with evidence at the crime scene, convinces Chief Tilson she needed to do so to fill in a missing piece of the information she has gathered. She is let go—but not without a stern reprimand.

7. Crime. Barb, a woman who appears to know more about the killing than she is letting on, feels something is not right; unknown to her she has become of interest to the Stranger (who is watching her).

8. Punishment. Figuring that she has stumbled onto something, Nicole approaches Cal with her information, hoping to convince him to follow her lead.

9. Give. As Mena begins her bid to become the town's new Mayor, Cal and Nicole piece together their information and deduct that a new suspect has entered the picture—the mysterious Allison Bridges.

10. Take. The truth behind her father's abusive behavior against her and her brother Michael comes to light when Katie breaks her silence and seeks help.

11. Venomous. As the Mayor begins his campaign for re-election, Cal and Nicole team with Barb, the woman who stole crime scene evidence, to help solve Jessica's murder.

12. Snake. A mole (John Commons) is revealed as using his position as the police department's tech

guy to gather information for? (possibly the Stranger, as he hears voices talking to him with captions on the screen for the viewer to understand).

13. Pomp. As Katie begins a search for Michael, who disappeared after Katie revealed they were being abused, preparations begin for a masquerade ball arranged by Mena to help support the Mayor. The program concludes unresolved.

343 *Stratford, Alabama.* webserieschannel.com. 2013 (Anthology).

A fictional place called Stratford, Alabama, provides the backdrop for re-imagined versions of Shakespearean plays that features the same characters and settings but in different time periods.

Cast: Bobby Bowman (Romeo), Ariel Richardson (Juliet), Josh Henry (Mercutio), Robert Jamerson (Tybalt), Marty Rogers (Benvolio), Tony Payne (Friar Lawrence). **Credits:** *Producer-Writer-Director:* Ty Fanning. **Comment:** The idea is good but the overall presentation suffers as the performers use the same dialogue as originally written by Shakespeare. Experienced actors have difficulty remembering and performing such lines and here, with amateurs (who do an overall good job) it appears obvious that some encountered difficulty (like flubbing lines). While attempts were made to be faithful to the 1960s (as with the music) cars seen in the background of outdoor scenes are modern and ruin the impression trying to be made. Adapting Shakespeare to any medium is not easy and here, using a modified version of the wording would have played better than using the Bard's original wording.

Episodes:

1. Romeo and Juliet (12 min., 1 sec.). A different twist on the immortal love story that is set during the race riots of the 1960s.

344 *Sundown.* westernsontheweb.com. 2013 (Western).

A revival (of sorts) of the classic 1950s and 60s television western series that tells the story of a stern Marshal (Jim Lane), his easy-going deputy (Bob McLynteck) and what happens when they attempt to escort a captured outlaw (Ben Reese) to the town of Sundown and he escapes, leaving Jim with a gunshot wound in the leg and Bob his only hope for survival when he leaves him alone to seek help.

Cast: R.W. Hampton (Marshal Jim Lane), Don Kay (Doc Brown), Moe Headrick (Frank), Scott Mendes (Jeb), Bobby Miles (Ben Reese), Sam Yoder (The Kid), Kirby Jonas (Gray), Faye Taylor (Mrs. Wallace), Johnie Terry (J.T. O'Mara), Bob Terry (Bob McLynteck), Jessie Robertson (Jessie Banks), Jimmy McCarley (Sheriff Buck Merritt), Kristyn Harris (Rose Waggoner), Chance Terry, Caz Wright (Cowhands). **Credits:** *Producer:* Bob Terry, Johnie Terry. **Comment:** Filmed in black and white and,

while not as action-packed or shoot-em-up as typical westerns, it is an interesting look at an aspect of the Old West—capturing a prisoner and attempting to get him to town. Those familiar with the TV series *The Rifleman* will immediately recognize that series background music as being incorporated here.

Episodes:

1. Lawman (6 min., 44 sec.; title from the 1958 ABC series). The epic begins with the Marshal and his deputy escorting a killer to justice.

2. Outlaws (7 min., 43 sec.; title from the 1960 NBC series). As the journey continues, Jim and Bob encounter Frank and Jeb, two outlaws (friends of Ben) posing as ranch hands.

3. Gunsmoke (7 min., 28 sec.; title from the 1955 CBS series). With Frank and Jed's help, Ben escapes, leaving Jim wounded (shot in the leg) and he and Bob without horses.

4. Two Faces West (5 min., 24 sec.; title from the 1960 Syndicated series). Although wounded and stranded, Jim and Bob decide it is best to walk to Sundown.

5. Overland Trail (7 min., 8 sec.; title from the 1960 Syndicated series). As the Marshal and his deputy begin their foot trek to Sundown, it soon becomes apparent that Jim cannot make the journey.

6. The Quest (6 min., 31 sec.; title from the 1976 NBC series). With Jim unable to travel, Bob leaves him in a safe place while he treks on alone to get help.

7. A Tale of Wells Fargo (8 min., 31 sec.; title from the 1956 pilot film for the NBC series *The Tales of Wells Fargo*). As Bob travels and crosses a ravine he finds a stash of stolen Wells Fargo money.

8. Sugarfoot (5 min., 30 sec.; title from the 1957 ABC series). With the money (which he plans to turn over to the Sheriff in Sundown), Bob hits the trail and encounters a young cowgirl (who calls him a "Sugarfoot" for walking when he should be riding). A conversation is exchanged and each goes their separate way shortly after.

9. Sundown Town (9 min., 8 sec.; uses an original title). Bob reaches Sundown and, after seeking the Sheriff (only to learn he is out of town) decides to have a meal before getting horses and heading back for the Marshal.

10. Pistols and Petticoats (10 min., 22 sec.; title from the 1966 CBS series). At the town saloon, Bob learns from the bartender where he can rent horses—but continual delays prevent him from doing so and helping the Marshal.

11. Gunslinger (7 min., 28 sec.; title from the 1961 CBS series). Suspicious eyes follow Bob (carrying the Wells Fargo money bag) as he finally checks into seeing about renting horses.

12. Cowboys (7 min., 28 sec.; title from the 1974 ABC series). Basically a look at a saloon card game and what happens when a card shark is caught.

13. Action in the Afternoon (4 min., 58 sec.; title from the 1953 CBS series). Bob returns to the saloon,

intervenes in and stops a fight—and is rewarded with a free stake dinner.

14. Trackdown (6 min., 8 sec.; title from the 1957 CBS series). A plan is set in motion from some bad guys to relieve Bob of the money bag.

15. Frontier Doctor (5 min., 11 sec.; title from the 1958 Syndicated series). Still in town, Bob faces the outlaws seeking the money.

16. Frontier Justice (9 min., 42 sec.; title from the 1958 CBS series which encompassed repeats of *Dick Powell's Zane Grey Theater*). With the outlaws defeated and the money safe, Bob finally gets the horses he needs and heads out of town. Unknown to him, he is being followed by a desperado seeking the money. The episode concludes with the desperado facing Bob but being bitten by a rattle snake and succumbing to its poison.

17. Boots and Saddles (8 min., 15 sec.; title from the 1957 Syndicated series *Boots and Saddles: The Story of the 5th Cavalry*). Two days have passed and the deputy finally reaches the now well-rested Marshal. The series concludes with the two men riding toward Sundown.

345 *Sunny Reign*. girlsmoove.wix. 2012–2013 (Crime Drama).

Sunny and Reign are lovers and con artists who thrive on devising small scams—nothing big and nothing that will get them caught (at least they hope). When Sunny and Reign have a falling out and each goes their separate way, a con worth a half-million dollars reunites them—not only as thieves but as lovers. The program charts their efforts to parlay a series of small scams into one complex hustle that will net them a small fortune.

Cast: Blaxx Casanova (Sunny), Kream Stalleion (Reign), Trice McKinney (Sway), Lorena Dali (Nelly), Tramaine Renee (Wiz), Bradford Haynes (Savage), Chantaille Elkerson (Dreya), Davinchii Woods (Marco). **Credits:** *Producer:* Bradford Haynes, Tramaine Renee. *Writer-Director:* Tramaine Renee. **Comment:** Fast-moving story with good acting and production values. The program, which contains vulgar language, is also unique in that it presents a lesson on how a scam (or racket) is performed and how one can protect themselves from it.

Episode List: *1.* Friendly Reminders. *2.* Choose Wisely. *3.* Learn to Adjust. *4.* Revamp the Team. *5.* Become the Connect. *6.* Confuse Reality. *7.* Run Game. *8.* Drive Slow (The Finale).

346 *Syd 2030*. syd2030.com.au. 2012 (Drama).

An Australian produced program (sort of a more adult version of America's *The Paper Chase* TV series) that explores the lives of first year law students not only struggling to survive the difficult first year but who will do anything "to get what their hearts desire."

Bridget Knox, born December 16, 1990, is single and proud of the fact that she is called "The Eastern Suburbs Bombshell." She is fearful of making a wrong decision and hates people who tell her to "relax" or "chill." She loves 1990's boy bands, traveling the world and will fight for what she believes in. Her favorite movie is *Cruel Intentions*.

Francesca Goldstein, born on June 28, 1990, is single and is called the school's "Eastern Suburbs Saucy Minx." *Pretty Woman* is her favorite film; hot chips covered in gravy are her favorite food. She hates people who wear socks with sandals; being alone is her greatest fear and she tries to not let anything get her down.

Leonardis Cassevetes, born May 7, 1990, claims he is "very single" but he fears contracting an STD and having to tell his recent "conquest" about it. He hates losing at board games; *The Godfather* is his favorite movie and claims his best quality is his ability to admit his faults.

Cameron Hunter, born November 21, 1990, is the school's ladies' man (or as he calls himself, a playboy). He is in a relationship with a fellow student (Lara) and hates people who share their ring tones in public. *Star Wars, Episode IV* is his favorite movie and he fears failing to live up to what is expected of him.

Lara Luhrman, born October 14, 1990, is called "The North Shore Princess Bitch." She is in a relationship with Cameron, hates Hippies, loves the movie *The Sound of Music* but fears doing poorly in class. She claims to have the ability to see the best in people.

Christopher L, the oldest of the friends (born January 3, 1986), is called "The Sydney City Underdog." His martial status, he claims, "is complicated" and hates Tom Hanks movies. His favorite feature film is *Eternal Sunshine of the Spotless Mind* and, while he fears heights, he claims his best quality is honesty.

Cast: Tatjana Alexis (Bridget Knox), Laura Benson (Lara Luhrman), Sophie Luck (Francesca Goldstein), David Anderson (McKenzie), George Harrison Xanthis (Leonardis Cassevetes), Johnny Emery (Christopher Luhrman), Jeff Gannon (Mr. Knox), Adam Hatzimanolis (The Dean), Aprille Lim (Victoria Lee), Ben Marks (Richard Watson), Abe Mitchell (Cameron Hunter). **Credits:** *Producer:* Suzie Smith. *Director:* Tatjana Alexis, Alex Barnett. *Writer:* Tatjana Alexis. **Comment:** Well photographed and portrayed program of more of what happens after class as opposed to what occurs in class. The cast is attractive and the stories play well and are not hindered by thick Australian accents.

Episodes:

1. She Came Back (5 min., 26 sec.). The two main characters are established: Bridget Knox and Cameron Hunter, the children of parents who own the business Knox and Hunter, as the heirs to the company.

2. Better the Devil You Know (9 min., 52 sec.). Bridget's return after a year's absence is a bit of a

shock to everyone especially when she decides to remain and enrolls in college.

3. Dirty Deeds Done Dirt Cheap (8 min., 19 sec.). Although Bridget and Cameron had broken off their relationship a year earlier, Cameron believes Bridget has come back for him to rekindle what they once had and set their future together as heads of the company.

4. Hearts a Mess (10 min., 34 sec.). A celebration of Cameron's 21st birthday is not all that happy an occasion when Bridget's return increasingly becomes unclear to Cameron.

5. On a Night Like This (8 min., 8 sec.). Cameron becomes a bit uneasy when Bridget confronts his current girlfriend (Lara).

6. Crash and Burn (9 min., 6 sec.). With the partying over, the students begin preparations for internship meetings and the upcoming swim team trials.

7. Need You Tonight (11 min., 19 sec.). With the swim trials over, the students prepare for the annual horse race.

8. Chase That Feeling (12 min., 18 sec.). Bridget threatens the future of Knox-Hunter when she resigns, leaving Cameron the lone heir and her father bitterly angry at her.

9. Truly, Madly, Deeply (11 min., 38 sec.). A shadow falls on the school when it is revealed that one the students (Vickie Lee), suffering from unnoticed depression, kills herself.

10. This Boy's in Love (9 min., 28 sec.). The upcoming gala, The Law Ball, has Cameron torn between Bridget and Lara—and his future happiness.

11. Are You Gonna Be My Girl? (11 min., 56 sec.). Cameron's dilemma continues, not only with Lara and Bridget, but over upcoming law exam finals and his inability to fully concentrate on his studies.

12. Big Jet Plane (12 min., 15 sec.). The concluding episode wherein the first semester ends but the doorway is left open to continue events in the students' lives (as happened with *The Paper Chase*, which continued for three more seasons and concluded with the graduation).

347 Tail of a Mermaid & Merman. youtube.com. 2013 (Comedy-Drama).

Jewel and Rin are a sister and brother (twins) and the merchildren of a Mermaid. Years ago an evil Shape Shifter (Davilin) kidnapped them and brought them to his world on the earth. Jewel and Rin lost their mer-powers and memories and began living life as ordinary humans. It is the day of their 16th birthday and Jewel is taking a bath when the water activates long-lost memories and abilities and transforms her into a Mermaid. Her screams bring Rin to her side and when he touches her tail, he too is transformed (into a Merman). As memories of their prior life slowly return they realize they are not human and must now defeat Davilin and return to their rightful world as a princess and a prince.

Cast: Nikki Crawford (Jewel Adams), Alexander Warren (Rin Adams), Heidi Fairgrive (Nixe Ocean), Nicole Katherine (Esther), L.J. Cleave (Makenna Seastar), Iona Worgan (Ruby Smith). **Comment:** Produced in Scotland and very difficult to understand (poor sound coupled with Scottish accents). It is also visually unimpressive (not very clear and a bit out of aspect ratio [stretched images]).

Episode List: *1.* A Magical Dream. *2.* Powers, Crazy Aunt & Another Mermaid. *3.* Demonic Possession. *4.* A Very Fishy Christmas.

348 The Tail of 2 Mermaids. youtube.com. 2012 (Comedy-Drama).

It is a warm summer's day and two young girls, Emma and Jackie, head to an area called Mako to cool off in its swimming pool. Everything appears to be normal until the water begins to bubble and the girls are magically transported back to Emma's house—but it doesn't seem to faze them as they go about their normal business. However, when Emma goes for a drink of water, she is transformed into a Mermaid. When Jackie attempts to dry her off, she too becomes a Mermaid when the water on Emma's tail touches her skin. Emma and Jackie quickly realize what has happened to them and must now accept the fact that contact with water will transform them into young Mermaids. The program charts their experiences, assisted by their friend Jack (an apparent expert on Mermaids) as they seek to conceal their secret and live as ordinary pre-teen girls.

Cast: Eiligh Rush (Emma), Alyssa Duncan (Jackie), Ian Rush (Jack). **Comment:** With the exception of episode 3, wherein Jackie's performance is embarrassing, the program plays well as kids (especially Jack) try to solve adult problems without help from adults. It is obvious that the child stars are non-professionals and do a good job of performing their roles.

Episodes:

1. Magic (3 min., 34 sec.). Emma and Jackie discover they have become Mermaids after mysterious bubbles erupt in a swimming pool.

2. Revealed! (4 min., 15 sec.). Unable to face the situation alone, Emma and Jackie seek the help of their friend Jack.

3. The Spell (4 min., 8 sec.). When Emma and Jackie return to the Mako pool, Emma finds a book of spells and reads one, altering Jackie's personality and body as she begins to develop scales (Jack is then introduced to help). The program concludes in an unresolved situation.

349 A Tail of Wonder. youtube.com. 2012 (Comedy Drama).

While swimming in the ocean, a young girl (Crystal) finds a magic necklace that has no effect on her at first, but when she returns home and comes in contact with water, the necklace transforms her into a Mermaid. Crystal has a best friend (Bella) and unable to contain her secret, she tells her what has happened. As the pilot film ends, Bella has learned Crystal's secret and it is assumed she will either become a Mermaid herself or provide the help Crystal needs to navigate life as both a Mermaid and ordinary girl. **Cast (as credited):** Hollie (Crystal), Emily (Bella). **Credits** are not given. **Comment:** Only a pilot film has been produced that has noticeable editing problems coupled with poor sound but good acting by the girls.

Episodes:

1. Tails. The pilot episode establishes the proposed series story line.

350 *Tail Us Bout It.* tailusboutit.weebly.com. 2012 (Comedy-Drama).

Six episode program about two young girls (Kenya and Loala) who magically become Mermaids while at the beach and whose adventures, while attempting to adjust to their new life, are experienced by Aqua, a life-long Mermaid who is still having difficulty adjusting to life on land as a human. **Cast (as credited):** Mirisa (Loala), Soleil (Kenya), Aysha (Aqua), Katelyn (Anne Thea). **Credits** are not given. **Comment:** All episodes and virtually all text information have been taken off-line. The program (correct with the word "Bout" in the title) is filmed in the Virgin Islands and, judging by the photographs on the website, it did appear to be an interesting variation on the Mermaid genre.

Episode List: *1.* Pilot. *2.* A Found Book. *3.* Forget-Me-Knot. *4.* Who Are You? *5.* The Fish Trap. *6.* Try and Catch Me.

351 *The Tails of a Wish.* youtube.com. 2013 (Comedy-Drama).

Two young girls, Livi and Tori, turned into Mermaids as the result of a wish, now struggle to navigate life as both humans and creatures of the sea. **Cast (as credited):** Emily (Livi), Abi (Tori), Monique (Monique). **Credits** are not given. **Comment:** Australian-produced program (where the TV series inspiration *H20: Just Add Water* was also produced) that has good underwater photography but, like American Mermaid series, suffers at times from poor sound quality.

Episodes: All six episodes, which have no titles (other than, Episode 1, Episode 2, etc.) have been taken off line.

352 *Tails of Hawaii.* youtube.com. 2011 (Comedy-Drama).

Hawaii provides the backdrop as two girls (Josephine and Jordan) walking by a very large tree, magically plunge into a water-filed cave beneath it.

But just as magically, the girls are propelled back to the surface where they have been transformed into Mermaids. Now with a secret they must keep, Josephine and Jordan must also navigate lives as ordinary girls. **Cast (as credited):** Chloe (Josephine), Victoria (Jordan), Isabelle (Gabrielle). **Credits** are not given. **Comment:** Slightly above the ordinary Mermaid series with decent acting and photography. Filmed in Hawaii.

Episodes:

1. Episode 1 (6 min., 58 sec.). The story line, as described above, is established.

2. Episode 2 (9 min., 29 sec.). As Gabrielle becomes grounded by her parents for failing her history test, Jordan and Josephine discover they have Mermaid powers.

3. Episode 3 (8 min., 22 sec.). The girls return to the cave where they each discover a necklace and find they can control water. But adding to their troubles is a book they find that states that if a Mermaid sees a crescent moon she will become wild and uncontrollable. The program ends with the girls realizing that it is the night of a crescent moon.

353 *Talent.* alloyentertainment.com. 2013 (Drama).

Harper Walker, a young woman who works as a singer in a ski lodge, is a talented singer who has dreams of becoming a recording artist, but thus far she has only dreams. One night the unthinkable happens. After performing a song, a patron of the lodge (pop singer Kenzie Walsh) recognizes that Harper is talented, has "a killer voice" and offers her the opportunity of a lifetime—the chance to sign a deal with a record label (Victous Records). Danielle, her best friend, who works as a bartender in the same lodge, becomes Harper's agent and their experiences as they head for Los Angeles becomes the focal point of stories as Harper and Danielle encounter the music industry sharks and discover that it takes more than talent to survive. **Cast:** Alexandra Chando (Danielle), BC Jean (Harper), Randy Wayne (Gabe), Juan Pope (Vic), Logen Hull (Kenzie Walsh), Mishell Livio (Bianca), Kavan Reece (Dylan). **Credits:** *Producer:* Leslie Morganstein, Josh Bank, Bob Levy, Tripp Reed. *Director:* Tripp Reed. *Writer:* Jessica Koosed Etting, Alyssa Embree Schwartz. **Comment:** Well acted and produced program that combines music with drama and very light comedy. The available episodes flow smoothly from beginning to end and the characters, especially Harper and Danielle are like-able from their first introduction at the ski lodge.

Episodes:

1. As Easy as Getting a Record Deal (9 min., 47 sec.). As Harper and Danielle arrive in Hollywood, they befriend Bianca, a rich girl who will soon change the course of their lives.

2. My Mansion Is Your Mansion (6 min., 45 sec.). At Victous Records, Danielle meets with executives who must now sign Harper with a producer for her album; meanwhile, Harper experiences her first VIP party.

3. Brilliant Rubbish (5 min., 47 sec.). The record company has given Harper and Danielle a rent free apartment but their luck may be running out when she is assigned a rather "insane" British producer named Marcus (A.J. Buckley) to transform her songs into an album.

4. How to Impress a Music Snob (6 min., 44 sec.). After hearing Harper perform, Marcus concludes that she has no talent and walks out on her. She must now convince him that she is talented.

5. U Don't Suck Like I Thought U Would (6 min., 17 sec.). As Harper makes her first demo, she also finds herself being treated to a new designer wardrobe.

6. Well, This Is Awkward (8 min., 37 sec.). Harper finds herself in an awkward position when she discovers that Kenzie, the girl who discovered her, will be singing the song she wrote.

7. Almost Like Being a Star (6 min., 32 sec.). Although upset that her song was sung by Kenzie, Harper and Danielle attend Kenzie's exclusive album release party.

8. Two Wrongs Make a Mess (5 min., 45 sec.). Harper's wild antics at the party have severe consequences when Gabe sees her in a new light and cancels her contract.

9. Misery Loves Music (6 min., 58 sec.). The loss of the record deal brings Harper and Danielle to an argument that apparently ends their friendship when Danielle gives up on her. Meanwhile Bianca has a plan to not only reunite Harper and Danielle, but change the direction in their quest.

10. Step Into My Office (6 min., 25 sec.). It can't be denied that Harper has talent and Danielle, realizing this, makes peace with Harper. It is then revealed that Bianca, Harper and Danielle have started (with Bianca's backing) their own record label—Roomies Records.

Note: Season 2 episodes have been taken off-line (but continue to relate Harper's efforts to become a recording artist through her own company while also helping other newcomers by producing their records). No explanation is given for their removal and either "This Video No Longer Exists" or a blue screen will appear when an attempt is made to watch them. While descriptions are on line for these episodes, they are rather vague and, even with editing, cannot produce a comprehensive series of events as has been done with the first season (which were compiled through watching). The second season episode titles are: *1.* Finding a Lost Dream (8 min., 58 sec.). *2.* Going Coco (6 min., 56 sec.). *3.* A Brand New Harper (6 min., 41 sec.). *4.* The Photo Shoot (6 min., 3 sec.). *5.* Harper's Debut Party (6 min., 3 sec.) introduces a song, written by Harper, for the

show: "I Don't Want Your Boyfriend." *6.* Back to Big Bear (8 min., 8 sec.). *7.* Dumping Coco (5 min., 55 sec.). *8.* The Music Video (8 min., 16 sec.) features a second song written for the show, "Stand Up." *9.* The Non-Wedding Party (7 min., 26 sec.).

354 *Tales of Tails.* youtube.com. 2013 (Comedy-Drama).

While boating on a lake, two girls (Zoe and Jessica) find two necklaces entangled in some lily pads. After retrieving them, they realize the bracelets are special when they come in contact with water in a swimming pool and they are transformed into Mermaids. Now with special abilities derived from water, Zoe and Jessica must guard their secret while at the same time continue life as ordinary girls. Originally titled *A Mermaid Secret: The Other Side of Us.*

Cast (as credited): Mermaidgirl1999 (Zoe), Cuteocelot (Jessica), Mermaidgirl1999's cousin (Rosabelle). **Credits** are not given. **Comment:** The girls are pretty, the underwater photography good but the sound can become difficult to understand at times.

Episode List: *1.* A Splash of Magic. *2.* Water + Water = Powers. *3.* Potion. *4.* Uncovered. *5.* Bye, Bye Fishies.

355 *Tanya X.* tanyax.com. 2010–2011 (Erotic Adventure).

The Bureau of Knowledge, Intelligence and Nonstandard Investigations (B.I.K.I.N.I. for short) is an organization run by the beautiful Director Martin and whose agents use sex as their main weapon. Tanya X, as she is called, is a gorgeous B.I.K.I.N.I. agent who finds women just as pleasing as men and uses her sexual abilities to foil evil wherever it exists. The program charts Tanya X's latest assignment: break up a counterfeiting ring run by Big Balls Parker, owner of BB's Nightclub, and his busty associate Knockers, fiends who will stop at nothing to flourish in the world of criminal activity.

Cast: Beverly Lynne (Tanya X), Christine Nguyen (Sandy Bottoms), Kylee Nash (Knockers), Monique Parent (Director Martin), Randy Spears (Cooper), Evan Stone (Big Balls Parker), Billy Chappell (Tony Baritone), Eric Masterson (Newton, Jr.), Robert Don (Ricardo). **Credits:** *Producer:* Rob Pyatt, Beverly Lynne, Dean McKendrick, Steve Fry, Brian David. *Writer-Director:* Dean McKendrick. **Comment:** With the exception of under 30-second episode previews on YouTube, the series has been taken off-line. The program is a spin off from the feature film *The Girl from B.I.K.I.N.I.* and features nudity and soft-core sexual situations (especially between Tanya and other girls). The series plays like the movie and is very adult-in-nature (although the situations are humorously presented).

Episodes:

1. Jungle Fever. Just as she completes an assignment

in the Amazon jungle, Tanya X returns to headquarters where she is assigned to break up a counterfeiting ring.

2. Is It Fake? A she prepares for her assignment Tanya X is equipped with sex-themed weapons.

3. Ye Olde Sex Shoppe. At a sex shop Tanya X meets with (and makes love to) undercover CIA agent Sandy Bottoms for information on BB.

4. Big Balls and Knockers. Armed with the information she needs about BB and Knockers, Tanya X begins the next phase of her assignment.

5. Fraternization. In her meeting with Director Martin (which is more than just talk) Tanya X believes going undercover to infiltrate BB's Nightclub may be the best tactic.

6. An Old Flame. A complication sets in when Tanya X learns that her former boyfriend, FBI Agent Cooper has also been assigned to the case.

7. Hitting the Mattresses. With Cooper as her partner on the case, Tanya begins the assignment by meeting with mobster Tony Baritone for training on how to act like a gangster (and deceive BB).

8. Lap Dance at BB's. As Tanya practices her 1930s movie-like gangster moves, Tony sets the stage with BB to meet Tanya X (in her disguise as Angie Paluzzi).

9. Tanya X Meets Big Balls. With the stage set, Tanya X (as the mobster Angie) prepares to meet BB for the first time.

10. Libido Enhancement. Director Martin gets some action of her own as Newton, Jr. (B.I.K.I.N.I.'s weapons creator), shows her his latest sex weapons.

11. Truth or Dare. Tanya X's meeting with BB goes well—until the truth serum she places in his drink to get him to reveal his counterfeiting plans are foiled when Knockers consumes it.

12. It Ends in a Smokin' Hot Three-Way. In the concluding episode Tanya X nabs BB and Knockers—but not before a sexual encounter precedes the arrest.

356 *TeleviSean.* blip.tv. 2103 (Drama).

Brady is a young man with only a short time to live. Rather than just sit around and wait for the end to come, Brady decides to make a list of what he would like to accomplish and, with the help of his friends, Em and Elstro, sets out to make the best of what time he has left. The program charts the rather rocky road that follows as Brady fights a losing battle to accomplish his goals.

Em is Brady's girlfriend and often questions some of the adventures he and Elstro have planned. Although she loves Brady, Brady is reluctant to make any sort of romantic commitment with her. Elstro is a bit of a jokester and a loyal friend who wants to be there for Brady every step of the way.

Other Characters: Molly is a psychic that appears to be able to predict Brady's future experiences. Caroline, a widow who comes to know Brady, raises

questions between his and Em's relationship when Caroline becomes just too close to Brady. Isabella is the trash-talking rocker that Elstro falls for during their travels. Amy is Brady's drug-addicted sister who is struggling (but failing) to overcome her addiction. Natasha is a dangerous, borderline psychotic drug addict who shares a home with Amy. Gabrielle Colby (called "Miss Colby") is, like Brady and Elstro, a schoolteacher, and so gorgeous that she is "the object of every man's dream"—including Brady's, whose uppermost wish is to date her.

Cast: Sean Robinson (Brady), Danielle Reverman (Em), Derek Elstro (Elstro), Katarina Leigh Waters (Natasha), Ashley Staples (Amy), Monika Balyan (Molly), Melissa Riso (Miss Colby), Nicole Stoehr (Isabella), Garrett Liggett (Troy), Gary Gunter (Stephen), Euni Lee (Lisa), Monika Balyan (Molly), Sam Migliozzi (Caroline), Jeff Trenkle (Tyler).

Credits: *Producer-Writer:* Sean Robinson. *Director:* Sean Robinson, Dane Story. **Comment:** While the subject matter has been done before and it is not to everyone's liking, *TeleviSean* is much more realistic and intriguing than say what the TV series *Run for Your Life* has offered (about a man with only two years left to live who decides to cram a lifetime of living into what time he has left). The characters, especially Brady, are realistically portrayed and, despite the abundant use of foul language and rather long episodes (for a web series) it does play well and is worth watching.

Episodes:

1. Confession (17 min., 47 sec.). Brady reveals to Em and Elstro that he is dying and needs to fulfill some fantasies before his time is up.

2. Oath (25 min., 9 sec.). With Em and Elstro's help, Brady makes a list of what he must accomplish.

3. Shoreline (16 min., 37 sec.). A day at the beach to relax before embarking on their journey has some unexpected results when a psychic (Molly) begins predicting future events in Brady's life.

4. Reflection (23 min., 49 sec.). As Brady, Em and Elstro plan their next move, Em becomes jealous when she sees Caroline kiss Brady.

5. Imprint (11 min., 39 sec.). A visit to the Clandestine Rabbit, a nightclub with a rather unsavory reputation, becomes the first destination for the friends.

6. Family (35 min., 37 sec.). Brady decides to visit his sister (Amy) only to encounter the contempt of Natasha, a psychotic who is overly protective of Amy.

7. Descent (31 min., 32 sec.). Natasha's verbal and physical attack on Brady is overshadowed by Amy when she succumbs to a drug seizure and almost dies.

8. Turbulence (50 min., 1 sec.). As Amy recovers from her seizure, Brady and Em appear to be growing close again; the group explores the next item on the list—white water rafting.

9. Anticipation (30 min., 24 sec.). The greatest moment of Brady's life has happened: he acquired a date with Miss Colby and the episode focuses on the preparations being made for that evening.

10. Unrequited (36 min., 31 sec.). The anticipation and reality of Brady's date with Miss Colby are explored.

11. Showdown (23 min., 26 sec.). Brady and Em's relationship appears to be torn apart when Brady discovers that Elstro kissed Em (or as he says, she kissed him). Although in failing health Brady challenges Elstro to a fight that he loses but bonds him with Em.

12. Reunion (42 min., 48 sec.). In the concluding episode Brady and Em's relationship is explored with Brady finally making a commitment.

357 *That's What She Said.* twssonline. com. 2010 (Comedy-Drama).

Five close friends (Nicole, Rae-Anne, Babette, Leslie and Shin) and their efforts to navigate life in Los Angeles.

Nicole Tran, nicknamed "Nic," is a slightly awkward young woman, born in Ohio and making the transition to life in California after a broken romance (with another woman) set her on the path to not face her problems, but run away from them. The L.A. lesbian scene is something totally new to Nicole and has opened up a new world of opportunities for her.

Rae-Anne Constantino, called "Rae," is Nicole's roommate, a caring girl and the glue that holds the friends together. She and Leslie work at a West Hollywood flower shop that is owned by Rae's family. Although she is attracted to other women, Rae prefers to be called "SGS" (Straight Girl Syndrome), as it depicts her problem of falling for women who are straight as opposed to being gay (as is her current involvement with Christina, who is straight).

Babette "Baby" Liu is the flirtatious, fun-loving girl who often gets herself overly involved in romantic situations that require the help of her friends to overcome. Babette, friends with Rae-Anne since high school, doesn't intentionally mean to find trouble but her efforts to seek fun with other women just mushroom into situations that get out of hand.

Leslie Park, an activist who will involve herself in any cause she feels worthy of, is an advocate for equal rights and what she calls "queer rights." Though as forceful and outspoken as she is, Leslie has a tendency to fall for gay men.

Shin Tanaka is a woman whose past is unknown and who prefers to keep it that way (it is best if one does not ask). She is mysterious, passionate about photography and has a difficult time expressing her emotions and tends to suppress them. Shin has an "in" with the "in crowd" lesbian scene but she never lets her encounters reach a point where she cannot control them.

Cast: Vicky Luu (Nicole Tran), Allison Santos (Rae-Anne Constantino), Claire Kim (Leslie Park), Narinda Heng (Shin Tanaka), Annigee (Babette Liu), Antoinette Reyes (Chloe), Aspen Clark (Ce-cilia). **Credits:** *Producer:* Pearl Girl Productions. *Director:* Vicky Luu. **Comment:** Although billed as "Queer Asian American Web Series," it is about lesbians and is better than its billing leads one to believe. Comedy mixes with light drama to relate events in the lives of the friends with good acting and production values. It is also one of the very few programs devoted to profiling Asian American lesbians and worth checking out (another example being, though in a more dramatic vein, *Give Me Grace*).

Season 1 Episode List: Episodes are no longer on-line. *1.* Just Friends. *2.* Body Language. *3.* On-Line Dating. *4.* The Valentine's Day Edition. *5.* Post Holiday Stress Disorder. *6.* Self Love. *7.* How to Break Up. *8.* Losing the Relationship Weight. *9.* Episode #1.9. *10.* The Makeover Show. *11.* Five Dollar Dates. *12.* Pheromones and Attraction. *13.* Celebrity Mail. *14.* The Five Senses. *15.* Dopamine and Pair Bonding. *16.* Long Distance Relationships. *17.* Episode #1.17. *18.* Good Conversation. *19.* How Not to Break Up. *20.* Answering Fan Mail.

Season 2 Episodes: Only four untitled episodes (2–5) remain on line: *2.* That's What She Said—S02E02 (Season 2 Episode 2). *3.* That's What She Said—S02E03. *4.* That's What She Said—S02E04. *5.* That's What She Said—S02E05.

358 *The Third Age.* thethirdagebegins.com. 2008 (Drama).

There is the Old Age, wherein people believed in magic. In the current second age, science is believed to be the answer to everything. But there is also a perceived third age which fuses everything that has come before. Jerrod Woolf, the owner of Woolf Pharmaceutical, is the third age. Thirty years ago he had a vision wherein he created a drug that could cure disease and save the world. That time has come and such a drug has been developed. But Jonathan now has second thoughts—is the drug the right thing for the world and does he have any say in his destiny (did that vision set the course for his future?).

Christopher Zionne is a high-class drug dealer (catering only to a wealthy clientele) who is also wondering if what he is doing is what he was meant to be.

Morning is a young, desperate woman, who has engaged in a dangerous quest to find her missing father, whom she believes is being held captive by a scientist. Fate appears to unite Morning and Christopher when, after a drug deal, he sees a woman crying on the street (Morning) and agrees to help her. As Jerrod begins a quest to reclaim his future and Morning and Christopher seek Morning's missing father, each will encounter the other and the program relates the twists and turns that occur as each seeks to fulfill a destiny.

Cast: Misti Garritano (Morning), Hallie Cooper-Novack (Holly), Brian Townes (Christopher Zionne),

Jerrod Woolf (Ted Spencer), Alex Berger (Mark), Charlie Miller (Alicia), Joel Seligmann (Milton), Dennis McNitt (Dennis), Ally Carillo (Cassie), Tom Macy (Seth). **Credits:** *Producer-Director:* Patrick Meaney. **Comment:** Intriguing, well acted and produced program that is psychedelic in a way as episodes begin with an alluring swirl of images and color that can peak one's interest as to what is happening—and what will happen.

Episodes:

1. Volume 1: Fall to Earth. A drug dealer (Christopher Zinone) begins to realize that something is just not right in his life.

2. Volume 1: Static. As events begin to alter Zinone's life, he encounters a strange woman (Morning) who appears to be suffering from the same condition.

3. Volume 1: Receives Transmissions. As Morning and Zinone discuss matters that are affecting each other, company owner Jerrod Woolf recalls the incidents that altered his life.

4. Volume 1: Cranial Sample. Morning begins to realize that her purpose, and others like her, is to save God in a world where science and magic are becoming the new "God."

5. Volume 1: Constructing Reality. As Morning begins her quest, Zinone seeks help in understanding his destiny from an old friend (Holly).

6. Volume 1: The Spiral Path. Jerrod has begun his quest to find the Divine while Holly and Zinone reacquaint themselves and learn that each is experiencing the same life-changing sensations.

7. Volume 1: The Tree of Life. With Morning apparently the key to what is happening, Holly conducts a ritual to discover that Morning is the essence of all that is good and she can control destiny.

8. Volume 1: Hyperopic. With the ritual completed, Holly now knows her mission—to join with Morning in her quest for the greater good.

9. Volume 1: Mission Control. With Jerrod's company behind the conspiracy, and Holly, Morning and Zinone able to expose it, they now find themselves on the run, seeking to avoid capture by company agents. It is also seen that Jerrod's continual use of drugs has warped his thinking.

10. Volume 1: In Exile. Woolf Pharmaceutical's influence is widespread and Holly, Morning and Zinone, still on the run, discover that Jerrod may have the upper hand.

11. Volume 1: A Very Generous Offer. Zinone, captured by Woolf Pharmaceutical agents, is brought to headquarters but apparently not as a prisoner—but as a guest. But why?

12/13. Volume 1: The Last Supper (Parts 1 and 2). Episodes 12 and 13 are combined as a one program season finale to explore the fate of Holly and Morning, but especially Zinone who has the ability to choose his own destiny and make a decision that could change the world—follow the path of good (angels) or evil (devils).

14. Volume 2: The Grand Illusion. Begins the series second season (although only this episode appears) with a focus on Morning, now married and the mother of a young daughter—and an uneasy feeling that what she is experiencing may not be real as she is haunted by faint memories of something (her former life) she cannot fully bring into focus.

359 *The Three Tails.* youtube.com. 2013 (Comedy-Drama).

Three young girls (Jackie, Selena and Emily) meet on a beach, become instant friends and decide to go swimming. It is the time of a half moon and, as the girls enter the water, strange sounds are heard (like whale "singing"). Suddenly, as the water becomes increasingly rough, they swim to the safety of an underwater cave. Here, Jackie spies writing on the wall and, as she reads it, she, Selena and Emily are transformed into Mermaids (with lime green tails and green bikini tops). Before the girls can even comprehend what has happened, they are magically transported to Emily's home and dressed as they were before the transformation. The situation does not seem to faze the girls until Emily accidentally spills water on herself and she is transformed into a Mermaid. When Jackie and Selena attempt to dry Emily's tail, they touch the water and are also transformed. When the water evaporates, the girls return to their normal selves but now must guard their secret, learn to encompass their developing Mermaid powers—and try to live a life as ordinary girls.

Season one episodes are basically an introduction to Jackie, Serena and Emily (and their nemesis, Mia) and their efforts to adjust to becoming Mermaids. The second season finds Mia attempting to adjust to the fact that she is now a Mermaid and her involvement with Jackie, Emily and Serena when Jackie finds a book once owned by a girl named Faith. Faith, an evil Siren who died 200 years ago, is awakened from her long sleep when Jackie begins reading passages from the book and finds the girls' the instruments through which to return to life—by acquiring their powers. Their effort to destroy Faith's spirit concludes the season when they concoct a potion that appears to accomplish their goal. However, Faith is a feline Mermaid and has nine lives—and to destroy her, they must literally kill her nine times (the plot of the concluding third season episodes). In season two, the Mermaid tail colors change to aqua and conclude in the third season with orange and purple colors.

Cast: Natasha Garreton (Emily Emery), Sofia Garreton (Jackie Sky), Marlena Lerner (Selena White), Julianna Goldsmith (Faith), Ruby Ray (Mia), Saga Dios (Nikki),

Comment: A bit more complex than an ordinary Mermaid tale that encompasses more than just young girls becoming Mermaids as they also have to battle an evil foe. The acting is acceptable and like most such series, the audio and video quality is poor at times.

Episodes:

1. Waters Change, Parts 1, 2 and 3. Establishes the story line as Jackie, Selena and Emily, trapped in an underwater cave, become Mermaids when Jackie reads a spell written on the wall.

2. The Fight. Curious to know why her friends (Emily, Selena and Jackie) are acting differently since their return from the beach, Mia sets her sights on to finding out why.

3. Cancun's Waters. On a trip to Mexico, Emily, Selena and Jackie risk revealing their secret when they go swimming, become Mermaids—and find the beach too crowded to exit the water. The episode has been removed due to music copyright violations.

4. Birthday Tail. Jackie's birthday party is not all that happy an occasion when water spills on Emily, transforms her into a Mermaid and Jackie has to do what she can to cover for her and prevent party guests from discovering her secret.

5. Charmed. Curious to know more about the cave in which they became Mermaids, Emily, Jackie and Selena decide to re-visit it and hopefully learn more about what has happened to them. Due to music copyright violations, only the video portion can be seen (the sound has been muted).

6. Halloween Horror Night. After enjoying an evening of trick-or-treating, the girls find trouble when the full moon rises and they become Mermaid vampires.

7. Study Hazard. Still determined to learn their secret, Mia pretends to need help studying and asks Selena for help in a devious plan to discover exactly what she is hiding.

8. Mia's Revenge. Mia's plan begins to take effect when Jackie and Emily join her and Selena and Mia doses them with water, takes a picture of them as Mermaids and runs off.

9. Christmas Disaster. Emily risks exposing her secret when she elects to go swimming rather than attend a family Christmas party.

10. The Attack. While hiking alone, Jackie attempts to cross a puddle when a tentacle rises from the water and attacks her. Worried that Jackie has not returned, Emily and Selena begin to search for her—and find and rescue her.

11. Sea Change. Still hoping to expose her friends as Mermaids, Mia follows Emily, Jackie and Selena to the ocean. As the girls go for a swim, Mia finds, in the rocks, a spell and reads it and instantly transforms into a Mermaid. Season 1 concludes.

12. Pressure Tail. Season 2 begins. Emily, Selena and Jackie attempt to help Mia who is having a difficult time learning how to live as a girl and a Mermaid at the same time.

13. Tail Trouble. While swimming Emily finds a strange liquid that she, Jackie and Selena are unable to figure out. In a rather dumb move, Emily drinks it. She transforms into a Mermaid—but now cannot turn back to a normal girl.

14. School Tail. With Emily returning to normal when the liquid potion wears off, she, Jackie, Mia and Selena face another problem: while at a school fair the girls are unaware that it is a half moon and its rays will transform them into Mermaids.

15. Fish Can't Swim. Overcoming her inhibitions about becoming a Mermaid, Mia takes the first step and, with her friends' help, makes her first transformation when she goes for an ocean swim.

16. Answers or Not. Selena, finding a rare book that was once owned by a Mermaid in the year 1831 learns that the book is not only alive, but it can make things happen for the greater good.

17. Power Outage. A vacation for Jackie, Selena and Emily at Emily's family's beach house turns out to be anything but relaxing when their powers go haywire and they find they cannot control them.

18. Scaly Troubles. Trouble enters the picture when Mia befriends a new girl at school (Nikki) and becomes jealous when she also takes a liking to Emily, Jackie and Selena.

19. Black Revenge. Christmas morning is anything but a happy occasion for Selena when she gets a mysterious present of chocolates, opens the box and comes under the spell of an evil being determined to absorb her powers.

20. 1871. A spell cast by Emily, saves Selena, but later, when Mia finds a necklace, the girls learn it belongs to Faith, an immortal girl (actually a Mermaid) who has been their age for hundreds of years. The second season concludes.

21. It's Back. Season 3 begins. Contact with the necklace has left Emily with strange dreams of visions of Faith and she, Selena and Jackie decide to return to the beach rocks, where the necklace was found, to search for answers.

22. Back Again. As the girls search, Selena mysteriously disappears. A clue to her discovery lies with Emily when she finds a note (background noise makes it very difficult to decipher) in her locker that has information that can bring her back. Meanwhile a mysterious figure, dressed in green has been stalking them.

23. Christmas Magic. With Christmas approaching, Emily, Selena and Jackie must contend with unusual problems as their powers appear to be acting up on their own.

24. Is This a Trick? When Selena finds that her Mermaid's book has been stolen, she, Jackie and Emily pursue Faith, believing that she is the culprit.

25. Spells and Magic. While at the beach, Jackie, Selena and Emily decide to investigate the Magic Caves under the ocean not realizing that Faith is observing their every move.

26. Secrets Aren't Safe. While swimming, Selena, Jackie and Emily find a necklace that belongs to Faith. If they destroy it, it can also rid their lives of Faith forever.

27. Somebody Is Hiding Something. Emily, Selena and Jackie get closer to uncovering the truth about Faith and her mysterious past in the concluding episode.

360 *The Three Water Girls.* youtube.com. 2011 (Comedy-Drama).

Nikki, Melissa and Selena (later Kylie) are young girls who can magically transform into Mermaids when touched by water (initiated when they found magic rings and lockets in a lake and activated their powers after using a waterslide). While the girls do develop powers and have to battle an evil Mermaid hunter, they also acquire strange side effects after watching an eclipse and must now navigate life as magical creatures of the sea.

Cast (as credited): Nikki, Melissa, Selena, Kylie. **Credits** are not given. **Comment:** A good idea (incorporating a Mermaid hunter) but the program has very poor sound coupled with equally bad photography (very jumpy picture).

Episode List: *1.* Something Fishy. *2.* Diving In. *3.* A Day at the Beach. *4.* Unknown Title. *6.* The Rings. *7.* Who Had Seen Them? *8.* Season Finale. *9.* Kylie Arrives (Begins Season 2). *10.* Heat Vision. *11.* The Lockets. *12.* Surprise!! *13.* Missing.

361 *Three Way.* onemorelesbian.com. 2008 (Comedy-Drama).

Siobhan is a bi-sexual woman who, after her divorce from aging motion picture action hero Dirk LaBonte, finds herself nearly broke and with no other choice moves in with her best friend, Roxie, a lesbian. All is progressing well for Siobhan until Roxie's girlfriend, Andrea, moves in with them (creating a sort of female version of the TV series *Three's Company*). Complications set in when Geri, Roxie's ex-girlfriend, decides to again become a part of Roxie's life and Siobhan finds herself becoming involved in all their craziness, including the lesbian scene. The program charts the events that spark the lives of all four women, especially Siobhan, as she learns that being with another woman may be the right choice for a mate.

Cast: Maeve Quinlan (Siobhan McGarry), Jill Bennett (Andrea Bailey), Cathy Shim (Roxie Lautzenheiser), Maile Flanagan (Geri O'Flanagan), Donna W. Scott (Winter Kote), Elizabeth Keener (Celia Sanderson), Liz Vassey (Mikki Majors), Christina Cox (Lara Lancaster), Kristy Swanson (Leslie Lapdalulu), Bridget McManus (Rhonda Rapid Delivery), Gabrielle Christian (Cindy Shimms), Linda Miller (Frankie), Elisa Dyann (Jamie). **Credits:** Producer: Paige Bernhardt, Nancylee Myatt, Maeve Quinlan, Joey Scott. *Director:* Mary Lou Belli, Courtney Rowe, Nancylee Myatt, Robert Ben Garant. *Writer:* Paige Bernhardt, Maile Flanagan, Nancylee Myatt, Maeve Quinn, Georgia Ragsdale. **Comment:**

Sexual situations coupled with mild profanity in a well produced and acted series. Its content is not new to what can be seen on TV and it is charmingly presented based on the episodes that remain on line.

Episodes: With the exception of the episodes *Let the Gaymes Begin* and *Fatal Distraction*, the episodes have been taken off line. Other episode titles: *Lady Cop, Psychodrama, Siobhan Sizzles, Rhonda Rapid Delivery, What's for Dinner, Friday Night Dykes, The Dinah Monologues.*

362 *The Throwaways.* onemorelesbian.com. 2012 (Drama).

For some, being gay or a lesbian is more of a curse than a declaration of who they are. Some find acceptance while others are considered weird and just not acceptable as a part of society. Olivia, a 17-year-old girl, is one such person, a lesbian whose family strongly disapproves of who she is. Olivia was the perfect daughter. She attended church, studied hard, never broke a curfew and had planned to attend Brown University. She never used drugs, never drank and even got along with her siblings. However, when her parents uncovered her sexuality, it was beyond their comprehending and literally disowned her when her mother caught Olivia and a girl "study buddy" engaging in more than books. To hopefully "cure her of the disease" it was decided to send Olivia to an institution in Utah "to fix her." Defiant, Olivia ran away and, on her seemingly endless journey to find herself, met Dorsey, a girl in the same position, who introduced her to a group of other such "Throwaways," misunderstood young women who have banned together to create their own little community. As Olivia adjusts to her new world she quickly learns that a darker side to society exists (a counter-culture of violence, crime and drug abuse) and that she must navigate it to survive—and hopefully make her way back home one day. The program follows Olivia's experiences as she and others like her struggle to enjoy a life with the girls they love no matter what others think.

Cast: Ashley Andersen (Olivia), Kate Black-Spence (Dorsey), Molly Pan (Jazzlyn), Hannah Aubry (Rynn), Mia Jones (Mia), Kristin Bennett (Olivia's aunt), Rocco Cataldo (Bill), Butch Jerinic (Olivia's mother), Michael Marsh (Olivia's father), Bridget McManus (Fiona), Ashley Nguyen (Nancy), Fawzia Mirza (Jayne), Jacqueline Salamack (Amy), Rachel Shapiro (Andrea), Luca Marsh (Bailey). **Credits:** *Producer:* Jessica King, Christin Mell. *Director:* Jessica King. *Writer:* Julie Keck, Jessica King.

Comment: Based on the only available episode, the program is well acted and produced. Ashley Andersen is appealing as Olivia and the story itself appears intriguing.

Episodes: Only episode 4 ("Room for One More") of 10 produced episodes and a teaser for the series remain on line.

363 Thurston the Western Web Series. thurston-series. com. 2011–2014 (Western).

Thurston, a remote town in the Kansas Ozarks founded by Garrett Thurston after the Civil War, was once a thriving mining town until a plague claimed the lives of many of its citizens. Now some 15 years later, the town has rebounded but become both a haven for lawlessness and a land where dreams of prosperity also exist. The program, set during the unrest of the 1880s (specifically 1881), follows incidents in the lives of the citizens of a growing but potentially dangerous town as they struggle for survival.

Thurston: Western Web Series. **Susannah Wells (left) and Catherine Frels (copyright Thurston, LLC, 2014).**

Maggie Callaway, a land owner who came west to escape an abusive marriage, is a symbol of the hardships women pioneers had to face in turbulent times in towns that were anything but respectable or crime free. Though independent and able to handle a gun, Maggie must fight to keep what is rightfully hers.

Perry Robinson, the town Marshal, is dedicated to his job but his somewhat mysterious background leads some townspeople to believe he may be hiding something.

Rosie MacGillicuddy, a woman who lost her family by the plague on her journey west, survives the only way she knows how—as a prostitute who will also conspire to learn what others want to know and sell those secrets at a price.

Cyrus McCormick, one of the first citizens of Thurston, runs the general store, though not as a legitimate enterprise as he has candle-stein relationships with traders beyond Thurston.

Agnes Snead, a former madam, and domineering woman who can not only take care of herself, but uses her sons (the Snead boys) to do her bidding. She is married to Edmund, a con artist and gambler who becomes violently dangerous when crossed. Harlan, the eldest of the Snead boys, is a former lawman turned cunning and cruel gunfighter. Amon, the second-born son, was a miner who now suffers from nightmares and delusions following an accident (fell down a mineshaft) and is considered to be mentally unstable. Owen, bullied by Harlan, but babied by Agnes, is the youngest son, a volcano waiting to erupt as he struggles to cope with life.

Josephine Maxwell, called Jo, possesses medical skills (learned during the Civil War) but now, after the death of her husband during a stagecoach robbery, does what is necessary to survive.

Benjamin Walkingstick, the town doctor, is what would be called a half-breed—part Cherokee Indian and part of the Western European settlers who came west.

Garrett Thurston, a pioneer who journeyed west is the town's founder. He is married to Pearl, a bitter woman who finds life in Thurston deplorable.

Cast: Catherine Frels (Maggie Callaway), Garry Westcott (Perry Robinson), Susannah Wells (Rosie MacGillicuddy), James O'Sullivan (Cyrus McCormick), Colleen Zenk (Agnes Snead), Walt Willey (Edmund Snead), Evan Casey (Harlan Snead), Felipe Cabezas (Amon Snead), Garrett Brennan (Owen Snead), Lisa Nanni-Messegee (Josephine Maxwell), Enrico Nassi (Dr. Benjamin Walkingstick), Bob Martin (Garrett Thurston), Kathryn Browning (Pearl Thurston), Autumn Morningstar Custalow Alfaro (Inolah Walkingstick), Todd Messegee (District Attorney Stewart), Dave Gamble (Judge William Richards), John C. Bailey (Frank Daniels, Pinkerton Detective), Peter Ponzini (Bailiff), Ariana Almajan (Marie Dumont), Richard Cutting (Preacher), Steve Quartell (Sheriff Nate Hart), Regen Wilson (John Callaway). **Credits:** *Producer:* Kathryn O'Sullivan, Paul Awad. *Writer:* Kathryn O'Sullivan. *Director:* Paul Awad. **Comment:** Westerns, once a major part of network television have virtually disappeared as first-run dramas. Certain series can be seen in syndicated reruns and to some these will be brand new. *Thurston* is a throwback to a time when westerns were the mainstay of ABC, CBS and NBC and well worth watching—even if you have never seen a TV western before. The cinematography is outstanding, the acting as good as any western television has produced and the locations well chosen to represent the harsh realization of how people lived and worked. Also unique about *Thurston* is that it is not a male-dominated western. It follows more along the lines of ABC's *The Big Valley* (where the importance of women, especially Victoria Barkley [Barbara Stanwyck] and her daughter Audra [Linda Evans]) were seen as much more than just store keepers or seamstresses. *Thurston* has opened up the possibility that the western has returned—although it may only be on the Internet.

Episodes:

1. Death Amongst Savages (7 min., 20 sec.). Introduces several of the regulars following the death of the town founder in the opening scene (suffers a heart attack while mining for gold).

2. Kill Me Tomorrow (6 min., 26 sec.). A stranger (Maggie's husband, John) arrives in town, accompanied by Marshal Perry Robinson seeking his wife.

3. The Bone Garden (6 min., 20 sec.). Maggie's reunion with John is not a pleasant one as she kills him when his abusive ways give her no other choice.

4. The Agony of Parting (8 min., 50 sec.). When John does not return to town after discovering where Maggie lives, Perry begins an investigation to find him. He uncovers the fact that Nate (the sheriff) and Maggie have been seeing each other.

5. Beating the Devil (6 min., 39 sec.). Nate, taking the blame for killing John to protect Maggie, faces Perry in a gun duel.

6. The Coldest End (5 min., 17 sec.). Unable to stop the duel Maggie watches as Nate is killed by Perry when he is outdrawn.

7. Something Wicked (7 min., 46 sec.). With Nate gone (and Maggie pregnant) Maggie returns to her life as a rancher while Perry decides to remain in Thurston, seeing it is now his duty to maintain the peace.

8. Pent-Up Guilts (9 min., 37 sec.). Amon Snead is introduced as he stands trial for the murder of a man. As the trial proceeds, his brothers free him, wounding only the judge's ego in the escape.

9. Hell Is Empty (9 min., 56 sec.). Reveals the back history of Rosie, the prostitute, who was taken in by the Snead family as a child after her parents' death and how, when she refused to leave Thurston with the Sneads, literally became their enemy.

10. And All the Devils Are Here (8 min., 58 sec.). The Snead brothers return to Thurston finds the townspeople banning together to confront them (Owen is knocked unconscious and captured; Rosie is shot by Harlan as he and Amon escape).

11. Trust a Few (9 min., 16 sec.). Perry jails Owen while Jo attempts to use her medical skills to help Rosie.

12. Lovely to the Dying (9 min., 10 sec.). Focuses on Jo and her efforts to remove the bullet and save Rosie's life.

13. Wrath of Love (10 min., 45 sec.). Time has passed since the prior episode and Rosie has recovered from her gunshot wound. Rosie reveals aspects of her past to Jo as does Jo to Rosie (while Rosie was taken in by Agnes, it was the Snead boys who killed Jo's husband during a stagecoach robbery). Harlan and Amon return home to Agnes and confess that they shot Rosie and left Owen back in Thurston.

14. What's Done Is Done (8 min., 1 sec.). As Maggie reflects on what has happened over the past few weeks, she begins to go into labor. Agnes departs for Thurston with Harlan and Amon to retrieve Owen.

15. Light in Darkness (6 min., 54 sec.). As Maggie's labor intensifies, Ben is called in to help. His reception from some is rather cold as he is Indian and not trusted. Agnes, Harlan and Amon arrive in Thurston.

16. Kin Will Have Kin (12 min., 37 sec.). As Maggie's labor intensifies, Ben enlists Perry's help. Meanwhile, Jo has taken a stand against Agnes's attempt to kidnap Rosie and retrieve Owen.

17. Bonds of Fate (12 min., 8 sec.). Maggie's baby is safely delivered but Jo's efforts to stop Agnes fail as Rosie is kidnapped (and later forced to marry Amon). Meanwhile, Edmund, Agnes's husband, is seen shooting a Pinkerton detective with the possibility being left open for additional episodes to follow to explore the lives of Maggie, Jo, the Sneads and other citizens of Thurston.

364 *To Kill a Princess*. tokillaprincess.com. 2013 (Mystery).

A beautiful young woman (Princess Ruby) is next in line to assume the royal throne as Queen. Not all are pleased at the prospect and Rose, the King's (Ruby's father) aide is the one most eager to see that Ruby does not live long enough to acquire the position, as she is seeking it for herself. To insure that Ruby does not become the Queen, Rose sets her up on a series of dates—seemingly normal to Ruby but the date (Morris) is actually an assassin hired by Rose to do away with Ruby. The program follows Rose's efforts to achieve her goal and Ruby's efforts to enjoy her dates without ever knowing that at any time Morris could strike and end her life.

Cast: Roxi Gregory (Princess Ruby), Hattie Morgan-Smith (Rose), Nick Hayles (Morris), Stephen Sheridan (Evil Bob), Sam Casserly (Ivor Innersteam), Chloe Wade (Mary). **Credits:** *Producer-Writer-Director:* Sam Casserly. **Comment:** Visually impressive (color and costumes), well acted and produced. But a bit bizarre at times with the unusual lengths Rose will go to become Queen. The program is produced in England and while there is mild violence, it also contains vulgar language.

Episodes:

1. Episode 1. Princess Ruby is introduced at the Royal New Year's Eve Gala.

2. Episode 2. Rose begins her behind-the-scenes treachery to betray the King and kill Ruby.

3. Episode 3. Rose hires Evil Bob (of the Royal Research Facility) to help in her cause by using his steam-powered technology to enhance Morris.

4. Episode 4. Evil Bob has produced a steam-powered subject (Ivor) that Rose hopes to use to enable Morris to complete his task.

5. Episode 5. It is the night of Ruby and Morris's date and Morris has lured her to the Castle but Ruby appears to be wiser than she seems and confronts Rose.

6. Episode 6. Ruby turns the tables on Rose and

Morris becomes the victim with the sweet Ruby now appearing as a sadistic woman torturing Morris to tell what he knows. The unresolved episode concludes with Rose appearing in what looks to be another confrontation between her and Ruby.

365 *Today and Tomorrow.* webserieschannel.com. 2012 (Drama).

Maria Estefan, a young woman living in Brazil and married to Ronaldo, wants only one thing: to escape from Ronaldo's mobster-controlled world and raise her children in a safer environment. With the help of her father (Bruno), Maria is able to escape from Ronaldo but had to leave her children behind. Although safe for the moment, and with a plan to rescue her children, the program charts the torment Maria endures until a time when she can be reunited with her children.

Cast: Anastasia Ampatzoglou (Maria Estefan), Victoria Delaney (Alexandra Petrova), Helen Cooke (Faye Saunders), Paul Newberry (Wayne Crawford), Edith Petersen (Lauren Baker), Emilie Miriam (Shirley Walker), Chris Kerry (Mother), Tim Rutherford (Gerrick Armstrong), Keith Bailey (Richard Newton), Lladel Brayant (Owen Parker), Adam Sean Butcher (Tony Hunter). **Credits:** *Producer-Writer-Director:* David Jones.

Comment: Only two episodes are on line to view for free. Others are only view-able through a rent or buy situation on the official website. The free episodes focus primarily on Maria and the desperation that surrounds her. The acting is good and the production values, based on the limited situations that are involved, are also good.

Episodes:
1. Online Episode 1 (3 min., 18 sec.). Maria has escaped from Ronaldo, but the sudden death of her father now leaves her all alone to battle her husband.
2. Online Episode 2 (3 min., 18 sec.). Relief comes in a way when Maria learns she has inherited a great deal of money from her father—money she hopes can help in the rescue of her children.

366 *Treasure Hunt.* youtube.com. 2014 (Adventure).

A breaking news report interrupts regular TV programming: "One year ago today, the only billion dollar lottery winner, Howard Kent, disappeared at sea." As the report continues it relates the fact that there are no heirs to the fortune and numerous scammers have tried to acquire it by pretending to be related to Kent. "But just now a last will and testament has been discovered and in a bizarre twist in the story it may be you!" The newscaster is referring to the viewer as the program is interactive and a prize can be won if a riddle is correctly solved.

Kent apparently hid his money before his disappearance and left a series of riddles behind that lead to its whereabouts—hidden somewhere in New York City (and in a public place). The program follows two people in particular, Hayden and Marlon, as they become part of a treasure hunt—seeking to unravel a series of clues that will eventually lead to a fortune in cash.

Cast: Melody Cheng (Hayden), Patrick Marlett (Marlon), Mark Ellmore (Howard Kent), Sam Reeder (Trevor), Caleb Wells (Frank), Erica Cho (Newscaster). **Credits:** *Producer:* Felipe Rosa. *Writer-Director:* Daniel Finley. **Comment:** Current at the time of publication but only the pilot episode has been released. An intriguing concept that, although not original (the feature film *It's a Mad, Mad, Mad, Mad World* comes to mind), is well acted and produced. There are numerous story possibilities and the characters are a nice blend of good and bad.

Episodes:
1. Pilot (8 min., 29 sec.). The story line is established with a group of people beginning a quest on the largest treasure hunt in U.S. history.

367 *The Trivial Pursuits of Arthur Banks.* amctv.com. 2011 (Drama).

Arthur Banks is a playwright and theater director with a serious problem: he is unfaithful and seduces other women (here, in the weeks leading to the opening of his play, the leading lady, an underage girl, the understudy and a Columbia University theater major). Arthur soon comes to realize what he is doing is wrong and seeks not only the help of his best friend (Chandler) but that of a therapist. The program relates Arthur's efforts to see what he is doing is wrong and someway learn how to deal with the issues that occur when he uncontrollably falls in love—especially when he writes plays based on his dysfunctional love life.

Cast: Adam Goldberg (Arthur Banks), Jeffrey Tambor (Therapist), Pete Chekvala (Chandler Brown), Larry Pine (Narrator), Wendy Glenn (Annette), Laura Clery (Cornelia Klein), Fabianne Therese (Chloe), Camille Cregan (Understudy), Barry Primus (George Epstein), Daffney Dawson (Sophie Liest). **Credits:** *Producer:* Peter Glanz, Juan Iglesias, Neda Armian. *Director:* Peter Glanz. *Writer:* Peter Glanz, Juan Iglesias. **Comment:** The first web series produced by the cable network AMC with acting and production values comparable to any TV series. The program, filmed in black and white, echoes the feature films *Annie Hall* and *Manhattan* for its seducing storyline and is a bit different in presentation than a typical TV series in that it encompasses a narrator to explain (in mocked Freud-like psychiatric language) what is happening.

Episodes:
1. I Pulled a Polanski (12 min., 43 sec.). As Arthur begins production on his most ambitious play to date, he finds himself becoming too involved with an underage girl.

2. Silent Treatment (13 min., 48 sec.). Again tempting fate, Arthur begins dating his leading lady.

3. The Latent Existentialist (15 min., 3 sec.). With two weeks before opening night Arthur finds that he must make a choice and focus on one woman—a woman he can love without his constant desire for sex.

368 Trouble Women. webserieschannel.com. 2013 (Drama).

Lisa, Josie and Veronica are three women who will stop at nothing to get what they want (mostly through the manipulation of men). Each woman has a story to tell and the program explores how and what they achieved by their addressing the camera.

Cast: Carolina Santos Read (Lisa Castillo), Jessica Castro (Josie Campolo), Natalie Freeman (Veronica Lawrence), Jorge Ferragut (Leonardo Velez). **Credits:** *Producer:* Jonathan Ago, Elspeth Brown, Rosie Hernandez. *Director:* Elspeth Brown, Daniel Tantalean. *Writer:* Elspeth Brown, Max Lehman. **Comment:** Well-paced program that draws the viewer right in as the profiled women relate aspects of who they are and what they need to accomplish. The acting and production values are good and episodes are just the right length so as not to become a chore to watch.

Episodes:

1. Lisa Castillo Confession, Part 1 (2 min., 46 sec.). Lisa reveals her motives to acquire money and power.

2. Lisa Castillo Confession, Part 2 (2 min.). Lisa's philosophies on life, business and love are explored.

3. Josie Campolo Confession (4 min., 29 sec.). Josie reveals her plans to move forward in her career—no matter what it takes to accomplish it.

4. Veronica Lawrence Confession (4 min., 44 sec.). Veronica, a spoiled woman who feels she is entitled to the finer things in life, reveals how she plans to find a man and be cared for like a princess.

5. Death in Colombia (6 min., 12 sec.). Portrays Lisa's efforts to prepare a feast and make her ill husband's last hours a happy occasion.

369 Truly Fishy. youtube.com. 2011 (Comedy-Drama).

Two girls (Carlee and Lauren), lost during a long walk, come across a river and decide to swim it upstream to get back home. Unknown to them, its waters are magic and has the power to make young girls Mermaids. Carlee and Lauren are unaffected at first, but once home and once they come in contact with water, their transformation begins and each becomes a Mermaid. Now, faced with living dual lives, Carlee and Lauren must keep secret their Mermaid abilities while trying to live as ordinary girls.

Cast (as credited): Brooke (Carlee Harper), Sierra (Becca Adams), Maddie (Lauren Stoll). **Cred-**

its are not given. **Comment:** The underwater photography is good, the girls seem to be enjoying themselves (acting natural) but the sound is poor and the above water scenes are somewhat shaky at times.

Episode List: *1.* Something Fishy. *2.* Blue Waters. *3.* Double Life. *4.* No Control. *5.* Tough Seashells. *6.* A Splash of Truth. *7.* The Last Goodbye? *8.* Too Much Sunlight. *9.* Three's a Charm. *10.* Falling in Sunset. *11.* Some Things Change.

370 Truly H20. youtube.com. 2013 (Comedy Drama).

"We have to keep it a secret. We don't want to become science experiments or something worse" is said by a young girl named Marina when she and her two girlfriends (Dylan and Sanna) find their lives changed forever after swimming in enchanted waters and being transformed into Mermaids (it occurred when Dylan and Marina's identical necklaces locked and they were transported to a mysterious underwater cave that endowed them with the unique ability to transform). With each there to help the other, Dylan, Sanna and Marina must now keep what happened to them a secret and convince the world they are ordinary girls.

Cast (as credited): Claudia (Marina), Genevieve (Dylan), Sara (Sanna). **Credits (as listed):** *Writer-Director:* Genevieve. **Comment:** Good acting, pretty girls and underwater photography coupled with adequate special effects (although they are quite obvious as being fake). Like most Mermaid series, the program suffers from poor sound at times.

Episode List: *1.* Changes in the Water. *2.* Miss Popularity's Pool. *3.* Frostbite. *4.* Moonstruck Mermaid. *5.* Boiling Over. *6.* Knowledge Is Power. *7.* Suspicions Rising. *8.* T Is for Trouble.

371 Twins of the Atlantic. youtube.com. 2011 (Comedy-Drama).

While walking to swim practice for school, Alice and Faith find two strange-looking necklaces that each contain several unusual gems. Thinking nothing of it, they keep the necklaces—but when they return home and come in contact with water, each transforms into a Mermaid. As they learn to accept what has happened to them, they must also lead double lives and protect their Mermaid abilities from being discovered by others.

Cast (as credited): Paige (Alice), Savannah (Faith), Sierra (Riley). **Credits** are not given. **Comment:** Poor sound quality but pretty girls coupled with good underwater photography.

Episode List: *1.* Sea Change. *2.* Fire and Ice. *3.* Party Time. *4.* Marilia. *5.* Babysitting Troubles. *6.* Ancestor Bracelet. *7.* Dance Camp.

372 Two Broken Girls. youtube.com. 2013 (Drama).

British-produced program about incidents in the lives of two beautiful women: Chloe, an actress, and Esther, a presenter (sort of like an entertainment reporter on programs like *Entertainment Tonight* and *Access Hollywood*).

Cast: Esther Shephard (Esther), Chloe Partridge (Chloe). **Credits:** *Producer-Writer:* Esther Shephard, Chloe Partridge. **Comment:** Programs that only feature one or two performers addressing the camera most often do not work as the viewer quickly loses interest. There have been some exceptions, like the horror Internet series *Pandora's Blog* where the lead is so like-able that you stay tuned. The same situation works here. Chloe and Esther are not only attractive, but captivating and can hold interest for the duration of each episode. It is a bit different and worth watching.

Episodes:

1. Just a Ride (6 min., 15 sec.). Chloe and Esther talk about their lives, especially their careers.

2. Drastic Measures (4 min., 56 sec.). The personal aspects of their lives are explored, including their vices, eating habits, wardrobes, and make-up techniques.

373 *The Two Silver Tails.* youtube.com. 2014 (Comedy-Drama).

While talking with her girlfriend Brooklyn, a young girl (Blaire) spots a bracelet hanging from the side of her home. After examining it, Brooklyn sees a similar bracelet just a few feet away and takes it. Each places her bracelet around her neck not realizing their lives are about to change forever. Later that day, when the girls touch water, they are transformed into Mermaids with specific powers: teleportation, shape-shifting and control over water (Blaire can heat water; Brooklyn can freeze it). The program charts their experiences as they struggle to guard their secret (especially from Blaire's stepsister, Katie) and pretend to be just ordinary girls.

Cast (as credited): Erin (Blaire), Julie (Brooklyn), Natalie (Katie). **Credits** are not given. **Comment:** The acting is acceptable, the girls pretty, the underwater photography good but poor sound (from camera microphones) hampers the production.

Episode List: *1.* Two Necklaces and One Big Secret. *2.* Power Hour. *3.* Splash from the Past. *4.* A Day at the Lake. *5.* Step Sister Trouble. *6.* Episode 6. *7.* Magical Tail Change and Bottle.

374 *The Two Tailed Mermaids.* youtube.com. 2012 (Comedy-Drama).

Annie and Emma, young girls playing soccer ball in a public park, find, when chasing a lost ball, an apparently hidden magical river that later transforms them into Mermaids (resulting from contact with the water). With their lives suddenly changed, Annie and Emma must now navigate life not only as magical Mermaids, but as ordinary girls as well.

Cast (as credited): Megan (Annie), Sam (Emma), Alyssa (Amber), Cassidy (Jamie). **Credits** are not given. **Comment:** Enjoyable story that is sometimes hampered by poor sound resulting from the use of only the microphone contained in the camera.

Episode List: *1.* Just the Beginning. *2.* Power Stones. *3.* Power Hour. *4.* One More Power. *5.* Sea Sick. *6.* Night of the Full Moon. *7.* Picture Perfect. *8.* Memory Loss. *9.* Double Crossed. *10.* Mermaid Amber. *11.* Birthday Wave. *12.* Lost on Shore. *13.* Washed Away. *14.* Power Storm.

375 *Two Tails, Three Wishes.* youtube.com. 2012 (Comedy-Drama).

April and Nidia are friends whose lives change forever when, during a sleepover, each experiences a strange dream involving monkeys. While the dream has no apparent affects (other than unnerving them) they just shrug it off until they come in contact with water and are transformed into Mermaids. How monkeys figure into such transformations is not explained and the program follows the girls as they attempt to live normal lives while concealing their true existences as Mermaids.

Cast (as credited): Sophie (April), Anna (Nidia), Lisa (Both mothers). **Credits** are not given. **Comment:** The program has very poor sound and is not in the proper aspect ratio (badly stretched picture that presents the girls in an unflattering "fat" image).

Episodes:

1. The Pilot. The story line is established as described above.

376 *An Undead Story: The Web Series.* youtube.com. 2013 (Drama).

In 2012 a young woman named Karen ran away from home following the death of her mother. A year later, an unknown infection spread across the world first causing madness then turning those infected into zombies. Karen, a survivor, now feels she needs to reconnect with her father and begins a trek across the U.S. to find him. The hope that her father is still alive instills in her the drive to begin her mission and the program charts her journey as she seeks to avoid zombies and reconnect with her father.

Cast: Jaz Kemp (Karen). Others include (but not shown on video): Kylie Contreary, Shondale Seymour, Michael Mullin, Tank Elinger, Haley Alvarado. **Credits:** *Producer-Writer-Director:* Patrick Sullivan. **Comment:** In her video, Jaz Kemp states that her show is a spin off from the movie *An Undead Story* wherein she played Lilith (such a movie, however, is not listed on the web site IMDB.com). Actually Jaz's introduction is the only viable information about what the web series is to be and from it, it appears to be very good (although anytime a pretty girl is placed in a perilous situation it is almost guaranteed an audience). Other than what Jaz mentions, there is no further information regarding the storyline or the cast.

Episodes:

1. Short Story Promo 1 (1 min., 21 sec.). Although labeled "Not a part of the story," it shows two people, a man and a woman with injuries possibly sustained from a zombie encounter, with the man leaving as the woman lies (dead?) on a bed.

2. Behind the Scenes with Jaz Kemp (1 min., 23 sec.). Star Jaz Kemp gives an introduction to the series.

3. Behind the Scenes Stunt Bloopers (1 min., 16 sec.). Several stunts are seen being performed.

377 *Under the Sea Secrets.* youtube.com. 2013 (Comedy-Drama).

Zanna, a young girl with fanciful dreams, decides to make a potion (from a recipe she found) that she believes will turn her into a Mermaid. She drinks the potion and when she first comes in contact with water she is transformed into a Mermaid—a secret she must keep as she struggles to also live life as an ordinary school girl. **Cast (as credited):** Jessie (Zanna), Tala (Scarlette). **Credits** are not given. **Comment:** A twist on how a young girl becomes a Mermaid, here using a home-brewed potion. The production suffers from poor audio quality but is acceptable in other aspects (acting, photography).

Episode List: *1.* I'm a What? *2.* The Forbidden Forest. *3.* Crazy Mermaid Stuff? *4.* Dangerous Waters. *5.* No Moon. *6.* Home Alone. *7.* Season Finale.

378 *Unfamous.* theunfamousseries.com. 2013 (Drama).

Rio Greene is a freshman at London's Brompton University. But a college education is not all that Rio wants. Dissatisfied with her lowly social status and yearning to become popular, she begins a quest to become Unfamous—a popular person of her generation or an "It Girl" (of the past, like actress Rita Hayworth in the 1940s). The program charts Rio's efforts to reinvent her life and the problems she encounters as she tries to become someone she really isn't for the sake of achieving status. Based on Shakira "Scotty Unfamous" Scott novel, *Unfamous, Book One.*

Cast: Busayo Ige (Rio Greene), Emmanuel Ogunjinmi (Tyson), Marcus Campbell (Nathaniel), Emma Malyszczuk (Georgia), Robert Griffiths (Carter), Leon Palmer (Leon), Sade Wright (Nadia), Natalie Fergus (Fontaine), Kassidy Chaplin (Ace), Michael Salami (Calvin), Michael Oba (Amari), Jason York (Manny), Kiell Smith-Byone (Shaquille), Nicole Abraham (Yoshi), Thea Gajic (Sky), Holly Brown (Robin). **Credits:** *Producer:* Scotty Unfamous, Deb

McKoy, Gemma Wedderburn. *Director:* Selina Osei. *Writer:* Scotty Unfamous. **Comment:** Interesting premise with good acting and production values. Although produced in England, the program is easily understandable and is not hampered (for American audience) by thick British accents that sometimes makes dialogue difficult to understand.

Episodes:

1. Welcome to Brompton (8 min., 33 sec.). Rio and her best friend, Tyson, begin their first day at Brompton.

2. The Fresher's Rave (9 min., 39 sec.). In her first step to achieve her goal, Rio attempts to start her own clique.

3. Unloyal Subjects (10 min., 20 sec.). Rio is forced to reevaluate her relatives when she feels they simply do not understand her.

4. Something for Sunday (16 min., 56 sec.). Rio and Tyson attend a weekly showcase called "Sunday Slam."

379 *Untitled Web Series About a Space Traveler Who Can Also Travel Through Time.* theinsepctor.tv. (Comedy-Adventure).

The Inspector, as he is called, is a traveler in time and space. B.O.O.T.H. (Bio Organic Omni-directional Time Helix) is a time ship that allows him, and his companion, Piper, to travel back in time or into the future. The program charts their adventures, most notably those as they battle Boyish the Extraordinary, the mad scientist and The Inspector's most diabolical enemy. **Cast:** Travis Richey (The Inspector), Carrie Keranen (Piper Tate), Eric Loya (Boyish), Mayim Bialik (Voice of B.O.O.T.H.), Robert Picardo (Bernard), Chase Masterson (Annabelle Wagner). **Credits:** *Producer:* Travis Richey, Golan Ramras. *Director:* Vincent Talenti, Nicholas Acosta. *Writer:* Eric Loya, Travis Richey. **Comment:** The program was inspired by an episode of the NBC series *Community* ("Biology 101") wherein a fictional TV series called *Inspector Spacetime* was mentioned. When the idea was formed to make an actual series but was rejected by NBC, it was funded as an Internet project although the original character name could not be used and was changed to The Inspector. The program is an obvious parody of the long-running British TV series *Doctor Who* and well done. While Doctor Who has the evil Master to contend with, The Inspector as his own version—Boyish the Extraordinary as well as a time machine similar to the Doctor's TARDIS (Time and Relative Dimensions in Space) blue phone booth (here a red phone booth).

Episodes:

1. Boyish the Extraordinary, Part 1 (3 min., 32 sec.). As The Inspector and Piper face danger from killer robots, The Inspector manages to destroy them with his sonic pocket knife (a take-off on Doctor's Who's sonic screwdriver).

Untitled Web Series About a Space Traveler... The Inspector (left) and Piper (photograph by Philip Martin; Copyright Siv-Art Productions, 2013).

2. Boyish the Extraordinary, Part 2 (3 min., 13 sec.). As The Inspector and Piper investigate their surroundings, they discover a laboratory from which the robots emerged.

3. Boyish the Extraordinary, Part 3 (4 min., 32 sec.). As they continue their search, The Inspector and Piper come face-to-face with the evil Boyish the Extraordinary, the mad scientist who has vowed to destroy The Inspector.

4. Boyish the Extraordinary, Part 4 (3 min., 34 sec.). Things take a turn for the worse when The Inspector learns that Boyish has created an android of him and seeks to replace the real Inspector with one programmed to do his bidding.

5. Boyish the Extraordinary, Part 5 (3 min., 32 sec.). As The Inspector and Piper manage to evade Boyish's attempts to capture them, Piper becomes confused as to which Inspector is real when Boyish dispatches his Inspector to retrieve them.

6. Boyish the Extraordinary, Part 6 (5 min., 48 sec.). Somehow The Inspector manages to create a duplicate of Boyish—who is amazed to see what he looks like. A standoff occurs and The Inspector and Piper escape—only to be warned that no matter how long it takes, he (Boyish) will destroy his mortal enemy (The Inspector).

Note: There is also one animated episode, a teaser for the series.

380 *Urban Wolf.* webserieschannel.com. 2009 (Mystery).

Surveillance cameras appear to be everywhere and capture everything. People are aware of them and accept them as they feel, despite the invasion of privacy it is for the greater good. One man, Justin Case, believes differently. He lives in Paris and becomes aware that something is not right—he is being watched and everything he does is being recorded. The program follows Justin as he seeks to unravel the mystery of why he is being stalked and by whom.

Cast: Vincent Size (Justin Case), Jean-Guillaume Le Dantec, Bill Dunn, Jacque Bounich. **Credits:** *Producer-Director-Writer:* Laurent Touil-Tartour. **Comment:** Although the episodes are off line, the program's official trailer is view-able on YouTube. Judging by it, it is filmed in Paris and appears very suspenseful as Justin tries to cope with and find out what is happening to him. The acting appears to be good and the photography well executed.

Episodes: 15 episodes have been produced but have been withdrawn (the message "This Video Is Private" will appear). The titles: *1.* Laying Plans. *2.* Waging War. *3.* Attack by Stratagem. *4.* Tactical Dispositions. *5.* Forces. *6.* Weak and Strong Points. *7.* Engaging the Force. *8.* Variations and Adaptability. *9.* The Army on the March. *10.* Terrain. *11.* The Nine

Battlegrounds. *12.* Attacking. *13.* The Use of Intelligence. *14.* The Purpose of the Trip. *15.* The Ends Justify the Means.

381 *The Ushers: A Dark Tale of a Bright Night.* youtube.com. 2013 (Drama).

Father Damien is a Catholic priest who, for reasons that he cannot explain, has become connected to people possessing strange powers; people who appear to not know each other and people with apparently no ties or anything in common. It appears that there are different forces in science, faith, darkness and light and when all such balances remain in tact, the world progresses as it should; however, when the balance is broken the forces are mutated and select people from around the world are suddenly possessed of strange powers that slowly begin to emerge within them. Father Damien appears to be a link between such people as he is now suffering from haunting hallucinations about the broken balance that he cannot explain or accept. But accept he must and the program charts his journey to unravel the mystery and discover why all such people are now connected to him.

Cast: Andrea Galata (Father Damien), Chiara De Caroli (Maria), Martin Rua (Martin), Jun Ichikawa (Jun), Tom Shaker (Ian Toth), Gerry Shanahan (Edgar Usher), Mai Soomeya (Mai), Kenjiro Otani (Ken), Marcel Romeign (Enno), Lavinia Guglielman (Lavinia), Raffaella Anzalone (Lilly), Rossana Colace (Roxy), Iaeli Anselmo (Iaeli). **Credits:** *Producer:* Andrea Galata, Chiara De Caroli. *Director:* Andrea Galata. *Writer:* Andrea Galata, Chiara De Caroli. **Comment:** Intriguing program with many twists and turns as it presents a mystery of global ramifications. The acting is good and the production itself was filmed on location in England, The Netherlands, Germany, Italy, Spain and Zambia.

Episodes:
1. Prologue (9 min., 6 sec.). Father Damien first experiences the effects of the broken alliance when a woman, based in Rome, asks for his help and a man in Berlin claims he will kill himself.
2. The Cursed Girl (11 min., 5 sec.). The signs continue to haunt Father Damien: a woman (Maria) confesses her unstoppable desire to have a baby drove her to a "curse" concealed in a Berlin hospital while a Madrid-based painter seeks help when he fears he is falling under the power of a symbol.
3. DNA (9 min., 4 sec.). A man approaches Father Damien (whom he calls My Son), claiming to have knowledge of the broken balance while people in several cities, including Los Angeles, are awakening to experience strange new abilities.
4. The Indigo Project (11 min., 1 sec.). As Father Damien tries to help Maria, he discovers that something called The Indigo Project appears to be the key to the events that are affecting people like Maria.
5. Dark Shadows. As Father Damien becomes haunted by visions of an unknown man named Edgar, he learns, by helping Maria, that an obscure symbol of a devious congregation (the Blackstone Order) are in some way connected to the Indigo Project.
6. Suicide Girls (14 min., 46 sec.). Father Damien envisions two Japanese sisters committing suicide (in Tokyo) while Maria's power (her curse) is rapidly manifesting itself to a point where she can destroy the lives of other people simply by touch.
7. Revelations (16 min., 12 sec.). Still journeying in the dark, Father Damien feels that he must go back to where it all started—an orphanage he oversaw with a girl named Lucia. Meanwhile, the mutations are causing affected people in Tokyo to commit suicide.
8. The Gathering (19 min., 48 sec.). The concluding episode that finds Father Damien facing the powers of the darkness and light and discovering that death can mean something different than just the end of something.

382 *The Vault.* youtube.com. 2011–2013 (Mystery).

It is the year 2016 and, in an effort to improve its ratings, a TV network devises a series called *The Vault*, a 24/7 reality game show wherein college students, chosen from around the country, are placed in a vault for seven days and presented with a series of clues that they must decipher to win the grand, multi-million-dollar prize. Each resides in a separate room (vault) that has been designed to test their individual abilities and to win, players must figure out the mystery of their room by the objects contained therein. They can communicate with each other but cannot physically go from one room to the other. As time passes they discover they have all been chosen for a specific reason and that they all need to work together, though separated, to discover those reasons. The players apparently know things about each other (their strengths and weaknesses) and that what appeared to be only a game is now progressing into something more sinister (the challenges have turned into situations where death is presented [for example, a hangman's noose]. But is that presentation only a challenge—or will it really kill?). What happens as the clock ticks is explored.

Cast: Shane Spalione (Henry), Alexia Dox (Alex), Adam Epelbaum (Eric), Carlo Maghirang (Ben), Rachel Leyco (Anne), Lilit Arakelyan (Amy), Barry Warrick (Bike Guy), Roy Rosell (The King), Steve Greene (Steve), Laura Waddell (Michelle), Omar Najam (Omar), Emily Evans (Ashley), Ashley Key (Nicole), Zach Hatch (Zach), Matthew Bridges (Matthew), Shawn Gray (Shawn), Rob Rush (Rob), Court Soto (Mark), Alison Vance (Rachel), Rebecca Brudzynski (Rebecca), Alyssa Carter (Jenna), J.R. Cox (James), Justin Marshall Elias (Justin), Sasha Feldman (Ryan), Chad Alligood (Angel), Amanda

Berning (Amanda), Natalie Montemayor (Natalie), Caslin Rose (Lauren), Taylore Murphy-Sinclair (Taylor). **Credits:** *Producer:* Mark Cuban, Aaron Hann, Ashley Key, Mario Miscione. *Writer-Director:* Aaron Hann, Mario Miscione.

Comment: While the program reads like an ordinary game show, it is actually quite intriguing as it presents twists and turns as it progresses and leads to a surprising (but cliff-hanging) conclusion. The acting and production values are good and well worth watching for something different.

Episodes: Each of the 19 episodes that have been produced shows what happens beginning on April 4, 2016 and counting down the 168 hours the game runs. With the exception of the cliff-hanging last episode, the other episodes are just a simple look at the contestants as they play what they think is a game to win money.

383 *Venator Elite.* webserieschannel.com. 2012 (Adventure).

In an attempt to produce specialized agents, the Scientific War Department of the U.S. Army (in Dunham, North Carolina), creates the CVR (Chemical Vision Reassignment) project. It is 1989 and three newborn infants become its first subjects (01ELT, 02ELT and 03ELT). All is progressing well until one test subject (02ELT) suffers a side effect when his eyes become sensitive to light (he can now see in the dark and his sight has been heightened by 300 percent). The CIA believe they have their first special agent (to perform sensitive missions in and outside of the U.S.) until 02ELT escapes from the test center and becomes a fugitive, now sought by the CIA. As the CIA begins refining its chemical process, 02ELT has secretly been in contact with 03ELT, a girl who keeps him informed of the CIA's movements. When 03ELT discovers that the CVR process has been perfected and three additional infants have been secured for testing, she contacts 02ELT. Unknown to her, communication is intercepted by 01ELT and brought to the attention of the CIA director (Merrimack). The news brings 02ELT out of hiding but the CIA has also dispatched its "Breach Team" to capture him. As 02ELT and 03ELT become a team, the program charts their efforts to stop the CVR program before the Breach Team apprehends them. **Cast:** Shannon Wallace (Ericson—02ELT), Donna Wilson-Mariscal (Mercy—03ELT), Bob Walz (Samuel Merrimack), Shuhei Kinoshita (Jackson—01ELT), D. Jus Riley (Sean Pryce III), Jae Woo Bong (Young Jackson), Amyris Colon (Young Mercy), Jaquay Rowe (Young Ericson). **Credits:** *Producer:* Michael Simmons, Jon Navarro, Jacki Zolezzi. *Director:* Michael Simmons. **Comment:** Intriguing story line with good acting and production values. The problem is—just how far can the story line be stretched with a fugitive on the run?

Episodes:

1. We're Going Hot! (6 min., 21 sec.). The story line is established with 02ELT already on the run and the CIA just tracking his whereabouts.

384 *Venger.* webserieschannel.com. 2011 (Action).

Anthony McCullough, the son of Francis and the brother of Michael, heads of a powerful crime family, has broken ties with his family opting to become a world-class race car driver. The situation doesn't sit well with the family, and in an effort to get Anthony back to where Francis believes he belongs, an attempt to persuade him goes wrong and his girlfriend is killed. Anthony, lured to the scene of the crime, finds a bullet next to the girl's body—a special bullet, one given to Michael and one to Anthony when they were children by their father, that leads him to believe Michael is the killer. But, before he is able to do anything, an FBI Swat team, lead by Agent Hollis, storms the crime scene and Anthony is arrested. Anthony now has only one thing on his mind—revenge. Hollis has only one thing on his mind—bring down the notorious McCullough Crime Syndicate. Believing that Anthony is the ticket he needs to accomplish his goal, Hollis sets Anthony free thus allowing him to get even but through Anthony, gather the evidence he needs to prove Michael is the killer. Anthony is anything but eager to return to a life he hates and the story follows Anthony as his efforts to seek vengeance involves him in world of secrecy and betrayal that could destroy his family. **Cast:** Christian Clark (Anthony McCullough), Henry Nixon (Agent Hollis), Bren Foster (Michael McCullough), James Caitlin (Francis McCullough), Jai Koutrae (Giovanni), Dan Mor (Jimmy), Amanda McConnell (Andrea), Jaylan Foster (Young Michael McCullough). **Credits:** *Producer:* Jesse Press, Matt Inglos, Simon Ritch, Marc Windon. *Director:* Marc Furmie. *Writer:* Marc Furmie, Shiyan Zheng, Vincent Andriano. **Comment:** Only one of three produced episodes remains on line (the pilot). The program is very violent although well acted and produced and rather unfulfilled as only mysteries are established with no resolutions.

Episodes:

1. Episode 1 of Venger (15 min.). The pilot film that sets the tone as Anthony begins his quest to find his girlfriend's killer.

385 *Venice: The Series.* venicetheseries. com. 2010–2014 (Drama).

Gina Brogno is a beautiful interior designer living in Venice Beach, California. She is also a lesbian and has thus far not been able to make a serious commitment. She has an addiction to alcohol and is very devoted to her brother Owen, a bond that developed in their childhood as they struggled to deal with a father (John) who disapproved of everything they did. Because of her fear of commitment, Gina lost the girl she believed was the love of her life (Ani Martin, a photographer). Stories, presented like a daytime TV soap opera, relate events in the lives of the people that are close to Gina—and her efforts to navigate a love life that becomes complicated when she begins seeing a new woman (Lara) but discovers that a business associate from London (Tracy) has also become sexually attracted to her. **Cast:** Crystal Chappell (Gina Brongo), Nadia Bjorlin (Lara Miller), Jessica Leccia (Ani Martin), Jordan Clarke (John Brogno), Galen Gering (Owen Brongo), Michael Sabatino (Alan Anders), Tina Sloan (Katherine Pierce), Hillary B. Smith (Guya), Harrison White (Jaime Smith), Adrienne Wilkinson (Adrienne), Michelle N. Carter (Michele King), Shawn Christian (Brandon), Aaron Hartzler (Drew), Gina Tognoni (Sami Nelson), Wes Ramsey (Van), Elizabeth Keifer (Amber), Peter Reckell (Richard), Judi Evans (Logan), Christian LeBlanc (Jake), Lesli Kay (Tracy Lansing), Annika Noelle (Sami Nelson). **Credits:** *Producer:* Hillary B. Smith, Crystal Chappell, Kim Turrisi, Christa Morros, Maria Macina. *Director:* Susan Flannery, Karen Wilkens, Crystal Chappell, Albert Alarr, Hope Royaley, Maria Macina. *Writer:* Crystal Chappell, Kim Turrisi, Jill Lorie Hurst, Leslie N. Johnson, Erika Schleich, Lindsay Harrison, Janet Iacobuzio, Penelope Koechl. **Comment:** The scenery is fabulous; the girl/girl kissing scenes very sexy and the acting comparable to most television series. *Venice* is a continuation from the Otalia story line that was begun on the CBS series *The Guiding Light* right before its cancellation and delves more into the main character's relationships and is enhanced by sexually provocative situations.

Venice: The Series. Crystal Chappell (creator and producer), left, and Jessica Leccia (co-star) (copyright Open Book Productions and Crystal Chappell).

Episodes:

1. Premiere. Gina and Ani are seen in bed indicating that, although they are intimate with each other, they have an emotional and troubled past. A mystery also begins when the body of a dead prostitute is mysteriously dropped off at a mortuary with no clues as to who she is or how or where she died.

2. Episode 2. Michele, Gina's assistant, and Guya, Gina's aunt, a tarot card reader, are introduced.

3. Episode 3. As Gina begins plans to decorate a hotel, she meets Tracy, the British interior decorator with whom she feels an immediate attraction.

4. Episode 4. As Tracy and Gina meet on the Rooftop Lounge, it appears that the two are becoming attracted to each other; meanwhile, Guya visits with Gina and Owens's father John (called The Colonel) hoping to get him to accept Gina for who she is (he cannot accept the fact that she is a lesbian).

5. Episode 5. While working out in a gym Gina is surprised to receive a phone call from her father, asking her to lunch. Although a bit unnerved, Gina agrees to do so as this is what her late mother (Katie) would want her to do.

6. Episode 6. Gina and Tracy are becoming closer (sharing an sensual kiss); Aunt Guya sets Owen up on a blind date (with Sami); Gina and Owen attend the luncheon arranged by Guya (but all does not go well as The Colonel not only belittles Gina, but Owen on his faltering acting career).

7. Episode 7. Feeling she needs someone to talk to, Gina calls Ani, who tries to tell her that she may never get her father's approval and should accept the situation and move on. As the two embrace, Gina admits to loving Ani but it is not quite sure if she loves her.

8. Episode 8. As Gina and Tracy continue with their plans for the hotel, it is becoming obvious they are more than just friends; later, with their Aunt Guya, Gina and Owen discuss past family relationships.

9. Episode 9. At a coffee shop Ani orders a coffee, realizes she left her money at home then meets Lara, a writer, who offers to pay for her coffee. They hit it off and agree to meet to have drinks.

10. Episode 10. Lara and Gina share a romantic dinner at a restaurant where each learns a bit about the other's past, including the fact that Lara is also a lesbian. As they talk, they also share a passionate kiss. Meanwhile, Owen and Sami, a Peace Corps worker, embark on their first date.

11. Episode 11. While Owen receives word that he has received a

part in a movie, it becomes obvious that Gina and Ani have broken up as Gina is now with Tracy and Ani is with Lara.

12. Episode 12. The season 1 finale wherein Tracy and Gina's relationship is now on the line as Gina does not know if she can make the commitment Tracy wants; later, meeting with Ani, Gina tries to mend their relationship by hoping they can be friends (but Ani insists they go their separate ways).

13. Episode 13. Lara, upset with her editor over a book deal, finds comfort from Ani while Gina, alone, reflects on her life and her lost love (Ani).

14. Episode 14. Introduces the characters Catherine, Jamie and Van as Owen learns that his father has collapsed and is now in the hospital. Gina, now alone since Tracy has returned to England, finds that she still has feelings for Ani, made more so when she meets her on the beach.

15. Episode 15. As Ani learns about The Colonel, she and Gina embrace and both admit to missing each other (although Ani is still seeing Lara). Meanwhile, Guya tries to persuade The Colonel to accept the therapy he must endure to get well; Van, Guya's son pays her a visit.

16. Episode 16. As Guya finds a new love interest (Brandon), Lara attempts to conceal the fact that she has turned to alcohol. At the soup kitchen where Sami works, she meets Van, unaware of his connection to Owen (his cousin).

17. Episode 17. Guya tries to make Gina forget the past and help her father while Ani begins to notice Lara's strange behavior (caused by drinking). That night Guya's thoughts turn to her sister, Katie (Gina's mother).

18. Episode 18. Taking Guya's advice, Gina attempts to help her father with his rehabilitation while Ani catches Lara drinking.

19. Episode 19. Sami discovers that Van and Owen are related while Gina crosses paths with an old high school friend (Richard) but doesn't reveal the fact that she is a lesbian.

20. Episode 20. Owen suspects Van is seeing Sami behind his back; Gina is still struggling to get her stubborn father to do his needed exercises and Ani becomes concerned about Lara when she sees an e-mail from her editor about missed deadlines.

21. Episode 21. As Gina and her father seem to be becoming close, Owen admits to his friend Jamie that he lost the film role; Ani finds Lara passed out on the couch (from drinking) and Michele finds herself under pressure from Alan to finish the hotel designs.

22. Episode 22. As Owen attempts to explain his relationship with Sami to his father, Michele continues to work under pressure to complete the designs. Meanwhile Gina and Jamie learn that Brandon (Guya's boyfriend) is a detective and investigating the death of a prostitute whose body mysteriously disappeared from a funeral home. Lara, continuing to drink, is saved by Gina and Ana after she falls into a swimming pool.

23. Episode 23. Katherine finds herself gazing at the beautiful women that surround her; Ani confronts Lara about her drinking; Owen sees Van and Sami kissing (but does not say anything).

24. Episode 24. Season 2 concludes with Lara and Ani attempting to come to terms with what is happening between them; Van telling Sami about Owen losing the movie roll; and The Colonel deciding it is time he became a part of Gina's life.

25. Episode 25. Season 3 begins with Gina having a sexy dream about Ani although Gina is not sure of her future with her. Gina later visits with her father to see that his health is improving and that he is actually happy to see her. Feeling that he and Sami are no longer a couple, Owen finds a new girl (Adrienne) although he still misses Sami (even though Sami values her relationship with Van).

26. Episode 26. Stella, The Colonel's nurse, plans a way to get him to continue therapy (challenge him to a game of arm wrestling. She wins as he continues). Owen approaches his father to tell him he lost the movie deal; Lara prepares to attend AA; Richard, still unaware that Gina is a lesbian, plans to re-connect with her.

27. Episode 27. Owen and Adrienne (the bartender at the Irish Mist Bar) spend the night together; Guya begins having visions of seeing her dead sister, Katie, and tells her she did her best to help raise Gina and Owen; Lara and Ani appear to be getting close again.

28. Episode 28. Gina discovers that, to help her in her time of need, Michele created designs and submitted them to Alan as Gina's. Brandon reveals that a household cleaning residue was found on the murdered prostitute's skin and that she was wearing two different shades of nail polish, indicating that the killer painted them. Stella and The Colonel begin to bond; at The Irish Mist, Jamie (the owner) tells Gina he overheard Brandon discussing the case of the prostitute with Guya; Guya becomes panicked when, at the police station she sees a picture of the prostitute on Brandon's laptop.

29. Episode 29. When Katie's spirit appears to Guya she tells Kate that the dead prostitute looked just like her and explains that spirits can transfer if they died within the vicinity of each other (she believes the prostitute must have died in The Colonel's neighborhood). Richard and Gina meet at the Rooftop Bar and begin reminiscing about their past. It is here that Gina reveals she is a lesbian and hopes to have a lasting relationship with Ani. Guya begins her own investigation into the dead prostitute and, hoping to find information from The Colonel, spies an earring on the floor.

30. Episode 30. Guya's conversation with Brandon reveals that only one earring was found on the prostitute and it is being held as evidence; when Katie again appears to Guya, Guya tells her that she believes the prostitute died in The Colonel's home and that is how the prostitute acquired Katie's soul.

Meanwhile Ani and Lara have gotten back together—but Lara is not the girl she once knew (Lara is now cold to her).

31. Episode 31. Lara and Ani discuss their situation with Ani telling Lara that she is proud of the fact that she is attending her AA meetings. As they talk their feelings for each other appear to be returning as they kiss and head for the bedroom. Guya questions Gina about the night of The Colonel's stroke hoping to learn what happened before he was taken to the hospital.

32. Episode 32. Guya receives another visit from Katie but they fail to figure out what the prostitute's connection was to The Colonel. Learning that a funeral has been planned for the prostitute (Amber), Guya also learns that Nurse Stella is accompanying The Colonel to the service. Meanwhile Brandon and his partner (Dana) have begun setting up surveillance equipment to record the people who show up for Amber's memorial service.

33. Episode 33. At the funeral, a mourner approaches The Colonel and tells him that Amber felt he was the father she never had. Gina, Owen, Richard and Amber's mother, Ms. Preston have also made an appearance. After seeing that Guya made an appearance at the funeral, Brandon approaches her to ask why. She reveals that Amber's spirit, manifesting itself through Katie, has been appearing to her in an effort to help her move on. Shortly after, Guya approaches Amber's mother to tell her that Amber never wanted to hurt her and had made the wrong choices. Guya then tells Brandon, off the record that Amber died in The Colonel's home.

34. Episode 34. Katie appears to be happy that Guya has Brandon but Guya wonders why Katie hasn't yet moved on. At a bar, where Lara and Sami discuss the book Lara is writing, Lara has a bit too much to drink and puts Sami in an awkward position when she becomes intoxicated.

35. Episode 35. The mystery surrounding Amber is revealed as dying of natural causes while with a client (The Colonel, who in turn panicked and dropped her body off at the mortuary before fleeing). Brandon feels the case is closed and will no longer pursue it (and implicate The Colonel). Still at the bar, Lara tells Sami that she is going home to Ani and face the consequences. Gina is relieved that the situation has been resolved while Owen relishes the fact that his father actually did something illegal (dispose of a body).

36. Episode 36. The concluding episode that opens the story for additional episodes: Kate is revealed to have had an affair with a man named Tubbs (who could actually be Owen's father and not The Colonel); Richard finding out that he may have a daughter he never knew existed; Michele receiving help from Ani regarding her designs; problems entering Sami and Owen's relationship; Katie revealing the reason why she has returned as a spirit.

386 La Verdad: Beginnings. blip.tv. 2012 (Thriller).

It is a time on Earth when all superheroes have perished (in an unexplained manner) and villains have taken over. In the city of Salvation, an evil, terrorist organization called Lazarus is relishing in the demise of heroes and seeking control of the world. Mysterious forces, however, change what has happened and bring to life Rocio Hernandez, an Hispanic heroine known as La Verdad, to battle evil. Rocio cannot explain her resurrection but she believes they are connected to a brewing storm that has brought her city to the brink of an all-out war. Her mission, it appears, is to stop it and the program charts her adventures as she encompasses her Hispanic culture to bring down Lazarus.

Cast: Blanca Estella Gomez (Rocio Hernandez/La Verdad), Cody Vaughan (Warren Bishop), Ian Roberts (Lazarus), D'Andre Lampkin (Alexander), Emily Dunham (Karma), Sourita Siri (Kay Roman), Timothy Oman (Terry Reynolds), Darrell Womack (Bullseye), Jesse L. Cyr (Sketch), Yesenia Juarez (Young Rocio), Paulette Lamori (Marie Hernandez), Krista Hazelwood (Reyna Hernandez), Clark Mitchell Long (Eldest King of Purgatory), Jaclyn Friedlander (Kendra Nolan), Tansy Alexander (Cynthia Bishop). **Credits:** *Producer:* Osokwe Tychicus Vasquez, Blanca Estella Gomez, Cody Vaughan. *Director:* Osokwe Tychicus Vasquez. *Writer:* Blanca Estella Gomez, Osokwe Tychicus Vasquez, Cody Vaughan. **Comment:** Good acting combines with a good story line to present an unusual take on super heroes. The program mixes black and white with color footage although some scenes are rather dark and difficult to see what is happening. The production values are also good although the program itself is violent and a bit bloody.

Episodes:

1. The Lion and the Lamb. It has been one year since superheroes perished and the terrorist cell, Lazarus, has begun to establish itself in Salvation, subjecting people to their demands.

2. The Second Coming. Rocio, alias La Verdad, is revived from her year-long "sleep" to encounter a new world in Salvation.

3. The Prologue. It is now six months since superheroes vanished and Warren Bishop, the mayor of Salvation, begins his quest to stop Lazarus from taking over his city.

4. Born Again. Still not her original self, Rocio recalls the events that led her to become a crime fighter.

5. A Sin Before Midnight. Rocio and her associate, Sketch, contemplate dealing with a deadly organization of killers known as The Hand.

6. Dark Side of the Moon. The confrontation fails dismally and Rocio faces the wrath of the King of Purgatory.

7. The Broad and Narrow Road, Part 1. Events in Rocio's past are further recalled.

8. The Broad and Narrow Road, Part 2. A figure from Rocio's past (Alexander) comes back into her life while the Mayor (Warren Bishop) continues his struggle against Lazarus.

9. My Sister's Keeper. Rocio, a prisoner in Purgatory, is released to continue her mission and bring down Lazarus.

10. Save Me, O God. The situation worsens in Salvation when Lazarus unleashes and all-out attack.

11. From Whence Cometh My Help, Part 1. How Lazarus came into being is revealed through a past conversation Warren had with his superhero mother, Cynthia.

12. From Whence Cometh My Help, Part 2. Rocio accepts her destiny and with Warren by her side, sets about to destroy Lazarus in the concluding episode.

387 Verdict. verdictseries.com. 2013 (Crime Drama).

In an alternate world, where crime and corruption have gotten out of control and criminals can beat the justice system, a court of public opinion has been established to replace the American system of justice. Cases are now tried and the public has become the juror. Cases are aired on television (on *Verdict*) and a suspect's guilt or innocence is determined by the majority of the vote of the public—not 12 jurors. Combining elements of *Law and Order* with the call-in voting of programs like *American Idol* viewers (at the time of original release) determined the outcome of each episode—whether the defendant was innocent or guilty based on the testimony presented. "Justice is now in the hands of the general public."

Kim Tollerton is the host of *Verdict*. She spearheaded a campaign for radical change in the justice system when the old system failed both her and her family. Three years ago, Kim's younger sister, Laura, an advocate for ending violence against women, was relentlessly stalked by her ex-boyfriend, Tyler Inglis, a ruthless investment banker with a penchant for controlling women. When Laura decided to stand up for herself and left Tyler, he vowed to make her life a living hell. He succeeded and even though he was charged with stalking, he managed to use his charm and, acting as his own lawyer, cleared himself of such charges (winning over a jury of 12 people in two separate trials). Shortly after, Tyler confronted Laura and gunned her down. The jury set Tyler free and Kim felt the justice system abandoned her. The killing however, outraged the country and the case became the first step in overhauling the judicial system. Kim then became a vocal crusader and when the system did change, she was selected to host *Verdict*.

Jason Mitchell is the son of a lawyer who is now a *Verdict* defense attorney, although his career choice was actually that of a baseball player (he pitched in the majors for seven seasons but an arm injury forced

him out of the league and a decision to follow in his father's footsteps). He is married to Chantelle and they are the patents of four-year-old Louise.

Tavia Booth has been a defense lawyer for 15 years and has recently joined *Verdict*. She is the single mother of two children and goes strictly-by-the-books.

Emily Ellison is a prosecutor and a recent law school graduate with a flair for garnishing publicity for herself—not just on *Verdict* but anything that will please the gossip columns and websites. She appears to live on energy drinks and is a fierce foe for the defense when she prosecutes those who have been convicted of a felony.

Michael Benoit, a seasoned prosecutor (over 30 years on the job), is regarded as one of the best. He has an encyclopedic knowledge of the law and knows the intricacies of every text. In the courtroom he is rather stubborn but direct when questioning suspects. He is married (to Ruth) and enjoys ballroom dancing.

Nathan Haim is a defense attorney with a gift of empathy (he can feel and understand a victim's pain and struggles and can paint vivid pictures of how his clients have suffered as a result of crime).

Cast: Sarah Allen (Kim Tollerton), Emy Aneke (Jason Mitchell), Tamara Gorski (Tavia Booth), Samantha Kendrick (Emily Ellison), Gord Tanner (Michael Benoit), Karl Thordarson (Nathan Haim). **Credits:** *Producer:* Tammy Marlowe Johnson, Jamie Brown, Shawn Watson. *Director:* Warren Sonoda. *Writer:* Mike McIntyre, Tammy Marlowe Johnson, Alex Levine. **Comment:** While not an original idea (NBC tried several similar pilots with *You Are the Jury*) it is an interesting concept that is well acted and produced. As originally presented, each Wednesday evening a new case was aired at www.verdictseries.com wherein the defense and prosecutor argued the case for the jury—the viewer. Over the next week hits of either guilty or not guilty were tabulated and the defendant's fate revealed in an afternoon edition of the show. On NBC's *You Are the Jury*, a case was presented and a special 900 telephone number issued during the show. At the end of the episode, the guilty or not guilty verdict was revealed based on the number of calls received.

Episodes: Each episode runs five minutes and details a court case: *1.* Driven to His Death. *2.* Shooting Stars. *3.* Boiling Point. *4.* The Devil Made Him Do It. *5.* What Gives You the Right? *6.* Tea Party. *7.* Tough Luck. *8.* Hired Gun. *10.* Judge on the Hot Seat. *11.* Till Death Do Us Part. *12.* Innocent Bystander? *13.* Miss Minx. *14.* Homegrown Terror. *15.* Unreasonable Doubt. *16.* Confessions.

388 Voracious. youtube.com. 2012 (Action).

"It was said the world would end in 2012. Instead humanity became extinct." A young woman (Cassie) states this as she and other people like her are now struggling for survival in a time when the unthinkable happens: a nuclear attack pollutes the world's supply of fresh water and those that drink it become zombie-like creatures with only one ambition: to kill those who have not turned. The program follows Cassie and a small group of survivors as they use whatever means possible to battle the increasingly army of zombie-like predators.

Cast: Cara Manuele (Cassie), Tim Kruse (Jared), Justine Leon (Audrey), Marcus Langston (Devin), Ed Spangler (Private Russell), Nathan Pata (Newscaster). *Zombies:* Darth Schuhe, Josh Munson, Colette Claire, David Fernandez, and Phoenix Lee Kiling. **Credits:** *Producer-Writer-Director:* Nick Griffo. **Comment:** The trailer does establish the story line and what to expect—violence as the survivors battle the zombies. The acting and production values appear to be good, but this is based only on what has been released, not what the actual episodes will produce.

Episodes:
1. The Official Trailer (2 min., 15 sec.). Aspects of the program are highlighted.

389 *The Wakefield Variation.* thewakefield variation.com. 2013 (Mystery).

A man, known only as Wakefield, and a girl (Eleanor) have been dating and apparently becoming very close. Suddenly, for reasons that are known only to him, Wakefield decides to leave Eleanor and, without telling her, vanishes. There are no clues to tell Eleanor where Wakefield is but Wakefield has not really left her. Although he now resides in a small, dingy apartment and keeps to himself, he has managed to keep tabs on Eleanor through hidden cameras and microphones. As time passes and Eleanor has moved on with her life, memories of his life with her begin to manifest themselves and Wakefield is overcome with feelings of remorse for what he did. Life changes for Wakefield when he discovers Eleanor is about to relocate thus putting Eleanor out of his reach. The program explores what happens when Wakefield decides to come out of the shadows and renter Eleanor's life. Based on the character created by Nathaniel Hawthorne.

Cast: Michael Brian (Wakefield), Kelsey Gillis (Eleanor). **Credits:** *Producer:* Gianluca Olmastroni, Alessandro DeNicola. *Writer-Director:* Gianluca Olmastroni. **Comment:** Produced in Italy with English speaking actors. Nicely filmed and acted but just how far the story can be stretched remains to be seen. The released pilot establishes that Wakefield has come back into Eleanor's life, but on the official website, the pilot cannot be seen: "The original pilot episode is currently not available for watching ... stay tuned for the new cut." What that reworked pilot will do to the story is unknown.

Episodes:
1. The Pilot (9 min., 56 sec.). Establishes the story line as Wakefield comes out of hiding and appears at Eleanor's front door. It concludes with Eleanor saying "You're here?"

390 *Ward 18.* webserieschannel.com. 2012 (Drama).

As part of a class assignment, five college students plan a project to document the history of a now abandoned hospital. With the guidance of their professor, the students begin filming but suddenly disappear, leaving only three video tapes behind. The program explores the possibilities of what happened to them—did they mysteriously disappear through unknown forces? Did they intentionally disappear (and for what reason)? Is there something evil lurking in the abandoned hospital?

Cast: Devin Camp (Bill), Jordan Jude (Veronica), Brett A. Newton (Tim), Leslie Ranne (Kerry), John M. Russell (Mike), Cody Cowel (Adam Williams), Sam Allen (Troy), Alison Lani (Chelsea), Greg Lewolt (Anthony), Justin Little (Alex), Paulina Logan (Rosie), Gininia Pulcinelli (Erin), Christy Sturza (Brigid O'Sullivan), Liam Tuohy (Father Bryne). **Credits:** *Producer-Director:* Ethen Lane. **Comment:** Based on the teaser, its presentation appeared to be done in the style of a reality TV series with people ("talking heads") reflecting on what has happened with clips from those found tapes being interspersed between theories (like, "It doesn't make any sense"). It also appears to have been a very annoying series as the camera movements are very shaky and the acting below par even for an Internet series.

Episodes: With the exception of a teaser, all 6 untitled episodes have been taken off-line ("This Video No Longer Exists" will appear).

391 *Wastelander Panda.* wastelanderpanda. com. 2013 (Adventure).

In an unknown time in a post-apocalyptic world, a seven-year-old girl (Rose), wanders into an area called the Wasteland after she witnesses the murder of her parents but escapes undetected. As she decides to rest for the night she is awakened from her sleep by a rustling sound in the bushes. She discovers the noise to be coming from Isaac, a rogue panda that has left his home to explore new territories. Unfortunately, before the two can become close, Isaac is killed and Rose, having previously learned that he has a brother (Arcayus), vows to find him and avenge Isaac's death. After days of searching Rose finds Arcayus but Arcayus has settled into a life of solitude and refuses at first to help her; he later heeds to Rose's pleas and agrees to assist her. The program charts their adventures in strange lands and encounters with fantasy-like creatures as Rose sets out to accomplish her goal.

Cast: Mandahla Rose (Rose), Sunny Heartfield (Young Rose), Marcus McKenzie (Arcayus), Roger

Newcombe (Voice of Arcayus), Marcel Blanch de Wilt (Isaac), Richard Magarey (Voice of Isaac), Ryan Cortazzo (Akira), Bob Ramos (Voice of Akira), Andreas Sobik (Sweet Pete), Aaron Schuppan (Leopard Jacket), Nathan Cain (Decks), Colin Gould (Slate). **Credits:** *Producer:* Sophie Hyde, Rebecca Summerton, Mike Jones, Kirsty Stark. *Writer-Director:* Victoria Cocks. **Comment:** Enjoyable fantasy with a well written story and good overall production values. Once achieving their goal, the program could continue as stories set in mystical lands are endless and often fascinating to watch.

Episodes:

1. Isaac and Rose (13 min., 36 sec.). Establishes how, after her family's murder, Rose encounters Isaac.

2. Arcayus and Rose (8 min., 40 sec.). Explores how Rose acquires Isaac's brother, Arcayus as an ally in the search for Isaac's killer.

392 *The Watcher.* blip.tv. 2011 (Thriller).

Dr. Gwen Clarke, married to John and mother to Avalon, is an expert physician who dreamed of becoming a doctor ever since she was a young girl (when she would "operate" on her plush animals). She is intelligent and a personable caregiver but has a seemingly irrational fear of letting anyone get close to her emotionally. She harbors a deep-seated urge for adventure and freedom but her need for control and safety prevents her from indulging in those ac-

tivities. Recently, Gwen has been experiencing strange and terrifying dreams that are triggering seemingly forgotten events from her past. Fearful and edgy, her dreams bleed into her waking hours as phantom flashbacks and she is no longer certain of what is real and who to trust. As Gwen struggles to come to terms with what is happening, she discovers that her every move is being watched by a person or persons unknown (using ultra-modern surveillance techniques and her online footprint). Is Gwen's fragile psyche breaking down or is The Watcher real? The program follows Gwen as she attempts to overcome her darkest fears (revisit her past) and use her wit and intelligence to find out who is watching her and why.

Dr. John Clarke, Gwen's ex-husband and Avalon's father, is a Bio-Genomic researcher with a specialty in assessing and predicting epidemic outbreaks and genetic engineering. Although John loves Gwen deeply, he chose science over his marriage and Gwen's repressed memories hint at an unimaginable betrayal that relates to their daughter, Avalon. The separation from Gwen hits John hard and although he attempts to bury his emotion and guilt in his teaching work, it also leads him to become an alcoholic. His only salvation appears to be Gwen, who out of desperation has turned to him for help in uncovering the mystery that is surrounding her.

Avalon Clarke, Gwen's daughter by John, is bright and possesses an intelligence and intuition that seems beyond her years. She has adjusted to the fact

The Watcher. Logo and poster art from the series (TM & © RSJ GROUP, LLC, 2010).

John is no longer an active part of her life and has accepted Aaron, Gwen's live-in boyfriend as her substitute father (although Aaron's intentions may be sinister as he seems to know too much about Gwen and conspires to keep John out of Gwen's reach). Gwen's changing personality has also caused Avalon to feel more secure with Aaron, something that begins to bother Gwen when she believes that Aaron may be conspiring to take Avalon away from her.

Cast: Sarah-Jane Dalby (Dr. Gwen Clarke), Taylor Hardik (Avalon Clarke), Tyler Brooks (Dr. John Clarke), Rob Hollocks (Michael Thompson), Nick Caballero (Aaron Walker). **Credits:** *Producer:* Rob Hollocks, Sarah-Jane Dalby. *Director:* Anthony Dalesandro, Rob Hollocks. *Writer:* Sarah-Jane Dalby. **Comment:** Intriguing, well produced and acted program that challenges viewers to piece together the puzzle pieces that are presented and solve the mystery.

Episodes:

1. Sweet Dreams (3 min., 10 sec.). Gwen's increasingly disturbing nightmares are beginning to affect her waking hours and changing her attitude toward those close to her.

2. Mr. Thompson (3 min., 34 sec.). Gwen begins to suspect that Mr. Thompson, her daughter's (Avalon) English teacher, may be the culprit as he appears to always be watching for her.

3. Taken (3 min., 51 sec.). A flashback to the year 2000 in North Korea reveals that Gwen was abducted and her about-to-be-born child delivered while she was sedated and taken away from her.

4. Love Letter (4 min., 15 sec.). Hoping to turn the tables on those who are watching her, Gwen sends a video message as a trap to expose her enemy. It works—but the viewer only sees a very brief glimpse of someone.

5. Every Breath You Take (4 min.). Gwen's uneasiness grows as she now fears that, even though she is alone in her apartment, she is being watched especially when a door she clicks closed continually opens.

6. The Good Doctor (5 min., 15 sec.). The concluding, unresolved episode wherein Gwen appears to be making progress with her therapist, Dr. Kramon (David Dean Botrell) in understanding her nightmares but her uneasiness over Aaron continues to grow when he suggests Kramon's intentions are not what they seem.

393 *We Have to Stop Now*. wehavetostopnow.com. 2009–2010 (Comedy-Drama).

Lesbians Dyna and Kit have written a book called *How to Succeed in Marriage Without Even Trying*. They are married and also therapists. But they have also grown apart over the years and even with the help of their own therapist (Susan) it appears that their marriage has ended. Unexpectedly, their book has become a number one best-seller and has stirred the interest of Guy, a film-maker who has contracted with them to produce a documentary based on their lives and the contents of their book. A breakup is now out of the question (as it could ruin their reputation and book sales) and the program follows their efforts to remain a couple despite the differences in their relationship.

Kit Janson is not always predictable in what she will do (sort of not sure if she sees a glass as half full or half empty). She is fun to be with, impulsive, honest and openly expresses her feelings. She maintains a strictly professional relationship with her clients (no matter how gorgeous one may be) and has come to realize that when she encounters a stumbling block to a relationship with another woman, she has a tendency to avoid facing the issues that are troubling her (or her lover).

Dyna Cella has a higher set of standards than Kit (classy and conservative). She prefers intellectual pursuits (such as reading books as opposed to surfing the Internet) and her high professional standards make her a more sympathetic when it comes to her patients. But like Kit, Dyna also has issues, the most personal being her tendency to conceal her loving and loyal side from those close to her (a situation that, if overcome, could possibly save her marriage to Kit).

Susan Dyson is Kit and Dyna's therapist, a compassionate woman with a knack for navigating her professional life, but just the opposite when it comes to her personal life, as she appears to not be able to maintain a steady relationship. She has been treating Kit and Dyna since the start of their breakup and has, in a way, changed her life: she is now prone to concealing her soft and compassionate side to focus on a straight forward, no-nonsense approach to counseling clients. She feels for Kit and Dyna and hopes that, through the documentary being made, she can reunite them as the happily married couple they once were.

Cindy Janson is Kit's younger sister, a girl who loves to get high or drunk, can't keep an apartment or a job and always finds "a home away from home" by crashing at Kit and Dyna's home. Dyna puts up with Cindy despite her loss of personal time with Kit. Cindy enjoys flirting with both men and women (her idea of having fun) and thrives on people's misconceptions regarding her sexuality and her motives.

Guy, the film-maker, has become like a member of the family, recording every aspect of Kit, Dyna and Cindy's life but also finding complications as he has fallen for Cindy and become involved in all the awkwardness as Kit and Dyna pretend to be a happy couple.

Cast: Jill Bennett (Kit Janson), Cathy DeBuono (Dyna Cella), Ann Nobe (Cindy Janson), Suzanne Westenhoefer (Susan Dyson), John W. McLaughlin (Guy), Meredith Baxter (Judy), Mary Frances Careccia (Dee Dee Cella), Shannan Leigh Reeve (Shauna), Maria Marini (Christy), Maia Madison (Sybil),

Catherine O'Connor (Mandy). **Credits:** *Producer:* Jill Bennett, Cathy DeBuono, Ann Noble, Donna Rucks, Libbie Shelton, Robyn Dettman, Rebecca S. Katz. *Director:* Robyn Dettman, Jill Bennett, Cathy DeBuono. *Writer:* Ann Noble. **Comment:** Well-acted and produced program that tries not to be more than it actually is—two lovers trying to understand and overcome the problems that are plaguing their relationship. There are moments of tenderness, but no nudity or vulgar language and a well worth watching program with characters that are as real as people you may actually know.

Season 1 Episodes:

1. The Pilot. Establishes the fact that Kit and Dyna are in therapy and trying to become a couple again.

2. The Golden Rules. The rules of being a good therapist are explored.

3. The Sock Puppets. Susan, Kit and Dyna's therapist, attempts to use sock puppets as a form of therapy.

Note: The following Season 1 episodes have been taken off line: *A Day at a Time, Transferential, Whose Side Are You On* and *Carnal Knowledge, Parts 1, 2 and 3.*

Season 2 Episodes:

1. The Baby and the Bathwater. As Kit and Dyna continue their therapy counseling with Susan, it is suggested that a baby may be the key to solving their problems.

2. The Grass Is Always Greener. Hoping to get other opinions about their relationship problems, Kit and Dyna each seek the advice of a different therapist.

3. Sisterhood-Winked. DeeDee, Dyna's younger sister, comes to visit Dyna at a time when Dyna and Kit have taken the advice of their substitute therapists to date other women.

4. How Sweet It Is. To begin their new dating experience, Kit and Dyna, accompanied by Dee Dee, decide to embark on an ocean cruise (the Sweet Cruise) hoping to meet other women. Meanwhile, Shauna, Guy's younger sister, has accompanied them to chronicle their adventures, while Guy becomes attracted to Cindy, Kit's kid sister.

5. Celesbianism. As Kit and Dyna find some relaxation during the cruise, Susan attempts to solve her own romantic problems by venturing into the world of speed dating.

6. Q&A. Kit and Dyna, recognized by passengers as the celebrities they have become, hold a question-and-answer session aboard ship and recall some of their more interesting clients.

7. The Truthyness of the Matter. Meeting other women did not help, the question-and-answer session brought about hidden feelings and now Kit and Dyna feel they must return to therapy and seek out Susan.

8. It's Not a Game. The concluding episode that revolves around a poker game wherein truths are revealed that could reunite Kit and Dyna as a couple.

394 *Welcome to Hell City.* webserieschannel.com. 2013 (Mystery).

Five children have disappeared in three days. The kidnapper is still at large and it appears that no child is safe. Clyde Lovell, an African-American ex–Marine, is believed to be the culprit (accused of killing an old white couple and stealing their children). But is he really guilty or has he been set up by someone else (supposedly a fellow ex–Marine, known only as the Video DJ, who is jealous of Clyde's success). Kate, Clyde's wife, knows he is innocent, and has begun an Internet hunt to clear her husband and rescue the kidnapped children, while Clyde, with no other choice, has begun a quest to track down the criminals "who have taken over Hell City." **Credits:** *Producer-Director-Writer:* Avi Schwartz. **Comment:** Only a 2 minute and 27 second teaser has been released that establishes what the series will be about. The production appears to be well done with good acting although it appears to be more of a social drama than a thriller or mystery as it deals with an African American and how he is manipulated by persons unknown (at least through what has been released). Unfortunately, a cast is not listed on its website or on the actual video.

395 *Welcome to Sanditon.* welcometosanditon.com. 2013 (Comedy-Drama).

A spin off from *The Lizzie Bennet Diaries* (which see) wherein the character Gigi Darcy was first introduced. Gigi is the younger sister of William Darcy, the CEO of a digital company called Pemberley Digital. The company has developed an app via an experimental video recording platform called Domino (which not only allows voice activation of telephones and computers but records all that happens while the unit is working). Sanditon is a small but growing California city that has been chosen as a test market for Domino. Its Mayor, Tom Parker, feels that doing so will transform his community into a health-conscious vacation resort and become prosperous for everyone, especially when its citizens share their lives through blogs, pictures and videos. William has chosen Gigi to tell the story of Domino (as she says, "I'm a helper. My job is to tell the story, not become the story") and keep track of Domino's progress through weekly video chats (what the viewer sees). Good ideas do not always appear as good as they seem and the program follows Gigi as she contends with all the problems that arise from the Domino test—from the reality that sets in when people's private lives are exposed to the technical problems that still need to be worked out to make Domino an effective (but not too intrusive) app.

Clara Breton is the ice cream parlor (Sanditon Scoops) owner; Tom Parker is the town Mayor; Ed Denham is the Mayor's assistant; Letitia is the owner of the gym, Spin Cycle; Beau Griffiths, Letitia's

Welcome to Sanditon. Kyle Walters (left inset) and Allison Paige (used by permission of Pemberley Digital).

husband, owns the stationary training facility Sit and Spin.

Cast: Allison Paige (Gigi Darcy), Joel Bryant (Tom Parker), Lenne Klingman (Clara Breton), Kyle Walters (Ed Denham), Vanessa Chester (Letitia "Griff" Griffiths), Vaughn Wilkinson (Beau Griffiths). **Credits:** *Producer:* Hank Green, Jenni Powell, Kate Rorick. *Director:* Bernie Su. *Writer:* Margaret Dunlap, Jay Bushman. **Comment:** Based on the unfinished novel by Jane Austen (but updated to the present), the program has all the charm and production values of its parent series. Allison Paige as Gigi is especially charming and a delight to watch as she struggles to keep Domino on track despite all the problems she encounters.

Episodes: (each is a video chat with Gigi as the main focus).

0. On My Way. May 9, 2013.
1. Home Away from Home. May 10, 2013.
2. Trick or Treat. May 15, 2013.
3. Domino 9000. May 17, 2013.
4. Domino, Start Recording. May 22, 2013.
5. The Map Is Not the Territory. May 23, 2013.
6. Chocolate Peanut Banana Juice. May 29, 2013.
7. Immovable Force, Meet Irresistible Object. June 3, 2013.
8. Save Sanditon Scoops. June 7, 2013.
9. Glitch. June 10, 2013.
10. Breakfast Sundae. June 13, 2013.
11. Occupational Hazards. June 17, 2013.
12. Domino Feels. June 20, 2013.
13. Sit and Spin Cycle. June 24, 2013.

14. Brownie Sandwich. June 26, 2013.
15. Business of Business. July 1, 2013.
16. Informed Decisions. July 4, 2013.
17. Futures. July 8, 2013.
18. Chocolate Dipped Cone with Raspberry Sorbet. July 11, 2013.
19. Red vs. Blue. July 15, 2013.
20. Care Packages. July 18, 2013.
21. Leave a Message. July 22, 2013.
22. Nutella Waffles for Two. July 25, 2013.
23. Almost Home. July 29, 2013.
24. Domino Season. Aug. 1, 2013.
25. Proper Sorting. Aug. 5, 2013.
26. Packet Loss. Aug. 8, 2013.
27. End Recording. Aug. 8, 2013.

396 Whatever. youtube.com. 2011–2012 (Comedy-Drama).

Three very pretty teenage girls (Grace, Mickey and Nola) and a look at their lives—not just their public lives, but their private lives—the ones nobody but themselves know about.

Grace is a fiercely independent 16 year old. She is the glue that holds everybody and everything together; she loves music and poetry and faced difficult challenges when she was 12 years old and cared for her two brothers and father when her mother died.

Mickey, 16 years old, loves everything about the 1970s and 80s (even the things that never made an impression). She is a fast thinker and continually bounces from one idea to another. Mickey practically raised herself as her single mother, a bartender, was often absent from her life. She considers her friends, especially Grace and Nola as her sisters.

Nola, the neglected 16-year-old daughter of wealthy parents, has been raised by nannies for most of her life. She doesn't know what it is like to really have parents and feels on the outside of everything. Her desperation to be needed led her to develop a passion to care and she now has a burning passion to save the world. She considers her friends the family she never had.

Cast: Elliott Stiles (Grace), Kate Morgan Chadwick (Mickey), Elisa Catherine Taylor (Nola), Skye Aspen (Jess; Grace's brother), Jayden Maddux (Jack, Grace's brother), Lisa Merkin (Maxine, Mickey's mother), Meredith Thomas (Amber, Nola's mother), Melvin Gregg (Derek, Grace's boyfriend), Shawn Conde (Marcus, Derek's brother), Scott Kennedy (James, Nola's father), Christian Hutcherson (Little Wally), Christy Keller (Little Crystal), Jamie Nocher (Tony, Mickey's boyfriend),Vitta Quinn (Big Crystal). **Comment:** While nicely acted and produced it is a bit more promiscuous than televised TV shows such as *Saved by the Bell* and *Sweet Valley High* as it goes beyond the norm to show Grace and Derek in bed (episode 1) and a party that gets out of hand when alcohol is introduced (episodes 6 and 7).

Episodes:

1. Close Call (3 min., 16 sec.). Grace and her boyfriend Derek, in bed together, have a close call but escape being seen together.

2. Mickey Rocks (4 min., 44 sec.). Mickey attempts to enjoy her rather loud music despite her mother's efforts to get her to turn down the sound.

3. Never Mind (3 min., 58 sec.). Nola balks at attending a cotillion—a tradition her mother wants to carry on in her family with her daughter.

4. Hello, My Name Is... (8 min., 8 sec.). A look at Grace's family coupled with Mickey's confronting her boyfriend about his drinking problem.

5. Just Another Day (10 min., 11 sec.). Grace finds herself in a precarious situation when she meets Derek's abusive brother (Marcus), who not only tries hitting on her, but causes a fight that leaves Derek with a head wound.

6. The Party, Part 1 (7 min., 34 sec.). A social gathering arranged by Mickey has her friends descending upon her home.

7. The Party, Part 2 (8 min., 15 sec.). Mickey and Grace attempt to get things under control when alcohol is introduced. The program's concluding episode.

397 *Whatever This Is.* whateverthisis.com. 2013 (Drama).

Sam and Ari are low paid production assistants who work for the owner (Oscar) of a video production company in New York City. Lisa is Sam's girlfriend, a public school teacher who becomes miser-

able each summer when school ends and she is without a job. Each is seeking a better life, but for the time being, they have to take what they can get until something better comes along. The program charts Lisa's efforts to find a job for the summer as well as Sam and Ari's video shoots—assignments that sound simple but are anything but.

Cast: Hunter Canning (Sam), Dylan Marron (Ari), Madeline Wise (Lisa), Sasha Winters (Dana), Ross Hamman (Oscar), Haley Rawson (Chris), Boo Killebrew (Alex), Tommy Heleringer (Toby), Lusia Strus (Donna), James Bailey Fletcher (Liam), Lucy Kaminsky (Tori). **Credits:** *Producer:* Amanda Warman, Vaughn Schoonmaker. *Director:* Adam Goldman. *Writer:* Elissa Bassist, Sam Denlinger, Adam Goldman, Charlie Reeves, Vaughn Schoonmaker, Jordan Seavey. **Comment:** Comedy mixes with drama to detail the adventures encountered by three young people just trying to find their place in the world. The acting and production values are good and the program is interesting as it explores the situations that Sam, Lisa and Ari encounter.

Episodes:

1. Reality. As Ari and Sam begin work as production assistants on a reality show about "real housewives," Lisa, a teacher seeks (with little success) a job for the summer.

2. Westchester. Lisa's job search is proving fruitless until she meets a law student (Dana) and accepts a job to become her apartment sitter while Ari and Sam are assigned to shoot a questionable music video for a rich teenager.

3. Ghost Cheaters. Lisa begins a new job while Sam and Ari become uneasy over filming on the set of a paranormal detective program.

4. Business. For their next assignment, Sam and Ari must film a corporate video for a big client—a venomous CEO (guest Alan Cumming as Oliver Powers).

5. Nature. A shoot in the country for a nature show sounds like an easy job for Ari and Sam until they become stranded in the wilderness and are unable to find their way home.

6. Broke. Sam and Ari decide to break away from Oscar (to begin their own business) but with Lisa undecided about joining them. The program's concluding episode.

398 *Who Killed Jessica Lane?* blip.tv. 2012 (Mystery).

On March 30, 2012, a 17-year-old girl named Jessica Lane held a party at her parents home in Eastdale (in Australia). Later that night tragedy struck when Jessica was found dead in the passenger seat of her car that had crashed into a tree. Who was driving? A friend of Jessica's, Alex Rowe, was found near the scene of the accident (?) and arrested, charged with her murder. Ruby, Kendra and Elle, although heartbroken over the loss of their friend, feel justified that the person responsible was caught. Their attitudes change shortly after when Alex is released, for a lack of evidence, leading them to believe that Alex beat the system and Jessica's killer is now free. Determined to solve a case that has baffled police, Ruby, Kendra and Elle become their own detectives and set out on a dangerous quest to bring Jessica's killer to justice.

Cast: Hannah Brauer (Ruby Brenner), Brianna Schlect (Elle Williams), Shanna Dib (Kendra Evans), Emily O'Connell (Madelyn Jones), Scott Lee (Damien Walker), Mitchell Fitzpatrick, Matthew Clarke, Neda Aslani, Alicia Kelly, Kaitlin Harasta, Julia Hunt, Samantha Doran. **Credits:** *Producer-Writer-Director:* Mitchell Fitzpatrick. **Comment:** Australian-produced program that is well acted and produced. The amateur sleuths are very attractive and the story provides enough intrigue to warrant interest in seeing what happens next.

Episodes:

1. What's He Doing Back? (5 min., 36 sec.). Just as Kendra, Ruby and Elle return from visiting Jessica's grave they are shocked to see and learn that Alex has been set free.

2. It Wasn't an Accident (4 min., 50 sec.). The girls surmise that if Alex is really innocent than the real killer is still on the loose.

3. Say Away from Me (3 min., 59 sec.). As the girls begin their investigation, Ruby questions Jessica's brother about the night of the party and, shortly afterward, finds a note left by persons unknown.

4. Who Wrote the Note? (3 min., 10 sec.). The note claims Alex is innocent. Believing she knows who wrote the note, Elle reveals that it may be Cassie, one of the guests at the party.

5. Cassie (2 min., 52 sec.). The girls approach Cassie and learn that she did write the note and reveals what she witnessed at the party, including the suspicious actions of a girl named Vivienne.

6. Vivienne (3 min., 49 sec.). Believing they now have s suspect, Kendra, Elle and Ruby approach Vivienne to question her about the night of the party.

7. You've Spoke to Him? (2 min., 51 sec.). Ruby makes her suspicions known to Vivienne that she believes Alex is responsible for Jessica's death.

8. The Text Message (3 min., 23 sec.). Now needing proof that Alex was at the scene of the car crash, Ruby uses Kendra to check Alex's cell phone.

9. Sarah (4 min., 50 sec.). Kendra's search reveals that Alex and Jessica were secretly seeing each other with suspicion now pointing to Sarah, Alex's ex-girlfriend.

10. Let It Go (2 min., 47 sec.). Following Ruby's questioning of Sarah, Elle suggests they should try and figure out who left the party with Jessica.

11. Local Boy Missing (3 min., 34 sec.). A local case involving a missing school boy takes police attention away from Jessica's case but Ruby believes she Kendra and Elle should continue their own investigation.

12. You're All Suspects Too (4 min., 29 sec.). When the girls begin questioning their latest suspect (Madeline) in an effort to find out who drove Jessica away from the party, they find the tables turned when they too are questioned.

13. Drugs (4 min., 1 sec.). A girl (Andrea) approaches Ruby to tell her that drugs may have led to Jessica's death (as she and fellow student Damien were involved with drugs).

14. Getting Somewhere (5 min., 6 sec.). Ruby learns that Andrea was hurt for revealing what she knows and now Ruby fears that she, Kendra and Elle may also be in danger as they continue their probe into Jessica's death. The program's concluding episode.

399 WIGS. watchwigs.com. 2012 (Anthology).

Women are depicted in a variety of roles, from comical to serious, in a series of short films designed to appeal to female viewers. **Credits:** *Producer:* Jake Avnet, Jon Avnet, Rodrigo Garcia, Effie Brown, Marsha Oglesby. **Comment:** Broadcast quality productions that not only encompass name performers but are well written and directed. While the age of anthology programs may have withered away from broadcast and cable TV, they could find a new home on the Internet if productions are as well done as those seen on *WIGS*. Casts are listed with episodes.

Episodes:

1. Ro. A woman, just released from prison, attempts to begin a new life, but encounters problems when she seeks a mate at a speed-dating event. Starring Melonie Diaz, Colleen Foy, Scott Michael Campbell, Christopher Carley; written by Mattie Brickman; directed by Patricia Cardoso.

2. Gumdrop. The life of a robot is depicted. Starring Venti Hristova; written by Kerry Conran; directed by Kerry Conran and Stephen Lawes.

3. Mary. The dilemma faced by an emergency room doctor when she encounters an ex-lover requiring treatment. Starring Melora Walters, Patrick Fabian, Eric Roberts; written by Rodrigo Garcia; directed by Tracey Gallacher.

4. Susanna. A young mother, developing postpartum depression, seeks help from her sister to care for her and her baby. Starring Anna Paquin and Maggie Grace; written and directed by Jon Avnet.

5. Paloma. A woman's efforts to deal with the relationships she encounters both on and off the job. Starring Grace Gunner, Garrett Dillahunt, Rhys Coiro; written and directed by Julia Stiles.

6. Lauren. The plight faced by a female soldier when she is assaulted: report the incident or keep it a secret to ensure her remaining in a job she loves. Starring Jennifer Beals, Troian Bellisario, Bradley Whitford, Mykelti Williamson, Sarah Jones; written by Jay Rodan; directed by Jon Avnet.

7. Blue. A mother, with a tainted past, struggles

to keep it from emerging and ruining the life of her son. Starring Julia Stiles, Holly Robinson Peete, Uriah Shelton, David Harbour; written by Rodrigo Garcia and Karen Graci; directed by Rodrigo Garcia.

8. Kendra. The reactions of a post-op nurse to the secrets she hears from patients under anesthesia. Starring Sarah Jones, Kate Beahan, Jason Isaacs, Bill Brochtrup; written and directed by Jon Avnet.

9. Audrey. A young woman attempts to curtail her flirtatious ways and concentrate on her ability as a cook to achieve her dream of becoming a chef. Starring Kim Shaw, Gary Cole, Arielle Kebbel, Amy Pietz, Bobby Campo; written by Leah Rachel; directed by Betty Thomas.

10. Celia. A doctor faces an uncomfortable situation when she is assigned to treat the daughter of an old friend. Starring Dakota Fanning, Allison Janney; written and directed by Rodrigo Garcia.

11. Ruth and Erica. A young woman struggles to deal with her mother, an aging woman who refuses to make the life changes that are needed to insure her well-being. Starring Maura Tierney, Lois Smith, Philip Baker Hall, Steven Weber; written and directed by Amy Lippman.

12. Vanessa and Jan. Two women encounter mishaps when trying speed dating for the first time. Starring Laura Spencer, Caitlin Gerard, Jimmy Wolk, Walton Goggins; written and directed by Jon Avnet.

13. Georgia. A psychotherapist attempts to incorporate the methods she uses on her clients to bring some serenity into her own life. Starring Mary Elizabeth Ellis, Debra Azar, Harold Perrineau, Mark Povinelli; written and directed by Martha Kaufman.

14. Jennifer. Futuristic tale of a young actress with a most unusual gig: pretending to be a parole officer at a prison to give comfort to treacherous felons—criminals who are unaware that are about to be executed for their crimes. Starring Dana Davis, Dawnn Lewis, Angelique Cabral, Mark Ivanir; written and directed by Mykelti Williamson.

15. Rochelle. The means plotted by a wife to achieve revenge on her ex-husband. Starring Rosanna Arquette, Nazanin Boniadi; written by Scott Turow; directed by Rose Troche.

16. Leslie. A middle-aged actress attempts to acquire the role of Mother Theresa in a film by becoming a real life Mother Theresa. Starring Catherine O'Hara, Anthony Castelow; written by Mitch Albom and Jesse Nesser; directed by Mitch Albon.

17. Christine. A young woman encounters anything but normal men at a speed dating event. Starring America Ferrera, Eric Balfour, Emily Rutherfurd, Gary Dourdan; written and directed by Rodrigo Garcia.

18. Dakota. A female poker player, facing a series of losing streaks, seeks a chance at overcoming her problems by entering a private, high-stakes game. Starring Jena Malone, Jason O'Mara, Michael Massee; written and directed by Ami Canaan Mann.

19. Allison. A young woman faces a romantic crisis when she finds herself unable to go all the way. Starring Marin Ireland, Joel Johnstone; written and directed by Paul Brickman.

20. Denise. A young woman's efforts to help a man come to terms with the lies he has been telling. Starring Alison Pill, T. Lynn Mikeska, Chris Messina; written by Neil LaBute; directed by Lee Toland Krieger.

21. Jan. A young woman attempts to deal with several situations—from a nagging boss to her ex, who still has designs on her. Starring Caitlin Gerard, Virginia Madsen, Stephen Moyer, Laura Spencer, Kyle Gallner; written and directed by Jon Avant.

22. Serena. The incidents encountered by a diverse group of people over the years. Starring Jennifer Garner, Alfred Molina; written and directed by Rodrigo Garcia.

400 Wunderland. youtube.com. 2012 (War Drama).

A rarity in an Internet series as it is a depiction of World War II on the battlefields of Europe and the islands of the South Pacific. Particular focus is on two brothers and their experiences with a squadron fighting Germans on the front lines.

Cast: Steve Luke (Lt. Cappa), Apostolos Gliarmis (Sgt. Rock), Aaron Courteau (Lt. Daniels), Graham Schuetzle (Pvt. Grace), Casey Sillas (Pvt. Kelly), Cody Fleury (Pvt. Williamson), Scott Steben (German Captain). **Credits:** *Producer-Writer:* Luke Schuetle. *Director:* Andrew Kightlinger. **Comment:** Not only a rarity, but very well produced and authentic. The acting and production values are good and, although it appears that only a pilot film will emerge, the program, although rather violent, has potential of becoming a modern-day version of ABC's 1960s TV series *Combat!*.

Episodes:
1. Wunderland Pilot (6 min., 47 sec.). Establishes the premise as the squadron takes on a platoon of Germans after a snow storm blankets the ground.

401 Xistance. webserieschannel.com. 2014 (Thriller).

Dion Chambers was a happily married woman with a good paying job. Becoming pregnant, however, could have possibly been the start of Dion losing control of her perception and questioning who she is. But what caused it? Was it her husband, the birth of her child or the loss of her job after giving birth? As Dion enters a nightmare world where sounds and images from her past merge with those of the present and an envisioned future, the program explores her efforts to find and accept who she has become and where and how she exists in the world— "xistance itself."

Cast: Melody Schroeder (Dion), Jane Sullivan

(Rachel), Chukwudi Onwere (Chris), Sandra Evans (Woman Stranger), Cleveland D. Herbert (Male Stranger), Kerry Ann White (Woman Visitor), Emma Sullivan (Rachel), Ravinder Gill (Female Housekeeper). **Credits:** *Producer-Writer-Director:* Eddie Saint-Jean. **Comment:** Interesting concept that is well acted and produced and reminiscent of *The Twilight Zone* style of presentation (images seen at angles that indicate something else may be happening than what is actually being seen).

Episodes:

1. Episode 1 (8 min., 15 sec.). Dion is introduced as she begins her plunge of self-doubt and efforts to determine the cause of her loss of perception.

2. Episode 2 (12 min., 5 sec.). As it is explained that Dion's case is not rare (it does happen to others) Dion seeks help from the only person she feels can help her, her sister Rachel. The program's concluding episode.

402 *The Year After.* theyearafterwebseries.com. 2012 (Drama).

Kerry and Jeff are recent college graduates with no real focus in life or what to do now that they have their degrees. The program traces their career choices as they set out to explore the opportunities that may be there for them and how they go about embracing them.

Cast: Bradley Gamble (Jeff), Wyvonne Hawkins (Kerry), Ini Inyang (Gloria), B.J. Abrams (Tina), David Havens (Tony), Tonio Junior (Ricky), Junia Massey (Tiffany). **Credits:** *Producer:* Edward Block, Wyvonne Hawkins. *Director:* Brian D. Lee. **Comment:** African-American production that is quite realistic in presentation. The acting is good and the production values standard for an Internet program.

Episodes:

1. Wake Up (4 min., 58 sec.). Jeff realizes that playing basketball is not the answer to the problems he is beginning to face.

2. What Now? (3 min., 47 sec.). Like Jeff, Kerry is now facing the same dilemma: what to do with her life—and her degree.

3. Classifieds (5 min., 9 sec.). Both Kerry and Jeff take the first step and begin a job search.

4. The Call (6 min., 25 sec.). Kerry and Jeff find a light at the end of the tunnel as Jeff gets a job offer and Kerry prepares for an interview.

5. New Job (9 min., 46 sec.). Jeff settles into a new job while Kerry faces her interview.

403 *Year Zero.* webserieschannel.com. 2013 (Action).

It is the future and America is under the dictatorship of the Orwellian government. While the seat of government still exists in Washington, D.C., rules must be obeyed or the punishment is harsh: imprisonment or death as dictated by the Bureau of Moral-

ity. Freedom of thought has been abolished and people live in constant fear. As with any society, there are resistance groups and the program charts the struggles of two underground factions as they struggle to defeat the new government and restore the rights and dignity of people.

Cast: Sara Giacobbe (Amber), Giuseppe Di Mauro (Brandon), Valeria Ricca (Susan), Gio Scarberg (Sniper), Claudio Agave (Novak Schecter), Ludavica Aliberti (Veronica Taylor), Fabrizio D'Angelo (Victor Sebastian), Giovanni Milo (Frank Taylor), Francesca Gatto (Thedora Jones). **Credits:** *Producer:* Foley Studios. *Director:* Gio Scarberg, Fabio Tango. *Writer:* Claudio Agave, Achille Conte, Gio Scarberg, Fabio Tango. **Comment:** America is the setting, but the program is produced in Italy with English subtitles. The subject has been done countless times before but it is interesting to see how a foreign country views America in a time of crisis. The acting and production values are good and it is worth watching (despite the distracting subtitles).

Episodes:

1. The Angry Sniper (8 min., 22 sec.). The story line is begun as the factions, based in Los Angeles, plot to overthrow the government.

2. Art Is Resistance (23 min., 18 sec.). Flyers opposing the government begin to appear throughout the city while Veronica, a chemist for Cedocore, discovers that her company may be responsible for distributing a street drug (Opal) that controls people's thoughts.

404 *Yu Solve.* yusolve.com. 2011 (Crime Drama).

"You see the crime. You see the suspects. Yu solve" is the tag line for the case investigations of Agatha Yu, a beautiful detective with the Los Angeles Missing Person's Unit (MPU) who, despite her dislike of firearms, does what she has to find missing people before time runs out. Agatha works with Anthony Kazantzakis and the program follows their efforts to locate a missing woman (Toni Atkins) who mysteriously disappeared without a trace.

Agatha was born in Hong Kong to a British mother and an American father. When she was six years old her mother simply walked out of her life and Agatha was raised primarily by her nanny, Lin Yu. Agatha embraced the Oriental culture and took Lin's last name as her own; she later relocated to Texas (beginning at age 14). She has blonde hair and is distinguished by two different colored eyes—one green and one blue (which suspects immediately notice and bring to her attention). Her one major flaw is that she is totally independent and if things are not going her way, her temper flares and she often faces discipline from her captain for losing control.

Anthony Kazantzakis is a sergeant and charming, but he has an addiction to gambling. Unlike Agatha, who likes to closely follow book procedure, Anthony is a bit hot headed and not one for following the rules. While he is an expert at examining evidence, he has a tendency to go off on his own and follow up on a clue.

Gabriel Thomas is the head of the MPU. He appears demure but takes abuse from no one, especially Agatha (whom he threatens to bust down to a beat cop if he doesn't change). He is responsible for initiating the Special Circumstances Division of the MPU (which handles especially sensitive cases involving high profile missing persons).

Cast: Mason Alexander (Det. Agatha Yu), Vince Lozano (Det. Anthony Kazantzakis), Lester Purry (Capt. Gabriel Thomas), Sean McHugh (Robert Costello), Linda Burzynski (Off. Ramsey), Tim Coultas (Det. Andre), Alex D'Lerma (Off. Nikos), Deidra Edwards (Cyndi Pryor), Kelly Knox (Eldridge Krumsky), Cesar Romos (Albert Shapiro), Amber Baleto (Toni Atkins), Sasha Van Duyn (Pristine Costello), Steve Wilcox (Det. Lars Welch). **Credits:** *Producer:* Mason Alexander, Marquez Lee, Alex D'Lerma, Lyvia Bydlowski, Nayoung Ahn. *Director:* Alex D'Lerma, Dexter N. Adriano, Belti Rivera. *Writer:* Mason Alexander. **Comment:** The program was interactive, and at the time viewers could choose what would happen. It is well acted with all the qualities of a network TV crime drama. There is a bit of vulgar language (when Agatha gets upset); although not really needed, it does fit in with the story based on Agatha's character.

Episodes:

1. Prologue (8 min., 34 sec.). Case Number SC 9252011 begins: The search for a missing woman (Toni Atkins).

2. Evidence (5 min., 44 sec.). As they investigate Agatha and Anthony find a wedding announcement for Toni and her fiancé Dan Owens.

3. Episode 3 (6 min., 35 sec.). Dan, brought in for questioning, proves to be a difficult task for Agatha as Dan is very evasive and violable.

4. Episode 4 (8 min., 25 sec.). A search of Toni's home brings Agatha in contact with Toni's nosey neighbor, Mrs. Pryor.

5. Episode 5 (8 min., 42 sec.). Agatha discovers that Toni worked for Councilman Costello and he appears to be hiding something about his relationship with her.

6. Episode 6 (6 min., 51 sec.). Agatha next turns to questioning Costello's wife, Pristine, regarding her knowledge of Toni.

Yu Solve. **Poster art from the series (poster artwork by Nick Piltch; copyright Yu Solve).**

7. Episode 7 (5 min., 5 sec.). Agatha breaks the rules and picks the lock to enter Costello's home. Inside she and Anthony find Toni—tied and gagged and confronted by an unknown woman holding a gun on them. A message then appears on screen: "You have 72 hours to choose. Shoot or Don't Shoot. Vote now at yusolve.com."

8. Episode 8. Because the episode was based on the outcome of viewer's voting, it has been withdrawn but the following message appears "Did viewers choose to shoot or not shoot. Watch the *Yu Solve* season finale to find out."

405 Zoochosis. youtube.com.com. 2013 (Drama).

"I'm a trained psychiatrist. But I've never seen cases like these: terror, obscurity, passion. What do I do with cases that are filled with so much of the unexpected?" These are the opening words spoken by Dr. Singer, a psychiatrist whose patients are anything but normal. Each episode presents a patient with a rather unusual problem—and explores not only the psychosis felt by the patient, but how Dr. Singer attempts to handle it.

Cast: Rick Steadman (Dr. Singer), Patrick Scott (Narration Voice of Dr. Singer). Other cast members are listed with the episodes in which they appear. **Credits:** *Producer:* Ryan Nicholson. *Writer-Director:* Patrick Scott. **Comment:** The term "zoochosis" relates to a psychological effect of being caged and can usually only be experienced by the person who possesses the problem although hand gestures and movements by patients can also present an idea as to what is happening. The program is, to say the least, quite unusual and very captivating; it is truly different and worth checking out.

Episodes:

1. Case 1: Aliens (5 min., 35 sec.). A young woman's wedding day may never happen when she believes squirmy, small aliens have invaded her wedding reception. *Cast:* Kelsey Nisbett (Bride), Jeff Larson (Groom).

2. Case 2: Love (2 min., 28 sec.). As he waits in the doctor's office, a man begins imagining he is embracing a beautiful woman. *Cast:* Mirna Rae (Lucky Gal), Brian James Hunt (Lucky Guy).

3. Case 3: Sex (5 min., 49 sec.). As the song "Bolero" plays in the background, a roofer imagines himself making love to a beautiful woman—and covering each other in tar. *Cast:* Anthony L. Fernandez (Roofer), Kate Pierson (Woman).

4. Case 4: Magic (2 min., 59 sec.). A female magician believes she has the power to prove that magic is not a trick but real. *Cast:* Elizabeth Bergstone (Madame Boudillia).

5. Case 5: Fate (4 min., 23 sec.). Episode has been taken off line. A story about scientists who believes fate is controlled by an army of rats. *Cast:* Kimberly Madison, John Livingston, Neil Sandilands (Scientists).

6. Case 6: Parenthood (2 min., 34 sec.). As a wife cuddles her new-born baby, the husband envisions himself as a baby and getting the same attention. *Cast:* Brett Davis (Father), Toni Torres (Mother).

7. Case 7: Revenge (2 min., 30 sec.). Believing that their pet parrot is ruining his marriage, a husband attempts to abandon it. As he drives, being guided by a GPS voice, he soon finds himself stuck on railroad tracks; the car is hit by a train just as the parrot (who imitated the voice and guided the driver) escapes. *Cast:* Dink O'Neal (Driver), Kat Feller (GPS voice).

8. Case 8: War (4 min., 6 sec.). When a small army of ants invades her home and take a liking to her fresh strawberries, the war begins—with the woman winning (by eating the ants with her strawberries). *Cast:* Alanna Swovelin (Woman).

9. Case 9: Celebration (4 min., 49 sec.). The doctor's exposure has him bedazzled—so much so that he begins having his own delusions—a wedding with Samba dancers occurring in his office. *Cast:* Diane Cavalcante, Andres Estrada, Eduardo Charmit, Kamilla Rodrigues deSousa, (Samba Dancers), Kelsey Nisbett (Bride), Jeff Larson (Groom).

INDEX TO ENTRY NUMBERS

www.ingramcontent.com/pod-product-compliance
Lightning Source LLC
Chambersburg PA
CBHW080551060326
40689CB00021B/4813

* 9 7 8 0 7 8 6 4 9 5 8 1 8 *